# STUDENT'S SOLUTIONS MANUAL

TO ACCOMPANY
JAMES T. McCLAVE AND P. GEORGE BENSON'S

# STATISTICS
## FOR BUSINESS AND ECONOMICS

FIFTH
EDITION

**NANCY S. BOUDREAU**
Bowling Green State University

DELLEN PUBLISHING COMPANY
an imprint of
MACMILLAN PUBLISHING COMPANY
NEW YORK

MAXWELL MACMILLAN CANADA
TORONTO

Printed in the United States of America



Macmillan Publishing Company
866 Third Avenue, New York, New York 10022

Macmillan Publishing Company is part of the Maxwell Communication Group of Companies.

Maxwell Macmillan Canada, Inc.
1200 Eglinton Avenue East
Suite 200
Don Mills, Ontario M3C 3N1

Permission: Dellen Publishing Company
400 Pacific Avenue
San Francisco, California 94133

Orders: Dellen Publishing Company
c/o Macmillan Publishing Company
Front and Brown Streets
Riverside, New Jersey 08075

PRINTING: 1 2 3 4 5 6 7 8 9, YEAR: 1 2 3 4 5 6

ISBN 0-02-379241-8

# P R E F A C E

This solutions manual is designed to accompany the text, *Statistics for Business and Economics, Fifth Edition,* by James T. McClave and P. George Benson (Dellen Publishing Company, 1991). It provides answers to most odd-numbered exercises for each chapter in the text. Other methods of solution may also be appropriate; however, the author has presented one that she believes to be most instructive to the beginning Statistics student. The student should first attempt to solve the assigned exercises without help from this manual. Then, if unsuccessful, the solution in the manual will clarify points necessary to the solution. The student who successfully solves an exercise should still refer to the manual's solution. Many points are clarified and expanded upon to provide maximum insight into and benefit from each exercise.

Instructors will also benefit from the use of this manual. It will save time in preparing presentations of the solutions and possibly provide another point of view regarding their meaning.

Some of the exercises are subjective in nature and thus omitted from the Answer Key at the end of *Statistics for Business and Economics, Fifth Edition*. The subjective decisions regarding these exercises have been made and are explained by the author. Solutions based on these decisions are presented; the solution to this type of exercise is often most instructive. When an alternative interpretation of an exercise may occur, the author has often addressed it and given justification for the approach taken.

ACKNOWLEDGMENTS

I would like to thank Brenda Dobson for her assistance and for typing this work.

Nancy S. Boudreau
Bowling Green State University
Bowling Green, Ohio

# CONTENTS

C H A P T E R 1

# WHAT IS STATISTICS?

1.1 Descriptive statistics utilizes numerical and graphical methods to look for patterns, to summarize, and to present the information in a set of data. Inferential statistics utilizes sample data to make estimates, decisions, predictions, or other generalizations about a larger set of data.

1.3 A population is a set of existing units such as people, objects, transactions, or events. A variable is a characteristic or property of an individual population unit such as height of a person, time of a reflex, amount of a transaction, etc.

1.5 An inference without a measure of reliability is nothing more than a guess. A measure of reliability separates statistical inference from fortune telling or guessing. Reliability gives a measure of how confident one is that the inference is correct.

1.7 a. The population of interest is all the students in the class. The variable of interest is the GPA of a student in the class.

b. Since the population of interest is all the students in the class and you obtained the GPA of every member of the class, this set of data would be a census.

c. Assuming the class had more than 10 students in it, the set of 10 GPAs would represent a sample. The set of ten students is only a subset of the entire class.

d. This average would have 100% reliability as an "estimate" of the class average, since it is the average of interest.

e. The average GPA of 10 members of the class will not necessarily be the same as the average GPA of the entire class. The reliability of the estimate will depend on how large the class is and how representative the sample is of the entire population.

1.9 a. The population of interest is all citizens of the United States.

b. The variable of interest is the view of each citizen as to whether the President is doing a good or bad job.

c. The sample is the 2000 individuals selected for the poll.

d. The inference of interest is to estimate the proportion of all citizens who believe the President is doing a good job.

1.11 a. There are two populations of interest to House. The first is the set of all trainees who have or will receive in the future the revised program. The second is the set of all trainees who have or will receive in the future the old program.

b. The variable he measured was the number of absences for each trainee in the course.

c. The first sample was the collection of 51 trainees who received the revised program. The second sample was the collection of 49 trainees who received the old program.

d. House concluded that the number of absences per person in the trainee group receiving the revised program was significantly less than that for the group trained under the old policies.

1.13 a. The population of interest is the set of 497 corporations listed on the New York Stock Exchange who acquired control of the assets of another firm that resulted in the listing of the acquired firms' stock during the period from 1958 - 1980.

b. The variable of interest is the change in the value of the holdings of the bidder firm's bondholders.

c. The sample is the set of 38 corporations selected.

d. Based on the information obtained from the 38 firms, one might want to estimate the proportion of all firms whose value of the holdings increased as a result of the merger. One might also want to estimate the average change in the value of the holdings as a result of the merger.

1.15 a. The population of interest is the collection of all department store executives.

b. Two variables are measured. The first is the job satisfaction of the executives and the second is the "Machiavellian" rating of each executive.

c. The sample is the collection of the 218 department store executives selected for the study.

d. The authors concluded that those executives with higher job satisfaction scores are likely to have a lower "Mach" rating.

1.17 a. The population of interest is all RV owners in the United States. The variables of interest are the preferences with respect to the features of a portable generator (e.g., size, manual or electric start, etc.). The sample is the collection of 1052 RV owners who returned the questionnaire. The inference of interest is to generalize the preferences of the 1052 sampled RV owners to the population of all RV owner preferences on the features of a portable generator. Specifically, the sample results will be used to decide what features should be included on a portable generator by estimating the proportion that like each feature suggested on the questionnaires.

b. One factor that may affect the reliability of inferences is the group of RV owners who return the questionnaire. Often, the people who return questionnaires have very strong opinions about the items on the questionnaire and may not be representative of the population in general. Another factor may be those receiving the questionnaire may no longer be RV owners.

1.19 a. The process of interest is the monitoring well for a coal-fired power plant in Miami, Florida. This is a process because it "generates" water quality over time.

b. The variables of interest are the levels of certain water quality parameters.

c. The sample is the collection of water samples taken from the monitoring well each quarter.

d. Based on the water quality parameters from the sample, the DER determines whether the water quality meets the State's guidelines.

e. When the water samples are taken may influence the reliability of the inference. If the water sample is taken when the plant is shut down or when the plant is running on low capacity the results may be quite different than when the plant is running at full capacity. The time of day the water samples are taken may also influence the results. Different operations may take place in the plant at different times during the day that may influence the quality of the water.

# CHAPTER 2

## GRAPHICAL DESCRIPTIONS OF DATA

2.1 a. Nominal data are measurements that simply classify the units of the sample or population into categories. These categories cannot be ranked. Ordinal data are measurements that enable the units of the sample or population to be ordered or ranked with respect to the variable of interest.

b. Interval data are measurements that enable the determination of the differential (how much more or less) of the characteristic being measured between one unit of the sample or population and another. Interval data will always be numerical, and the numbers assigned to the two units can be subtracted to determine the difference between the units. However, the zero point is not meaningful for these data. Thus, these data cannot be multiplied or divided. Ratio data are measurements that enable the determination of the multiple (how many times as much) of the characteristic being measured between one unit of the sample or population and another. All the characteristics of interval data are included in ratio data. In addition, the zero point for ratio data is meaningful

c. Qualitative data have no meaningful numbers associated with them. Qualitative data include nominal and ordinal data. Quantitative data have meaningful numbers associated with them. Quantitative data include interval and ratio data.

2.3 The data consisting of the classifications A, B, C, and D are qualitative. These data are nominal and thus are qualitative. After the data are input as 1, 2, 3, and 4, they are still nominal and thus qualitative. The only difference between the two data sets are the names of the categories. The numbers associated with the four groups are meaningless.

2.5 a. Nominal; possible brands are "Guess," "Levis," "Lee," etc., each of which represents a nonranked category.

b. Ratio; the number of hours of sports programming carried in a typical week is measured on a numerical scale where the zero point has meaning. Ten hours of sports programming is five times as much as two hours of sports programming.

c. Ratio; the percentage of their workdays spent in meetings is measured on a numerical scale where the zero point has meaning. Forty percent of workdays spent in meetings is twice as much as twenty percent.

d. Ratio; the number of long distance telephone calls is measured on a numerical scale where the zero point has meaning. Twenty phone calls is four times as many as five phone calls.

e. Interval; SAT scores are measured on a numerical scale where the zero point has no meaning. A score of 500 is not twice as good as a score of 250.

2.7 a. Nominal; brand of stereo speaker would be measured using nonranked categories.

b. Ratio; loss (in dollars) is measured on a numerical scale where the zero point has meaning. A loss of $600 is three times as much as a loss of $200.

c. Nominal; color is measured using nonranked categories.

d. Ordinal; ranking of football teams orders the teams, but does not indicate how much better one team is than another.

2.9 The frequency for a category is the total number of measurements that fall in the category. The relative frequency for a category is the proportion of the total number of measurements that fall in the category. The relative frequency is found by dividing the number of measurements in a category by the total number of measurements.

2.11 a. The defects are classified into four categories. Thus, the data are nominal.

b. The frequency of Type C defectives is the total number of Type C defectives, which is 6. The relative frequency is the frequency divided by the total number of chips, which is 6/1000 = .006.

c.

| CATEGORY | FREQUENCY | RELATIVE FREQUENCY |
|---|---|---|
| A | 3 | 3/1000 = .003 |
| B | 21 | 21/1000 = .021 |
| C | 6 | 6/1000 = .006 |
| D | 34 | 34/1000 = .034 |
| No Defect | 936 | 936/1000 = .936 |
| Total | 1000 | 1.000 |

The relative frequencies add to 1.0.

The frequency bar chart is constructed by placing the type of defect on the horizontal axis and the frequency on the vertical axis.

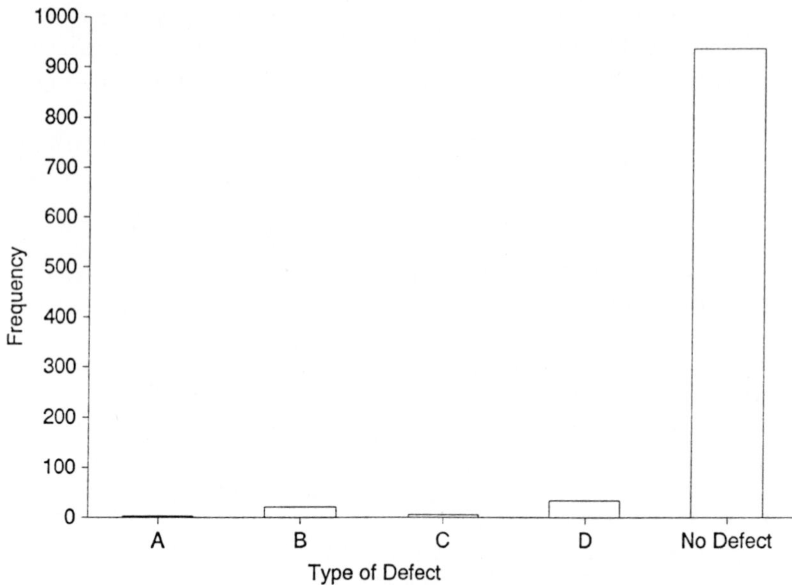


The relative frequency bar chart is constructed by placing the type of defect on the horizontal axis and the relative frequency on the vertical axis.

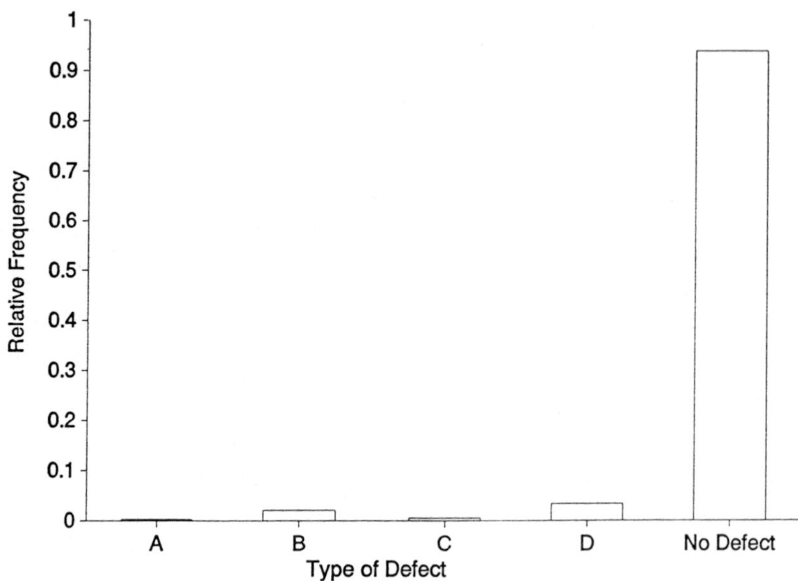

d. The frequency of Type C defectives among the defective chips is the total number of chips with the Type C defect, which is 6. The relative frequency of the Type C defectives among the defective chips is the frequency divided by the total number of defectives and is 6/64 = .094.

e.

| CATEGORY | FREQUENCY | RELATIVE FREQUENCY |
|---|---|---|
| A | 3 | 3/64 = .047 |
| B | 21 | 21/64 = .328 |
| C | 6 | 6/64 = .094 |
| D | 34 | 34/64 = .531 |
| Total | 64 | 1.000 |

The relative frequencies add to 1.0.

The frequency bar chart is constructed by placing the type of defect on the horizontal axis and the frequency on the vertical axis.

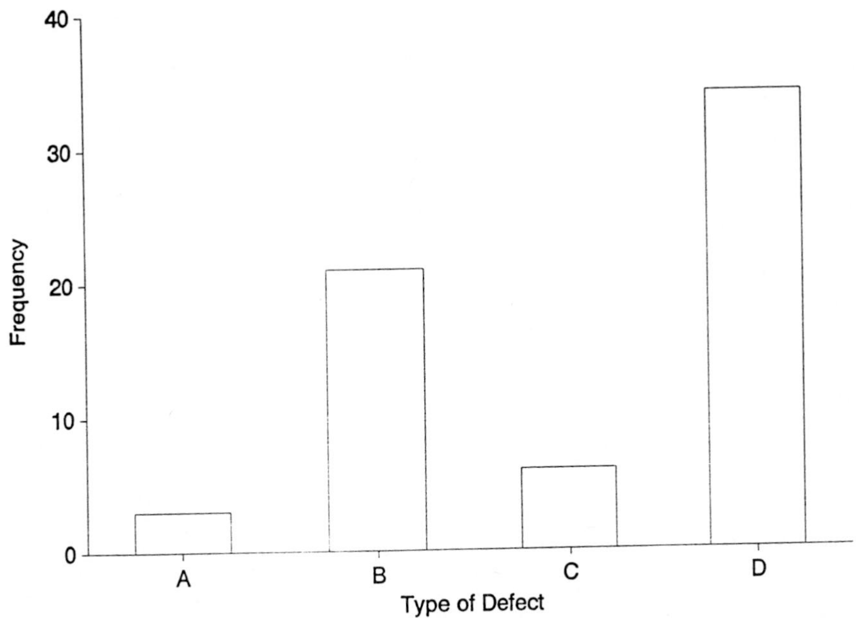


The relative frequency bar chart is constructed by placing the type of defect on the horizontal axis and the relative frequency on the vertical axis.

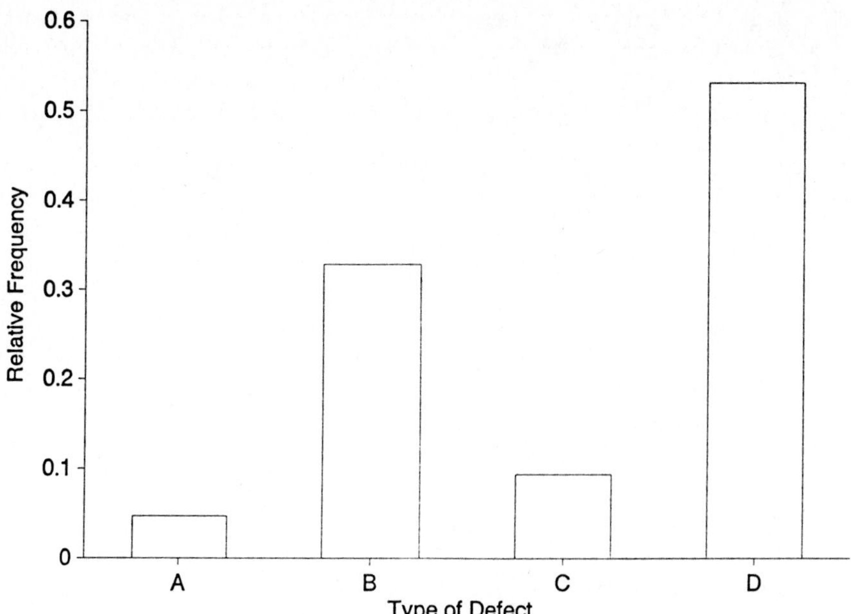


f. The Pareto diagram is similar to the frequency bar chart. The only difference is that the categories are arranged in order from the highest to the lowest on the horizontal axis.

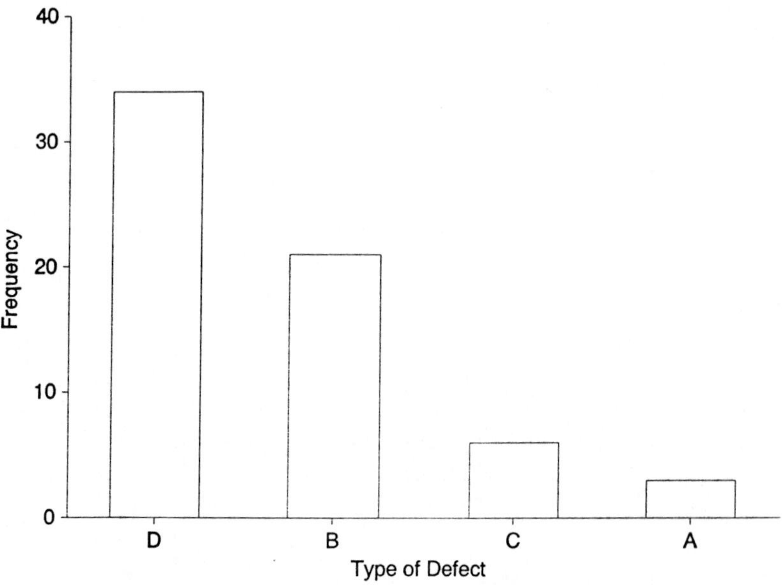


2.13 a. The bar chart describes the cigarette sales for six companies in 1985.

b. The Philip Morris Company sold the most cigarettes; approximately 211.8 billion.

c. To convert the bar chart to a relative frequency bar chart, we must compute the sample size by summing the sales for each company.

$$n = 211.8 + 189.7 + 69.1 + 48.6 + 43.9 + 29.8 = 592.9$$

Calculate the relative frequencies for each company by dividing the sales by n, $f_i/n$.

| COMPANY | FREQUENCY | RELATIVE FREQUENCY $f_i/n$ |
|---|---|---|
| Philip Morris | 211.8 | .36 |
| Reynolds | 189.7 | .32 |
| Brown & Williamson | 69.1 | .12 |
| Lorillard | 48.6 | .08 |
| American | 43.9 | .07 |
| Liggett | 29.8 | .05 |
| | 592.9 | 1.00 |

The relative frequency bar chart is constructed by placing the company on the vertical axis and the relative frequency on the horizontal axis.

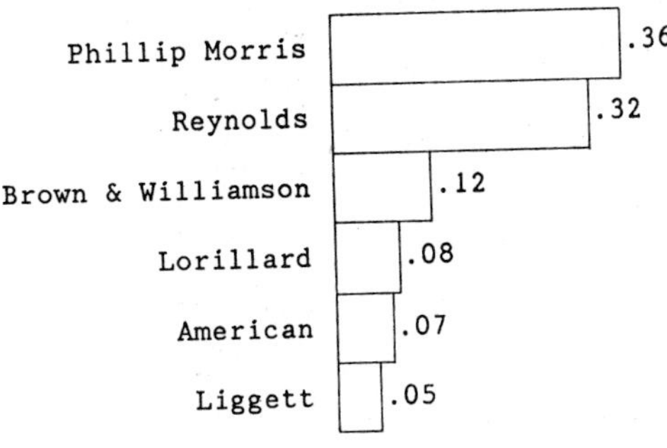


2.15 a. A frequency bar chart is constructed by placing the cities in Ramsey County on the horizontal axis and the frequencies on the vertical axis. The frequencies represent the number of apartments converted to condominiums.

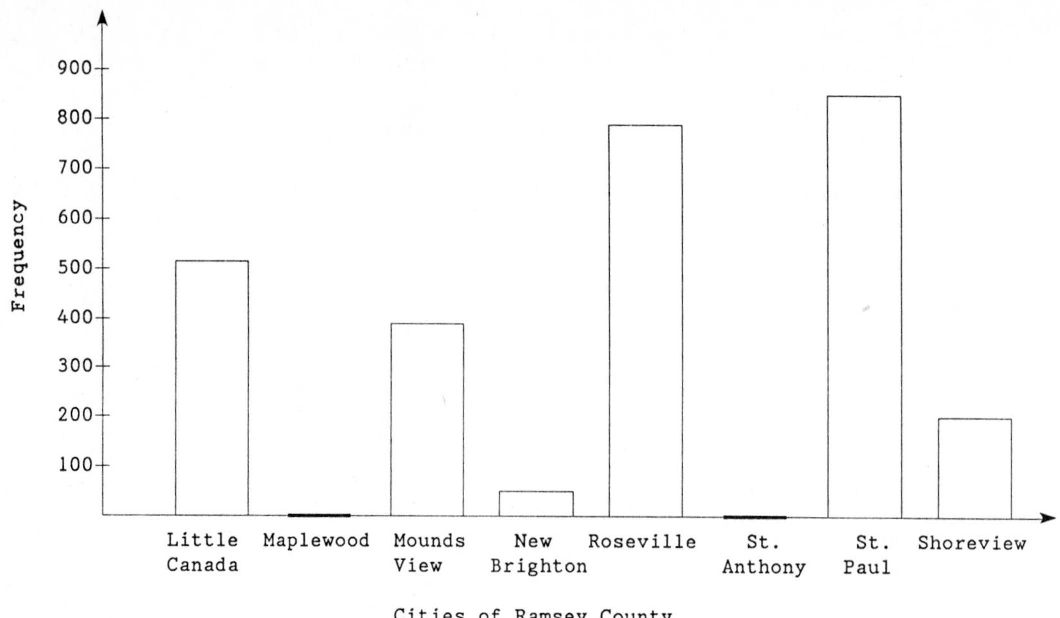


b. First we need to compute the total number of condominiums in each city of Ramsey County and find the relative frequencies.

RAMSEY COUNTY

| City | Total Number of Condominiums | Relative Frequency $f_i/n$ |
|---|---|---|
| Little Canada | 511 + 101 = 612 | 612/3723 = .164 |
| Maplewood | 0 + 252 = 252 | .068 |
| Mounds View | 385 + 0 = 385 | .103 |
| New Brighton | 54 + 0 = 54 | .015 |
| Roseville | 767 + 30 = 797 | .214 |
| St. Anthony | 0 + 148 = 148 | .040 |
| St. Paul | 832 + 443 = 1275 | .342 |
| Shoreview | 192 + 8 = 200 | .054 |
| | n = 3723 | 1.000 |

A relative frequency bar chart is constructed by placing the cities of Ramsey County on the horizontal axis and the relative frequencies on the vertical axis.

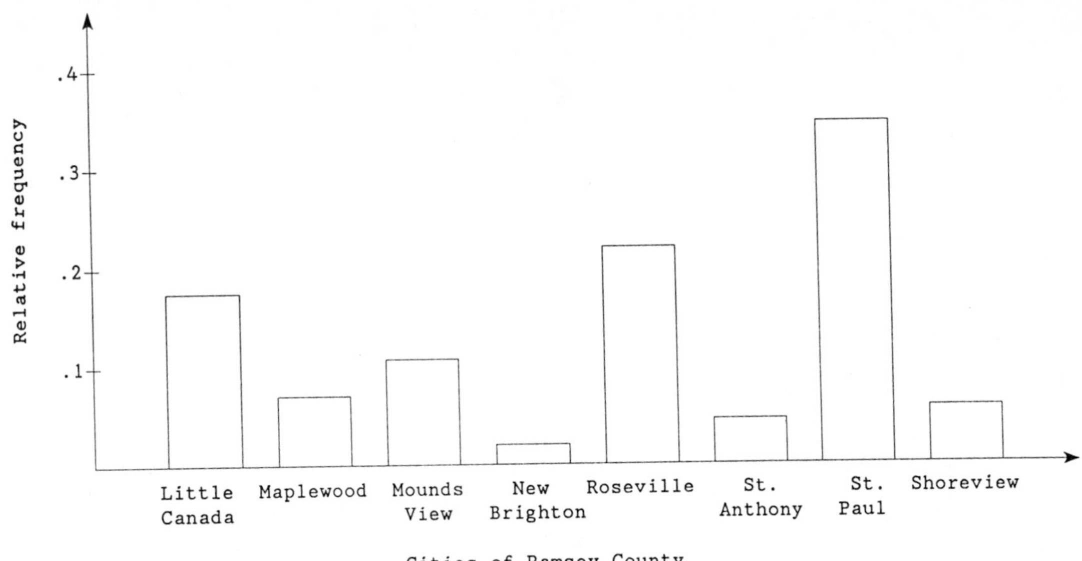


Now we need to compute the total number of condominiums in each city of Dakota County and find the relative frequencies.

DAKOTA COUNTY

| City | Total Number of Condominiums | Relative Frequency $f_i/n$ |
|---|---|---|
| Burnsville | 409 + 135 = 544 | 544/1213 = .4485 |
| Eagan | 8 + 128 = 136 | .1121 |
| Farmington | 0 + 36 = 36 | .0297 |
| Inver Grove Heights | 0 + 84 = 84 | .0692 |
| Lilydale | 0 + 139 = 139 | .1146 |
| Mendota Heights | 0 + 200 = 200 | .1649 |
| West St. Paul | 66 + 8 = 74 | .0610 |
| | n = 1213 | 1.0000 |

A relative frequency bar chart is constructed by placing the cities of Dakota County on the horizontal axis and the relative frequencies on the vertical axis.

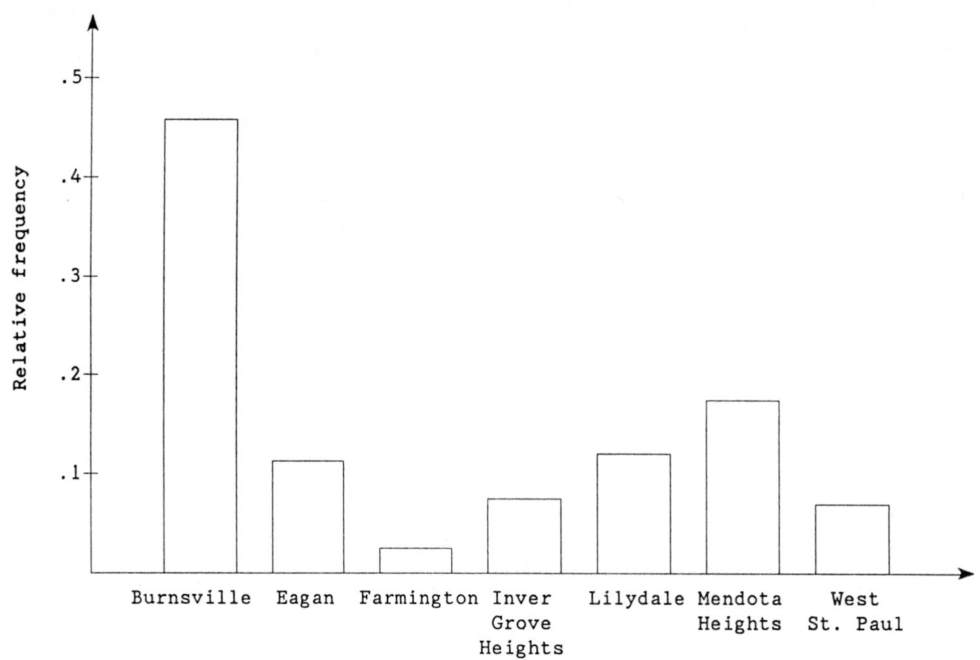


c. By referring the bar charts in part (b):

In Ramsey County, St. Paul had the largest share of the county's condominiums (1275 out of 3723).

In Dakota County, Burnsville had the largest share of the county's condominiums (544 out of 1213).

2.17 a. To construct the relative frequency bar charts, we must first calculate the relative frequencies for barrels added and barrels withdrawn.

| | BARRELS ADDED | | BARRELS WITHDRAWN | |
|---|---|---|---|---|
| COMPANY | Frequency $f_i$ | Relative Frequency $f_i/n$ | Frequency $f_i$ | Relative Frequency $f_i/n$ |
| Exxon | 124 | 124/270 = .46 | 270 | 270/621 = .43 |
| Texaco | 55 | 55/270 = .20 | 127 | 127/621 = .21 |
| Socal | 57 | 57/270 = .21 | 121 | 121/621 = .19 |
| Mobil | 34 | 34/270 = .13 | 103 | 103/621 = .17 |
| | n = 270 | 270/270 = 1.00 | n = 621 | 621/621 = 1.00 |

A relative frequency bar chart is constructed by placing categories along the horizontal axis and relative frequency on the vertical axis.

b.

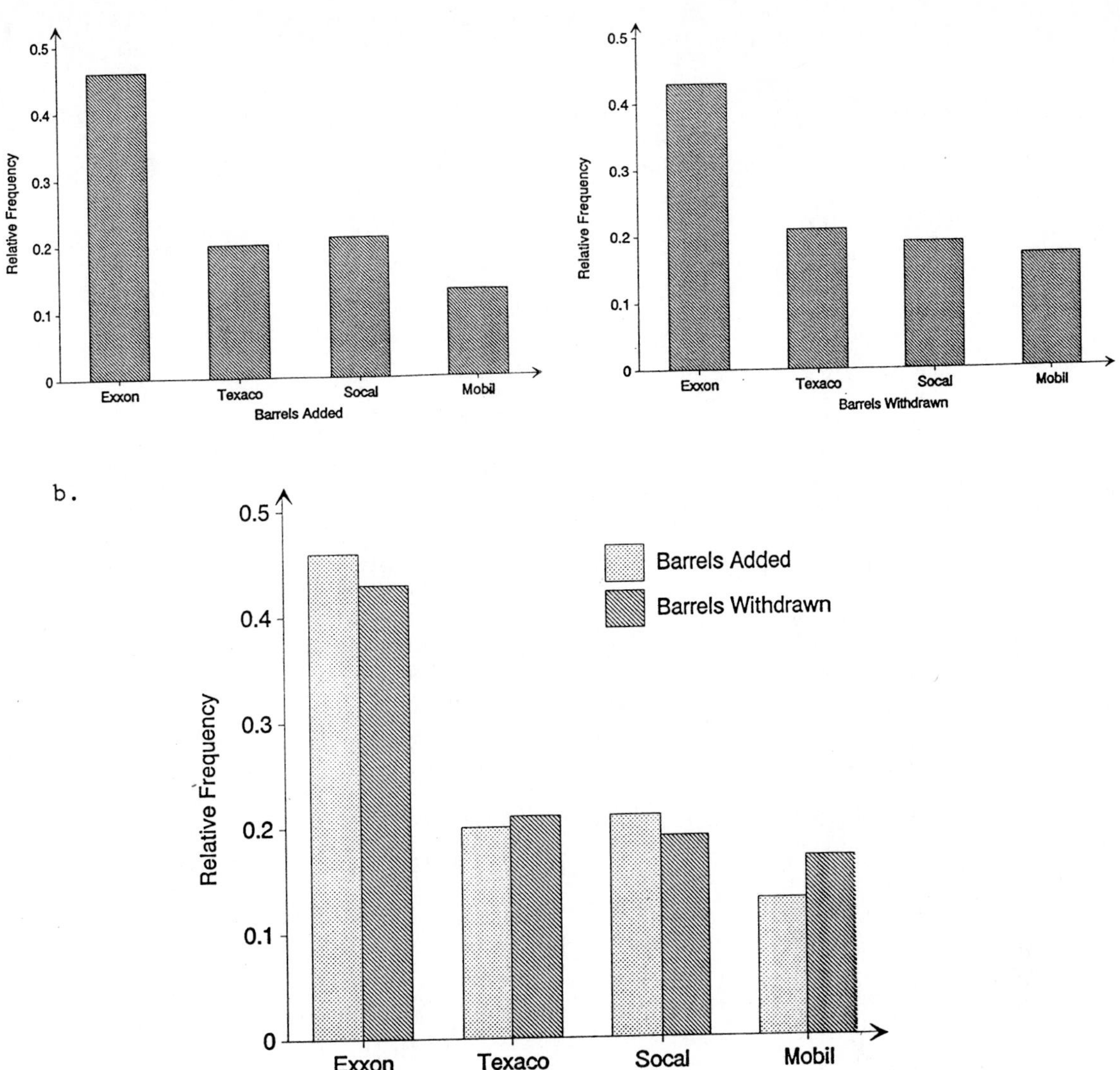


c. The bar charts show you that each company used and found oil with the same relative frequency. However, by looking at the data, you can see that each company withdrew more than double what they found.

2.19 First, find the angle corresponding to each category by multiplying the relative frequency by 360°.

| CATEGORY | RELATIVE FREQUENCY | ANGLE | |
|---|---|---|---|
| 1 | .10 | .10 × 360 = | 36 |
| 2 | .15 | .15 × 360 = | 54 |
| 3 | .40 | .40 × 360 = | 144 |
| 4 | .35 | .35 × 360 = | 126 |
| | | Total | 360 |

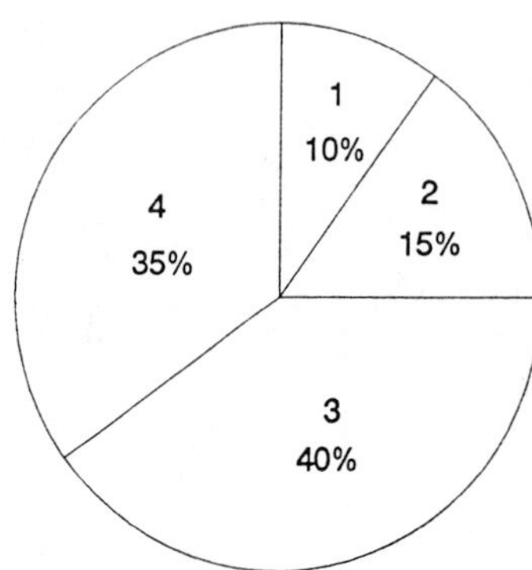


2.21 a. To construct the pie charts, we must calculate the relative frequency and the size of the pie slice for each year.

1960

| LIVING AREA | (Millions) FREQUENCY $f_i$ | RELATIVE FREQUENCY $f_i/n$ | SIZE OF PIE SLICE $(f_i/n) \times 360°$ |
|---|---|---|---|
| Suburbs | 54.9 | .3062 | 110.232° |
| Cities | 58.0 | .3235 | 116.46° |
| Other | 66.4 | .3703 | 133.308° |
| | n = 179.3 | 1.0000 | 360° |

1970

| LIVING AREA | (Millions) FREQUENCY $f_i$ | RELATIVE FREQUENCY $f_i/n$ | SIZE OF PIE SLICE $(f_i/n) \times 360°$ |
|---|---|---|---|
| Suburbs | 75.6 | .372 | 133.92° |
| Cities | 63.8 | .314 | 113.04° |
| Other | 63.8 | .314 | 113.04° |
| | n = 203.2 | 1.000 | 360° |

| LIVING AREA | 1980 (Millions) FREQUENCY $f_i$ | RELATIVE FREQUENCY $f_i/n$ | SIZE OF PIE SLICE $(f_i/n) \times 360°$ |
|---|---|---|---|
| Suburbs | 101.5 | .448 | 161.28° |
| Cities | 67.9 | .300 | 108.00° |
| Other | 57.1 | .252 | 90.72° |
| | n = 226.5 | 1.000 | 360° |

The pie charts are given below.

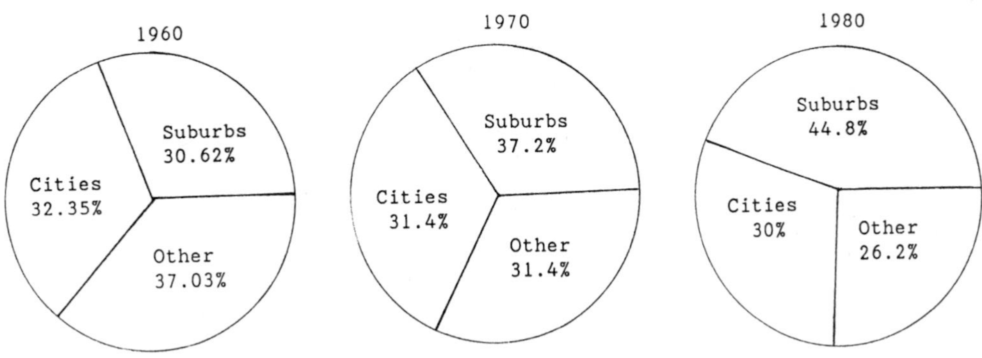


b. The percentage of people living in the cities decreased slightly from 1960 to 1980. The percentage of people living in the suburbs grew considerably (from 30.62% to 44.8%) and the percentage living in other areas decreased considerably over this period.

2.23 a. The pie chart shows where each dollar spent on breakfast cereal goes. The complete circle represents one dollar spent on breakfast cereal while each slice is proportional to the relative frequency of that expense or profit. It also points out that 60¢ of each dollar goes to the manufacturer of the cereal and 40¢ goes to the retailer.

b. The pie chart shows the ingredients cost 8¢ and the packaging 11¢ out of each dollar. Therefore, the package costs more than the cereal.

c. The pie chart gives the cost per $1.00 spent on cereal. Therefore, the 'cents' corresponds to the proportion of money spent on each expense or profit. If a box of cereal costs $1.75, the ingredients would cost $1.75 x .08 = $.14.

2.25 The stem will consist of the digit to the left of the decimal point while the leaf will consist of the digit to the right of the decimal point.

| Stem | Leaf |
|---|---|
| 0 | 8 |
| 1 | 1 6 7 9 |
| 2 | 0 4 5 6 6 8 9 9 |
| 3 | 3 4 5 9 |
| 4 | 1 5 |
| 5 | 0 |

Key: Leaf units are in tenths

2.27 The stem will consist of the left most digit while the leaf will consist of the right most digit.

| Stem | Leaf |
|---|---|
| 0 | 1 1 2 2 3 6 7 8 8 9 |
| 1 | 1 2 4 8 |
| 2 | 0 2 7 |
| 3 | 2 3 |
| 4 | 2 |

Key: Leaf units are in hundredths

2.29 a. The stem will consist of the digits to the left of the one's column, while the leaf will consist of the right most digit.

| Stem | Leaf |
|---|---|
| 3 | 2 3 9 |
| 4 | 3 4 9 9 |
| 5 | 0 0 1 1 4 6 9 |
| 6 | 3 4 4 5 (8) |
| 7 | (1) 3 |
| 8 | 2 (6) |
| 9 | (5) |
| 10 | (2) |

Key: Leaf units are ones

c. Since there were only two customers with delivery times of 68 days or longer that placed additional orders, I would say the maximum tolerable delivery time is about 65 to 67 days. Everyone with delivery times less than 67 days placed additional orders.

2.31 a. For both sets of data, the stem will consist of the digits to the left of the one's column, while the leaf will consist of the right most digit.

NUMBER OF ITEMS ARRIVING AT WORK CENTER PER HOUR

| Stem | Leaf |
|---|---|
| 09 | |
| 10 | |
| 11 | 5 |
| 12 | 9 |
| 13 | 5 8 9 |
| 14 | 0 3 8 8 |
| 15 | 0 1 2 5 6 9 9 |
| 16 | 1 3 6 |
| 17 | 2 5 |

Key: Leaf units are ones

NUMBER OF ITEMS DEPARTING WORK CENTER PER HOUR

| Stem | Leaf |
|---|---|
| 09 | 9 |
| 10 | 6 7 9 |
| 11 | 1 5 9 |
| 12 | 2 3 5 7 7 |
| 13 | 5 5 7 |
| 14 | 0 8 |
| 15 | 2 6 |
| 16 | 1 |
| 17 | 1 |

Key: Leaf units are ones

b. Yes. Most of the numbers of items arriving at the work center per hour are in the 140 to 166 area. Most of the numbers of items departing the work center per hour are in the 110 and 137 area. Thus, more items are arriving than departing.

2.33 a. The stem will consist of the digits to the left of the comma, while the leaf will consist of the right three most digits. We will drop the right two most digits of the leaves.

| Stem | Leaf |
|---|---|
| 33 | 5 |
| 34 | 0 0 |
| 35 | 6 |
| 36 | 3 3 5 6 7 9 |
| 37 | 0 0 1 8 |
| 38 | 0 1 |
| 39 | 0 2 9 |
| 40 | 4 5 8 |
| 41 | 0 2 |
| 42 | 5 8 |
| 43 | 0 3 |
| 44 | |
| 45 | 8 |
| 46 | |
| 47 | |
| 48 | 5 |

Key: Leaf units are hundreds

b. The circles tend to be around numbers that are larger than the numbers that the boxes are around. This implies the MIS students tend to have higher offers them marketing students.

c. Using MINITAB, the stem and leaf display is:

```
Stem-and-leaf of C1          N = 30
Leaf Unit = 1000

  1     3 3
  4     3 445
 14     3 6666667777
 (5)    3 88999
 11     4 00011
  6     4 2233
  2     4 5
  1     4
  1     4  8
```

2.35 The measurement classes, class frequencies, and class relative frequencies for the data are shown in the following table.

| CLASS | MEASUREMENT CLASS | CLASS FREQUENCY | CLASS RELATIVE FREQUENCY |
|---|---|---|---|
| 1 | 8.05 - 9.25 | 3 | 3/30 = .100 |
| 2 | 9.25 - 10.45 | 8 | 8/30 = .267 |
| 3 | 10.45 - 11.65 | 7 | .233 |
| 4 | 11.65 - 12.85 | 6 | .200 |
| 5 | 12.85 - 14.05 | 3 | .100 |
| 6 | 14.05 - 15.25 | 1 | .033 |
| 7 | 15.25 - 16.45 | 1 | .033 |
| 8 | 16.45 - 17.65 | 1 | .033 |
| | | n = 30 | 30/30 = 1.000 |

The relative frequency histogram for this data is shown below.

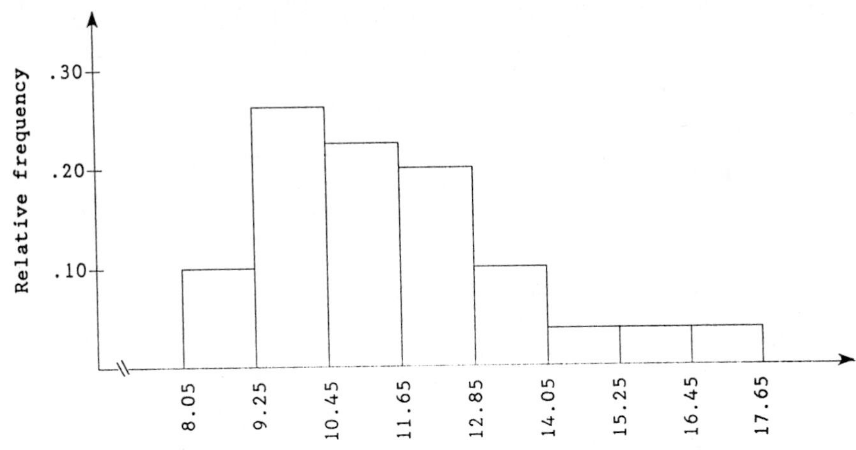


2.37 a. Since there are only 24 observations, 6 measurement classes would be sufficient. (This is just one example of a relative frequency histogram.)

$$\text{The class interval width} = \frac{\text{Largest measurement - Smallest measurement}}{\text{Number of intervals}}$$

$$= \frac{12 - (-5)}{6} = \frac{17}{6} = 2.83$$

Rounding upward, the class width is 3.

The lower boundary for the for the first class is -5.5 (.5 below the smallest measurement).

The measurement classes, class frequencies, and class relative frequencies for the data are shown in the following table.

| CLASS | MEASUREMENT CLASS | CLASS FREQUENCY | CLASS RELATIVE FREQUENCY |
|---|---|---|---|
| 1 | -5.5 - -2.5 | 2 | 2/24 = .08 |
| 2 | -2.5 - 0.5 | 6 | .25 |
| 3 | 0.5 - 3.5 | 5 | .21 |
| 4 | 3.5 - 6.5 | 8 | .33 |
| 5 | 6.5 - 9.5 | 2 | .08 |
| 6 | 9.5 - 12.5 | 1 | .04 |
| | | n = 24 | .99 |

The relative frequency histogram for this data is shown below.

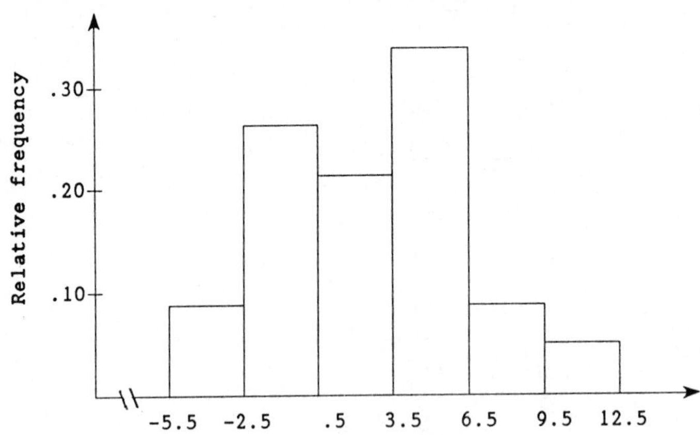


b. We could summarize these 24 predictions by computing the average, the range, the maximum number, the minimum number, etc.

2.39 a. There are 20 observations, so we will select 5 measurement classes. The class interval width

$$= \frac{\text{Largest measurement - Smallest measurement}}{\text{Number of intervals}}$$

$$= \frac{28 - 6}{5} = 4.4 \approx 5$$

The lower boundary for the first class is 5.5 (.5 below the smallest measurement). The measurement classes, class frequencies, and class relative frequencies for the data are shown in the following table.

| CLASS | MEASUREMENT CLASS | CLASS FREQUENCY | CLASS RELATIVE FREQUENCY |
|---|---|---|---|
| 1 | 5.5 - 10.5 | 3 | 3/20 = .15 |
| 2 | 10.5 - 15.5 | 10 | .50 |
| 3 | 15.5 - 20.5 | 5 | .25 |
| 4 | 20.5 - 25.5 | 1 | .05 |
| 5 | 25.5 - 30.5 | 1 | .05 |
| | | n = 20 | 1.00 |

The relative frequency histogram for this data is shown below:

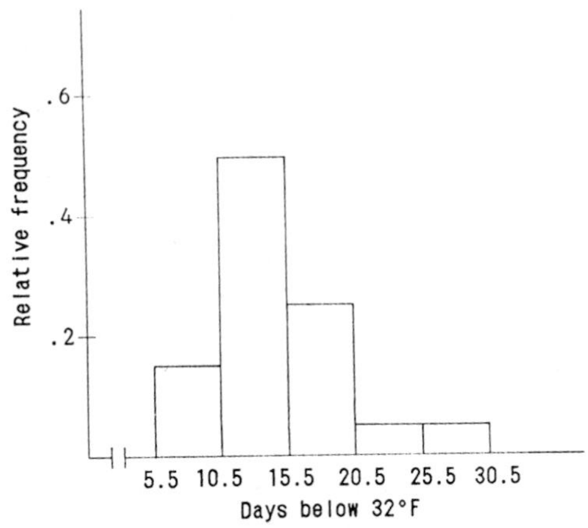


b. From the sample, there are 13 years out of 20 where 15 or fewer days had the temperature fall below 32°F. Thus, we would estimate the proportion of years in which the pots have to be lit 15 days or less with the sample proportion 13/20 = .65.

2.41 b. In all three histograms, most of the observed times were less than 45.5 minutes. There were proportionately more observations in the lower measurement classes in histogram (2) than in histogram (3). This indicates that the time spent when a purchase was made is somewhat shorter than when a purchase is not made.

c. One possible explanation is that when the purchase is made may not be the first time the customer has been in the store. These customers may have come to the store at an earlier date and spent more time with the salesperson.

2.43 The sum of the cumulative relative frequencies over all the measurement classes will be more than 1.0. The cumulative relative frequency for the last measurement class will equal 1.0.

2.45 a. To construct a frequency distribution for this data, we will use 8 measurement classes. (This is one example of a frequency distribution.)

$$\text{The class interval width} = \frac{\text{Largest measurement - Smallest measurement}}{\text{Number of intervals}}$$

$$= \frac{8.3 - 1.0}{8} = \frac{7.3}{8} = .9125$$

Rounding upward, the class width is 1.0.

The lower boundary for the first class is .95 (.05 below the smallest measurement).

The frequency is shown below.

| CLASS | MEASUREMENT CLASS | CLASS FREQUENCY |
|---|---|---|
| 1 | .95 - 1.95 | 8 |
| 2 | 1.95 - 2.95 | 11 |
| 3 | 2.95 - 3.95 | 6 |
| 4 | 3.95 - 4.95 | 5 |
| 5 | 4.95 - 5.95 | 4 |
| 6 | 5.95 - 6.95 | 3 |
| 7 | 6.95 - 7.95 | 2 |
| 8 | 7.95 - 8.95 | 1 |

b. The class cumulative frequency is found by summing the frequency for each class plus the frequencies of all classes above it.

| CLASS | CLASS CUMULATIVE FREQUENCY |
|---|---|
| 1 | 8 |
| 2 | 19 |
| 3 | 25 |
| 4 | 30 |
| 5 | 34 |
| 6 | 37 |
| 7 | 39 |
| 8 | 40 |

c. The class cumulative relative frequency is found by dividing the cumulative frequency by n.

| CLASS | CLASS CUMULATIVE RELATIVE FREQUENCY |
|---|---|
| 1 | .200 |
| 2 | .475 |
| 3 | .625 |
| 4 | .750 |
| 5 | .850 |
| 6 | .925 |
| 7 | .975 |
| 8 | 1.000 |

d. A class frequency tells how many of the observations in the data set fall in the measurement class.

A class cumulative frequency tells how many of the observations in the data set fall below or in the measurement class.

A class cumulative relative frequency tells the proportion of observations in the data set that are below or in the measurement class.

2.47 a. There are 35 observations, so we will select 6 measurement classes. The class interval width

$$= \frac{\text{Largest measurement - Smallest measurement}}{6}$$

$$= \frac{283.8 - 3.8}{6} = 46.667 \approx 47$$

The lower boundary for the first class is 3.75 (.05 below the smallest measurement). The measurement classes and class frequencies are shown in the following table:

| CLASS | MEASUREMENT CLASS | FREQUENCY | CUMULATIVE FREQUENCY | CUMULATIVE RELATIVE FREQUENCY |
|---|---|---|---|---|
| 1 | 3.75 - 50.75 | 16 | 16 | 16/35 = .457 |
| 2 | 50.75 - 97.75 | 7 | 23 | 23/35 = .657 |
| 3 | 97.75 - 144.75 | 7 | 30 | .857 |
| 4 | 144.75 - 191.75 | 1 | 31 | .886 |
| 5 | 191.75 - 238.75 | 3 | 34 | .971 |
| 6 | 238.75 - 285.75 | 1 | 35 | 1.000 |
| | | n = 35 | | |

b. The cumulative frequency is found by summing all frequencies of measurement classes up to and including the class of interest. The cumulative relative frequency is found by dividing the cumulative frequency by n.

c. The cumulative relative frequency histogram is:

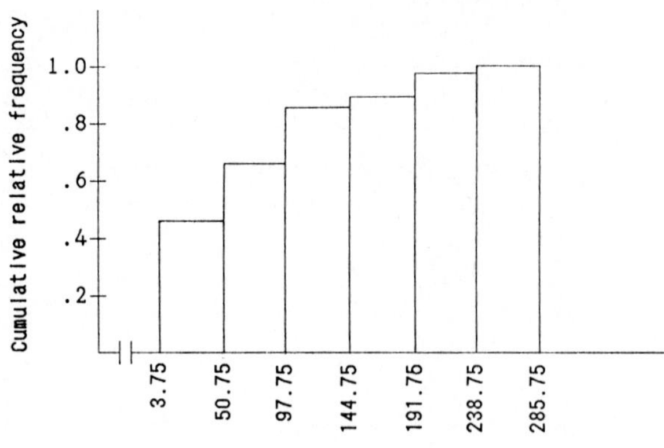


d. From the graph, the proportion of firms that had sales less than or equal to $80 million is between .457 and .657.

The proportion that had sales more than $100 million is between 1 - .857 = .143 and 1 - .657 = .343.

e. From the data, 21 of the 35 or 21/35 = .6 of the firms had sales less than or equal to $80 million.

From the data, 12 of the 35 or 12/35 = .343 of the firms had sales greater than $100 million.

f. Once the data have been put into measurement classes, the exact proportions can no longer be found.

2.49 a. From Exercise 2.38, find the cumulative frequency by adding the frequency of the category to all the frequencies in categories above it. Find the cumulative relative frequency by dividing the cumulative frequency by the total number of observations, n = 25.

| MEASUREMENT CLASS | FREQUENCY | CUMULATIVE FREQUENCY | CUMULATIVE RELATIVE FREQUENCY |
|---|---|---|---|
| 46.5 - 49.5 | 2 | 2 | .08 |
| 49.5 - 52.5 | 2 | 4 | .16 |
| 52.5 - 55.5 | 5 | 9 | .36 |
| 55.5 - 58.5 | 8 | 17 | .68 |
| 58.5 - 61.5 | 5 | 22 | .88 |
| 61.5 - 64.5 | 3 | 25 | 1.00 |
| | n = 25 | | |

The cumulative relative frequency histogram is:

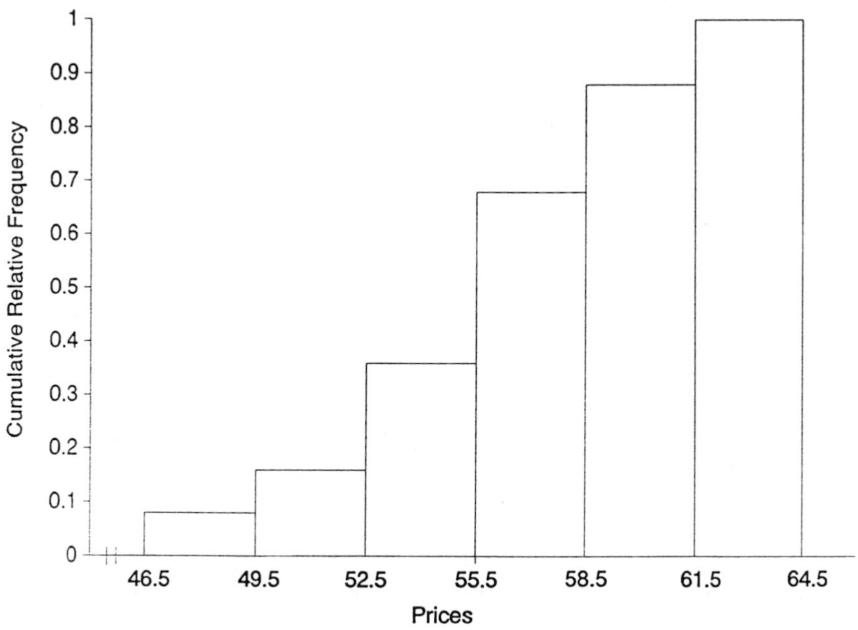


b. From the cumulative relative frequency histogram, 36% of the wellhead prices are less than 55¢. Thus, 100% - 36% = 64% of the wellhead prices exceed 55¢. It is usually easier to make this determination from the cumulative histogram.

2.51 a. Ratio; time is measured on a numerical scale where the zero point has meaning. A time of 20 minutes is four times as long as a time of 5 minutes.

b. Normal; style of music is measured with nonranked categories such as rock, classical, big band, etc.

c. Interval; arrival time is measured on a numerical scale where the zero point has no meaning. An arrival time of 5:00 p.m. is not twice as long as an arrival time of 2:30 p.m.

d. Ordinal; a rating is measured on a nonnumerical scale that can be ranked. Good is better than fair, and fair is better than poor.

e. (a) Quantitative; time is measured on a numerical scale.

(b) Qualitative; style is measured on a nonnumerical scale.

(c) Quantitative; arrival time is measured on a numerical scale.

(d) Qualitative; rating is measured on a nonnumerical scale.

2.53. In Exercise 2.52, we found the relative frequency by dividing the percent by 100%. To form a pie chart, we must find the angle associated with each category by multiplying 360° by the relative frequency.

| LEVEL OF EDUCATION | PERCENT | RELATIVE FREQUENCY | ANGLE |
|---|---|---|---|
| High school or less | 4.5 | .045 | .045 × 360 = 16.2 |
| Attended college | 9.3 | .093 | .093 × 360 = 33.5 |
| College graduate | 27.9 | .279 | .279 × 360 = 100.4 |
| Postgraduate study | 18.6 | .186 | .186 × 360 = 67.0 |
| Master's degree | 24.2 | .242 | .242 × 360 = 87.1 |
| Doctorate | 15.5 | .155 | .155 × 360 = 55.8 |

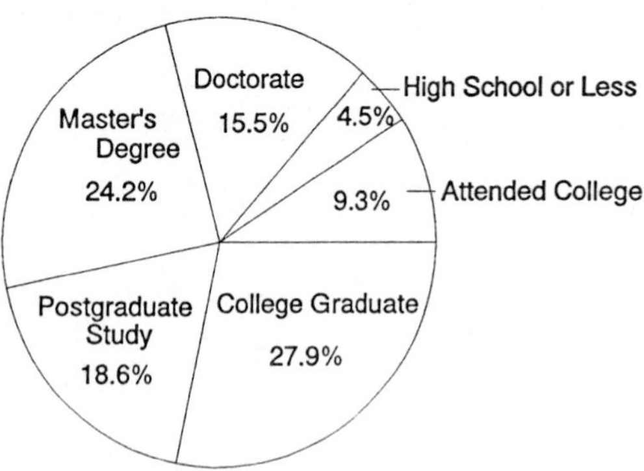


2.55 a. One reason the plot may be interpreted differently is that no scale is given on the vertical axis. Also, since the plot almost reaches the horizontal axis at 3 years, it is obvious that the bottom of the plot has been cut off. Another important factor omitted is who responded to the survey.

b. A scale should be added to the vertical axis. Also, that scale should start at 0.

2.57 We will construct six measurement classes for the data on the length of golf tees.

$$\text{The class interval width} = \frac{\text{Largest measurement - Smallest measurement}}{\text{Number of intervals}}$$

$$\frac{1.57 - 1.47}{6} = \frac{.10}{6} = .0167$$

Rounding upward, the class width is .02.

The boundary for the first class is 1.465 (.005 below the smallest measurement).

The measurement classes, class frequencies, and class relative frequencies for the data are shown in the following table.

| CLASS | MEASUREMENT CLASS | CLASS FREQUENCY | CLASS RELATIVE FREQUENCY |
|---|---|---|---|
| 1 | 1.465 - 1.485 | 3 | 3/30 = .100 |
| 2 | 1.485 - 1.505 | 10 | 10/30 = .333 |
| 3 | 1.505 - 1.525 | 10 | .333 |
| 4 | 1.525 - 1.545 | 4 | .133 |
| 5 | 1.545 - 1.565 | 2 | .067 |
| 6 | 1.565 - 1.585 | 1 | .033 |
| | | n = 30 | 1.000 |

The relative frequency histogram describing the length of the golf tees is shown below.

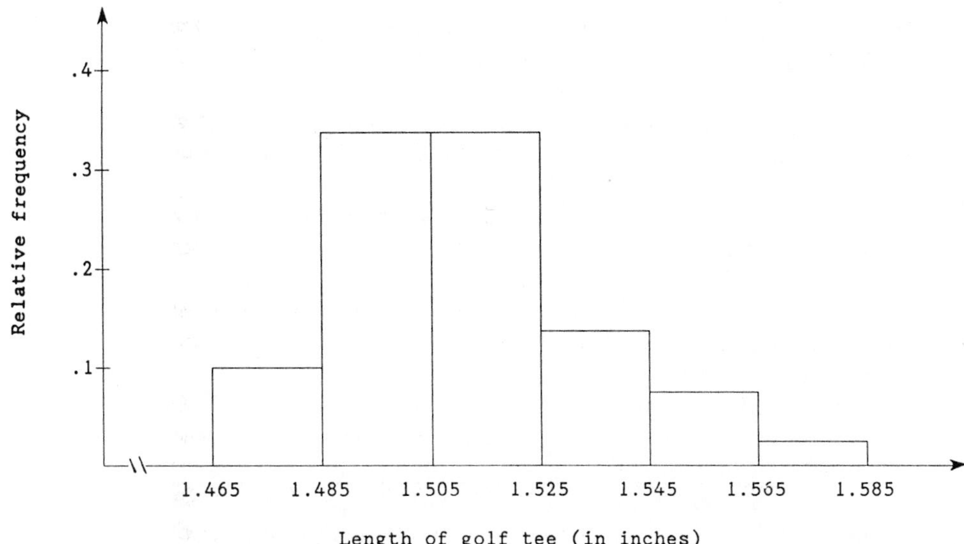


2.59 a. Both the height and width of the bars (peanuts) change. Thus, some readers may tend to equate the *area of the peanuts with the frequency for each year.

b. The frequency bar chart is:

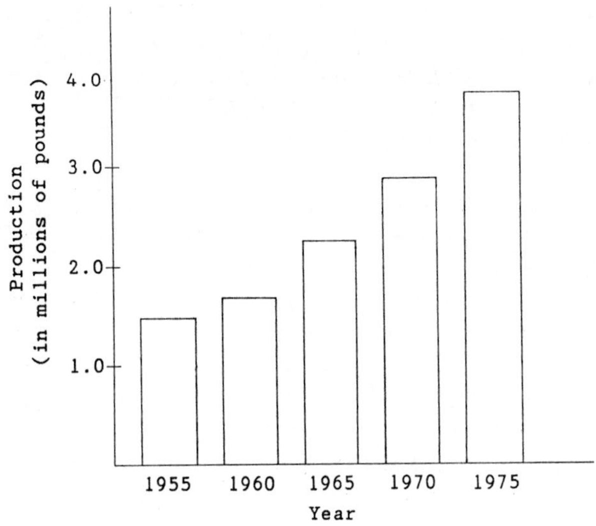


2.61 a. Frequency bar chart.

b. It presents the number of napkins (out of 1000) that fall into each of 4 categories.

c. Of the 1000 napkins printed, 700 were successful. Another way of saying this is 700/1000 x 100% = 70% of the imprints were successful.

2.63 a. Three pie charts are shown for the comparison of 1975, 1983, and 1987 data.

b. The pie charts describe the regional share of Single-Family Housing Starts in the United States. One pie chart is given for 1975, one for 1983, and one for 1987.

c. I would calculate the relative frequency for each region for the three years (separately) by dividing the number of housing starts in the region by the total number of housing starts for that year.

Then I would find the degree measurement for each region by multiplying the relative frequency by 360°.

Then, by using the compass and protractor, I could construct the three pie charts shown.

d. The shift for Single-Family Housing Starts in the United States from 1975 to 1983 has been basically from the Midwest to the South. The other two regions have remained about the same. From 1983 to 1987, the shift has been basically from the South to both the Midwest and Northeast.

2.65 a. To construct a pie chart for the data, calculate the relative frequency and the size of the pie slice for each response.

| RESPONSE | PERCENTAGE OF SAMPLE | RELATIVE FREQUENCY | SIZE OF PIE SLICE |
|---|---|---|---|
| Assigns real value | 32% | .32 | .33 x 360 = 115.2° |
| Undervalues | 60% | .60 | 216° |
| Overvalues | 2% | .02 | 7.2° |
| Not sure | 6% | .06 | 21.6° |
| | | 1.00 | 360° |

The pie chart for the responses is shown below.

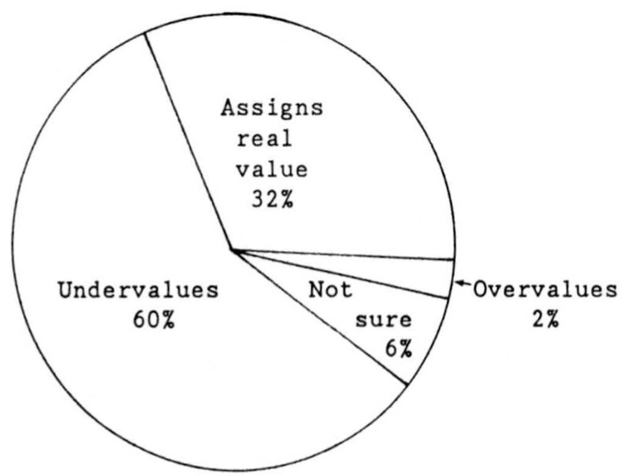


b. To construct a frequency bar chart for the data, calculate the frequency for each response when n = 700, by multiplying the relative frequency by n.

| RESPONSE | RELATIVE FREQUENCY | FREQUENCY |
|---|---|---|
| Assigns real value | .32 | .32 x 700 = 224 |
| Undervalues | .60 | 420 |
| Overvalues | .02 | 14 |
| Not sure | .06 | 42 |
| | 1.00 | n = 700 |

The frequency bar chart for the responses is shown below.

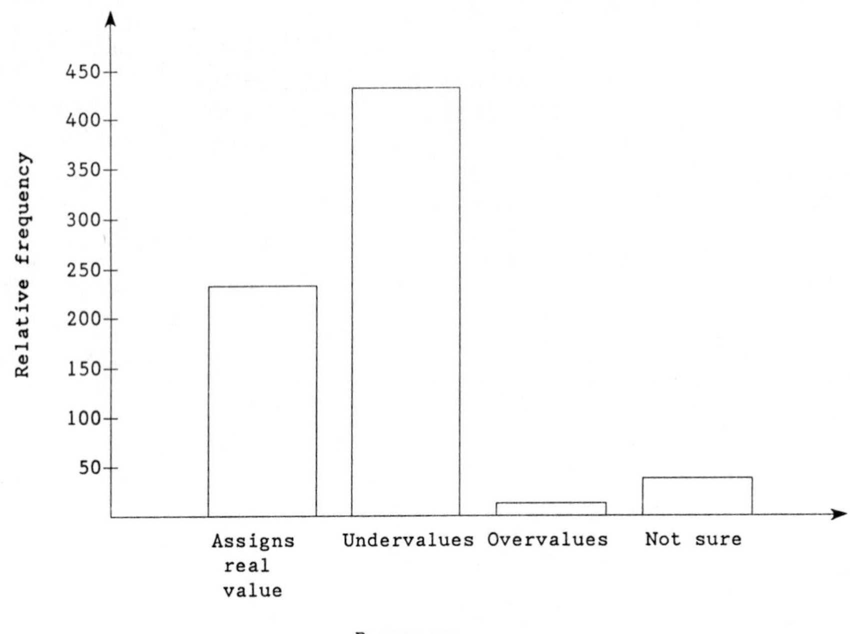


2.67 First, calculate the total processing time for the individual price quotes in Exercise 2.66 by summing the processing times for the marketing, the engineering and the accounting departments.

| REQUEST NUMBER | TOTAL PROCESSING TIME | REQUEST NUMBER | TOTAL PROCESSING TIME |
|---|---|---|---|
| 1 | 13.3 | 26 | 3.3 |
| 2 | 5.7 | 27 | 8.0 |
| 3 | 7.6 | 28 | 6.9 |
| 4 | 20.0 | 29 | 17.2 |
| 5 | 6.1 | 30 | 10.2 |
| 6 | 1.8 | 31 | 16.0 |
| 7 | 13.5 | 32 | 9.5 |
| 8 | 13.0 | 33 | 23.4 |
| 9 | 15.6 | 34 | 14.2 |
| 10 | 10.9 | 35 | 14.3 |
| 11 | 8.7 | 36 | 24.0 |
| 12 | 14.9 | 37 | 6.1 |
| 13 | 3.4 | 38 | 7.4 |
| 14 | 13.6 | 39 | 17.7 |
| 15 | 14.6 | 40 | 15.4 |
| 16 | 14.4 | 41 | 16.4 |
| 17 | 19.4 | 42 | 9.5 |
| 18 | 4.7 | 43 | 8.1 |
| 19 | 9.4 | 44 | 18.2 |
| 20 | 30.2 | 45 | 15.3 |
| 21 | 14.9 | 46 | 13.9 |
| 22 | 10.7 | 47 | 19.9 |
| 23 | 36.2 | 48 | 15.4 |
| 24 | 6.5 | 49 | 24.3 |
| 25 | 10.4 | 50 | 19.0 |

We will construct 8 measurement classes for the data on the total processing time (in days).

$$\text{The class interval width} = \frac{\text{Largest measurement - Smallest measurement}}{\text{Number of intervals}}$$

$$= \frac{36.2 - 1.8}{8} = \frac{34.4}{8} = 4.3$$

Rounding upward, the class width is 4.4.

The lower boundary of the first class is 1.75 (.05 below the smallest measurement).

The measurement classes, class frequencies, and class cumulative frequencies for the total processing time are shown in the following table:

| CLASS | MEASUREMENT CLASS | CLASS FREQUENCY | CLASS CUMULATIVE FREQUENCY |
|---|---|---|---|
| 1 | 1.75 - 6.15 | 7 | 7 |
| 2 | 6.15 - 10.55 | 12 | 19 |
| 3 | 10.55 - 14.95 | 13 | 32 |
| 4 | 14.95 - 19.35 | 10 | 42 |
| 5 | 19.35 - 23.75 | 4 | 46 |
| 6 | 23.75 - 28.15 | 2 | 48 |
| 7 | 28.15 - 32.55 | 1 | 49 |
| 8 | 32.55 - 36.95 | 1 | 50 |

A cumulative frequency distribution answers the question: How many measurements fall in or below class i?

2.69 Pareto Analysis involves the categorization of items and the determination of which categories contain the most observations. These are the "vital few" categories. Pareto analysis is used in industry today as a problem identification tool. Managers and workers use it to identify the most important problems or causes of problems that plague them. Knowledge of the "vital few" problems permits management to prioritize and focus their problem-solving efforts.

2.71 In the United Kingdom, conglomerates have increased in each period, from 5% to 9% to 11% to 17%. Companies that have diversified either horizontally or vertically increased from 1950 to 1970 (from 20% to 28% to 49%), and then dropped slightly in 1980 (48%). Companies with a dominant business activity that accounts for more than 70% of revenues stayed relatively the same from 1950 to 1960 (40% to 43%), dropped in 1970, and held relatively the same from 1950 to 1960 (40% to 43%), dropped in 1970, and held relatively constant in 1980 (29% and 27%). Companies with a single business activity held the highest percentage in 1950 (35%) and then dropped steadily until 1980 (20% to 11% to 8%).

In the United States, conglomerates have increased in each period, from 3% to 5% to 13% to 24%. Companies that have diversified either horizontally or vertically increased from 1950 to 1960 (from 27% to 39%), held relatively constant from 1960 to 1970 (39% to 36%), and then increased again from 1970 to 1980 (36% to 54%). Companies with a dominant business activity that accounts for more than 70% of revenues stayed relatively the same from 1950 to 1970 (44% to 40% to 41%), and then dropped in 1980 to 22%. Companies with a single business activity held the highest percentage in 1950 (28%) and then dropped steadily until 1980 (16% to 10% to 0%).

2.73 a. The time series plot is:

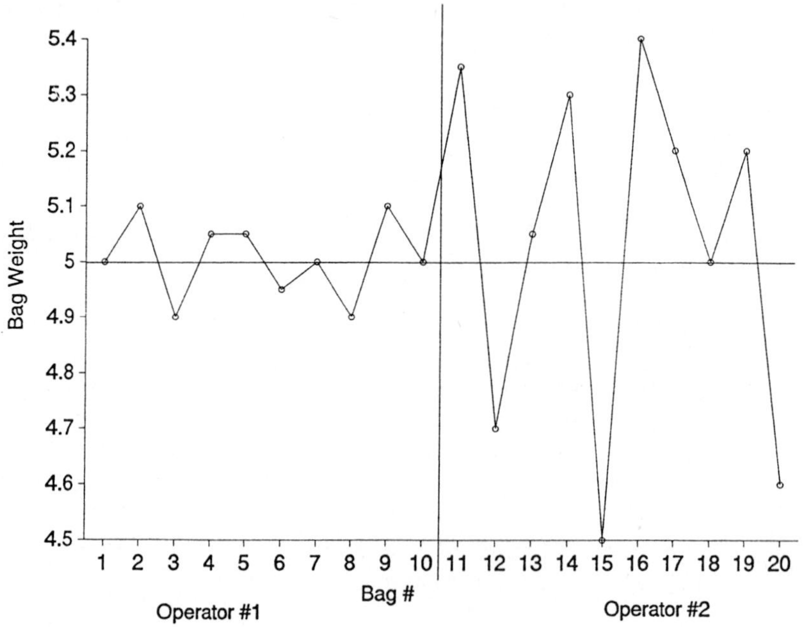


b. From the plot, it is evident that there is more variability in the fill weights of operator #2 than in those of operator #1. The fill weights of operator #2 vary from 4.50 to 5.40 while the fill weights of operator #1 vary from 4.90 to 5.10. However, each operator had only 3 fill weights less than 5 pounds.

c. From the plot, 30% or 6 of the 20 bags were underfilled, while 50% or 10 of the 20 bags were overfilled. Of the bags underfilled, only 3 were underfilled by more than .1 pound. All three of these bags were filled by operator #2. Thus, this could account for the customer complaints.

d. Again, it appears that operator #1 is much more consistent filling the bags than is operator #2. Even though operator #2 tends to underfill bags by more than operator #1, operator #2 also tends to overfill the bags by more than operator #1.

# CHAPTER 3

## NUMERICAL DESCRIPTIVE MEASURES

3.1 Assume the data are a sample. The mode is the observation that occurs most frequently. For this sample, the mode is 15, which occurs 3 times.

The sample mean is:

$$\bar{x} = \frac{\sum_{i=1} x_i}{n} = \frac{18 + 10 + 15 + 13 + 17 + 15 + 12 + 15 + 18 + 16 + 11}{11}$$

$$= \frac{160}{11} = 14.545$$

The median is the middle number when the data are arranged in order. The data arranged in order are: 10, 11, 12, 13, 15, 15, 15, 16, 17, 18, 18. The middle number is the 6th number, which is 15.

3.3 The median is the middle number once the data have been arranged in order. If n is even, there is not a single middle number. Thus, to compute the median, we take the average of the middle two numbers. If n is odd, there is a single middle number. The median is this middle number.

A data set with 5 measurements arranged in order is 1, 3, 5, 6, 8. The median is the middle number, which is 5.

A data set with 6 measurements arranged in order is 1, 3, 5, 5, 6, 8. the median is the average of the middle two numbers which is

$$\frac{5 + 5}{2} = \frac{10}{2} = 5$$

3.5 Quite often when dealing with opinions, guesses, and estimates, there tend to be some very high or very low answers. Since the mean is more sensitive to extreme values, the median would represent a more accurate description of the responses.

3.7 a. We can identify the sample observations using the notation:

$$x_1 = 110, \; x_2 = 90, \; \ldots \; , \; x_{19} = 162$$

Then, the sample mean is

$$\bar{x} = \frac{\sum_{i=1}^{n} x_i}{n} = \frac{110 + 90 + \ldots + 162}{19} = \frac{3420}{19} = 180$$

Since $n = 19$ is odd, the median will be the middle observation ($x_{10}$) when the data are arranged from smallest to largest.

The data arranged from smallest to largest are:

| | |
|---|---|
| 90 | 162 |
| 110 | 176 |
| 110 | 181 |
| 114 | 187 |
| 125 | 200 |
| 129 | 200 |
| 158 | 230 |
| 159 | 274 |
| 162 | 290 |
| | 363 |

The median is 162.

b. Since the median is less than the mean, the data set is skewed to the right.

c. No, the median will not always be an actual value in the data set. When n is odd, it will always be an actual value; but when n is even, we average the two middle values in the data set. If these two values are not the same value, the median will not be an actual value of the data set.

3.9 a. The sample mean is

$$\bar{x} = \frac{\sum_{i=1}^{n} x_i}{n} = \frac{92.5 + 63.3 + \ldots + 69.7}{20} = \frac{1400.2}{20} = 70.01$$

Since $n = 20$ is even, the median is the average of the middle two numbers when the data are arranged from smallest to largest.

The data arranged from smallest to largest are:

| | | | |
|---|---|---|---|
| 63.3 | 64.9 | 69.0 | 74.9 |
| 63.4 | 65.5 | 69.7 | 74.9 |
| 63.9 | 65.7 | 70.6 | 76.8 |
| 64.6 | 67.6 | 70.8 | 76.8 |
| 64.6 | 68.5 | 72.4 | 92.5 |

The median is $\frac{x_{(10)} + x_{(11)}}{2} = \frac{68.5 + 69.0}{2} = \frac{137.5}{2} = 68.75$

The mode is the measurement that occurs with the greatest frequency. In this data set, 64.6 and 76.8 are both modes. (They both occur twice.)

b. The highest price in the data set is 92.5. By eliminating this price from the data set,

$$\text{the sample mean} = \bar{x} = \frac{\sum x}{n} = \frac{1307.7}{19} = 68.83$$

Since n = 19 is odd, the median is the middle number $(x_{(10)})$ when the data are arranged from smallest to largest.

$$\text{The median} = x_{(10)} = 69.0$$

The modes are 64.6 and 76.8.

By dropping the highest value in the data set, the mean and median decreased while the mode did not change.

c. By eliminating the highest two prices (92.5 and 76.8) and the lowest two prices (63.3 and 63.4), the 80% trimmed mean is

$$\bar{x} = \frac{\sum_{i=1}^{n} x_i}{n} = \frac{1104.2}{16} = 69.0125$$

3.11 The mean value per coupon is the total value of the coupons $\left(\sum_{i=1}^{n} x\right)$ divided by the number of coupons redeemed (n).

$$\bar{x} = \frac{\sum_{i=1}^{n} x_i}{n} = \frac{2.24 \text{ billion}}{6.49 \text{ billion}} = 0.35$$

3.13 a. The sample mean is

$$\bar{x} = \frac{\sum_{i=1}^{n} x_i}{n} = \frac{3342}{100} = 33.42$$

Since n = 100 is even, the median is the average of the middle two numbers when the data are arranged from smallest to largest.

The data arranged from smallest to largest are:

| | | | | | | | | | | |
|---|---|---|---|---|---|---|---|---|---|---|
| 1 | 2 | 5 | 6 | 7 | 8 | 8 | 9 | 10 | 10 | 10 |
| 11 | 11 | 12 | 12 | 13 | 15 | 15 | 17 | 18 | 19 | 19 |
| 19 | 19 | 20 | 20 | 20 | 20 | 21 | 21 | 22 | 22 | 23 |
| 24 | 24 | 24 | 24 | 25 | 25 | 25 | 26 | 27 | 27 | 27 |
| 28 | 28 | 28 | 28 | 29 | 29 | 29 | 29 | 30 | 30 | 30 |
| 30 | 30 | 31 | 32 | 32 | 33 | 33 | 33 | 33 | 34 | 34 |
| 35 | 35 | 36 | 36 | 37 | 38 | 39 | 40 | 41 | 42 | 43 |
| 43 | 44 | 44 | 45 | 45 | 48 | 48 | 49 | 52 | 55 | 55 |
| 58 | 58 | 63 | 66 | 70 | 75 | 80 | 88 | 90 | 92 | 110 |
| 126 | | | | | | | | | | |

The median is $\frac{x_{(50)} + x_{(51)}}{2} = \frac{29 + 29}{2} = \frac{58}{2} = 29$

Since the median (29) is less than the mean (33.42), the data are skewed to the right.

b. To construct a frequency histogram, we can use 10 measurement classes.

$$\text{The class interval width} = \frac{\text{Largest measurement} - \text{Smallest measurement}}{\text{Number of intervals}}$$

$$= \frac{126 - 1}{10} = \frac{125}{10} = 12.5$$

Rounding upward, the class width is 13.

The lower boundary of the first measurement class is .5 below the smallest number, or 1 - .5 = .5.

The measurement classes and class frequencies are shown in the following table.

| CLASS | MEASUREMENT CLASS | CLASS FREQUENCY |
|---|---|---|
| 1 | .5 - 13.5 | 16 |
| 2 | 13.5 - 26.5 | 25 |
| 3 | 26.5 - 39.5 | 32 |
| 4 | 39.5 - 52.5 | 13 |
| 5 | 52.5 - 65.5 | 5 |
| 6 | 65.5 - 78.5 | 3 |
| 7 | 78.5 - 91.5 | 3 |
| 8 | 91.5 - 104.5 | 1 |
| 9 | 104.5 - 117.5 | 1 |
| 10 | 117.5 - 130.5 | 1 |
| | | n = 100 |

The frequency histogram for the data set is illustrated below.

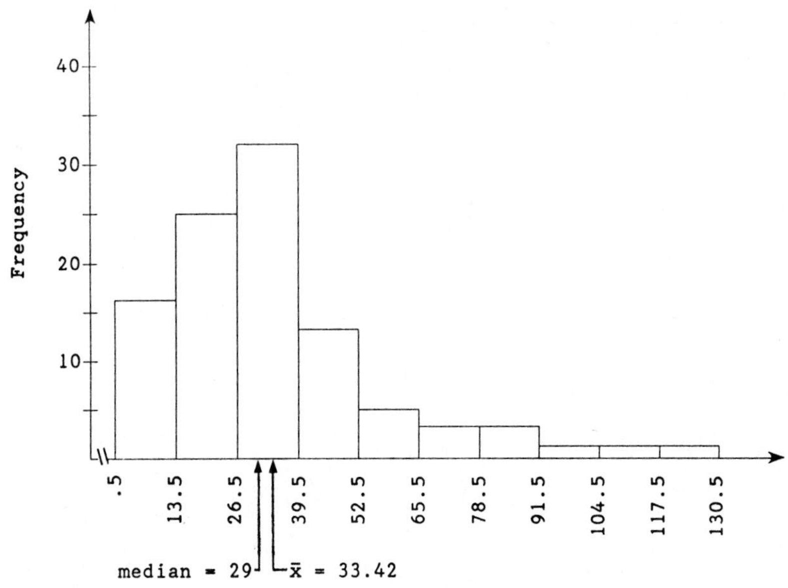


c. If the two total sales figures (\$20 and \$250) were included in the data set, the median would not be affected since one of the values is below the original median and one is above it. Therefore, the median is still 29. The new mean would be

$$\bar{x} = \frac{\sum_{i=1}^{n} x_i}{n} = \frac{3342 + 20 + 250}{102} = \frac{3612}{102} = 35.41$$

The new mean is higher than the original mean since the value \$250 is quite a bit larger than the other sales figures in the data set.

3.15 a. $\sum_{i=1}^{n} x_i = 5 + 9 + 6 + 3 + 7 = 30$

$\sum_{i=1}^{n} x_i^2 = 5^2 + 9^2 + 6^2 + 3^2 + 7^2 = 200$

$\left(\sum_{i=1}^{n} x_i\right)^2 = 30^2 = 900$

b. $\sum_{i=1}^{n} x_i = 3 + 1 + 4 + 3 + 0 + (-2) = 9$

$\sum_{i=1}^{n} x_i^2 = 3^2 + 1^2 + 4^2 + 3^2 + 0^2 + (-2)^2 = 39$

$\left(\sum_{i=1}^{n} x_i\right)^2 = 9^2 = 81$

c. $\sum_{i=1}^{n} x_i = 90 + 12 + 40 + 15 = 157$

$\sum_{i=1}^{n} x_i^2 = 90^2 + 12^2 + 40^2 + 15^2 = 10{,}069$

$\left(\sum_{i=1}^{n} x_i\right)^2 = 157^2 = 24{,}649$

d. $\sum_{i=1}^{n} x_i = -1 + 4 + 1 + 0 + 5 = 9$

$\sum_{i=1}^{n} x_i^2 = (-1)^2 + 4^2 + 1^2 + 0^2 + 5^2 = 43$

$\left(\sum_{i=1}^{n} x_i\right)^2 = 9^2 = 81$

e. $\sum_{i=1}^{n} x_i = 1 + 0 + 0 + 1 + 0 + 10 = 12$

$\sum_{i=1}^{n} x_i^2 = 1^2 + 0^2 + 0^2 + 1^2 + 0^2 + 10^2 = 102$

$\left(\sum_{i=1}^{n} x_i\right)^2 = 12^2 = 144$

3.17 a. $\sum_{i=1}^{n} x_i = 10 + 1 + 0 + 0 + 20 = 31$

$\sum_{i=1}^{n} x_i^2 = 10^2 + 1^2 + 0^2 + 0^2 + 20^2 = 501$

$$\bar{x} = \frac{\sum_{i=1}^{n} x_i}{n} = \frac{31}{5} = 6.2$$

$$s^2 = \frac{\sum_{i=1}^{n} x_i^2 - \frac{\left(\sum_{i=1}^{n} x_i\right)^2}{n}}{n - 1} = \frac{501 - \frac{31^2}{5}}{5 - 1} = \frac{308.8}{4} = 77.2$$

$s = \sqrt{77.2} = 8.786$

b. $\sum_{i=1}^{n} x_i = 5 + 9 + (-1) + 100 = 113$

$\sum_{i=1}^{n} x_i^2 = 5^2 + 9^2 + (-1)^2 + 100^2 = 10,107$

$$\bar{x} = \frac{\sum_{i=1}^{n} x_i}{n} = \frac{113}{4} = 28.25$$

$$s^2 = \frac{\sum_{i=1}^{n} x_i^2 - \frac{\left(\sum_{i=1}^{n} x_i\right)^2}{n}}{n - 1} = \frac{10107 - \frac{113^2}{4}}{4 - 1} = \frac{6914.75}{3} = 2304.92$$

$s = \sqrt{2304.92} = 48.010$

3.19 a. The range, variance, and standard deviation measure the variability of the data set. They give a measure of the spread of the data. The larger the value, the more spread out the data. The range gives you an idea how wide the data set is, the standard deviation tells you approximately how far the values are from the mean, and the variance gives the sum of the squared distances form the mean divided by the number of observations.

b. An advantage of using the range is that it is so easy to compute. A disadvantage is that it only uses the smallest and largest values of the data set. No information is used from the other observations of the data set.

An advantage of the variance is that it does take all of the values of the data set into account. It gives the sum of the squared distances from the mean divided by the number of observations. A disadvantage is that it is expressed in square units. This makes it hard to interpret. It is also harder to calculate than the range.

An advantage of the standard deviation is that it also takes all of the observations into account. It is also expressed in the original units of the problem so that it is easier to interpret than the variance. It gives a measure of the distance the observations are from the mean. A disadvantage is that it is hard to calculate.

3.21 This is one possibility for the two data sets.

Data Set 1: 0, 1, 2, 3, 4, 5, 6, 7, 8, 9

Data Set 2: 0, 0, 1, 1, 2, 2, 3, 3, 9, 9

The two sets of data above have the same range = largest measurement - smallest measurement = 9 - 0 = 9.

The means for the two data sets are:

$$\bar{x}_1 = \frac{\sum_{i=1}^{n} x_i}{n} = \frac{0 + 1 + 2 + 3 + 4 + 5 + 6 + 7 + 8 + 9}{10} = \frac{45}{10} = 4.5$$

$$\bar{x}_2 = \frac{\sum_{i=1}^{n} x_i}{n} = \frac{0 + 0 + 1 + 1 + 2 + 2 + 3 + 3 + 9 + 9}{10} = \frac{30}{10} = 3$$

The dot diagrams for the two data sets are shown below.

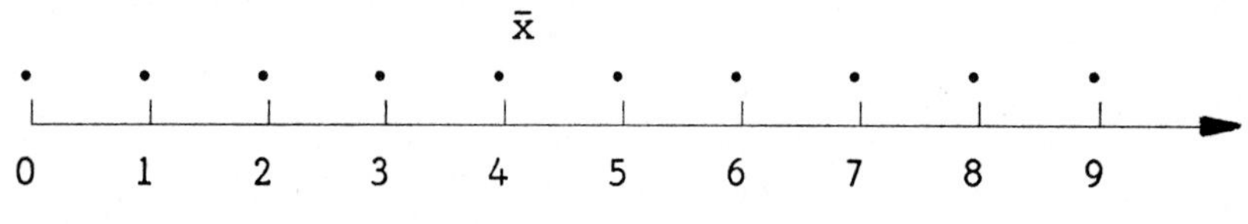


Data Set 1

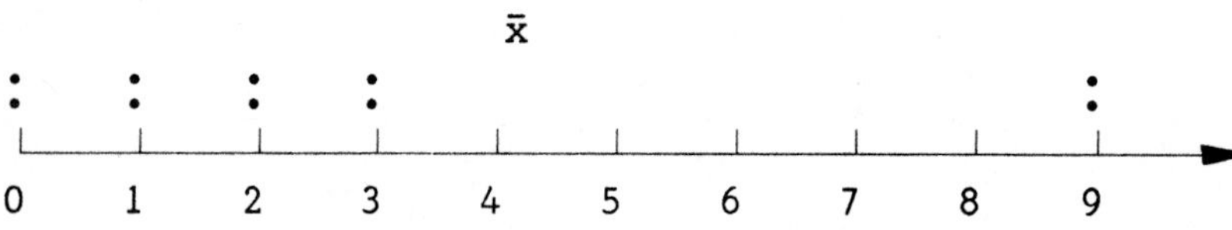


Data Set 2

3.23 a. The mean value for the U.S. City Average Index for the data in the table is

$$\bar{x} = \frac{\sum_{i=1}^{n} x_i}{n} = \frac{2654.6}{21} = 126.4095$$

The mean value for the Chicago Index for the data in the table is

$$\bar{x} = \frac{\sum_{i=1}^{n} x_i}{n} = \frac{2678.4}{21} = 127.5429$$

b. For the U.S. City Average Index, the range = largest measurement - smallest measurement = 132.7 - 121.1 = 11.6.

For the Chicago Index, the range = largest measurement - smallest measurement = 133.8 - 121.5 = 12.3.

c. The standard deviation for the Chicago Index for the data in the table is

$$s = \sqrt{\frac{\sum_{i=1}^{n} x_i^2 - \frac{\left(\sum_{i=1}^{n} x_i\right)^2}{n}}{n - 1}} = \sqrt{\frac{341867.18 - \frac{2678.4^2}{21}}{21 - 1}}$$

$$= \sqrt{12.81957} = 3.5804$$

d. The Chicago Index displays the greater variation about its mean for this time period. This is evident by the larger standard deviation and range for the Chicago Index.

3.25 a. Germany - The range is 7.9 - 6.5 = 1.4
Italy - The range is 26.5 - 21.8 = 4.7
France - The range is 23.2 - 19.1 = 4.1
United Kingdom - The range is 20.1 - 11.3 = 8.8
Belgium - The range is 12.3 - 10.8 = 1.5

b. <u>Germany</u>

$$s^2 = \frac{\sum_{i=1}^{n} x_i^2 - \frac{\left(\sum_{i=1}^{n} x_i\right)^2}{n}}{n - 1} = \frac{157.95 - \frac{21.7^2}{3}}{3 - 1} = .4933$$

$$s = \sqrt{.4933} = .7024$$

Italy

$$s^2 = \frac{\sum_{i=1}^{n} x_i^2 - \frac{\left(\sum_{i=1}^{n} x_i\right)^2}{n}}{n - 1} = \frac{1748.7 - \frac{72.2^2}{3}}{3 - 1} = 5.5433$$

$$s = \sqrt{5.5433} = 2.3544$$

France

$$s^2 = \frac{\sum_{i=1}^{n} x_i^2 - \frac{\left(\sum_{i=1}^{n} x_i\right)^2}{n}}{n - 1} = \frac{1365.8 - \frac{63.8^2}{3}}{3 - 1} = 4.2433$$

$$s = \sqrt{4.2433} = 2.0599$$

United Kingdom

$$s^2 = \frac{\sum_{i=1}^{n} x_i^2 - \frac{\left(\sum_{i=1}^{n} x_i\right)^2}{n}}{n - 1} = \frac{778.19 - \frac{47.1^2}{3}}{3 - 1} = 19.36$$

$$s = \sqrt{19.36} = 4.4$$

Belgium

$$s^2 = \frac{\sum_{i=1}^{n} x_i^2 - \frac{\left(\sum_{i=1}^{n} x_i\right)^2}{n}}{n - 1} = \frac{402.49 - \frac{34.7^2}{3}}{3 - 1} = .5633$$

$$s = \sqrt{.5633} = .7506$$

c. Using the ranges from part (a), the ranks of the countries are:

1. Germany (range = 1.4)
2. Belgium (range = 1.5)
3. France (range = 4.1)
4. Italy (range = 4.7)
5. United Kingdom (range = 8.8)

Using the standard deviations from part (b), the ranks of the countries are:

1. Germany (s = .7024)
2. Belgium (s = .7506)
3. France (s = 2.0599)
4. Italy (s = 2.3544)
5. United Kingdom (s = 4.4)

d. Yes, the two sets of rankings in part (c) are in agreement. But no, the range and standard deviation will not always yield the same rankings. A data set could have a large range due to one extreme value. Another data set could have a slightly smaller range but more values near the extreme, thus having a larger standard deviation.

3.27 Chebyshev's theorem can be applied to any data set. The Empirical Rule applies only to data sets that are mound shaped--that are approximately symmetric, with a clustering of measurements about the midpoint of the distribution and that tail off as one moves away from the center of the distribution.

3.29 a. $\bar{x} = \frac{\sum_{i=1}^{n} x_i}{n} = \frac{1442}{36} = 40.0556$

$$s^2 = \frac{\sum_{i=1}^{n} x_i^2 - \frac{\left(\sum_{i=1}^{n} x_i\right)^2}{n}}{n - 1} = \frac{57926 - \frac{1442^2}{36}}{36 - 1} = 4.7397$$

$s = \sqrt{4.7397} = 2.1771$

b. A visual inspection of the data indicates that more than half of the measurements are 40 or over. The manufacturer would react favorably to this observation. Also, the mean is 40.0556 which is greater than 40.

c. Using Chebyshev's theorem, at least 8/9 of the measurements will fall within 3 standard deviations of the mean. Thus, the range of the data would be around 6 standard deviations. Using the Empirical Rule, approximately 95% of the observations are within 2 standard deviations of the mean. Thus, the range of the data would be around 4 standard deviations. We would expect the standard deviation to be somewhere between Range/6 and Range/4. For our data, Range/6 = (45 - 35)/6 = 1.667 and Range/4 = 10/4 = 2.5. Our computed value of s is 2.1771 which does fall between 1.667 and 2.5.

d. To construct a relative frequency histogram of the data set, we can use 6 measurement classes.

$$\text{The class interval width} = \frac{\text{Largest measurement - Smallest measurement}}{\text{Number of intervals}}$$

$$= \frac{45 - 35}{6} = 1.667$$

Rounding upward, the class width is 2.

The lower class boundary of the first measurement class is .5 below the smallest number or 35 - .5 = 34.5

The measurement classes, class frequencies, and class relative frequencies are shown in the following table.

| CLASS | MEASUREMENT CLASS | CLASS FREQUENCY | CLASS RELATIVE FREQUENCY |
|---|---|---|---|
| 1 | 34.5 - 36.5 | 2 | .056 |
| 2 | 36.5 - 38.5 | 6 | .167 |
| 3 | 38.5 - 40.5 | 13 | .361 |
| 4 | 40.5 - 42.5 | 11 | .306 |
| 5 | 42.5 - 44.5 | 3 | .083 |
| 6 | 44.5 - 46.5 | 1 | .028 |
| | | n = 36 | 36/36 = 1.000 |

The relative frequency histogram for this data set is illustrated below.

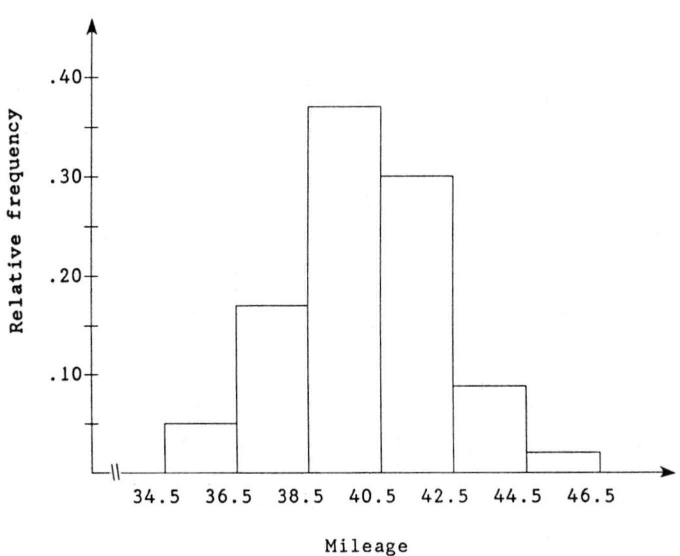


Yes, the data set does look mound-shaped.

e. Since the data set does look mound-shaped, by the Empirical Rule we would expect approximately 68% of the measurements to fall within $\bar{x} \pm s$, 95% within $\bar{x} \pm 2s$, and essentially all or 100% within $\bar{x} \pm 3s$.

f. $\bar{x} \pm s \Rightarrow 40.0556 \pm 2.1771 \Rightarrow (37.8785, 42.2327)$

In this data set, 27/36 x 100 = 75% of the measurements fall within $\bar{x} \pm s$.

$$\bar{x} \pm 2s \Rightarrow 40.0556 - 2(2.1771) \Rightarrow 40.0556 \pm 4.3542 \Rightarrow (35.7014, 44.4098)$$

In this data set, 34/36 x 100 = 94.4% of the measurements fall within $\bar{x} \pm 2s$.

$$\bar{x} \pm 3x \Rightarrow 40.0556 \pm 3(2.1771) \Rightarrow 40.0556 \pm 6.5313 \Rightarrow (33.5243, 46.5869)$$

All of the measurements, 100% of them, fall within $\bar{x} \pm 3s$.

These results compare very well with the Empirical Rule used in part (e).

3.31 a. $$\bar{x} = \frac{\sum_{i=1}^{n} x_i}{n} = \frac{2078}{20} = 103.9$$

b. $$s^2 = \frac{\sum_{i=1}^{n} x_i^2 - \frac{\left(\sum_{i=1}^{n} x_i\right)^2}{n}}{n - 1} = \frac{451432 - \frac{2078^2}{20}}{20 - 1} = \frac{235527.8}{19} = 12,396.2$$

$s = \sqrt{12396.2} = 111.3$

c. Using Chebyshev's theorem, at least 8/9 of the measurements will fall within 3 standard deviations of the mean. Thus, the range of the data would be around 6 standard deviations. Using the Empirical Rule, approximately 95% of the observations are within 2 standard deviations of the mean. Thus, the range of the data would be around 4 standard deviations. We would expect the standard deviation to be somewhere between Range/6 and Range/4. For our data, Range/6 = (400 - 0)/6 = 66.67 and Range/4 = 400/4 = 100. Our computed value of s is 111.3. This is close to the above estimates. It is not in between them as would be expected since the data are not mound-shaped.

d. According to Chebyshev's theorem:

It is possible that none of the measurements will fall within the interval $\bar{x} \pm s$. Therefore, at most 100% will fall outside the interval $\bar{x} \pm s$.

At least 3/4 of the measurements will fall within $\bar{x} \pm 2s$. Therefore, at most $1/4 \times 100\% = 25\%$ will fall outside the interval $\bar{x} \pm 2s$.

At least 8/9 of the measurements will fall within $\bar{x} \pm 3s$. Therefore, at most $1/9 \times 100\% = 11.1\%$ will fall outside the interval $\bar{x} \pm 3s$.

e. $\bar{x} \pm s \Rightarrow 103.9 \pm 111.3 \Rightarrow (-7.4, 215.2)$

In this data set, $3/20 \times 100\% = 15\%$ of the measurements fall outside $\bar{x} \pm s$.

$$\bar{x} \pm 2s \Rightarrow 103.9 \pm 2(111.3) \Rightarrow 103.9 \pm 222.6 \Rightarrow (-118.7, 326.5)$$

In this data set, $1/20 \times 100\% = 5\%$ of the measurements fall outside $\bar{x} \pm 2s$.

$$\bar{x} \pm 3s \Rightarrow 103.9 \pm 3(111.3) \Rightarrow 103.9 \pm 333.9 \Rightarrow (-230, 437.8)$$

In this data set, none of the measurements (0%) fall outside $\bar{x} \pm 3s$.

These results seem to be comparable with the results of part (d).

3.33 a. To decide if Chebyshev's theorem or the Empirical Rule is more appropriate, we need to know if the sample has a mound-shaped distribution.

To construct a relative frequency histogram for the data set, we will use 7 measurement classes.

$$\text{The class interval width} = \frac{\text{Largest measurement - Smallest measurement}}{\text{Number of intervals}}$$

$$= \frac{290{,}000 - 65{,}000}{7} = 32142.857$$

Rounding upward, the class width is 32150.

The measurement classes, class frequencies, and class relative frequencies are shown in the following table.

| CLASS | MEASUREMENT CLASS | CLASS FREQUENCY | CLASS RELATIVE FREQUENCY |
|---|---|---|---|
| 1 | 64,999 - 97,149 | 26 | .722 |
| 2 | 97,149 - 129,299 | 5 | .139 |
| 3 | 129,299 - 161,449 | 1 | .028 |
| 4 | 161,449 - 193,599 | 3 | .083 |
| 5 | 193,599 - 225,749 | 0 | .000 |
| 6 | 225,749 - 257,899 | 0 | .000 |
| 7 | 257,899 - 290,049 | 1 | .028 |
| | | n = 36 | 1.000 |

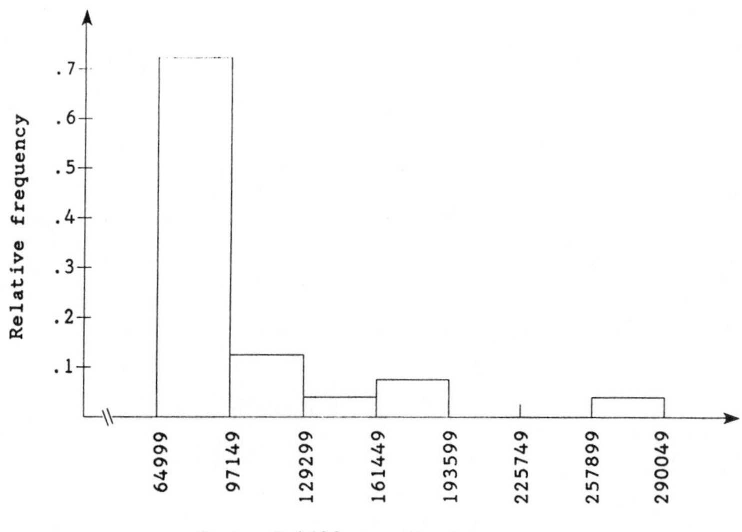


The relative frequency histogram above is not mound-shaped. Therefore, Chebyshev's theorem would be more appropriate.

b. The average price of a 1600 square-foot home in a desirable neighborhood is $96,732. The standard deviation is $45,322. At least 3/4 of all 1600 square-foot homes in desirable neighborhoods will be priced between $96,732 ± 2(45.322) or $6,088 and $187,376.

c. $\bar{x} \pm 2s \Rightarrow 96{,}731.94 \pm 2(45{,}322.18) \Rightarrow (6{,}087.58,\ 187{,}376.30)$

Using Chebyshev's theorem, we would expect at least $1 - \frac{1}{2^2} = .75$ of the sale prices to fall within this interval. For this data set, $\frac{34}{36} = .944$ of the sales prices actually fall in the interval. This is at least .75.

$\bar{x} \pm 3s \Rightarrow 96{,}731.94 \pm 3(45{,}322.18) \Rightarrow (-39{,}234.60,\ 232{,}698.48)$

Using Chebyshev's theorem, we would expect at least $1 - \frac{1}{3^2} = .889$ of the sale prices to fall within this interval. Thus, at most $1 - .889 = .111$ of the sale prices will fall outside this interval. For this data set, $\frac{1}{36} = .028$ of the sale prices actually fall outside the interval. This is at most .111.

d. The sale price of a home in Darien, Connecticut, is \$290,000. The number of standard deviations \$290,000 is from the mean is

$$\frac{\$290{,}000 - 96731.94}{45322.18} = 4.26$$

3.35 Since the distribution is approximately mound-shaped, we can use the Empirical Rule.

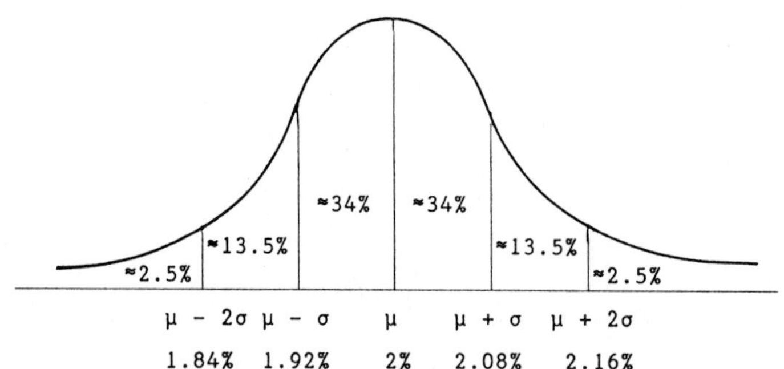


Percentage of zinc phosphide

As illustrated in the figure above, approximately 2.5% will contain less than 1.84% zinc phosphide. Therefore, the approximate probability is .025.

3.37 Since $\bar{x} = 385$ and $s = 15$,

$\bar{x} \pm 3s \Rightarrow 385 \pm 3(15) \Rightarrow 385 \pm 45 \Rightarrow (340, 430)$

According to Chebyshev's theorem, at least $1 - \frac{1}{3^2} = \frac{8}{9}$ or .889 of the days the number of vehicles on the road falls within this interval.

3.39 $\bar{x} = 125$, $s = 15$

a. $\bar{x} \pm 3s \Rightarrow 125 \pm 3(15) \Rightarrow 125 \pm 45 \Rightarrow (80, 170)$

Since nothing is known about the distribution of utility bills, we need to apply Chebyshev's Theorem. According to Chebyshev's theorem, the fraction of all three-bedroom homes with gas or electric energy that have bills within this interval is at least

$$1 - \frac{1}{3^2} = \frac{8}{9}$$

b. If it is reasonable to assume the distribution of utility bills is mound-shaped, we can apply the Empirical Rule.

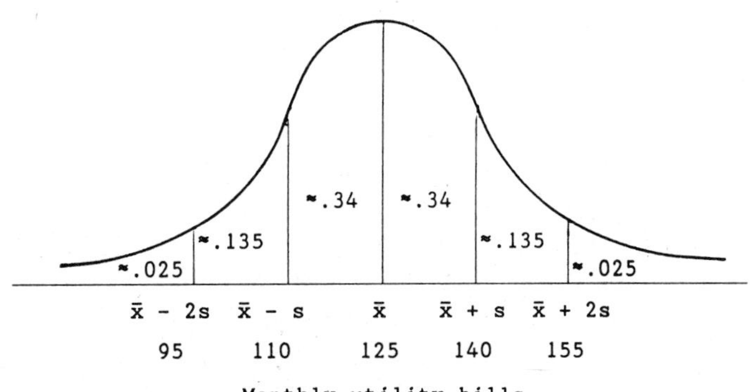


As illustrated in the figure above, approximately .135 + .025 = .16 of three-bedroom homes would have monthly bills less than $110.

c. Yes, these three values do suggest that solar energy units might result in lower utility bills. This is evident since if the solar energy units do not decrease the utility bills, only approximately .025 of the utility bills would be under $95. But all three of the sampled bills from houses with solar energy units were under $95.

3.41 Since we do not know if the distribution of the heights of the trees is mound-shaped, we need to apply Chebyshev's theorem. We know $\mu = 30$ and $\sigma = 3$. Therefore,

$$\mu \pm 3\sigma \Rightarrow 30 \pm 3(3) \Rightarrow 30 \pm 9 \Rightarrow (21, 39)$$

According to Chebyshev's theorem, at least $1 - \frac{1}{3^2} = \frac{8}{9}$ or .89 of the tree heights on this piece of land fall within this interval. However, the buyer will only purchase the land if at least $\frac{1000}{5000}$ or .20 of the tree heights are at least 40 feet tall. Therefore, the buyer should not buy the piece of land.

3.43 a. Since we know $\bar{x}$ and s, the sample z-score is

$$z = \frac{x - \bar{x}}{s} = \frac{31 - 24}{7} = \frac{7}{7} = 1$$

b. Since we know $\bar{x}$ and s, the sample z-score is

$$z = \frac{x - \bar{x}}{s} = \frac{95 - 101}{4} = \frac{-6}{4} = -1.5$$

c. Since we know μ and σ, the population z-score is

$$z = \frac{x - \mu}{\sigma} = \frac{5 - 2}{1.7} = \frac{3}{1.7} = 1.765$$

d. Since we know μ and σ, the population z-score is

$$z = \frac{x - \mu}{\sigma} = \frac{14 - 17}{5} = \frac{-3}{5} = -.6$$

3.45 a. From the problem, $\mu = 2.7$ and $\sigma = .5$

$$z = \frac{x - \mu}{\sigma} \Rightarrow z\sigma = x - \mu \Rightarrow x = \mu + z\sigma$$

For $z = 2.0$, $x = 2.7 + 2.0(.5) = 3.7$

For $z = -1.0$, $x = 2.7 - 1.0(.5) = 2.2$

For $z = .5$, $x = 2.7 + .5(.5) = 2.95$

For $z = -2.5$, $x = 2.7 - 2.5(.5) = 1.45$

b. For $z = -1.6$, $x = 2.7 - 1.6(.5) = 1.9$

c. If we assume the distribution of GPAs is approximately mound shaped, we can use the Empirical Rule.

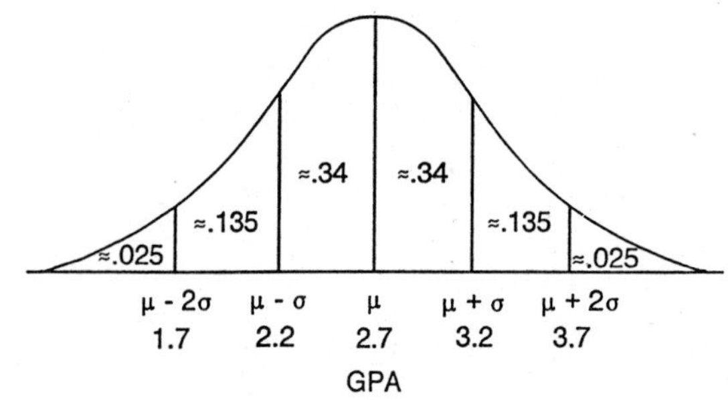


From the Empirical Rule, we know that ≈.025 or ≈2.5% of the students will have GPAs above 3.7 (with $z = 2$). Thus, the GPA corresponding to summa cum laude (top 2.5%) will be greater than 3.7 ($z > 2$).

We know that ≈.16 or 16% of the students will have GPAs above 3.2 ($z = 1$). Thus, the limit on GPAs for cum laude (top 16%) will be greater than 3.2 ($z > 1$).

We must assume the distribution is mound shaped.

3.47 a. To calculate the U.S. merchandise trade balance for each of the ten countries, take the exports minus imports.

| COUNTRY | U.S. MERCHANDISE TRADE BALANCE (in billions) |
|---|---|
| Brazil | -3.825 |
| Egypt | 1.745 |
| France | -2.787 |
| Italy | -5.510 |
| Japan | -56.326 |
| Mexico | -5.689 |
| Panama | 0.387 |
| Soviet Union | 1.055 |
| Sweden | -2.864 |
| Turkey | 0.622 |

b. To find the z-scores, we must first calculate the sample mean and standard deviation.

$$\bar{x} = \frac{\sum_{i=1}^{n} x_i}{n} = \frac{-73.152}{10} = -7.3152$$

$$s^2 = \frac{\sum_{i=1}^{n} x_i^2 - \frac{\left(\sum_{i=1}^{n} x_i\right)^2}{n}}{n - 1} = \frac{3270.68965 - \frac{(-73.152)^2}{10}}{10 - 1} = \frac{2735.56814}{9}$$

$$= 303.952$$

$$s = \sqrt{303.952} = 17.4342$$

Japan: $z = \frac{x - \bar{x}}{s} = \frac{-56.326 - (-7.3152)}{17.4342} = -2.81$

The relative position of the U.S. trade balance with Japan is 2.81 standard deviations below the mean. This indicates that this measurement is small compared to the other U.S. trade balances.

Soviet Union: $z = \frac{x - \bar{x}}{s} = \frac{1.055 - (-7.3152)}{17.4342} = .48$

The relative position of the U.S. trade balance with the Soviet Union is .48 standard deviation above the mean. This indicates that this measurement is larger than the average of the U.S. trade balances.

3.49 In 1989, Control Data Corporation ranked 153 out of 500. Therefore, (500 - 153)/500 x 100% = 69.4% of the corporations were ranked below Control Data Corporation. Control Data Corporation was at the $69.4^{th}$ percentile. In 1984, Control Data Corporation ranked 71 out of 500. Thus, (500 - 71)/500 x 100% = 85.8% of the corporations were ranked below Control Data Corporation. Control Data Corporation was at the 85.8th percentile.

In 1981, Control Data Corporation ranked 144 out of 500. Therefore, (500 - 144)/500 x 100 = 71.2% of the corporations were ranked below Control Data Corporation. Control Data Corporation was at the $71.2^{th}$ percentile.

3.51 a. From the Empirical Rule, we know that approximately 68% of the measurements will fall within $\bar{x} \pm s$, 95% within $\bar{x} \pm 2s$, and almost all within $\bar{x} \pm 3s$.

Since $\bar{x} = 35$ and $s = \sqrt{9} = 3$,

$\bar{x} \pm s \Rightarrow 35 \pm 3 \Rightarrow (32, 38)$

Therefore, approximately 68% of the measurements should fall between 32 and 38.

$\bar{x} \pm 3s \Rightarrow 35 \pm 3(3) \Rightarrow 35 \pm 9 \Rightarrow (26, 34)$

Therefore, almost all (100%) of the measurements should fall between 26 and 44.

b. $z = \frac{x - \bar{x}}{s}$

$-1.33 = \frac{x - 35}{3}$

$-3.99 = x - 35$

$31.01 = x$ due to rounding

The store sold 31 VCRs.

c. We will calculate the z-score for x = 41 for both stores.

Large department store:

$$z = \frac{x - \bar{x}}{s} = \frac{41 - 35}{3} = \frac{6}{3} = 2$$

Rival department store:

$$z = \frac{x - \bar{x}}{s} = \frac{41 - 35}{2} = \frac{6}{2} = 3$$

The store with the lowest z-score is more likely to sell more than 41 VCRs. Thus, the first store is more likely to sell 41 or more VCRs.

3.53 a. When the income x is \$190,

$$z = \frac{x - \mu}{\sigma} = \frac{190 - 170}{10} = 2$$

Using Chebyshev's theorem, at least 3/4 of the incomes fall within 2 standard deviations of the mean. Therefore, at most 1/4 x 100% = 25% of the employees should expect an income over \$190 per week.

When x = 160,

$$z = \frac{x - \mu}{\sigma} = \frac{160 - 170}{10} = -1$$

Using Chebyshev's theorem, it is possible that none of the incomes will fall within 1 standard deviation of the mean. Therefore, we cannot determine the percentage of employees that should expect an income under \$160 per week.

When x = 200,

$$z = \frac{x - \mu}{\sigma} = \frac{200 - 170}{10} = 3$$

At least 8/9 of the incomes fall within 3 standard deviations of the mean. Therefore, at most, 1/9 x 100% = 11.1% of the employees should expect an income over \$200 per week.

b. When your income x is \$185,

$$z = \frac{x - \mu}{\sigma} = \frac{185 - 170}{10} = 1.5$$

My salary would be 1.5 standard deviations above the mean salary.

3.55 The 25th percentile, or lower quartile, is the measurement that has 25% of the measurements below it and 75% of the measurements above it. The 50th percentile, or median, is the measurement that has 50% of the measurements below it and 50% of the measurements above it. The 75th percentile, or upper quartile, is the measurements that has 75% of the measurements below it and 25% of the measurements above it.

3.57 a. Median is approximately 39.

b. $Q_L$ is approximately 31.5 (Lower Quartile)

$Q_U$ is approximately 45 (Upper Quartile)

c. IQR = $Q_U - Q_L \approx 45 - 31.5 \approx 13.5$

d. The data set is skewed to the left since the left whisker is longer.

e. 50% of the measurements are to the right of the median and 75% are to the left of the upper quartile.

*3.59 Using Minitab, the box plot for the sample is given below.

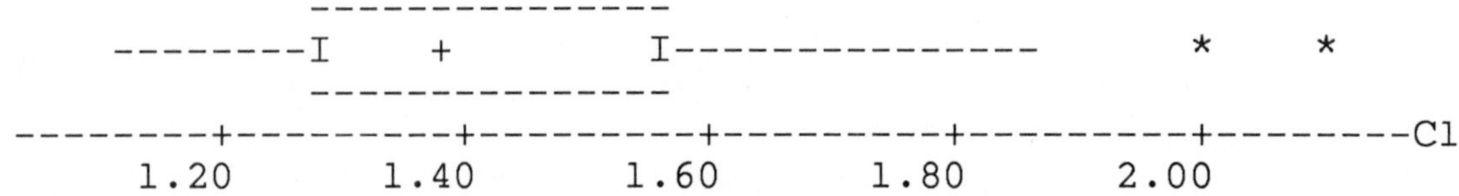

```
                 ----------------
         --------I     +        I---------------        *     *
                 ----------------
    --------+---------+---------+---------+---------+--------C1
          1.20      1.40      1.60      1.80      2.00
```

3.61 Owens-Illinois sales are at the upper quartile or the 75th percentile. This means that 75% of the nation's largest companies' 1989 sales were below \$3,692 million and 25% were above \$3,692 million.

*3.63 a. Using Minitab, the box plot for the earnings per share for the 30 firms is given below.

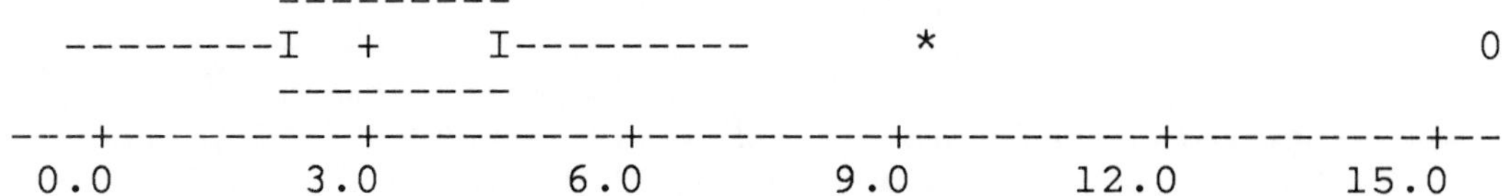

```
                 ---------
         --------I  +    I---------         *                    0
                 ---------
      ---+----------+----------+----------+----------+----------+--
        0.0        3.0        6.0        9.0       12.0       15.0
```

In the sample of 30 firms, the E/S for Washington Post (15.50) is an outlier. This measurement falls outside the outer fence.

In addition, the E/S for Reynolds Metals (9.20) may be an outlier. It lies outside the inner fence.

b. To determine the number of standard deviations a measurement is from the mean (the z-score), we must first calculate the sample mean and standard deviation.

$$\bar{x} = \frac{\sum_{i=1}^{n} x_i}{n} = \frac{110.84}{30} = 3.695$$

$$s^2 = \frac{\sum_{i=1}^{n} x_i^2 - \frac{\left(\sum_{i=1}^{n} x_i\right)^2}{n}}{n - 1} = \frac{697.4438 - \frac{110.84^2}{30}}{30 - 1} = 9.9285$$

$$s = \sqrt{9.9285} = 3.151$$

For the E/S for Washington Post, $x = 15.50$, the z-score is:

$$z = \frac{x - \bar{x}}{s} = \frac{15.50 - 3.695}{3.151} = 3.75$$

For the E/S for Reynolds Metals, $x = 9.20$, the z-score is:

$$z = \frac{x - \bar{x}}{s} = \frac{9.20 - 3.695}{3.151} = 1.74$$

3.65 a. For Ford the median is approximately 23.5, while Honda's median is approximately 27.3. Therefore, Honda has the higher median mileage estimate.

b. For Ford the range is approximately 41 - 17 = 24, while Honda's range is approximately 51.1 - 22.4 = 28.7. Therefore, Honda has the greater range.

c. For Ford,

$$IQR = Q_U - Q_L \approx 27 - 19 \approx 8$$

For Honda,

$$IQR = Q_U - Q_L \approx 29.4 - 23.8 \approx 5.6$$

Therefore, Ford's mileage estimates have the greater interquartile range.

d. For Ford the highest mileage estimate is approximately 41, while Honda's highest mileage estimate is approximately 51.1. Therefore, Honda has the model with the highest mileage estimate.

3.67 a. $\sum_{i=1}^{n} x_i^2 = 11^2 + 1^2 + 2^2 + 8^2 + 7^2 = 239$

$$\sum_{i=1}^{n} x_i = 11 + 1 + 2 + 8 + 7 = 29$$

$$\left(\sum_{i=1}^{n} x_i\right)^2 = 29^2 = 841$$

b. $\sum_{i=1}^{n} x_i^2 = 15^2 + 15^2 + 2^2 + 6^2 + 12^2 = 634$

$\sum_{i=1}^{n} x_i = 15 + 15 + 2 + 6 + 12 = 50$

$\left(\sum_{i=1}^{n} x_i\right)^2 = 50^2 = 2500$

c. $\sum_{i=1}^{n} x_i^2 = (-1)^2 + 2^2 + 0^2 + (-4)^2 + (-8)^2 + 13^2 = 254$

$\sum_{i=1}^{n} x_i = -1 + 2 + 0 + (-4) + (-8) + 13 = 2$

$\left(\sum_{i=1}^{n} x_i\right)^2 = 2^2 = 4$

d. $\sum_{i=1}^{n} x_i^2 = 100^2 + 0^2 + 0^2 + 2^2 = 10,004$

$\sum_{i=1}^{n} x_i = 100 + 0 + 0 + 2 = 102$

$\left(\sum_{i=1}^{n} x_i\right)^2 = 102^2 = 10,404$

3.69 a. $s^2 = \dfrac{\sum_{i=1}^{n} x_i^2 - \dfrac{\left(\sum_{i=1}^{n} x_i\right)^2}{n}}{n - 1} = \dfrac{246 - \dfrac{63^2}{22}}{22 - 1} = 3.1234$

b. $s^2 = \dfrac{\sum_{i=1}^{n} x_i^2 - \dfrac{\left(\sum_{i=1}^{n} x_i\right)^2}{n}}{n - 1} = \dfrac{666 - \dfrac{106^2}{25}}{25 - 1} = 9.0233$

c. $s^2 = \dfrac{\sum_{i=1}^{n} x_i^2 - \dfrac{\left(\sum_{i=1}^{n} x_i\right)^2}{n}}{n - 1} = \dfrac{76 - \dfrac{11^2}{7}}{7 - 1} = 9.7857$

3.71 a. $\sum_{i=1}^{n} x_i = 4 + 6 + 6 + 5 + 6 + 7 = 34$

$\sum_{i=1}^{n} x_i^2 = 4^2 + 6^2 + 6^2 + 5^2 + 6^2 + 7^2 = 198$

$$\bar{x} = \frac{\sum_{i=1}^{n} x_i}{n} = \frac{34}{6} = 5.67$$

$$s^2 = \frac{\sum_{i=1}^{n} x_i^2 - \frac{\left(\sum_{i=1}^{n} x_i\right)^2}{n}}{n - 1} = \frac{198 - \frac{34^2}{6}}{6 - 1} = \frac{5.3333}{5} = 1.067$$

$s = \sqrt{1.067} = 1.03$

b. $\sum_{i=1}^{n} x_i = -1 + 4 + (-3) + 0 + (-3) + (-6) = -9$

$\sum_{i=1}^{n} x_i^2 = (-1)^2 + 4^2 + (-3)^2 + 0^2 + (-3)^2 + (-6)^2 = 71$

$$\bar{x} = \frac{\sum_{i=1}^{n} x_i}{n} = \frac{-9}{6} = -\$1.5$$

$$s^2 = \frac{\sum_{i=1}^{n} x_i^2 - \frac{\left(\sum_{i=1}^{n} x_i\right)^2}{n}}{n - 1} = \frac{71 - \frac{(-9)^2}{6}}{6 - 1} = \frac{57.5}{5} = 11.5 \text{ dollars squared}$$

$s = \sqrt{11.5} = \$3.39$

c. $\sum_{i=1}^{n} x_i = \frac{3}{5} + \frac{4}{5} + \frac{2}{5} + \frac{1}{5} + \frac{1}{16} = 2.0625$

$\sum_{i=1}^{n} x_i^2 = \left(\frac{3}{5}\right)^2 + \left(\frac{4}{5}\right)^2 + \left(\frac{2}{5}\right)^2 + \left(\frac{1}{5}\right)^2 + \left(\frac{1}{16}\right)^2 = 1.2039$

$$\bar{x} = \frac{\sum_{i=1}^{n} x_i}{n} = \frac{2.0625}{5} = .4125 \text{ pounds}$$

$$s^2 = \frac{\sum_{i=1}^{n} x_i^2 - \frac{\left(\sum_{i=1}^{n} x_i\right)^2}{n}}{n - 1} = \frac{1.2039 - \frac{2.0625^2}{5}}{5 - 1} = \frac{.3531}{4}$$

$= .088$ pounds squared

$s = \sqrt{.088} = .30\%$

d. (a) Range = 7 - 4 = 3

(b) Range = \$4 - (\$-6) = \$10

(c) Range $= \frac{4}{5}$ pound $- \frac{1}{16}$ pound $= \frac{64}{80}$ pound $- \frac{5}{80}$ pound $= \frac{59}{80}$ pound

$= .7375$ pound

3.73 a. The population of interest is the set of all gasoline stations in the United States.

b. The sample of interest is the set of 200 stations selected.

c. The variable of interest is the price of regular unleaded gasoline at each station.

d. $\mu$ = the mean price of regular unleaded gasoline at all stations in the United States.

$\sigma$ = the standard deviation of the price of regular unleaded gasoline at all stations in the United States.

$\bar{x}$ = the mean price of regular unleaded gasoline at the 200 selected stations.

s = the standard deviation of the price of regular unleaded gasoline at the 200 selected stations.

e. The mean price of a gallon of regular unleaded gasoline at the 200 selected stations is \$1.39, and the standard deviation is \$0.12. The distribution of the prices is probably approximately mound shaped. About half of the stations probably have prices above \$1.39 and about half have prices below \$1.39.

f. For x = \$1.09, $z = \frac{x - \bar{x}}{s} = \frac{1.09 - 1.39}{.12} = \frac{-.30}{.12} = -2.5$

A price of \$1.09 per gallon is 2.5 standard deviations below the mean. Not many stations will have prices below this value.

3.75 The standard deviation is expressed in the units of the problem while the variance is in square units. Therefore, it is easier to interpret the standard deviation than the variance.

3.77 A z-score locates a measurement in a data set by expressing the measurement in terms of the number of standard deviations it is above or below the mean.

3.79 The mode is often not an acceptable measure of central tendency. If the data set has few observations, no value may occur more than one time. If the data set is of moderate size, several different values may occur the same number of times, giving little information about the center of the distribution.

3.81 $\bar{x} = 75$, $s^2 = 36$, $s = 6$

a. $\bar{x} \pm s \Rightarrow 75 \pm 6 \Rightarrow (69, 81)$

Since we do not know the shape of the distribution, using Chebyshev's theorem we can say that at least $1 - \frac{1}{1^2} = 0$ will fall within this interval.

b. $\bar{x} \pm 2s \Rightarrow 75 \pm 2(6) \Rightarrow 75 \pm 12 \Rightarrow (63, 87)$

By Chebyshev's theorem, at least $1 - \frac{1}{2^2} = .75$ of the measurements should fall within this interval. So at most, $.25 \times 100\% = 25\%$ of the trainees would be expected to fail.

*3.83 a. Using MINITAB, the box plot is:

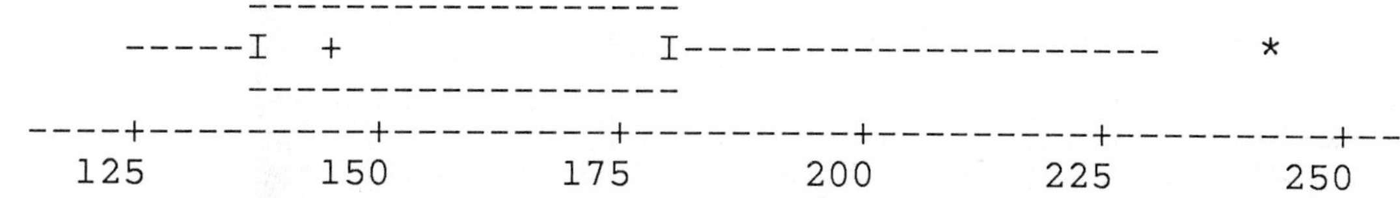


b. The frequency distribution of the data set is skewed right, since the right whisker is longer than the left whisker in the box plot.

c. There is one potential outlier in the data set. The observation 242 corresponding to UTL lies outside the inner fence.

d. The mean of the data is $\bar{x} = \frac{\sum_{i=1}^{n} x_i}{n} = \frac{3217}{20} = 160.85$

For x = 242, $z = \frac{x - \bar{x}}{s} = \frac{242 - 160.85}{34.3} = \frac{81.15}{34.3} = 2.37$

e. No. Since we know from part (b) that the data are skewed, we must use Chebyshev's theorem. We know at least

$1 - \frac{1}{k^2} = 1 - \frac{1}{2.37^2} = .82$ of the observations will fall within 2.37 standard deviations of the mean. It is not real likely one would observe a value larger than 242.

*3.85 a. $s \approx \frac{\text{Range}}{4} \approx \frac{30000}{4} \approx \$7500$

b. It is more likely that division B's sales next month will be over $120,000 since it is fewer standard deviations from the mean of $110,000.

$$(z = \frac{120,000 - 110,000}{7500} = 1.33 \text{ is smaller than}$$

$$z = \frac{90,000 - 220,000}{7500} = 2.67)$$

c. Yes, it is possible for division B's sales next month to be over $160,000. But it very unlikely since

$$z = \frac{x - \bar{x}}{s} = \frac{160,000 - 110,000}{7500} = 6.67$$

This is a very large z-score.

3.87 $\bar{x} = 35000$, $s = 9000$

Based only on this information, all we know is the mean salary is $35,000 and the standard deviation is $9000. We have no information about the shape of the distribution.

$$\bar{x} \pm 3s \Rightarrow 35,000 \pm 3(9000) \Rightarrow 35,000 \pm 27,000 \Rightarrow (8,000, 62,000)$$

Since we do not know the shape of the distribution, we will use Chebyshev's theorem. At least $1 - \frac{1}{3^2} = \frac{8}{9}$ of the manufacturer's sales people's incomes will fall within this interval.

3.89 No information about the variability of a data set can be obtained from this formula, because $\sum(x_i - \bar{x}) = 0$ for all data sets. The data set from Exercise 3.67(a) is 11, 1, 2, 8, 7.

$$\bar{x} = \frac{\sum_{i=1}^{n} x_i}{n} = \frac{29}{5} = 5.8$$

$$\begin{aligned}\sum_{i=1}^{n} (x_i - \bar{x}) &= (11 - 5.8) + (1 - 5.8) + (2 - 5.8) + (8 - 5.8) + (7 - 5.8) \\ &= 5.2 + (-4.8) + (-3.8) + 2.2 + 1.2 \\ &= 0\end{aligned}$$

$$\text{So, } V = \frac{\sum_{i=1}^{n}(x_i - \bar{x})}{n} = \frac{0}{5} = 0$$

V will always be 0 regardless of the data set.

3.91 a. From looking at the box plot's scales and shapes, the expenditures are the highest for magazines. The lower quartile for magazines is 900 which is larger than the upper quartiles of the other two mediums.

b. The range is the largest measurement minus the smallest measurement.

Magazines: The range is approximately 4700 - 0 = 4700

Billboards: The range is approximately 2500 - 0 = 2500

Newspapers: The range is approximately 920 - 0 = 920

The range of expenditures is largest for magazines and smallest for newspapers.

c. The interquartile range = IQR = $Q_U - Q_L$

Magazines: The interquartile range is approximately 3100 - 900 = 2200.

Billboards: The interquartile range is approximately 650 - 0 = 650.

Newspapers: The interquartile range is approximately 500 - 60 = 440.

The interquartile range is largest for magazines and smallest for newspapers.

d. Magazines: The frequency distribution is slightly skewed to the right since the right whisker is longer.

Billboards: The frequency distribution is skewed to the right since the right whisker is longer (there is no left whisker).

Newspapers: The frequency distribution is skewed to the right since the right whisker is longer.

e. No, none of the 3 media receive expenditures from all 16 brands. This is evident since all three box plots have 0 as their smallest measurement.

3.93 a.

| CLASS | CLASS MIDPOINT $x_i$ | CLASS FREQUENCY $f_i$ |
|---|---|---|
| 10-19 | 14.5 | 15 |
| 20-29 | 24.5 | 12 |
| 30-39 | 34.5 | 8 |
| 40-49 | 44.5 | 5 |
| 50-59 | 54.5 | 2 |
| | | n = 42 |

$$\bar{x} = \frac{\sum_{i=1}^{k} x_i f_i}{n} = \frac{14.5(15) + 24.5(12) + 34.5(8) + 44.5(5) + 54.5(2)}{42}$$

$$= \frac{1119}{42} = 26.6429$$

$$\sum_{i=1}^{k} x_i^2 f_i = (14.5)^2 15 + (24.5)^2 12 + (34.5)^2 8 + (44.5)^2 5 + (54.5)^2 2$$

$$= 35720.5$$

$$s^2 = \frac{\sum_{i=1}^{k} x_i^2 f_i - \frac{\left(\sum_{i=1}^{n} x_i f_i\right)^2}{n}}{n - 1} = \frac{35720.5 - \frac{1119^2}{42}}{42 - 1} = \frac{5907.1429}{41} = 144.0767$$

$$s = \sqrt{144.0767} = 12.0032$$

b.

| CLASS | CLASS MIDPOINT $(x_i)$ | CLASS FREQUENCY $(f_i)$ |
|---|---|---|
| -99 to -50 | -74.5 | 20 |
| -49 to 0 | -24.5 | 55 |
| 1 to 50 | 25.5 | 102 |
| 51 to 100 | 75.5 | 63 |
| 101 to 150 | 125.5 | 18 |
| | | n = 258 |

$$\bar{x} = \frac{\sum_{i=1}^{k} x_i f_i}{n} = \frac{(-74.5)20 + (-24.5)55 + 25.5(102) + 75.5(63) + 125.5(18)}{258}$$

$$= \frac{6779}{258} = 26.2752$$

$$\sum_{i=1}^{k} x_i^2 f_i = (-74.5)^2 20 + (-24.5)^2 55 + (25.5)^2 102 + (75.5)^2 63 + (125.5)^2 18$$

$$= 852964.5$$

$$s^2 = \frac{\sum_{i=1}^{k} x_i^2 f_i - \frac{\left(\sum_{i=1}^{k} x_i f_i\right)^2}{n}}{n - 1} = \frac{852964.5 - \frac{6779^2}{258}}{258 - 1} = \frac{674844.9613}{257} = 2625.8559$$

$$s = \sqrt{2625.8559} = 51.2431$$

3.95 a. For June, the range = 10 - 0 = 10.
For August, the range = 11 - 0 = 11.

Since the range for June is smaller than the range for August, the month of August exhibits more variability in the number of machine breakdowns.

For June, the sample variance is

$$s^2 = \frac{\sum_{i=1}^{n} x_i^2 - \frac{\left(\sum_{i=1}^{n} x_i\right)^2}{n}}{n - 1} = \frac{270 - \frac{34^2}{7}}{7 - 1} = 17.4762$$

For August, the sample variance is

$$s^2 = \frac{\sum_{i=1}^{n} x_i^2 - \frac{\left(\sum_{i=1}^{n} x_i\right)^2}{n}}{n - 1} = \frac{168 - \frac{26^2}{7}}{7 - 1} = 11.9048$$

Since the variance for August is smaller than the variance for June, the month of June exhibits more variability in the number of machine breakdowns.

The variance better represents the variability of these two data sets. Note that August only has one extreme value (11), while the other values are quite close together; but the numbers in June are spread out. The variance detects this while the range does not. The range is affected by the extreme value of 11.

b. The following "new" data set is obtained for June:

11, 6, 3, 3, 13, 7, 12

Hence, $\sum x = 55$, $\sum x^2 = 537$, and

$$s^2 = \frac{537 - \frac{(55)^2}{7}}{6} = 17.4762$$

Adding (or subtracting) a constant to (or from) each of the sample measurements has no effect on the value of $s^2$.

c. Multiplying by 3 generates the following data set:

24, 9, 0, 0, 30, 12, 27

Hence, $\sum x = 102$, $\sum x^2 = 2430$, and

$$s^2 = \frac{2430 - \frac{(102)^2}{7}}{6} = 157.2857$$

Since $9 \times 17.4762 = 157.2857$, we conclude that multiplying each sample measurement by a constant, c, inflates the original variance by a factor of $c^2$.

# CHAPTER 4

# PROBABILITY

4.1 A simple event is an outcome of an experiment that cannot be decomposed into a simpler outcome. An event is a collection of one or more simple events.

4.3 a.

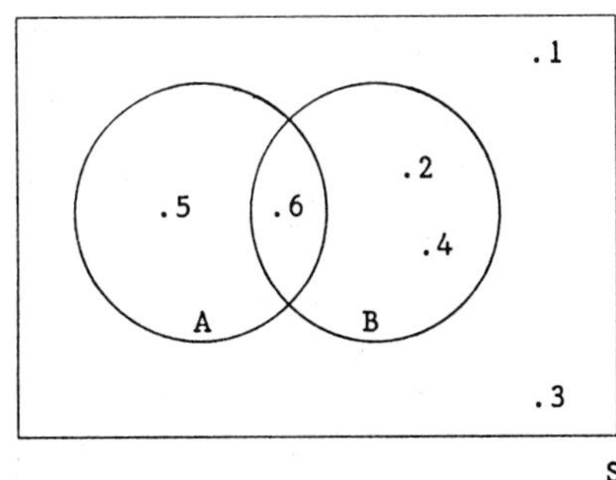


b. If a die is "fair," then there is an equal chance that any of the six numbers will be observed when the die is rolled.

If the die is "fair," then you have an equal chance of observing any of the six numbers on the die. Therefore, the probability of observing a three is 1/6 since there is one three out of the six numbers.

c. $P(A) = P(5) + P(6) = \frac{1}{6} + \frac{1}{6} = \frac{2}{6} = \frac{1}{3}$

$P(B) = P(2) + P(4) + P(6) = \frac{1}{6} + \frac{1}{6} + \frac{1}{6} = \frac{3}{6} = \frac{1}{2}$

d. You could determine the probability of a 3 occurring by tossing the die a large number of times and counting the number of 3's that appear. Divide the number of 3's by the total number of tosses and this would be an estimate of the probability of observing a 3.

4.5 a. $\binom{10}{3} = \frac{10!}{3!(10-3)!} = \frac{10!}{3!7!} = \frac{10 \cdot 9 \cdot 8 \cdot 7 \cdot 6 \cdot 5 \cdot 4 \cdot 3 \cdot 2 \cdot 1}{(3 \cdot 2 \cdot 1)(7 \cdot 6 \cdot 5 \cdot 4 \cdot 3 \cdot 2 \cdot 1)}$

$= 120$

b. $\binom{6}{2} = \frac{6!}{2!(6-2)!} = \frac{6!}{2!4!} = \frac{6 \cdot 5 \cdot 4 \cdot 3 \cdot 2 \cdot 1}{(2 \cdot 1)(4 \cdot 3 \cdot 2 \cdot 1)} = 15$

c. $\binom{8}{3} = \frac{8!}{3!(8-3)!} = \frac{8!}{3!5!} = \frac{8 \cdot 7 \cdot 6 \cdot 5 \cdot 4 \cdot 3 \cdot 2 \cdot 1}{(3 \cdot 2 \cdot 1)(5 \cdot 4 \cdot 3 \cdot 2 \cdot 1)} = 56$

d. $\binom{5}{5} = \frac{5!}{5!(5-5)!} = \frac{5!}{5!0!} = \frac{5 \cdot 4 \cdot 3 \cdot 2 \cdot 1}{(5 \cdot 4 \cdot 3 \cdot 2 \cdot 1)(1)} = 1$

e. $\binom{4}{0} = \frac{4!}{0!(4-0)!} = \frac{4!}{0!4!} = \frac{4 \cdot 3 \cdot 2 \cdot 1}{(1)(4 \cdot 3 \cdot 2 \cdot 1)} = 1$

4.7 $P(A) = P(S_1, S_2) = .16$

$P(B) = P(S_1, S_2) + P(S_1, F_2) + P(F_1, S_2) = .16 + .24 + .24 = .64$

4.9 $P(A) = P(G_1, G_2) = \frac{1}{6}$

$P(B) = P(G_1, P_1) + P(G_1, P_2) + P(G_2, P_1) + P(G_2, P_2) + P(P_1, P_1)$

$= \frac{1}{6} + \frac{1}{6} + \frac{1}{6} + \frac{1}{6} + \frac{1}{6} = \frac{5}{6}$

4.11 We will denote the five successful utility companies as $S_1$, $S_2$, $S_3$, $S_4$, and $S_5$ and the two failing companies as $F_1$ and $F_2$. There are

$$\binom{7}{3} = \frac{7!}{3!4!} = 35$$

possible ways to choose three companies from the seven, as shown below:

$(S_1, S_2, S_3)$ $(S_1, S_3, S_4)$ $(S_1, S_4, S_5)$ $(S_1, S_5, F_1)$
$(S_1, S_2, S_4)$ $(S_1, S_3, S_5)$ $(S_1, S_4, F_1)$ $(S_1, S_5, F_2)$
$(S_1, S_2, S_5)$ $(S_1, S_3, F_1)$ $(S_1, S_4, S_2)$
$(S_1, S_2, F_1)$ $(S_1, S_3, F_2)$ $(S_1, F_1, F_2)$
$(S_1, S_2, F_2)$

$(S_2, S_3, S_4)$ $(S_2, S_4, S_5)$ $(S_2, S_5, F_1)$ $(S_2, F_1, F_2)$
$(S_2, S_3, S_5)$ $(S_2, S_4, F_1)$ $(S_2, S_5, F_2)$
$(S_2, S_3, F_1)$ $(S_2, S_4, F_2)$
$(S_2, S_3, F_2)$

$(S_3, S_4, S_5)$ $(S_3, S_5, F_1)$ $(S_3, F_1, F_2)$
$(S_3, S_4, F_1)$ $(S_3, S_5, F_2)$
$(S_3, S_4, F_2)$

$(S_4, S_5, F_1)$ $(S_5, F_1, F_2)$
$(S_4, S_5, F_2)$
$(S_4, F_1, F_2)$

a. From the 35 events listed, 10 do not contain $F_1$ or $F_2$. Therefore, P(selecting none) = 10/35.

b. From the 35 events listed, 20 contain either $F_1$ or $F_2$, but not both. Therefore, P(selecting one) = 20/35.

c. From the 35 events listed, 5 contain both $F_1$ and $F_2$. Therefore, P(selecting both) = 5/35.

4.13 Define L: {Draw a Lenient Judge}

a. Since Judge A (a strict judge) is leaving to go home, there are 3 strict judges ($S_1$, $S_2$, and $S_3$) and 3 lenient judges ($L_1$, $L_2$, and $L_3$) left. If you have an equally-likely chance of getting any of the 6 judges,

$$P(L) = P(L_1) + P(L_2) + P(L_3)$$
$$= \frac{1}{6} + \frac{1}{6} + \frac{1}{6}$$
$$= \frac{3}{6}$$
$$= \frac{1}{2}$$

b. P(Judge B) = $P(S_1)$ = .3 and P(Judge C) = $P(S_2)$ = .4

Thus, $P(S_3) + P(L_1) + P(L_2) + P(L_3) = 1 - P(S_1) - P(S_2)$

Since $P(S_3) = P(L_1) = P(L_2) = P(L_3)$,

$$4P(S_3) = 1 - .3 - .4 = .3$$

$$\Rightarrow \quad P(S_3) = \frac{.3}{4} = .075$$

$$\Rightarrow \quad P(L_1) = P(L_2) = P(L_3) = .075$$

$P(L) = P(L_1) + P(L_2) + P(L_3) = .075 + .075 + .075 = .225$

c. Since Judge D (a lenient judge, $L_1$) never follows Judge A,

P(Judge D) = $P(L_1)$ = 0

P(Judge B) = $P(S_1)$ = .3

P(Judge C) = $P(S_2)$ = .4

Since the other three judges are equally likely,

$$P(S_3) + P(L_2) + P(L_3) = 1 - .3 - .4 = .3$$

$$\Rightarrow \quad 3P(S_3) = .3$$

$$\Rightarrow \quad P(S_3) = \frac{.3}{3} = .1$$

$$\Rightarrow \quad P(L_2) = P(L_3) = .1$$

Thus, $P(L) = P(L_2) + P(L_3) = .1 + .1 = .2$

4.15 a. Since each of the 15 states has an equal probability of being selected,

P(Pennsylvania will be selected) = P(Florida will be selected) = P(Virginia will be selected) = 1/15.

b. Since all of the states had a change in their unemployment rate, the probability of selecting a state that had no change is $0/15 = 0$.

c. By looking at the change in the unemployment rates in the table for each of the 15 Atlantic coast states, 10 states had an increase in the unemployment rate from 1983 to 1984.

Therefore, the probability of selecting a state with an increase = $10/15 = 2/3$, while the probability of selecting a state with a decrease = $5/15 = 1/3$.

d. Three of the states had an increase of 1% or more. The probability of selecting a state with an increase $\geq$ 1% = $3/15 = .2$.

One of the states had a decrease of 1% or more. The probability of selecting a state with a decrease $\geq$ 1% = $1/15$.

4.17 a. The odds in favor of a Snow Chief win are $\frac{1}{3}$ to $1 - \frac{1}{3} = \frac{2}{3}$ or 1 to 2.

b. If the odds in favor of Snow Chief are 1 to 1, then the probability the Snow Chief wins is $\frac{1}{1 + 1} = \frac{1}{2}$.

c. If the odds against Snow Chief are 3 to 2, then the odds in favor of Snow Chief are 2 to 3. Therefore, the probability the Snow Chief wins is $\frac{2}{2 + 3} = \frac{2}{5}$.

4.19 a. $A = \{(1, 4), (4, 1), (2, 3), (3, 2)\}$

$B = \{(2, 3), (3, 2), (1, 3), (3, 1), (3, 3), (4, 3), (3, 4),$
$(5, 3), (3, 5), (6, 3), (3, 6)\}$

$A \cap B = \{(2, 3), (3, 2)\}$

$A \cup B = \{(1, 4), (4, 1), (2, 3), (3, 2), (1, 3), (3, 1), (3, 3),$
$(4, 3), (3, 4), (5, 3), (3, 5), (6, 3), (3, 6)\}$

b. There are 36 possible combinations from tossing two dice, so the probability of each simple event is 1/36. Thus,

$P(A) = \frac{4}{36}$ $\quad P(B) = \frac{11}{36}$

c. $P(A \cap B) = \frac{2}{36}$ $\quad P(A \cup B) = \frac{13}{36}$

4.21 The relative frequencies found by dividing the frequencies by n = 8000, are given in table form.

| | | INCOME | | |
|---|---|---|---|---|
| | | (D) | (E) | (F) |
| | | Under \$20,000 | \$20,000-\$50,000 | Over \$50,000 |
| AGE | (A) Under 25 | $\frac{950}{8000}$ | $\frac{1000}{8000}$ | $\frac{50}{8000}$ |
| | (B) 25-45 | $\frac{450}{8000}$ | $\frac{2050}{8000}$ | $\frac{1500}{8000}$ |
| | (C) Over 45 | $\frac{50}{8000}$ | $\frac{950}{8000}$ | $\frac{1000}{8000}$ |

a. $P(B) = \frac{450}{8000} + \frac{2050}{8000} + \frac{1500}{8000} = \frac{4000}{8000}$

b. $P(F) = \frac{50}{8000} + \frac{1500}{8000} + \frac{1000}{8000} = \frac{2550}{8000}$

c. $P(C \cap F) = \frac{1000}{8000}$

d. $P(B \cup C) = \frac{450}{8000} + \frac{2050}{8000} + \frac{1500}{8000} + \frac{50}{8000} + \frac{950}{8000} + \frac{1000}{8000} = \frac{6000}{8000}$

e. $$P(A^c) = 1 - P(A) = 1 - \left(\frac{950}{8000} + \frac{1000}{8000} + \frac{50}{8000}\right)$$
$$= 1 - \frac{2000}{8000}$$
$$= \frac{6000}{8000}$$

f. $P(A^c \cap F) = \frac{1500}{8000} + \frac{1000}{8000} = \frac{2500}{8000}$

4.23 a. $B \cap C$ b. $A^c$ c. $C \cup B$ d. $A \cap C^c$

4.25 a. A simple event is an event that cannot be decomposed into two or more other events. In this example, there are nine simple events. Let 1 be Warehouse 1, 2 be Warehouse 2, 3 be Warehouse 3, and let R be Regular, S be Stiff, and E be Extra stiff. The simple events are:

(1, R) (1, S) (1, E)
(2, R) (2, S) (2, E)
(3, R) (3, S) (3, E)

b. The *sample space* of an experiment is the collection of all its simple events.

c. $P(C) = P(3, R) + P(3, S) + P(3, E)$
$= .28 + .18 + 0$
$= .46$

d. $P(F) = P(1, E) + P(2, E) + P(3, E)$
$= .03 + .02 + 0$
$= .05$

e. $P(A) = P(1, R) + P(1, S) + P(1, E)$
$= .19 + .08 + .03$
$= .30$

f. $P(D) = P(1, R) + P(2, R) + P(3, R)$
$= .19 + .14 \quad .28$
$= .61$

g. $P(E) = P(1, S) + P(2, S) + P(3, S)$
$= .08 + .08 + .18$
$= .34$

4.27 a. The 20 simple events may be listed as follows:

$E_1$: (Under 1000, 12)
$E_2$: (Under 1000, 24)
$E_3$: (Under 1000, 36)
$E_4$: (Under 1000, 42)
$E_5$: (Under 1000, 48)
$E_6$: (1000-3999, 12)
$E_7$: (1000-3999, 24)
$E_8$: (1000-3999, 36)
$E_9$: (1000-3999, 42)
$E_{10}$: (1000-3999, 48)
$E_{11}$: (4000-5999, 12)
$E_{12}$: (4000-5999, 24)
$E_{13}$: (4000-5999, 36)
$E_{14}$: (4000-5999, 42)
$E_{15}$: (4000-5999, 48)
$E_{16}$: (6000 or more, 12)
$E_{17}$: (6000 or more, 24)
$E_{18}$: (6000 or more, 36)
$E_{19}$: (6000 or more, 42)
$E_{20}$: (6000 or more, 48)

where the first entry within the parentheses indicates the amount of the loan (in dollars), and the second entry indicates the length of the loan (in months).

b. P(Selected loan will be for $6000 or more)

$$= P(E_{16}) + P(P(E_{17}) + P(E_{18}) + P(E_{19}) + P(E_{20})$$

$$= 0 + 0 + \frac{2}{500} + \frac{50}{500} + \frac{24}{500} = \frac{76}{500} = .152$$

Yes, this is the same answer obtained in part (b) of Exercise 4.6.

c. $P(E_{18}) = \dfrac{2}{500} = .004$

d. P(Selected loan is for three or four years)

$= P(\text{Selected loan is for 36 or 48 months})$

$= P(E_3) + P(E_5) + P(E_8) + P(E_{10}) + P(E_{13}) + P(E_{15}) + P(E_{18}) + P(E_{20})$

$$= 0 + 0 + \frac{27}{500} + 0 + \frac{92}{500} + \frac{112}{500} + \frac{2}{500} + \frac{24}{500} = \frac{257}{500} = .514$$

e. P(Selected loan is a 42-month loan for $1000 or more)

$= P(E_9) + P(E_{14}) + P(E_{19})$

$$= \frac{53}{500} + \frac{93}{500} + \frac{50}{500} = \frac{196}{500} = .392$$

4.29 a. The employee is a male, or the highest degree obtained by the employee is a Ph.D.

b. The employee is a female, or the highest degree obtained by the employee is a high school diploma.

c. The employee is a male, and the highest degree obtained by the employee is a Master's Degree.

d. The employee is a female, and the highest degree obtained by the employee is a Bachelor's Degree.

4.31 a. The sale was paid by credit card, or the merchandise purchased was women's wear.

$P(A \cup B) = .04 + .37 + .11 + .04 + .18 = .74$

b. The merchandise purchased was women's wear or men's wear.

$P(B \cup C) = .04 + .37 + .07 + .11 = .59$

c. The merchandise purchased was women's wear, and it was paid by credit card.

$P(B \cap A) = .37$

d. The merchandise purchased was men's wear, and it was paid by credit card.

$P(C \cap A) = .11$

4.33 The following events are defined:

A: {male worker}
B: {female worker}
C: {service worker}
D: {managerial/professional worker}
E: {operator/fabricator worker}
F: {technical/sales/administrative worker}

a. $P(A \cap C) = .053$

b. $P(D) = P(A \cap D) + P(B \cap D)$
$= .137 + .109$
$= .246$

c. $P[(B \cap D) \cup (B \cap E)] = .109 + .040$
$= .149$

d. $P(F^C) = 1 - P(F) = 1 - [P(A \cap F) + P(A \cap F)]$
$= 1 - (.110 + .202)$
$= 1 - .312$
$= .688$

4.35 a. $P(A) = P(E_1) + P(E_2) + P(E_3)$
$= .1 + .1 + .3$
$= .5$

$P(B) = P(E_2) + P(E_3) + P(E_5)$
$= .1 + .3 + .1$
$= .5$

$P(A \cap B) = P(E_2) + P(E_3)$
$= .1 + .3$
$= .4$

b. $P(E_1|A) = \frac{P(E_1 \cap A)}{P(A)} = \frac{P(E_1)}{P(A)} = \frac{.1}{.5} = .2$

$P(E_2|A) = \frac{(P(E_2 \cap A)}{P(A)} = \frac{P(E_2)}{P(A)} = \frac{.1}{.5} = .2$

$P(E_3|A) = \frac{P(E_3 \cap A)}{P(A)} = \frac{P(E_3)}{P(A)} = \frac{.3}{.5} = .6$

The original simple event probabilities are in the proportion .1 to .1 to .3 or 1 to 1 to 3.

The conditional probabilities for these simple events are in the proportion .2 to .2 to .6 or 1 to 1 to 3.

c. (1) $P(B|A) = P(E_2|A) + P(E_3|A)$
$= .2 + .6$ (from part (b))
$= .8$

(2) $P(B|A) = \frac{P(A \cap B)}{P(A)} = \frac{.4}{.5} = .8$ (from part (a))

The two methods do yield the same result.

d. If A and B are independent events, $P(B|A) = P(B)$.

From part (c), $P(B|A) = .8$. From part (a), $P(B) = .5$.

Since $.8 \neq .5$, A and B are not independent events.

4.37 a. If A and B are independent, then $P(A|B) = P(A)$.

$$P(A|B) = \frac{P(A \cap B)}{P(B)} = \frac{P(E_3)}{P(E_2,\ E_3,\ E_4)} = \frac{.15}{.31 + .15 + .22} = \frac{.15}{.68} = .221$$

$P(A) = P(E_1) + P(E_3) = .22 + .15 = .37$

$.221 \neq .37$; therefore, A and B are not independent.

b. If A and C are independent, then $P(A|C) = P(A)$.

$$P(A|C) = \frac{P(A \cap C)}{P(C)} = \frac{P(E_1)}{P(E_1) + P(E_5)} = \frac{.22}{.22 + .10} = .688$$

$P(A) = P(E_1) + P(E_3) = .22 + .15 = .37$

$.37 \neq .688$; therefore, A and C are not independent.

c. If B and C are independent, then $P(B|C) = P(B)$.

$$P(B|C) = \frac{P(B \cap C)}{P(C)} = \frac{0}{.32} = 0$$

$P(B) = P(E_2) + P(E_7) + P(E_4) = .31 + .15 + .22 = .680$

$0 \neq .680$; therefore, B and C are not independent.

4.39 $P(R) = \frac{1}{3}$, $P(S) = \frac{1}{3}$

Since R and S are mutually exclusive, $P(R \cap S) = 0$

$$P(R|S) = \frac{P(R \cap S)}{P(S)} = \frac{0}{\frac{1}{3}} = 0$$

$$P(S|R) = \frac{P(R \cap S)}{P(R)} = \frac{0}{\frac{1}{3}} = 0$$

4.41 We define the following events:

A: {saw ad}
B: {shopped at X}

a. $P(A) = \frac{100}{200} + \frac{25}{200} = \frac{125}{200} = \frac{5}{8}$

b. $P(A \cap B) = \frac{100}{200} = \frac{1}{2}$

c. $P(B|A) = \frac{P(B \cap A)}{P(A)} = \frac{\frac{100}{200}}{\frac{125}{200}} = \frac{100}{125} = \frac{4}{5}$

d. $P(B) = \frac{100}{200} + \frac{25}{200} = \frac{125}{200} = \frac{5}{8}$

e. If A and B are independent events, $P(A \cap B) = P(A)P(B)$

From part (a), $P(A) = \frac{5}{8}$ From part (b), $P(A \cap B) = \frac{1}{2}$

From part (d), $P(B) = \frac{5}{8}$

$$P(A)P(B) = \frac{5}{8} \times \frac{5}{8} = \frac{25}{64}$$

$$\frac{1}{2} \neq \frac{25}{64}$$

Therefore, the events A and B are dependent events.

f. If the events "Did not see the ad" and "Did not shop at X" are mutually exclusive,

$$P(A^c \cap B^c) = 0$$

But $P(A^c \cap B^c) = \frac{50}{200} = \frac{1}{4} \neq 0$

Therefore, the 2 events are not mutually exclusive.

4.43 a. We will define the following events:

A: {The first activation device works properly; i.e., activates the sprinkler when it should}

B: {The second activation device works properly}

From the statement of the problem, we know

$P(A) = .91$ and $P(B) = .87$.

Furthermore, since the activation devices work independently, we conclude that

$P(A \cap B) = P(A)P(B) = (.91)(.87) = .7917$.

Now, if a fire starts near a sprinkler head, the sprinkler will be activated if either the first activation device or the second activation device, or both, operates properly. Thus,

$$\begin{aligned} P(\text{Sprinkler head will be activated}) &= P(A \cup B) \\ &= P(A) + P(B) - P(A \cap B) \\ &= .91 + .87 - .7917 \\ &= .9883 \end{aligned}$$

b. The event that the sprinkler head will not be activated is the complement of the event that the sprinkler will be activated. Thus,

P(Sprinkler head will not be activated)
= 1 - P(Sprinkler head will be activated)
= 1 - .9883
= .0117

c. From part (a), $P(A \cap B) = .7917$

d. In terms of the events we have defined, we wish to determine

$$
\begin{aligned}
P(A \cap B^c) &= P(A)P(B^c) \text{ (by independence)} \\
&= .91(1 - .87) \\
&= .91(.13) \\
&= .1183
\end{aligned}
$$

4.45 Define the following events.

A: {A defective case gets by inspector 1}
B: {A defective case gets by inspector 2}

We want to know

$A \cap B$: {A defective case gets by inspector 1 and inspector 2}.

We know that the two inspectors check the cases independently. Therefore,

$$P(A \cap B) = P(A)P(B) = (.05)(.10) = .005$$

4.47 Define the following events:

A: {Population under 10,000}
B: {Population 10,000-100,000}
C: {Population over 100,000}
D: {NE Region}
E: {SE Region}
F: {SW Region}
G: {NW Region}

a. $P(D|C) = \dfrac{P(C \cap D)}{P(C)} = \dfrac{.25}{.25 + .04 + .05 + .1} = \dfrac{.25}{.44} = .568$

b. $P(A|E) = \dfrac{P(A \cap E)}{P(E)} = \dfrac{.06}{.06 + .15 + .04} = \dfrac{.06}{.25} = .24$

c. $P[(A \cup B)|F] = \dfrac{P[(A \cup B) \cap F]}{P(F)} = \dfrac{.03 + .12}{.03 + .12 + .05} = \dfrac{.15}{.2} = .75$

d. $P[(B \cup C) | G] = \frac{P[(B \cup C) \cap G]}{P(G)} = \frac{.05 + .10}{0 + .05 + .1} = \frac{.15}{.15} = 1$

4.49 Define the following events:

A: {Product A is profitable}
B: {Product B is profitable}

We know that

P(Individual product profitable) = .18,

and

P(Two products profitable) = .05.

a. $P(A) = .18$

b. $P(B^C) = 1 - P(B) = 1 - .18 = .82$

c. $P(A \cup B) = P(A) + P(B) - P(A \cap B)$
$= .18 + .18 - .05$
$= .31$

d. $P((A \cup B)^C) = 1 - P(A \cup B)$
$= 1 - .31$
$= .69$

e. $P(A \cup B) - P(A \cap B)$
$= .31 - .05$
$= .26$

4.51 Define the following events:

A: {saw the advertisement}
$S_1$: {stage 1 decision to purchase}
$S_2$: {stage 2 decision to purchase}
$S_3$: {stage 3 decision to purchase}
$S_4$: {stage 4 decision to purchase}
$S_5$: {stage 5 decision to purchase}

$P(A \cap S_1 \cap S_2 \cap S_3 \cap S_3 \cap S_5)$

$= P(A)P(S_1)P(S_2)P(S_3)P(S_4)P(S_5)$
$= .9(.7)(.7)(.7)(.7)(.7)$
$= .151263$

4.53 Starting in row 5, column 2, of Table I of Appendix B and reading across, take the first 20 single digit numbers.

The 20 digits selected for the random sample are:

3, 9, 9, 7, 5, 8, 1, 8, 3, 7, 1, 6, 6, 5, 6, 0, 6, 1, 2, 1

4.55 a. In a random sample, all 12 people have an equal chance of being selected. Therefore the probability of selecting any one of the 12 people in the population is 1/12.

Since only one person in the population has a weekly income of $900 (Jerry), the probability of selecting a person with a weekly income of $900 is 1/12.

Two people in the population have weekly incomes of $1500 (Carl and Paul). Therefore the probability of selecting a person with a weekly income of $1500 is $\frac{1}{12} + \frac{1}{12} = \frac{2}{12} = \frac{1}{6}$

b. Since there are 12 people in the population, the number of samples of size 3 is a combination of 12 things taken 3 at a time or

$$\binom{12}{3} = \frac{12!}{3!(12-3)!} = \frac{12!}{3!9!}$$

$$= \frac{12 \cdot 11 \cdot 10 \cdot 9 \cdot 8 \cdot 7 \cdot 6 \cdot 5 \cdot 4 \cdot 3 \cdot 2 \cdot 1}{(3 \cdot 2 \cdot 1)(9 \cdot 8 \cdot 7 \cdot 6 \cdot 5 \cdot 4 \cdot 3 \cdot 2 \cdot 1)} = 220$$

c. Since there are 220 possible samples of size 3 that can be selected, the probability of any one of them being selected is 1/220.

The probability of selecting Norm, Art, and John is 1/220.

The probability of selecting Rema, Shawn, and David is 1/220.

d. First, assign each person in the population a number from 01 to 12.

| | | | |
|---|---|---|---|
| Norm | 01 | Art | 07 |
| Carl | 02 | John | 08 |
| Maureen | 03 | David | 09 |
| Paul | 04 | George | 10 |
| Rema | 05 | Chris | 11 |
| Shawn | 06 | Jerry | 12 |

Using Table I of Appendix B, start in row 15, column 1 and read across. Group the numbers in sets of two digits and take the first three numbers from 01 to 12.

The following two digit numbers were found in Table I using the above procedure.

07, 11, 99, 73, 36, 71, 04

The random sample of size 3 from this population is Art (07), Chris (11), and Paul (04).

4.57 a. Decide on a starting point on the random number table. Then take the first n numbers reading down, and this would be the sample. Group the digits on the random number table into groups of 7 (for part (b)) or groups of 4 (for part (c)). Eliminate any duplicates and numbers that begin with zero since they are not valid telephone numbers.

b. Starting in Row 6, column 5, take the first 10 seven-digit numbers reading down. The telephone numbers are:

277-5653
988-7231
188-7620
174-5318
530-6059
709-9779
496-2669
889-7433
482-3752
772-3313

c. Starting in Row 10, column 7, take the first 5 four-digit numbers reading down. The 5 telephone numbers are:

373-3886
373-5686
373-1866
373-3632
373-6768

4.59 b. On page 1 of your local telephone directory, give each nonbusiness telephone subscriber a number (from 1 to n). Using Table I of Appendix B, pick a starting point and read down until you have 5 different numbers. If n is less than 1000, you need to look at groups of 3 digits. If n is more than 999, then you need to look at groups of 4 digits.

c. It would be very time consuming to go through the entire telephone directory and number each nonbusiness telephone subscriber.

4.61 (1) The probabilities of all simple events must lie between 0 and 1, inclusive.

(2) The probabilities of all the simple events in the sample space must sum to 1.

4.63 $P(A \cap B) = .4$, $P(A|B) = .8$

Since the $P(A|B) = \frac{P(A \cap B)}{P(B)}$, substitute the given probabilities into the formula and solve for P(B).

$$.8 = \frac{.4}{P(B)}$$

Therefore, $P(B) = .50$.

4.65 Define the following events:

A: {the watch is accurate}
N: {the watch is not accurate}

Assuming the manufacturer's claim is correct,

$$P(N) = .05 \text{ and } P(A) = 1 - P(N) = 1 - .05 = .95$$

The sample space for the purchase of 4 of the manufacturer's watches is listed below.

| | | | |
|---|---|---|---|
| (A, A, A, A) | (A, N, A, A) | (N, A, A, A) | (N, N, A, A) |
| (A, A, A, N) | (A, N, A, N) | (N, A, A, N) | (N, N, A, N) |
| (A, A, N, A) | (A, N, N, A) | (N, A, N, A) | (N, N, N, A) |
| (A, A, N, N) | (A, N, N, N) | (N, A, N, N) | (N, N, N, N) |

a. All 4 watches being accurate as claimed is the simple event (A, A, A, A).

Assuming the watches purchased operate independently and the manufacturer's claim is correct,

$$P(A, A, A, A) = P(A)P(A)P(A)P(A) = (.95)^4 = .8145$$

b. The simple events in the sample space that consist of exactly two watches failing to meet the claim are listed below.

| | |
|---|---|
| (A, A, N, N) | (N, A, A, N) |
| (A, N, A, N) | (N, A, N, A) |
| (A, N, N, A) | (N, N, A, A) |

The probability that exactly two of the four watches fail to meet the claim is the sum of the probabilities of these six simple events.

Assuming the watches purchased operate independently and the manufacturer's claim is correct,

$$P(A, A, N, N) = P(A)P(A)P(N)P(N) = (.95)(.95)(.05)(.05)$$
$$= .00225625$$

All six of the simple events will have the same probability. Therefore, the probability that exactly two of the four watches fail to meet the claim when the manufacturer's claim is correct is

$$6(0.00225625) = .0135$$

c. The simple events in the sample space that consist of three of the four watches failing to meet the claim are listed below.

(A, N, N, N)  (N, N, A, N)
(N, A, N, N)  (N, N, N, A)

The probability that three of the four watches fail to meet the claim is the sum of the probabilities of the four simple events.

Assuming the watches purchased operate independently and the manufacturer's claim is correct,

$$P(A, N, N, N) = P(A)P(N)P(N)P(N) = (.95)(.05)(.05)(.05) = .00011875$$

All four of the simple events will have the same probability. Therefore, the probability that three of the four watches fail to meet the claim when the manufacturer's claim is correct is

$$4(.00011875) = .000475$$

If this event occurred, we would tend to doubt the validity of the manufacturer's claim since its probability of occurring is so small.

d. All 4 watches tested failing to meet the claim is the simple event (N, N, N, N).

Assuming the watches purchased operate independently and the manufacturer's claim is correct,

$$P(N, N, N, N) = P(N)P(N)P(N)P(N) = (.05)^4 = .00000625$$

Since the probability of observing this event is so small if the claim is true, we have strong evidence against the validity of the claim. However, we do not have conclusive proof that the claim is false. There is still a chance the event can occur (with probability .00000625) although it is extremely small.

4.67 Define the following events:

T: {Technical staff}
N: {Nontechnical staff}
U: {Under 20 years with company}
O: {Over 20 years with company}
$R_1$: {Retire at age 65}
$R_2$: {Retire at age 68}

The probabilities for each simple event are given in table form.

| | U | | O | |
|---|---|---|---|---|
| | T | N | T | N |
| $R_1$ | $\frac{31}{200}$ | $\frac{5}{200}$ | $\frac{45}{200}$ | $\frac{12}{200}$ |
| $R_2$ | $\frac{59}{200}$ | $\frac{25}{200}$ | $\frac{15}{200}$ | $\frac{8}{200}$ |

Each simple event consists of 3 characteristics: type of staff (T or N), years with the company, (U or O), and age plan to retire ($R_1$ or $R_2$).

a. $P(T) = P(T \cap U \cap R_1) + P(T \cap U \cap R_2) + P(T \cap O \cap R_1) + P(T \cap O \cap R_2)$

$$= \frac{31}{200} + \frac{59}{200} + \frac{45}{200} + \frac{15}{200} = \frac{150}{200}$$

b. $P(O) = P(O \cap T \cap R_1) + P(O \cap T \cap R_2) + P(O \cap N \cap R_1) + P(O \cap N \cap R_2)$

$$= \frac{45}{200} + \frac{15}{200} + \frac{12}{200} + \frac{8}{200} = \frac{80}{200}$$

$$P(R_2 \cap O) = P(R_2 \cap O \cap T) + P(R_2 \cap O \cap N) = \frac{15}{200} + \frac{8}{200} = \frac{23}{200}$$

Thus, $P(R_2|O) = \frac{P(R_2 \cap O)}{P(O)} = \frac{\frac{23}{200}}{\frac{80}{200}} = \frac{23}{80}$

c. $P(T) = \frac{150}{200}$ from a.

$$P(U \cap T) = P(U \cap T \cap R_1) + P(U \cap T \cap R_2) = \frac{31}{200} + \frac{59}{200} = \frac{90}{200}$$

Thus, $P(U|T) = \frac{P(U \cap T)}{P(T)} = \frac{\frac{90}{200}}{\frac{150}{200}} = \frac{90}{150}$

d. $P(O \cap N \cap R_1) = \frac{12}{200}$

4.69 The number of different ways to select 5 stocks from 10 stocks is a combination of 10 things taken 5 at a time or

$$\binom{10}{5} = \frac{10!}{5!(10 - 5)!} = \frac{10 \cdot 9 \cdot 8 \cdot 7 \cdot 6 \cdot 5 \cdot 4 \cdot 3 \cdot 2 \cdot 1}{5 \cdot 4 \cdot 3 \cdot 2 \cdot 1 \cdot 5 \cdot 4 \cdot 3 \cdot 2 \cdot 1} = 252$$

4.71 Define the following events:

L: {under 30}
M: {30-50}
H: {over 50}
N: {Noticed the ad}
$N^c$: {Did not notice the ad}

a. The simple events are:

(L, N), (M, N), (H, N), (L, $N^c$), (M, $N^c$), (H, $N^c$)

b. The set of all possible simple events is called the sample space.

c. P(L, N) = .25     P(L, $N^c$) = .05
P(M, N) = .20     P(M, $N^c$) = .15
P(H, N) = .10     P(H, $N^c$) = .25

4.73 Define the following events:

G: {regularly use the golf course}
T: {regularly use the tennis courts}

Given: P(G) = .7 and P(T) = .5

The event 'uses neither facility' can be written as $G^c \cap T^c$ or $(G \cup T)^c$. We are given $P(G^c \cap T^c) = P[(G \cup T)^c] = .05$. The complement of the event 'uses neither facility' is the event 'uses at least one of the two facilities' which can be written as $G \cup T$.

$$P(G \cup T) = 1 - P[(G \cup T)^c] = 1 - .05 = .95$$

From the additive rule, $P(G \cup T) = P(G) + P(T) - P(G \cap T)$

$\Rightarrow .95 = .7 + .5 - P(G \cap T)$
$\Rightarrow P(G \cap T) = .25$

a. The Venn Diagram is:

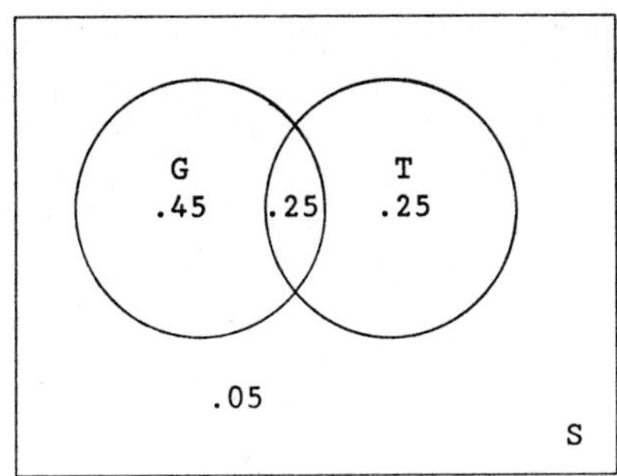


b. $P(G \cup T) = .95$ from above.

c. $P(G \cap T) = .25$ from above.

d. $P(G|T) = \frac{P(G \cap T)}{P(T)} = \frac{.25}{.5} = .5$

4.75 The statement would be valid if 1/50th of all U.S. citizens reside in New Hampshire. However, this is not true. Therefore, the statement is invalid.

4.77 Define the following events:

$O_1$: Component #1 operates properly
$O_2$: Component #2 operates properly
$O_3$: Component #3 operates properly

$P(O_1) = 1 - P(O_1^c) = 1 - .12 = .88$
$P(O_2) = 1 - P(O_2^c) = 1 - .09 = .91$
$P(O_3) = 1 - P(O_3^c) = 1 - .11 = .89$

a. P(system operates properly) $= P(O_1 \cap O_2 \cap O_3)$
$= P(O_1)P(O_2)P(O_3)$ (since the three components operate independently)
$= (.88)(.91)(.89)$
$= .7127$

b. P(system fails) = 1 - P(system operates properly)
= 1 - .7127 (see part (a))
= .2873

4.79 Define the following events:

A: {product A is accepted by the public}
B: {product B is accepted by the public}

Given:

$P(A \cap B^c) = .3$
$P(A^c \cap B) = .4$
$P(A \cap B) = .2$

The simple events of the sample space are.

A, B
A, $B^c$
$A^c$, B
$A^c$, $B^c$

Since the sum of the probabilities of these 4 events is 1,

$$P(A^c \cap B^c) = 1 - P(A \cap B) - P(A \cap B^c) - P(A^c \cap B)$$
$$= 1 - .2 - .3 - .4 = .1$$

This probability is not equal to .01. Therefore, we would disagree with the manager.

4.81 Let $M_1$, $M_2$, $M_3$, and $M_4$ represent the four minority applicants, and $N_1$ and $N_2$ represent the two nonminority applicants. The sample space for choosing two of the six applicants is:

| | | |
|---|---|---|
| $(M_1, M_2)$ | $(M_2, M_3)$ | $(M_3, N_1)$ |
| $(M_1, M_3)$ | $(M_2, M_4)$ | $(M_3, N_2)$ |
| $(M_1, M_4)$ | $(M_2, N_1)$ | $(M_4, N_1)$ |
| $(M_1, N_1)$ | $(M_2, N_2)$ | $(M_4, N_2)$ |
| $(M_1, N_2)$ | $(M_3, M_4)$ | $(N_1, N_2)$ |

Since the choice is random, all 15 of the simple events listed are equally likely. Therefore, they all have probability 1/15 of occurring.

a. $P(A) = P(N_1, N_2) = \frac{1}{15}$

b. $$P(B) = P(M_1, M_2) + P(M_1, M_3) + P(M_1, M_4) + P(M_2, M_3) + P(M_2, M_4) + P(M_3, M_4)$$
$$= \frac{1}{15} + \frac{1}{15} + \frac{1}{15} + \frac{1}{15} + \frac{1}{15} + \frac{1}{15}$$
$$= \frac{6}{15}$$

c. $P(C) = 1 - P(A) = 1 - \frac{1}{15} = \frac{14}{15}$

d. $P(B|C) = \frac{P(B \cap C)}{P(C)} = \frac{P(B)}{P(C)} = \frac{\frac{6}{15}}{\frac{14}{15}} = \frac{6}{14}$

e. $P(D|C) = \frac{P(D \cap C)}{P(C)}$

$= \frac{P(M_1, M_2) + P(M_1, M_3) + P(M_1, M_4) + P(M_1, N_1) + P(M_1, N_2)}{P(C)}$

$= \frac{\frac{5}{15}}{\frac{14}{15}} = \frac{5}{14}$

4.83 $P(A) = .06 + .15 + .04 = .25$

$P(B) = .05 + .06 + .03 + 0 = .14$

$P(A \cap B) = .06$

$P(A|B) = \frac{P(A \cap B)}{P(B)} = \frac{.06}{.14} = .4286$

$P(B|A) = \frac{P(A \cap B)}{P(A)} = \frac{.06}{.25} = .24$

$P(A \cap B) = P(A)P(B|A) = P(B)P(A|B) = .06$

$.06 = .25(.24) = .14\left(\frac{.06}{.14}\right) = .06$

4.85 a. We will first determine the number of ways n = 5 candidates may be selected from the N = 30 finalists:

$$\binom{30}{5} = \frac{30!}{5!25!} = 142{,}506$$

Thus, there are 142,506 simple events for this experiment. Furthermore, since the candidates are to be selected at random, each simple event is equally likely, with probability 1/142,506.

The next step is to determine the number of simple events which satisfy the event that none of the minority candidates is hired. The event of interest will occur if 0 of the 7 minority candidates is selected and 5 of the 23 nonminority candidates are selected. The number of ways this can occur is:

$$\binom{7}{0}\binom{23}{5} = \frac{7!}{0!7!} \cdot \frac{23!}{5!18!} = 33{,}649$$

Of the 142,506 simple events, 33,649 constitute the event of interest and thus the probability that none of the minority candidates is selected is:

$$\frac{33{,}649}{142{,}506} = .2361$$

b. The event that no more than one minority candidate is hired will occur if no minority candidate is hired or if one minority candidate is hired. Thus,

$$P(\text{No more than one minority candidate is hired}) = P(\text{No minority candidate is hired}) + P(\text{One minority candidate is hired}).$$

In part (a), we computed

$$P(\text{No minority candidate is hired}) = \frac{33,649}{142,506}$$

and it remains to compute the probability that exactly one minority candidate is hired.

The experiment contains 142,506 simple events, as shown in part (a). The number of these simple events for which 1 of the 7 minority candidates and 4 of the 23 nonminority candidates will be selected is

$$\binom{7}{1}\binom{23}{4} = \frac{7!}{1!6!} \cdot \frac{23!}{4!19!} = 61,985$$

and the probability that exactly one minority candidate will be hired is

$$\frac{61,985}{142,506} = .4350$$

Finally, the probability that no more than one minority candidate is hired is

$$\frac{33,649}{142,506} =+ \frac{61,985}{142,506} = .2361 + .4350 = .6711$$

4.87 Define the following events:

A: {salesperson sells computer on first visit}
B: {salesperson sells computer on second visit}

Given: $P(A) = .4$ and $P(B|A^c) = .65$

$$P(A^c) = 1 - P(A) = 1 - .4 = .6$$

$$P(\text{Sale}) = P(A) + P(B \cap A^c) = P(A) + P(B|A^c)P(A^c)$$

$$= .4 + .65(.6) = .4 + .390 = .79$$

4.89

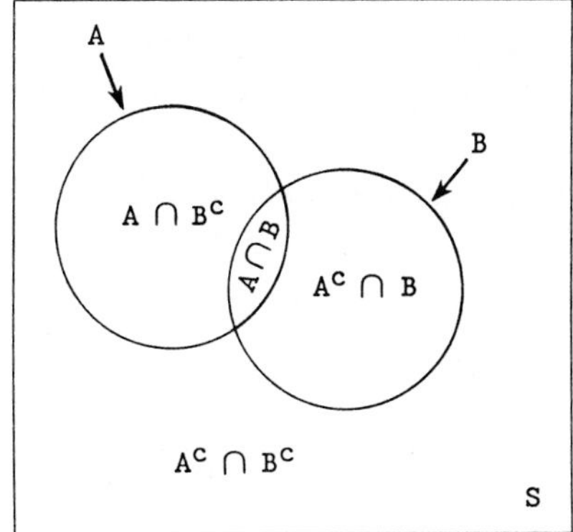


From the Venn Diagram, you can see that

$$P(A) = P(A \cap B^c) + P(A \cap B).$$

Thus, $P(A \cap B^c) = P(A) = P(A \cap B)$

4.91 This statement is false. The outcomes of the first 20 tosses are independent of any future tosses. Anytime a fair coin is tossed, the probability of a head is 1/2 and the probability of a tail is 1/2.

# CHAPTER 5

## DISCRETE RANDOM VARIABLES

5.1 A random variable is a rule that assigns one and only one value to each simple event of an experiment.

5.3 a. The number of houses sold by a real estate developer is countable (1, 2, 3, ...), so this is a *discrete* random variable.

b. This is a *continuous* random variable because we cannot count all the possible values.

c. Although a quart of milk is supposed to be 32 ounces, it can take on any value within an acceptable limit of 32 ounces, e.g., 32.09 ounces. Therefore, this is a *continuous* random variable.

d. The possible values for this random variable can be counted (e.g., 0, 7, 10, etc.). Hence, the variable is *discrete.*

5.5 The number of occupied units in an apartment complex at any time is a discrete random variable, as is the number of shares of stock traded on the New York Stock Exchange on a particular day. Two examples of continuous random variables are the length of time to complete a building project and the weight of a truckload of oranges.

5.7 An economist might be interested in the percentage of the work force that is unemployed, or the current inflation rate, both of which are continuous random variables.

5.9 The manager of a clothing store might be concerned with the number of employees on duty at a specific time of day, or the number of articles of a particular type of clothing that are on hand.

5.11 The probability distribution of a discrete random variable is a graph, table, or formula that specifies the probability associated with each possible value the random variable can assume.

5.13 a. When a die is tossed, the number of spots observed on the upturned face can be 1, 2, 3, 4, 5, or 6. Since the 6 simple events are equally likely, each one has a probability of 1/6.

The probability distribution of x may be summarized in tabular form:

| x | 1 | 2 | 3 | 4 | 5 | 6 |
|---|---|---|---|---|---|---|
| p(x) | $\frac{1}{6}$ | $\frac{1}{6}$ | $\frac{1}{6}$ | $\frac{1}{6}$ | $\frac{1}{6}$ | $\frac{1}{6}$ |

b. The probability distribution of x may also be presented in graphical form:

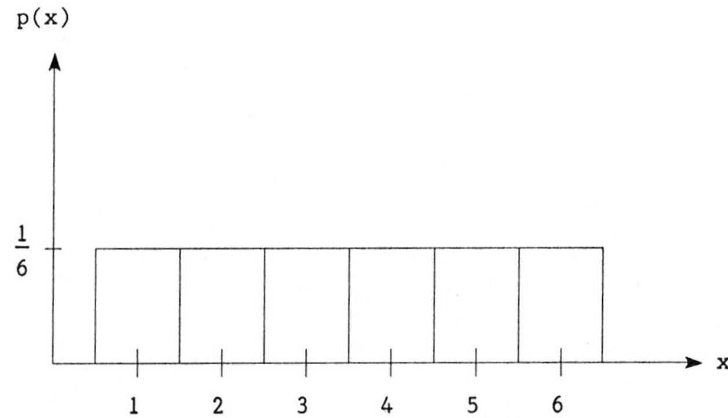


5.15 a. $P(x \leq 12) = p(10) + p(11) + p(12)$
$= .1 + .2 + .5$
$= .8$

b. $P(x > 12) = p(13) + p(14)$
$= .1 + .1$
$= .2$

c. $P(x \leq 14) = p(10) + p(11) + p(12) + p(13) + p(14)$
$= .1 + .2 + .5 + .1 + .1$
$= 1$

d. $P(x = 14) = p(14) = .1$

e. $P(x \leq 11 \text{ or } x > 12) = p(10) + p(11) + p(13) + p(14)$
$= .1 + .2 + .1 + .1$
$= .5$

5.17 a. The probability distribution for x in graphical form:

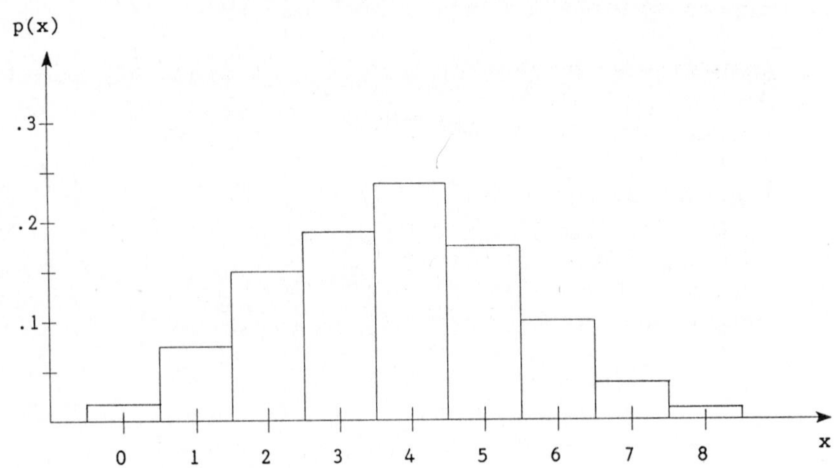


b. $P(x > 3) = p(4) + p(5) + p(6) + p(7) + p(8)$
$= .24 + .17 + .10 + .04 + .01$
$= .56$

$P(x > 4) = p(5) + p(6) + p(7) + p(8)$
$= .17 + .10 + .04 + .01 = .32$

5.19 a. Let x equal the value of the prize. Since there are 300,000 brochures mailed, 3 people will win $5,000, 3 will win a microwave oven, 3 will win a television, 3 will win a computer, 3 will win a video recorder, 3 will win a moped, and 299,982 will win a raft. Since the winning numbers are randomly assigned to brochures, the probability distribution of x is given below in tabular form:

| x | 5000 | 795 | 769 | 699 | 500 | 49.95 |
|---|---|---|---|---|---|---|
| p(x) | $\frac{3}{300,000}$ | $\frac{3}{300,000}$ | $\frac{3}{300,000}$ | $\frac{6}{300,000}$ | $\frac{3}{300,000}$ | $\frac{299,982}{300,000}$ |

b. P(not win an inflatable raft)
= 1 - P(will win an inflatable raft)
= 1 - p(49.95)

$= 1 - \frac{299,982}{300,000}$

$= \frac{18}{300,000} = .00006$

c. No, the answer would not change if 1,000,000 instead of 300,000 brochures are mailed. When the number of brochures is increased, the number of winners also increases, but the ratio always stays the same. Therefore, the probability of winning the prizes will not change.

b. $\sigma = \sqrt{\sigma^2}$ $\quad \sigma^2 = \sum_{\text{All } x} (x - \mu)^2 p(x)$

Firm A:

$$\begin{aligned}\sigma^2 &= (0 - 2450)^2(.01) + (500 - 2450)^2(.01) + \ldots \\ &\quad + (5000 - 2450)^2(.01) \\ &= 60{,}025 + 38{,}025 + 21{,}025 + 18{,}050 + 70{,}875 + 750 \\ &\quad + 75{,}625 + 22{,}050 + 24{,}025 + 42{,}025 + 65{,}025 \\ &= 437{,}500 \\ \sigma &= 661.44\end{aligned}$$

Firm B:

$$\begin{aligned}\sigma^2 &= (0 - 2450)^2(.00) + (200 - 2450)^2(.01) + \ldots \\ &\quad + (4700 - 2450)^2(.01) \\ &= 0 + 50{,}625 + 61{,}250 + 31{,}250 + 84{,}375 + 18{,}750 \\ &\quad + 84{,}375 + 31{,}250 + 61{,}250 + 50{,}625 \\ &= 492{,}500 \\ \sigma &= 701.78\end{aligned}$$

Firm B faces greater risk of physical damage because it has a higher variance and standard deviation.

c. Part (b) is concerned with measuring pure risk since there is a chance of incurring an economic loss with the delivery trucks but no chance of a gain.

5.27 a. Let x = change in price of ABC at the close of business. First we need to find the probability distribution for x.

Since we are assuming that when stock ABC's price changes it is by \$2, the probability distribution of x is:

| x | -2 | 0 | 2 |
|---|---|---|---|
| p(x) | .2 | .2 | .6 |

The expected change in ABC's price is

$$\begin{aligned}E(x) = \sum_{\text{All } x} xp(x) &= -2(.2) + 0(.2) + 2(.6) \\ &= -.4 + 0 + 1.2 \\ &= .80\end{aligned}$$

b. We are assuming that ABC's price changes by exactly \$2 when it changes. Therefore, the change in ABC's price cannot equal its expected value of \$.80. The change must be -\$2, \$0, or \$2.

5.29 a. $E(x) = \sum_{\text{All } x} xp(x)$

$= 1.5(.055) + 2.5(.211) + 3.5(.226) + 4.5(.147) + 5.5(.10)$
$+ 6.5(.079) + 7.5(.046) + 8.5(.03) + 9.5(.028)$
$+ 10.5(.027) + 11.5(.022) + 15.5(.029)$
$= .0825 + .5275 + .791 + .6615 + .55 + .5135 + .345 + .255$
$+ .266 + .2835 + .253 + .4495$
$= 4.978$

b. $\sigma = \sqrt{\sigma^2}$

$\sigma^2 = \sum(x - \mu)^2 p(x)$

$= (1.5 - 4.978)^2(.055) + (2.5 - 4.978)^2(.211) + \ldots$
$+ (15.5 - 4.978)^2(.029)$
$= .665 + 1.296 + .494 + .034 + .027 + .183 + .293 + .372$
$+ .573 + .823 + .936 + 3.211$
$= 8.907$

$\sigma = \sqrt{8.907} = 2.984$

c. $\mu \pm 2\sigma \Rightarrow 4.978 \pm 2(2.984) \Rightarrow (-.99, 10.949)$

$P(-.99 < x < 10.946) = p(1.5) + p(2.5) + p(3.5) + p(4.5) + p(5.5)$
$+ p(6.5) + p(7.5) + p(8.5) + p(9.5)$
$+ p(10.5)$
$= .055 + .211 + .226 + .147 + .100 + .079$
$+ .046 + .030 + .028 + .027$
$= .949$

5.31 We need to find E(x).

$E(x) = \sum_{\text{All } x} xp(x)$

$= -5000(.2) + 10,000(.5) + 30,000(.3)$
$= -1000 + 5000 + 9000$
$= 13,000$

Since the expected contribution to profit is over $10,000, the company should market the new line.

5.33 a. Let x = profit from the concert. The probability distribution for the random variable x is

| | (Rain) | (No Rain) |
|---|---|---|
| x | -12,000 | 20,000 |
| p(x) | .4 | .6 |

The producer's expected profit from the concert is

$$E(x) = \sum_{\text{All } x} xp(x) = -12000(.4) + 20000(.6)$$
$$= -4800 + 12000$$
$$= \$7200$$

b. Let x = profit from the concert. The probability distribution for the random variable x if the producer buys insurance is

| | (Rain) | (No Rain) |
|---|---|---|
| x | -1,000 | 19,000 |
| p(x) | .4 | .6 |

The producer's expected profit form the concert if she buys insurance is

$$E(x) = \sum_{\text{All } x} xp(x) = -1000(.4) + 19000(.6)$$
$$= -400 + 11400$$
$$= \$11,000$$

c. The insurance company has charged too little for the policy since the producer's expected profit has increased by 11000 - 7200 = \$3800 by buying insurance.

5.35 a. $\frac{5!}{3!(5-3)!} = \frac{5!}{3!2!} = \frac{5 \cdot 4 \cdot 3 \cdot 2 \cdot 1}{3 \cdot 2 \cdot 1 \cdot 2 \cdot 1} = 10$

b. $\binom{6}{3} = \frac{6!}{3!(6-3)!} = \frac{6!}{3!3!} = \frac{6 \cdot 5 \cdot 4 \cdot 3 \cdot 2 \cdot 1}{3 \cdot 2 \cdot 1 \cdot 3 \cdot 2 \cdot 1} = 20$

c. $\binom{8}{0} = \frac{8!}{0!(8-0)!} = \frac{8!}{0!8!} = \frac{8 \cdot 7 \cdot 6 \cdot 5 \cdot 4 \cdot 3 \cdot 2 \cdot 1}{1 \cdot 8 \cdot 7 \cdot 6 \cdot 5 \cdot 4 \cdot 3 \cdot 2 \cdot 1} = 1$

(Note: $0! = 1$)

d. $\binom{5}{5} = \frac{5!}{5!(5-5)!} = \frac{5!}{5!0!} = \frac{5 \cdot 4 \cdot 3 \cdot 2 \cdot 1}{5 \cdot 4 \cdot 3 \cdot 2 \cdot 1 \cdot 1} = 1$

e. $\binom{6}{1} = \frac{6!}{1!(6-1)!} = \frac{6!}{1!5!} = \frac{6 \cdot 5 \cdot 4 \cdot 3 \cdot 2 \cdot 1}{1 \cdot 5 \cdot 4 \cdot 3 \cdot 2 \cdot 1} = 6$

5.37 a. $p(x) = \binom{n}{x} p^x(1-p)^{n-x}$

$P(x = 0) = p(0) = \binom{5}{0}.2^0.8^5 = \frac{5!}{0!5!}.2^0.8^5 = 1(1)(.32768) = .32768$

$P(x = 1) = p(1) = \binom{5}{1}.2^1.8^4 = \frac{5!}{1!4!}.2^1.8^4 = 5(.2)(.4096) = .4096$

$P(x = 2) = p(2) = \binom{5}{2}.2^2.8^3 = \frac{5!}{2!3!}.2^2.8^3 = 10(.04)(.512) = .2048$

$P(x = 3) = p(3) = \binom{5}{3}.2^3.8^2 = \frac{5!}{3!2!}.2^3.8^2 = 10(.008)(.64) = .0512$



$P(6) = \binom{36}{6}(.17)^6(.83)^{30}$

$P(x = 4) = p(4) = \binom{5}{4}.2^4.8^1 = \frac{5!}{4!1!}.2^4.8^1 = 5(.0016)(.8) = .0064$

$P(x = 5) = p(5) = \binom{5}{5}.2^5.8^0 = \frac{5!}{5!0!}.2^5.8^0 = 1(.00032)(1) = .00032$

In tabular form, the probability distribution for x is

| x | 0 | 1 | 2 | 3 | 4 | 5 |
|---|---|---|---|---|---|---|
| p(x) | .32768 | .4096 | .2048 | .0512 | .0064 | .00032 |

b.

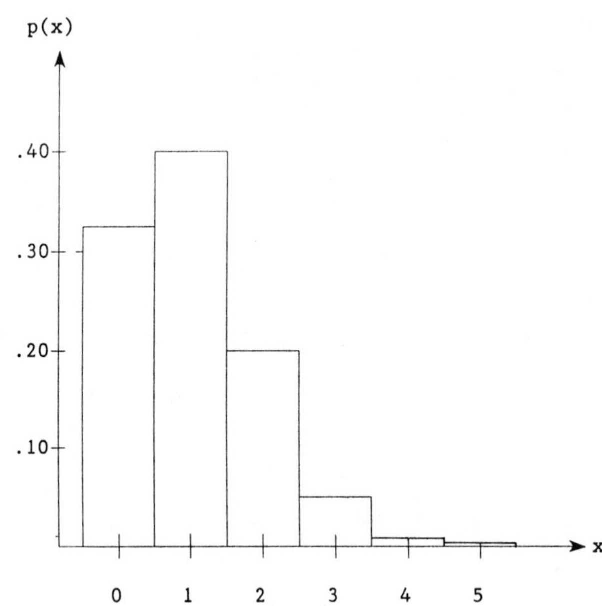


5.39 a. $p(x) = \binom{11}{x}.5^x.5^{11-x} \quad x = 0, 1, 2, \ldots, 11$

$P(x = 0) = p(0) = \binom{11}{0}.5^0.5^{11} = \frac{11!}{0!11!}.5^{11} = (.5)^{11} = .000488$

$P(x = 1) = p(1) = \binom{11}{1}.5^1.5^{10} = \frac{11!}{1!10!}.5^{11} = 11(.5)^{11} = .005371$

$P(x = 2) = p(2) = \binom{11}{2}.5^2.5^9 = \frac{11!}{2!9!}.5^{11} = 55(.5)^{11} = .026855$

$P(x = 3) = p(3) = \binom{11}{3}.5^3.5^8 = \frac{11!}{3!8!}.5^{11} = 165(.5)^{11} = .080566$

$P(x = 4) = p(4) = \binom{11}{4}.5^4.5^7 = \frac{11!}{4!7!}.5^{11} = 330(.5)^{11} = .161133$

$P(x = 5) = p(5) = \binom{11}{5}.5^5.5^6 = \frac{11!}{5!6!}.5^{11} = 462(.5)^{11} = .225586$

$P(x = 6) = p(6) = \binom{11}{6}.5^6.5^5 = \frac{11!}{6!5!}.5^{11} = 462(.5)^{11} = .225586$

$$P(x = 7) = p(7) = \binom{11}{7}.5^7.5^4 = \frac{11!}{7!4!}.5^{11} = 330(.5)^{11} = .161133$$

$$P(x = 8) = p(8) = \binom{11}{8}.5^8.5^3 = \frac{11!}{8!3!}.5^{11} = 165(.5)^{11} = .080566$$

$$P(x = 9) = p(9) = \binom{11}{9}.5^9.5^2 = \frac{11!}{9!2!}.5^{11} = 55(.5)^{11} = .026855$$

$$P(x = 10) = p(10) = \binom{11}{10}.5^{10}.5^1 = \frac{11!}{10!1!}.5^{11} = 11(.5)^{11} = .005371$$

$$P(x = 11) = p(11) = \binom{11}{11}.5^{11}.5^0 = \frac{11!}{11!0!}.5^{11} = (.5)^{11} = .000488$$

In tabular form, the probability distribution for x is:

| x | 0 | 1 | 2 | 3 | 4 | 5 | 6 |
|---|---|---|---|---|---|---|---|
| p(x) | .000488 | .005371 | .026855 | .080566 | .161133 | .225586 | .225586 |

| 7 | 8 | 9 | 10 | 11 |
|---|---|---|---|---|
| .161133 | .080566 | .026855 | .005371 | .000488 |

b. $$\begin{aligned}\mu = \sum_{\text{All } x} x(px) &= 0(.000488) + 1(.005371) + 2(.026855) + 3(.080566) \\ &\quad + 4(.161133) + 5(.225586) + 6(.225586) \\ &\quad + 7(.161133) + 8(.080566) + 9(.026855) \\ &\quad + 10(.005371) + 11(.000488) \\ &= 0 + .005371 + .05371 + .241698 + .644532 + 1.12793 \\ &\quad + 1.353516 + 1.127931 + .644528 + .241695 \\ &\quad + .05371 + .005368 \\ &= 5.5.\end{aligned}$$

$$\begin{aligned}\sigma^2 = \sum_{\text{All } x} (x - \mu)^2 p(x) &= (0 - 5.5)^2(.000488) + (1 - 5.5)^2(.005371) \\ &\quad + (2 - 5.5)^2(.026855) + (3 - 5.5)^2(.080566) \\ &\quad + (4 - 5.5)^2(.161133) + (5 - 5.5)^2(.225586) \\ &\quad + (6 - 5.5)^2(.225586) + (7 - 5.5)^2(.161133) \\ &\quad + (8 - 5.5)^2(.080566) + (9 - 5.5)^2(.026855) \\ &\quad + (10 - 5.5)^2(.005371) \\ &\quad + (11 - 5.5)^2(.000488) \\ &= .014762 + .10876275 + .32897375 + .5035375 \\ &\quad + .36254925 + .05363965 + .0563965 \\ &\quad + .36254925 + .5035375 + .32897375 \\ &\quad + .10876275 + .014762 \\ &= 2.75\end{aligned}$$

c.

p(x)

.25 .20 .15 .10 .05

0 1 2 3 4 5 6 7 8 9 10 11 x

$\mu - 2\sigma = 2.18$ $E(x) = 5.5$ $\mu \pm 2\sigma = 8.82$

$$\mu \pm 2\sigma \Rightarrow 5.5 \pm 2\sqrt{2.75} \Rightarrow 5.5 \pm 2(1.6583)$$
$$\Rightarrow 5.5 \pm 3.3166$$
$$\Rightarrow (2.1834,\ 8.8166)$$

d. $\mu \pm 2\sigma \Rightarrow (2.18,\ 8.82)$ (part (c))

$$P(2.18 < x < 8.82) = \sum_{x=3}^{8} p(x)$$
$$= .080566 + .161133 + .225586 + .225586 + .161133 + .080566$$
$$= .93457$$

5.41 Using Table II in Appendix B with n = 15 and p = .40:

a. $P(x \le 1) = \sum_{x=0}^{1} p(x) = .005$

b. $P(x \ge 3) = 1 - P(x \le 2) = 1 - \sum_{x=0}^{2} p(x) = 1 - .027 = .973$

c. $P(x \le 5) = \sum_{x=0}^{5} p(x) = .403$

d. $P(x < 10) = P(x \le 9) = \sum_{x=0}^{9} p(x) = .966$

e. $P(x > 10) = 1 - P(x \le 10) = 1 - \sum_{x=0}^{10} p(x) = 1 - .991 = .009$

f. $P(x = 6) = P(x \le 6) - p(x \le 5) = .610 - .403 = .207$

5.43 Define x as the number of invoices in the sample that contain arithmetic errors. The random variable x is a binomial random variable since it fits the characteristics (the invoices are independently chosen with only two possible outcomes). If the accountant's theory is valid, n = 25 and p = .10.

$$P(x \geq 7) = 1 - P(x \leq 6) = 1 - \sum_{x=0}^{6} p(x)$$
$$= 1 - .991 \quad \text{(Table II)}$$
$$= .009$$

5.45 Define x as the number of components that operate successfully. The random variable x is a binomial random variable (the components operate independently and there are only two possible outcomes) with n = 4 and p = .85.

$$P(\text{system fails}) = P(x = 0)$$
$$= \binom{4}{0}.85^0(.15)^{4-0}$$
$$= \frac{4!}{0!4!}\ .85^0(.15)^4$$
$$= .15^4 = .0005$$

5.47 Define the following events:

J: Stock market is up in January
Y: Stock market is up for the whole year

If there is no truth to the "January" theory, there are four equally likely events that could occur in any a given year:

$J, Y \qquad J, Y^c \qquad J^c, Y \qquad J^c, Y^c$

Thus, the probability of perfect agreement with the "January" theory if, in fact, there is no truth to the theory is

$$P(J, Y) + P(J^c, Y^c) = \frac{1}{4} + \frac{1}{4} = \frac{1}{2}$$

Let x equal the number of years that the January and annual movements are in perfect agreement during a period of 15 years.

The random variable x is a binomial random variable with p = .5, q = 5, and n = 15.

a. $p(x) = \binom{n}{x}p^x q^{n-x}$

$$P(x = 15) = \binom{15}{15}.5^{15}.5^0 = \frac{15!}{15!0!}\ .5^{15}.5^0$$
$$= 1(.5^{15})(1) = .00003052 \approx 0$$

b. $P(x \geq 10) = 1 - P(x \leq 9)$

$$= 1 - \sum_{x=0}^{9} p(x)$$

$= 1 - .849$ (Table II, Appendix B)

$= .151$

5.49 a. We must assume that the probability that a specific type of ball meets the requirements is always the same from trial to trial and the trials are independent. To use the binomial probability distribution, we need to know the probability that a specific type of golf ball meets the requirements.

b. For a binomial distribution,

$$\mu = np$$
$$\sigma = \sqrt{npq}$$

In this example, n = two dozen = 2 • 12 = 24.

$p = .10$ (Success here means the golf ball *does not* meet
$q = .90$ standards.)

$$\mu = np = 24(.10) = 2.4$$

$$\sigma = \sqrt{npq} = \sqrt{24(.10)(.90)} = 1.47$$

c. In this situation,

$p$ = Probability of success
= Probability golf ball *does* meet standards
= .90
$q = 1 - .90 = .10$
$n = 24$
$\mu = np = 24(.90) = 21.60$

$\sigma = \sqrt{npq} = \sqrt{24(.10)(.90)} = 1.47$ (Note that this is the same as in part (b).)

5.51 The random variable x = number of defective fuses is a binomial random variable with n = 25. We will accept a lot if $x < 3$.

Using Table II, Appendix B:

a. $P(\text{accepting a lot}) = P(x < 3) = \sum_{x=0}^{2} p(x) = 0$ when $p = 1$

b. $P(\text{accepting a lot}) = P(x < 3) = \sum_{x=0}^{2} p(x) \approx 0$ when $p = .8$

c. P(accepting a lot) = $P(x < 3) = \sum_{x=0}^{2} p(x) \approx 0$ when $p = .5$

d. P(accepting a lot) = $P(x < 3) = \sum_{x=0}^{2} p(x) = .098$ when $p = .2$

e. P(accepting a lot) = $P(x < 3) = \sum_{x=0}^{2} p(x) = .873$ when $p = .05$

f. P(accepting a lot) = $P(x < 3) = \sum_{x=0}^{2} p(x) = 1$ when $p = 0$

A graph of the operating characteristic curve for this sampling plan is shown below.

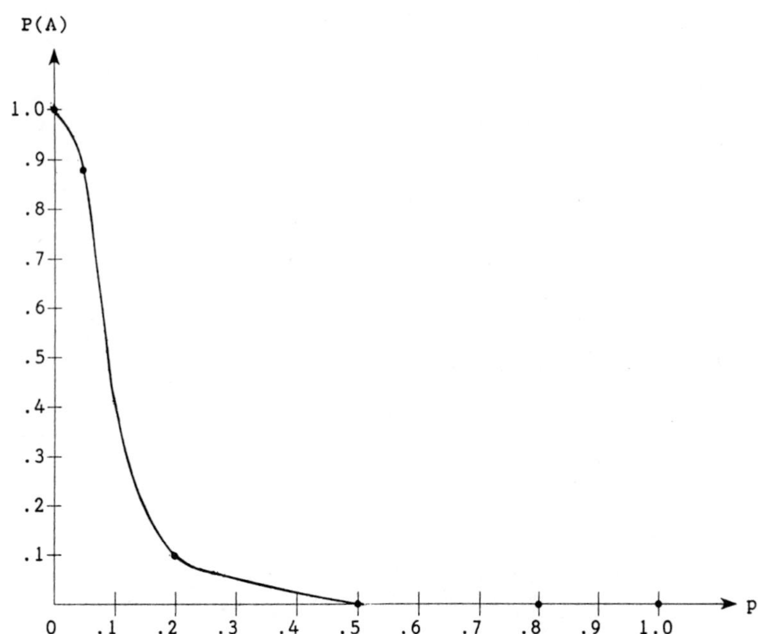


5.53 The random variable x (the number that prefer the beverage) is a binomial random variable with n = 400, p = .12, and q = .88 if the market analyst's claim is correct.

$$\mu = np = 400(.12) = 48$$

$$\sigma = \sqrt{npq} = \sqrt{400(.12)(.88)} = \sqrt{42.24} = 6.4992$$

If the market analyst's claim is true, it is not likely we would observe a value of $x \leq 31$. The value 31 is almost 3 standard deviations below the mean value of 48. Therefore, the survey does not agree with the market analyst's claim.

5.55 a. When $\lambda = 1$, $P(x \leq 2) = .920$

b. When $\lambda = 2$, $P(x \leq 2) = .677$

c. When $\lambda = 3$, $P(x \leq 2) = .423$

d. It decreases. As the expected value $\lambda$ gets larger, the $P(x \leq 2)$ would decrease.

5.57 a. To graph the Poisson probability distribution with $\lambda = 2$, we need to calculate p(x) for x = 0 to 10. Using Table III, Appendix B,

$p(0) = .135$
$p(1) = P(x \leq 1) - P(x = 0) = .406 - .135 = .271$
$p(2) = P(x \leq 2) - P(x \leq 1) = .677 - .406 = .271$
$p(3) = P(x \leq 3) - P(x \leq 2) = .857 - .677 = .180$
$p(4) = P(x \leq 4) - P(x \leq 3) = .947 - .857 = .090$
$p(5) = P(x \leq 5) - P(x \leq 4) = .983 - .947 = .036$
$p(6) = P(x \leq 6) - P(x \leq 5) = .995 - .983 = .012$
$p(7) = P(x \leq 7) - P(x \leq 6) = .999 - .995 = .004$
$p(8) = P(x \leq 8) - P(x \leq 7) \approx 1.000 - .999 \approx .001$
$p(9) = P(x \leq 9) - P(x \leq 8) \approx 1.000 - 1.000 \approx 0$
$p(10) = P(x \leq 10) - P(x \leq 9) \approx 1.000 - 1.000 \approx 0$

The graph is shown below.

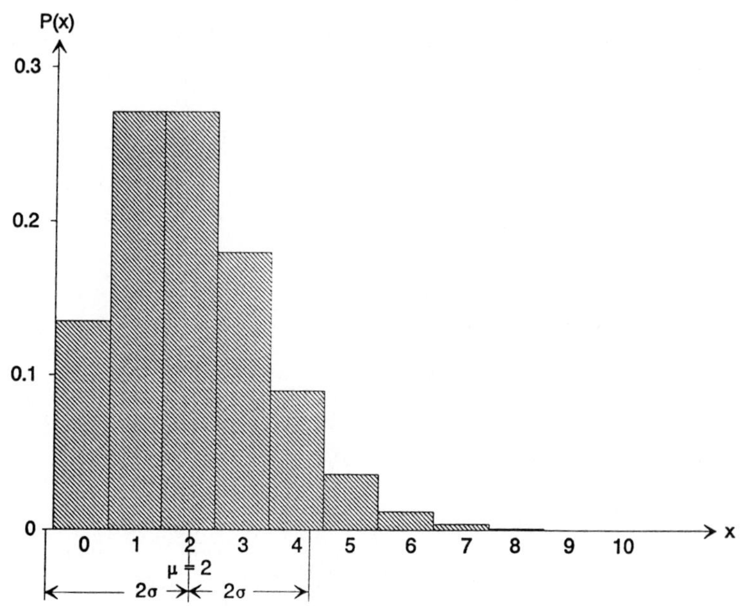

b. $\mu = \lambda = 2$

$\sigma = \sqrt{\lambda} = \sqrt{2} = 1.414$

$\mu \pm 2\sigma \Rightarrow 2 \pm 2(1.414)$
$\Rightarrow (-.828, 4.828)$

c. $P(\mu - 2\sigma < x < \mu + 2\sigma)$

$= P(-.828 < x < 4.828)$
$= P(x \leq 4)$
$= .947$

5.59 The random variable x is a binomial random variable with n = 25, p = .05, and q = 1 - .05 = .95.

Using Table II, Appendix B,

$p(0) = P(x = 0) = .277$
$p(1) = P(x = 1) = P(x \leq 1) - P(x = 0) = .642 - .277 = .365$
$p(2) = P(x = 2) = P(x \leq 2) - P(x \leq 1) = .873 - .642 = .231$

When $\lambda = \mu = np = 25(.05) = 1.25$, the corresponding Poisson approximations are given below.

Using the formula,

$$p(0) = P(x = 0) = \frac{\lambda^x e^{-\lambda}}{x!} = \frac{1.25^0(2.71828)^{-1.25}}{0!} = .287$$

$$p(1) = P(x = 1) = \frac{1.25^1(2.71828)^{-1.25}}{1!} = .358$$

$$p(2) = P(x = 2) = \frac{1.25^2(2.71828)^{-1.25}}{2!} = .224$$

5.61 a. $\sigma = \sqrt{\sigma^2} = \sqrt{\lambda} = \sqrt{4} = 2$

b. $P(x > 10) = 1 - P(x \leq 10)$
$= 1 - .977$ (Table III, Appendix B)
$= .003$

No. The probability that a sample of air from the plant exceeds the EPA limit is only .003. Since this value is very small, it is not very likely that this will occur.

c. The experiment consists of counting the number of parts per million of vinyl chloride in air samples. We must assume the probability of a part of vinyl chloride appearing in a million parts of air is the same for each million parts of air. We must also assume the number of parts of vinyl chloride in one million parts of air is independent of the number in any other one million parts of air.

5.63 $\mu = \lambda = 3.4$, using Table III, Appendix B:

$$P(x = 2) = P(x \leq 2) - P(x \leq 1) = .340 - .147 = .193$$

$$P(x \geq 3) = 1 - P(x \leq 2) = 1 - .340 = .660$$

We need to assume that the probability that an accident occurs in a particular month is the same for all months. The number of accidents that occur in a particular month must all be independent of the number occurring in other months.

5.65 $\mu = \lambda = 1.5$, using Table III, Appendix B:

$$P(x = 2) = P(x \leq 2) - P(x \leq 1) = .809 - .558 = .251$$

$$P(x < 2) = P(x \leq 1) = .558$$

The probability of no breakdowns on one shift is

$$P(x = 0) = .223$$

Therefore, the probability of no breakdowns for 3 consecutive 8-hour shifts

$$= P(x = 0 \cap x = 0 \cap x = 0)$$
$$= P(x = 0)P(x = 0)P(x = 0) \qquad \text{(by independence)}$$
$$= .223(.223)(.223)$$
$$= .011$$

5.67 Let $x$ = the number of major medical claims the health insurance company must pay.

The random variable $x$ is a binomial random variable with $n = 1000$, $p = .001$, and $q = 1 - .001 = .999$.

$$np = 1000(.001) = 1 \text{ which is } \leq 7$$

Therefore, the Poisson probability distribution provides a good approximation to the binomial probability distribution.

$$P(x \geq 1) = 1 - P(x = 0)$$
$$= 1 - .368 \qquad \text{Table III, Appendix B, with } \lambda = 1$$
$$= .632$$

5.69 a. The random variable x is a Poisson random variable with $\lambda = .5$

b. The random variable x is a binomial random variable with $n = 6$ and $p = .2$.

c. The random variable x is a binomial random variable with $n = 10$ and $p = .9$.

5.71 a. This experiment consists of 100 trials. Each trial results in one of two outcomes: chip is defective or not defective. If the number of chips produced in one hour is much larger than 100, then we can assume the probability of a defective chip is the same on each trial and that the trials are independent. Thus, x is a binomial. If, however, the number of chips produced in an hour is not much larger than 100, the trials would not be independent. Then x would not be a binomial random variable.

b. This experiment consists of 2 trials. Each trial results in one of two outcomes: applicant qualified or not qualified. However, the trials are not independent. The probability of selecting a qualified applicant on the first trial is 3 out of 5. The probability of selecting a qualified applicant on the second trial depends on what happened on the first trial. Thus, x is not a binomial random variable.

c. The number of trials is not a specified number in this experiment, thus x is not a binomial random variable. In this experiment, x is counting the number of calls received.

d. The number of trials in this experiment is 1000. Each trial can result in one of two outcomes: favor state income tax or not favor state income tax. Since 1000 is small compared to the number of registered voters in Florida, the probability of selecting a voter in favor of the state income tax is the same from trial to trial, and the trials are independent of each other. Thus, x is a binomial random variable.

5.73 x is a Poisson random variable with $\lambda = 4$. Using Table III, Appendix B,

a. $P(x = 0) = .018$

b. $P(x = 3) = P(x \leq 3) - P(x \leq 2) = .433 - .238 = .195$

c. $P(x = 1) = P(x \leq 1) - P(x = 0) = .092 - .018 = .074$

d. $P(x = 5) = P(x \leq 5) - P(x \leq 4) = .785 - .629 = .156$

e. $P(x \leq 2) = .238$

f. $P(x \geq 2) = 1 - P(x \leq 1) = 1 - .092 = .908$

5.75 The variable y has the largest variance since the data are more spread out in the graph of p(y). There are more data on the outside and less in the middle, as indicated in the graph. The variable z would have the next largest variance. The variable x would have the smallest variance since the data are not as spread out in the graph of p(x). The data are grouped in the middle at the mean.

5.77 a. The random variable x is a binomial random variable (the boards are chosen independently and there are two possible outcomes) with $n = 5$ and $p = 20/200 = .1$.

In order to graph the probability distribution for x, we need to know the probabilities for each possible value of x. Using Table II, Appendix B, with $n = 5$ and $p = .1$:

$$
\begin{aligned}
P(x = 0) &= .590 \\
P(x = 1) &= P(x \leq 1) - P(x = 0) = .919 - .590 = .329 \\
P(x = 2) &= P(x \leq 2) - P(x \leq 1) = .991 - .919 = .072 \\
P(x = 3) &= P(x \leq 3) - P(x \leq 2) \approx 1 - .991 = .009 \\
P(x = 4) &= P(x \leq 4) - P(x \leq 3) \approx 1 - 1 = .000 \\
P(x = 5) &= P(x \leq 5) - P(x \leq 4) \approx 1 - 1 = .000
\end{aligned}
$$

The probability distribution for x in tabular form is:

| x | 0 | 1 | 2 | 3 | 4 | 5 |
|---|---|---|---|---|---|---|
| p(x) | .590 | .329 | .072 | .009 | .000 | .000 |

The probability distribution for x in graphical form is:

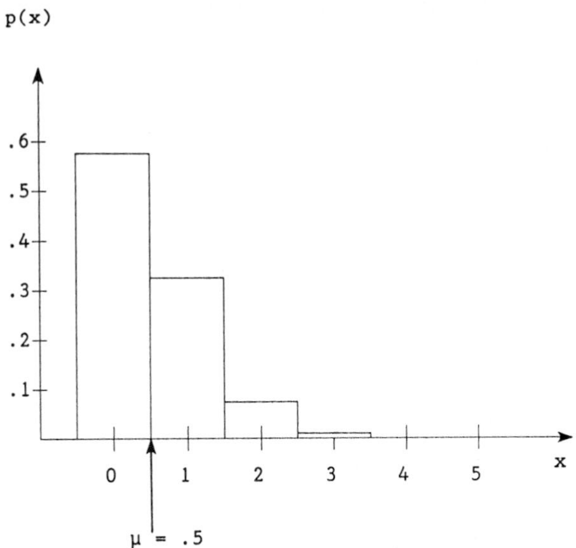


b. $\mu = np = 5(.1) = .5$

$\sigma^2 = npq = 5(.1)(.9) = .45$

5.79 a. The number of cars that have mileages within 2 miles per gallon of their EPA projections in a sample of 20 chosen from a population of 842 is not a binomial random variable since the sample is chosen without replacement from a finite population. However, since the sample is small compared to the population, we could treat it like a binomial random variable for convenience. Therefore, the statement is true.

b. Let x be the number of cars that have mileages within 2 miles per gallon of their EPA projections. For convenience, assume the random variable x is binomial with n = 20 and p = .68. Using Table II, Appendix B, with n = 20 and p = .70,

$$P(x < 10) = P(x \leq 9) = .017$$

Therefore, the probability is approximately .017.

5.81 a. For company A,

$$\begin{aligned} E(x) = \sum_{\text{All } x} xp(x) &= 2(.05) + 3(.15) + 4(.20) + 5(.35) + 6(.25) \\ &= .10 + .45 + .80 + 1.75 + 1.50 \\ &= 4.60 \end{aligned}$$

For company B,

$$E(x) = \sum_{\text{All } x} xp(x) = 2(.15) + 3(.30) + 4(.30) + 5(.20) + 6(.05)$$
$$= .30 + .90 + 1.20 + 1.00 + .30$$
$$= 3.70$$

b. The expected profit equals the expected value of x times the profit for each job.

For company A,

$$4.6(\$10{,}000) = \$46{,}000$$

For company B,

$$3.7(\$15{,}000) = \$55{,}500$$

c. For company A,

$$\sigma^2 = \sum_{\text{All } x} (x - \mu)^2 p(x) = (2 - 4.6)^2.05 + (3 - 4.6)^2.15 + (4 - 4.6)^2.20 + (5 - 4.6)^2.35 + (6 - 4.6)^2.25$$
$$= .338 + .384 + .072 + .056 + .49$$
$$= 1.34$$

$$\sigma = \sqrt{\sigma^2} = \sqrt{1.34} = 1.16$$

For company B,

$$\sigma^2 = \sum_{\text{All } x} (x - \mu)^2 p(x) = (2 - 3.7)^2.15 + (3 - 3.7)^2.30 + (4 - 3.7)^2.30 + (5 - 3.7)^2.20 + (6 - 3.7)^2.05$$
$$= .4335 + .147 + .027 + .338 + .2645$$
$$= 1.21$$

$$\sigma = \sqrt{\sigma^2} = \sqrt{1.21} = 1.10$$

d. For company A, the graph of p(x) is given below.

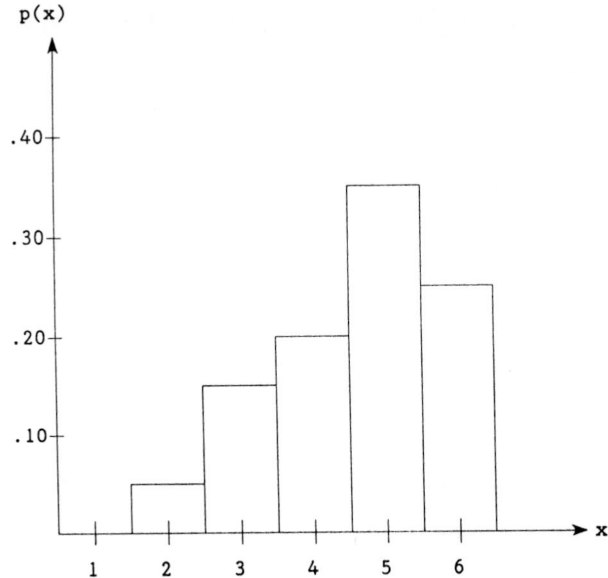


For company A,

$$\mu \pm 2\sigma \Rightarrow 4.6 \pm 2(1.16) \Rightarrow 4.6 \pm 2.32 \Rightarrow (2.28, 6.92)$$

$$\begin{aligned} P(2.28 < x < 6.92) &= p(3) + p(4) + p(5) + p(6) \\ &= .15 + .20 + .35 + .25 \\ &= .95 \end{aligned}$$

For company B, the graph of p(x) is given below.

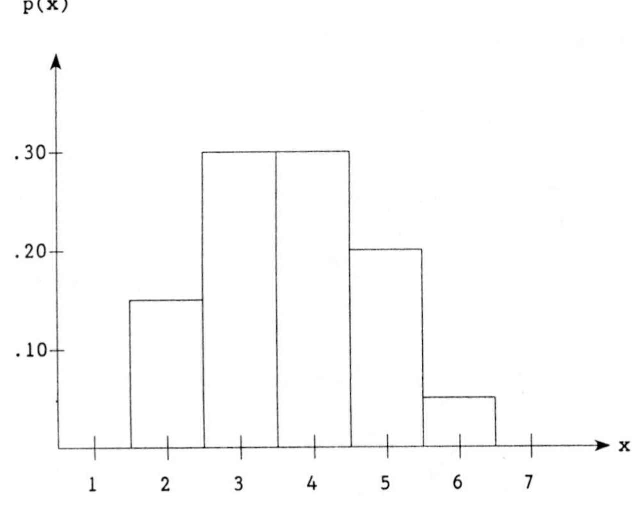

For company B,

$$\mu \pm 2\sigma \Rightarrow 3.70 \pm 2(1.10) \Rightarrow 3.67 \pm 2.2 \Rightarrow (1.5,\ 5.9)$$

$$\begin{aligned} P(1.5 < x < 5.9) &= p(2) + p(3) + p(4) + p(5) \\ &= .15 + .30 + .30 + .20 \\ &= .95 \end{aligned}$$

5.83 Let $x$ = the number of calls that are a hoax; then $x$ is a binomial random variable with $n = 5$, $p = \frac{1}{6}$, and $q = \frac{5}{6}$.

$$p(x) = \binom{5}{x}\left(\frac{1}{6}\right)^x\left(\frac{5}{6}\right)^{5-x} \qquad x = 0, 1, 2, 3, 4, 5$$

The probability that none of the calls was a hoax is:

$$P(x = 0) = p(0) = \binom{5}{0}\left(\frac{1}{6}\right)^0\left(\frac{5}{6}\right)^{5-0} = \frac{5!}{0!5!}\left(\frac{1}{6}\right)^0\left(\frac{5}{6}\right)^5 = 1(1)(.4019) = .4019$$

The probability that three of the callers really needed assistance is the probability that two of the calls were hoaxes:

$$P(x = 2) = p(2) = \binom{5}{2}\left(\frac{1}{6}\right)^2\left(\frac{5}{6}\right)^{5-2} = \frac{5!}{2!3!}\left(\frac{1}{6}\right)^2\left(\frac{5}{6}\right)^3 = 10(.02778)(.5787)$$

$$= .1608$$

We must assume that the characteristics of a binomial experiment are satisfied. That is, the five calls received are independent with the same probability of a hoax on each call.

5.85 We are interested in the number of calls from roadside boxes occurring in one hour. Let $x$ = the number of calls per hour. The random variable $x$ has a Poisson distribution with $\mu = \lambda = 1.1$.

$$P(x > 2) = 1 - P(x \leq 2) = 1 - .900 = .100$$

$$\begin{aligned} P(x = 3) &= P(x \leq 3) - P(x \leq 2) \\ &= .974 - .900 \\ &= .074 \end{aligned}$$

5.87 Let $x$ = the number of defective units in the sample. The random variable $x$ is a binomial random variable with $n = 10$ and $p = .11$.

$$p(x) = \binom{10}{x}.11^x.89^{10-x} \qquad x = 0, 1, 2, \ldots, 10$$

P(correct decision)
= P(reject the lot) (since more than 10% of the units are defective)
= $P(x \geq 2)$
= $1 - P(x \leq 1)$
= $1 - [p(0) + p(1)]$
= $1 - [\binom{10}{0}.11^0.89^{10} + \binom{10}{1}.11^1.89^9]$

= $1 - [.312 + .385]$
= $1 - .697$
= $.303$

5.89 Let x = the number of typewriters the outlet sells tomorrow. The random variable x is a Poisson random variable with $\mu = \lambda = 2.4$. Using Table III, Appendix B:

P(outlet runs out of typewriters tomorrow)
= $P(x > 5)$
= $1 - P(x \leq 5)$
= $1 - .964$
= $.036$

5.91 Let x = the number of delivery truck breakdowns today and y = the number of delivery truck breakdowns tomorrow. The random variables x and y are Poisson with $\mu = \lambda = 1.5$. Using Table III, Appendix B:

$P(x = 2 \cap y = 3)$
= $P(x = 2)P(y = 3)$ (by independence)

= $[P(x \leq 2) - P(x \leq 1)][P(y \leq 3) - P(y \leq 2)]$
= $(.809 - .558)(.934 - .809)$
= $.251(.125)$
= $.0314$

$P(x < 2 \cap y > 2)$
= $P(x < 2)P(y > 2)$ (by independence)
= $P(x \leq 1)[1 - P(y \leq 2)]$
= $.558(1 - .809)$
= $.558(.191)$
= $.1066$

5.93 Let x = the number of defective products in a sample of four products. In order to solve this problem, we need to assume the following:

1) Whether one product is defective is independent of whether the other product is defective.

2) The probability of a product being defective is the same ($p = .05$) for all the products.

With the above assumptions, x is a binomial random variable with $n = 4$, $p = .05$, and $q = .95$.

$$p(x) = \binom{n}{x}p^x q^{n-x} = \binom{4}{x}.05^x .95^{4-x} \qquad x = 0, 1, 2, 3, 4$$

$$P(x = 1) = p(1) = \binom{4}{1}.05^1 .95^3 = \frac{4!}{1!3!}(.05)(.95)^3$$

$$= 4(.05)(.95)^3$$
$$= .1715$$

5.95 The random variable x is a binomial random variable with $n = 25$, $p = .20$, and $q = 1 - p = .80$. (Assuming that whether a person refuses to take part in the poll is independent of any other person refusing.)

a. $\mu = np = 25(.20) = 5$
$\sigma^2 = npq = 25(.20)(.80) = 4$

b. $P(x \leq 5) = .617$ Table II, Appendix B

c. $P(x > 10) = 1 - P(x \leq 10)$
$= 1 - .994$
$= .006$

5.97 Let y = percentage of tax on sale.

The values y can take on are:

$y = 0$ if $x = 0, 1, 2, \ldots, 9$

$y = \frac{1}{x}(100)$ if $x = 10, 11, \ldots, 25$

$y = \frac{2}{x}(100)$ if $x = 26, 27, \ldots, 50$

$y = \frac{3}{x}(100)$ if $x = 51, 52, \ldots, 75$

$y = \frac{4}{x}(100)$ if $x = 76, 77, \ldots, 99$

Assuming $p(x) = .01$ for $x = 0, 1, 2, \ldots, 99$, the probability distribution for y is:

| y | p(y) | y p(y) |
|---|---|---|
| 0.00000 | 0.10 | 0.00000 |
| 4.00000 | 0.13 | 0.12000 |
| 4.04040 | 0.01 | 0.04040 |
| 4.05405 | 0.01 | 0.04054 |
| 4.08163 | 0.02 | 0.08163 |
| 4.10959 | 0.01 | 0.04110 |
| 4.12371 | 0.01 | 0.04124 |
| 4.16667 | 0.04 | 0.16667 |
| 4.21053 | 0.01 | 0.04211 |
| 4.22535 | 0.01 | 0.04225 |
| 4.25532 | 0.02 | 0.08511 |
| 4.28571 | 0.01 | 0.04286 |
| 4.30108 | 0.01 | 0.04301 |
| 4.34783 | 0.04 | 0.17391 |
| 4.39560 | 0.01 | 0.04396 |
| 4.41176 | 0.01 | 0.04412 |
| 4.44444 | 0.02 | 0.08889 |
| 4.47661 | 0.01 | 0.04478 |
| 4.49438 | 0.01 | 0.04494 |
| 4.54545 | 0.04 | 0.18182 |
| 4.59770 | 0.01 | 0.04598 |
| 4.61538 | 0.01 | 0.04615 |
| 4.65116 | 0.02 | 0.09302 |
| 4.68750 | 0.01 | 0.04688 |
| 4.70588 | 0.01 | 0.04706 |
| 4.76190 | 0.04 | 0.19048 |
| 4.81928 | 0.01 | 0.04819 |
| 4.83871 | 0.01 | 0.04839 |
| 4.87805 | 0.02 | 0.09756 |
| 4.91803 | 0.01 | 0.04918 |
| 4.93827 | 0.01 | 0.04938 |
| 5.00000 | 0.04 | 0.20000 |
| 5.06329 | 0.01 | 0.05063 |
| 5.08475 | 0.01 | 0.05085 |
| 5.12821 | 0.02 | 0.10256 |
| 5.17241 | 0.01 | 0.05172 |
| 5.19481 | 0.01 | 0.05195 |
| 5.26316 | 0.04 | 0.21053 |
| 5.35714 | 0.01 | 0.05357 |
| 5.40541 | 0.01 | 0.05405 |
| 5.45455 | 0.01 | 0.05455 |
| 5.55556 | 0.03 | 0.16667 |
| 5.66038 | 0.01 | 0.05660 |
| 5.71429 | 0.01 | 0.05714 |
| 5.76923 | 0.01 | 0.05769 |
| 5.88235 | 0.03 | 0.17647 |
| 6.06061 | 0.01 | 0.06061 |
| 6.25000 | 0.02 | 0.12500 |
| 6.45161 | 0.01 | 0.06452 |
| 6.66667 | 0.02 | 0.13333 |
| 6.89655 | 0.01 | 0.06897 |
| 7.14286 | 0.02 | 0.14286 |
| 7.40741 | 0.01 | 0.07407 |
| 7.69231 | 0.02 | 0.15385 |
| 8.33333 | 0.01 | 0.08333 |
| 9.09091 | 0.01 | 0.09091 |
| 10.00000 | 0.01 | 0.10000 |
| | 1.00 | 4.66402 |

The expected value of y is $E(y) = \sum_{\text{All } y} yp(y) = 4.66402$.

# CHAPTER 6

# CONTINUOUS RANDOM VARIABLES

6.1 a. $f(x) = \dfrac{1}{d - c} \quad (c \leq x \leq d)$

$$\frac{1}{d - c} = \frac{1}{45 - 20} = \frac{1}{25} = .04$$

So, $f(x) = .04 \ (20 \leq x \leq 45)$.

b. $\mu = \dfrac{c + d}{2} = \dfrac{20 + 45}{2} = \dfrac{65}{2} = 32.5$

$$\sigma = \frac{d - c}{\sqrt{12}} = \frac{45 - 20}{\sqrt{12}} = 7.2169$$

$$\sigma^2 = (7.2169)^2 = 52.0833$$

c.

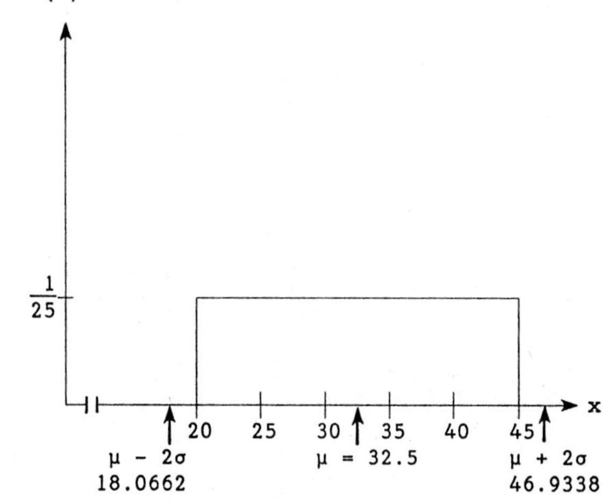


$\mu \pm 2\sigma \Rightarrow 32.5 \pm 2(7.2169) \Rightarrow (18.0662, 46.9338)$

$$P(18.0662 < x < 49.9338) = P(20 < x < 45)$$

$$= (45 - 20)\frac{1}{25} = 1$$

6.3 a. $f(x) = \frac{1}{d - c} \quad (c \leq x \leq d)$

$$\frac{1}{d - c} = \frac{1}{5 - 2} = \frac{1}{3}$$

$$f(x) = \frac{1}{3} \quad (2 \leq x \leq 5)$$

b. $\mu = \frac{c + d}{2} = \frac{2 + 5}{2} = \frac{7}{2} = 3.5$

$$\sigma = \frac{d - c}{\sqrt{12}} = \frac{5 - 2}{\sqrt{12}} = \frac{3}{\sqrt{12}} = .866$$

$$\sigma^2 = (.866)^2 = .75$$

c.

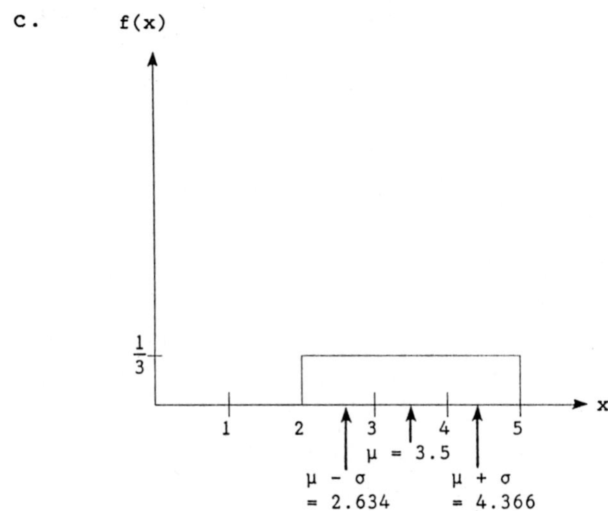


$\mu \pm \sigma \Rightarrow 3.5 \pm .866 \Rightarrow (2.634, 4.366)$

$$P(a < x < b) = P(2.634 < x < 4.366) = \frac{b - a}{d - c} = \frac{4.366 - 2.634}{5 - 2}$$

$$= \frac{1.732}{3} = .577$$

6.5 $f(x) = \frac{1}{d - c} = \frac{1}{200 - 100} = \frac{1}{100} = .01 \quad (100 \leq x \leq 200)$

f(x)

.01

100 200 x

$$\mu = \frac{c + d}{2} = \frac{100 + 200}{2} = \frac{300}{2} = 150$$

$$\sigma = \frac{d - c}{\sqrt{12}} = \frac{200 - 100}{\sqrt{12}} = \frac{100}{\sqrt{12}} = 28.8675$$

a. $\mu \pm 2\sigma \Rightarrow 150 \pm 2\left(\frac{100}{\sqrt{12}}\right) \Rightarrow 150 \pm 57.735$

$\Rightarrow (92.265, 207.735)$

$$P(x < 92.265) + P(x > 207.735) = P(x < 100) + P(x > 200) = 0 + 0 = 0$$

b. $\mu \pm 3\sigma \Rightarrow 150 \pm 3\left(\frac{100}{\sqrt{12}}\right) \Rightarrow 150 \pm 86.6025$

$\Rightarrow (63.3975, 236.6025)$

$$P(63.3975 < x < 236.6025) = P(100 < x < 200) = (200 - 100)(.01) = 1$$

c. From (a), $\mu \pm 2\sigma = (92.265, 207.735)$.

$$P(92.265 < x < 207.735) = P(100 < x < 200) = (200 - 100)(.01) = 1$$

6.7 To construct a relative frequency histogram for the data, we can use 7 measurement classes.

$$\text{Interval width} = \frac{\text{Largest number - smallest number}}{\text{Number of classes}} = \frac{98.0716 - .7434}{7} = 13.9$$

We will use an interval width of 14 and a starting value of .74335.

The measurement classes, frequencies, and relative frequencies are given in the table below.

| CLASS | MEASUREMENT CLASS | CLASS FREQUENCY | CLASS RELATIVE FREQUENCY |
|---|---|---|---|
| 1 | .74335 - 14.74335 | 6 | 6/40 = .15 |
| 2 | 14.74335 - 28.74335 | 4 | .10 |
| 3 | 28.74335 - 42.74335 | 6 | .15 |
| 4 | 42.74335 - 56.74335 | 6 | .15 |
| 5 | 56.74335 - 70.74335 | 5 | .125 |
| 6 | 70.74335 - 84.74335 | 4 | .10 |
| 7 | 84.74335 - 98.74335 | 9 | .225 |
| | | 40 | 1.000 |

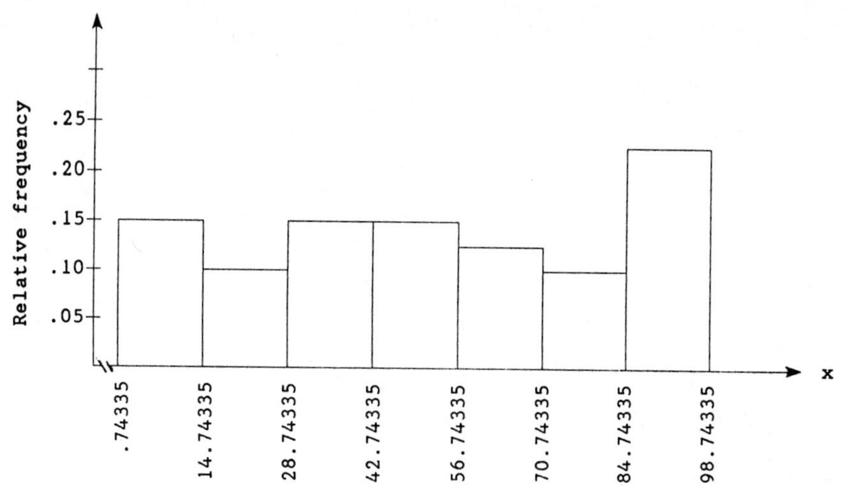


The histogram looks like the data could be from a uniform distribution. The last class (84.74335 - 98.74335) has a few more observations in it. However, we cannot expect a perfect graph from a sample of only 40 observations.

6.9 a.

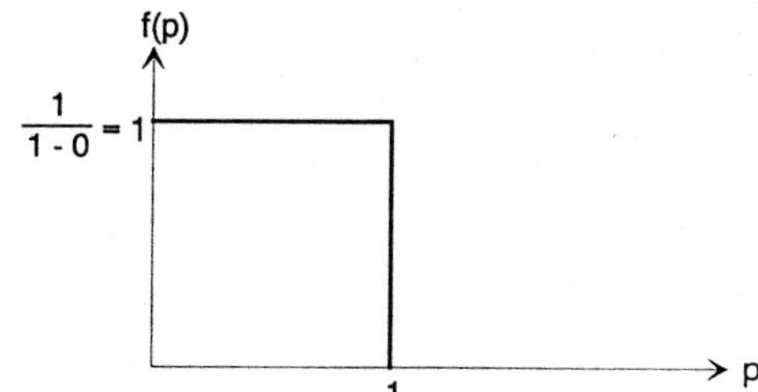


b. $\mu = \frac{c + d}{2} = \frac{0 + 1}{2} = .5$

$\sigma = \frac{d - c}{\sqrt{12}} = \frac{1 - 0}{\sqrt{12}} = .289 \qquad \sigma^2 = .289^2 = .083$

c. $P(p > .95) = (1 - .95)(1) = .05$
$P(p < .95) = (.95 - 0)(1) = .95$

d. The analyst should use a uniform probability distribution with $c = .90$ and $d = .95$.

$$f(p) = \frac{1}{d - c} = \frac{1}{.95 - .90} = \frac{1}{.05} = 20 \quad (.90 \leq p \leq .95)$$

6.11 Let x = the number of minutes you wait for the bus. The random variable x is best described by a uniform probability distribution with $c = 0$ and $d = 30$.

$$f(x) = \frac{1}{d - c} = \frac{1}{30 - 0} = \frac{1}{30} = .0333 \quad (0 \leq x \leq 30)$$

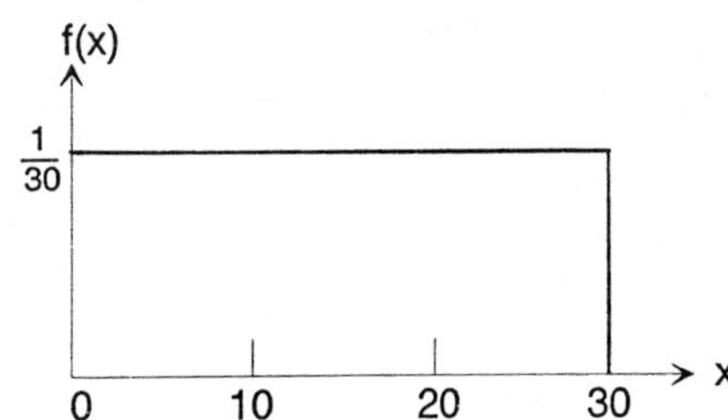


$P(x > 20) = (30 - 20)\left(\frac{1}{30}\right) = \frac{10}{30} = .333$

$\mu = \frac{c + d}{2} = \frac{0 + 30}{2} = 15$

You would expect to wait 15 minutes for the bus.

6.13 Table IV in the text gives the area between $z = 0$ and $z = z_0$. In this exercise, the answers may thus be read directly from the table by looking up the appropriate z.

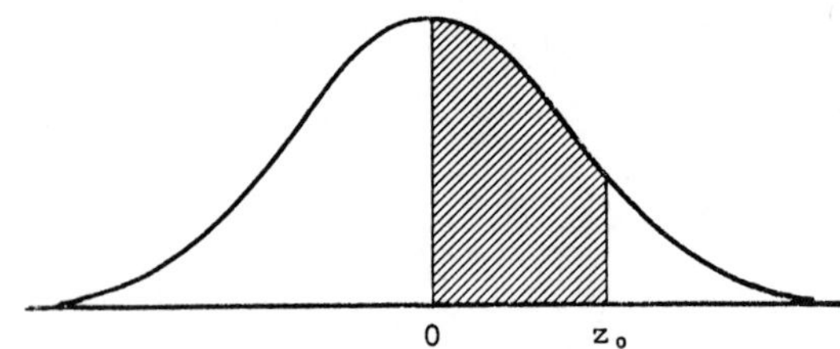


a. $P(0 < z < 2) = .4772$

b. $P(0 < z < 3.0) = .4987$

c. $P(0 < z < 1.5) = .4332$

d. $P(0 < z < .80) = .2881$

6.15 It is helpful to draw sketches to assist in finding the required areas. The areas can be found by using Table IV, Appendix B.

a. The area between $z = -1.5$ and $z = -1.0$ is equal to $A_1 - A_2$, where $A_1$ = area between -1.5 and 0 = .4332
$A_2$ = area between -1.0 and 0 = .3413

Thus, the required area is
.4332 - .3413 = .0919

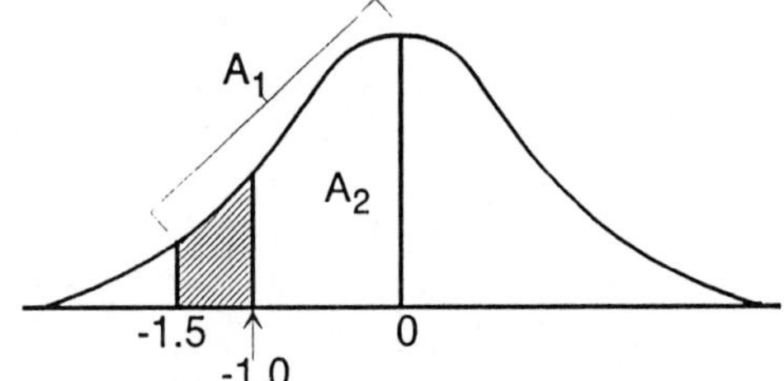

b. The area between −.45 and .90 is

$A_1 + A_2 = .1736 + .3159$
$= .4895$

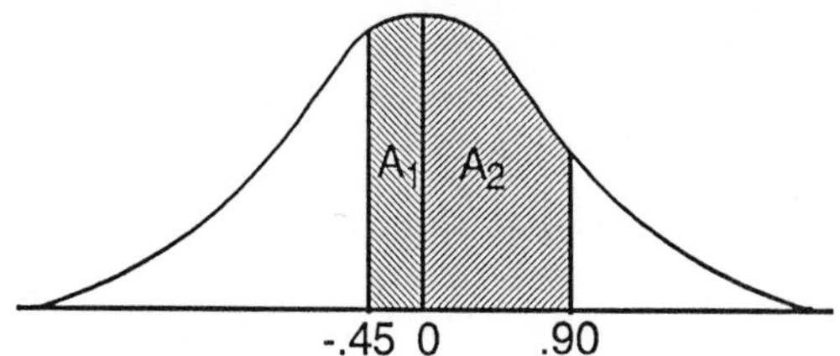


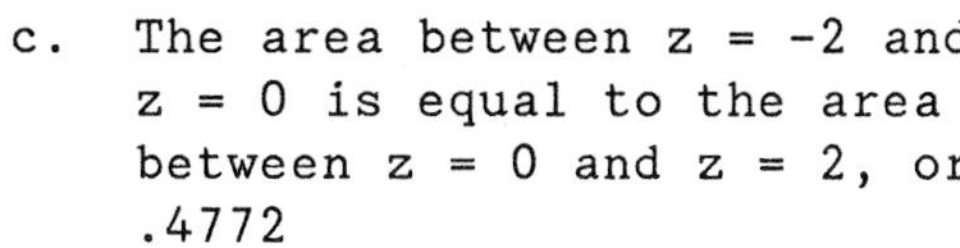
c. The area between z = −2 and z = 0 is equal to the area between z = 0 and z = 2, or .4772

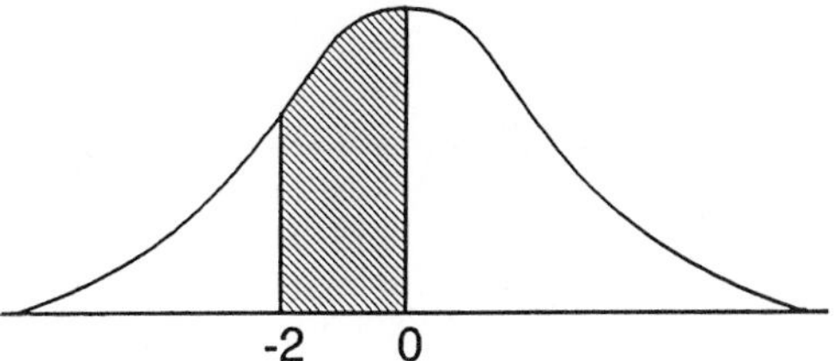


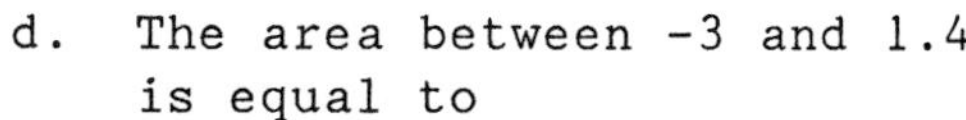
d. The area between −3 and 1.4 is equal to

$A_1 + A_2 = .4987 + .4192$
$= .9179$

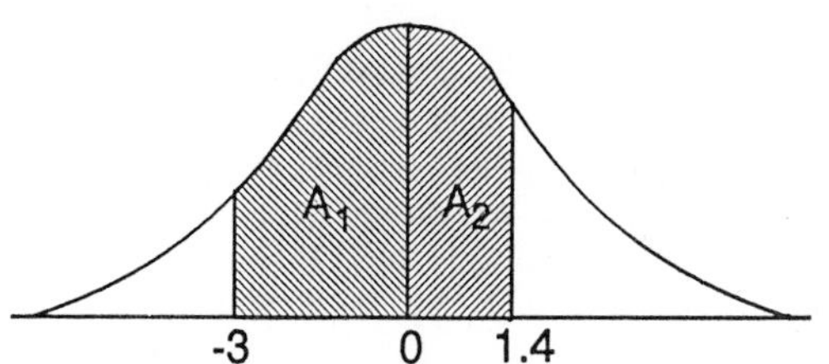


e. The area between z = .5 and z = 1.5 is equal to

$A_1 - A_2$, where
$A_1$ = area between 0 and 1.5
= .4332

and

$A_2$ = area between 0 and .5
= .1915

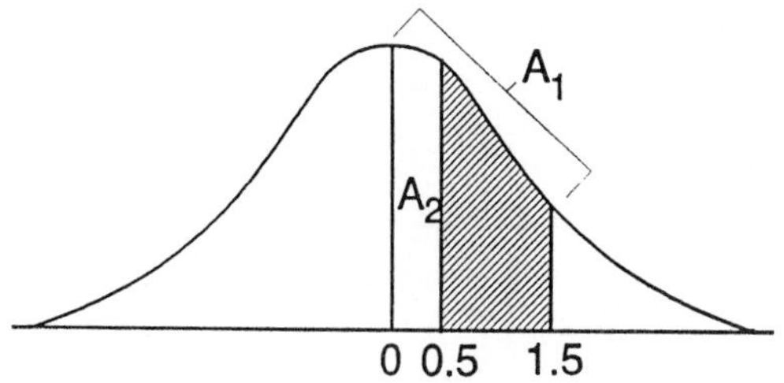


Thus, the shaded area is .4332 − .1915 = .2417

f. The shaded area is $A_1 - A_2$, where

$A_1$ = area between z = −2 and z = 0
= area between z = 0 and z = 2
= .4772

and

$A_2$ = area between z = −.5 and z = 0
= area between z = 0 and z = .5
= .1915

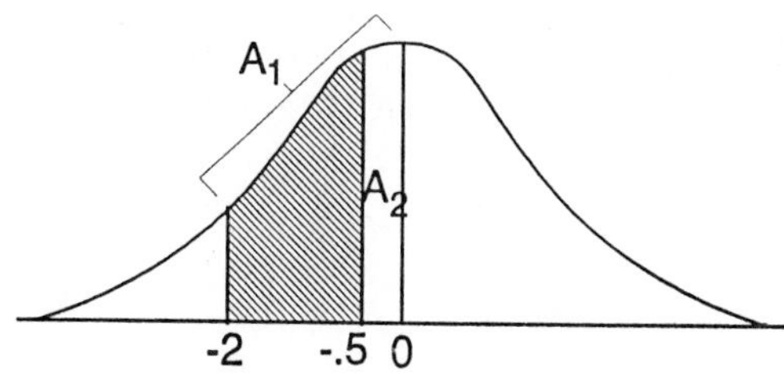


Thus, the required area is .4772 − .1915 = .2857

6.17 a. $P(z = 1) = 0$, since a single point does not have an area.

b. $P(z \leq 1) = P(z \leq 0) + P(0 < z \leq 1) = A_1 + A_2$
$= .5 + .3413$ (Table IV, Appendix B)
$= .8413$

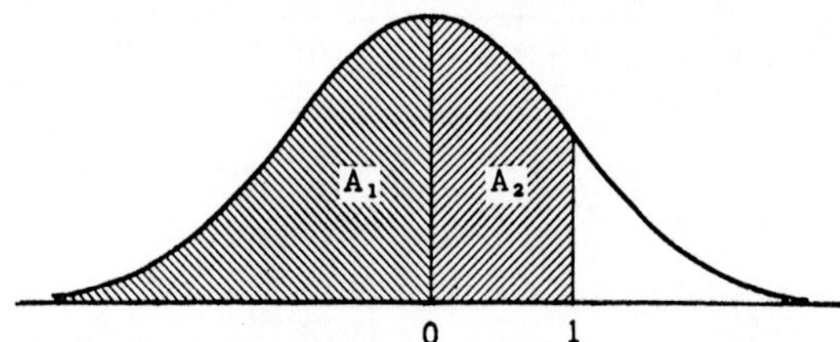


c. $P(z < 1) = P(z \leq 1) = .8413$ (Refer to part (b).)

d. $P(z > 1) = 1 - P(z \leq 1) = 1 - .8413 = .1587$ (Refer to part (b).)

6.19 Using Table IV in Appendix B:

a. $P(-1 \leq z \leq 1) = 2P(0 \leq z \leq 1) = 2(.3413) = .6826$

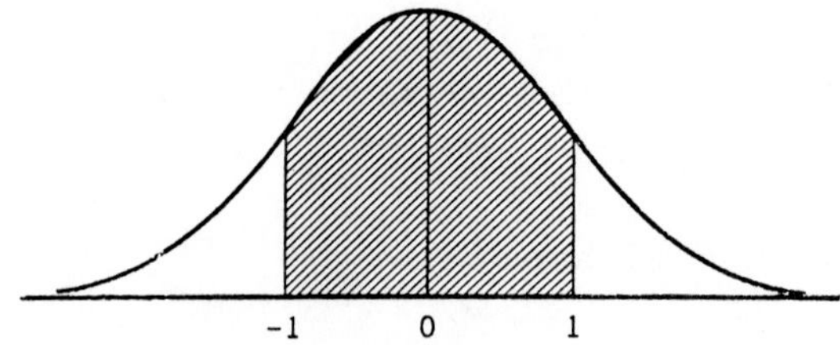


b. $P(-1.96 < z < 1.96) = 2P(0 < z < 1.96) = 2(.4750) = .95$

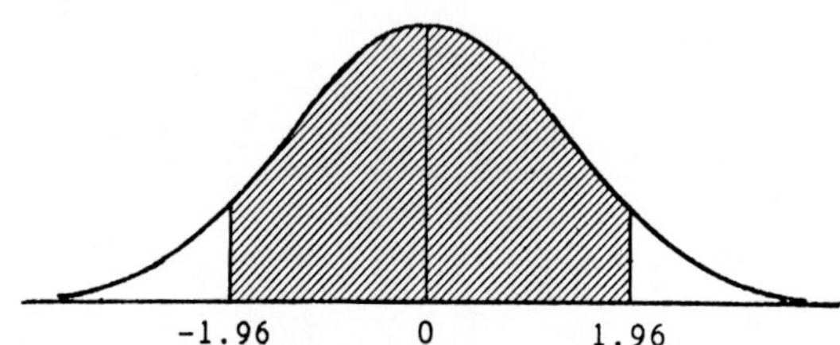


c. $P(-1.645 < z \leq 1.645) = 2P(0 \leq z \leq 1.645) = 2(.45) = .90$

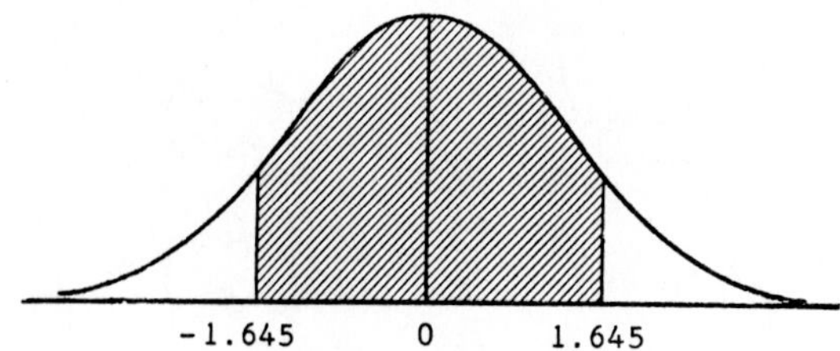

d. $P(-2 < z < 2) = 2P(0 < z < 2) = 2(.4772) = .9544$

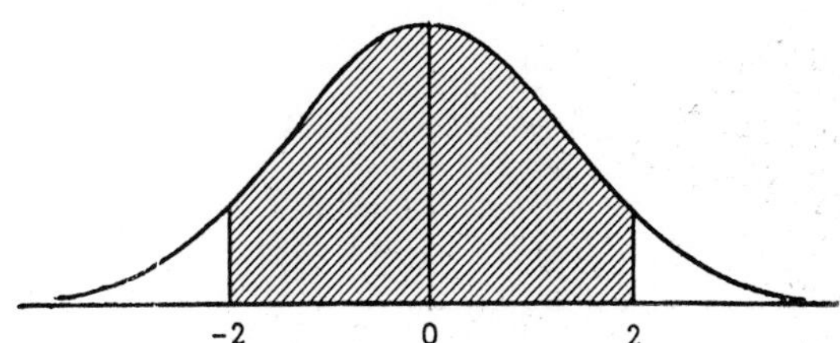


The answers for each part in Exercises 6.18 and 6.19 are the same. The questions only differ by the sign ("<" or "≤"). These are equivalent events when using the normal distribution.

6.21 Using Table IV of Appendix B:

a. $P(z \leq z_0) = .0301$

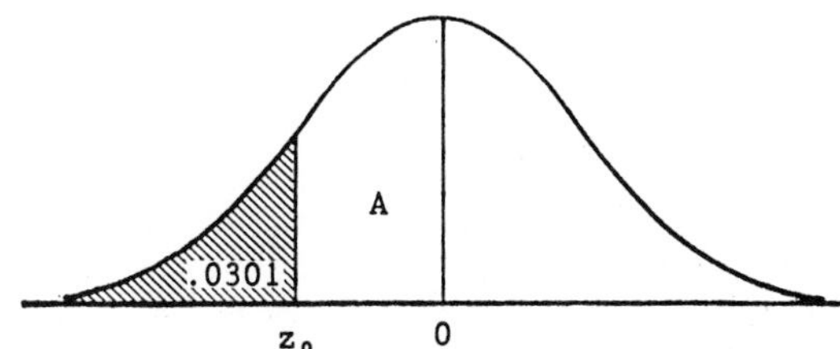


$A = .5000 - .0301 = .4699$

Look up the area .4699 in the body of Table IV; $z_0 = -1.88$.

($z_0$ is negative since the graph shows $z_0$ is on the left side of 0.)

b. $P(-z_0 \leq z \leq z_0) = .95$

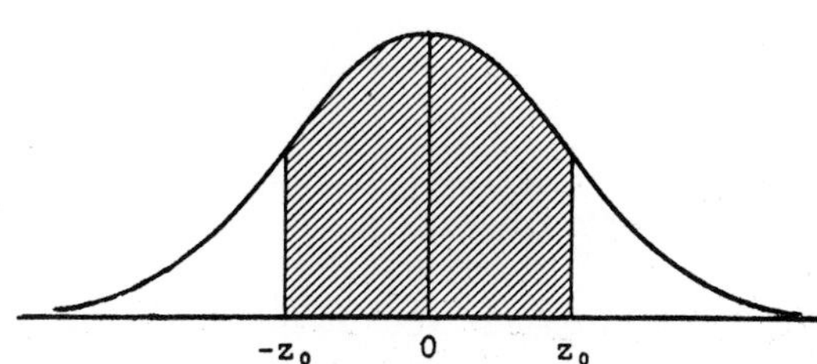


$P(-z_0 \leq z \leq z_0) = 2P(0 \leq z \leq z_0)$
$2P(0 \leq z \leq z_0) = .95$

Therefore, $p(0 \leq z \leq z_0) = .4750$.

Look up the area .4750 in the body of Table IV; $z_0 = 1.96$.

c. $P(-z_0 \leq z < z_0) = .90$

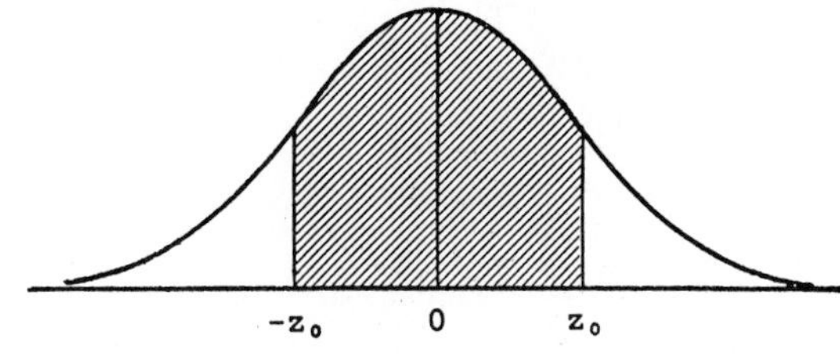


$P(-z_0 \leq z < z_0) = 2P(0 \leq z < z_0)$
$2P(0 \leq z < z_0) = .90$

Therefore, $P(0 \leq z \leq z_0) = .45$. Look up the area .45 in the body of Table IV; $z_0 = 1.645$. (.45 is half way between .4495 and .4505; therefore, we average the z-scores $\frac{1.64 + 1.65}{2} = 1.645$)

d. $P(-z_0 \leq z \leq z_0) = .6826$

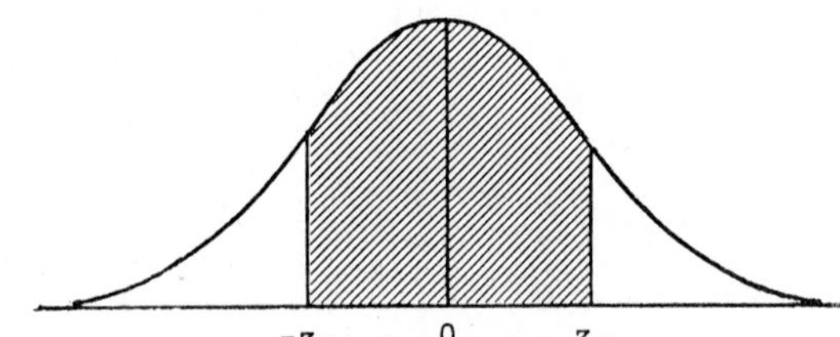


$P(-z_0 \leq z \leq z_0) = 2P(0 \leq z \leq z_0)$
$2P(0 \leq z \leq z_0) = .6826$

Therefore, $P(0 \leq z \leq z_0) = .3413$.

Look up the area .3413 in the body of Table IV; $z_0 = 1.0$

e. $P(z_0 \leq z \leq 0) = .1628$

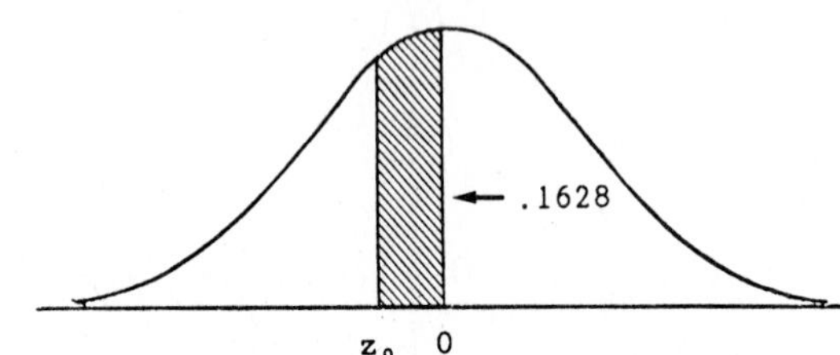


$P(z_0 \leq z \leq 0) = P(0 \leq z \leq -z_0)$

Look up the area .1628 in the body of Table IV; $z_0 = -.42$

f. $P(-.75 < z < z_0) = .7026$

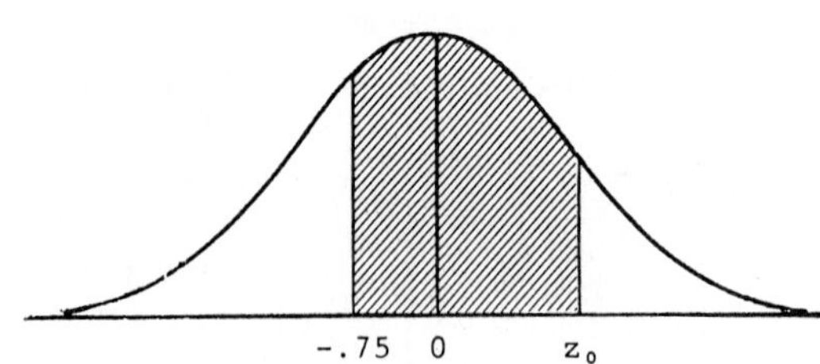


$$\begin{aligned} P(-.75 < z < z_0) &= P(-.75 < z < 0) \\ &\quad + P(0 < z < z_0) \\ &= .7026 \end{aligned}$$

$$\begin{aligned} P(0 < z < .75) + P(0 < z < z_0) \\ = .7026 \end{aligned}$$

Thus, $P(0 < z < z_0)$
$= .7026 - .2734 = .4292$

Look up the area .4292 in the body of Table IV; $z_0 = 1.47$

6.23 From Exercise 6.22, x is described by a normal distribution with $\mu = 30$ and $\sigma = 4$. The number of standard deviations away from the mean of x is the z-score for the given x value.

a. If $x = 25$, $z = \frac{x - \mu}{\sigma} = \frac{25 - 30}{4} = \frac{-5}{4} = -1.25$

Therefore, x is 1.25 standard deviations below the mean.

b. If $x = 37.5$, $z = \frac{x - \mu}{\sigma} = \frac{37.5 - 30}{4} = \frac{7.5}{4} = 1.875$

Therefore, x is 1.875 standard deviations above the mean.

c. If $x = 30$, $z = \frac{x - \mu}{\sigma} = \frac{30 - 30}{4} = 0$

Therefore, x is 0 standard deviations from the mean (x is the mean).

d. If $x = 36$, $z = \frac{x - \mu}{\sigma} = \frac{36 - 30}{4} = \frac{6}{4} = 1.5$

Therefore, x is 1.5 standard deviations above the mean.

6.25 Using Table IV of Appendix B:

a. To find the probability that x assumes a value more than 2 standard deviations from $\mu$:

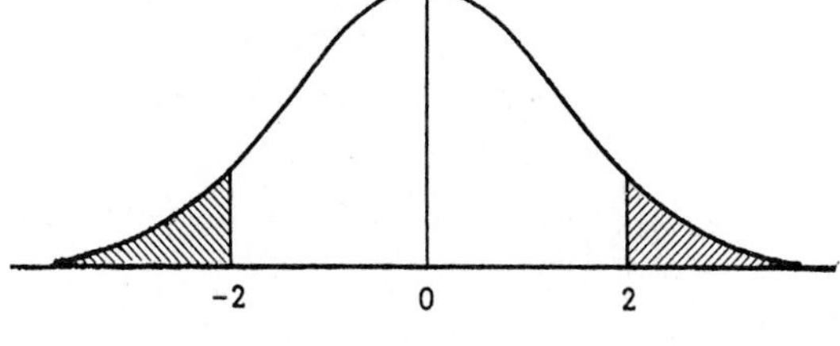


$$
\begin{aligned}
P(x < \mu - 2\sigma) &+ P(x > \mu + 2\sigma) \\
&= P(z < -2) + P(z > 2) \\
&= 2P(z > 2) \\
&= 2(.5000 - .4772) \\
&= 2(.0228) = .0456
\end{aligned}
$$

To find the probability that x assumes a value more than 3 standard deviations from $\mu$:

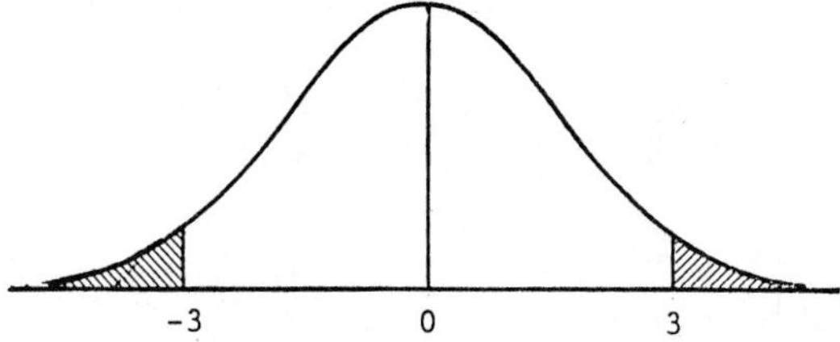


$$
\begin{aligned}
P(x < \mu - 3\sigma) &+ P(x > \mu + 3\sigma) \\
&= P(z < -3) + P(z > 3) \\
&= 2P(z > 3) \\
&= 2(.5000 - .4987) \\
&= 2(.0013) = .0026
\end{aligned}
$$

b. To find the probability that x assumes a value within 1 standard deviation of its mean:

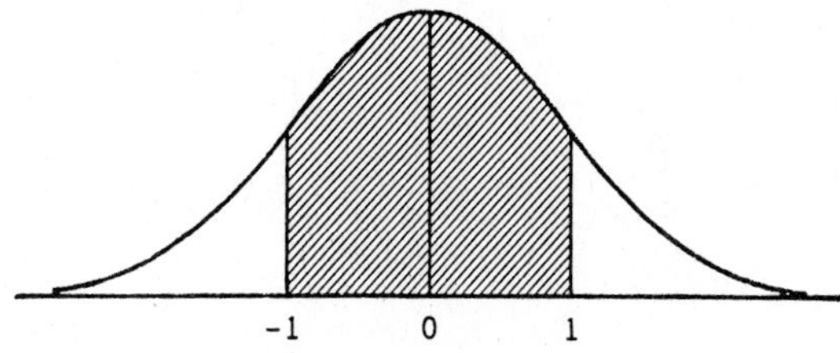


$$
\begin{aligned}
P(\mu - \sigma &< x < \mu + \sigma) \\
&= P(-1 < z < 1) \\
&= 2P(0 < z < 1) \\
&= 2(.3413) \\
&= .6826
\end{aligned}
$$

To find the probability that x assumes a value within 2 standard deviations of $\mu$:

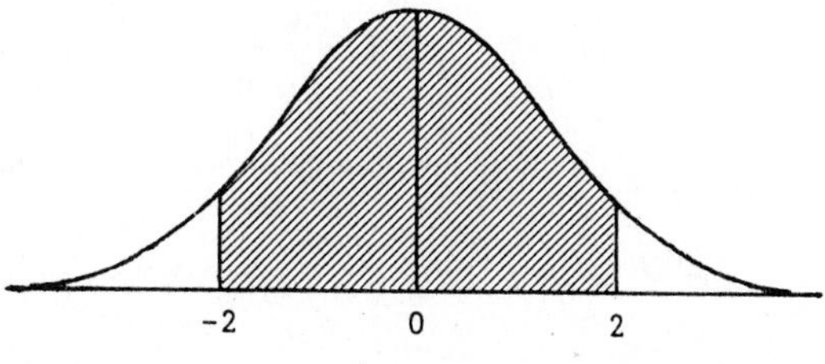


$$
\begin{aligned}
P(\mu - 2\sigma &< x < \mu + 2\sigma) \\
&= P(-2 < z < 2) \\
&= 2P(0 < z < 2) \\
&= 2(.4772) \\
&= .9544
\end{aligned}
$$

c. To find the value of x that represents the 80th percentile, we must first find the value of z that corresonds to the 80th percentile.

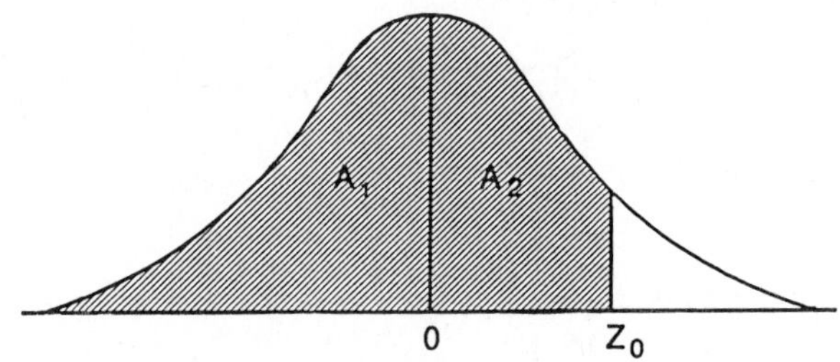


$P(z < z_0) = .80$. Thus, $A_1 + A_2 = .80$. Since $A_1 = .50$, $A_2 = .80 - .50 = .30$. Using the body of Table IV, $z_0 = .84$. To find x, we substitute the values into the z-score formula:

$$z = \frac{x - \mu}{\sigma}$$

$$.84 = \frac{x - 1000}{10} \Rightarrow x = .84(10) + 1000 = 1008.4$$

To find the value of x that represents the 10th percentile, we must first find the value of z that corresponds to the 10th percentile.

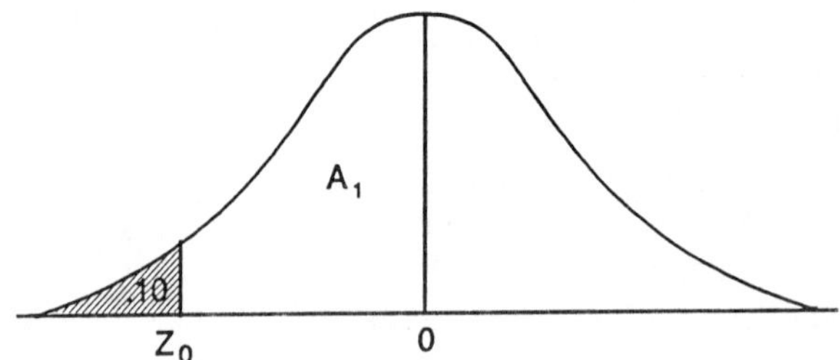


$P(z < z_0) = .10$. Thus, $A_1 = .50 - .10 = .40$. Using the body of Table IV, $z_0 = -1.28$. To find x, we substitute the values into the z-score formula:

$$z = \frac{x - \mu}{\sigma}$$

$$-1.28 = \frac{x - 1000}{10} \Rightarrow x = -1.28(10) + 1000 = 987.2$$

6.27 The random variable x has a normal distribution with $\sigma = 25$.

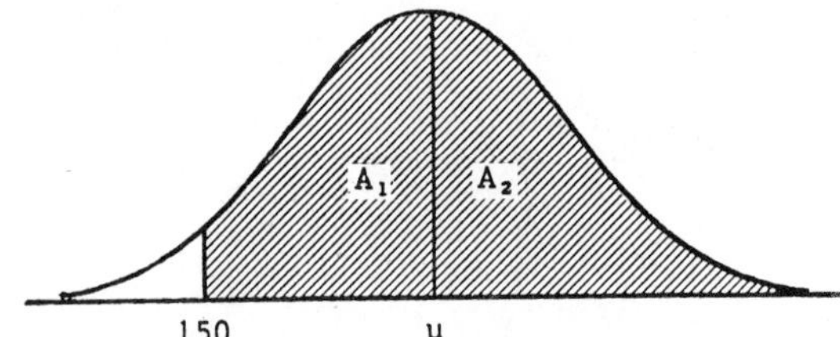

We know $P(x > 150) = .90$. So, $A_1 + A_2 = .90$. Since $A_2 = .50$, $A_1 = .90 - .50 = .40$. Look up the area .40 in the body of Table IV; (take the closest value) $z_0 = -1.28$.

To find $\mu$, substitute all the values into the z-score formula:

$$z = \frac{x - \mu}{\sigma}$$

$$-1.28 = \frac{150 - \mu}{25}$$

$$\mu = 150 + 25(1.28) = 182$$

6.29 Let x = the wage rates. Then x is normally distributed with $\mu = 10.50$ and $\sigma = 1.25$.

a. $z = \frac{x - \mu}{\sigma} = \frac{12 - 10.5}{1.25} = 1.2$

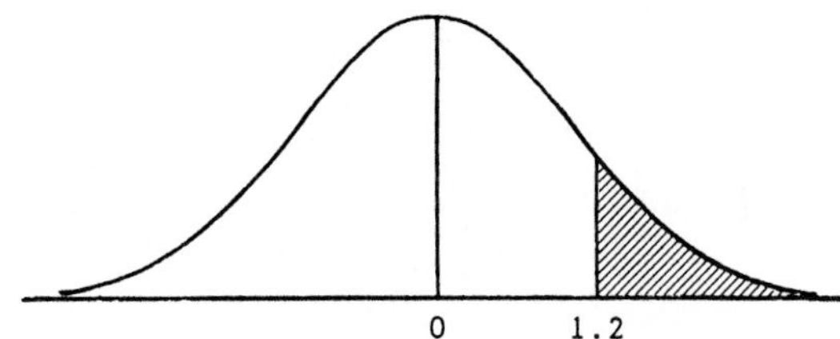


Thus,

$P(x > 12) = P(z > 1.2)$
$= .5000 - .3849$ (Table IV, Appendix B)
$= .1151$

b. $z = \frac{x - \mu}{\sigma} = \frac{10 - 10.50}{1.25} = -.40$

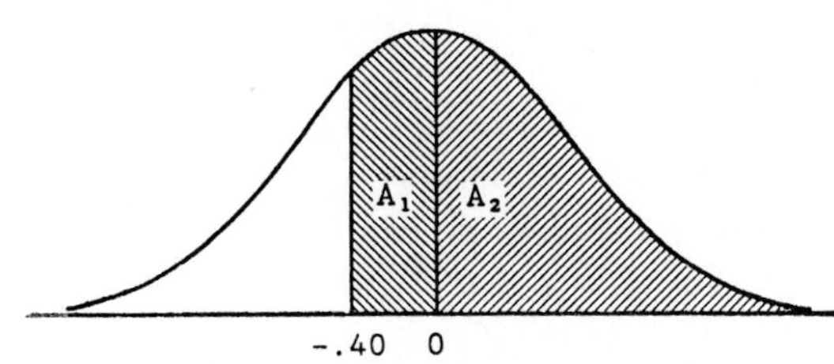


Thus,

$P(x > 10) = P(z > -.40)$
$= A_1 + A_2$
$= P(-.40 < z < 0) + P(z > 0)$
$= P(0 < z < .40) + .5000$ (Table IV, Appendix B)
$= .6554$

c. $P(x \geq x_m) = P(x \leq x_m) = .5$

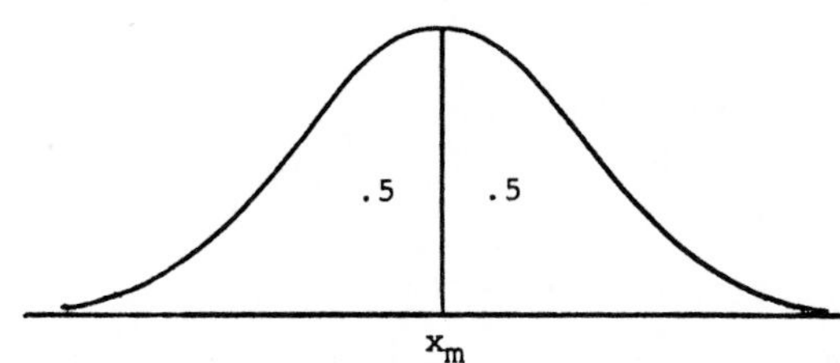


Therefore, $x_m = \mu = 10.50$

(Recall from Section 3.3 that in a symmetric distribution, the mean equals the median.)

6.31 Let x = the number of ounces of soft drink injected into 8-ounce bottles. The random variable x is approximately normally distributed with $\mu = 8.00$ and $\sigma = .05$.

a. The probability that one randomly selected bottle fails to meet the quality standard is:

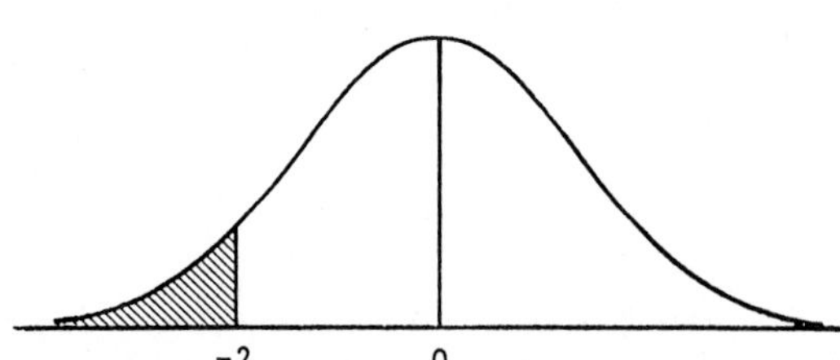


$$z = \frac{x - \mu}{\sigma} = \frac{7.9 - 8.0}{.05} = -2$$

$$P(x < 7.9) = P(z < -2) = .5000 - .4772 = .0228 \quad \text{(Table IV, Appendix B)}$$

Therefore, out of 20,000 bottles, approximately 20,000(.0228) = 456 will fail to meet the quality standard.

b. (This problem can be solved the same way as part (a) with $\mu = 7.95$ instead of 8.)

The probability that one randomly selected bottle fails to meet the quality standard is:

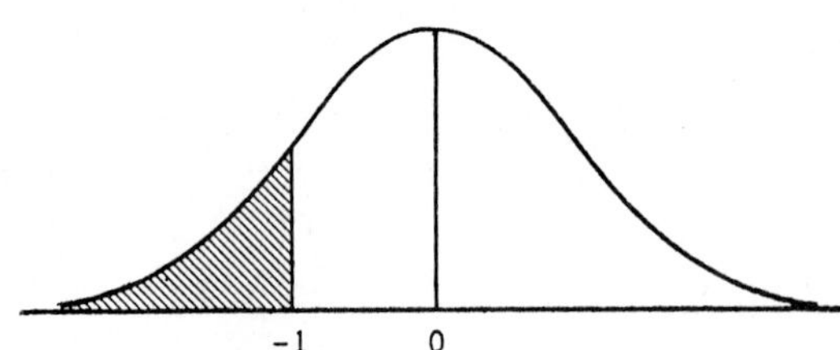


$$z = \frac{x - \mu}{\sigma} = \frac{7.9 - 7.95}{.05} = -1$$

$$P(x < 7.9) = P(z < -1) = .5000 - .3413 = .1587 \quad \text{(Table IV, Appendix B)}$$

Therefore, out of 20,000 bottles, approximately 20,000(.1587) = 3174 will fail to meet the quality standard.

c. (This problem can be solved the same was as part (a) with $\sigma = .10$ instead of .05.)

The probability that one randomly selected bottle fails to meet the quality standard is:

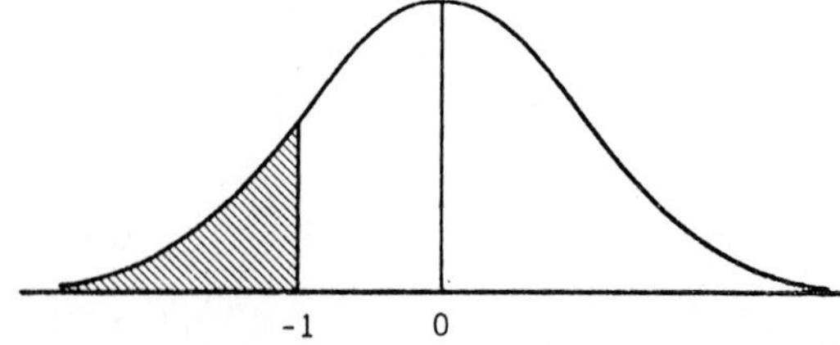


$$z = \frac{x - \mu}{\sigma} = \frac{7.9 - 8.0}{.1} = -1$$

$$P(x < 7.9) = P(z < -1) = .5000 - .3413 = .1587 \quad \text{(Table IV, Appendix B)}$$

Therefore, out of 20,000 bottles, approximately 20,000(.1587) = 3174 will fail to meet the quality standard.

6.33 Let x = the analysts' forecast errors. The random variable x is normally distributed with $\mu$ = 31.3% and $\sigma$ = 10%.

a.

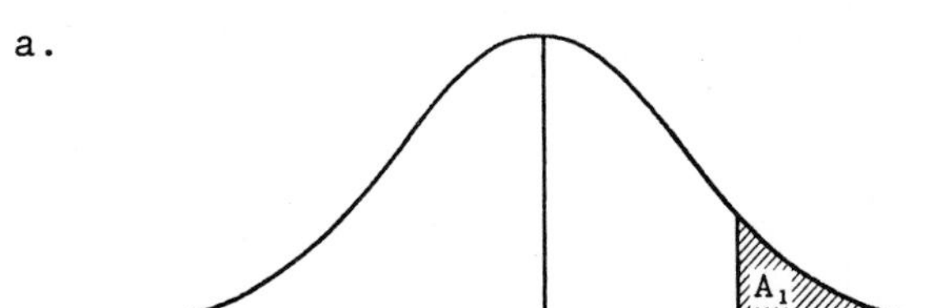


$$z = \frac{x - \mu}{\sigma} = \frac{50 - 31.3}{10} = 1.87$$

$$\begin{aligned} P(x > 50) &= P(z > 1.87) \\ &= .5000 - .4693 \\ &= .0307 \quad \text{(Table IV, Appendix B)} \end{aligned}$$

b. Let y = the number of analysts that will err by more than 50% out of 3. The random variable y is a binomial random variable (assuming whether one analyst errs is independent of whether the other analyst errs) with n = 3 and p = .0307 (found in part (a)).

$$\begin{aligned} P(y \geq 1) = 1 - p(0) &= 1 - \binom{3}{0}(.0307)^0(.9693)^3 \\ &= 1 - (1)(1)(.9693)^3 \\ &= 1 - .9107 = .0893 \end{aligned}$$

6.35 Let x = the lifetimes of the participants in the plan. The random variable x is approximately normal with $\mu$ = 68 and $\sigma$ = 3.5.

a.

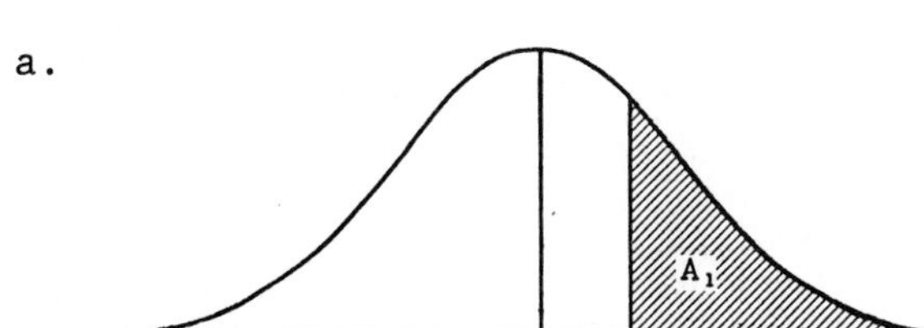


$$z = \frac{x - \mu}{\sigma} = \frac{70 - 68}{3.5} = .57$$

$$\begin{aligned} P(x > 70) &= P(z > .57) \\ &= .5000 - .2157 \\ &= .2843 \quad \text{(Table IV, Appendix B)} \end{aligned}$$

b.

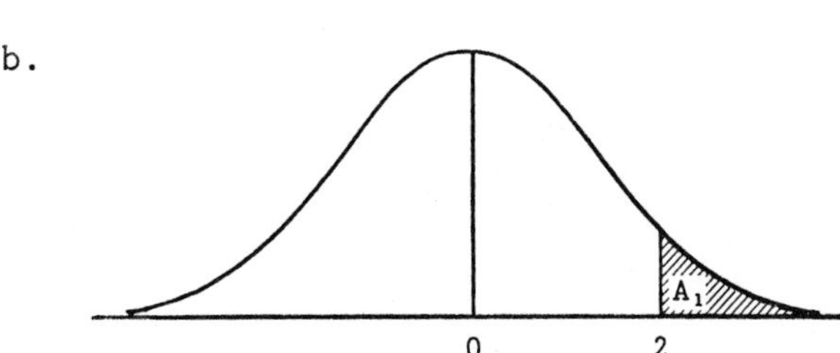


$$z = \frac{x - \mu}{\sigma} = \frac{75 - 68}{3.5} = 2$$

$$\begin{aligned} P(x > 75) &= P(z > 2) \\ &= .5000 - .4772 \\ &= .0228 \quad \text{(Table IV, Appendix B)} \end{aligned}$$

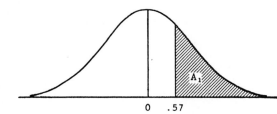

c. Only 15% of plan participants will receive payment beyond age 71.64.

We must find the age, $x_0$, such that $P(x > x_0) = P(z > z_0) = .15$. $A_1 = .5 - .15 = .35$. From the body of Table IV, $z_0 = 1.04$.

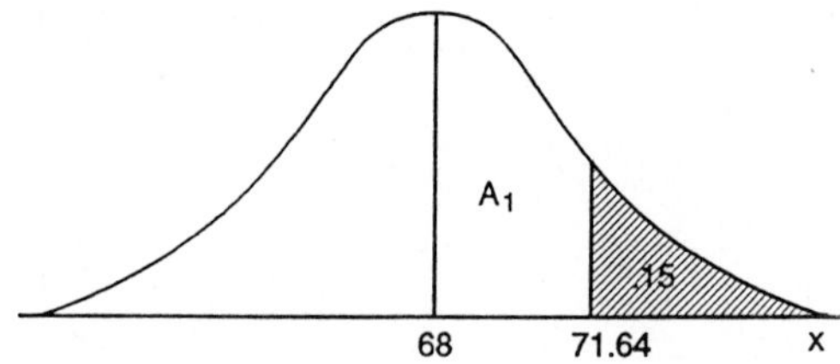


Using the z-score formula,

$$z = \frac{x - \mu}{\sigma}$$

$$1.04 = \frac{x - 68}{3.5} \Rightarrow x = 1.04(3.5) + 68 = 71.64$$

6.37 a. If z is a standard normal random variable,

$Q_L = z_L$ is the value of the standard normal distribution which has 25% of the data to the left and 75% to the right.

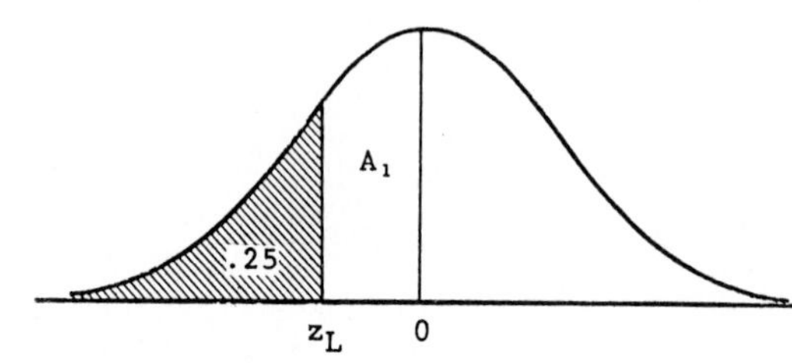


Find $z_L$ such that $P(z < z_L) = .25$

$A_1 = .50 - .25 = .25$

Look up the area $A_1 = .25$ in the body of Table IV of Appendix B; $z_L = -.67$ (take the closest value).

$Q_U = z_U$ is the value of the standard normal distribution which has 75% of the data to the left and 25% to the right.

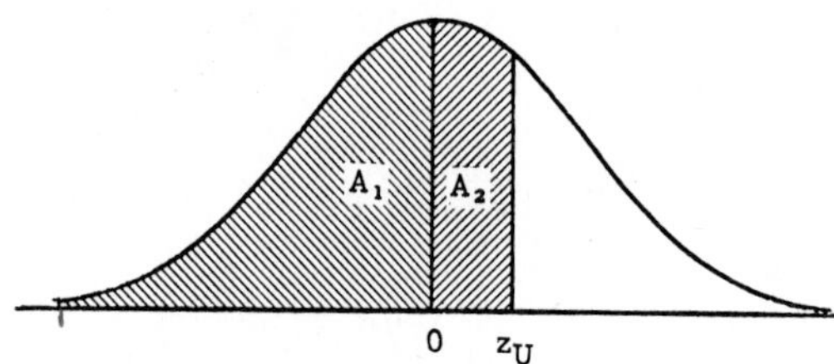


Find $z_U$ such that $P(z < z_U) = .75$

$$\begin{aligned} A_1 + A_2 &= P(z \leq 0) \\ &\quad + P(0 \leq z \leq z_U) \\ &= .5 + P(0 \leq z \leq z_U) \\ &= .75 \end{aligned}$$

Therefore, $P(0 \leq z \leq z_U) = .25$.

Look up the area .25 in the body of Table IV of Appendix B; $z_U = .67$ (take the closest value).

b. Recall that the inner fences of a boxplot are located $1.5(Q_U - Q_L)$ outside the hinges ($Q_L$ and $Q_U$).

To find the lower inner fence,

$$\begin{aligned} Q_L - 1.5(Q_U - Q_L) &= -.67 - 1.5(.67 - (-.67)) \\ &= -.67 - 1.5(1.34) \\ &= -2.68 \end{aligned}$$

The upper inner fence is:

$$\begin{aligned} Q_U + 1.5(Q_U - Q_L) &= .67 + 1.5(.67 - (-.67)) \\ &= .67 + 1.5(1.34) \\ &= 2.68 \end{aligned}$$

c. Recall that the outer fences of a boxplot are located $3(Q_U - Q_L)$ outside the hinges ($Q_L$ and $Q_U$).

To find the lower outer fence,

$$\begin{aligned} Q_L - 3(Q_U - Q_L) &= -.67 - 3(.67 - (.67)) \\ &= -.67 - 3(1.34) \\ &= -4.69 \end{aligned}$$

The upper outer fence is:

$$\begin{aligned} Q_U + 3(Q_U - Q_L) &= .67 + 3(.67 - (-.67)) \\ &= .67 + 3(1.34) \\ &= 4.69 \end{aligned}$$

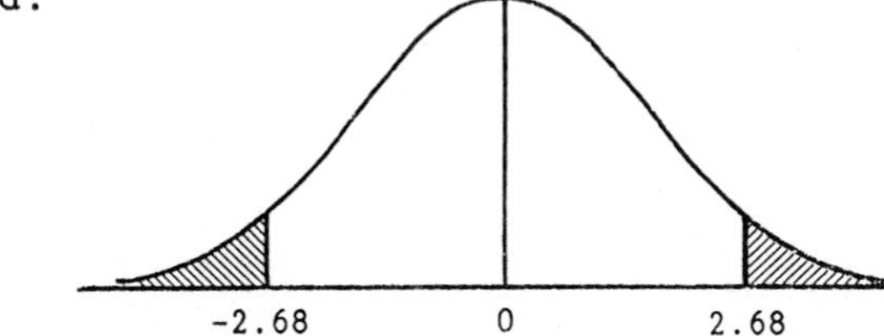


$$\begin{aligned} &P(z < -2.68) + P(z > 2.68) \\ &= 2P(z > 2.68) \\ &= 2(.5000 - .4963) \quad \text{(Table IV, Appendix B)} \\ &= 2(.0037) \\ &= .0074 \end{aligned}$$

-4.69 0 4.69

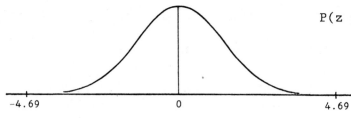

$$\begin{aligned} &P(z < -4.69) + P(z > 4.69) \\ &= 2P(z > 4.69) \\ &\approx 2(.5000 - .5000) \\ &\approx 0 \end{aligned}$$

e. In a normal probability distribution, the probability of an observation being beyond the inner fences is only .0074 and the probability of an observation being beyond the outer fences is approximately zero. Since the probability is so small, there should not be any observations beyond the inner and outer fences. Therefore, they are probably outliers.

6.39 a. If $\lambda = 1$, $a = 1$, then $e^{-\lambda a} = e^{-1} = .367879$

b. If $\lambda = 1$, $a = 2.5$, then $e^{-\lambda a} = e^{-2.5} = .082085$

c. If $\lambda = 2.5$, $a = 3$, then $e^{-\lambda a} = e^{-7.5} = .000553$

d. If $\lambda = 5$, $a = .3$, then $e^{-\lambda a} = e^{-1.5} = .223130$

6.41 Using Table V in Appendix B:

a. $P(x \leq 3) = 1 - P(x > 3) = 1 - e^{-2.5(3)} = 1 - e^{-7.5} = 1 - .000553$
$= .999447$

b. $P(x \leq 4) = 1 - P(x > 4) = 1 - e^{-2.5(4)} = 1 - e^{-10} = 1 - .000045$
$= .999955$

c. $P(x \leq 1.6) = 1 - P(x > 1.6) = 1 - e^{-2.5(1.6)} = 1 - e^{-4}$
$= 1 - .018316$
$= .981684$

d. $P(x \leq .4) = 1 - P(x > .4) = 1 - e^{-2.5(.4)} = 1 - e^{-1} = 1 - .367879$
$= .632121$

6.43 $f(x) = \lambda e^{-\lambda x} = e^{-x} \qquad (x > 0)$

$\mu = \frac{1}{\lambda} = \frac{1}{1} = 1, \; \sigma = \frac{1}{\lambda} = \frac{1}{1} = 1$

a. $\mu \pm 3\sigma \Rightarrow 1 \pm 3(1) \Rightarrow (-2, 4)$

Since $\mu - 3\sigma$ lies below 0, find the probability that x is more than $\mu + 3\sigma = 4$.

$P(x > 4) = e^{-1(4)} = e^{-4} = .018316$ (using Table V in Appendix B)

b. $\mu \pm 2\sigma \Rightarrow 1 \pm 2(1) \Rightarrow (-1, 3)$

Since $\mu - 2\sigma$ lies below 0, find the probability that x is between 0 and 3.

$P(x < 3) = 1 - P(x \geq 3) = 1 - e^{-1(3)} = 1 - e^{-3} = 1 - .049787$
$= .950213$
(using Table V in Appendix B)

c. $\mu \pm .5\sigma \Rightarrow 1 \pm .5(1) \Rightarrow (.5, 1.5)$

$$P(.5 < x < 1.5) = P(x > .5) - P(x > 1.5)$$
$$= e^{-.5} - e^{-1.5}$$
$$= .606531 - .223130$$
$$= .383401 \quad \text{(using Table V in Appendix B)}$$

6.45 Let x = the shelf-life of bread. The mean of an exponential distribution is $\mu = 1/\lambda$. We know that $\mu = 2$; therefore, $\lambda = .5$. We want to find:

$$P(x > 3) = e^{-.5(3)} = e^{-1.5} = .223130 \quad \text{(using Table V in Appendix B)}$$

6.47 Let x = the number of minutes to treat a patient in the emergency room. The mean of an exponential distribution is $\mu = 1/\lambda$. We know that $\mu = 58$; therefore, $\lambda = 1/58 = .0172$.

a. $P(x > 58) = e^{-.0172(58)} = e^{-1} = .367879$

$$P(x > 1.5(60)) = P(x > 90) = e^{-\lambda a} = e^{-.0172(90)}$$
$$= e^{-1.55} = .212248$$
(using Table V in Appendix B)

b. $P(x > 58)P(x > 58)P(x > 58) = .367879^3 = .049787$
(using Table V in Appendix B)

c. The median time to treat a patient is less than 58 minutes since $P(x > 58) = .367879$ and the probability gets larger for smaller x values.

d. $e^{-.7}$ is closest to .5 on Table V in Appendix B.

Therefore, $.7 = \lambda a$
$.7 = .01724a$
$a = 40.6$

Thus, the median is approximately 40.6.

6.49 a. To construct a relative frequency histogram of the data, we can use 8 measurement classes.

$$\text{Class width} = \frac{\text{Largest measurement - smallest measurement}}{\text{Number of classes}}$$
$$= \frac{37 - 1}{8} = \frac{36}{8} = 4.5$$

We will round up and use a width of 5.

The measurement classes, frequencies, and relative frequencies are given in the following table.

| CLASS | MEASUREMENT CLASS | CLASS FREQUENCY | CLASS RELATIVE FREQUENCY |
|---|---|---|---|
| 1 | 0.5 - 5.5 | 20 | 20/50 = .40 |
| 2 | 5.5 - 10.5 | 12 | .24 |
| 3 | 10.5 - 15.5 | 7 | .14 |
| 4 | 15.5 - 20.5 | 4 | .08 |
| 5 | 20.5 - 25.5 | 3 | .06 |
| 6 | 25.5 - 30.5 | 2 | .04 |
| 7 | 30.5 - 35.5 | 1 | .02 |
| 8 | 35.5 - 40.5 | 1 | .02 |
| | | n = 50 | 1.00 |

The relative frequency histogram for the data is given below:

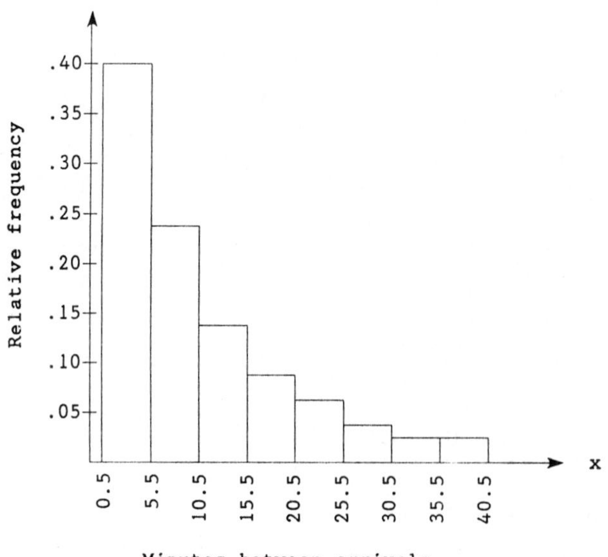


Yes, it does look like an exponential distribution could be used to characterize the length of time between arrivals since the relative frequency histogram for the data looks like an exponential curve.

b. I would find the mean time between arrivals over a long period of time. Then I could find $\lambda$ since $\mu = 1/\lambda$.

6.51 The calculation of binomial probabilities becomes extremely tedious as the sample size increases. Under certain situations, a normal random variable may provide satisfactory approximations to exact binomial probabilities.

6.53 In order to approximate the binomial distribution with the normal distribution, the interval $\mu \pm 3\sigma \Rightarrow np \pm 3\sqrt{npq}$ should lie in the range 0 to n.

a. When n = 50 and p = .01,

$$\begin{aligned} np \pm 3\sqrt{npq} &\Rightarrow 50(.01) \pm 3\sqrt{50(.01)(1 - .01)} \\ &\Rightarrow .5 \pm 3\sqrt{.495} \\ &\Rightarrow 8.5 \pm 2.1107 \\ &\Rightarrow (-1.6107,\ 2.6107) \end{aligned}$$

Since the interval calculated does not lie in the range 0 to 50, we should not use the normal approximation.

b. When n = 20, p = .45

$$\begin{aligned} np \pm 3\sqrt{npq} &\Rightarrow 20(.45) \pm 3\sqrt{20(.45)(1 - .45)} \\ &\Rightarrow 9 \pm 3\sqrt{4.95} \\ &\Rightarrow 9 \pm 6.6746 \\ &\Rightarrow (2.3254,\ 15.6746) \end{aligned}$$

Since the interval calculated does lie in the range 0 to 20, we can use the normal approximation.

c. When n = 10, p = .40

$$\begin{aligned} np \pm 3\sqrt{npq} &\Rightarrow 10(.40) \pm 3\sqrt{10(.40)(1 - .40)} \\ &\Rightarrow 4 \pm 3\sqrt{2.4} \\ &\Rightarrow 4 \pm 4.6479 \\ &\Rightarrow (-.6479,\ 8.6479) \end{aligned}$$

Since the interval calculated does not lie in the range 0 to 10, we should not use the normal approximation.

d. If n = 1000 and p = .1,

$$\begin{aligned} np \pm 3\sqrt{npq} &\Rightarrow 1000(.1) \pm 3\sqrt{1000(.1)(1 - .1)} \\ &\Rightarrow 100 \pm 3\sqrt{90} \\ &\Rightarrow 100 \pm 28.4605 \\ &\Rightarrow (71.5395,\ 128.4605) \end{aligned}$$

Since the interval calculated does lie in the range 0 to 1000, we can use the normal approximation.

e. If n = 200 and p = .8,

$$\begin{aligned} np \pm 3\sqrt{npq} &\Rightarrow 200(.8) \pm 3\sqrt{200(.8)(1 - .8)} \\ &\Rightarrow 160 \pm 3\sqrt{32} \\ &\Rightarrow 160 \pm 16.9706 \\ &\Rightarrow (143.0294,\ 166.9706) \end{aligned}$$

Since the interval calculated does lie in the range 0 to 200, we can use the normal approximation.

f. If $n = 35$ and $p = .7$,

$$np \pm 3\sqrt{npq} \Rightarrow 35(.7) \pm 3\sqrt{35(.7)(1 - .7)}$$
$$\Rightarrow 24.5 \pm 3\sqrt{7.35}$$
$$\Rightarrow 24.5 \pm 8.1333$$
$$\Rightarrow (16.3667, 32.6333)$$

Since the interval calculated does lie in the range 0 to 35, we can use the normal approximation.

6.55 x is a binomial random variable with $n = 25$ and $p = .5$. Therefore, $\mu = np = 25(.5) = 12.5$ and

$$\sigma = \sqrt{npq} = \sqrt{25(.5)(.5)} = 2.5$$

a. $P(x \leq 12) = .500$ (using Table II in Appendix B)

To find the approximate probability with the normal approximation,

$$z = \frac{(a + .5) - \mu}{\sigma} = \frac{12.5 - 12.5}{2.5} = 0$$

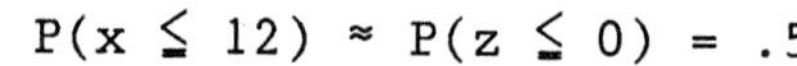

$P(x \leq 12) \approx P(z \leq 0) = .5$

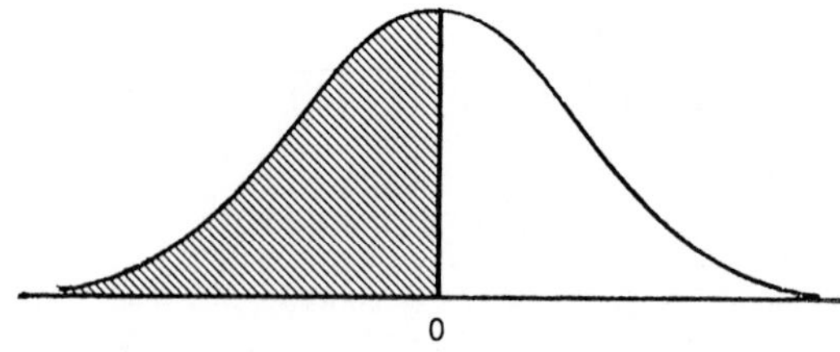


b. $P(x \geq 15) = 1 - P(x \leq 14) = 1 - .788 = .212$
(using Table II in Appendix B)

To find the approximate probability with the normal approximation,

$$z = \frac{(a - .5) - \mu}{\sigma} = \frac{14.5 - 12.5}{2.5} = .8$$

$P(x \geq 15) \approx P(z \geq .8)$
$= .5000 - .2881 = .2119$
(using Table IV in Appendix B)

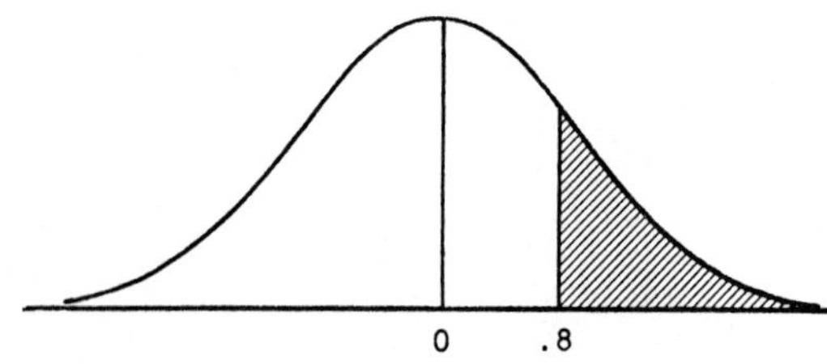

c. $P(9 \leq x \leq 15) = P(x \leq 15) - P(x \leq 8) = .885 - .054 = .831$
(using Table II in Appendix B)

To find the approximate probability with the normal approximation,

$$z = \frac{(a - .5) - \mu}{\sigma} = \frac{8.5 - 12.5}{2.5} = -1.6$$

$$z = \frac{(a + .5) - \mu}{\sigma} = \frac{15.5 - 12.5}{2.5} = 1.2$$

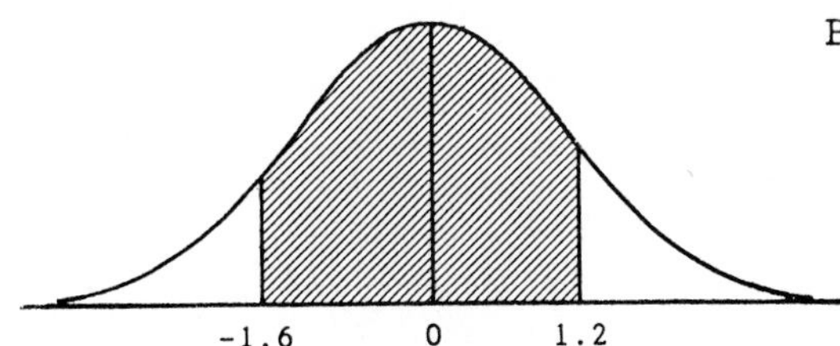


$$\begin{aligned} P(9 \leq x \leq 15) &\approx P(-1.6 \leq z \leq 1.2) \\ &= P(-1.6 \leq z \leq 0) + P(0 \leq z \leq 1.2) \\ &= P(0 \leq z \leq 1.6) + P(0 \leq z \leq 1.2) \\ &= .4452 + .3849 \\ &= .8301 \end{aligned}$$

(using Table IV in Appendix B)

6.57 x is a binomial random variable with n = 1000 and p = .50.

$$\begin{aligned} \mu \pm 3\sigma = np \pm 3\sqrt{npq} &= 1000(.50) \pm 3\sqrt{1000(.5)(.5)} \\ &= 500 \pm 3(15.8114) \\ &= (452.5658, 547.4342) \end{aligned}$$

Since the interval lies in the range 0 to 1000, we can use the normal approximation to approximate the probabilities.

a. $$z = \frac{(a + .5) - \mu}{\sigma} = \frac{500.5 - 500}{15.8114} = .03$$

(Using Table IV in Appendix B)

$$\begin{aligned} P(x > 500) &\approx P(z > .03) \\ &= .5000 - .012 = .488 \end{aligned}$$

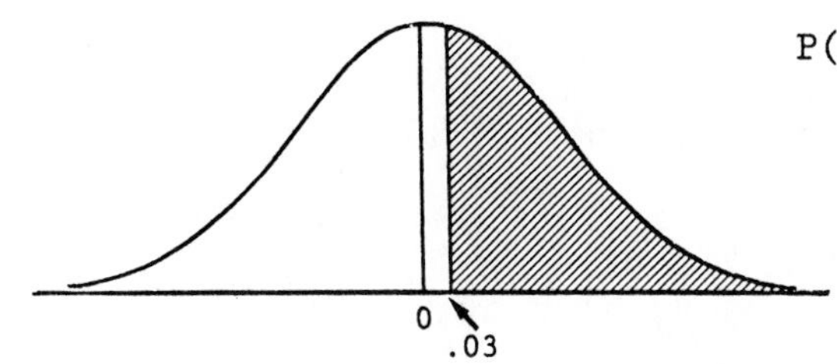


b. $$z = \frac{(a - .5) - \mu}{\sigma} = \frac{489.5 - 500}{15.8114} = -.66$$

$$z = \frac{(a - .5) - \mu}{\sigma} = \frac{499.5 - 500}{15.8114} = -.03$$

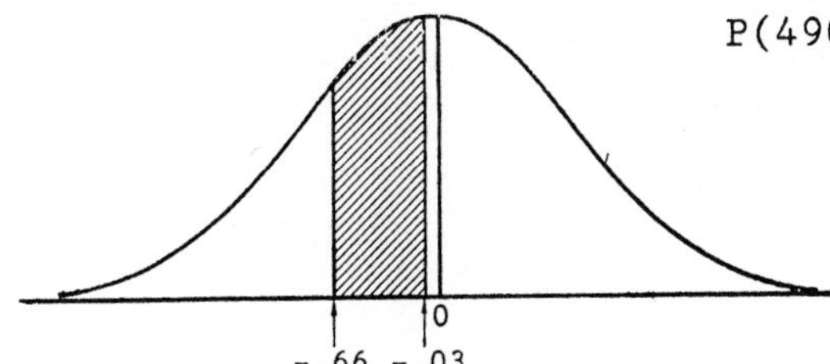


$$\begin{aligned} P(490 \leq x < 500) &\approx P(-.66 \leq z < -.03) \\ &= P(-.66 \leq z \leq 0) - P(-.03 \leq z \leq 0) \\ &= P(0 \leq z \leq .66) - P(0 \leq z \leq .03) \\ &= .2454 - .012 = .2334 \end{aligned}$$

(Using Table IV in Appendix B)

c. $P(x > 1000) = 0$

Since $n = 1000$, the random variable x can only take on the values 0, 1, 2, ... , 1000.

6.59 a. Let x = the number of workers on the job on a particular day out of 50 workers. The random variable x is a binomial random variable with $n = 50$ and $p = .80$ (if 20% are absent, 80% are on the job).

90% of 50 workers = .9(50) = 45

$$\mu = np = 50(.8) = 40$$
$$\sigma^2 = npq = 50(.8)(.2) = 8$$
$$\sigma = \sqrt{\sigma^2} = \sqrt{8} = 2.8284$$

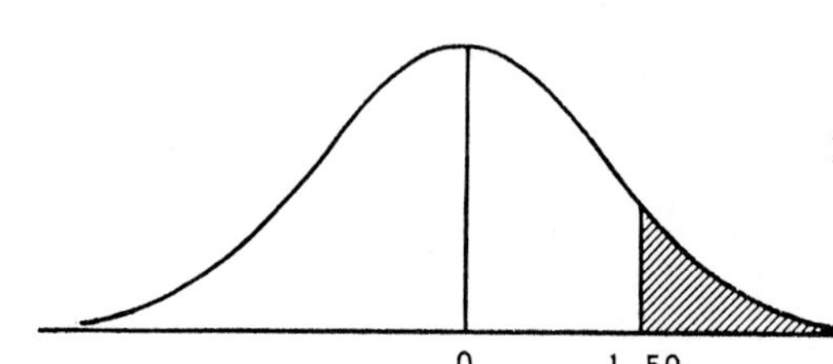


$$z = \frac{(a + .5) - \mu}{\sigma} = \frac{44.5 - 40}{2.8284} = 1.59$$

$$P(x \geq 45) \approx P(z \geq 1.59) = .5000 - .4441 = .0559$$

b. $\mu \pm 3\sigma \Rightarrow np \pm 3\sqrt{npq} \Rightarrow 40 \pm 3(2.8284)$ (part (a)) $\Rightarrow (31.5148, 48.4852)$

Since the interval lies in the range 0 to 50, we can use the normal approximation to approximate the probability in part (a).

c. If the absentee rate is 2%, then 98% of the workers are on the job. Hence, x is a binomial random variable with $n = 50$ and $p = .98$.

$$\mu \pm 3\sigma \Rightarrow np \pm 3\sqrt{npq} \Rightarrow 50(.98) \pm 3\sqrt{50(.98)(1 - .98)}$$
$$\Rightarrow 49 \pm 2.9698$$
$$\Rightarrow (46.0302, 51.9698)$$

Since the interval does not lie in the range 0 to 50, we should not use the normal approximation to approximate the probability in part (a).

6.61 a. We must assume that whether one smoke detector is defective is independent of whether any other smoke detector is defective. Also the probability of a smoke detector being defective must remain constant for all smoke detectors. These assumptions seem to be satisfied since a random sample was taken.

b. The random variable x is a binomial random variable with n = 2000 and p = .40.

$$\mu \pm 3\sigma \Rightarrow np \pm 3\sqrt{npq} \Rightarrow 2000(.40) \pm 3\sqrt{2000(.40)(1 - .40)}$$
$$\Rightarrow 800 \pm 65.7267$$
$$\Rightarrow (734.2733, 865.7267)$$

Since the interval does lie in the range 0 to 2000, we can use the normal approximation to approximate the probability.

$$z = \frac{(a + .5) - \mu}{\sigma} = \frac{4.5 - 800}{\sqrt{2000(.4)(1 - .4)}} = \frac{4.5 - 800}{21.9089} = -.36.31$$

$$P(x \leq 4) \approx P(z \leq -36.31)$$
$$\approx .5 - .5 = 0$$

c. No, it is not likely that 40% of their detectors are defective. If 40% really were defective, then the probability of four or fewer defectives is approximately zero. But there were only four defectives. Therefore, it is very unlikely that 40% are defective.

d. Yes, it is possible that 40% of the detectors are defective. The probability of four or fewer defectives is approximately zero. It is possible but very unlikely.

6.63 Let x equal the number of consumers that learned about the product through sources attributable to the campaign. The random variable x is a binomial random variable with n = 2000 and p = .30.

$$\mu \pm 3\sigma \Rightarrow np \pm 3\sqrt{npq} \Rightarrow 2000(.30) \pm 3\sqrt{2000(.3)(1 - .3)}$$
$$\Rightarrow 600 \pm 61.4817$$
$$\Rightarrow (538.5183, 661.4817)$$

Since the interval does lie in the range 0 to 2000, we can use the normal approximation to approximate the probability.

$$z = \frac{(a + .5) - \mu}{\sigma} = \frac{527.5 - 600}{\sqrt{2000(.3)(1 - .3)}} = -3.54$$

$$P(x \leq 527) \approx P(z \leq -3.54)$$
$$\approx .5 - .5 = 0$$

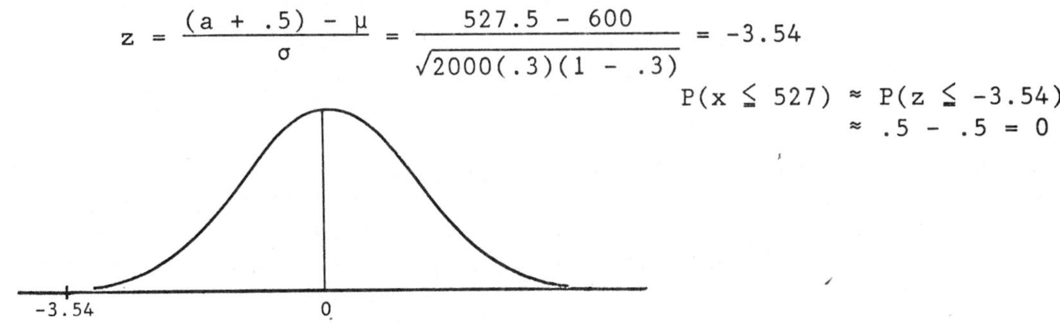

6.65 a. $f(x) = \frac{1}{d - c} = \frac{1}{90 - 10} = \frac{1}{80}, \quad 10 \leq x \leq 90$

b. $\mu = \frac{c + d}{2} = \frac{10 + 90}{2}$

$= 50$

$\sigma = \frac{d - c}{\sqrt{12}} = \frac{90 - 10}{\sqrt{12}}$

$= 23.094011$

c. The interval $\mu \pm 2\sigma \Rightarrow (50 \pm 2(23.1))$
$\Rightarrow (3.8, 96.2)$
is indicated on the graph.

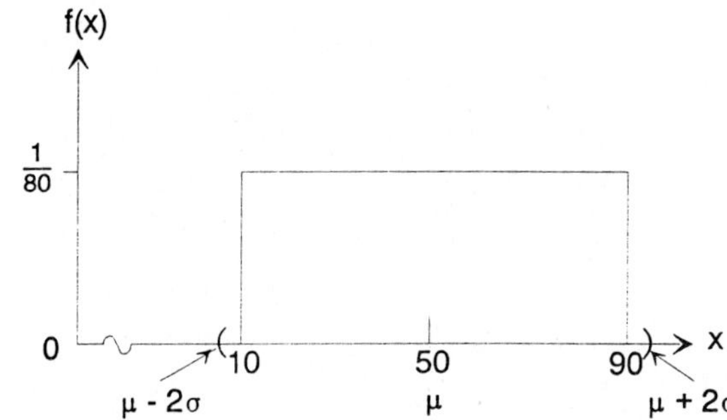


d. $P(x \leq 60) = \text{Base(height)} = (60 - 10)\frac{1}{80} = \frac{5}{8} = .625$

e. $P(x \geq 90) = 0$

f. $P(x \leq 80) = \text{Base(height)} = (80 - 10)\frac{1}{80} = \frac{7}{8} = .875$

g. $P(\mu - \sigma \leq x \leq \mu + \sigma) = P(50 - 23.1 \leq x \leq 50 + 23.1)$
$= P(26.9 \leq x \leq 73.1)$
$= \text{Base(height)}$
$= (73.1 - 26.9)(\frac{1}{80}) = \frac{46.2}{80} = .5775$

h. $P(x > 75) = \text{Base(height)} = (90 - 75)\frac{1}{80} = \frac{15}{80} = .1875$

6.67 a. $P(z \geq .4) = .5000 - P(0 \leq z \leq .4) = .5000 - .1554 = .3446$

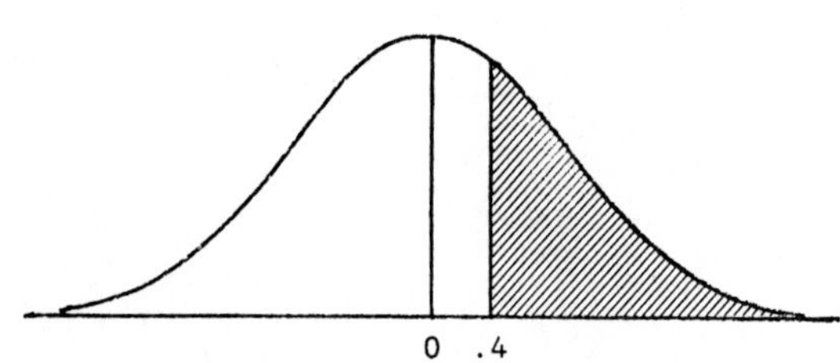

b. $P(z \leq .3) = P(z \leq 0) + P(0 \leq z \leq .3) = .5000 + .1179 = .6179$

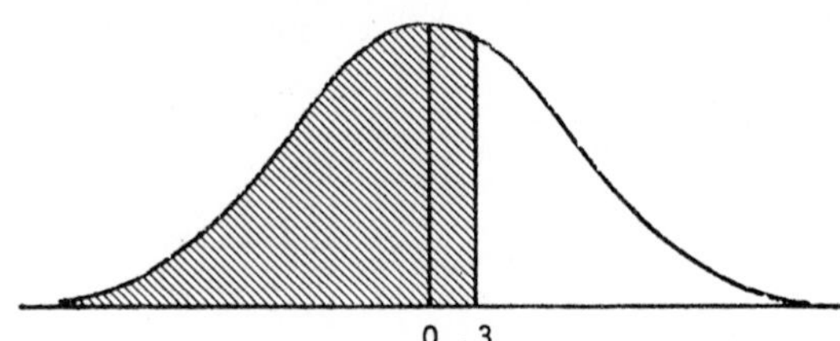


c. $P(z \geq -3.05) = P(-3.05 \leq z \leq 0) + P(z \geq 0)$
$= P(0 \leq z \leq 3.05) + P(z \geq 0)$
$= .4989 + .5000$
$= .9989$

-3.05 0

d. $P(-1.75 \leq z \leq -.25) = P(-1.75 \leq z \leq 0) - P(-.25 \leq z \leq 0)$
$= P(0 \leq z \leq 1.75) - P(0 \leq z \leq .25)$
$= .4599 - .0987$
$= .3612$

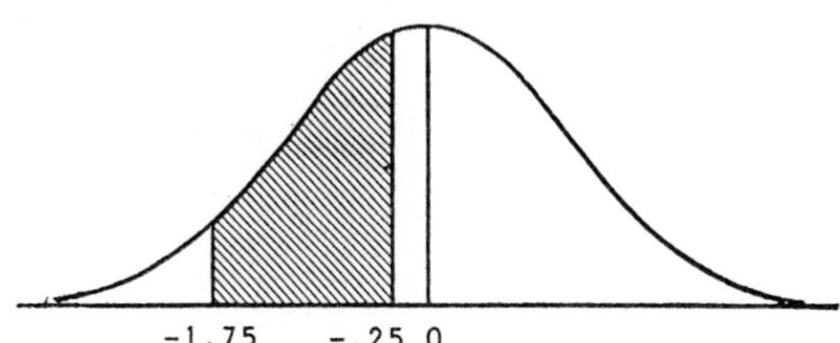


6.69 a. $P(z \geq z_0) = .5517$
$\Rightarrow P(z_0 \leq z \leq 0) = .0517$
$\Rightarrow z_0 = -.13$

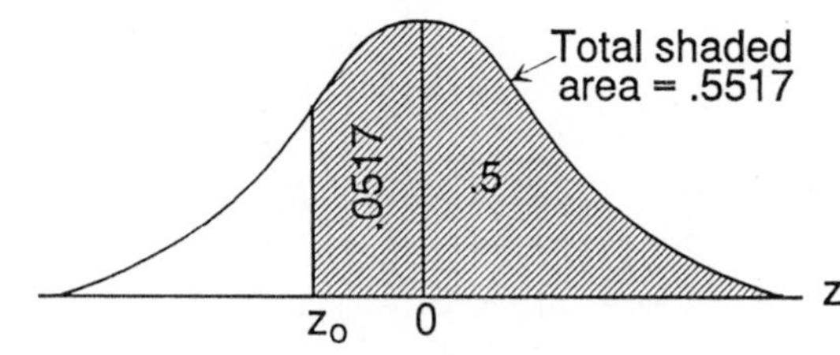

b. $P(z \leq z_0) = .5080$
$\Rightarrow P(0 \leq z \leq z_0) = .0080$
$\Rightarrow z_0 = .02$

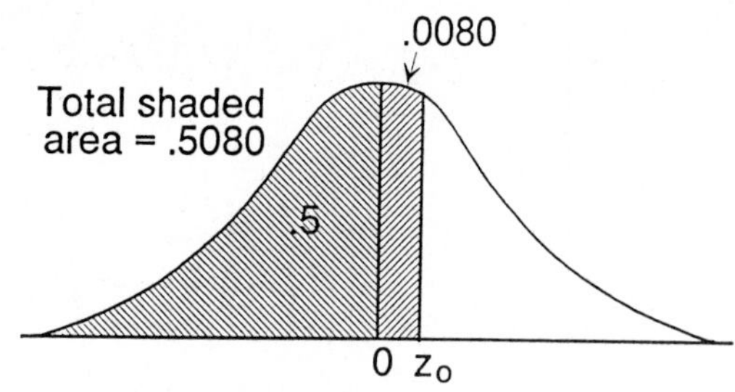


c. $P(z \geq z_0) = .1492$
$\Rightarrow P(0 \leq z \leq z_0) = .5 - .1492 = .3508$
$\Rightarrow z_0 = 1.04$

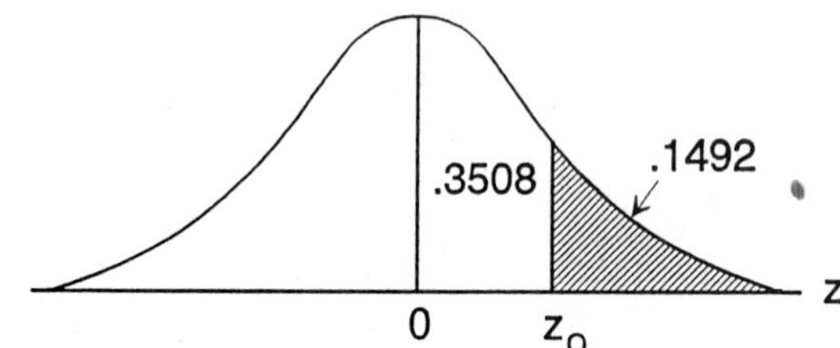


d. $P(z_0 \leq z \leq .59) = .4773$
$\Rightarrow P(z_0 \leq z \leq 0) = .4773 - .2224 = .2549$
$\Rightarrow z_0 = -.69$

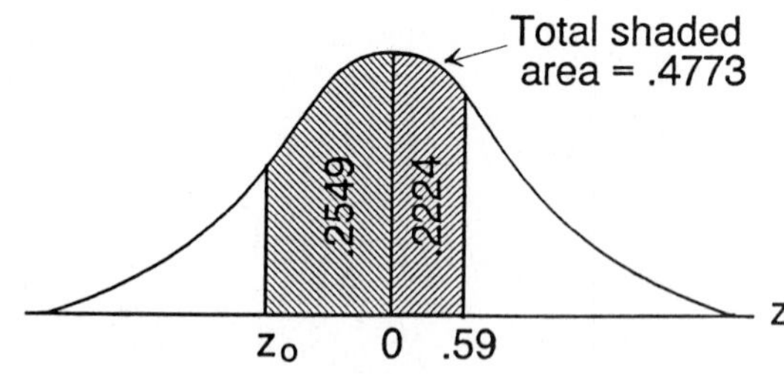


6.71 x has an exponential distribution with $\lambda = .3$.

a. $P(x \leq 2) = 1 - P(x > 2) = 1 - e^{-.3(2)}$
$= 1 - e^{-.6} = 1 - .548812$
$= .451188$

b. $P(x > 3) = e^{-.3(3)} = e^{-.9} = .406570$

c. $P(x = 1) = 0$. Since x is continuous, there is no probability at a single point.

d. $P(x \leq 7) = 1 - P(x > 7) = 1 - e^{-.3(7)}$
$= 1 - e^{-2.1} = 1 - .122456$
$= .877544$

e. $P(4 \leq x \leq 12) = P(x \geq 4) - P(x > 12)$

$= e^{-.3(4)} - e^{-.3(12)}$

$= e^{-1.2} - e^{-3.6}$

$= .301194 - .027324$

$= .27387$

f. $P(x = 2.5) = 0$. Since x is continuous, there is no probability at a single point.

6.73 Let x be the noise level per jet takeoff in a neighborhood near the airport. The random variable x is approximately normally distributed with $\mu = 100$ and $\sigma = 6$.

a. $z = \frac{x - \mu}{\sigma} = \frac{108 - 100}{6} = 1.33$

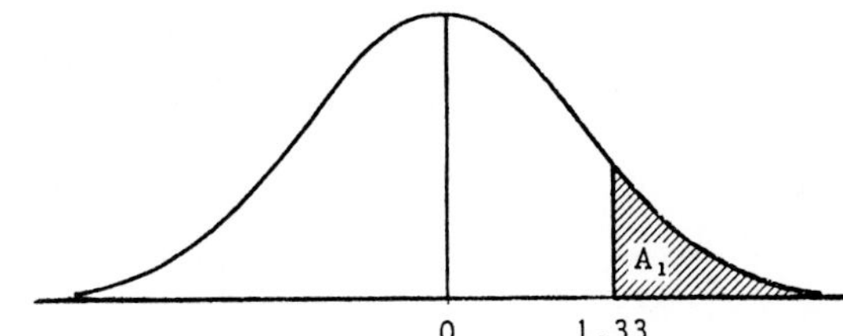


$P(x > 108) = P(z > 1.33)$
$= .5000 - P(0 \leq z \leq 1.33)$
$= .5000 - .4082$
$= .0918$

b. $P(x = 100) = 0$

c. Given $P(x < 105) = .95$ and $\sigma = 6$,

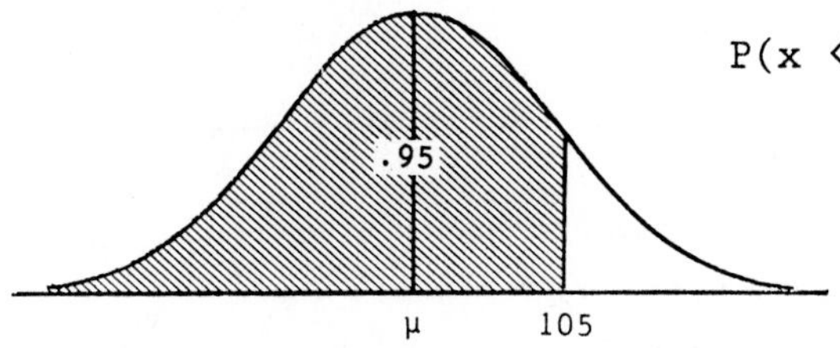


$P(x < 105) = P(x < \mu) + P(\mu < x < 105)$
$= .5 + .45$
$= .5000 + P(0 < z < 1.645)$

Since $z = 1.645$, $x = 105$ and $\sigma = 6$,

$$z = \frac{x - \mu}{\sigma}$$

$$\Rightarrow 1.645 = \frac{105 - \mu}{6}$$

$$\Rightarrow 9.87 = 105 - \mu$$

Hence, $\mu = 95.13$

Since $\mu = 100$, the mean level of noise must be lowered $100 - 95.13 = 4.87$ decibels.

6.75 Let y be the profit on a metal part that is produced. Then y is \$10, \$-2, or \$-1, depending where it falls with respect to the tolerance limits.

Let x be the tensile strength of a particular metal part. The random variable x is normally distributed with $\mu = 25$ and $\sigma = 2$.

$$z = \frac{x - \mu}{\sigma} = \frac{21 - 25}{2} = -2$$

$$z = \frac{x - \mu}{\sigma} = \frac{30 - 25}{2} = 2.5$$

$P(y = 10) = P(x \text{ falls within the tolerance limits})$

$= P(21 < x < 30) = P(-2 < z < 2.5)$
$= P(-2 < z < 0) + P(0 < z < 2.5)$
$= P(0 < z < 2) + P(0 < z < 2.5)$
$= .4772 + .4938$
$= .9710$

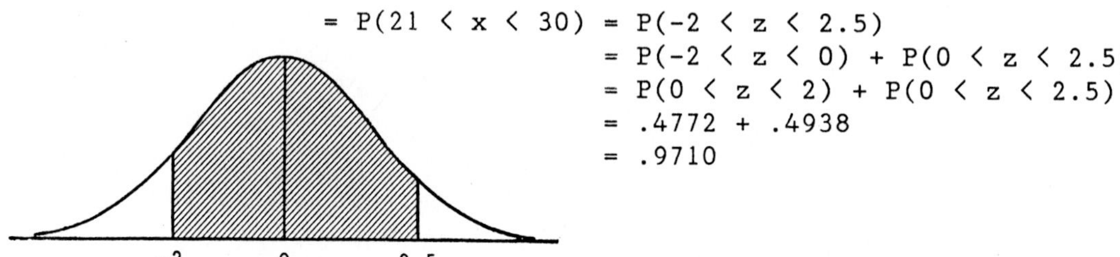


$P(y = -2) = P(x \text{ falls below the lower tolerance limit})$

$= P(x < 21) = P(z < -2)$
$= .5000 - P(-2 < z < 0)$
$= .5000 - P(0 < z < 2)$
$= .5000 - .4772$
$= .0228$

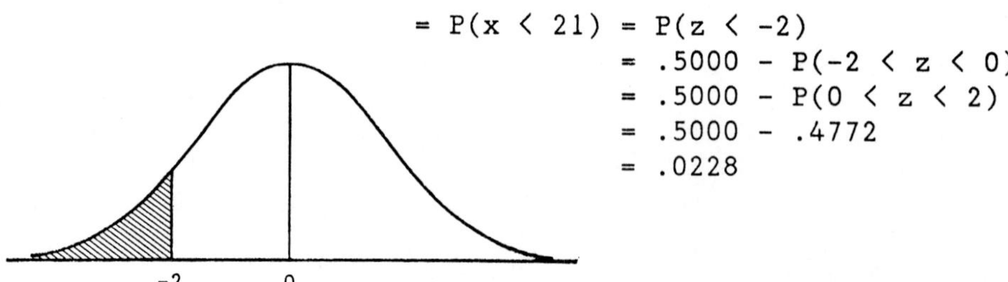


$P(y = -1) = P(x \text{ falls above the upper tolerance limit})$

$= P(x > 30) = P(z > 2.5)$
$= .5000 - P(0 < z < 2.5)$
$= .5000 - .4938$
$= .0062$

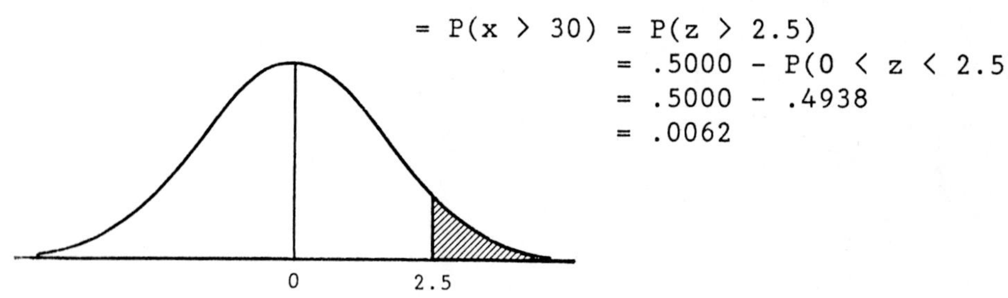

The probability distribution of y is given below:

| y | 10 | -2 | -1 |
|---|---|---|---|
| p(y) | .9710 | .0228 | .0062 |

$$E(y) = \sum yp(y) = 10(.9710) + -2(.0228) + -1(.0062)$$
$$= 9.71 - .0456 - .0062$$
$$= 9.6582$$

6.77 a. There are 36 quality control inspectors who each have one observation for 8 weeks. Thus, the number of observations is 8 x 36 = 288.

b. Let x be the weekly average earnings.

$$z = \frac{x - \mu}{\sigma} = \frac{8.5 - 7.65}{1.25} = .68$$

$$P(x > 8.5) = P(z > .68)$$
$$= .5000 - P(0 < z < .68)$$
$$= .5000 - .2517$$
$$= .2483$$

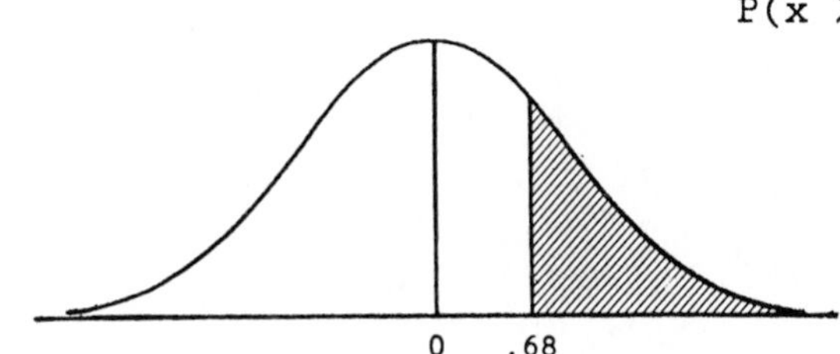


c. No, it is not possible to determine how many of the inspectors average over \$8.50 per hour. In order to determine the number of inspectors who average over \$8.50 per hour, we have to know the total number of inspectors.

6.79 Let x be the time a worker is unemployed in weeks. The random variable x is an exponential random variable with $\lambda = .075$.

a. $\mu = 1/\lambda = 1/.075 = 13.33$ weeks

b. $P(x \geq 2) = e^{-2\lambda} = e^{-2(.075)} = e^{-.15} = .860708$

$P(x > 6) = e^{-6\lambda} = e^{-6(.075)} = e^{-.45} = .637628$

c. $P(x < 12) = 1 - P(x \geq 12) = 1 - e^{-12(.075)}$

$$= 1 - e^{-.9} = 1 - .40657$$
$$= .59343$$

6.81 The summary statistics were computed for each bank as follows:

| | Range | $s = \sqrt{\dfrac{\sum x^2 - \dfrac{(\sum x)^2}{n}}{n-1}}$ | Coefficient of Variation $(s/\bar{x})$ |
|---|---|---|---|
| Bank 1 | 31 - 10 = 21 | $\sqrt{\dfrac{2554 - \dfrac{116^2}{6}}{5}} = 7.8909$ | $\dfrac{7.8909}{19.3333} = .408$ |
| Bank 2 | 70 - 54 = 16 | $\sqrt{\dfrac{22974 - \dfrac{370^2}{6}}{5}} = 5.6095$ | $\dfrac{5.6095}{61.6667} = .091$ |
| Bank 3 | 129 - 81 = 48 | $\sqrt{\dfrac{64791 - \dfrac{617^2}{6}}{5}} = 16.3880$ | $\dfrac{16.3880}{102.8333} = .159$ |

The rankings (from high to low) based on each measure are:

(a) Range: Bank 3, Bank 1 Bank 2

(b) Standard deviation: Bank 3, Bank 1, Bank 2

(c) Coefficient of variation: Bank 1, Bank 3, Bank 2

6.83 The random variable x is a binomial random variable with n = 4000 and p = .001.

$$\mu = np = 4000(.001) = 4$$
$$\sigma^2 = npq = 4000(.001)(.999) = 3.996$$

$$\sigma = \sqrt{\sigma^2} = \sqrt{3.996} = 1.999$$

Using the normal approximation of the binomial,

$$z = \frac{(a - .5) - \mu}{\sigma} = \frac{.5 - 4}{1.999} = -1.75$$

$$\begin{aligned} P(x \geq 1) &\approx P(z \geq -1.75) \\ &= P(-1.75 \leq z \leq 0) + P(z \geq 0) \\ &= P(0 \leq z \leq 1.75) + .5000 \\ &= .4599 + .5000 \text{ (Table IV)} \\ &= .9599 \end{aligned}$$

-1.75 0

Using the Poisson approximation of the binomial, $\lambda = \mu = np = 4$

$$P(x > 0) = 1 - P(x = 0) = 1 - .018 = .982$$

(Using Table III, Appendix B)

6.85 a. Define x = the number of serious accidents per month. Then x has a Poisson distribution with $\lambda = 2$. If we define y = the time between adjacent serious accidents, then y has an exponential distribution with $\mu = 1/\lambda = 1/2$ and $\lambda = 2$. If an accident occurs today, the probability that the next serious accident will <u>not</u> occur during the next month is:

$$P(y > 1) = e^{-1(2)} = e^{-2} = .135335$$

Alternatively, we could solve the problem in terms of the random variable x by noting that the probability that the next serious accident will <u>not</u> occur during the next month is the same as the probability that the number of serious accident next month is zero, i.e.,

$$P(y > 1) = P(x = 0) = \frac{e^{-2}2^0}{0!} = e^{-2} = .135335$$

b. $P(x > 1) = 1 - P(x \leq 1) = 1 - .406 = .594$

(Using Table III in Appendix B with $\lambda = 2$)

6.87 The random variable x is a binomial random variable with n = 1600 and p = .20.

$$\mu = np = 1600(.20) = 320$$

$$\sigma = \sqrt{npq} = \sqrt{1600(.20)(1 - .20)} = \sqrt{256} = 16$$

We observe that x = 400 out of the 1600 customers. This value is much larger than the mean value. It is 5 standard deviations above the mean.

The probability of observing a value this high or higher when p = .2 is (using the normal approximation)

$$P(x \geq 400) \approx P(z \geq 4.97) \approx 0$$

where $z = \frac{(a - .5) - \mu}{\sigma} = \frac{399.5 - 320}{16} = 4.97$

This would lead me to believe that p is really larger than .2 since x is 400.

6.89 Using Minitab, the following relative frequency histograms were obtained for the data sets:

a.

```
Midpoint   Count
     0.0      15   ***************
     0.2      14   **************
     0.4       9   *********
     0.6       5   *****
     0.8       1   *
     1.0       1   *
     1.2       1   *
     1.4       0
     1.6       1   *
     1.8       1   *
```

It appears the data came from an exponential probability distribution with $\lambda \approx 2$.

b.

```
Midpoint   Count
    10.0       2   **
    10.5      10   **********
    11.0       6   ******
    11.5       5   *****
    12.0       8   ********
    12.5       6   ******
    13.0       4   ****
    13.5       4   ****
    14.0       3   ***
```

It appears the data came from a uniform probability distribution with $c \approx 10$ and $d \approx 14$.

c.

```
Midpoint   Count
      45       1   *
      50       1   *
      55       0
      60       4   ****
      65       8   ********
      70       9   *********
      75      11   ***********
      80       6   ******
      85       6   ******
      90       2   **
```

It appears the data came from a normal distribution with $\mu \approx 75$ and $\sigma \approx 6$.

# CHAPTER 7

## SAMPLING DISTRIBUTIONS

7.1 a. "The sampling distribution of the sample statistic A" is the probability distribution of the variable A.

b. "A" is an unbiased estimator of $\alpha$ because the mean of the sampling distribution of A is $\alpha$.

c. If both A and B are unbiased estimators of $\alpha$, then the statistic whose standard deviation is smaller is a better estimator of $\alpha$.

d. No. The Central Limit Theorem applies only to the sample mean. If A is the sample mean, $\bar{x}$, and n is sufficiently large, then the Central Limit Theorem will apply. However, both A and B cannot be sample means. Thus, we cannot apply the Central Limit Theorem to both A and B.

7.3 a. $\mu_{\bar{x}} = \mu = 20 \qquad \sigma_{\bar{x}} = \frac{\sigma}{\sqrt{n}} = \frac{3}{\sqrt{10}} = .949$

b. $\mu_{\bar{x}} = \mu = 100 \qquad \sigma_{\bar{x}} = \frac{\sigma}{\sqrt{n}} = \frac{10}{\sqrt{40}} = 1.581$

c. $\mu_{\bar{x}} = \mu = 25 \qquad \sigma_{\bar{x}} = \frac{\sigma}{\sqrt{n}} = \frac{2}{\sqrt{12}} = .577$

d. $\mu_{\bar{x}} = \mu = 400 \qquad \sigma_{\bar{x}} = \frac{\sigma}{\sqrt{n}} = \frac{9}{\sqrt{100}} = .900$

7.5 We know that the sampling distribution of $\bar{x}$ will be normal since the sampled population is normal. We also know that the sampling distribution will have mean and standard deviation

$$\mu_{\bar{x}} = \mu = 15 \qquad \sigma_{\bar{x}} = \frac{\sigma}{\sqrt{n}} = \frac{3}{\sqrt{25}} = .6$$

a. $P(\bar{x} > 16) = P\left(z > \frac{16 - \mu}{\sigma_{\bar{x}}}\right) = P\left(z > \frac{16 - 15}{.6}\right) = P(z > 1.67)$

$= .5 - P(0 < z < 1.67) = .5 - .4525 = .0475$

b. $P(\bar{x} < 16) = P\left(z < \frac{16 - \mu}{\sigma_{\bar{x}}}\right) = P\left(z < \frac{16 - 15}{.6}\right) = P(z < 1.67)$

$= .5 + P(0 < z < 1.67) = .5 + .4525 = .9525$

Note: $\bar{x} < 16$ is the complement of $\bar{x} > 16$; therefore, $P(\bar{x} < 16) = 1 - P(\bar{x} > 16) = 1 - .0475 = .9525$.

c. $P(\bar{x} > 14.2) = P\left(z > \frac{14.2 - \mu}{\sigma_{\bar{x}}}\right) = P\left(z > \frac{14.2 - 15}{.6}\right) = P(z > -1.33)$

$= .5 + P(-1.33 < z < 0) = .5 + P(0 < z < 1.33)$
$= .5 + .4082 = .9082$

d. $P(14 < \bar{x} < 16) = P\left(\frac{14 - \mu}{\sigma_{\bar{x}}} < z < \frac{16 - \mu}{\sigma_{\bar{x}}}\right) = P\left(\frac{14 - 15}{.6} < z < \frac{16 - 15}{.6}\right)$

$= P(-1.67 < z < 1.67) = 2P(0 < z < 1.67)$
$= 2(.4525) = .9050$

e. $P(\bar{x} < 14) = P\left(z < \frac{14 - \mu}{\sigma_{\bar{x}}}\right) = P\left(z < \frac{14 - 15}{.6}\right) = p(z < -1.67)$

$= .5 - P(-1.67 < z < 0) = .5 - P(0 < z < 1.67)$
$= .5 - .4525 = .0475$

Note: Because the normal distribution is symmetric, $p(\bar{x} < 14) = P(\bar{x} > 16)$ (see part (a)).

7.7 Though we do not know the relative frequency distribution of the sampled population, we know by the Central Limit Theorem that the sampling distribution of $\bar{x}$ will be approximately normal since $n \geq 30$. Also the sampling distribution will have mean and standard deviation

$$\mu_{\bar{x}} = \mu = 200 \qquad \sigma_{\bar{x}} = \frac{\sigma}{\sqrt{n}} = \frac{20}{\sqrt{49}} = 2.86$$

a. $P(\bar{x} \leq 200) = P\left(z \leq \frac{200 - \mu}{\sigma_{\bar{x}}}\right) = P\left(z \leq \frac{200 - 200}{2.86}\right) = P(z \leq 0) = .5$

b. $P(\bar{x} < 200) = P\left(z \leq \frac{200 - \mu}{\sigma_{\bar{x}}}\right) = P\left(z \leq \frac{200 - 200}{2.86}\right) = P(z < 0) = .5$

Recall that $p(x = a) = 0$ for a continuous distribution; hence (a) and (b) are identical problems. Also, notice that the probability of observing a sample mean greater than or less than $\mu$ is .5 as the symmetric normal distribution is split into two equal parts by its mean.

c. $P(\bar{x} < 205) = P\left(z < \frac{205 - \mu}{\sigma_{\bar{x}}}\right) = P\left(z \leq \frac{205 - 200}{2.86}\right) = P(z < 1.75)$

$= .5 + P(0 < z < 1.75) = .5 + .4599 = .9599$

d. $P(\bar{x} > 190) = P\left(z < \frac{190 - \mu}{\sigma_{\bar{x}}}\right) = P\left(z > \frac{190 - 200}{2.86}\right) = P(z > -3.50)$

$= .5 + P(-3.50 < z < 0) = .5 + P(0 < z < 3.50)$
$= .5 + \text{approx. } .5 = \text{approx. } 1$

e. $P(\bar{x} > 209) = P\left(z > \frac{209 - \mu}{\sigma_{\bar{x}}}\right) = P\left(z > \frac{209 - 200}{2.86}\right) = P(z > 3.15)$

$= .5 - P(0 < z < 3.15) = .5 - \text{approx. } .5 = \text{approx. } 0$

f. $P(193 \leq \bar{x} \leq 200) = P\left(\frac{193 - \mu}{\sigma_{\bar{x}}} \leq z \leq \frac{200 - \mu}{\sigma_{\bar{x}}}\right)$

$= P\left(\frac{193 - 200}{2.86} \leq z \leq \frac{200 - 200}{2.86}\right)$

$= P(-2.45 \leq z \leq 0) = P(0 \leq z \leq 2.45) = .4929$

g. $P(197.1 \leq \bar{x} \leq 202.9) = P\left(\frac{197.1 - \mu}{\sigma_{\bar{x}}} \leq z \leq \frac{202.9 - \mu}{\sigma_{\bar{x}}}\right)$

$= P\left(\frac{197.1 - 200}{2.86} \leq z \leq \frac{202.9 - 200}{2.86}\right)$

$= P(-1.01 \leq z \leq 1.01) = 2P(0 \leq z \leq 1.01)$
$= 2(.3438) = .6876$

h. $P(205 \leq \bar{x} \leq 210) = P\left(\frac{205 - \mu}{\sigma_{\bar{x}}} \leq z \leq \frac{210 - \mu}{\sigma_{\bar{x}}}\right)$

$= P\left(\frac{205 - 200}{2.86} \leq z \leq \frac{210 - 200}{2.86}\right)$

$= P(1.75 \leq z \leq 3.50) = P(0 \leq z \leq 3.50) - P(0 \leq z \leq 1.75)$
$= \text{approx } .5 - .4599 = \text{approx. } .0401$

7.9 Recall that $\bar{x} = \frac{\sum x}{n}$. The following sample means are computed. The results are arranged in the same manner as the data sets in the exercise.

| | | | |
|---|---|---|---|
| 4.83 | 4.50 | 4.50 | 5.67 |
| 4.67 | 5.00 | 4.17 | 5.00 |
| 5.17 | 4.67 | 5.33 | 4.17 |
| 4.50 | 5.33 | 3.83 | 2.50 |
| 5.67 | 3.83 | 4.33 | 2.67 |
| 5.00 | 4.17 | 4.83 | 5.50 |
| 7.33 | 4.00 | 3.50 | 2.17 |
| 5.83 | 3.33 | 3.50 | 7.00 |
| 4.00 | 4.33 | 6.83 | 5.83 |
| 6.17 | 4.00 | 6.83 | 2.67 |
| 3.17 | 3.83 | 5.83 | 5.67 |
| 4.83 | 5.17 | 3.83 | 5.50 |
| 5.50 | 3.50 | | |

a. The following relative frequency histogram can be obtained.

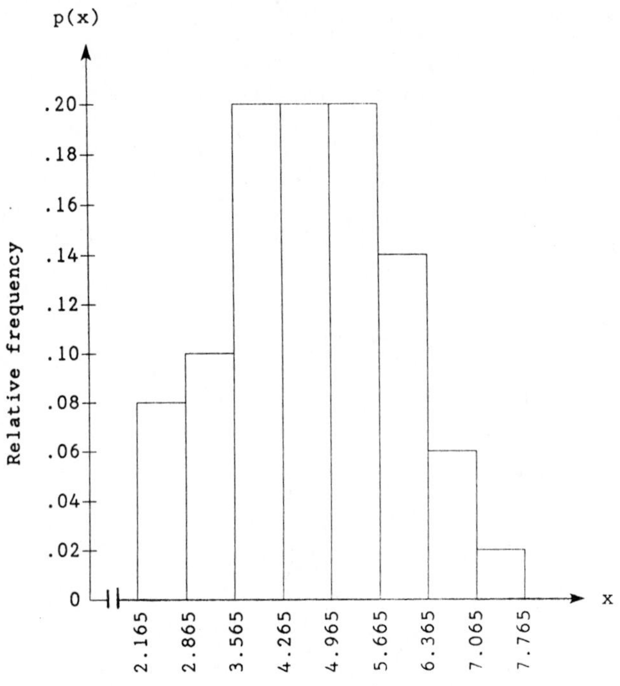


b. $\mu_{\bar{x}} = \mu = 4.5$ $\qquad \sigma_{\bar{x}} = \frac{\sigma}{\sqrt{n}} = \frac{\sqrt{8.25}}{\sqrt{6}} = 1.172$

The center of the histogram appears to be around 4.5, and the standard deviation of 1.172 appears reasonable.

c. The mean and standard deviation of the 50 medians are 4.78 and 1.642, respectively.

The actual mean and standard deviation of the 50 means are 4.68 and 1.172, respectively.

From this information, it appears the sample means are closer to the true mean than the sample medians.

7.11 The sample means are:

| | | | |
|---|---|---|---|
| 4.75 | 4.83 | 4.33 | 5.33 |
| 4.83 | 4.58 | 4.58 | 3.33 |
| 5.33 | 4.08 | 4.58 | 4.08 |
| 6.58 | 3.83 | 3.50 | 4.58 |
| 5.08 | 3.92 | 6.83 | 4.25 |
| 4.00 | 4.33 | 4.83 | 5.58 |
| 5.00 | | | |

a. We will graph the relative frequency histogram using the same measurement classes used in Exercise 7.7 to provide a good comparison.

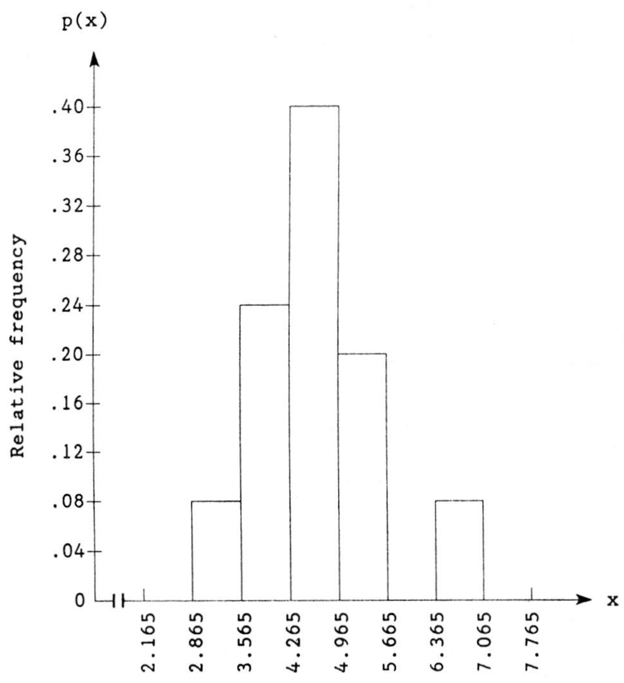


The means based on n = 12 are much less variable than those based on n = 6.

b. Let $\bar{\bar{x}}$ = mean of the 25 sample means, $\bar{\bar{x}} = \frac{\sum \bar{x}_i}{n} = \frac{116.94}{25} = 4.68$

Let $s^2_{\bar{x}}$ = variance of the 25 sample means.

$$s^2_{\bar{x}} = \frac{\sum \bar{x}_i^2 - \frac{(\sum \bar{x}_i)^2}{n}}{n - 1} = \frac{563.388 - \frac{116.94^2}{25}}{25 - 1} = \frac{16.389456}{24} = .682894$$

$$s_{\bar{x}} = \sqrt{s^2_{\bar{x}}} = \sqrt{.682894} = .8264$$

Notice that the standard deviation of the means is close to

$$\sigma_{\bar{x}} = \frac{\sigma}{\sqrt{n}} = \frac{2.872}{\sqrt{12}} = .829$$

The standard deviation of the mean, $\sigma_{\bar{x}} = \frac{\sigma}{\sqrt{n}}$ will decrease as the sample size increases. In this case, as n doubled, we expect $\sigma_{\bar{x}}$ to decrease by $\frac{1}{\sqrt{2}}$. Notice that $\frac{1.172}{\sqrt{2}} = .829$

7.17 a. The number of samples of size n = 2 that could be selected without replacement from a population of size N = 4 is:

$$\binom{N}{n} = \binom{4}{2} = \frac{4!}{2!(4 - 2)!} = 6$$

The samples are:

| | |
|---|---|
| chip 1, chip 2 | chip 2, chip 3 |
| chip 1, chip 3 | chip 2, chip 4 |
| chip 1, chip 4 | chip 3, chip 4 |

where chip 1 is marked 1, chips 2 and 3 are marked 2, and chip 4 is marked 3.

b. Each of the six outcomes is equally likely since the chips are chosen at random; therefore, each has probability 1/6.

c.

| Sample (Number marked on chip) | $\bar{x}$ |
|---|---|
| 1, 2 | 1.5 |
| 1, 2 | 1.5 |
| 1, 3 | 2 |
| 2, 2 | 2 |
| 2, 3 | 2.5 |
| 2, 3 | 2.5 |

d.

| $\bar{x}$ | $p(\bar{x})$ |
|---|---|
| 1.5 | $\frac{2}{6} = \frac{1}{3}$ |
| 2 | $\frac{2}{6} = \frac{1}{3}$ |
| 2.5 | $\frac{2}{6} = \frac{1}{3}$ |

e. Population Probability Distribution

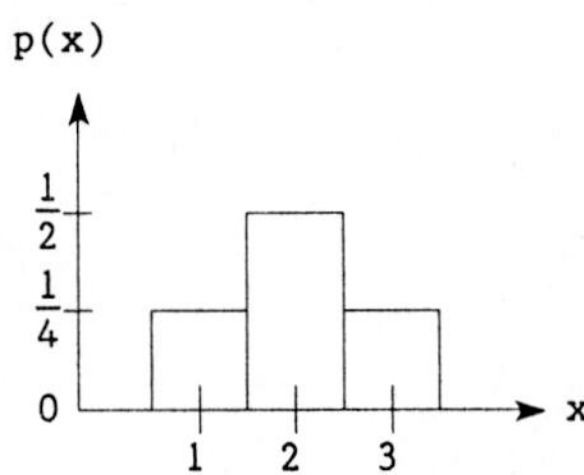


Sampling Distribution

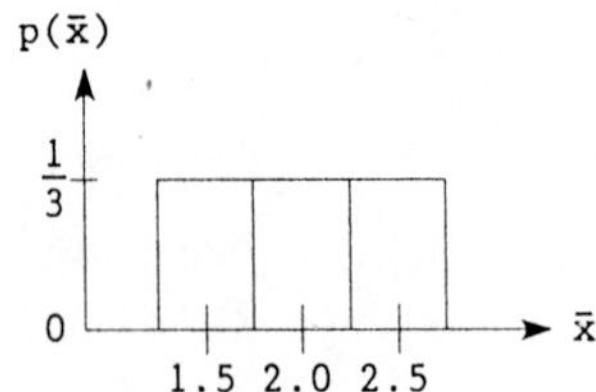

a. For confidence coefficient .90, $\alpha = 1 - .90 = .10$ and $\alpha/2 = .10/2 = .05$. From Table VI, Appendix B, with $df = n - 1 = 6 - 1 = 5$, $t_{.05} = 2.015$. The 90% confidence interval is:

$$\bar{x} \pm t_{.05}\frac{s}{\sqrt{n}}$$

$$\Rightarrow 4.833 \pm 2.015\,\frac{2.137}{\sqrt{6}}$$

$$\Rightarrow 4.833 \pm 1.758 \Rightarrow (3.075,\ 6.591)$$

b. For confidence coefficient .95, $\alpha = 1 - .95 = .05$ and $\alpha/2 = .05/2 = .025$. From Table VI, Appendix B, with $df = n - 1 = 6 - 1 = 5$, $t_{.025} = 2.571$. The 95% confidence interval is:

$$\bar{x} \pm t_{.025}\frac{s}{\sqrt{n}}$$

$$\Rightarrow 4.833 \pm 2.571\,\frac{2.137}{\sqrt{6}}$$

$$\Rightarrow 4.833 \pm 2.243 \Rightarrow (2.590,\ 7.076)$$

c. For confidence coefficient .99, $\alpha = 1 - .99 = .01$ and $\alpha/2 = .01/2 = .005$. From Table VI, Appendix B, with $df = n - 1 = 6 - 1 = 5$, $t_{.005} = 4.032$. The 99% confidence interval is:

$$\bar{x} \pm t_{.005}\frac{s}{\sqrt{n}}$$

$$\Rightarrow 4.833 \pm 4.032\,\frac{2.137}{\sqrt{6}}$$

$$\Rightarrow 4.833 \pm 3.518 \Rightarrow (1.315,\ 8.351)$$

d. a) For confidence coefficient .90, $\alpha = 1 - .90 = .10$ and $\alpha/2 = .10/2 = .05$. From Table VI, Appendix B, with $df = n - 1 = 25 - 1 = 24$, $t_{.05} = 1.711$. The 90% confidence interval is:

$$\bar{x} \pm t_{.05}\,\frac{s}{\sqrt{n}}$$

$$\Rightarrow 4.833 \pm 1.711\,\frac{2.137}{\sqrt{25}}$$

$$\Rightarrow 4.833 \pm .731 \Rightarrow (4.102,\ 5.564)$$

b) For confidence coefficient .95, $\alpha = 1 - .95 = .05$ and $\alpha/2 = .05/2 = .025$. From Table VI, Appendix B, with df = n - 1 = 25 - 1 = 24, $t_{.025} = 2.064$. The 95% confidence interval is:

$$\bar{x} \pm t_{.025} \frac{s}{\sqrt{n}}$$

$$\Rightarrow 4.833 \pm 2.064 \frac{2.137}{\sqrt{25}}$$

$$\Rightarrow 4.833 \pm .882 \Rightarrow (3.951,\ 5.715)$$

c) For confidence coefficient .99, $\alpha = 1 - .99 = .01$ and $\alpha/2 = .01/2 = .005$. From Table VI, Appendix B, with df = n - 1 = 25 - 1 = 24, $t_{.005} = 2.797$. The 99% confidence interval is:

$$\bar{x} \pm t_{.005} \frac{s}{\sqrt{n}}$$

$$\Rightarrow 4.833 \pm 2.797 \frac{2.137}{\sqrt{25}}$$

$$\Rightarrow 4.833 \pm 1.195 \Rightarrow (3.638,\ 6.028)$$

Increasing the sample size decreases the width of the confidence interval.

8.33 a. For confidence coefficient .90, $\alpha = 1 - .90 = .10$ and $\alpha/2 = .10/2 = .05$. From Table VI, Appendix B, with df = n - 1 = 20 - 1 = 19, $t_{.05} = 1.729$. The 90% confidence interval is:

$$\bar{x} \pm t_{.05} \frac{s}{\sqrt{n}}$$

$$\Rightarrow 3.8 \pm 1.729 \frac{1.2}{\sqrt{20}}$$

$$\Rightarrow 3.8 \pm .464 \Rightarrow (3.336,\ 4.264)$$

b. We are 90% confident that the mean LOS in 1990 will be between 3.336 and 4.264 days.

c. "90% confidence interval" means that if repeated samples of size n are selected from a population and 90% confidence intervals are constructed, 90% of all intervals thus constructed will contain the population mean.

8.35 a. The population of interest is the balance of all home mortgages foreclosed by the bank due to default by the borrower during the last 3 years. This population should be normally distributed to use the t distribution.

b. First, compute the sample mean and standard deviation.

$$\bar{x} = \frac{\sum x}{n} = \frac{811783}{12} = 67,648.58$$

$$s = \sqrt{\frac{\sum x^2 - \frac{(\sum x)^2}{n}}{n - 1}} = 19171.28$$

For confidence coefficient .90, $\alpha$ = .10 and $\alpha/2$ = .05. From Table VI, Appendix B, with df = n - 1 = 12 - 1 = 11, $t_{.05}$ = 1.796. The 90% confidence interval is:

$$\bar{x} \pm t_{.05} \frac{s}{\sqrt{n}}$$

$$\Rightarrow 67,648.58 \pm 1.796 \frac{19171.28}{\sqrt{12}}$$

$$\Rightarrow 67,648.58 \pm 9939.55 \Rightarrow (57,709.03,\ 77,588.13)$$

c. We are 90% confident that the true mean outstanding principal lies in the interval $57,709.03 to $77,588.13.

8.37 First, compute the sample mean and standard deviation:

$$\bar{x} = \frac{\sum x}{n} = \frac{487,514}{7} = 69,644.8571$$

$$s^2 = \frac{\sum x^2 - \frac{(\sum x)^2}{n}}{n - 1} = \frac{43,523,214,550 - \frac{487,514^2}{7}}{7 - 1} = 1,595,061,944$$

$$s = \sqrt{s^2} = 39,938.2266$$

For confidence coefficient .90, $\alpha$ = .10 and $\alpha/2$ = .05. From Table VI, Appendix B, with df = n - 1 = 7 - 1 = 6, $t_{.05}$ = 1.943. The 90% confidence interval is:

$$\bar{x} \pm t_{.05} \frac{s}{\sqrt{n}}$$

$$\Rightarrow 69,644.86 \pm 1.943 \frac{39,938.2266}{\sqrt{7}}$$

$$\Rightarrow 69,644.86 \pm 29,330.03 \Rightarrow (40,314.83,\ 98,974.89)$$

Assumption: the sample is a random sample selected from a normally distributed population.

8.39 a. For confidence coefficient .95, $\alpha = 1 - .95 = .05$ and $\alpha/2 = .05/2 = .025$. From Table VI, Appendix B, with $df = n - 1 = 23 - 1 = 22$, $t_{.025} = 2.074$. The 95% confidence interval is:

$$\bar{x} \pm t_{.025} \frac{s}{\sqrt{n}}$$

$$\Rightarrow 135 \pm 2.074 \frac{32}{\sqrt{23}}$$

$$\Rightarrow 135 \pm 13.839 \Rightarrow (121.161, 148.839)$$

b. We must assume a random sample was selected and that the population of all health insurance costs per worker per month is normally distributed.

c. "95%" confidence interval" means that if repeated samples of size 23 were selected from the population and 95% confidence intervals formed, 95% of all confidence intervals will contain the true value of $\mu$.

8.41 An unbiased estimator is one in which the mean of the sampling distribution is the parameter of interest, i.e., $E(\hat{p}) = p$.

8.43 a. The sample size is large enough if the interval $\hat{p} \pm 3\sigma_{\hat{p}}$ does not include 0 or 1.

$$\hat{p} \pm 3\sigma_{\hat{p}} \Rightarrow \hat{p} \pm 3\sqrt{\frac{pq}{n}}$$

$$\Rightarrow \hat{p} \pm 3\sqrt{\frac{\hat{p}\hat{q}}{n}}$$

$$\Rightarrow .76 \pm 3\sqrt{\frac{.76(1 - .76)}{144}}$$

$$\Rightarrow .76 \pm .107 \Rightarrow (.653, .867)$$

Since the interval lies within the interval (0, 1), the normal approximation will be adequate.

b. For confidence coefficient .90, $\alpha$ = .10 and $\alpha/2$ = .05. From Table IV, Appendix B, $z_{.05}$ = 1.645. The 90% confidence interval is:

$$\hat{p} \pm z_{.05}\sqrt{\frac{pq}{n}}$$

$$\Rightarrow \hat{p} \pm 1.645\sqrt{\frac{\hat{p}\hat{q}}{n}}$$

$$\Rightarrow .76 \pm 1.645\sqrt{\frac{.76(.24)}{144}}$$

$$\Rightarrow .76 \pm .059 \Rightarrow (.701,\ .819)$$

c. We must assume that the sample is a random sample from the population of interest.

8.45 a. Since p is the proportion of consumers who like the snack food, $\hat{p}$ will be:

$$\hat{p} = \frac{\text{number of 1's in sample}}{n} = \frac{15}{50} = 0.3$$

Check to see if the normal approximation is appropriate.

$$\hat{p} \pm 3\sigma_{\hat{p}} \Rightarrow \hat{p} \pm 3\sqrt{\frac{pq}{n}} \Rightarrow \hat{p} \pm 3\sqrt{\frac{\hat{p}\hat{q}}{n}}$$

$$\Rightarrow .3 \pm 3\sqrt{\frac{.3(.7)}{50}}$$

$$\Rightarrow .3 \pm .194 \Rightarrow (.106,\ .494)$$

This interval lies within the interval (0, 1), so the normal approximation is adequate.

For confidence coefficient .80, $\alpha$ = .20 and $\alpha/2$ = .10. From Table IV, Appendix B, $z_{.10}$ = 1.28. The 80% confidence interval is:

$$\hat{p} \pm z_{.10}\sqrt{\frac{pq}{n}}$$

$$\Rightarrow \hat{p} \pm 1.28\sqrt{\frac{\hat{p}\hat{q}}{n}}$$

$$\Rightarrow .3 \pm 1.28\sqrt{\frac{.3(.7)}{50}}$$

$$\Rightarrow .3 \pm .083 \Rightarrow (.217,\ .383)$$

b. We are 80% confident the true proportion of consumers who like the snack food lies in the interval .217 to .383.

8.47 $\hat{p} = \frac{x}{n} = \frac{55}{71} = .775$

a. We first check to see if the sample size is sufficiently large.

$$\hat{p} \pm 3\sigma_{\hat{p}} \Rightarrow \hat{p} \pm 3\sqrt{\frac{\hat{p}\hat{q}}{n}}$$

$$\Rightarrow .775 \pm 3\sqrt{\frac{(.775)(.225)}{71}}$$

$$\Rightarrow .775 \pm .149 \Rightarrow (.626, .924)$$

Since the interval is wholly contained in the interval (0, 1), we may conclude that the normal approximation is reasonable.

For confidence coefficient .95, $\alpha = 1 - .95 = .05$ and $\alpha/2 = .05/2 = .025$. From Table IV, Appendix B, $z_{.025} = 1.96$. The 95% confidence interval is:

$$\hat{p} \pm z_{.025}\sqrt{\frac{\hat{p}\hat{q}}{n}}$$

$$\Rightarrow .775 \pm 1.96\sqrt{\frac{(.775)(.225)}{71}}$$

$$\Rightarrow .775 \pm .097 \Rightarrow (.678, .872)$$

b. We are 95% confident the proportion of all Illinois banks who used microcomputers at the time of the survey is between .678 and .872.

c. The interval in this problem is wider than the interval in Exercise 8.46. This is because the sample size in Exercise 8.46 ($n = 122$) is larger than that in this problem ($n = 71$).

8.49 a. The population of interest is all owners and managers of small U.S. businesses.

b. The sample size is large enough if $\hat{p} \pm 3\sigma_{\hat{p}}$ lies within the interval (0, 1).

$$\hat{p} \pm 3\sigma_{\hat{p}} \Rightarrow \hat{p} \pm 3\sqrt{\frac{pq}{n}} \Rightarrow \hat{p} \pm 3\sqrt{\frac{\hat{p}\hat{q}}{n}}\,t$$

$$\Rightarrow .4 \pm 3\sqrt{\frac{.4(.6)}{258}}$$

$$\Rightarrow .4 \pm .091 \Rightarrow (.309, .491)$$

Since the interval lies completely in the interval (0, 1), the normal approximation will be adequate.

c. For confidence coefficient .95, $\alpha$ = .05 and $\alpha/2$ = .025. From Table IV, Appendix B, $z_{.025}$ = 1.96. The 95% confidence interval is:

$$\hat{p} \pm z_{.025}\sqrt{\frac{pq}{n}}$$

$$\Rightarrow \hat{p} \pm 1.96\sqrt{\frac{\hat{p}\hat{q}}{n}}$$

$$\Rightarrow .4 \pm 1.96\sqrt{\frac{.4(.6)}{258}}$$

$$\Rightarrow .4 \pm .06 \Rightarrow (.34, .46)$$

d. The interval would be narrower for $\hat{p}$ = .30 rather than $\hat{p}$ = .40. As $\hat{p}$ approaches .5, the standard error, $\sigma_{\hat{p}}$, gets larger; therefore, a smaller $\hat{p}$ produces a smaller $\sigma_{\hat{p}}$ and a narrower confidence interval.

8.51 Check to see if the normal approximation will be adequate:

$$\hat{p} \pm 3\sigma_{\hat{p}} \Rightarrow \hat{p} \pm 3\sqrt{\frac{pq}{n}} \Rightarrow \hat{p} \pm 3\sqrt{\frac{\hat{p}\hat{q}}{n}} \quad \text{where } \hat{p} = \frac{24}{400} = .06$$

$$\Rightarrow .06 \pm 3\sqrt{\frac{.06(.94)}{400}}$$

$$\Rightarrow .06 \pm .0356 \Rightarrow (.0244, .0956)$$

Since the interval lies within in the interval (0, 1), the normal approximation will be adequate.

For confidence coefficient .90, $\alpha$ = .10 and $\alpha/2$ = .05. From Table IV, Appendix B, $z_{.05}$ = 1.645. The 90% confidence interval is:

$$\hat{p} \pm z_{.05}\sqrt{\frac{pq}{n}}$$

$$\Rightarrow \hat{p} \pm 1.645\sqrt{\frac{\hat{p}\hat{q}}{n}}$$

$$\Rightarrow .06 \pm 1.645\sqrt{\frac{.06(.94)}{400}}$$

$$\Rightarrow .06 \pm .0195 \Rightarrow (.0405, .0795)$$

8.53 The sample size will be larger than necessary for any p other than .5.

8.55 a. To compute the needed sample size, use:

$$n = \frac{4(z_{\alpha/2})^2pq}{w^2} \quad \text{where } z_{.025} = 1.96 \text{ from Table IV, Appendix B.}$$

Thus,

$$n = \frac{4(1.96)^2(.3)(.7)}{.12^2}$$

$$= 224.1$$

You would need to take n = 225 samples.

b. To compute the needed sample size, use:

$$n = \frac{4(z_{\alpha/2})^2pq}{w^2} = \frac{4(1.96)^2(.5)(.5)}{.12^2}$$

$$= 266.8$$

You would need to take 267 samples.

8.57 a. To compute the needed sample size, use:

$$n = \frac{4(z_{\alpha/2})^2pq}{w^2}$$ where $z_{.05} = 1.645$ from Table IV, Appendix B.

Thus,

$$n = \frac{4(1.645)^2(.17)(.83)}{.06^2}$$

$$= 424.2$$

You would need to sample 425 IRS offices.

8.59 a. To compute the necessary sample size, use:

$$n = \frac{4(z_{\alpha/2})^2(pq)}{w^2}$$ where $z_{.025} = 1.96$ from Table IV, Appendix B.

Thus,

$$n = \frac{4(1.96)^2(.3)(.7)}{.01^2}$$

$$= 32{,}269.4$$

You would need to sample 32,270 viewers.

8.61 a. To compute the necessary sample size, use:

$$n = \frac{4(z_{\alpha/2})^2(pq)}{w^2}$$ where $z_{.05} = 1.645$ from Table IV, Appendix B.

Thus,

$$n = \frac{4(1.645)^2(.05)(.95)}{.02^2}$$

$$= 321.3$$

You would need to observe 322 customers.

8.63 a. For a small sample from a normal distribution with unknown standard deviation, we use the t statistic. For confidence coefficient .95, $\alpha = 1 - .95 = .05$ and $\alpha/2 = .05/2 = .025$. From Table VI, Appendix B, with df = n - 1 = 23 - 1 = 22, $t_{.025} = 2.074$.

b. For a large sample from a distribution with an unknown standard deviation, we can estimate the population standard deviation with s and use the z statistic. For confidence coefficient .95, $\alpha = 1 - .95 = .05$ and $\alpha/2 = .05/2 = .025$. From Table IV, Appendix B, $z_{.025} = 1.96$.

c. For a small sample from a normal distribution with known standard deviation, we use the z statistic. For confidence coefficient .95, $\alpha = 1 - .95 = .05$ and $\alpha/2 = .05/2 = .025$. From Table IV, Appendix B, $z_{.025} = 1.96$.

d. For a large sample from a distribution about which nothing is known, we can estimate the population standard deviation with s and use the z statistic. For confidence coefficient .95, $\alpha = 1 - .95 = .05$ and $\alpha/2 = .05/2 = .025$. From Table IV, Appendix B, $z_{.025} = 1.96$.

e. For a small sample from a distribution about which nothing is known, we can use neither z nor t.

8.65 a. The average number of checks the bank processed per week for the 50 randomly sampled weeks.

b. The proportion of weeks the bank processed more than 100,000 checks in the 50 randomly sampled weeks.

c. The standard deviation of the number of checks the bank processes each week.

d. The average number of checks the bank processes per week.

e. The number of weeks that are randomly sampled (n = 50).

f. The standard deviation of the average number of checks the bank processed each week for the 50 randomly selected weeks.

g. The proportion of weeks the bank processes more than 100,000 checks.

h. The standard deviation of the number of checks the bank processed each week in the 50 randomly sampled weeks.

8.67 a. For confidence coefficient .90, $\alpha$ = .10 and $\alpha/2$ = .05. From Table IV, Appendix B, $z_{.05}$ = 1.645. The 90% confidence interval is:

$$\bar{x} \pm z_{.05} \frac{\sigma}{\sqrt{n}}$$

$$=> \bar{x} \pm 1.645 \frac{s}{\sqrt{n}}$$

$$=> 12.2 \pm 1.645 \frac{0}{100}$$

$$=> 12.2 \pm 1.6 \quad => (10.555, 13.845)$$

b. To compute the cessary sample size, use:

$$n = \frac{(z_{\alpha/2}-)^2}{B} \quad \text{where } z_{.005} = 2.575 \text{ from Table IV, Appendix B.}$$

Thus,

$$n = \frac{(75)^2(10)^2}{2^2}$$

$$= 5.8$$

You w dleed to sample 166 personnel files.

8.69 a. To c putthe needed sample size, use:

$$n = \frac{/2)^2(pq)}{B^2} \quad \text{where } z_{.05} = 1.645 \text{ from Table IV, Appendix B.}$$

Thus,

$$n = \frac{45)^2(.6)(.4)}{.03^2}$$

$$= 61 \approx 722$$

b. To compu e needed sample size, use:

$$n = \frac{)^2\sigma^2}{2}$$

Thus,

$$n = \frac{)^2(2)}{5^2}$$

$$= \approx 174$$

Therefo sample size determined in part (a) is large enough to also e $\mu$ with the desired specifications.

8.71 a. For confidence coefficient .95, $\alpha$ = .05 and $\alpha/2$ = .025. From Table IV, Appendix B, $z_{.025}$ = 1.96. The 95% confidence interval is:

$$\bar{x} \pm z_{.025} \frac{\sigma}{\sqrt{n}} \Rightarrow \bar{x} \pm 1.96 \frac{s}{\sqrt{n}}$$

$$\Rightarrow 12522 \pm 1.96 \frac{4000}{\sqrt{100}}$$

$$\Rightarrow 12522 \pm 784 \Rightarrow (11760, 13328)$$

b. The fact that both values are positive indicates that the actual income was larger than reported income. Also, we can be 95% confident the true mean error in reported income lies in the interval \$11,760 to \$13,328.

8.73 $\hat{p} = \frac{x}{n} = \frac{212}{346} = .613$

For confidence coefficient .95, $\alpha$ = .05 and $\alpha/2$ = .05/2 = .025. From Table IV, Appendix B, $z_{.025}$ = 1.96. The 95% confidence interval is:

$$\hat{p} \pm z_{.025} \sqrt{\frac{\hat{p}\hat{q}}{n}}$$

$$\Rightarrow .613 \pm 1.96\sqrt{\frac{(.613)(.387)}{346}}$$

$$\Rightarrow .613 \pm .051 \Rightarrow (.562, .664)$$

We are 95% confident the proportion of households in the city who are using available recycling facilities is between .562 and .664.

8.75 a. The point estimate for the mean wear is $\bar{x}$ = 42,250 miles.

b. For confidence coefficient .90, $\alpha$ = 1 - .90 = .10 and $\alpha/2$ = .10/2 = .05. From Table IV, Appendix B, $z_{.05}$ = 1.645. The 90% confidence interval is:

$$\bar{x} \pm z_{.05}\sigma_{\bar{x}}$$

$$\bar{x} \pm 1.645 \frac{\sigma}{\sqrt{n}}$$

$$\Rightarrow 42,250 \pm 1.645 \frac{4355}{\sqrt{200}}$$

$$\Rightarrow 42,250 \pm 506.570 \Rightarrow (41,743.430, 42,756.57)$$

c. Interval estimation is better. The choice of estimating the true mean exactly with a single number is 0. With a confidence interval, we can estimate the true mean using a range of values. We are then fairly confident the true mean will fall in this range.

The interval in this problem is smaller than the one in Exercise 8.74, because the sample size is larger. In Exercise 8.74, we had to use the t statistic, while in this problem, we used the z statistic.

8.77 To compute the needed sample size, use:

$$n = \frac{4(z_{\alpha/2})^2pq}{W^2} \quad \text{where } z_{.025} = 1.96 \text{ from Table IV, Appendix B.}$$

Thus, $n = \frac{4(1.96)^2(.094)(.906)}{.04^2} \approx 817.9 \approx 818$

8.79 a. To compute the necessary sample size, use:

$$n = \frac{(z_{\alpha/2})^2\sigma^2}{B^2} \quad \text{where } \alpha = 1 - .99 = .01 \text{ and } \alpha/2 = .01/2 = .005$$

From Table IV, Appendix B, $z_{.005} = 2.575$. Thus,

$$n = \frac{(2.575)^2 11.34^2}{1^2} = 852.7 \approx 853.$$

b. We would have to assume the sample was a random sample.

# CHAPTER 9

# INFERENCES BASED ON A SINGLE SAMPLE: TESTS OF HYPOTHESES

9.1 The null hypothesis is the "status quo" hypothesis, while the alternative hypothesis is the research hypothesis.

9.3 The "level of significance" of a test is $\alpha$. This is the probability that the test statistic will fail in the rejection region when the null hypothesis is true.

9.5 The four possible results are:

1. Rejecting the null hypothesis when it is true. This would be a Type I error.

2. Accepting the null hypothesis when it is true. This would be a correct decision.

3. Rejecting the null hypothesis when it is false. This would be a correct decision.

4. Accepting the null hypothesis when it is false. This would be a Type II error.

9.7 When you reject the null hypothesis in favor of the alternative hypothesis, this does not prove the alternative hypothesis is correct. We are $100(1 - \alpha)\%$ confident that there is sufficient evidence to conclude that the alternative hypothesis is correct.

If we were to repeatedly draw samples from the population and perform the test each time, approximately $100(1 - \alpha)\%$ of the tests performed would yield the correct decision.

9.9 a. Since the company must give proof the drug is safe, the null hypothesis would be the drug is unsafe. The alternative hypothesis would be the drug is safe.

b. A Type I error would be concluding the drug is safe when it is not safe. A Type II error would be concluding the drug is not safe when it is. $\alpha$ is the probability of concluding the drug is safe when it is not. $\beta$ is the probability of concluding the drug is not safe when it is.

c. In this problem, it would be more important for $\alpha$ to be small. We would want the probability of concluding the drug is safe when it is not to be as small as possible.

9.11 a. $H_0$: $\mu = 100$
$H_a$: $\mu > 100$

The test statistic is $z = \frac{\bar{x} - \mu_0}{\sigma_{\bar{x}}} = \frac{\bar{x} - \mu_0}{\sigma/\sqrt{n}} = \frac{110 - 100}{60/\sqrt{100}} = 1.67$

The rejection region requires $\alpha = .05$ in the upper tail of the z distribution. From Table IV, Appendix B, $z_{.05} = 1.645$. The rejection region is $z > 1.645$.

Since the observed value of the test statistic falls in the rejection region, ($z = 1.67 > 1.645$), $H_0$ is rejected. There is sufficient evidence to indicate the true population mean is greater than 100 at $\alpha = .05$.

b. $H_0$: $\mu = 100$
$H_a$: $\mu \neq 100$

The test statistic is $z = \frac{\bar{x} - \mu_0}{\sigma_{\bar{x}}} = \frac{110 - 100}{60/\sqrt{100}} = 1.67$

The rejection region requires $\alpha/2 = .05/2 = .025$ in each tail of the z distribution. From Table IV, Appendix B, $z_{.025} = 1.96$. The rejection region is $z < -1.96$ or $z > 1.96$.

Since the observed value of the test statistic does not fall in the rejection region, ($z = 1.67 \not> 1.96$), $H_0$ is not rejected. There is insufficient evidence to indicate $\mu$ does not equal 0 at $\alpha = .05$.

c. In part (a), we rejected $H_0$ and concluded the mean was greater than 100. In Part (b), we did not reject $H_0$. There was insufficient evidence to conclude the mean was different from 100. Because the alternative hypothesis in part (a) is more specific than the one in (b), it is easier to reject $H_0$.

c. First, compute the sample mean and standard deviation.

$$\bar{x} = \frac{\sum x}{n} = \frac{446}{48} = 9.2917$$

$$s^2 = \frac{\sum x^2 - \frac{(\sum x)^2}{n}}{n - 1} = \frac{4352 - \frac{446^2}{48}}{48 - 1} = 4.4238$$

$$s = \sqrt{s^2} = 2.1033$$

The test statistic is $z = \frac{\bar{x} - \mu_0}{\sigma_{\bar{x}}} = \frac{\bar{x} - \mu_0}{\sigma/\sqrt{n}} \approx \frac{\bar{x} - \mu_0}{s/\sqrt{n}} = \frac{9.2917 - 10}{2.1033/\sqrt{48}}$

$= -2.33$

The rejection region requires $\alpha = .05$ in the lower tail of the z distribution. From Table IV, Appendix B, $z_{.05} = 1.645$. The rejection region is $z < -1.645$.

Since the observed value of the test statistic falls in the rejection region ($z = -2.33 < -1.645$), $H_0$ is rejected. There is sufficient evidence to indicate the equipment can inspect less than 10 joints per second on the average at $\alpha = .05$.

9.21 We will reject $H_0$ if the p-value $< \alpha$.

a. $.06 \nless .05$, do not reject $H_0$

b. $.10 \nless .05$, do not reject $H_0$

c. $.01 < .05$, reject $H_0$

d. $.001 < .05$, reject $H_0$

e. $.251 \nless .05$, do not reject $H_0$

f. $.042 < .05$, reject $H_0$

9.25 p-value $= P(z \geq 2.26) = .5 - P(0 < z < 2.26)$

$= .5 - .4881$

$= .0119$

9.27 p-value $= P(z \leq -1.11) = .5 - P(0 < z < 1.11)$

$= .5 - .3665$

$= .1335$

9.29 First, find the value of the test statistic:

$$z = \frac{\bar{x} - \mu_0}{\sigma_{\bar{x}}} = \frac{\bar{x} - \mu_0}{\sigma/\sqrt{n}} \approx \frac{\bar{x} - \mu_0}{s/\sqrt{n}}$$

$$= \frac{9.5 - 10}{2.1/\sqrt{50}}$$

$$= -1.68$$

$$\begin{aligned} \text{p-value} &= P(z \leq -1.68 \text{ or } z \geq 1.68) \\ &= 2P(z \geq 1.68) \\ &= 2[.5 - P(0 < z < 1.68)] \\ &= 2(.5 - .4535) \\ &= 2(.0465) = .093 \end{aligned}$$

9.31 From Exercise 9.16, z = 7.02 for a two-tailed test.

$$\begin{aligned} \text{p-value} &= P(z \leq -7.02 \text{ or } z \geq 7.02) \\ &= 2P(z \geq 7.02) \\ &= 2[.5 - P(0 < z < 7.02)] \\ &= 2[.5 - \text{approx. } .5] \\ &= 2[\text{approx. } 0] \\ &\approx 0 \end{aligned}$$

9.33 a. $H_0$: $\mu = \$90,380$
$H_a$: $\mu > \$90,380$

b. First, find the value of the test statistic:

$$z = \frac{\bar{x} - \mu_0}{\sigma_{\bar{x}}} = \frac{\bar{x} - \mu_0}{\sigma/\sqrt{n}} \approx \frac{\bar{x} - \mu_0}{s/\sqrt{n}}$$

$$= \frac{93,290 - 90,380}{6,500/\sqrt{30}}$$

$$= 2.45$$

$$\begin{aligned} \text{p-value} = P(z \geq 2.45) &= .5 - P(0 < z < 2.45) \\ &= .5 - .4929 \\ &= .0071 \end{aligned}$$

There is a strong indication that the mean cost of a new home in Florida is greater than $90,380, since we would observe a test statistic this extreme or more extreme only 71 in 10,000 times if the mean is $90,380.

9.35 From Exercise 9.20, we want to test $H_0$: $\mu$ = \$30,000 against $H_a$: $\mu$ > \$30,000, z = 2.44.

$$\text{p-value} = P(z \geq 2.44)$$
$$= .5 - P(0 \leq z \leq 2.44)$$
$$= .5 - .4927 = .0073$$

9.37 We may use the t distribution in testing a hypothesis about a population mean when the relative frequency distribution of the sampled population is approximately normal and $\sigma$ is unknown.

9.39 $\alpha$ = P(Type I error) = P(Reject $H_0$ when $H_0$ is true)

a. $\alpha = P(t > 1.440)$ where df = 6

$= .10$ Table VI, Appendix B

b. $\alpha = P(t < -1.782)$ where df = 12

$= P(t > 1.782)$

$= .05$ Table VI, Appendix B

c. $\alpha = P(t < -2.060 \text{ or } t > 2.060)$ where df = 25

$= 2P(t > 2.060)$

$= 2(.025)$

$= .05$ Table VI, Appendix B

9.41 From Exercise 9.40, t = -1.63 with df = 4.

a. To test

$H_0$: $\mu = 6$
$H_a$: $\mu < 6$

p-value $= P(t \leq -1.63)$ where df = 4

$= P(t \geq 1.63)$

$.05 < \text{p-value} < .10$

b. To test

$H_0$: $\mu = 6$
$H_a$: $\mu \neq 6$

p-value $= P(t \leq -1.63 \text{ or } t \geq 1.63)$ where df = 4

$= 2P(t \geq 1.63)$

$2(.05) < \text{p-value} < 2(.10)$

$\Rightarrow .10 < \text{p-value} < .20$

9.43 For this sample,

$$\bar{x} = \frac{\sum x}{n} = \frac{11}{6} = 1.8333$$

$$s^2 = \frac{\sum x^2 - \frac{(\sum x)^2}{n}}{n - 1} = \frac{41 - \frac{11^2}{6}}{6 - 1} = 4.1667$$

$$s = \sqrt{s^2} = 2.0412$$

a. $H_0$: $\mu = 3$
$H_a$: $\mu < 3$

The test statistic is $t = \frac{\bar{x} - \mu_0}{s/\sqrt{n}} = \frac{1.8333 - 3}{2.0412/\sqrt{6}} = -1.40$

The rejection region requires $\alpha = .05$ in the lower tail of the t distribution with df = n - 1 = 6 - 1 = 5. From Table VI, Appendix B, $t_{.05} = 2.015$. The rejection region is $t < -2.015$.

Since the observed value of the test statistic does not fall in the rejection region ($t = -1.40 \not< -2.015$), $H_0$ is not rejected. There is insufficient evidence to indicate $\mu$ is less than 3.

b. $H_0$: $\mu = 3$
$H_a$: $\mu \neq 3$

Test statistic: $t = -1.40$ (Refer to part (a).)

The rejection region requires $\alpha/2 = .05/2 = .025$ in each tail of the t distribution with df = n - 1 = 6 - 1 = 5. From Table VI, Appendix B, $t_{.025} = 2.571$. The rejection region is $t < -2.571$ or $t > 2.571$.

Since the observed value of the test statistic does not fall in the rejection region ($t = -1.40 \not< -2.571$), $H_0$ is not rejected. There is insufficient evidence to indicate $\mu$ differs from 3.

9.45 To determine if the sample information disagrees with the manufacturer's claim, we test:

$H_0$: $\mu = 4$
$H_a$: $\mu > 4$

The test statistic is $t = \frac{\bar{x} - \mu_0}{s/\sqrt{n}} = \frac{4.16 - 4}{.3/\sqrt{25}} = 2.67$

The rejection region requires $\alpha = .05$ in the upper tail of the t distribution with df = n - 1 = 25 - 1 = 24. From Table VI, Appendix B, $t_{.05} = 1.711$. The rejection region is $t > 1.711$.

Since the observed value of the test statistic falls in the rejection region ($t = 2.67 > 1.711$), $H_0$ is rejected. There is sufficient evidence to indicate the average milligrams of tar in the cigarette is more than 4. That is, the sample information disagrees with the manufacturer's claim at $\alpha = .05$.

Assumption: The sample is a random sample selected from a normally distributed population.

9.47 a. First, compute the sample mean and standard deviation:

$$\bar{x} = \frac{\sum x}{n} = \frac{37663}{12} = 3138.5833$$

$$s^2 = \frac{\sum x^2 - \frac{(\sum x)^2}{n}}{n - 1} = \frac{119161829 - \frac{37663^2}{12}}{12 - 1} = 86669.53818$$

$$s = \sqrt{s^2} = 294.3969$$

To determine if the sample data provides evidence that the average interest deduction in 1986 is greater than in 1980 for taxpayers in the \$25,000-\$30,000 bracket, we test:

$H_0$: $\mu = \$3,011$
$H_a$: $\mu > \$3,011$

The test statistic is $t = \dfrac{\bar{x} - \mu_0}{s/\sqrt{n}} = \dfrac{3138.5833 - 3011}{294.3969/\sqrt{12}} = 1.50$

The rejection region requires $\alpha = .05$ in the upper tail of the t distribution with df $= n - 1 = 12 - 1 = 11$. From Table VI, Appendix B, $t_{.05} = 1.796$. The rejection region is $t > 1.796$.

Since the observed value of the test statistic does not fall in the rejection region ($t = 1.50 \not> 1.796$), $H_0$ is not rejected. There is insufficient evidence to indicate the average interest deduction in 1986 is greater than in 1980 for taxpayers in the \$25,000-\$30,000 bracket at $\alpha = .05$.

Assumption: The sample is a random sample selected from a population with a relative frequency distribution that is approximately normal.

b. p-value $= P(t \geq 1.50)$ where df $= 11$

$.05 < \text{p-value} < .10$ (Table VI, Appendix B)

The results are not highly significant, but at $\alpha = .10$, we would reject $H_0$.

9.49 a. First, compute the sample mean and standard deviation for plant 1's arsenic level:

$$\bar{x} = \frac{\sum x}{n} = \frac{.015}{2} = .0075$$

$$s^2 = \frac{\sum x^2 - \frac{(\sum x)^2}{n}}{n - 1} = \frac{.000125 - \frac{.015^2}{2}}{2 - 1} = .0000125$$

$$s = \sqrt{s^2} = .003536$$

To determine if plant 1 fails to meet OSHA standards, we test:

$H_0\colon \mu = .004$
$H_a\colon \mu > .004$

The test statistic is $t = \frac{\bar{x} - \mu_0}{s/\sqrt{n}} = \frac{.0075 - .004}{.003536/\sqrt{2}} = 1.40$

The rejection region requires $\alpha = .05$ in the upper tail of the t distribution with df $= n - 1 = 2 - 1 = 1$. From Table VI, Appendix B, $t_{.05} = 6.314$. The rejection region is $t > 6.314$.

Since the observed value of the test statistic does not fall in the rejection region ($t = 1.40 \not> 6.314$), $H_0$ is not rejected. There is insufficient evidence to indicate the mean level of exposure to arsenic per cubic meter of air is more than .004 milligrams. Thus, there is insufficient evidence that plant 1 fails to meet the OSHA standard at $\alpha = .05$.

Assumption: The sample is a random sample selected from a population with a relative frequency distribution that is approximately normal.

b. First, compute the sample mean and standard deviation for plant 2's arsenic level:

$$\bar{x} = \frac{\sum x}{n} = \frac{.14}{2} = .07$$

$$s^2 = \frac{\sum x^2 - \frac{(\sum x)^2}{n}}{n - 1} = \frac{.0106 - \frac{.14^2}{2}}{2 - 1} = .0008$$

$$s = \sqrt{s^2} = .0283$$

To determine if plant 2 fails to meet OSHA standards, we test:

$H_0\colon \mu = .004$
$H_a\colon \mu > .004$

The test statistic is $t = \frac{\bar{x} - \mu_0}{s/\sqrt{n}} = \frac{.07 - .004}{.0283/\sqrt{2}} = 3.3$

The rejection region is $t > 6.314$. (Refer to part (a).)

Since the observed value of the test statistic does not fall in the rejection region ($t = 3.3 \not> 6.314$), $H_0$ is not rejected. There is insufficient evidence to indicate the mean level of exposure to arsenic per cubic meter of air is more than .004 milligrams. Thus, there is insufficient evidence that plant 2 fails to meet the OSHA standard at $\alpha = .05$.

Assumption: The sample is a random sample selected from a population with a relative frequency distribution that is approximately normal.

c. Part (a) (plant 1)

p-value = $P(t \geq 1.40)$ where df = 1

p-value > .10 (Table VI, Appendix B)

The results are not statistically significant.

Part (b) (plant 2)

p-value = $P(t \geq 3.30)$ where df = 1

$.05 <$ p-value $< .10$ (Table VI, Appendix B)

The results are not highly significant, but at $\alpha = .10$ we would reject $H_0$.

9.51 b. First, check to see if n is large enough.

$$p_0 \pm 3\sigma_{\hat{p}} \Rightarrow p_0 \pm 3\sqrt{\frac{pq}{n}} \Rightarrow p_0 \pm 3\sqrt{\frac{p_0 q_0}{100}}$$

$$\Rightarrow .70 \pm 3\sqrt{\frac{.70(.30)}{100}}$$

$$\Rightarrow .70 \pm .137 \Rightarrow (.563, .837)$$

Since the interval lies within the interval (0, 1), the normal approximation will be adequate.

$H_0$: $p = .70$
$H_a$: $p < .70$

The test statistic is $z = \frac{\hat{p} - p_0}{\sigma_{\hat{p}}} = \frac{\hat{p} - p_0}{\sqrt{\frac{pq}{n}}} \approx \frac{\hat{p} - p_0}{\sqrt{\frac{p_0 q_0}{n}}}$

$$= \frac{.63 - .70}{\sqrt{\frac{.70(.30)}{100}}}$$

$$= -1.53$$

The rejection region requires $\alpha = .05$ in the lower tail of the z distribution. From Table IV, Appendix B, $z_{.05} = 1.645$. The rejection region is $z < -1.645$.

Since the observed value of the test statistic does not fall in the rejection region, ($z = -1.53 \not< -1.645$), $H_0$ is not rejected. There is insufficient evidence to indicate p is less than .70.

c. p-value $= P(z \leq -1.53) = .5 - P(0 < z < 1.53)$

$$= .5 - .4370$$

$$= .0630$$

9.53 Since p is the proportion of consumers who do not like the snack food, $\hat{p}$ will be:

$$\hat{p} = \frac{\text{number of 0's in sample}}{n} = \frac{29}{50} = .58$$

First, check to see if the normal approximation will be adequate:

$$p_0 \pm 3\sigma_{\hat{p}} \Rightarrow p_0 \pm 3\sqrt{\frac{pq}{n}} \Rightarrow p_0 \pm 3\sqrt{\frac{p_0 q_0}{n}}$$

$$\Rightarrow .5 \pm 3\sqrt{\frac{.5(1 - .5)}{50}}$$

$$\Rightarrow .5 \pm .2121 \Rightarrow (.2879, .7121)$$

Since the interval lies completely in the interval (0, 1), the normal approximation will be adequate.

a. $H_0$: $p = .5$
$H_a$: $p > .5$

The test statistic is $z = \frac{\hat{p} - p_0}{\sigma_{\hat{p}}} = \frac{\hat{p} - p_0}{\sqrt{\frac{pq}{n}}} \approx \frac{\hat{p} - p_0}{\sqrt{\frac{p_0 q_0}{n}}}$

$$= \frac{.58 - .5}{\sqrt{\frac{.5(1 - .5)}{50}}} = 1.13$$

The rejection region requires $\alpha = .10$ in the upper tail of the z distribution. From Table IV, Appendix B, $z_{.10} = 1.28$. The rejection region is $z > 1.28$.

Since the observed value of the test statistic does not fall in the rejection region ($z = 1.13 \not> 1.28$), $H_0$ is not rejected. There is insufficient evidence to indicate the proportion of customers who do not like the snack food is greater than .5 at $\alpha = .10$.

b. $$\text{p-value} = P(z \geq 1.13) = .5 - P(0 < z < 1.13) = .5 - .3708 = .1292$$

9.55 a. Yes, it does appear that more than 50% of the public has an unfavorable opinion since more than 50% of the sampled people felt this way.

b. Check to see if the normal approximation is appropriate.

$$p_0 \pm 3\sigma_{\hat{p}} \Rightarrow p_0 \pm 3\sqrt{\frac{pq}{n}} \Rightarrow p_0 \pm 3\sqrt{\frac{p_0 q_0}{n}}$$

$$\Rightarrow .5 \pm 3\sqrt{\frac{.5(.5)}{6788}}$$

$$\Rightarrow .5 \pm .0182 \Rightarrow (.4818, .5182)$$

This interval lies within the interval (0, 1), so the normal approximation is adequate.

To determine if more than 50% of the general public hold unfavorable opinions, we test:

$H_0$: $p = .5$
$H_a$: $p > .5$

The test statistic is $z = \dfrac{\hat{p} - p_0}{\sigma_{\hat{p}}} = \dfrac{\hat{p} - p_0}{\sqrt{\frac{pq}{n}}} \approx \dfrac{\hat{p} - p_0}{\sqrt{\frac{p_0 q_0}{n}}}$

$$= \frac{.51046 - .50}{\sqrt{\frac{.5(.5)}{6788}}} = 1.72 \quad \text{where } \hat{p} = \frac{3,465}{6,788} = .51046$$

The rejection region requires $\alpha = .05$ in the upper tail of the z distribution. From Table IV, Appendix B, $z_{.05} = 1.645$. The rejection region is $z > 1.645$.

Since the observed value of the test statistic falls in the rejection region ($z = 1.72 > 1.645$), $H_0$ is rejected. There is sufficient evidence to indicate the proportion of the general public that hold unfavorable opinions is greater than .5 at $\alpha = .05$.

c. Check to see if the normal approximation will be adequate:

$$\hat{p} \pm 3\sigma_{\hat{p}} \Rightarrow \hat{p} \pm 3\sqrt{\frac{pq}{n}} \Rightarrow \hat{p} \pm 3\sqrt{\frac{p_0q_0}{n}} \text{ where } \hat{p} = \frac{821}{6,788} = .1209$$

$$\Rightarrow .1209 \pm 3\sqrt{\frac{.1209(.8791)}{6,788}}$$

$$\Rightarrow .1209 \pm .0119 \Rightarrow (.109, .1328)$$

Since the interval lies within in the interval (0, 1), the normal approximation will be adequate.

For confidence coefficient .90, $\alpha = .10$ and $\alpha/2 = .05$. From Table IV, Appendix B, $z_{.05} = 1.645$. The 90% confidence interval is:

$$\hat{p} \pm z_{.05}\sqrt{\frac{pq}{n}}$$

$$\Rightarrow \hat{p} \pm 1.645\sqrt{\frac{\hat{p}\hat{q}}{n}}$$

$$\Rightarrow .1209 \pm 1.645\sqrt{\frac{.1209(.8791)}{6788}}$$

$$\Rightarrow .1209 \pm .0065 \Rightarrow (.1144, .1274)$$

d. The experiment must be binomial. Therefore, the people surveyed were independently chosen from the general public.

9.57 a. To determine if brand A is perceived by consumers as being superior to brand B in softness, we test:

$H_0$: $p = .5$
$H_a$: $p > .5$ where $p$ = proportion of consumers who rank brand A as softer

First, check to see if the normal approximation is adequate:

$$p_0 \pm 3\sigma_{\hat{p}} \Rightarrow p_0 \pm 3\sqrt{\frac{pq}{n}} \Rightarrow p_0 \pm 3\sqrt{\frac{p_0q_0}{n}}$$

$$\Rightarrow .5 \pm 3\sqrt{\frac{.5(.5)}{205}}$$

$$\Rightarrow .5 \pm .1048 \Rightarrow (.3952, .6048)$$

Since the interval does not include 0 or 1, the normal approximation will be adequate.

The test statistic is $z = \dfrac{\hat{p} - p_0}{\sigma_{\hat{p}}} = \dfrac{\hat{p} - p_0}{\sqrt{\dfrac{pq}{n}}} \approx \dfrac{\hat{p} - p_0}{\sqrt{\dfrac{p_0 q_0}{n}}}$

$$= \frac{.58049 - .5}{\sqrt{\dfrac{.5(.5)}{205}}} = 2.30, \text{ where } \hat{p} = \frac{119}{205} = .58049$$

The rejection region requires $\alpha = .05$ in the upper tail of the z distribution. From Table IV, Appendix B, $z_{.05} = 1.645$. The rejection region is $z > 1.645$.

Since the observed value of the test statistic falls in the rejection region ($z = 2.30 > 1.645$), $H_0$ is rejected. There is sufficient evidence to indicate the proportion of consumers that think brand A is softer is larger than .5. That is, there is sufficient evidence that consumers perceive brand A to be softer at $\alpha = .05$.

b. $$\text{p-value} = P(z \geq 2.30) = .5 - P(0 < z < 2.30)$$
$$= .5 - .4893$$
$$= .0107$$

The smallest value $\alpha$ could assume where the conclusion is to reject $H_0$ is .0107. The results are highly significant.

9.59 a. First, check to see if the normal approximation is adequate:

$$p_0 \pm 3\sigma_{p_0} \Rightarrow p_0 \pm 3\sqrt{\frac{p_0 q_0}{n}} \Rightarrow .90 \pm 3\sqrt{\frac{(.90)(.10)}{350}}$$
$$\Rightarrow .90 \pm .048 \Rightarrow (.852, .958)$$

Since the interval falls completely in the interval (0, 1), the normal distribution will be adequate.

To determine if the results support the claim of the union, we test:

$H_0$: $p = .90$
$H_a$: $p > .90$

The test statistic is $z = \dfrac{\hat{p} - p_0}{\sigma_{\hat{p}}} = \dfrac{\hat{p} - p_0}{\sqrt{\dfrac{pq}{n}}} \approx \dfrac{\hat{p} - p_0}{\sqrt{\dfrac{p_0 q_0}{n}}}$

$$= \frac{.92 - .90}{\sqrt{\dfrac{.90(.10)}{350}}} = 1.25, \text{ where } \hat{p} = \frac{350 - 28}{350} = \frac{322}{350} = .92$$

The rejection region requires $\alpha = .10$ in the upper tail of the z distribution. From Table IV, Appendix B, $z_{.10} = 1.28$. The rejection region is $z > 1.28$.

Since the observed value of the test statistic does not fall in the rejection region ($z = 1.25 \not> 1.28$), $H_0$ is not rejected. There is insufficient evidence to indicate at least 90% of firms in the manufacturing sector still do not offer any childcare benefits to their workers at $\alpha = .10$.

b. $\text{p-value} = P(z \geq 1.25) = .5 - P(0 \leq z \leq 1.25)$

$$= .5 - .3944 = .1056$$

9.61 The power of a test increases when:

1. The distance between the null and alternative values of $\mu$ increases.

2. The value of $\alpha$ increases.

3. The sample size increases.

9.63 From Exercise 9.62 we want to test $H_0: \mu = 1{,}000$ against $H_a: \mu > 1{,}000$ using $\alpha = .05$, $\sigma = 120$, $n = 36$, and $\bar{x}_0 = 1032.9$.

a. $\beta = P(\bar{x}_0 < 1032.9 \text{ when } \mu = 1040)$.

$$z = \frac{\bar{x}_0 - \mu_a}{\sigma_{\bar{x}}} = \frac{\bar{x}_0 - \mu_a}{\sigma/\sqrt{n}}$$

$$= \frac{1032.9 - 1040}{120/\sqrt{36}}$$

$$= -.36$$

$$\beta = P(z < -.36) = .5 - P(-.36 < z < 0)$$

$$= .5 - .1406$$

$$= .3594$$

b. $\text{power} = 1 - \beta$

$$= 1 - .3594$$

$$= .6406$$

c. In Exercise 9.62, $\beta = .74055$ and the power is .25945. The value of $\beta$ has decreased in this exercise since $\mu = 1040$ is further from the hypothesized value than $\mu = 1020$. As a result, the power of the test in this exercise has increased (when $\beta$ decreases, the power of the test increases).

.65 From Exercise 9.64, we want to test $H_0$: $\mu = 50$ against $H_a$: $\mu < 50$ using $\alpha = .10$, $\sigma = 20$, $n = 64$, and $\bar{x}_0 = 46.8$.

Now, find

$$\beta = P(\bar{x}_0 > 46.8 \text{ when } \mu = 48)$$

$$z = \frac{\bar{x}_0 - \mu_a}{\sigma_{\bar{x}}} = \frac{\bar{x}_0 - \mu_a}{\sigma/\sqrt{n}} = \frac{46.8 - 48}{20/\sqrt{64}} = -.48$$

$$\beta = P(z > -.48) = .5 + P(-.48 < z < 0) = .5 + .1844 = .6844$$

$$\text{power} = 1 - \beta = 1 - .6844 = .3156$$

In Exercise 9.64, when $\mu = 45$, the power was .7642. The power of the test decreased with $\mu = 48$ since the distance between the null and alternative values decreased. ($\mu = 48$ is closer to $\mu_0 = 50$ than $\mu = 45$).

.67 a. From Exercise 9.64, we want to test $H_0$: $\mu = 50$ against $H_a$: $\mu < 50$ using $\alpha = .10$, $\sigma = 20$, $n = 64$, and $\bar{x}_0 = 46.8$.

<u>If $\mu = 49$</u>,

$$\beta = P(\bar{x}_0 > 46.8 \text{ when } \mu = 49)$$

$$z = \frac{\bar{x}_0 - \mu_a}{\sigma_{\bar{x}}} = \frac{\bar{x}_0 - \mu_a}{\sigma/\sqrt{n}} = \frac{46.8 - 49}{20/\sqrt{64}} = -.88$$

$$\beta = P(z > -.88) = .5 + P(-.88 < z < 0) = .5 + .3106 = .8106$$

<u>If $\mu = 47$</u>,

$$\beta = P(\bar{x}_0 > 46.8 \text{ when } \mu = 47)$$

$$z = \frac{\bar{x}_0 - \mu_a}{\sigma_{\bar{x}}} = \frac{\bar{x}_0 - \mu_a}{\sigma/\sqrt{n}}$$

$$= \frac{46.8 - 47}{20/\sqrt{64}}$$

$$= -.08$$

$$\beta = P(z > -.08) = .5 + P(-.08 < z < 0)$$

$$= .5 + .0319$$

$$= .5319$$

<u>If $\mu = 45$</u>,

$$\beta = P(\bar{x}_0 > 46.8 \text{ when } \mu = 45)$$

$$= .2358$$

(Refer to Exercise 9.64, part (c)).

<u>If $\mu = 43$</u>,

$$\beta = P(\bar{x}_0 > 46.8 \text{ when } \mu = 43)$$

$$z = \frac{\bar{x}_0 - \mu_a}{\sigma_{\bar{x}}} = \frac{\bar{x}_0 - \mu_a}{\sigma/\sqrt{n}}$$

$$= \frac{46.8 - 43}{20/\sqrt{64}}$$

$$= 1.52$$

$$\beta = P(z > 1.52) = .5 - P(0 < z < 1.52)$$

$$= .5 - .4357$$

$$= .0643$$

<u>If $\mu = 41$</u>,

$$\beta = P(\bar{x}_0 > 46.8 \text{ when } \mu = 41)$$

$$z = \frac{\bar{x}_0 - \mu_a}{\sigma_{\bar{x}}} = \frac{\bar{x}_0 - \mu_a}{\sigma/\sqrt{n}}$$

$$= \frac{46.8 - 41}{20/\sqrt{64}}$$

$$= 2.32$$

$$\beta = P(z > 2.32) = .5 - P(0 < z < 2.32)$$
$$= .5 - .4898$$
$$= .0102$$

In summary,

| $\mu$ | 49 | 47 | 45 | 43 | 41 |
|---|---|---|---|---|---|
| $\beta$ | .8106 | .5319 | .2358 | .0643 | .0102 |

b.

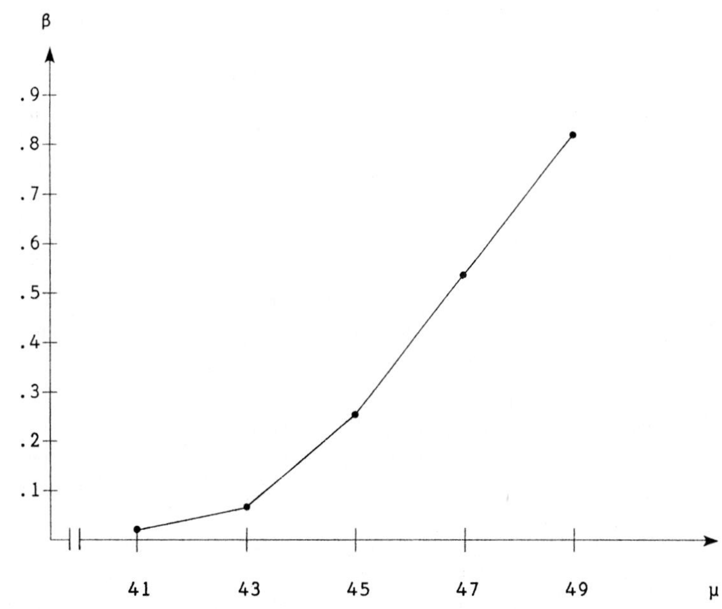


c. Looking at the graph, $\beta$ is approximately .7 when $\mu = 48$.

In Exercise 9.65, we found $\beta = .6844$ when $\mu = 48$.

d. power = $1 - \beta$

Therefore,

| $\mu$ | 49 | 47 | 45 | 43 | 41 |
|---|---|---|---|---|---|
| $\beta$ | .8106 | .5319 | .2358 | .0643 | .0102 |
| power | .1894 | .4681 | .7642 | .9357 | .9898 |

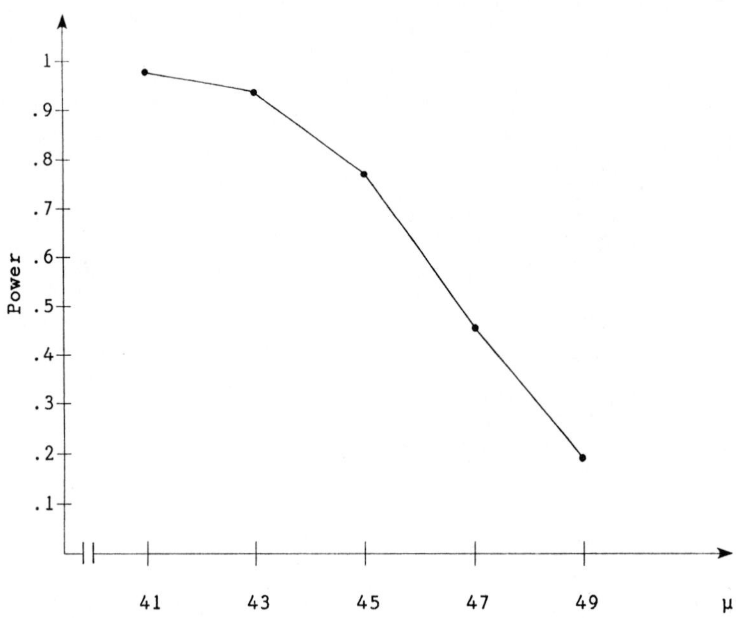


The power curve starts out close to 1 when $\mu = 41$ and decreases as $\mu$ increases, while the $\beta$ curve is close to 0 when $\mu = 41$ and increases as $\mu$ increases.

e. As the distance between the true mean $\mu$ and the null hypothesized mean $\mu_0$ increases, $\beta$ decreases and the power increases. We can also see that as $\beta$ increases, the power decreases.

9.69 Referring to Exercise 9.19, we want to test $H_0: \mu = 10$ against $H_a: \mu < 10$.

First, find

$$\bar{x}_0 = \mu_0 - z_\alpha \sigma_{\bar{x}} = \mu_0 - z_\alpha \frac{\sigma}{\sqrt{n}}$$ where $z_{.05} = 1.645$ from Table IV, Appendix B.

Thus, $\bar{x}_0 = 10 - 1.645 \dfrac{1.2}{\sqrt{48}}$

$= 9.7151$

Now, find

$$\beta = P(\bar{x}_0 > 9.7151 \text{ when } \mu = 9.5)$$

$$z = \frac{\bar{x}_0 - \mu_a}{\sigma_{\bar{x}}} = \frac{\bar{x}_0 - \mu_a}{\sigma/\sqrt{n}}$$

$$= \frac{9.7151 - 9.5}{1.2/\sqrt{48}}$$

$$= 1.24$$

$$\beta = P(z > 1.24) = .5 - P(0 < z < 1.24)$$

$$= .5 - .3925$$

$$= .1075$$

9.71 First, find:

$\bar{x}_0 = \mu_0 + z_\alpha \sigma_{\bar{x}} \approx \mu_0 + z_\alpha \frac{\sigma}{\sqrt{n}}$ where $z_{.05} = 1.645$ from Table IV, Appendix B.

$$\text{Thus, } \bar{x}_0 = 35 + 1.645 \frac{6}{\sqrt{100}}$$

$$= 35.987$$

Now, find $\beta$ for each value of $\mu_a$.

$\underline{\mu = 35.5}$

$$\beta = P(\bar{x}_0 < 35.987 \text{ when } \mu = 35.5)$$

$$z = \frac{\bar{x}_0 - \mu_a}{\sigma_{\bar{x}}} = \frac{\bar{x}_0 - \mu_a}{\sigma/\sqrt{n}} = \frac{35.987 - 35.5}{6/\sqrt{100}} = .81$$

$$\beta = P(z < .81) = .5 + P(0 < z < .81)$$

$$= .5 + .291$$

$$= .791$$

$$\text{power} = 1 - \beta = 1 - .791 = .209$$

$\underline{\mu = 36.0}$

$$\beta = P(\bar{x}_0 < 35.987 \text{ when } \mu = 36.0)$$

$$z = \frac{\bar{x}_0 - \mu_a}{\sigma_{\bar{x}}} = \frac{\bar{x}_0 - \mu_a}{\sigma/\sqrt{n}} = \frac{35.987 - 36}{6/\sqrt{100}} = -.02$$

$$\beta = P(z < -.02) = .5 - P(0 < z < .02)$$
$$= .5 - .008$$
$$= .492$$

$$\text{power} = 1 - \beta = 1 - .492 = .508$$

$\underline{\mu = 36.5}$

$$\beta = P(\bar{x}_0 < 35.987 \text{ when } \mu = 36.5)$$

$$z = \frac{\bar{x}_0 - \mu_a}{\sigma_{\bar{x}}} = \frac{\bar{x}_0 - \mu_a}{\sigma/\sqrt{n}} = \frac{35.987 - 36.5}{6/\sqrt{100}} = -.855$$

$$\beta = P(z < -.855) = .5 - P(0 < z < .855)$$
$$= .5 - \frac{.3023 + .3051}{2}$$
$$= .1963$$

$$\text{power} = 1 - \beta = 1 - .1963 = .8037$$

$\underline{\mu = 37.0}$

$$\beta = P(\bar{x}_0 < 35.987 \text{ when } \mu = 37.0)$$

$$z = \frac{\bar{x}_0 - \mu_a}{\sigma_{\bar{x}}} = \frac{\bar{x}_0 - \mu_a}{\sigma/\sqrt{n}} = \frac{35.987 - 37}{6/\sqrt{100}} = -1.69$$

$$\beta = P(z < -1.69) = .5 - P(0 < z < 1.69)$$
$$= .5 - .4545$$
$$= .0455$$

$$\text{power} = 1 - \beta = 1 - .0455 = .9545$$

$\underline{\mu = 37.5}$

$$\beta = P(\bar{x}_0 < 35.987 \text{ when } \mu = 37.5)$$

$$z = \frac{\bar{x}_0 - \mu_a}{\sigma_{\bar{x}}} = \frac{\bar{x}_0 - \mu_a}{\sigma/\sqrt{n}} = \frac{35.987 - 37.5}{6/\sqrt{100}} = -2.52$$

$$\beta = P(z < -2.52) = .5 - P(0 < z < 2.52)$$
$$= .5 - .4941$$
$$= .0059$$

$$\text{power} = 1 - \beta = 1 - .0059 = .9941$$

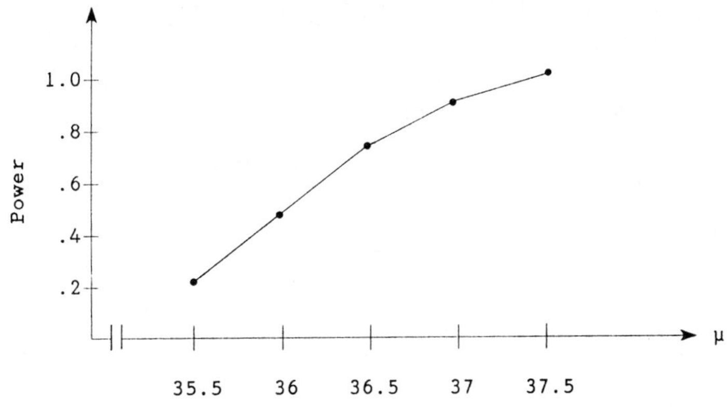


When n = 100 instead of n = 36, the power curve shifts upward; the power becomes larger in each case.

9.73 The smaller the p-value associated with a test of hypothesis, the stronger the support for the alternative hypothesis. The p-value is the probability of observing your test statistic or anything more unusual, given the null hypothesis is true. If this value is small, it would be very unusual to observe this test statistic if the null hypothesis were true. Thus, it would indicate the alternative hypothesis is true.

9.75 a. The hypotheses would be:

$H_0$: Individual does not have the disease
$H_a$: Individual does have the disease

b. A Type I error would be: Conclude the individual has the disease when in fact he/she does not. This would be a false positive test.

A Type II error would be: Conclude the individual does not have the disease when in fact he/she does. This would be a false negative test.

c. If the disease is serious, either error would be grave. Arguments could be made for either error being more grave. However, I believe a Type II error would be more grave: Concluding the individual does not have the disease when he/she does. This person would not receive critical treatment, and may suffer very serious consequences. Thus, it is more important to minimize $\beta$.

9.77 The larger the p-value associated with a test of hypothesis, the stronger the support for the null hypothesis. The p-value is the probability of observing your test statistic or anything more unusual, given the null hypothesis is true. If this value is large, it would not be very unusual to observe this test statistic if the null hypothesis were true. Thus, it would lend support that the null hypothesis is true.

9.79 a. A Type II error results if we decide not to halt production when we should have since the mean amount of PCB exceeds 3 parts per million.

b. First, find

$$\bar{x}_0 = \mu_0 + z_\alpha \sigma_{\bar{x}} \approx \mu_0 + z_{.01} \frac{s}{\sqrt{n}}$$ where $z_{.01} = 2.33$ from Table IV, Appendix B.

$$\bar{x}_0 = 3 + 2.33 \frac{.5}{\sqrt{50}}$$

$$= 3.1648$$

Then, compute

$$\beta = P(\bar{x}_0 < 3.1648 \text{ when } \mu = 3.1)$$

$$z = \frac{\bar{x}_0 - \mu_a}{\sigma_{\bar{x}}} \approx \frac{\bar{x}_0 - \mu_a}{s/\sqrt{n}}$$

$$= \frac{3.1648 - 3.1}{.5/\sqrt{50}}$$

$$= .92$$

$$\beta = P(z < .92) = .5 + P(0 < z < .92)$$

$$= .5 + .3212$$

$$= .8212$$

c. power $= 1 - \beta = 1 - .8212 = .1788$

d. From part (b), $\bar{x}_0 = 3.165$

Then, compute

$$\beta = P(\bar{x}_0 < 3.165 \text{ when } \mu = 3.2)$$

$$z = \frac{\bar{x}_0 - \mu_a}{\sigma_{\bar{x}}} \approx \frac{\bar{x}_0 - \mu_a}{s/\sqrt{n}}$$

$$= \frac{3.165 - 3.2}{.5/\sqrt{50}}$$

$$= -.49$$

$$\beta = P(z < -.49) = .5 - .1879$$

$$= .3121$$

power $= 1 - \beta = 1 - .3121 = .6879$

The power becomes larger as the plant's mean PCB departs further from the standard.

9.81 To determine if the proportion of defective can openers in the shipment exceeds .02, we test:

$H_0$: $p = .02$
$H_a$: $p > .02$

First, check to see if the normal approximation will be adequate:

$$p_0 \pm 3\sigma_{\hat{p}} \Rightarrow p_0 \pm 3\sqrt{\frac{pq}{n}} \Rightarrow p_0 \pm 3\sqrt{\frac{p_0 q_0}{n}}$$

$$\Rightarrow .02 \pm 3\sqrt{\frac{.02(.98)}{400}}$$

$$\Rightarrow .02 \pm .021 \Rightarrow (-.001, .041)$$

Since the interval does not lie completely in the interval (0, 1), the normal approximation will not be adequate.

We will use the approximation to get an idea of the answer.

The test statistic is $z = \frac{\hat{p} - p_0}{\sigma_{\hat{p}}} = \frac{\hat{p} - p_0}{\sqrt{\frac{pq}{n}}} \approx \frac{\hat{p} - p_0}{\sqrt{\frac{p_0 q_0}{n}}}$

$$= \frac{.0275 - .02}{\sqrt{\frac{.02(.98)}{400}}} = 1.07, \text{ where } \hat{p} = \frac{11}{400} = .0275$$

$$\begin{aligned} \text{p-value} = P(z \geq 1.07) &= .5 - P(0 < z < 1.07) \\ &= .5 - .3577 \\ &= .1423 \end{aligned}$$

Reject $H_0$ if p-value $< \alpha$
$.1423 \not< .05$

Fail to reject $H_0$. There is insufficient evidence to indicate the proportion of defective can openers exceeds .02 at $\alpha = .05$.

9.83 To compute the necessary sample size, use:

$$n = \frac{4(z_{\alpha/2})^2(pq)}{W^2} \text{ where } z_{.025} = 1.96 \text{ from Table IV, Appendix B.}$$

If we use $p = .02$ (refer to Exercise 9.81):

$$n = \frac{4(1.96)^2(.02)(.98)}{.08^2}$$

$$= 47.06 \approx 48$$

If we have no knowledge about p, use $p = .5$.

Thus,

$$n = \frac{4(1.96)^2(.5)(.5)}{.08^2}$$

$$= 600.25 \approx 601$$

9.85 From Exercise 9.84, the test statistic is $t = -1.28$. From Table VI, Appendix B, with $df = n - 1 = 20 - 1 = 19$, $P(t \leq -1.28) > .10$. Thus, the p-value $> .10$.

9.87 From Exercise 9.86, $z = -3.03$ for a one-tailed, lower tail test.

$$\text{p-value} = P(z \leq -3.03) = .5 - P(0 < z < 3.03)$$
$$= .5 - .4988$$
$$= .0012$$

$\alpha$ could be as small as .0012 and we would still reject $H_0$. The results of this experiment are highly significant.

9.89 To determine if the discount chain's tires are more resistant to wear, we test:

$H_0: p = .5$
$H_a: p > .5$ where p = proportion of cars in which the discount tire shows less wear.

First, check to see if the normal approximation will be adequate:

$$p_0 \pm 3\sigma_{\hat{p}} \Rightarrow p_0 \pm 3\sqrt{\frac{pq}{n}} \Rightarrow p_0 \pm 3\sqrt{\frac{p_0q_0}{n}}$$

$$\Rightarrow .5 \pm 3\sqrt{\frac{.5(.5)}{40}}$$

$$\Rightarrow .5 \pm .237 \Rightarrow (.263, .737)$$

Since the interval lies completely in the interval (0, 1), the normal approximation will be adequate.

$H_0: p = .5$
$H_a: p > .5$

The test statistic is $z = \frac{\hat{p} - p_0}{\sigma_{\hat{p}}} = \frac{\hat{p} - p_0}{\sqrt{\frac{pq}{n}}} \approx \frac{\hat{p} - p_0}{\sqrt{\frac{p_0q_0}{n}}}$

$$= \frac{.8 - .5}{\sqrt{\frac{.5(.5)}{40}}} = 3.79, \text{ where } \hat{p} = \frac{32}{40} = .8$$

$$\text{p-value} = P(z \geq 3.79) = .5 - P(0 < z < 3.79)$$
$$\approx .5 - .5$$
$$= 0$$

Reject $H_0$ if p-value $< \alpha$.

Reject $H_0$ no matter what $\alpha$ is used. There is sufficient evidence to conclude the discount chain's claim is correct ($p > .5$).

9.91 a. The value of the test statistic is $t = 2.408$. The p-value is .0304, which corresponds to a two-tailed test. $P(t \geq 2.408) + P(t \leq -2.408) = .0304$. Since the p-value is less than $\alpha = .10$, $H_0$ is rejected. There is sufficient evidence to indicate the mean beta coefficient of high technology stock is different than 1.

b. The p-value would be $.0304/2 = .0152$.

9.93 Using Table IV, Appendix B, the p-value is $P(z > 1.41) = .5 - .4207 = .0793$. The probability of observing a test statistic of 1.41 or anything more unusual is .0793. This is not particularly small. There is no evidence to reject $H_0$.

# CHAPTER 10

## TWO SAMPLES: ESTIMATION AND TESTS OF HYPOTHESES

10.1 a. From Chapter 7, $\sigma_{\bar{x}_1} = \dfrac{\sigma_1}{\sqrt{n_1}} = \dfrac{\sqrt{900}}{\sqrt{100}} = \dfrac{30}{10} = 3$

$\mu_1 \pm 2\sigma_{\bar{x}_1} \Rightarrow 150 \pm 2(3) \Rightarrow 150 \pm 6 \Rightarrow (144, 156)$

b. $\sigma_{\bar{x}_2} = \dfrac{\sigma_2}{\sqrt{n_2}} = \dfrac{\sqrt{1600}}{\sqrt{100}} = \dfrac{40}{10} = 4$

$\mu_2 \pm 2\sigma_{\bar{x}_2} \Rightarrow 150 \pm 2(4) \Rightarrow 150 \pm 8 \Rightarrow (142, 158)$

c. $\mu_{\bar{x}_1-\bar{x}_2} = \mu_1 - \mu_2 = 150 - 150 = 0$

$\sigma_{\bar{x}_1-\bar{x}_2} = \sqrt{\dfrac{\sigma_1^2}{n_1} + \dfrac{\sigma_2^2}{n_2}} = \sqrt{\dfrac{900}{100} + \dfrac{1600}{100}} = \sqrt{25} = 5$

d. $\mu_{\bar{x}_1-\bar{x}_2} \pm 2\sigma_{\bar{x}_1-\bar{x}_2} \Rightarrow 0 \pm 2(5) \Rightarrow 0 \pm 10 \Rightarrow (-10, 10)$

e. In general, the variability of the difference between independent sample means is larger than the variability of individual sample means.

10.3 From Exercise 10.2, $\sigma_{\bar{x}_1-\bar{x}_2} = \sqrt{\dfrac{\sigma_1^2}{n_1} + \dfrac{\sigma_2^2}{n_2}} = \sqrt{\dfrac{4^2}{64} + \dfrac{3^2}{64}} = \sqrt{\dfrac{25}{64}} = \dfrac{5}{8}$

$\mu_{\bar{x}_1-\bar{x}_2} = \mu_1 - \mu_2 = 12 - 10 = 2$

a. $z = \dfrac{(\bar{x}_1 - \bar{x}_2) - (\mu_1 - \mu_2)}{\sigma_{\bar{x}_1-\bar{x}_2}} = \dfrac{1.5 - 2}{\frac{5}{8}} = -.8$

b. $P[(\bar{x}_1 - \bar{x}_2) > 1.5] = P(z > -.8) = .5 + .2881 = .7881$ (from Table IV, Appendix B).

c. $P[(\bar{x}_1 - \bar{x}_2 < 1.5] = P(z < -.8) = .5 - .2881 = .2119$ (from Table IV, Appendix B).

d. $z = \frac{1 - 2}{\frac{5}{8}} = -1.6$ $\qquad z = \frac{-1 - 2}{\frac{5}{8}} = -4.8$

$P[(\bar{x}_1 - \bar{x}_2) < -1] + P[(\bar{x}_1 - \bar{x}_2) > 1] = P(z < -4.8) + P(z > -1.6)$

$= (.5 - .5) + (.5 + .4452) = .9452$ (from Table IV, Appendix B).

10.5 The form of the confidence interval is:

$$(\bar{x}_1 - \bar{x}_2) \pm z_{\alpha/2} \sqrt{\frac{\sigma_1^2}{n_1} + \frac{\sigma_2^2}{n_2}}$$

For confidence coefficient .95, $\alpha = 1 - .95 = .05$ and $\alpha/2 = .05/2 = .025$. From Table IV, Appendix B, $z_{.025} = 1.96$. The confidence interval is:

$$(70 - 50) \pm 1.96 \sqrt{\frac{100}{100} + \frac{64}{100}} \Rightarrow 20 \pm 2.51 \Rightarrow (17.49, 22.51)$$

We are 95% confident that the difference in the two means is between 17.49 and 22.51.

10.7 a. To determine if the merged firms generally have smaller price earnings ratios, we test:

$H_0: \mu_1 = \mu_2$
$H_a: \mu_1 < \mu_2$

where $\mu_1$ = mean price earnings ratio for merged firms, and
$\mu_2$ = mean price earnings ratio for nonmerged firms.

The test statistic is $z = \frac{(\bar{x}_1 - \bar{x}_2) - 0}{\sqrt{\frac{\sigma_1^2}{n_1} + \frac{\sigma_2^2}{n_2}}} = \frac{(7.295 - 14.666) - 0}{\sqrt{\frac{7.374^2}{44} + \frac{16.089^2}{44}}}$

$= \frac{-7.371}{2.6681} = -2.76$

The rejection region requires $\alpha = .05$ in the lower tail of the z distribution. From Table IV, Appendix B, $z_{.05} = -1.645$. The rejection region is $z < -1.645$.

Since the observed value of the test statistic falls in the rejection region ($z = -2.76 < -1.645$), $H_0$ is rejected. There is sufficient evidence to indicate the mean price earnings ratio for merged firms is smaller than that for nonmerged firms at $\alpha = 05$.

b. The p-value is $P(z \le -2.76) = .5 - .4971 = .0029$.

c. We must assume the samples are randomly selected.

d. No. If the price-earnings ratios cannot be negative, the populations cannot be normal because the standard deviations for both groups are larger than the means. Thus, there can be no observations more than one standard deviation below the mean.

10.9 For confidence coefficient .90, $\alpha = 1 - .90 = .1$ and $\alpha/2 = .1/2 = .05$. From Table IV, Appendix B, $z_{.05} = 1.645$. The confidence interval is:

$$(\bar{x}_1 - \bar{x}_2) \pm z_{\alpha/2}\sqrt{\frac{\sigma_1^2}{n_1} + \frac{\sigma_2^2}{n_2}} \Rightarrow (25.4 - 27.3) \pm 1.645\sqrt{\frac{3.1^2}{50} + \frac{3.7^2}{50}}$$

$$\Rightarrow -1.9 \pm 1.123 \Rightarrow (-3.023, -.777)$$

10.11 To determine if there is a difference in job satisfaction for the 2 groups, we test:

$H_0$: $\mu_1 - \mu_2 = 0$
$H_a$: $\mu_1 - \mu_2 \neq 0$

where $\mu_1$ = mean rating for workers that believe in an existence of a class system, and
$\mu_2$ = mean rating for workers that do not believe in an existence of a class system.

The test statistic is $z = \dfrac{(\bar{x}_1 - \bar{x}_2) - 0}{\sqrt{\dfrac{\sigma_1^2}{n_1} + \dfrac{\sigma_2^2}{n_2}}} \approx \dfrac{(5.42 - 5.19) - 0}{\sqrt{\dfrac{1.24^2}{175} + \dfrac{1.17^2}{277}}} = 1.96$

The rejection region requires $\alpha/2 = .10/2 = .05$ in each tail of the z distribution. From Table IV, Appendix B, $z_{.05} = 1.645$. The rejection region is $z < -1.645$ or $z > 1.645$.

Since the observed value of the test statistic falls in the rejection region ($z = 1.96 > 1.645$), $H_0$ is rejected. There is sufficient evidence to indicate a difference in job satisfaction for the two different sociocultural types of workers at $\alpha = .10$.

Since the test statistic is positive, workers with belief in class systems are more satisfied with their jobs.

10.13 From Exercise 10.12, $\bar{x}_1 = 51.4$, $\bar{x}_2 = 49.5$, $s_1 = 2.1$, $s_2 = 1.8$, $n_1 = 35$, and $n_2 = 45$.

For confidence coefficient .95, $\alpha = 1 - .95 = .05$ and $\alpha/2 = .05/2 = .025$. From Table IV, Appendix B, $z_{.025} = 1.96$. The confidence interval is:

$$(\bar{x}_1 - \bar{x}_2) \pm z_{\alpha/2}\sqrt{\frac{\sigma_1^2}{n_1} + \frac{\sigma_2^2}{n_2}} \Rightarrow (51.4 - 49.5) \pm 1.96\sqrt{\frac{2.1^2}{35} + \frac{1.8^2}{45}}$$

$$\Rightarrow 1.9 \pm .87 \Rightarrow (1.03,\ 2.77)$$

A 99% confidence interval would be wider than the 95% confidence interval calculated above. When the confidence level increases, the interval gets wider.

10.15 From Exercise 10.14, $\bar{x}_1 = 365$, $s_1 = 23$, and $n_1 = 100$.

To determine if the mean strength of firm A's corrugated fiberboard is more than 360 pounds, we test:

$H_0$: $\mu_1 = 360$
$H_a$: $\mu_1 > 360$

The test statistic is $z = \dfrac{\bar{x}_1 - \mu_0}{\sigma_{\bar{x}_1}} = \dfrac{\bar{x}_1 - \mu_0}{\sigma_1/\sqrt{n_1}} = \dfrac{\bar{x}_1 - \mu_0}{s_1/\sqrt{n_1}}$

$$= \frac{365 - 360}{23/\sqrt{100}} = 2.17$$

The rejection region requires $\alpha = .10$ in the upper tail of the z distribution. From Table IV, Appendix B, $z_{.10} = 1.28$. The rejection region is $z > 1.28$.

Since the observed value of the test statistic falls in the rejection region ($z = 2.17 > 1.28$), $H_0$ is rejected. There is sufficient evidence to indicate the mean strength of firm A's corrugated fiberboard is more than 360 pounds at $\alpha = .10$.

10.17 The two populations must have relative frequency distributions that are approximately normal and the population variances must be equal.

The samples must be randomly and independently selected from the populations.

10.19 The pooled variance ($s_p^2$) is simply a weighted average of the two sample variances, $s_1^2$ and $s_2^2$. The pooled variance, $s_p^2$, should be closer to $\sigma^2$ than $s_1^2$ or $s_2^2$ since it is based on a larger sample size.

10.21 a. First, compute the mean and variance for each sample.

$$\bar{x}_1 = \frac{\sum x_1}{n_1} = \frac{16.2}{6} = 2.7 \qquad \bar{x}_2 = \frac{\sum x_2}{n_2} = \frac{17.9}{5} = 3.58$$

$$s_1^2 = \frac{\sum x_1^2 - \frac{(\sum x_1)^2}{n}}{n_1 - 1} = \frac{46.98 - \frac{16.2^2}{6}}{6 - 1} = .648$$

$$s_2^2 = \frac{\sum x_2^2 - \frac{(\sum x_2)^2}{n_2}}{n_2 - 1} = \frac{64.83 - \frac{17.9^2}{5}}{5 - 1} = .187$$

$$s_p^2 = \frac{(n_1 - 1)s_1^2 + (n_2 - 1)s_2^2}{n_1 + n_2 - 2} = \frac{(6 - 1).648 + (5 - 1)(.187)}{6 + 5 - 2} = \frac{3.988}{9}$$

$$= .443$$

b. $H_0: \mu_1 = \mu_2$
$H_a: \mu_1 < \mu_2$

The test statistic is $t = \dfrac{(\bar{x}_1 - \bar{x}_2) - D_0}{\sqrt{s_p^2\left(\frac{1}{n_1} + \frac{1}{n_2}\right)}} = \dfrac{(2.7 - 3.58) - 0}{\sqrt{.443\left(\frac{1}{6} + \frac{1}{5}\right)}}$

$$= \frac{-.88}{.403} = -2.18$$

The rejection region requires $\alpha = .10$ in the lower tail of the t distribution with df $= n_1 + n_2 - 2 = 6 + 5 - 2 = 9$. From Table VI, Appendix B, $t_{.10} = 1.383$. The rejection region is $t < -1.383$.

Since the observed value of the test statistic falls in the rejection region ($t = -2.18 < -1.383$), $H_0$ is rejected. There is sufficient evidence to indicate that $\mu_1 < \mu_2$ ($\mu_2 > \mu_1$) at $\alpha = .10$.

Assumption: the population variances are equal.

c. The approximate observed significance level is $P(t \leq -2.18) = P(t \geq 2.18)$. From Table VI, Appendix B, with df = 9, $.025 <$ p-value $< .05$.

The results are statistically significant. We would reject $H_0$ if $\alpha$ is larger than .05.

10.23 a. $s_p^2 = \dfrac{(n_1 - 1)s_1^2 + (n_2 - 1)s_2^2}{n_1 + n_2 - 2} = \dfrac{(12 - 1)4.2^2 + (16 - 1)3.7^2}{12 + 16 - 2}$

$$= \frac{399.39}{26} = 15.36$$

b. $H_0: \mu_1 = \mu_2$
$H_a: \mu_1 \neq \mu_2$

The test statistic is $t = \dfrac{(\bar{x}_1 - \bar{x}_2) - D_0}{\sqrt{s_p^2\left(\dfrac{1}{n_1} + \dfrac{1}{n_2}\right)}} = \dfrac{(35 - 43) - 0}{\sqrt{15.36\left(\dfrac{1}{12} + \dfrac{1}{16}\right)}}$

$$= \frac{-8}{1.4967} = -5.35$$

The rejection region requires $\alpha/2 = .05/2$ in each tail of the t distribution with df $= n_1 + n_2 - 2 = 12 + 16 - 2 = 26$. From Table VI, Appendix B, $t_{.025} = 2.056$. The rejection region is $t < -2.056$ or $t > 2.056$.

Since the observed value of the test statistic falls in the rejection region ($t = -5.35 < -2.056$), $H_0$ is rejected. There is sufficient evidence to indicate that $\mu_1 \neq \mu_2$ at $\alpha = .05$.

Assumption: the population variances are equal.

c. The approximate p-value is $P(t \leq -5.35 \text{ or } t \geq 5.35)$
$\Rightarrow 2P(t \geq 5.35)$.
From Table VI, Appendix B, with df = 26,
p-value $= 2P(t \geq 5.35) < 2(.005)$ (Approximately 0)
$\Rightarrow$ p-value $< .01$.

The results are highly significant.

10.25 Some preliminary calculations are:

$$\bar{x}_1 = \frac{\sum x_1}{n_1} = \frac{654}{15} = 43.6 \qquad \bar{x}_2 = \frac{\sum x_2}{n_2} = \frac{858}{16} = 53.625$$

$$s_1^2 = \frac{\sum x_1^2 - \frac{(\sum x_1)^2}{n_1}}{n_1 - 1} = \frac{28934 - \frac{654^2}{15}}{15 - 1} = 29.9714$$

$$s_2^2 = \frac{\sum x_2^2 - \frac{(\sum x_2)^2}{n_2}}{n_2 - 1} = \frac{46450 - \frac{858^2}{16}}{16 - 1} = 29.3167$$

$$s_p^2 = \frac{(n_1 - 1)s_1^2 + (n_2 - 1)s_2^2}{n_1 + n_2 - 2} = \frac{(15 - 1)29.9714 + (16 - 1)29.3167}{15 + 16 - 2}$$

$$= \frac{859.3501}{29} = 29.6328$$

a. $H_0$: $\mu_2 - \mu_1 = 10$
$H_a$: $\mu_2 - \mu_1 > 10$

The test statistic is $t = \dfrac{(\bar{x}_2 - \bar{x}_1) - D_0}{\sqrt{s_p^2\left(\frac{1}{n_1} + \frac{1}{n_2}\right)}} = \dfrac{(53.625 - 43.6) - 10}{\sqrt{29.6328\left(\frac{1}{15} + \frac{1}{16}\right)}}$

$= .013$

The rejection region requires $\alpha = .01$ in the upper tail of the t distribution with df $= n_1 + n_2 - 2 = 15 + 16 - 2 = 29$. From Table VI, Appendix B, $t_{.01} = 2.462$. The rejection region is $t > 2.462$.

Since the observed value of the test statistic does not fall in the rejection region ($t = .013 \not> 2.462$), $H_0$ is not rejected. There is insufficient evidence to indicate $\mu_2 - \mu_1 > 10$ at $\alpha = .01$.

Assumption: the population variances are equal. (Note: this assumption is also needed for part (b).)

b. For confidence coefficient .98, $\alpha = 1 - .98 = .02$ and $\alpha/2 = .02/2 = .01$. From Table VI, Appendix B, with df = 29, $t_{.01} = 2.462$. The confidence interval is:

$$(\bar{x}_2 - \bar{x}_1) \pm t_{.01}\sqrt{s_p^2\left(\frac{1}{n_1} + \frac{1}{n_2}\right)}$$

$$\Rightarrow (53.625 - 43.6) \pm 2.462\sqrt{29.6328\left(\frac{1}{15} + \frac{1}{16}\right)}$$

$$\Rightarrow 10.025 \pm 4.817 \Rightarrow (5.208,\ 14.842)$$

We are 98% confident $\mu_2$ exceeds $\mu_1$ by anywhere from 5.208 to 14.842.

10.27 a. Let $\mu_1$ = mean daily output for operator 1, and
$\mu_2$ = mean daily output for operator 2.

$$s_p^2 = \frac{(n_1 - 1)s_1^2 + (n_2 - 1)s_2^2}{n_1 + n_2 - 2} = \frac{(10 - 1)17.2 + (10 - 1)19.1}{10 + 10 - 2} = \frac{326.7}{18}$$

$$= 18.15$$

To determine if there is a difference in the mean daily outputs for the two operators, we test:

$H_0$: $\mu_1 - \mu_2 = 0$
$H_a$: $\mu_1 - \mu_2 \neq 0$

The test statistic is $t = \dfrac{(\bar{x}_1 - \bar{x}_2) - D_0}{\sqrt{s_p^2\left(\frac{1}{n_1} + \frac{1}{n_2}\right)}} = \dfrac{(35 - 31) - 0}{\sqrt{18.15\left(\frac{1}{10} + \frac{1}{10}\right)}}$

$= 2.099$

The rejection region requires $\alpha/2 = .05/2 = .025$ in each tail of the t distribution with df $= n_1 + n_2 - 2 = 10 + 10 - 2 = 18$. From Table VI, Appendix B, $t_{.025} = 2.101$. The rejection region is $t < -2.101$ or $t > 2.101$.

Since the observed value of the test statistic does not fall in the rejection region ($t = 2.099 \not> 2.101$), $H_0$ is not rejected. There is insufficient evidence to indicate there is a difference in the mean daily outputs of the machine operators at $\alpha = .05$.

b. The necessary assumptions are:

1. Both sampled populations are approximately normal.
2. The population variances are equal.
3. The samples are randomly and independently sampled.

c. For confidence coefficient .90, $\alpha = 1 - .90 = .10$ and $\alpha/2 = .10/2 = .05$. From Table VI, Appendix B, with df = 18, $t_{.05} = 1.734$. The confidence interval is:

$$(\bar{x}_1 - \bar{x}_2) \pm t_{.05}\sqrt{s_p^2\left(\frac{1}{n_1} + \frac{1}{n_2}\right)}$$

$$\Rightarrow (35 - 31) \pm 1.734\sqrt{18.15\left(\frac{1}{10} + \frac{1}{10}\right)}$$

$$\Rightarrow 4 \pm 3.304 \Rightarrow (.696,\ 7.304)$$

I am 90% confident the mean daily output for operator 1 exceeds that for operator 2 by anywhere from .696 to 7.304 units.

10.29 a. Let $\mu_1$ = mean change in bond prices handled by underwriter 1 and $\mu_2$ = mean change in bond prices handled by underwriter 2.

$$s_p^2 = \frac{(n_1 - 1)s_1^2 + (n_2 - 1)s_2^2}{n_1 + n_2 - 2} = \frac{(27 - 1).0098 + (23 - 1).002465}{27 + 23 - 2}$$

$$= \frac{.30903}{48} = .006438$$

To determine if there is a difference in the mean change in bond prices handled by the 2 underwriters, we test:

$H_0$: $\mu_1 - \mu_2 = 0$
$H_a$: $\mu_1 - \mu_2 \neq 0$

The test statistic is $t = \frac{(\bar{x}_1 - \bar{x}_2) - D_0}{\sqrt{s_p^2(\frac{1}{n_1} + \frac{1}{n_2})}} = \frac{-.0491 - (-.0307) - 0}{\sqrt{.006438(\frac{1}{27} + \frac{1}{23})}}$

$= -.81$

The rejection region requires $\alpha/2 = .05/2 = .025$ in each tail of the t distribution with df $= n_1 + n_2 - 2 = 27 + 23 - 2 = 48$. From Table VI, Appendix B, $t_{.025} \approx 1.96$. The rejection region is $t < -1.96$ or $t > 1.96$.

Since the observed value of the test statistic does not fall in the rejection region ($t = -.81 \not< -1.96$), $H_0$ is not rejected. There is insufficient evidence to indicate there is a difference in the mean change in bond prices handled by the 2 underwriters at $\alpha = .05$.

b. For confidence coefficient .95, $\alpha = 1 - .95 = .05$ and $\alpha/2 = .05/2 = .025$. From Table VI, Appendix B, with df = 48, $t_{.025} \approx 1.96$. The confidence interval is:

$(\bar{x}_1 - \bar{x}_2) \pm t_{.025}\sqrt{s_p^2(\frac{1}{n_1} + \frac{1}{n_2})}$

$\Rightarrow (-.0491 - (-.0307) \pm 1.96\sqrt{.006438(\frac{1}{27} + \frac{1}{23})}$

$\Rightarrow -.0184 \pm .0446 \Rightarrow (-.063, .0262)$

I am 95% confident the mean difference in bond prices handled by underwriter 1 and underwriter 2 is somewhere between -.063 and .0262.

10.31 a. $s_1^2 = \frac{\sum x_1^2 - \frac{(\sum x_1)^2}{n_1}}{n_1 - 1} = \frac{2436 - \frac{128^2}{10}}{10 - 1} = 88.6222$

$s_2^2 = \frac{\sum x_2^2 - \frac{(\sum x_2)^2}{n_2}}{n_2 - 1} = \frac{1698 - \frac{104^2}{10}}{10 - 1} = 68.4889$

b. $s_p^2 = \frac{(n_1 - 1)s_1^2 + (n_2 - 1)s_2^2}{n_1 + n_2 - 2} = \frac{(10 - 1)88.6222 + (10 - 1)68.4889}{10 + 10 - 2}$

$= 78.5556$

$s_p = \sqrt{s_p^2} = 8.86$

The estimate of $\sigma(s_p = 8.86)$ appears to be a reasonable value for $\sigma$.

c. $H_0$: $\mu_1 = \mu_2$
$H_a$: $\mu_1 > \mu_2$

The test statistic is $t = \dfrac{(\bar{x}_1 - \bar{x}_2) - D_0}{\sqrt{s_p^2\left(\frac{1}{n_1} + \frac{1}{n_2}\right)}} = \dfrac{(12.8 - 10.4) - 0}{\sqrt{78.5556\left(\frac{1}{10} + \frac{1}{10}\right)}}$

$= .61$

The rejection region requires $\alpha = .05$ in the upper tail of the t distribution with df $= n_1 + n_2 - 2 = 10 + 10 - 2 = 18$. From Table VI, Appendix B, $t_{.05} = 1.734$. The rejection region is $t > 1.734$.

Since the observed value of the test statistic does not fall in the rejection region ($t = .61 \not> 1.734$), $H_0$ is not rejected. There is insufficient evidence to indicate that $\mu_1 > \mu_2$. That is, there is insufficient evidence to indicate the mean number of sick days is larger for the night shift at $\alpha = .05$.

d. The necessary assumptions are:

1. Both sampled populations are approximately normal.
2. The population variances are equal.
3. The samples are randomly and independently sampled.

e. If the assumptions are not satisfied, use the Wilcoxon rank sum test for independent samples to test for a shift in population distributions (see Chapter 18).

10.33 The necessary conditions are:

1. Both sampled populations are normally distributed.
2. The samples are random and independent.

10.35 a. With $\nu_1 = 2$ and $\nu_2 = 30$,
$P(F \geq 5.39) = .01$ (Table X, Appendix B)

b. With $\nu_1 = 24$ and $\nu_2 = 10$,
$P(F \geq 2.74) = .05$ (Table VIII, Appendix B)
Thus, $P(F < 2.74) = 1 - P(F \geq 2.74) = 1 - .05 = .95$.

c. With $\nu_1 = 7$ and $\nu_2 = 1$,
$P(F \geq 236.8) = .05$ (Table VIII, Appendix B)
Thus, $P(F < 236.8) = 1 - P(F \geq 236.8) = 1 - .05 = .95$.

d. With $\nu_1 = 40$ and $\nu_2 = 40$,
$P(F > 2.11) = .01$ (Table X, Appendix B)

10.37 To test $H_0$: $\sigma_1^2 = \sigma_2^2$ against $H_a$: $\sigma_1^2 \neq \sigma_2^2$, the rejection region is $F > F_{\alpha/2}$ with $\nu_1 = 10$ and $\nu_2 = 12$.

a. $\alpha = .20$, $\alpha/2 = .10$
Reject $H_0$ if $F > F_{.10} = 2.19$ (Table VII, Appendix B)

b. $\alpha = .10$, $\alpha/2 = .05$
Reject $H_0$ if $F > F_{.05} = 2.75$ (Table VIII, Appendix B)

c. $\alpha = .05$, $\alpha/2 = .025$
Reject $H_0$ if $F > F_{.025} = 3.37$ (Table IX, Appendix B)

d. $\alpha = .02$, $\alpha/2 = .01$
Reject $H_0$ if $F > F_{.01} = 4.30$ (Table X, Appendix B)

10.39 a. Some preliminary calculations are:

$$s_1^2 = \frac{\sum x_1^2 - \frac{(\sum x_1)^2}{n_1}}{n_1 - 1} = \frac{45.35 - \frac{14.5^2}{6}}{6 - 1} = 2.062$$

$$s_2^2 = \frac{\sum x_2^2 - \frac{(\sum x_2)^2}{n_2}}{n_2 - 1} = \frac{130.4 - \frac{21.8^2}{5}}{5 - 1} = 8.838$$

To determine if a difference exists between the population variances, we test:

$H_0$: $\sigma_1^2 = \sigma_2^2$
$H_a$: $\sigma_1^2 \neq \sigma_2^2$

The test statistic is $F = \frac{s_2^2}{s_1^2} = \frac{8.838}{2.062} = 4.29$

The rejection region requires $\alpha/2 = .05/2 = .025$ in the upper tail of the F distribution with $\nu_1 = n_2 - 1 = 5 - 1 = 4$ and $\nu_2 = n_1 - 1 = 6 - 1 = 5$. From Table IX, Appendix B, $F_{.025} = 7.39$. The rejection region is $F > 7.39$.

Since the observed value of the test statistic does not fall in the rejection region ($F = 4.29 \not> 7.39$), $H_0$ is not rejected. There is insufficient evidence to indicate a difference between the population variances at $\alpha = .05$.

b. The p-value is $2P(F \geq 4.29)$. From Tables VII and VIII, with $\nu_1 = 4$ and $\nu_2 = 5$,

$2(.05) < 2P(F \geq 4.29) < 2(.10)$
$\Rightarrow .10 <$ p-value $< .20$

10.41 To determine if the variances of the number of units produced per day differ for the two arrangements, we test:

$H_0$: $\sigma_1^2 = \sigma_2^2$
$H_a$: $\sigma_1^2 \neq \sigma_2^2$

The test statistic is $F = \dfrac{s_2^2}{s_1^2} = \dfrac{3761}{1432} = 2.63$

The rejection region requires $\alpha/2 = .10/2 = .05$ in the upper tail of the F distribution with $\nu_1 = n_2 - 1 = 21 - 1 = 20$ and $\nu_2 = n_1 - 1 = 21 - 1 = 20$. From Table VIII, Appendix B, $F_{.05} = 2.12$. The rejection region is $F > 2.12$.

Since the observed value of the test statistic falls in the rejection region ($F = 2.63 > 2.12$), $H_0$ is rejected. There is sufficient evidence to indicate the variances of the number of units produced per day differ for the 2 arrangements at $\alpha = .10$.

Since Assembly line 1 has the smaller variance, you should choose Assembly line 1.

10.43 a. Let $\sigma_1^2$ = variance of completion times with the time guideline issued, and
$\sigma_2^2$ = variance of completion times without the time guideline issued.

Some preliminary calculations are:

$$s_1^2 = \frac{\sum x_1^2 - \frac{(\sum x_1)^2}{n_1}}{n_1 - 1} = \frac{7455.34 - \frac{270.8^2}{10}}{10 - 1} = 13.564$$

$$s_2^2 = \frac{\sum x_2^2 - \frac{(\sum x_2)^2}{n_2}}{n_2 - 1} = \frac{11366.33 - \frac{327.9^2}{10}}{10 - 1} = 68.2766$$

To determine if the variance in completion times for the 2 groups is equal, we test:

$H_0$: $\sigma_1^2 = \sigma_2^2$
$H_a$: $\sigma_1^2 \neq \sigma_2^2$

The test statistic is $F = \dfrac{s_2^2}{s_1^2} = \dfrac{68.2766}{13.564} = 5.03$

The rejection region requires $\alpha/2 = .05/2 = .025$ in the upper tail of the F distribution with $\nu_1 = n_2 - 1 = 10 - 1 = 9$ and $\nu_2 = n_1 - 1 = 10 - 1 = 9$. From Table IX, Appendix B, $F_{.025} = 4.03$. The rejection region is $F > 4.03$.

Since the observed value of the test statistic falls in the rejection region ($F = 5.03 > 4.03$), $H_0$ is rejected. There is sufficient evidence to indicate that the population variances are not equal at $\alpha = .05$.

The two-sample t is not appropriate in this situation. In order to use the two-sample t, you need to assume the population variances are equal. We just showed that there is evidence to indicate that the population variances are not equal.

b. The necessary assumptions are:

1. Both sampled populations are normally distributed.
2. The samples are random and independent.

c. A Type I error is rejecting $H_0$ when $H_0$ is true. In this case, you decide there is a difference in the variances of the completion times for the 2 groups, but there is not a difference.

A Type II error is accepting $H_0$ when it is false. In this case, you decide there is not a difference in the variances of the completion times for the 2 groups, but there is a difference.

d. The p-value is $2P(F \geq 5.03)$. From Tables IX and X, with $\nu_1 = 9$ and $\nu_2 = 9$,

$$2(.01) < 2P(F \geq 5.03) < 2(.025)$$
$$\Rightarrow .02 < \text{p-value} < .05$$

10.45 a. To determine if the data violates the assumption of equal population variances, we test:

$$H_0: \sigma_1^2 = \sigma_2^2$$
$$H_a: \sigma_1^2 \neq \sigma_2^2$$

The test statistic is $F = \frac{s_2^2}{s_1^2} = \frac{19.1}{17.2} = 1.11$

The rejection region requires $\alpha/2 = .10/2 = .05$ in the upper tail of the F distribution with $\nu_1 = n_2 - 1 = 10 - 1 = 9$ and $\nu_2 = n_1 - 1 = 10 - 1 = 9$. From Table VIII, Appendix B, $F_{.05} = 3.18$. The rejection region is $F > 3.18$.

Since the observed value of the test statistic does not fall in the rejection region ($F = 1.11 \not> 3.18$), $H_0$ is not rejected. There is insufficient evidence to indicate the variances in the number of units produced per day by the 2 operators is different at $\alpha = .10$.

Therefore, the two-sample t is appropriate in this situation. The test in Exercise 10.27 was valid.

b. If the conclusion in part (a) were incorrect, a Type II error would have been committed since we accepted $H_0$ when $H_0$ was false.

10.47 Some preliminary calculations are:

| PERSON | DIFFERENCE (BEFORE - AFTER) |
|---|---|
| 1 | -9 |
| 2 | -11 |
| 3 | -1 |
| 4 | -5 |
| 5 | -12 |

a. $\bar{x}_D = \frac{\sum x_D}{n_D} = \frac{-38}{5} = -7.6$

$$s_D^2 = \frac{\sum x_D^2 - \frac{(\sum x_D)^2}{n_D}}{n_D - 1} = \frac{372 - \frac{(-38)^2}{5}}{5 - 1} = 20.8$$

$s_D = \sqrt{s_D^2} = 4.56$

b. $\bar{x}_1 = \frac{\sum x_1}{n_1} = \frac{374}{5} = 74.8$

$\bar{x}_2 = \frac{\sum x_2}{n_2} = \frac{412}{5} = 82.4$

$\bar{x}_1 - \bar{x}_2 = 74.8 - 82.4 = -7.6 = \bar{x}_D$

c. $H_0$: $\mu_1 = \mu_2$
$H_a$: $\mu_1 \neq \mu_2$

The test statistic is $t = \frac{\bar{x}_D - 0}{\frac{s_D}{\sqrt{n_D}}} = \frac{-7.6 - 0}{\frac{4.56}{\sqrt{5}}} = -3.73$

The rejection region requires $\alpha/2 = .05/2 = .025$ in each tail of the t distribution with df $= n_D - 1 = 5 - 1 = 4$. From Table VI, Appendix B, $t_{.025} = 2.776$. The rejection region is $t < -2.776$ or $t > 2.776$.

Since the observed value of the test statistic falls in the rejection region ($t = -3.73 < -2.776$), $H_0$ is rejected. There is sufficient evidence to indicate that $\mu_1 \neq \mu_2$ at $\alpha = .05$.

d. p-value $= P(t \leq -3.73 \text{ or } t \geq 3.73)$
$= 2P(t \geq 3.73)$

From Table VI, Appendix B, with df = 4,
$2(.01) < 2P(t \geq 3.73) < 2(.025)$
$\Rightarrow .02 <$ p-value $< .05$.

e. The necessary assumptions are:

1. The population of differences is normal.
2. The differences are randomly selected.

10.49 a. $H_0: \mu_1 - \mu_2 = 0$
$H_a: \mu_1 - \mu_2 < 0$

The rejection region requires $\alpha = .10$ in the lower tail of the t distribution with df $= n_D - 1 = 18 - 1 = 17$. From Table VI, Appendix B, $t_{.10} = 1.333$. The rejection region is $t < -1.333$.

b. $H_0: \mu_1 - \mu_2 = 0$
$H_a: \mu_1 - \mu_2 < 0$

The test statistic is $t = \dfrac{\bar{x}_D - 0}{\dfrac{s_D}{\sqrt{n_D}}} = \dfrac{-3.5 - 0}{\dfrac{\sqrt{21}}{\sqrt{18}}} = -3.24$

The rejection region is $t < -1.333$. (Refer to part (a).)

Since the observed value of the test statistic falls in the rejection region ($t = -3.24 < -1.333$), $H_0$ is rejected. There is sufficient evidence to indicate $\mu_1 - \mu_2 < 0$ at $\alpha = .10$.

c. The necessary assumptions are:

1. The population of differences is normal.
2. The differences are randomly selected.

d. For confidence coefficient .90, $\alpha = 1 - .90 = .10$ and $\alpha/2 = .10/2 = .05$. From Table VI, Appendix B, with df = 17, $t_{.05} = 1.740$. The confidence interval is:

$$\bar{x}_D \pm t_{.05}\frac{s_D}{\sqrt{n_D}} \Rightarrow -3.5 \pm 1.740\frac{\sqrt{21}}{\sqrt{18}}$$

$$\Rightarrow -3.5 \pm 1.88 \Rightarrow (-5.38, -1.62)$$

e. The confidence interval provides more information since it gives an interval of possible values for the difference between the population means.

10.51 Some preliminary calculations are:

| PAIR | DIFFERENCE x - y |
|---|---|
| 1 | 11 |
| 2 | 13 |
| 3 | 15 |
| 4 | -1 |
| 5 | 13 |
| 6 | 14 |
| 7 | 18 |

$$\bar{x}_D = \frac{\sum x_D}{n_D} = \frac{83}{7} = 11.857$$

$$s_D^2 = \frac{\sum x_D^2 - \frac{(\sum x_D)^2}{n_D}}{n_D - 1} = \frac{1205 - \frac{83^2}{7}}{7 - 1} = 36.8095$$

$$s_D = \sqrt{s_D^2} = 6.067$$

a. $H_0$: $\mu_D = 10$
$H_a$: $\mu_D \neq 10$

The test statistic is $t = \frac{\bar{x}_D - 10}{\frac{s_D}{\sqrt{n_D}}} = \frac{11.857 - 10}{\frac{6.067}{\sqrt{7}}} = .81$

The rejection region requires $\alpha/2 = .05/2 = .025$ in each tail of the t distribution with df $= n_D - 1 = 7 - 1 = 6$. From Table VI, Appendix B, $t_{.025} = 2.447$. The rejection region is $t < -2.447$ or $t > 2.447$.

Since the observed value of the test statistic does not fall in the rejection region ($t = .81 \not> 2.447$), $H_0$ is not rejected. There is insufficient evidence to indicate $\mu_1 - \mu_2 \neq 10$ at $\alpha = .05$.

b. The p-value $= P(t \leq -.81 \text{ or } t \geq .81)$
$= 2P(t \geq .81)$

From Table VI, Appendix B, with df = 6,
$2P(t \geq .81) > 2(.10)$
$\Rightarrow$ p-value $> .20$

The probability of observing our test statistic or anything more unusual if the difference in the means is 10 is greater than .20. This is not unusual, so $H_0$ is not rejected.

10.53 Some preliminary calculations are:

| EMPLOYEE ID NUMBER | DIFFERENCE (1986 - 1987) |
|---|---|
| 1011 | 1 |
| 0033 | -2 |
| 0998 | -2 |
| 0006 | -1 |
| 1802 | 1 |
| 0246 | -3 |
| 0777 | - |
| 1112 | -2 |

$$\bar{x}_D = \frac{\sum x_D}{n_D} = \frac{-8}{7} = -1.14$$

$$s_D^2 = \frac{\sum x_D^2 - \frac{(\sum x_D)^2}{n_D}}{n_D - 1} = \frac{24 - \frac{(-8)^2}{7}}{7 - 1} = 2.4762$$

$$s_D = \sqrt{s_D^2} = 1.5736$$

a. To determine if the program has helped increase worker productivity, we test:

$H_0$: $\mu_D = 0$
$H_a$: $\mu_D < 0$

The test statistic is $t = \frac{\bar{x}_D - 0}{\frac{s_D}{\sqrt{n_D}}} = \frac{-1.14 - 0}{\frac{1.5736}{\sqrt{7}}} = -1.92$

The rejection region requires $\alpha = .10$ in the lower tail of the t distribution with df $= n_D - 1 = 7 - 1 = 6$. From Table VI, Appendix B, $t_{.10} = 1.44$. The rejection region is $t < -1.44$.

Since the observed value of the test statistic falls in the rejection region ($t = -1.92 < -1.44$), $H_0$ is rejected. There is sufficient evidence to indicate that the program has helped to increase worker productivity at $\alpha = .10$.

The necessary assumptions are:

1. The population of differences is normal.
2. The differences are randomly selected.

b. We could lose some of the workers along the way (promotion, no longer employed, etc.). In this particular problem, we did lose one worker which gave us a smaller sample size.

10.55 Some preliminary calculations are:

| FIRM | DIFFERENCE 1970's - 1960's |
|---|---|
| 1 | 0 |
| 2 | 4 |
| 3 | -1 |
| 4 | 9 |
| 5 | 6 |
| 6 | -1 |
| 7 | 5 |
| 8 | 3 |
| 9 | 3 |
| 10 | 5 |

$$\bar{x}_D = \frac{\sum x_D}{n_D} = \frac{33}{10} = 3.3$$

$$s_D^2 = \frac{\sum x_D^2 - \frac{(\sum x_D)^2}{n_D}}{n_D - 1} = \frac{203 - \frac{(33)^2}{10}}{10 - 1} = 10.4556$$

$$s_D = \sqrt{s_D^2} = 3.2335$$

a. To determine if we can reject Beckenstein, Gabel, and Roberts' claim, we test:

$H_0$: $\mu_D = 3.22$
$H_a$: $\mu_D \neq 3.22$

The test statistic is $t = \dfrac{\bar{x}_D - 3.22}{\frac{s_D}{\sqrt{n_D}}} = \dfrac{3.3 - 3.22}{\frac{3.2335}{\sqrt{10}}} = .078$

p-value = $2P(t \geq .078)$

From Table VI, Appendix B, with df = $n_D - 1 = 10 - 1 = 9$,
p-value > 2(.10) = .20

This is not significant.

Therefore, there is insufficient evidence to indicate that the difference in the number of litigations between 1970 and 1960 is different from 3.22 on the average. We would not reject Beckenstein, Gabel, and Roberts' claim.

b. For confidence coefficient .90, $\alpha = 1 - .90 = .10$ and $\alpha/2 = .10/2 = .05$. From Table VI, Appendix B, with df = 9, $t_{.05} = 1.833$. The confidence interval is:

$$\bar{x}_D \pm t_{.05}\frac{s_D}{\sqrt{n_D}} \Rightarrow 3.3 \pm 1.833\frac{3.2335}{\sqrt{10}}$$

$$\Rightarrow 3.3 \pm 1.874 \Rightarrow (1.426, 5.174)$$

Beckenstein, Gabel, and Roberts found they faced 3.22 more litigations in the 1970's than in the 1960's. This agrees with our findings since 3.22 is in the confidence interval.

10.57 Some preliminary calculations are:

$$\bar{x}_1 = \frac{\sum x_1}{n_1} = \frac{64.3}{6} = 10.7167 \qquad \bar{x}_2 = \frac{\sum x_2}{n_2} = \frac{61.8}{6} = 10.3$$

$$s_1^2 = \frac{\sum x_1^2 - \frac{(\sum x_1)^2}{n_1}}{n_1 - 1} = \frac{704.43 - \frac{64.3^2}{6}}{6 - 1} = 3.0697$$

$$s_2^2 = \frac{\sum x_2^2 - \frac{(\sum x_2)^2}{n_2}}{n_2 - 1} = \frac{653.06 - \frac{61.8^2}{6}}{6 - 1} = 3.304$$

$$s_p^2 = \frac{(n_1 - 1)s_1^2 + (n_2 - 1)s_2^2}{n_1 + n_2 - 2} = \frac{(6 - 1)3.0697 + (6 - 1)3.304}{6 + 6 - 2}$$

$$= 3.18685$$

a. To determine if there is a difference in the mean strength of the two types of shocks, we test:

$H_0\colon \mu_1 - \mu_2 = 0$
$H_a\colon \mu_1 - \mu_2 \neq 0$

The test statistic is $t = \dfrac{(\bar{x}_1 - \bar{x}_2) - D_0}{\sqrt{s_p^2\left(\frac{1}{n_1} + \frac{1}{n_2}\right)}} = \dfrac{(10.717 - 10.3) - 0}{\sqrt{3.18685\left(\frac{1}{6} + \frac{1}{6}\right)}}$

$$= .40$$

The rejection region requires $\alpha/2 = .05/2 = .025$ in each tail of the t distribution with df $= n_1 + n_2 - 2 = 6 + 6 - 2 = 10$. From Table VI, Appendix B, $t_{.025} = 2.228$. The rejection region is $t < -2.228$ or $t > 2.228$.

Since the observed value of the test statistic does not fall in the rejection region ($t = .40 \not> 2.228$), $H_0$ is not rejected. There is insufficient evidence to indicate a difference between the mean strengths for the two types of shocks at $\alpha = .05$.

b. For confidence coefficient .95, $\alpha = 1 - .95 = .05$ and $\alpha/2 = .05/2 = .025$. From Table VI, Appendix B, with df $= n_1 + n_2 - 2 = 6 + 6 - 2 = 10$, $t_{.025} = 2.228$. The confidence interval is:

$$(\bar{x}_1 - \bar{x}_2) \pm t_{.025}\sqrt{s_p^2\left(\frac{1}{n_1} + \frac{1}{n_2}\right)}$$

$$\Rightarrow (10.717 - 10.3) \pm 2.228\sqrt{3.18685\left(\frac{1}{6} + \frac{1}{6}\right)}$$

$$\Rightarrow .417 \pm 2.2963 \Rightarrow (-1.8793,\ 2.7133)$$

I am 95% confident the mean strength of the manufacturer's shock exceeds the mean strength of the competitor's shock by anywhere from -1.8793 to 2.7133.

c. The confidence interval obtained in part (b) is wider than that found in Exercise 10.56. This interval is wider because the standard deviation is larger for the independent samples than for the matched-pair design.

d. The results of an unpaired analysis are not valid when the data are collected from a paired experiment. The assumption of independent samples is not valid.

10.59 Some preliminary calculations are:

| CONSUMER | DIFFERENCE PATTERN 1 - PATTERN 2 | CONSUMER | DIFFERENCE PATTERN 1 - PATTERN 2 |
|---|---|---|---|
| 1 | .2 | 9 | .07 |
| 2 | .31 | 10 | .36 |
| 3 | .23 | 11 | .25 |
| 4 | .21 | 12 | .12 |
| 5 | -.04 | 13 | .27 |
| 6 | .21 | 14 | .20 |
| 7 | .51 | 15 | .10 |
| 8 | .59 | | |

$$\bar{x}_D = \frac{\sum x_D}{n_D} = \frac{3.59}{15} = .239$$

$$s_D^2 = \frac{\sum x_D^2 - \frac{(\sum x_D)^2}{n_D}}{n_D - 1} = \frac{1.2213 - \frac{3.59^2}{15}}{15 - 1} = .0259$$

$$s_D = \sqrt{s_D^2} = .1608$$

a. For confidence coefficient .90, $\alpha = 1 - .90 = .10$ and $\alpha/2 = .10/2 = .05$. From Table VI, Appendix B, with $df = n_D - 1 = 15 - 1 = 14$, $t_{.05} = 1.761$. The confidence interval is:

$$\bar{x}_D \pm t_{.05}\frac{s_D}{\sqrt{n_D}} \Rightarrow .239 \pm 1.761\frac{.1608}{\sqrt{15}}$$

$$\Rightarrow .239 \pm .0731 \Rightarrow (.1659, .3121)$$

b. I am 90% confident that the mean amount of pupil dilation per consumer for silverware pattern 1 exceeds the mean amount for pattern 2 by between .1659 and .3121. Therefore, the consumers are more interested in pattern 1, on the average.

c. Since all the values in the confidence interval are greater than .1, the confidence interval in part (a) supports the inference.

d. $H_0\colon \mu_D = .1$
$H_a\colon \mu_D > .1$ where $\mu_D = \mu_1 - \mu_2$

The test statistic is $t = \frac{\bar{x}_D - .1}{\frac{s_D}{\sqrt{n_D}}} = \frac{.239 - .1}{\frac{.1608}{\sqrt{15}}} = 3.35$

The rejection region requires $\alpha = .05$ in the upper tail of the t distribution with $df = n_D - 1 = 15 - 1 = 14$. From Table VI, Appendix B, $t_{.05} = 1.761$. The rejection region is $t > 1.761$.

Since the observed value of the test statistic falls in the rejection region ($t = 3.35 > 1.761$), $H_0$ is rejected. There is sufficient evidence to indicate the mean dilation for pattern 1 exceeds that for pattern 2 by more than .1 millimeter at $\alpha = .05$.

10.61 $x_1$ and $x_2$ are both binomial random variables which represent the number of successes in sample 1 and sample 2, respectively.

The sampling distributions of $\hat{p}_1$ and $\hat{p}_2$ are approximately normal with means of $p_1$ and $p_2$, respectively, and standard deviations of

$\sqrt{\frac{p_1q_1}{n_1}}$ and $\sqrt{\frac{p_2q_2}{n_2}}$, respectively.

10.63 For testing $H_0$: $p_1 - p_2 = 0$ against $H_a$: $p_1 - p_2 < 0$, we would reject $H_0$ in favor of $H_a$ if $z < -z_\alpha$. Using Table IV, Appendix B:

a. When $\alpha = .01$,
reject $H_0$ if $z < -z_{.01} = -2.33$.

b. When $\alpha = .025$,
reject $H_0$ if $z < -z_{.025} = -1.96$.

c. When $\alpha = .05$,
reject $H_0$ if $z < -z_{.05} = -1.645$.

d. When $\alpha = .10$,
reject $H_0$ if $z < -z_{.10} = -1.28$.

10.65 From Exercise 10.64,

$$\hat{p}_1 = \frac{x_1}{n_1} = \frac{38}{200} = .19, \qquad \hat{p}_2 = \frac{x_1}{n_2} = \frac{71}{220} = .323$$

For confidence coefficient .98, $\alpha = 1 - .98 = .02$ and $\alpha/2 = .02/2 = .01$. From Table IV, Appendix B, $z_{.01} = 2.33$. The confidence interval is:

$$(\hat{p}_1 - \hat{p}_2) \pm z_{.01}\sqrt{\frac{\hat{p}_1\hat{q}_1}{n_1} + \frac{\hat{p}_2\hat{q}_2}{n_2}}$$

$$\Rightarrow (.19 - .323) \pm 2.33\sqrt{\frac{.19(.81)}{200} + \frac{.323(.677)}{220}}$$

$$\Rightarrow -.133 \pm .0978 \Rightarrow (-.2308, -.0352)$$

I am 98% confident that $p_2$ exceeds $p_1$ by between .0352 and .2308.

10.67 From Exercise 10.66,

$$\hat{p}_1 = \frac{x_1}{n_1} = \frac{140}{500} = .28 \qquad \hat{p}_2 = \frac{x_2}{n_2} = \frac{192}{500} = .384$$

For confidence coefficient .80, $\alpha = 1 - .80 = .20$ and $\alpha/2 = .20/2 = .10$. From Table IV, Appendix B, $z_{.10} = 1.28$. The confidence interval is:

$$(\hat{p}_1 - \hat{p}_2) \pm z_{.10}\sqrt{\frac{\hat{p}_1\hat{q}_1}{n_1} + \frac{\hat{p}_2\hat{q}_2}{n_2}}$$

$$\Rightarrow (.28 - .384) \pm 1.28\sqrt{\frac{.28(.72)}{500} + \frac{.384(.616)}{500}}$$

$$\Rightarrow -.104 \pm .0379 \Rightarrow (-.1419, -.0661)$$

I am 80% confident that $p_2$ exceeds $p_1$ by between .0661 and .1419.

10.69 a. The sample sizes for each of the 3 areas are large enough to use the methods of this section if the intervals

$$\hat{p}_i \pm 3\sigma_{\hat{p}_i} \Rightarrow \hat{p}_i \pm 3\sqrt{\frac{\hat{p}_i\hat{q}_i}{n_i}}$$ do not contain 0 or 1.

<u>For Age</u>:

$$\hat{p}_1 = \frac{x_1}{n_1} = \frac{19}{207} = .092 \qquad \hat{p}_2 = \frac{x_2}{n_2} = \frac{96}{153} = .627$$

$$\hat{p}_1 \pm 3\sigma_{\hat{p}_1} \Rightarrow .092 \pm 3\sqrt{\frac{.092(.908)}{207}} \Rightarrow .092 \pm .06 \Rightarrow (.032, .152)$$

$$\hat{p}_2 \pm 3\sigma_{\hat{p}_2} \Rightarrow .627 \pm 3\sqrt{\frac{.627(.373)}{153}} \Rightarrow .627 \pm .117 \Rightarrow (.51, .744)$$

Since neither interval contains 0 or 1, the sample sizes are large enough to use the methods of this section in the area age.

<u>For Education</u>:

$$\hat{p}_1 = \frac{x_1}{n_1} = \frac{195}{207} = .942 \qquad \hat{p}_2 = \frac{x_2}{n_2} = \frac{116}{153} = .758$$

$$\hat{p}_1 \pm 3\sigma_{\hat{p}_1} \Rightarrow .942 \pm 3\sqrt{\frac{.942(.058)}{207}} \Rightarrow .942 \pm .049 \Rightarrow (.893, .991)$$

$$\hat{p}_2 \pm 3\sigma_{\hat{p}_2} \Rightarrow .758 \pm 3\sqrt{\frac{.758(.242)}{153}} \Rightarrow .758 \pm .104 \Rightarrow (.654, .862)$$

Since neither interval contains 0 or 1, the sample sizes are large enough to use the methods of this section in the area education.

<u>For Employment</u>:

$$\hat{p}_1 = \frac{x_1}{n_1} = \frac{19}{207} = .092 \qquad \hat{p}_2 = \frac{x_2}{n_2} = \frac{47}{153} = .307$$

$$\hat{p}_1 \pm 3\sigma_{\hat{p}_1} \Rightarrow .092 \pm 3\sqrt{\frac{.092(.908)}{207}} \Rightarrow .092 \pm .06 \Rightarrow (.032, .152)$$

$$\hat{p}_2 \pm 3\sigma_{\hat{p}_2} \Rightarrow .307 \pm 3\sqrt{\frac{.307(.693)}{153}} \Rightarrow .307 \pm .112 \Rightarrow (.195, .419)$$

Since neither interval contains 0 or 1, the sample sizes are large enough to use the methods of this section in the area employment.

b. To determine if Fortune 500 CEO's and entrepreneurs differ in terms of education, we test:

$H_0: p_1 - p_2 = 0$
$H_a: p_1 - p_2 \neq 0$

The test statistic is $z = \dfrac{(\hat{p}_1 - \hat{p}_2) - 0}{\sqrt{\hat{p}\hat{q}\left(\frac{1}{n_1} + \frac{1}{n_2}\right)}}$

where $\hat{p}_1 = .942$, $\hat{p}_2 = .758$, and

$$\hat{p} = \frac{x_1 + x_2}{n_1 + n_2} = \frac{195 + 116}{207 + 153} = .864$$

$$\text{Thus, } z = \frac{(.942 - .758) - 0}{\sqrt{.864(.136)\left(\frac{1}{207} + \frac{1}{153}\right)}} = 5.03$$

The rejection region requires $\alpha/2 = .05/2 = .025$ in each tail of the z distribution. From Table IV, Appendix B, $z_{.025} = 1.96$. The rejection region is $z < -1.96$ or $z > 1.96$.

Since the observed value of the test statistic falls in the rejection region ($z = 5.03 > 1.96$), $H_0$ is rejected. There is sufficient evidence to indicate that Fortune 500 CEO's and entrepreneurs differ in terms of education at $\alpha = .05$.

c. We must assume the 2 samples are independent random samples from binomial distributions. Both samples should be large enough that the normal distribution provides an adequate approximation to the sampling distributions of $\hat{p}_1$ and $\hat{p}_2$. This was checked in part (a).

10.71 a. To determine if CEO's and entrepreneurs differ in the proportion that have been fired or dismissed from a job, we test:

$H_0: p_1 - p_2 = 0$
$H_a: p_1 - p_2 \neq 0$

The test statistic is $z = \dfrac{(\hat{p}_1 - \hat{p}_2) - 0}{\sqrt{\hat{p}\hat{q}\left(\frac{1}{n_1} + \frac{1}{n_2}\right)}}$

where $\hat{p}_1 = \dfrac{x_1}{n_1} = \dfrac{19}{207} = .092$, $\quad \hat{p}_2 = \dfrac{x_2}{n_2} = \dfrac{47}{153} = .307$, and

$$\hat{p} = \frac{x_1 + x_2}{n_1 + n_2} = \frac{19 + 47}{207 + 153} = .183$$

Thus, $z = \dfrac{(.092 - .307) - 0}{\sqrt{.183(.817)\left(\frac{1}{207} + \frac{1}{153}\right)}} = -5.22$

The rejection region requires $\alpha/2 = .01/2 = .005$ in each tail of the z distribution. From Table IV, Appendix B, $z_{.005} = 2.575$. The rejection region is $z < -2.575$ or $z > 2.575$.

Since the observed value of the test statistic falls in the rejection region ($z = -5.22 < -2.575$), $H_0$ is rejected. There is sufficient evidence to indicate there is a difference in the fraction of CEO's and entrepreneurs who have been fired or dismissed from job at $\alpha = .01$.

b. For confidence coefficient .99, $\alpha = 1 - .99 = .01$ and $\alpha/2 = .01/2 = .005$. From Table IV, Appendix B, $z_{.005} = 2.575$. The confidence interval is:

$$(\hat{p}_1 - \hat{p}_2) \pm z_{\alpha/2}\sqrt{\frac{\hat{p}_1\hat{q}_1}{n_1} + \frac{\hat{p}_2\hat{q}_2}{n_2}}$$

$$\Rightarrow (.092 - .307) \pm 2.575\sqrt{\frac{.092(.908)}{207} + \frac{.307(.693)}{153}}$$

$$\Rightarrow -.215 \pm .109 \Rightarrow (-.324, -.106)$$

c. The confidence interval in part (b) provides more information about employment records. The confidence interval gives an interval of possible values for the difference in the proportions while the hypothesis test only tells us that they differ.

10.73 Some preliminary calculations are:

$$\hat{p}_1 = \frac{x_1}{n_1} = \frac{475}{1000} = .475 \qquad \hat{p}_2 = \frac{x_2}{n_2} = \frac{305}{1000} = .305$$

a. For confidence coefficient .90, $\alpha = 1 - .90 = .10$ and $\alpha/2 = .10/2 = .05$. From Table IV, Appendix B, $z_{.05} = 1.645$. The confidence interval is:

$$(\hat{p}_1 - \hat{p}_2) \pm z_{\alpha/2}\sqrt{\frac{\hat{p}_1\hat{q}_1}{n_1} + \frac{\hat{p}_2\hat{q}_2}{n_2}}$$

$$\Rightarrow (.475 - .305) \pm 1.645\sqrt{\frac{.475(.525)}{1000} + \frac{.305(.695)}{1000}}$$

$$\Rightarrow .17 \pm .0353 \Rightarrow (.1347, .2053)$$

b. I am 90% confident the proportion of households that use the firm's salt before the packaging switch exceeds the proportion that use it after the switch by between .1347 and .2053.

10.75 a. A confidence interval reflects the reliability of an estimate.

For confidence coefficient .95, $\alpha = 1 - .95 = .05$ and $\alpha/2 = .05/2 = .025$. From Table IV, Appendix B, $z_{.025} = 1.96$. The confidence interval is:

$$\hat{p}_1 \pm z_{.025}\sqrt{\frac{\hat{p}_1\hat{q}_1}{n_1}} \qquad \text{where } \hat{p}_1 = \frac{x_1}{n_1} = \frac{1653}{9542} = .1732$$

$$\Rightarrow .1732 \pm 1.96\sqrt{\frac{.1732(.8268)}{9542}}$$

$$\Rightarrow .1732 \pm .0076 \Rightarrow (.1656, .1808)$$

b. A 95% confidence interval for $p_2$ is:

$$\hat{p}_2 \pm z_{.025}\sqrt{\frac{\hat{p}_2\hat{q}_2}{n_2}} \qquad \text{where } \hat{p}_2 = \frac{x_2}{n_2} = \frac{501}{6631} = .0756$$

$$\Rightarrow .0756 \pm 1.96\sqrt{\frac{.0756(.9244)}{6631}}$$

$$\Rightarrow .0756 \pm .0064 \Rightarrow (.0692, .082)$$

c. A 95% confidence interval for $p_1 - p_2$ is:

$$(\hat{p}_1 - \hat{p}_2) \pm z_{.025}\sqrt{\frac{\hat{p}_1\hat{q}_1}{n_1} + \frac{\hat{p}_2\hat{q}_2}{n_2}}$$

$$\Rightarrow (.1732 - .0756) \pm 1.96\sqrt{\frac{.1732(.8268)}{9542} + \frac{.0756(.9244)}{6631}}$$

$$\Rightarrow .0976 \pm .0099 \Rightarrow (.0877, .1075)$$

10.77 In Exercise 10.76, we used $\alpha = .05$. If $\alpha$ were set at .01 instead, we would be less likely to reject the null hypothesis if in fact it is true. Recall $\alpha$ = P(Type I error) = P(Reject $H_0$ when $H_0$ is true). Therefore, the smaller $\alpha$ is, the less likely we are of committing a Type I error.

10.79 Some preliminary calculations are:

$$\hat{p}_1 = \frac{x_1}{n_1} = \frac{61}{307} = .1987 \qquad \hat{p}_2 = \frac{x_2}{n_2} = \frac{5}{35} = .1429$$

$$\hat{p} = \frac{x_1 + x_2}{n_1 + n_2} = \frac{61 + 5}{307 + 35} = .193$$

To determine whether a higher proportion of breathing irregularities exist among miners than Duluth men, we test:

$H_0$: $p_1 - p_2 = 0$
$H_a$: $p_1 - p_2 > 0$

The test statistic is $z = \dfrac{(\hat{p}_1 - \hat{p}_2) - 0}{\sqrt{\hat{p}\hat{q}\left(\frac{1}{n_1} + \frac{1}{n_2}\right)}}$

$$= \frac{(.1987 - .1429) - 0}{\sqrt{.193(.807)\left(\frac{1}{307} + \frac{1}{35}\right)}} = .79$$

$$\text{p-value} = P(z \geq .79) = .5 - P(0 < z < .79) = .5 - .2852 = .2148$$

This is not significant. We would reject $H_0$ if $\alpha > .2148$. Since this is unrealistic, we fail to reject $H_0$. There is insufficient evidence to conclude the miners have a higher proportion of breathing irregularities than Duluth men.

10.81 For confidence coefficient .90, $\alpha = 1 - .90 = .10$ and $\alpha/2 = .10/2 = .05$. From Table IV, Appendix B, $z_{.05} = 1.645$. We estimate $p_1 = p_2 = .5$ to be conservative.

$$n_1 = n_2 = \frac{4(z_{\alpha/2})^2(p_1q_1 + p_2q_2)}{W^2} = \frac{4(1.645)^2(.5(.5) + .5(.5))}{.06^2}$$

$$= 1503.35 \approx 1504$$

10.83 First, find the sample sizes needed for width 4:

For confidence coefficient .9, $\alpha = 1 - .9 = .1$ and $\alpha/2 = .1/2 = .05$. From Table IV, Appendix B, $z_{.05} = 1.645$.

$$n_1 = n_2 = \frac{4(z_{\alpha/2})^2(\sigma_1^2 + \sigma_2^2)}{W^2} = \frac{4(1.645)^2(10^2 + 10^2)}{4^2} = 135.30$$

Thus, the necessary sample size from each population is 136. Therefore, sufficient funds have not been allocated to meet the specifications since $n_1 = n_2 = 100$ are not large enough samples.

10.85 From Exercise 10.43, $n_1 = 10$, $n_2 = 10$, $s_1^2 = 13.564$, and $s_2^2 = 68.2766$.

First, find the sample sizes needed to meet the desired specifications.

For confidence coefficient .80, $\alpha = 1 - .80 = .20$ and $\alpha/2 = .20/2 = .10$. From Table IV, Appendix B, $z_{.10} = 1.28$.

$$n_1 = n_2 = \frac{(z_{\alpha/2})^2(\sigma_1^2 + \sigma_2^2)}{B^2} = \frac{1.28^2(13.564 + 68.2766)}{2^2} = 33.52$$

You need 34 completion times. Therefore, 24 additional completion times are needed.

10.87 For confidence coefficient .95, $\alpha = 1 - .95 = .05$ and $\alpha/2 = .05/2 = .025$. From Table IV, Appendix B, $z_{.025} = 1.96$. We estimate $p_1 = p_2 = .5$ to be conservative.

$$n_1 = n_2 = \frac{(z_{\alpha/2})^2(p_1q_1 + p_2q_2)}{B^2} = \frac{1.96^2(.5(.5) + .5(.5))}{.02^2} = 4802$$

10.89 Some preliminary calculations are:

| FIRM | DIFFERENCE 1989 - 1988 |
|---|---|
| Adams-Russell | -1.2 |
| Harris | -12.9 |
| Aydin | -1.9 |
| Andrew | 2.9 |
| Compudyn | -.5 |
| Raytheon | 3.7 |
| Varian Assoc. | 2.9 |
| General Instr. | 9.4 |

$$\bar{x}_D = \frac{\sum x_D}{n_D} = \frac{2.4}{8} = .3$$

$$s_D^2 = \frac{\sum x_D^2 - \frac{(\sum x_D)^2}{n_D}}{n_D - 1} = \frac{290.58 - \frac{2.4^2}{8}}{8 - 1} = 41.4086$$

$$s_D = \sqrt{s_D^2} = 6.4349$$

a. To determine if the R&D expenditures have increased, we test:

$H_0$: $\mu_D = 0$
$H_a$: $\mu_D > 0$

The test statistic is $t = \dfrac{\bar{x}_D - 0}{\frac{s_D}{\sqrt{n_D}}} = \dfrac{.3 - 0}{\frac{6.4349}{\sqrt{8}}} = .13$

The rejection region requires $\alpha = .10$ in the upper tail of the t distribution with df $= n_D - 1 = 10 - 1 = 9$. From Table VI, Appendix B, $t_{.10} = 1.383$. The rejection region is $t > 1.383$.

Since the observed value of the test statistic does not fall in the rejection region ($t = .13 \not> 1.383$), $H_0$ is not rejected. There is insufficient evidence to indicate the R&D expenditures have increased at $\alpha = .10$. That is, the data do not support the analyst's beliefs.

b. A Type I error is rejecting $H_0$ when $H_0$ is true. In this case, you decide the R&D expenditures have increased when they have not.

A Type II error is accepting $H_0$ when it is false. In this case, you decide the R&D expenditures have not increased when they have increased.

c. The necessary assumptions are:

1. The population of differences is normal.
2. The differences are randomly selected.

10.91 Some preliminary calculations are:

$$\hat{p}_1 = \frac{x_1}{n_1} = \frac{12}{500} = .024 \qquad \hat{p}_2 = \frac{x_2}{n_2} = \frac{15}{450} = .0333$$

$$\hat{p} = \frac{x_1 + x_2}{n_1 + n_2} = \frac{12 + 15}{500 + 450} = .0284$$

To determine if there is a difference in the proportions preferring the new brand between the 2 regions, we test:

$H_0: p_1 - p_2 = 0$
$H_a: p_1 - p_2 \neq 0$

The test statistic is $z = \dfrac{(\hat{p}_1 - \hat{p}_2) - 0}{\sqrt{\hat{p}\hat{q}\left(\frac{1}{n_1} + \frac{1}{n_2}\right)}}$

$$= \frac{(.024 - .0333) - 0}{\sqrt{.0284(.9716)\left(\frac{1}{500} + \frac{1}{450}\right)}} = -.86$$

The rejection region requires $\alpha/2 = .05/2 = .025$ in each tail of the z distribution. From Table IV, Appendix B, $z_{.025} = 1.96$. The rejection region is $z < -1.96$ or $z > 1.96$.

Since the observed value of the test statistic does not fall in the rejection region ($z = -.86 \nless -1.96$), $H_0$ is not rejected. There is insufficient evidence to indicate there is a difference in the proportions preferring the new brand between the two regions at $\alpha = .05$.

Since there is no evidence to indicate a difference in the proportions preferring the new brand, the two advertising agencies are equally effective.

10.93 Let $p_1$ = proportion of shoppers that are exposed to the commercial that purchase XYZ, and
$p_2$ = proportion of shoppers that are not exposed to the commercial that purchase XYZ.

Some preliminary calculations are:

$$\hat{p}_1 = \frac{x_1}{n_1} = \frac{84}{387} = .2171 \qquad \hat{p}_2 = \frac{x_2}{n_2} = \frac{57}{392} = .1454$$

$$\hat{p} = \frac{x_1 + x_2}{n_1 + n_2} = \frac{84 + 57}{387 + 392} = .181$$

a. To determine if the new commercial motivates shoppers to purchase the XYZ brand, we test:

$H_0$: $p_1 = p_2$
$H_a$: $p_1 > p_2$

The test statistic is $z = \dfrac{(\hat{p}_1 - \hat{p}_2) - 0}{\sqrt{\hat{p}\hat{q}\left(\frac{1}{n_1} + \frac{1}{n_2}\right)}}$

$$= \frac{(.2171 - .1454) - 0}{\sqrt{.181(.819)\left(\frac{1}{387} + \frac{1}{392}\right)}} = 2.60$$

The rejection region requires $\alpha = .05$ in the upper tail of the z distribution. From Table IV, Appendix B, $z_{.05} = 1.645$. The rejection region is $z > 1.645$.

Since the observed value of the test statistic falls in the rejection region ($z = 2.60 > 1.645$), $H_0$ is rejected. There is sufficient evidence to indicate the new XYZ commercial motivates shoppers to purchase the XYZ brand at $\alpha = .05$.

b. The p-value is $P(z \geq 2.60) = .5 - P(0 < z < 2.60)$
$= .5 - .4953$
$= .0047$ (Table IV, Appendix B)

This is highly significant. The probability of observing a test statistic of 2.60 or higher is .0047 if the proportions are equal. We would reject $H_0$ for $\alpha > .0047$.

10.95 For confidence coefficient .90, $\alpha = 1 - .90 = .10$ and $\alpha/2 = .10/2 = .05$. From Table IV, Appendix B, $z_{.05} = 1.645$. We estimate $p_1 = p_2 = .5$.

$$n_1 = n_2 = \frac{(z_{\alpha/2})^2(p_1q_1 + p_2q_2)}{B^2} = \frac{1.645^2(.5(.5) + .5(.5))}{.05^2}$$

$$= 541.205 \approx 542$$

10.97 From Exercise 10.96, $s_1 = 1.1$, $s_2 = 1$, $n_1 = 10$, and $n_2 = 10$.

$H_0$: $\sigma_1^2 = \sigma_2^2$
$H_a$: $\sigma_1^2 \neq \sigma_2^2$

The test statistic is $F = \frac{s_1^2}{s_2^2} = \frac{1.1^2}{1.0^2} = 1.21$

The rejection region requires $\alpha/2 = .10/2 = .05$ in the upper tail of the F distribution with $\nu_1 = n_1 - 1 = 10 - 1 = 9$ and $\nu_2 = n_2 - 1 = 10 - 1 = 9$. From Table VIII, Appendix B, $F_{.05} = 3.18$. The rejection region is $F > 3.18$.

Since the observed value of the test statistic does not fall in the rejection region ($F = 1.21 \not> 3.18$), $H_0$ is not rejected. There is insufficient evidence to indicate the population variances differ at $\alpha = .10$.

Therefore, the sample data do not cast a doubt on the assumption of equal variances.

The necessary assumptions are:

1. Both sampled populations are normally distributed.
2. The samples are random and independent.

10.99 For confidence coefficient .90, $\alpha = 1 - .90 = .10$ and $\alpha/2 = .10/2 = .05$. From Table IV, Appendix B, $z_{.05} = 1.645$.

An estimate of $\sigma_1$ and $\sigma_2$ is obtained from:

$$\text{range} \approx 4s$$
$$s \approx \frac{\text{range}}{4} = \frac{6}{4} = 1.5$$

$$n_1 = n_2 = \frac{4(z_{\alpha/2})^2(\sigma_1^2 + \sigma_2^2)}{W^2} = \frac{4(1.645^2)(1.5^2 + 1.5^2)}{1^2} = 48.71 \approx 49$$

10.101 From Exercise 10.100, $\hat{p}_1 = .2$, $\hat{p}_2 = .1$, $n_1 = 387$, and $n_2 = 311$.

$$\hat{p} = \frac{n_1\hat{p}_1 + n_2\hat{p}_2}{n_1 + n_2} = \frac{387(.2) + 311(.1)}{387 + 311} = .1554$$

To determine if a difference exists between the proportions of the two types of executives who do not know how much poor quality costs their company, we test:

$H_0$: $p_1 - p_2 = 0$
$H_a$: $p_1 - p_2 \neq 0$

The test statistic is $z = \frac{(\hat{p}_1 - \hat{p}_2) - 0}{\sqrt{\hat{p}\hat{q}\left(\frac{1}{n_1} + \frac{1}{n_2}\right)}}$

$$= \frac{(.2 - .1) - 0}{\sqrt{.1554(.8446)\left(\frac{1}{387} + \frac{1}{311}\right)}} = 3.62$$

The rejection region requires $\alpha/2 = .10/2 = .05$ in each tail of the z distribution. From Table IV, Appendix B, $z_{.05} = 1.645$. The rejection region is $z < -1.645$ or $z > 1.645$.

Since the observed value of the test statistic falls in the rejection region ($z = 3.62 > 1.645$), $H_0$ is rejected. There is sufficient evidence to indicate there is a difference in the proportions of the two types of executives who do not know how much poor quality costs their company at $\alpha = .10$.

10.103 To determine if the average number of services used by bank 1's customers is greater than that for bank 2's customers, we test:

$H_0\colon \mu_1 - \mu_2 = 0$
$H_a\colon \mu_1 - \mu_2 > 0$

The test statistic is $z = \frac{(\bar{x}_1 - \bar{x}_2) - 0}{\sqrt{\frac{\sigma_1^2}{n_1} + \frac{\sigma_2^2}{n_2}}} \approx \frac{(2.2 - 1.8) - 0}{\sqrt{\frac{1.15^2}{40} + \frac{1.10^2}{50}}} = 1.67$

The rejection region requires $\alpha = .10$ in the upper tail of the z distribution. From Table IV, Appendix B, $z_{.10} = 1.28$. The rejection region is $z > 1.28$.

Since the observed value of the test statistic falls in the rejection region ($z = 1.67 > 1.28$), $H_0$ is rejected. There is sufficient evidence to indicate the mean number of services used by bank 1's customers is greater than that for bank 2's customers at $\alpha = .10$.

10.105 To determine if the mean housing price per square foot differs in the two locales, we test:

$H_0\colon \mu_1 - \mu_2 = 0$
$H_a\colon \mu_1 - \mu_2 \neq 0$

The test statistic is $z = \frac{(\bar{x}_1 - \bar{x}_2) - 0}{\sqrt{\frac{\sigma_1^2}{n_1} + \frac{\sigma_2^2}{n_2}}} \approx \frac{(50.4 - 53.7) - 0}{\sqrt{\frac{4.5^2}{63} + \frac{5.3^2}{78}}} = -4.00$

The rejection region requires $\alpha/2 = .01/2 = .005$ in each tail of the z distribution. From Table IV, Appendix B, $z_{.005} = 2.575$. The rejection region is $z < -2.575$ or $z > 2.575$.

Since the observed value of the test statistic falls in the rejection region ($z = -4.00 < -2.575$), $H_0$ is rejected. There is sufficient evidence to indicate the mean housing price per square foot differs for the two locales at $\alpha = .01$.

10.107 For confidence coefficient .95, $\alpha = 1 - .95 = .05$ and $\alpha/2 = .05/2 = .025$. From Table IV, Appendix B, $z_{.025} = 1.96$.

An estimate of $\sigma_1$ and $\sigma_2$ is obtained from:

$$\text{range} \approx 4s$$

$$s \approx \frac{\text{range}}{4}$$

$$= \frac{4}{4} = 1$$

$$n_1 = n_2 = \frac{4(z_{\alpha/2})^2(\sigma_1^2 + \sigma_2^2)}{W^2} = \frac{4(1.96^2)(1^2 + 1^2)}{.4^2} = 192.08 \approx 193$$

You need to take 193 measurements at each site.

10.109 From Exercise 10.108, $\bar{x}_1 = 106.4$, $\bar{x}_2 = 96.5$, $s_1 = 10.3$, $s_2 = 13.4$, $n_1 = 15$, $n_2 = 15$, and $s_p^2 = 142.825$.

For confidence coefficient .95, $\alpha = 1 - .95 = .05$ and $\alpha/2 = .05/2 = .025$. From Table IV, Appendix B, with $df = n_1 + n_2 - 2 = 15 + 15 - 2 = 28$, $t_{.025} = 2.048$. The confidence interval is:

$$(\bar{x}_1 - \bar{x}_2) \pm t_{.025}\sqrt{s_p^2\left(\frac{1}{n_1} + \frac{1}{n_2}\right)}$$

$$\Rightarrow (106.4 - 96.5) \pm 2.048\sqrt{142.825\left(\frac{1}{15} + \frac{1}{15}\right)}$$

$$\Rightarrow 9.9 \pm 8.937 \Rightarrow (.963, 18.837)$$

The necessary assumptions are:

1. Both sampled populations are approximately normal.
2. The population variances are equal.
3. The samples are randomly and independently sampled.

10.111 Some preliminary calculations are:

| MONTH | DIFFERENCE MEN'S - SPORT | MONTH | DIFFERENCE MEN'S - SPORT |
|---|---|---|---|
| 1 | -1,807 | 7 | -1,249 |
| 2 | 348 | 8 | -424 |
| 3 | 2,876 | 9 | 314 |
| 4 | 1,994 | 10 | -841 |
| 5 | -6,249 | 11 | 1,403 |
| 6 | -7,934 | 12 | -2,131 |

$$\bar{x}_D = \frac{\sum x_D}{n_D} = \frac{-13700}{12} = -1,141.67$$

$$s_D^2 = \frac{\sum x_D^2 - \frac{(\sum x_D)^2}{n_D}}{n_D - 1} = \frac{126687346 - \frac{(-13700)^2}{12}}{12 - 1} = 10,095,137.51$$

$$s_D = \sqrt{s_D^2} = 3,177.2846$$

a. For confidence coefficient .95, $\alpha = 1 - .95 = .05$ and $\alpha/2 = .05/2 = .025$. From Table VI, Appendix B, with df $= n_D - 1 = 12 - 1 = 11$, $t_{.025} = 2.201$. The confidence interval is:

$$\bar{x}_D \pm t_{.025} \frac{s_D}{\sqrt{n_D}} \Rightarrow -1,141.67 \pm 2.201\left(\frac{3,177.2846}{\sqrt{12}}\right)$$

$$\Rightarrow -1,141.67 \pm 2,018.76 \Rightarrow (-3,160.43,\ 877.09)$$

b. We cannot make a decision based on the confidence interval in part (a) since we cannot determine which department has the greater mean sales.

c. The necessary assumptions are:

1. The population of differences is normal.
2. The differences are randomly selected.

10.113 a. $$s_p^2 = \frac{(n_1 - 1)s_1^2 + (n_2 - 1)s_2^2}{n_1 + n_2 - 2} = \frac{(15 - 1)2300^2 + (22 - 1)3100^2}{15 + 22 - 2}$$

$$= 7,882,000$$

To determine if the mean salary of male first-level managers exceeds that of females, we test:

$H_0$: $\mu_1 - \mu_2 = 0$
$H_a$: $\mu_1 - \mu_2 < 0$

The test statistic is $$t = \frac{(\bar{x}_1 - \bar{x}_2) - 0}{\sqrt{s_p^2\left(\frac{1}{n_1} + \frac{1}{n_2}\right)}} = \frac{(33,400 - 34,700) - 0}{\sqrt{7,882,000\left(\frac{1}{15} + \frac{1}{22}\right)}}$$

$$= -1.38$$

The rejection region requires $\alpha = .05$ in the lower tail of the t distribution with df $= n_1 + n_2 - 2 = 15 + 22 - 2 = 35$. From Table VI, Appendix B, $t_{.05} \approx 1.645$. The rejection region is $t < -1.645$.

Since the observed value of the test statistic does not fall in the rejection region ($t = -1.38 \not< -1.645$), $H_0$ is not rejected. There is insufficient evidence to indicate the mean salary of male first-level managers exceeds the mean salary of females at $\alpha = .05$.

b. The necessary assumptions are:

1. Both sampled populations are approximately normal.
2. The population variances are equal.
3. The samples are randomly and independently sampled.

CHAPTER 11

# SIMPLE LINEAR REGRESSION

11.1 a.

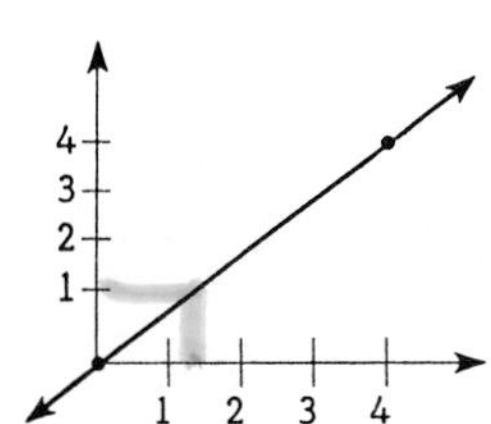


b.

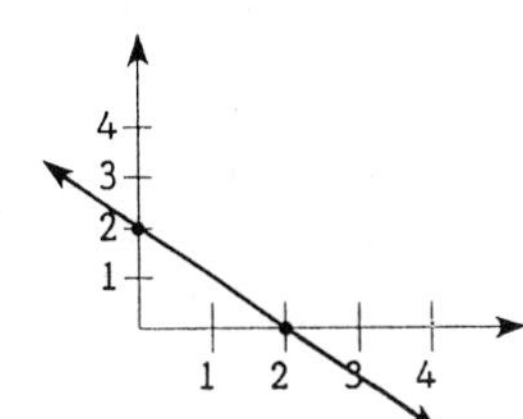


c.

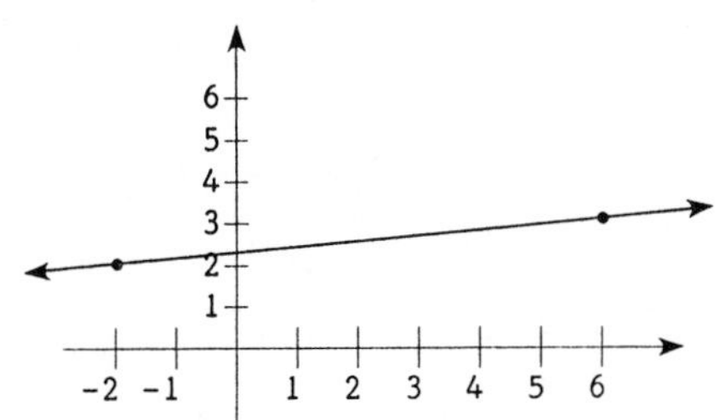


d.

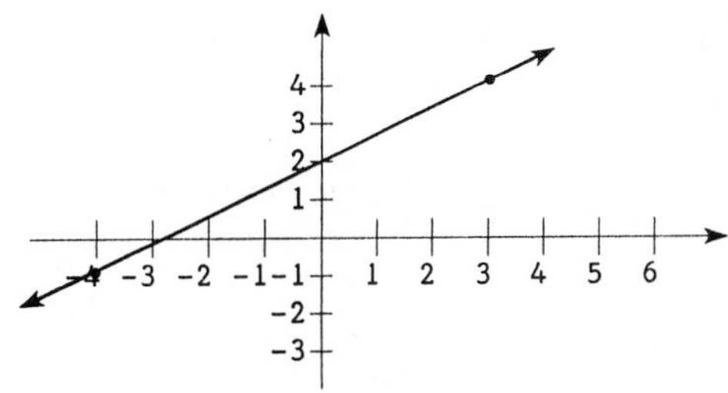


11.3 a. The equation for a straight line (deterministic) is

$$y = \beta_0 + \beta_1 x$$

If the line passes through (0, 0), then

$$0 = \beta_0 + \beta_1(0) \Rightarrow 0 = \beta_0$$

Likewise, through (4, 4),

$$4 = \beta_0 + \beta_1(4)$$

$$4 = \beta_1(4) \Rightarrow \beta_1 = 1$$

Thus, $y = 0 + 1x$ or $y = x$

b. The equation for a straight line is $y = \beta_0 + \beta_1 x$. If the line passes through (0, 2), then $2 = \beta_0 + \beta_1(0)$, which implies $\beta_0 = 2$. Likewise, through the point (2, 0), then $0 = \beta_0 + 2\beta_1$ or $-\beta_0 = 2\beta_1$. Substituting $\beta_0 = 2$, we get $-2 = 2\beta_1$ or $\beta_1 = -1$. Therefore, the line passing through (0, 2) and (2, 0) is $y = 2 - x$.

c. The equation for a straight line is $y = \beta_0 + \beta_1 x$. If the line passes through (-2, 2), then $2 = \beta_0 + \beta_1(-2)$. Likewise through the point (6, 3), $3 = \beta_0 + \beta_1(6)$. Solving for these 2 equations

$$\begin{array}{rcl} 3 & = & \beta_0 + \beta_1 6 \\ -(2 & = & \beta_0 - \beta_1 2) \\ \hline 1 & = & 8\beta_1 \quad \text{or} \quad \beta_1 = \frac{1}{8} \end{array}$$

Solving for $\beta_0$, $2 = \beta_0 + \frac{1}{8}(-2)$ or $2 = \beta_0 - \frac{1}{4}$ or $\beta_0 = 2 + \frac{1}{4} = \frac{9}{4}$

The equation, with $\beta_0 = \frac{9}{4}$ and $\beta_1 = \frac{1}{8}$, is $y = \frac{9}{4} + \frac{1}{8}x$

d. The equation for a straight line is $y = \beta_0 + \beta_1 x$. If the line passes through (-4, -1), then $-1 = \beta_0 - \beta_1 4$. Likewise, through the point (3, 4), $4 = \beta_0 + \beta_1 3$. Solving these equations simultaneously,

$$\begin{array}{rcl} 4 & = & \beta_0 + \beta_1 3 \\ -[(-1) & = & \beta_0 - \beta_1 4] \\ \hline 5 & = & 7\beta_1 \quad \text{or} \quad \beta_1 = \frac{5}{7} \end{array}$$

Solving for $\beta_0$, $4 = \beta_0 + 3\left(\frac{5}{7}\right) \Rightarrow 4 - \frac{15}{7} = \beta_0$ or $\beta_0 = \frac{13}{7}$.

Therefore, $y = \frac{13}{7} + \frac{5}{7}x$.

11.5 a. $y = 3 + 2x$. The slope is the value for $\beta_1$ or $\beta_1 = 2$. The intercept is that value for $\beta_0$ or $\beta_0 = 3$.

b. $y = 3 - 2x$. The slope is the value for $\beta_1$, which is -2; the intercept is the value for $\beta_0$ or 3.

c. $y = -3 + 2x$. The slope is the value for $\beta_1$, which is 2; the intercept is the value $\beta_0$ or -3.

d. $y = -x$. We note $\beta_0 = 0$, so the intercept is 0. The slope, $\beta_1 = -1$.

e. $y = 2x$. We note $\beta_0 = 0$, so the intercept is 0. The slope, $\beta_1 = 2$.

f. $y = .5 + 1.25x$. The slope, $\beta_1 = 1.25$, and the intercept $\beta_0 = .5$.

11.7 The "line of means" is the deterministic component of the probabilistic model, because the mean of y, E(y), is equal to the straight-line component of the model. That is, $E(y) = \beta_0 + \beta_1 x$.

11.9 a.

| $x_i$ | $y_i$ | $x_i^2$ | $x_i y_i$ |
|---|---|---|---|
| 7 | 2 | $7^2 = 49$ | $7(2) = 14$ |
| 4 | 4 | $4^2 = 16$ | $4(4) = 16$ |
| 6 | 2 | $6^2 = 36$ | $6(2) = 12$ |
| 2 | 5 | $2^2 = 4$ | $2(5) = 10$ |
| 1 | 7 | $1^2 = 1$ | $1(7) = 7$ |
| 1 | 6 | $1^2 = 1$ | $1(6) = 6$ |
| 3 | 5 | $3^2 = 9$ | $3(5) = 15$ |

Totals: $\sum x_i = 7 + 4 + 6 + 2 + 1 + 1 + 3 = 24$

$\sum y_i = 2 + 4 + 2 + 5 + 7 + 6 + 5 = 31$

$\sum x_i^2 = 49 + 16 + 36 + 4 + 1 + 1 + 9 = 116$

$\sum x_i y_i = 14 + 16 + 12 + 10 + 7 + 6 + 15 = 80$

b. $$SS_{xy} = \sum_{i=1}^{n} x_i y_i - \frac{\left(\sum_{i=1}^{n} x_i\right)\left(\sum_{i=1}^{n} y_i\right)}{n} = 80 - \frac{(24)(31)}{7} = 80 - 106.2857$$

$$= -26.2857$$

c. $$SS_{xx} = \sum x_i^2 - \frac{(\sum x_i)^2}{7} = 116 - \frac{(24)^2}{7} = 116 - 82.2857 = 33.7143$$

d. $$\hat{\beta}_1 = \frac{SS_{xy}}{SS_{xx}} = \frac{-26.2857}{33.7143} = -.7796$$

e. $$\bar{x} = \frac{\sum x_i}{n} = \frac{24}{7} = 3.4286 \qquad \bar{y} = \frac{\sum y_i}{n} = \frac{31}{7} = 4.4286$$

f. $$\hat{\beta}_0 = \bar{y} - \hat{\beta}_1 \bar{x} = 4.4286 - (-.7796)(3.4286) = 4.4286 - (-2.6729)$$

$$= 7.102$$

g. The least squares line is $\hat{y} = \hat{\beta}_0 + \hat{\beta}_1 x = 7.102 - .7796x$

11.11 a.

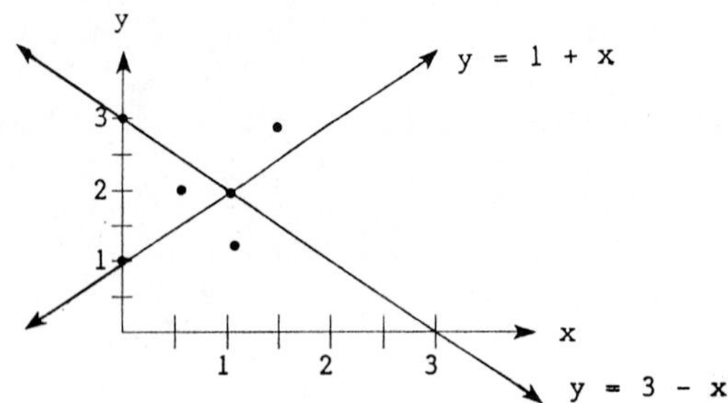


b. Choose y = 1 + x since it best describes the relation of x and y.

c.

| y | x | $\hat{y} = 1 + x$ | $y - \hat{y}$ |
|---|---|---|---|
| 2 | .5 | 1.5 | 2 - 1.5 = .5 |
| 1 | 1 | 2 | 1 - 2 = -1 |
| 3 | 1.5 | 2.5 | 3 - 2.5 = .5 |
| | | | Sum of errors = 0 |

| y | x | $\hat{y} = 3 - x$ | $y - \hat{y}$ |
|---|---|---|---|
| 2 | .5 | 3 - .5 = 2.5 | 2 - 2.5 = .5 |
| 1 | 1 | 3 - 1 = 2 | 1 - 2 = -1 |
| 3 | 1.5 | 3 - 1.5 = 1.5 | 3 - 1.5 = 1.5 |
| | | | Sum of errors = 0 |

d. $SSE = \sum(y - \hat{y})^2$

SSE for 1st model: $y = 1 + x$, $SSE = (.5)^2 + (-1)^2 + (.5)^2 = 1.5$

SSE for 2nd model: $y = 3 - x$, $SSE = (.5)^2 + (-1)^2 + (1.5)^2 = 3.5$

e. The best fitting straight line is the one that has the least squares. The model y = 1 + x has a smaller SSE, and therefore it verifies the visual check in part (a). The least squares line,

$$\hat{\beta}_1 = \frac{SS_{xy}}{SS_{xx}} \quad \sum x_i = 3 \quad \sum y_i = 6 \quad \sum x_i y_i = 6.5 \quad \sum x_i^2 = 3.5 \quad \sum y_i^2 = 14$$

$$SS_{xy} = \sum x_i y_i - \frac{(\sum x_i)(\sum y_i)}{n} = 6.5 - \frac{(3)(6)}{3} = .5$$

$$SS_{xx} = \sum x_i^2 - \frac{(\sum x_i)^2}{n} = 3.5 - \frac{(3)^2}{3} = .5$$

$$\hat{\beta}_1 = \frac{.5}{.5} = 1 \qquad \bar{x} = \frac{\sum x_i}{3} = \frac{3}{3} = 1 \qquad \bar{y} = \frac{\sum y_i}{3} = \frac{6}{3} = 2$$

$$\hat{\beta}_0 = \bar{y} - \hat{\beta}_1\bar{x} = 2 - 1(1) = 1 \Rightarrow \hat{y} = \hat{\beta}_0 + \hat{\beta}_1 x = 1 + x$$

11.13 a. $y = \beta_0 + \beta_1 x + \varepsilon$. The model implies that mean sales price and square feet of living space are linearly related.

b. The estimate of the y-intercept is $\hat{\beta}_0 = -30{,}000$ and the estimate of the slope is $\hat{\beta}_1 = 70$.

c. The interpretation of the estimate of the y-intercept is not meaningful in this problem because x = 0 is not in the range of values for the square footage, x, which is 1500 to 4000.

d. For each additional square foot of living space, the mean selling price of a house is estimated to increase by $70.

e. $\hat{y} = -30{,}000 + 70(3000) = \$180{,}000$. This is meaningful because x = 3000 is in the observed range of x.

f. $\hat{y} = -30{,}000 + 70(5000) = \$320{,}000$. This is not meaningful because x = 5000 is not in the observed range of x.

11.15 a. $\bar{x} = \frac{\sum x}{n} = \frac{235.92}{14} = 16.8514 \qquad \bar{y} = \frac{\sum y}{n} = \frac{1257}{14} = 89.7857$

$$SS_{xy} = \sum xy - \frac{(\sum x)(\sum y)}{n} = 24{,}654.87 - \frac{235.92(1257)}{14}$$
$$= 24{,}654.87 - 21{,}182.24571$$
$$= 3{,}472.62429$$

$$SS_{xx} = \sum x^2 - \frac{(\sum x)^2}{n} = 5{,}074.0898 - \frac{235.92^2}{14}$$
$$= 5{,}074.0898 - 3975.589029$$
$$= 1{,}098.500771$$

$$\hat{\beta}_1 = \frac{SS_{xy}}{SS_{xx}} = \frac{3{,}472.62429}{1{,}098.500771} = 3.161239738 \approx 3.1612$$

$$\hat{\beta}_0 = \bar{y} - \hat{\beta}_1\bar{x} = 89.7857 - 3.161239738(16.8514)$$
$$= 89.7857 - 53.2713532$$
$$= 36.5144$$

The least squares line is $\hat{y} = 36.5144 + 3.1612x$.

b.

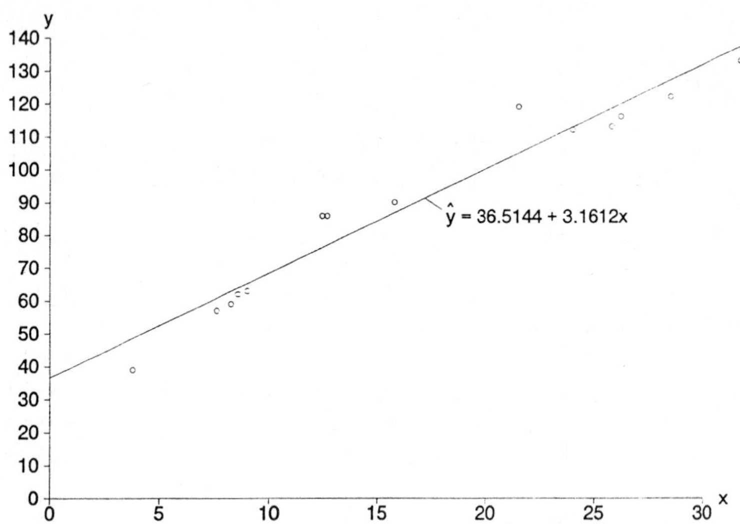


The least squares line fits the data fairly well.

c. Using the least squares line with x = 8,

$$\hat{y} = 36.5144 + 3.1612(8) = 61.8040$$

The price of regular gasoline would fall to approximately 61.80 cents per gallon.

11.17 a.

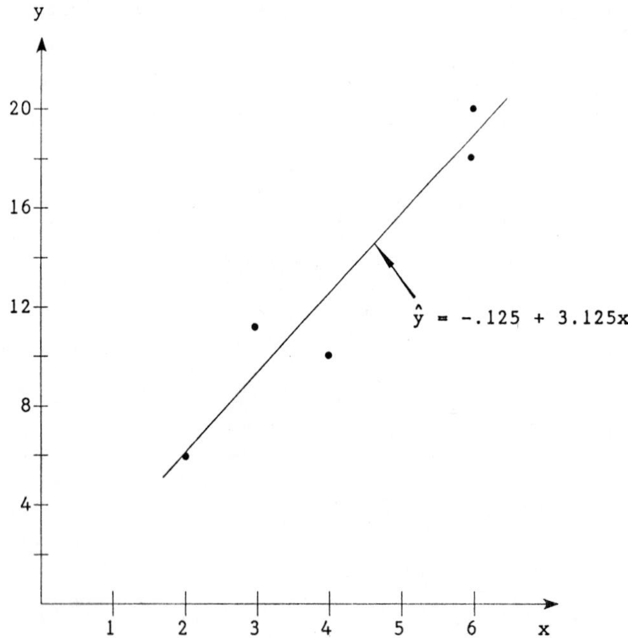

b. $\sum x = 21$ $\quad \sum y = 65$ $\quad \sum xy = 313$ $\quad \sum x^2 = 101$

$$\bar{x} = \frac{\sum x}{n} = \frac{21}{5} = 4.2 \qquad \bar{y} = \frac{\sum y}{n} = \frac{65}{5} = 13$$

$$SS_{xy} = \sum xy - \frac{(\sum x)(\sum y)}{n} = 313 - \frac{21(65)}{5} = 313 - 273 = 40$$

$$SS_{xx} = \sum x^2 - \frac{(\sum x)^2}{n} = 101 - \frac{21^2}{5} = 101 - 88.2 = 12.8$$

$$\hat{\beta}_1 = \frac{SS_{xy}}{SS_{xx}} = \frac{40}{12.8} = 3.125$$

$$\hat{\beta}_0 = \bar{y} - \hat{\beta}_1\bar{x} = 13 - 3.125(4.2) = -.125$$

c. Refer to graph in part (a).

d. $\hat{\beta}_0 = -.125$. The estimated mean number of cars sold when 0 salespeople are on duty is $-.125$. This is not meaningful because $x = 0$ is not in the observed range.

$\hat{\beta}_1 = 3.125$. For every additional salesperson on duty, it is estimated that the mean number of cars sold will increase by 3.125. This is true for values of x between 2 and 6.

e. Using the least squares line with $x = 5$,

$$\begin{aligned}\hat{y} &= -.125 + 3.125(5) \\ &= 15.5\end{aligned}$$

11.19 a. $$\hat{\beta}_1 = \frac{SS_{xy}}{SS_{xx}} = \frac{-2,393.3333}{9,043.3333} = -.26465$$

$$\begin{aligned}\hat{\beta}_0 = \bar{y} - \hat{\beta}_1\bar{x} &= 36.6667 - (-.26465)(364.3333) \\ &= 36.6667 + 96.4208 \\ &= 133.0875\end{aligned}$$

The least squares line is $\hat{y} = 133.09 - .265x$

b.

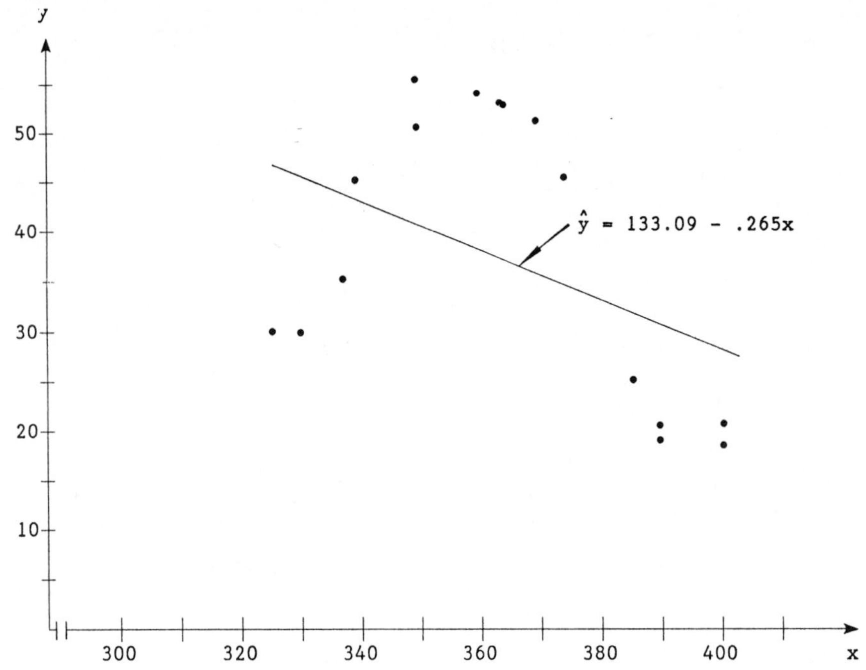

$\hat{y} = 133.09 - .265x$

Note: The line goes through the data but the scattergram does not look linear.

c. $\hat{\beta}_0 = 133.09$. The estimated mean number of TV sets sold is 133.09 when priced at \$0. This is not meaningful because x = 0 is not in the observed range.

$\hat{\beta}_1 = -.265$. For each additional \$1 in price, it is estimated that the mean number of TV sets sold will decrease by .265. This is meaningful for x in the range of \$325 to \$400.

11.21 a.

$$SSE = SS_{yy} - \hat{\beta}_1 SS_{xy}$$
$$= 95 - .75(50)$$
$$= 57.5$$

$$s^2 = \frac{SSE}{n - 2} = \frac{57.5}{18 - 2} = 3.59375$$

b.

$$SS_{yy} = \sum y^2 - \frac{(\sum y)^2}{n} = 860 - \frac{50^2}{35} = 788.57143$$

$$SSE = SS_{yy} - \hat{\beta}_1 SS_{xy}$$
$$= 788.57143 - .2(2700)$$
$$= 248.57143$$

$$s^2 = \frac{SSE}{n - 2} = \frac{248.57143}{35 - 2} = 7.53247$$

c. $SS_{yy} = \sum(y_i - \bar{y})^2 = 58$

$$\hat{\beta}_1 = \frac{SS_{xy}}{SS_{xx}} = \frac{91}{170} = .535294$$

$$SSE = SS_{yy} - \hat{\beta}_1 SS_{xy}$$

$$= 58 - .535294(91)$$

$$= 9.2882$$

$$s^2 = \frac{SSE}{n - 2} = \frac{9.2882}{20 - 2} = .5160$$

11.23 Scattergram (c) would have the smallest variance since the data are not as spread out as in the other two scattergrams.

11.25 From Exercise 11.15, $\sum y = 1257$, $\sum y^2 = 124{,}459$, $n = 14$, and $SS_{xy} = 3{,}472.62429$

a. $SS_{yy} = \sum y^2 - \frac{(\sum y)^2}{n} = 124{,}459 - \frac{1257^2}{14}$

$$= 124{,}459 - 112{,}860.6429$$
$$= 11{,}598.3571$$

$$SSE = SS_{yy} - \hat{\beta}_1 SS_{xy}$$

$$= 11{,}598.3571 - 3.1612(3{,}472.62429)$$
$$= 11{,}598.3571 - 10{,}977.6599$$
$$= 620.6972$$

$$s^2 = \frac{SSE}{n - 2} = \frac{620.6972}{14 - 2} = 51.7248$$

$$s = \sqrt{s^2} = 7.192$$

b. The least squares line is $\hat{y} = 36.514 + 3.1612x$.

When $x = 15$,

Estimate of $E(y) = \hat{y} = 36.514 + 3.1612(15) = 83.932$ cents

Standard deviation of $\varepsilon$ = standard deviation of $y$

Estimate of $\sigma = s = 7.192$ cents (Refer to part (a).)

c. When $x = 30$,

Estimate of $E(y) = \hat{y} = 36.514 + 3.1612(30) = 131.35$ cents or \$1.3135

The average price of gasoline is \$1.3135.

Standard deviation of $\varepsilon$ = standard deviation of $y$

Estimate of $\sigma = s = 7.192$ cents (Refer to part (a).)

d. The necessary assumptions are:

1. The mean of the probability distribution of $\varepsilon$ is 0.
2. The variance of the probability distribution of $\varepsilon$ is constant for all values of the independent variables, x.
3. The probability distribution of $\varepsilon$ is normal.
4. The errors associated with any two different observations are independent.

11.27 a. $\hat{\beta}_1 = \frac{SS_{xy}}{SS_{xx}} = \frac{236.5}{21,752} = .01087$

$\hat{\beta}_0 = \bar{y} - \hat{\beta}_1\bar{x} = 22.5 - .01087(332) = 18.89$

The least squares line is $\hat{y} = 18.89 + .01087x$.

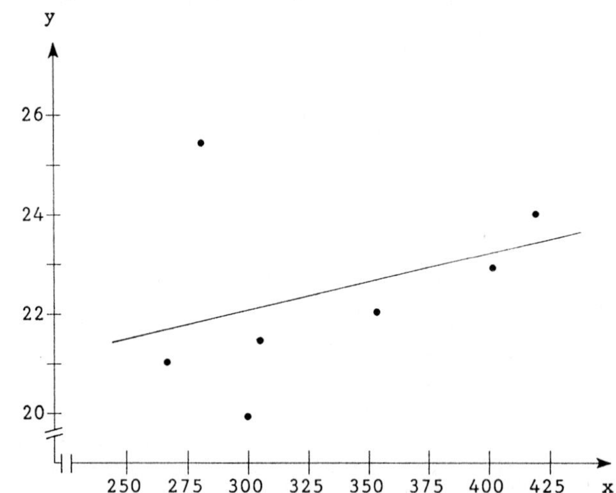


Note: The data point (279, 25.5) does not seem to fit the rest of the data. As a result, the least squares line is pulled up to minimize the sum of the squared errors. This point should be investigated.

b. When x = 400,

$$\hat{y} = 18.89 + .01087(400) = 23.238 \approx 23.24 \text{ years}$$

c. $SS_{yy} = \sum y^2 - \frac{(\sum y)^2}{n} = 3,565.75 - \frac{157.5)^2}{7} = 22$

$SSE = SS_{yy} - \hat{\beta}_1 SS_{xy} = 22 - .01087(236.5) = 19.43$

$s^2 = \frac{SSE}{n - 2} = \frac{19.43}{7 - 2} = 3.886$

d. The standard deviation s represents the spread of the life lengths about the least squares line. Approximately 95% of the life lengths of the horses should lie within $2s = 2\sqrt{3.886} = 3.943$ years of the least squares line.

11.29 a. For confidence coefficient .95, $\alpha = 1 - .95 = .05$ and $\alpha/2 = .05/2 = .025$. From Table VI, Appendix B, with $df = n - 2 = 10 - 2 = 8$, $t_{.025} = 2.306$.

The 95% confidence interval for $\beta_1$ is:

$$\hat{\beta}_1 \pm t_{.025} s_{\hat{\beta}_1} \text{ where } s_{\hat{\beta}_1} = \frac{s}{\sqrt{SS_{xx}}} = \frac{3}{\sqrt{35}} = .5071$$

$$\Rightarrow 31 \pm 2.306(.5071) \Rightarrow 31 \pm 1.17 \Rightarrow (29.83, 32.17)$$

For confidence coefficient .90, $\alpha = 1 - .90 = .10$ and $\alpha/2 = .10/2 = .05$. From Table VI, Appendix B, with df = 8, $t_{.05} = 1.860$.

The 90% confidence interval for $\beta_1$ is:

$$\hat{\beta}_1 \pm t_{.05} s_{\hat{\beta}_1}$$

$$\Rightarrow 31 \pm 1.860(.5071) \Rightarrow 31 \pm .94 \Rightarrow (30.06, 31.94)$$

b. $$s^2 = \frac{SSE}{n - 2} = \frac{1,960}{14 - 2} = 163.3333, \quad s = \sqrt{s^2} = 12.7802$$

For confidence coefficient .95, $\alpha = 1 - .95 = .05$ and $\alpha/2 = .05/2 = .025$. From Table VI, Appendix B, with $df = n - 2 = 14 - 2 = 12$, $t_{.025} = 2.179$. The 95% confidence interval for $\beta_1$ is:

$$\hat{\beta}_1 \pm t_{.025} s_{\hat{\beta}_1} \text{ where } s_{\hat{\beta}_1} = \frac{s}{\sqrt{SS_{xx}}} = \frac{12.7802}{\sqrt{30}} = 2.3333$$

$$\Rightarrow 64 \pm 2.179(2.3333) \Rightarrow 64 \pm 5.08 \Rightarrow (58.92, 69.08)$$

For confidence coefficient .90, $\alpha = 1 - .90 = .10$ and $\alpha/2 = .10/2 = .05$. From Table VI, Appendix B, with df = 12, $t_{.05} = 1.782$.

The 90% confidence interval for $\beta_1$ is:

$$\hat{\beta}_1 \pm t_{.05} s_{\hat{\beta}_1}$$

$$\Rightarrow 64 \pm 1.782(2.3333) \Rightarrow 64 \pm 4.16 \Rightarrow (59.84, 68.16)$$

c. $s^2 = \frac{SSE}{n - 2} = \frac{146}{20 - 2} = 8.1111$, $s = \sqrt{s^2} = 2.848$

For confidence coefficient .95, $\alpha = 1 - .95 = .05$ and $\alpha/2 = .05/2 = .025$. From Table VI, Appendix B, with $df = n - 2 = 20 - 2 = 18$, $t_{.025} = 2.776$. The 95% confidence interval for $\beta_1$ is:

$$\hat{\beta}_1 \pm t_{.025} s_{\hat{\beta}_1} \text{ where } s_{\hat{\beta}_1} = \frac{s}{\sqrt{SS_{xx}}} = \frac{2.848}{\sqrt{64}} = .356$$

$$\Rightarrow -8.4 \pm 2.101(.356) \Rightarrow -8.4 \pm .75 \Rightarrow (-9.15, -7.65)$$

For confidence coefficient .90, $\alpha = 1 - .90 = .10$ and $\alpha/2 = .10/2 = .05$. From Table VI, Appendix B, with df = 18, $t_{.05} = 1.734$.

The 90% confidence interval for $\beta_1$ is:

$$\hat{\beta}_1 \pm t_{.05} s_{\hat{\beta}_1}$$

$$\Rightarrow -8.4 \pm 1.734(.356) \Rightarrow -8.4 \pm .62 \Rightarrow (-9.02, -7.78)$$

11.31 From Exercise 11.30, $\hat{\beta}_1 = .8214$, $s = 1.1922$, $SS_{xx} = 28$, and $n = 7$.

For confidence coefficient .80, $\alpha = 1 - .80 = .20$ and $\alpha/2 = .20/2 = .10$. From Table VI, Appendix B, with $df = n - 2 = 7 - 2 = 5$, $t_{.10} = 1.476$. The 80% confidence interval for $\beta_1$ is:

$$\hat{\beta}_1 \pm t_{.10} s_{\hat{\beta}_1} \text{ where } s_{\hat{\beta}_1} = \frac{s}{\sqrt{SS_{xx}}} = \frac{1.1922}{\sqrt{28}} = .2253$$

$$\Rightarrow .8214 \pm 1.476(.2253) \Rightarrow .8214 \pm .3325 \Rightarrow (.4889, 1.1539)$$

For confidence coefficient .98, $\alpha = 1 - .98 = .02$ and $\alpha/2 = .02/2 = .01$. From Table VI, Appendix B, with df = 5, $t_{.01} = 3.365$.

The 98% confidence interval for $\beta_1$ is:

$$\hat{\beta}_1 \pm t_{.01} s_{\hat{\beta}_1}$$

$$\Rightarrow .8214 \pm 3.365(.2253) \Rightarrow .8214 \pm .7581 \Rightarrow (.0633, 1.5795)$$

11.33 a. For n = 100, df = n - 2 = 100 - 2 = 98. From Table VI with df = 98, p-value = $2P(t \geq 6.572) < 2(.0005) = .0010$. Since this p-value is very small, we would reject $H_0$. There is sufficient evidence to indicate the slope is not 0. Thus, there is evidence to indicate sales price and square feet of living space are linearly related.

11.39 Some preliminary calculations are:

$$\sum x_i = 206 \qquad \sum x_i^2 = 7590 \qquad \sum x_i y_i = 47{,}035$$

$$\sum y_i = 1285 \qquad \sum y_i^2 = 292{,}211$$

$$SS_{xy} = \sum x_i y_i - \frac{\sum x_i \sum y_i}{n} = 47{,}035 - \frac{206(1285)}{6} = 2916.6667$$

$$SS_{xx} = \sum x_i^2 - \frac{(\sum x_i)^2}{n} = 7590 - \frac{206^2}{6} = 517.3333$$

$$SS_{yy} = \sum y_i^2 - \frac{(\sum y_i)^2}{n} = 292{,}211 - \frac{1285^2}{6} = 17006.8333$$

$$\hat{\beta}_1 = \frac{SS_{xy}}{SS_{xx}} = \frac{2916.6667}{517.3333} = 5.637887$$

$$SSE = SS_{yy} - \hat{\beta}_1 SS_{xy} = 17006.8333 - 5.637887(2916.6667)$$

$$= 562.99567$$

$$s^2 = \frac{SSE}{n - 2} = \frac{562.99567}{6 - 2} = 140.74891 \qquad s = \sqrt{140.74891} = 11.8638$$

The confidence interval for $\beta_1$ is

$$\hat{\beta}_1 \pm t_{\alpha/2} s_{\hat{\beta}_1} \quad \text{where } s_{\hat{\beta}_1} = \frac{s}{\sqrt{SS_{xx}}} = \frac{11.8638}{\sqrt{517.3333}} = .5216$$

For confidence coefficient .95, $\alpha = 1 - .95 = .05$ and $\alpha/2 = .05/2 = .025$. From Table VI, Appendix B, with df $= n - 2 = 6 - 2 = 4$, $t_{.025} = 2.776$. The 95% confidence interval is

$$5.638 \pm 2.776(.5216) \Rightarrow 5.638 \pm 1.448 \Rightarrow (4.190,\ 7.086)$$

11.41 a. $$\sigma_{\hat{\beta}} = \frac{\sigma}{\sqrt{SS_{xx}}} = \frac{\sigma}{\sqrt{\sum(x_i - \bar{x})^2}}$$

If there is a lot of variability in the independent variable, $\sigma_{\hat{\beta}}$ will be small. If there is little variability in the independent variable, $\sigma_{\hat{\beta}}$ will be large.

b. We would want to pick display areas that cover a wide range. This will force $\sum(x_i - \bar{x})^2$ to be large and $\sigma_{\hat{\beta}}$ to be small.

11.43 a. Some preliminary calculations are:

$\sum x_i = 750$ $\sum x_i^2 = 47,750$ $\sum x_i y_i = 24,282.5$

$\sum y_i = 390.4$ $\sum y_i^2 = 12,725.68$

$$SS_{xy} = \sum x_i y_i - \frac{\sum x_i \sum y_i}{n} = 24282.5 - \frac{750(390.4)}{12} = -117.5$$

$$SS_{xx} = \sum x_i^2 - \frac{(\sum x_i)^2}{n} = 47750 - \frac{750^2}{12} = 875$$

$$SS_{yy} = \sum y_i^2 - \frac{(\sum y_i)^2}{n} = 12,725.68 - \frac{390.4^2}{12} = 24.66667$$

$$\hat{\beta}_1 = \frac{SS_{xy}}{SS_{xx}} = \frac{-117.5}{875} = -.1342857$$

$$\hat{\beta}_0 = \bar{y} - \hat{\beta}_1\bar{x} = \frac{390.4}{12} - (-.1342857)\left(\frac{750}{12}\right) = 32.533333 + 8.3928571$$
$$= 40.92619$$

$$SSE = SS_{yy} - \hat{\beta}_1 SS_{xy} = 24.66667 - (-.1342857)(-117.5) = 8.8881$$

$$s^2 = \frac{SSE}{n - 2} = \frac{8.8881}{12 - 2} = .88881, \quad s = \sqrt{.88881} = .94277$$

The fitted line is $\hat{y} = 40.926 - .1343x$

b. To determine if a straight-line model provides useful information about the relationship between gasoline consumption and speed, we test:

$H_0$: $\beta_1 = 0$
$H_a$: $\beta_1 \neq 0$

The test statistic is $t = \dfrac{\hat{\beta}_1 - 0}{s_{\hat{\beta}_1}} = \dfrac{-.1342857}{\frac{.94277}{\sqrt{875}}} = \dfrac{-.1342857}{.03187}$

$= -4.21$

The rejection region requires $\alpha/2 = .05/2 = .025$ in each tail of the t distribution with df $= n - 2 = 12 - 2 = 10$. From Table VI, Appendix B, $t_{.025} = 2.228$. The rejection region is $t > 2.228$ or $t < -2.228$.

Since the observed value of the test statistic falls in the rejection region ($t = -4.21 < -2.228$), $H_0$ is rejected. There is sufficient evidence to indicate the straight-line model provides useful information about the relationship between gasoline consumption and speed at $\alpha = .05$.

c. The form of the confidence interval for $\beta_1$ is

$$\hat{\beta}_1 \pm t_{\alpha/2} s_{\hat{\beta}_1} \quad \text{where } s_{\hat{\beta}_1} = \frac{s}{\sqrt{SS_{xx}}} = \frac{.94277}{\sqrt{875}} = .03187$$

For confidence coefficient .90, $\alpha = 1 - .90 = .10$ and $\alpha/2 = .10/2 = .05$. From Table VI, Appendix B, $t_{.05} = 1.812$ with df = n - 2 = 12 - 2 = 10. The confidence interval is

$$-.1343 \pm 1.812(.03187) \Rightarrow -.1343 \pm .0577 \Rightarrow (-.1920, -.0766)$$

We are 90% confident the change in mean miles per gallon for each additional mile per hour is between -.1920 and -.0766.

11.45 a. If r = .7, there is a positive relationship between x and y. As x increases, y tends to increase.

b. If r = -.7, there is a negative relationship between x and y. As x increases, y tends to decrease.

c. If r = 0, there is a 0 slope. There is no relationship between x and y.

d. If $r^2 = .64$, then r is either .8 or -.8. The relationship between x and y could be either positive or negative.

11.47 a. From Exercises 11.9 and 11.22,

$$r^2 = 1 - \frac{SSE}{SS_{yy}} = 1 - \frac{1.2203662}{21.714286} = 1 - .0562 = .9438$$

94.38% of the sample variability around $\bar{y}$ is explained by the linear relationship between y and x.

b. From Exercises 11.12 and 11.22,

$$r^2 = 1 - \frac{SSE}{SS_{yy}} = 1 - \frac{5.1348681}{41.714286} = .877$$

87.7% of the sample variability around $\bar{y}$ is explained by the linear relationship between y and x.

c. From Exercise 11.30,

$$r^2 = 1 - \frac{SSE}{SS_{yy}} = 1 - \frac{7.1071422}{26} = 1 - .273 = .727$$

72.7% of the sample variability around $\bar{y}$ is explained by the linear relationship between y and x.

11.49 $r = \frac{SS_{xy}}{\sqrt{SS_{xx}SS_{yy}}} = \frac{49,153.00}{\sqrt{13,143,088(1,552,011.334)}} = .0109$

The relationship between x and y is positive because $r > 0$. However, because $r = .0109$ is very close to 0, the relationship between gross national product and new housing starts is very weak.

$r^2 = (.0109)^2 = .0001$

.01% of the sample variability around the sample mean new housing starts is explained by the linear relationship between new housing starts and GNP.

11.51 a. From Exercise 11.18, $SS_{xy} = .6972857$, $SS_{xx} = .001334857$

$$SS_{yy} = \sum y_i^2 - \frac{(\sum y_i)^2}{n} = 92,703 - \frac{1133^2}{14} = 1010.92857$$

$$r = \frac{SS_{xy}}{\sqrt{SS_{xx}SS_{yy}}} = \frac{.6972857}{\sqrt{.001334857(1010.92857)}} = .600$$

The relationship between number of games won and team batting average is positive since $r > 0$. The relationship is not particularly strong because .6 is not that close to 1.

$r^2 = .600^2 = .360$

36.0% of the sample variability around the sample mean number of games won is explained by the linear relationship between number of games won and team batting average.

b. To determine if a correlation exists, we test:

$H_0$: $\rho = 0$
$H_a$: $\rho \neq 0$

The test statistic is $t = \frac{r}{\sqrt{(1 - r^2)/(n - 2)}} = \frac{.600}{\sqrt{(1 - .36)/(14 - 2)}}$
$= 2.60$

The rejection region requires $\alpha/2 = .05/2 = .025$ in each tail of the t distribution with df $= n - 2 = 14 - 2 = 12$. From Table VI, Appendix B, $t_{.025} = 2.179$. The rejection region is $t > 2.179$ or $t < -2.179$.

Since the observed value of the test statistic falls in the rejection region ($t = 2.60 > 2.179$), $H_0$ is rejected. There is sufficient evidence to indicate a correlation exists between number of games and team batting average at $\alpha = .05$.

11.53 a.

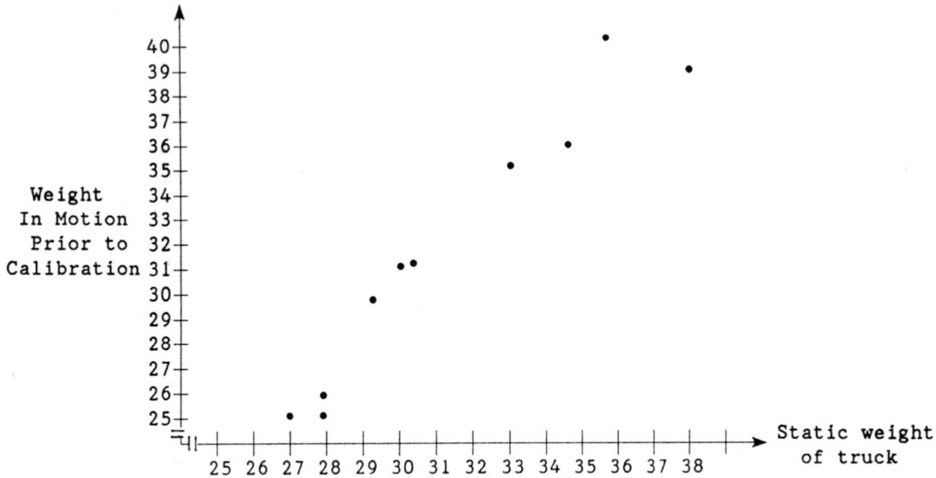


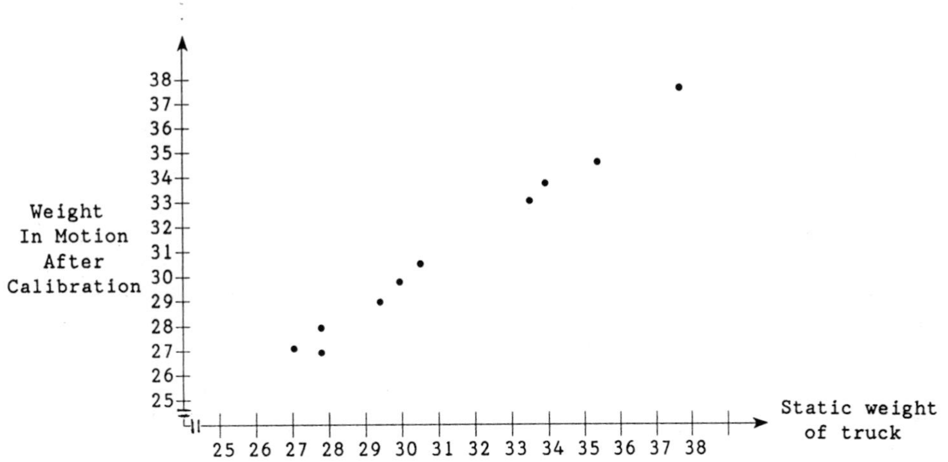


b. We note there is a much stronger linear relationship after calibration than prior, because the points fall closer to a straight line.

c. Some preliminary calculations are:

$\sum x_i = 312.8$ $\quad \sum y_{i1} = 320.2$ $\quad \sum x_i y_{i1} = 10201.41$ $\quad \sum y_{i2} = 311.2$

$\sum x_i^2 = 9911.42$ $\quad \sum y_{i1}^2 = 10543.68$ $\quad \sum x_i y_{i2} = 9859.84$ $\quad \sum y_{i2}^2 = 9809.52$

$$SS_{xy_1} = \sum x_i y_{i1} - \frac{\sum x_i \sum y_{i1}}{n} = 10201.41 - \frac{312.8(320.2)}{10} = 185.554$$

$$SS_{xx} = \sum x_i^2 - \frac{(\sum x_i)^2}{n} = 9911.42 - \frac{312.8^2}{10} = 127.036$$

$$SS_{y_1y_1} = \sum y_{i1}^2 - \frac{(\sum y_{i_1})^2}{n} = 10543.68 - \frac{320.2^2}{10} = 290.876$$

$$SS_{xy_2} = \sum x_i y_{i2} - \frac{\sum x_i \sum y_{i_2}}{n} = 9859.84 - \frac{312.8(311.2)}{14} = 125.504$$

$$SS_{y_2y_2} = \sum y_{i2}^2 - \frac{(\sum y_{i_2})^2}{n} = 9809.52 - \frac{311.2^2}{14} = 124.976$$

For prior adjustment,

$$r = \frac{SS_{xy_1}}{\sqrt{SS_{xx}SS_{y_1y_1}}} = \frac{185.554}{\sqrt{127.036(290.876)}} = .965$$

The correlation between weight and weight-in-motion prior to adjustment is .965. This relationship is positive since $r > 0$. Since $r = .965$ is close to 1, the relationship is very strong.

For after adjustment,

$$r = \frac{SS_{xy_2}}{\sqrt{SS_{xx}SS_{y_2y_2}}} = \frac{125.504}{\sqrt{127.036(124.976)}} = .996$$

The correlation between weight and weight-in-motion after adjustment is .996. This relationship is positive since $r > 0$. Since $r = .996$ is almost 1, the relationship is almost a perfect relationship.

d. Yes, it could happen. If the difference between the static weights and weight-in-motion readings was constant for every pair, the correlation would be 1.

11.55 a. Some preliminary calculations are:

$\sum x_i = 10,166$ $\sum x_i^2 = 37,987,830$ $\sum x_i y_i = 45,986,410$

$\sum y_i = 10,595$ $\sum y_i^2 = 57,142,963$

$$SS_{xy} = \sum x_i y_i - \frac{\sum x_i \sum y_i}{n} = 45,986,410 - \frac{10166(10595)}{10} = 35,215,533$$

$$SS_{xx} = \sum x_i^2 - \frac{(\sum x_i)^2}{n} = 37,987,830 - \frac{10166^2}{10} = 27,653,074.4$$

$$SS_{yy} = \sum y_i^2 - \frac{(\sum y_i)^2}{n} = 57{,}142{,}963 - \frac{10595^2}{10} = 45{,}917{,}560.5$$

$$\hat{\beta}_1 = \frac{SS_{xy}}{SS_{xx}} = \frac{35{,}215{,}533}{27{,}653{,}074.4} = 1.273476232$$

$$\hat{\beta}_0 = \bar{y} - \hat{\beta}_1\bar{x} = \frac{10595}{10} - (1.273476232)\left(\frac{10166}{10}\right) = -235.115937$$

$$SSE = SS_{yy} - \hat{\beta}_1 SS_{xy} = 45{,}917{,}560.5 - 1.273476232(35{,}215{,}533)$$
$$= 1{,}071{,}416.23$$

$$s^2 = \frac{SSE}{n-2} = \frac{1071416.23}{10-2} = 133927.0288$$

$$s = \sqrt{133927.0288} = 365.9604$$

The fitted line is $\hat{y} = -235.1 + 1.273x_2$

b. To determine if the number of arrests increase as the number of law enforcement employees increase, we test:

$H_0$: $\beta_1 = 0$
$H_a$: $\beta_1 > 0$

The test statistic is $t = \dfrac{\hat{\beta}_1 - 0}{s_{\hat{\beta}_1}} = \dfrac{1.2735}{\frac{365.9604}{\sqrt{27653074.4}}} = \dfrac{1.2735}{.06959} = 18.30$

The rejection region requires $\alpha/2 = .05$ in the upper tail of the t distribution with df = n - 2 = 10 - 2 = 8. From Table VI, Appendix B, $t_{.05} = 1.860$. The rejection region is $t > 1.860$.

Since the observed value of the test statistic falls in the rejection region ($t = 18.30 > 1.860$), $H_0$ is rejected. There is sufficient evidence to indicate that as the number of law enforcement employees increases, the number of arrests increases at $\alpha = .05$.

c. $r^2 = 1 - \dfrac{SSE}{SS_{yy}} = 1 - \dfrac{1{,}071{,}416.23}{45{,}917{,}560.5} = .977$

97.7% of the variability in the number of arrests is explained by the linear relationship between number of arrests and number of law enforcement employees.

d. SSE from Exercise 11.54 is 19,082,078.13. SSE from Exercise 11.55 is 1,071,416.23. Thus, SSE from Exercise 11.55 is smaller.

e. $r^2 = .584$ from Exercise 11.54; $r^2 = .977$ from Exercise 11.55. Thus, $x_2$ explains more of the variation in y because its $r^2$ is larger.

11.57 Some preliminary calculations are

$\sum x_i = 230$ $\sum x_i^2 = 12150$ $\sum x_i y_i = 9850$

$\sum y_i = 215$ $\sum y_i^2 = 12781$

$$SS_{xy} = \sum x_i y_i - \frac{\sum x_i \sum y_i}{n} = 9850 - \frac{230(215)}{5} = -40$$

$$SS_{xx} = \sum x_i^2 - \frac{(\sum x_i)^2}{n} = 12150 - \frac{230^2}{5} = 1570$$

$$SS_{yy} = \sum y_i^2 - \frac{(\sum y_i)^2}{n} = 12781 - \frac{215^2}{5} = 3536$$

$$\hat{\beta}_1 = \frac{SS_{xy}}{SS_{xx}} = \frac{-40}{1570} = -.025477707$$

$$\hat{\beta}_0 = \bar{y} - \hat{\beta}_1\bar{x} = \frac{215}{5} - (-.025477707)\left(\frac{230}{5}\right) = 44.17197452$$

$$SSE = SS_{yy} - \hat{\beta}_1 SS_{xy} = 3536 - (-.025477707)(-40) = 3534.980892$$

$$s^2 = \frac{SSE}{n-2} = \frac{3534.980892}{5-2} = 1178.326964$$

$$s = \sqrt{1178.326964} = 34.3268$$

a. The fitted line is $\hat{y} = 44.17 - .0255x$

b.

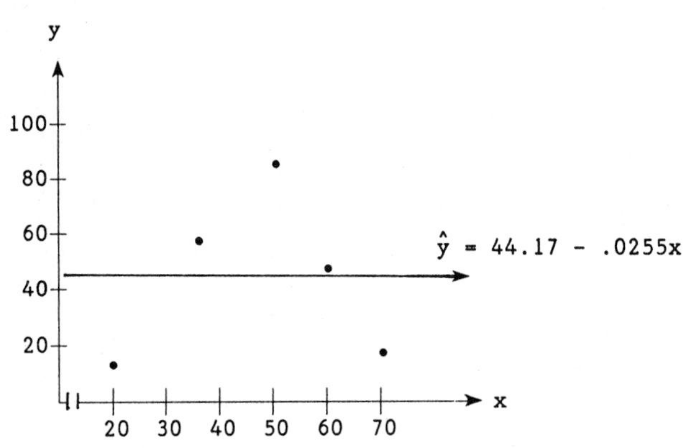

c. $H_0$: $\beta_1 = 0$
$H_a$: $\beta_1 \neq 0$

The test statistic is $t = \dfrac{\hat{\beta}_1 - 0}{s_{\hat{\beta}_1}} = \dfrac{-.0255}{\dfrac{34.3268}{\sqrt{1570}}} = -.03$

The rejection region requires $\alpha/2 = .05/2 = .025$ in each tail of the t distribution with df = n - 2 = 5 - 2 = 3. From Table VI, Appendix B, $t_{.025} = 3.182$. The rejection region is $t > 3.182$ or $t < -3.182$.

Since the observed value of the test statistic does not fall in the rejection region ($t = -.03 \not< -3.182$), $H_0$ is not rejected. There is insufficient evidence to indicate the number of tires sold and tire price are linearly related.

d. No. It implies tire price and number of tires sold are not <u>linearly</u> related.

e. $r^2 = 1 - \dfrac{SSE}{SS_{yy}} = 1 - \dfrac{3534.980892}{3536} = .0003$

.03% of the sample variability in the number of tires sold is explained by the linear relationship between number of tires sold and tire price.

11.59 a.

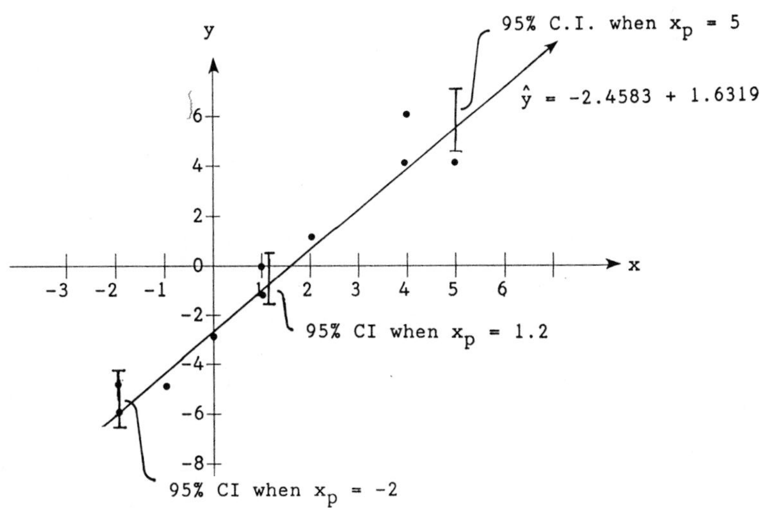

c. The form of the confidence interval is

$$\hat{y} \pm t_{\alpha/2}\, s\sqrt{\frac{1}{n} + \frac{(x_p - \bar{x})^2}{SS_{xx}}}$$

where $s = \sqrt{\frac{SSE}{n-2}} = \sqrt{\frac{SS_{yy} - \hat{\beta}_1 SS_{xy}}{n-2}} = \sqrt{\frac{162.5 - 1.6319(94)}{10-2}}$

$= 1.0666$

$\hat{y} = -2.4583 + 1.6319(5) = 5.7012$ and $\bar{x} = \frac{\sum x}{n} = \frac{12}{10} = 1.2$

For confidence coefficient .95, $\alpha = 1 - .95 = .05$ and $\alpha/2 = .05/2 = .025$. From Table VI, Appendix $\beta$, $t_{.025} = 2.036$ with df $= n - 2 = 10 - 2 = 8$. The 95% confidence interval is:

$$5.7012 \pm 2.306(1.0666)\sqrt{\frac{1}{10} + \frac{(5 - 1.2)^2}{57.6}}$$

$\Rightarrow 5.7012 \pm 1.4565 \Rightarrow (4.2447, 7.1577)$

d. For $x_p = 1.2$, $\hat{y} = -2.4583 + 1.6319(1.2) = -.5000$

The 95% confidence interval is

$$-.5000 \pm 2.306(1.0666)\sqrt{\frac{1}{10} + \frac{(1.2 - 1.2)^2}{57.6}}$$

$\Rightarrow -.5000 \pm .7778 \Rightarrow (-1.2778, .2778)$

For $x_p = -2$, $\hat{y} = -2.4583 + 1.6319(-2) = -5.7221$

The 95% confidence interval is

$$-5.7222 \pm 2.306(1.0666)\sqrt{\frac{1}{10} + \frac{(-2 - 1.2)^2}{57.6}}$$

$\Rightarrow -5.7222 \pm 1.2963 \Rightarrow (-7.0185, -4.4259)$

e. When $x_p = 5$, the width of the confidence interval is $7.1577 - 4.2447 = 2.913$.

When $x_p = 1.2$, the width of the confidence interval is $.2778 - (-1.2778) = 1.5556$.

When $x_p = -2$, the width of the confidence interval is $-4.4259 - (-7.0185) = 2.5926$.

The smallest interval will always be when $x_p = \bar{x}$. In this case, $\bar{x} = 1.2$, so the smallest interval is the one for $x_p = 1.2$ and has a width of 1.5556. The further $x_p$ is from $\bar{x}$, the larger the interval width will be. This is reflected in this problem.

11.61 a. $\hat{\beta}_1 = \frac{SS_{xy}}{SS_{xx}} = \frac{20}{25} = .8$

$\hat{\beta}_0 = \bar{y} - \hat{\beta}_1\bar{x} = 3 - .8(2) = 1.4$

The least squares line is $\hat{y} = 1.4 + .8x$

b.

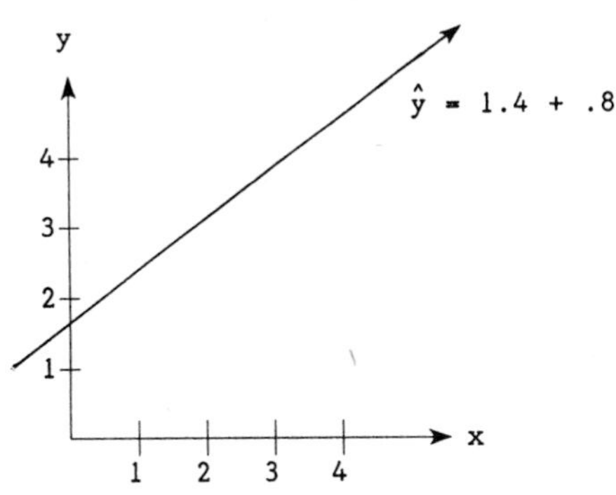


c. $SSE = SS_{yy} - \hat{\beta}_1 SS_{xy} = 17 - .8(20) = 1$

d. $s^2 = \frac{SSE}{n - 2} = \frac{1}{12 - 2} = .1$

e. The form of the confidence interval is

$$\hat{y} \pm t_{\alpha/2}\, s\sqrt{\frac{1}{n} + \frac{(x_p - \bar{x})^2}{SS_{xx}}}$$

where $\hat{y} = 1.4 + .8(1) = 2.2$

For confidence coefficient .95, $\alpha = 1 - .95 = .05$ and $\alpha/2 = .05/2 = .025$. From Table VI, Appendix B, $t_{.025} = 2.228$ with df = n - 2 = 10 - 2 = 8.

The confidence interval is

$$2.2 \pm 2.228\sqrt{.1}\sqrt{\frac{1}{12} + \frac{(1 - 2)^2}{25}} \Rightarrow 2.2 \pm .247 \Rightarrow (1.953, 2.447)$$

f. The form of the prediction interval is

$$\hat{y} \pm t_{\alpha/2}\, s\sqrt{1 + \frac{1}{n} + \frac{(x_p - \bar{x})^2}{SS_{xx}}}$$

where $\hat{y} = 1.4 + .8(1.5) = 2.6$

The prediction interval is

$$2.6 \pm 2.228\sqrt{.1}\sqrt{1 + \frac{1}{12} + \frac{(1.5 - 2)^2}{25}} \Rightarrow 2.6 \pm .737$$

$$\Rightarrow (1.863, 3.337)$$

11.63 From Exercise 11.15, the least squares line is $\hat{y} = 36.514 + 3.1612x$

$\bar{x} = 16.8514$

$SS_{xy} = 3472.624 \qquad SS_{xx} = 1098.500771 \qquad SS_{yy} = 11,598.3571$

$SSE = SS_{yy} - \hat{\beta}_1 SS_{xy} = 11,598.3571 - 3.1612(3472.62429) = 620.6972$

$s^2 = \frac{SSE}{n - 2} = \frac{620.6972}{14 - 2} = 51.7248 \qquad s = \sqrt{51.7248} = 7.192$

For confidence coefficient .95, $\alpha = 1 - .95 = .05$ and $\alpha/2 = .05/2 = .025$. From Table VI, Appendix B, $t_{.025} = 2.179$ with df $= n - 2 = 14 - 2 = 12$. The confidence interval is

$\hat{y} \pm t_{\alpha/2}\, s\sqrt{\frac{1}{n} + \frac{(x_p - \bar{x})^2}{SS_{xx}}}$ where $\hat{y} = 36.514 + 3.1612(30)$
$= 131.35$

$\Rightarrow 131.35 \pm 2.179(7.192)\sqrt{\frac{1}{14} + \frac{(30 - 16.8514)^2}{1098.500771}}$

$\Rightarrow 131.35 \pm 7.496 \Rightarrow (123.854, 138.846)$

11.65 a. From Exercise 11.24,

| Brand A | | Brand B | |
|---|---|---|---|
| | $\hat{y} = 6.62 - .0727x$ | | $\hat{y} = 9.31 - .1077x$ |
| | $s = 1.211$ | | $s = .610$ |
| | $\bar{x} = 50$ | | $\bar{x} = 50$ |
| | $n = 15$ | | $n = 15$ |
| | $SS_{xx} = 3000$ | | $SS_{xx} = 3000$ |

For $x_p = 45$ and Brand A,
$\hat{y} = 6.62 - .0727(45) = 3.3485$

For $x_p = 45$ and Brand B,
$\hat{y} = 9.31 = .1077(45) = 4.4635$

The form of the confidence interval is

$\hat{y} \pm t_{\alpha/2}\, s\sqrt{\frac{1}{n} + \frac{(x_p - \bar{x})^2}{SS_{xx}}}$

For confidence coefficient .90, $\alpha = 1 - .90 = .10$ and $\alpha/2 = .10/2 = .05$. From Table VI, Appendix B, $t_{.05} = 1.771$ with df $= n - 2 = 15 - 2 = 13$.

For Brand A,

$3.3485 \pm 1.771(1.211)\sqrt{\frac{1}{15} + \frac{(45 - 50)^2}{3000}}$

$\Rightarrow 3.3485 \pm .5873 \Rightarrow (2.7612, 3.9358)$

For Brand B,

$$4.4635 \pm 1.771(.610)\sqrt{\frac{1}{15} + \frac{(45 - 50)^2}{3000}}$$

$\Rightarrow 4.4635 \pm .2959 \Rightarrow (4.1676, 4.7594)$

The width for the confidence interval for Brand B is smaller than that for Brand A because the estimate of the standard deviation (s = .610) is smaller.

b. The form of the prediction interval is

$$\hat{y} \pm t_{\alpha/2}\, s\sqrt{1 + \frac{1}{n} + \frac{(x_p - \bar{x})^2}{SS_{xx}}}$$

For Brand A,

$$3.3485 \pm 1.771(1.211)\sqrt{1 + \frac{1}{15} + \frac{(45 - 50)^2}{3000}}$$

$\Rightarrow 3.3485 \pm 2.2237 \Rightarrow (1.1248, 5.5722)$

For Brand B,

$$4.4635 \pm 1.771(.610)\sqrt{1 + \frac{1}{15} + \frac{(45 - 50)^2}{3000}}$$

$\Rightarrow 4.4635 \pm 1.1201 \Rightarrow (3.3434, 5.5836)$

Again the width of the prediction interval for Brand B is smaller than that for Brand A because the estimate of the standard deviation is smaller. The width of the prediction intervals are always larger than the width of the confidence interval for the mean.

c. For $x_p = 100$ and Brand A,

$\hat{y} = 6.62 - .0727(100) = -.65$

For confidence coefficient .95, $\alpha = 1 - .95 = .05$ and $\alpha/2 = .05/2 = .025$. From Table VI, Appendix B, $t_{.025} = 2.160$ with df = n - 2 = 15 - 2 = 13.

The prediction interval is

$$-.65 \pm 2.160(1.211)\sqrt{1 + \frac{1}{15} + \frac{(100 - 50)^2}{3000}}$$

$\Rightarrow -.65 \pm 3.606 \Rightarrow (-4.256, 2.956)$

We have to assume that the relationship observed between x and y extends to x = 100.

11.67 a.

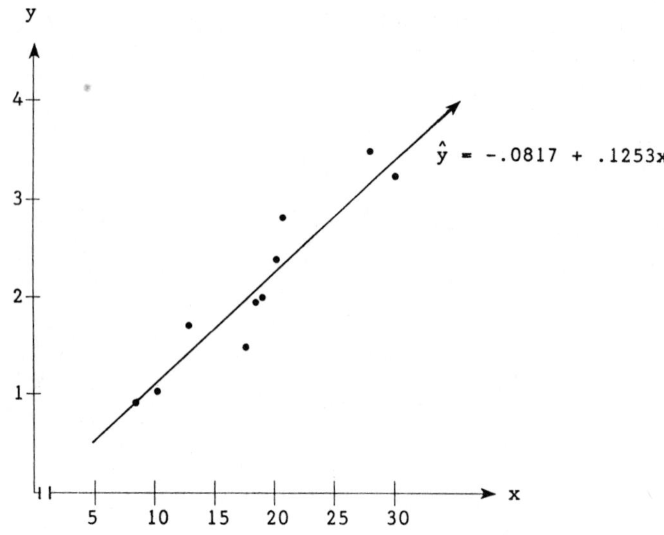


b. Some preliminary calculations are:

$\sum x_i = 180.7$ $\quad\sum x_i^2 = 3696.71$ $\quad\sum x_i y_i = 448.543$

$\sum y_i = 21.83$ $\quad\sum y_i^2 = 55.2359$

$$SS_{xy} = \sum x_i y_i - \frac{\sum x_i \sum y_i}{n} = 448.543 - \frac{(180.7)(21.83)}{10} = 54.0749$$

$$SS_{xx} = \sum x_i^2 - \frac{(\sum x_i)^2}{n} = 3696.71 - \frac{180.7^2}{10} = 431.461$$

$$SS_{yy} = \sum y_i^2 - \frac{(\sum y_i)^2}{n} = 55.2359 - \frac{21.83^2}{10} = 7.58101$$

$$\hat{\beta}_1 = \frac{SS_{xy}}{SS_{xx}} = \frac{54.0749}{431.461} = .125329751$$

$$\hat{\beta}_0 = \bar{y} - \hat{\beta}_1\bar{x} = \frac{21.83}{10} - (.125329751)\left(\frac{180.7}{10}\right) = -.0817086$$

$$SSE = SS_{yy} - \hat{\beta}_1 SS_{xy} = 7.58101 - (.125329751)(54.0749) = .803816$$

$$s^2 = \frac{SSE}{n-2} = \frac{.803816}{10-2} = .100477 \qquad s = \sqrt{.100477} = .31698$$

The least squares line is $\hat{y} = -.0817 + .1253x$

c. To determine if the number of nights stayed in Florida contributes information for the prediction of total quarterly tourist expenditures, we test:

$H_0$: $\beta_1 = 0$
$H_a$: $\beta_1 \neq 0$

The test statistic is $t = \dfrac{\hat{\beta}_1 - 0}{s_{\hat{\beta}_1}} = \dfrac{.1253}{\dfrac{.31698}{\sqrt{431.461}}} = 8.21$

The rejection region requires $\alpha/2 = .05/2 = .025$ in each tail of the t distribution with df = n - 2 = 10 - 2 = 8. From Table VI, Appendix B, $t_{.025} = 2.306$. The rejection region is $t > 2.306$ or $t < -2.306$.

Since the observed value of the test statistic falls in the rejection region ($t = 8.21 > 2.306$), $H_0$ is rejected. There is sufficient evidence to indicate the number of nights stayed in Florida contributes information for the prediction of quarterly tourist expenditures at $\alpha = .05$.

d. $r = \dfrac{SS_{xy}}{\sqrt{SS_{xx}SS_{yy}}} = \dfrac{54.0749}{\sqrt{431.461(7.58101)}} = .9455$

The relationship between number of nights stayed in Florida and quarterly tourist expenditures is positive and very strong since $r > 0$ and r is close to 1.

$r^2 = .9455^2 = .894$

89.4% of the sample variation in total expenditures is explained by the linear relationship between total expenditures and number of nights stayed.

e. For confidence coefficient .90, $\alpha = 1 - .90 = .10$ and $\alpha/2 = .10/2 = .05$. From Table VI, Appendix B, $t_{.05} = 1.860$ with df = n - 2 = 10 - 2 = 8.

For $x_p = 15$, $\hat{y} = -.0817 + .1253(15) = 1.7978$

The confidence interval is

$$\hat{y} \pm t_{\alpha/2}\, s\sqrt{\frac{1}{n} + \frac{(x_p - \bar{x})^2}{SS_{xx}}}$$

$$\Rightarrow 1.7978 \pm 1.860(.31698)\sqrt{\frac{1}{10} + \frac{(15 - 18.07)^2}{431.461}}$$

$$\Rightarrow 1.7978 \pm .2058 \Rightarrow (1.5920,\ 2.0036)$$

f. The prediction interval is

$$\hat{y} \pm t_{\alpha/2} s \sqrt{1 + \frac{1}{n} + \frac{(x_p - \bar{x})^2}{SS_{xx}}}$$

$$\Rightarrow 1.7978 \pm 1.860(.31698)\sqrt{1 + \frac{1}{10} + \frac{(15 - 18.07)^2}{431.461}}$$

$$\Rightarrow 1.7978 \pm .6245 \Rightarrow (1.1733, 2.4223)$$

11.69 a. From the printout,

$\hat{\beta}_0$(INTERCEP) = 44.130454

$\hat{\beta}_1$(SALARY) = .23617

Thus, $\hat{y} = 44.13 + .2366x$

b. s = Root MSE = 19.40375

The estimate standard deviation of managerial success index scores is 19.40375.

c. $r^2$ = R-SQUARE = .0865

8.65% of the sample variability in the managerial success index is explained by the linear relationship between the success index and the number of interactions with outsiders.

d. To determine if the model is useful, we test:

$H_0$: $\beta_1 = 0$
$H_a$: $\beta_1 \neq 0$

The test statistic is t = 1.269

The observed significance level is .2216.

For $\alpha = .05$, the observed significance level is greater than $\alpha$. Therefore, we do not reject $H_0$. There is insufficient evidence to indicate the model is useful for predicting y at $\alpha = .05$.

11.71 a.

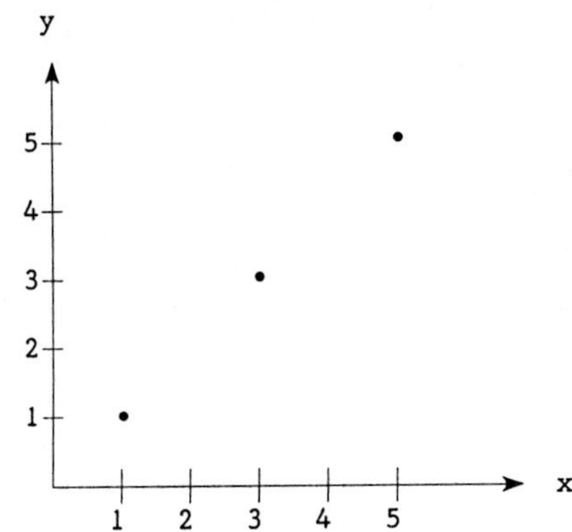


b. One possible line is $\hat{y} = x$.

| x | y | $\hat{y}$ | $y - \hat{y}$ |
|---|---|---|---|
| 1 | 1 | 1 | 0 |
| 3 | 3 | 3 | 0 |
| 5 | 5 | 5 | 0 |
| | | | 0 |

For this example $\sum(y - \hat{y}) = 0$

A second possible line is $\hat{y} = 3$.

| x | y | $\hat{y}$ | $y - \hat{y}$ |
|---|---|---|---|
| 1 | 1 | 3 | -2 |
| 3 | 3 | 3 | 0 |
| 5 | 5 | 3 | 2 |
| | | | 0 |

For this example $\sum(y - \hat{y}) = 0$

c. Some preliminary calculations are:

$\sum x_i = 9$ $\quad \sum x_i^2 = 35$ $\quad \sum x_i y_i = 35$

$\sum y_i = 9$ $\quad \sum y_i^2 = 35$

$$SS_{xy} = \sum x_i y_i - \frac{\sum x_i \sum y_i}{n} = 35 - \frac{9(9)}{3} = 8$$

$$SS_{xx} = \sum x_i^2 - \frac{(\sum x_i)^2}{n} = 35 - \frac{9^2}{3} = 8$$

$$SS_{yy} = \sum y_i^2 - \frac{(\sum y_i)^2}{n} = 35 - \frac{9^2}{3} = 8$$

$$\hat{\beta}_1 = \frac{SS_{xy}}{SS_{xx}} = \frac{8}{8} = 1 \qquad \hat{\beta}_0 = \bar{y} - \hat{\beta}_1\bar{x} = \frac{9}{3} - 1\left(\frac{9}{3}\right) = 0$$

The least squares line is $\hat{y} = 0 + 1x = x$

d. For $\hat{y} = x$, SSE = $SS_{yy} - \hat{\beta}_1 SS_{xy} = 8 - 1(8) = 0$

For $\hat{y} = 3$, SSE = $\sum(y_i - \hat{y}_i)^2 = (1 - 3)^2 + (3 - 3)^2 + (5 - 3)^2 = 8$

The least squares line has the smallest SSE of all possible lines.

11.73 a. $\hat{\beta}_0$(INTERCEP) = -99045

$\hat{\beta}_1$(AREA) = 102.814048

b. To determine if energy consumption is positively linearly related to the shell area, we test:

$H_0$: $\beta_1 = 0$
$H_a$: $\beta_1 > 0$

The test statistic is t = 6.483 (from printout).

The rejection region requires $\alpha = .10$ in the upper tail of the t distribution with df = n - 2 = 22 - 2 = 20. From Table VI, Appendix B, $t_{.10} = 1.325$. The rejection region is t > 1.325.

Since the observed value of the test statistic falls in the rejection region (t = 6.483 > 1.325), $H_0$ is rejected. There is sufficient evidence to indicate energy consumption is positively linearly related to the shell area at $\alpha = .10$.

c. The observed significance level is $\frac{1}{2}(\text{Prob} > |T|) < \frac{1}{2}(.0001) = .00005$.

d. $r^2$ = R-SQUARE = .6776

67.76% of the sample variability in energy consumption is explained by the linear relationship between energy consumption and shell area.

e. From the printout, for x = 8000, $\hat{y} = 723467$ (observation 23).

The 95% prediction interval is (-631,806, 2,078,740).

This interval is so large, it probably is not very useful.

11.75 a. Some preliminary calculations are:

$\sum x_i = 3753$ $\sum x_i^2 = 1,231,085$ $\sum x_i y_i = 609,902$

$\sum y_i = 2160$ $\sum y_i^2 = 502,080$

$$SS_{xy} = \sum x_i y_i - \frac{\sum x_i \sum y_i}{n} = 609,902 - \frac{3753(2160)}{12} = -65,638$$

$$SS_{xx} = \sum x_i^2 - \frac{(\sum x_i)^2}{n} = 1231085 - \frac{3753^2}{12} = 57,334.25$$

$$SS_{yy} = \sum y_i^2 - \frac{(\sum y_i)^2}{n} = 502080 - \frac{2160^2}{12} = 113280$$

$$r = \frac{SS_{xy}}{\sqrt{SS_{xx} SS_{yy}}} = \frac{-65638}{\sqrt{57334.25(113280)}} = -.8145$$

This implies that the number of passengers carried by air carriers and by railroad are negatively related. Since $r = -.8145$ is close to $-1$, the relationship is fairly strong.

$$r^2 = (-.8145)^2 = .6634$$

66.34% of the sample variability in number of passengers carried by air carriers is explained by the linear relationship between the number of passengers carried by air carriers and by railroad.

b. To determine if x and y are correlated, we test:

$H_0$: $\rho = 0$
$H_a$: $\rho \neq 0$

The test statistic is $t = \dfrac{r}{\sqrt{(1 - r^2)/(n - 2)}}$

$$= \frac{-.8145}{\sqrt{(1 - (-.8145)^2/(12 - 2)}} = -4.44$$

The rejection region requires $\alpha/2 = .05/2 = .025$ in each tail of the t distribution with df $= n - 2 = 12 - 2 = 10$. From Table VI, Appendix B, $t_{.025} = 2.228$. The rejection region is $t > 2.228$ or $t < -2.228$.

Since the observed value of the test statistic falls in the rejection region ($t = -4.44 < -2.228$), $H_0$ is rejected. There is sufficient evidence to indicate that x and y are correlated at $\alpha = .05$.

11.77 a. Some preliminary calculations are:

$\sum x_i = 4305$ $\sum x_i^2 = 1{,}652{,}025$ $\sum x_i y_i = 76{,}652{,}695$

$\sum y_i = 201{,}558$ $\sum y_i^2 = 3{,}571{,}211{,}200$

$$SS_{xy} = \sum x_i y_i - \frac{\sum x_i \sum y_i}{n} = 76{,}652{,}695 - \frac{4305(201558)}{15} = 18{,}805{,}549$$

$$SS_{xx} = \sum x_i^2 - \frac{(\sum x_i)^2}{n} = 1{,}652{,}025 - \frac{4305^2}{15} = 416{,}490$$

$$SS_{yy} = \sum y_i^2 - \frac{(\sum y_i)^2}{n} = 3{,}571{,}211{,}200 - \frac{201558^2}{15} = 862{,}836{,}042$$

$$\hat{\beta}_1 = \frac{\sum x_i y_i}{\sum x_i^2} = \frac{76{,}652{,}695}{1{,}652{,}025} = 46.39923427$$

The least squares line is $\hat{y} = 46.399x$

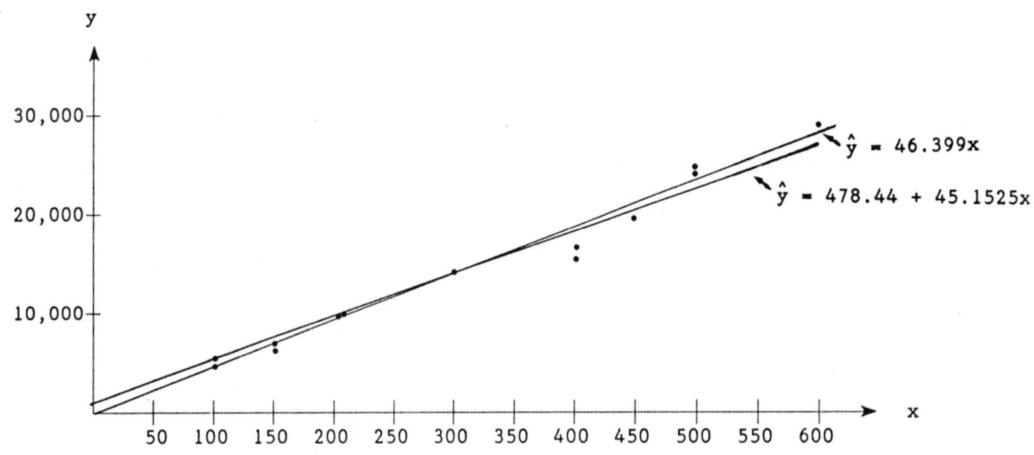


b. $$\hat{\beta}_1 = \frac{SS_{xy}}{SS_{xx}} = \frac{18805549}{416490} = 45.15246224$$

$$\hat{\beta}_0 = \bar{y} - \hat{\beta}_1\bar{x} = \frac{201558}{15} - 45.15246224\left(\frac{4305}{15}\right) = 478.44334$$

The least squares line is $\hat{y} = 478.44 + 45.1525x$

c. Because $x = 0$ is not in the observed range. Also, $\hat{\beta}_0$ is only a point estimate for $\beta_0$.

d. $$SSE = SS_{yy} - \hat{\beta}_1 SS_{xy} = 862{,}836{,}042 - (45.15246224)(18{,}805{,}549)$$
$$= 13{,}719{,}200.88$$

$$s^2 = \frac{SSE}{n - 2} = \frac{13,719,200}{15 - 2} = 1,055,323.145$$

$$s = \sqrt{1055323.145} = 1027.28922$$

To determine if $\beta_0$ is different from zero, we test:

$H_0\colon\ \beta_0 = 0$
$H_a\colon\ \beta_0 \neq 0$

The test statistic is $t = \dfrac{\hat{\beta}_0 - 0}{s\sqrt{\dfrac{1}{n} + \dfrac{\bar{x}^2}{SS_{xx}}}}$

$$= \frac{478.44334}{1027.2892\sqrt{\dfrac{1}{15} + \dfrac{287^2}{416490}}} = .91$$

The rejection region requires $\alpha/2 = .10/2 = .05$ in each tail of the t distribution with df = n - 2 = 15 - 2 = 13. From Table VI, Appendix B, $t_{.05} = 1.771$. The rejection region is $t > 1.771$ or $t < -1.771$.

Since the observed value of the test statistic does not fall in the rejection region ($t = .91 \not> 1.771$), $H_0$ is not rejected. There is insufficient evidence to indicate $\beta_0$ is not 0. Thus, $\beta_0$ should not be included in the model at $\alpha = .10$.

11.79 Some preliminary calculations are:

$\sum x_i = 109.3$ $\qquad \sum x_i^2 = 2061.79$ $\qquad \sum x_i y_i = 6063.69$

$\sum y_i = 324.8$ $\qquad \sum y_i^2 = 17915.2$

$$SS_{xy} = \sum x_i y_i - \frac{\sum x_i \sum y_i}{n} = 6063.69 - \frac{109.3(324.8)}{6} = 146.916667$$

$$SS_{xx} = \sum x_i^2 - \frac{(\sum x_i)^2}{n} = 2061.79 - \frac{109.3^2}{6} = 70.708333$$

$$SS_{yy} = \sum y_i^2 - \frac{(\sum y_i)^2}{n} = 17915.2 - \frac{324.8^2}{6} = 332.69333$$

a. $\hat{\beta}_1 = \dfrac{SS_{xy}}{SS_{xx}} = \dfrac{146.916667}{70.708333} = 2.07778434$

$$\hat{\beta}_0 = \bar{y} - \hat{\beta}_1\bar{x} = \frac{324.8}{6} - 2.07778434\left(\frac{109.3}{6}\right) = 16.2830286$$

$$SSE = SS_{yy} - \hat{\beta}_1 SS_{xy} = 332.69333 - 2.07778434(146.916667)$$
$$= 27.43218$$

$$s^2 = \frac{SSE}{n-2} = \frac{27.43218}{6-2} = 6.858045 \qquad s = \sqrt{6.858045} = 2.6188$$

The least squares line is $\hat{y} = 16.283 + 2.0778x$

b.

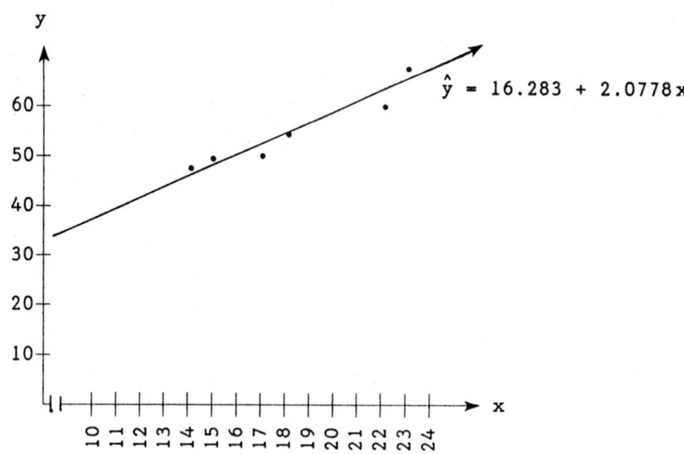


c. To determine if total sales during the trial period contribute information for predicting total sales during the first month, we test:

$H_0$: $\beta_1 = 0$
$H_a$: $\beta_1 \neq 0$

The test statistic is $t = \frac{\hat{\beta}_1 - 0}{s_{\hat{\beta}_1}} = \frac{2.0778}{\frac{2.6188}{\sqrt{70.708333}}} = 6.67$

The rejection region requires $\alpha/2 = .10/2 = .05$ in each tail of the t distribution with df = n - 2 = 6 - 2 = 4. From Table VI, Appendix B, $t_{.05} = 2.132$. The rejection region is $t > 2.132$ or $t < -2.132$.

Since the observed value of the test statistic falls in the rejection region ($t = 6.67 > 2.132$), $H_0$ is rejected. There is sufficient evidence to indicate sales during the trial period contribute information for predicting total sales during the first month at $\alpha = .10$.

d. The p-value is $2 \cdot P(t > 6.67)$. From Table VI, Appendix B, with df = n - 2 = 6 - 2 = 4, $P(t > 6.67) < .005$.

The p-value is less than 2(.005) = .010.

e. For \$2000 sales, $x_p = 20$. $\hat{y} = 16.283 + 2.0778(20) = 57.839$.

$$\bar{x} = \frac{\sum x_i}{n} = \frac{109.3}{6} = 18.2167$$

For confidence coefficient .90, $\alpha = 1 - .90 = .10$ and $\alpha/2 = .10/2 = .05$. From Table VI, Appendix B, $t_{.05} = 2.132$ with df $= n - 2 = 6 - 2 = 4$.

The prediction interval is

$$\hat{y} \pm t_{\alpha/2}\, s\sqrt{1 + \frac{1}{n} + \frac{(x_p - \bar{x})^2}{SS_{xx}}}$$

$$\Rightarrow 57.839 \pm 2.132(2.6188)\sqrt{1 + \frac{1}{6} + \frac{(20 - 18.2167)^2}{70.708333}}$$

$$\Rightarrow 57.839 \pm 6.146 \Rightarrow (51.693, 63.985)$$

11.81 a.

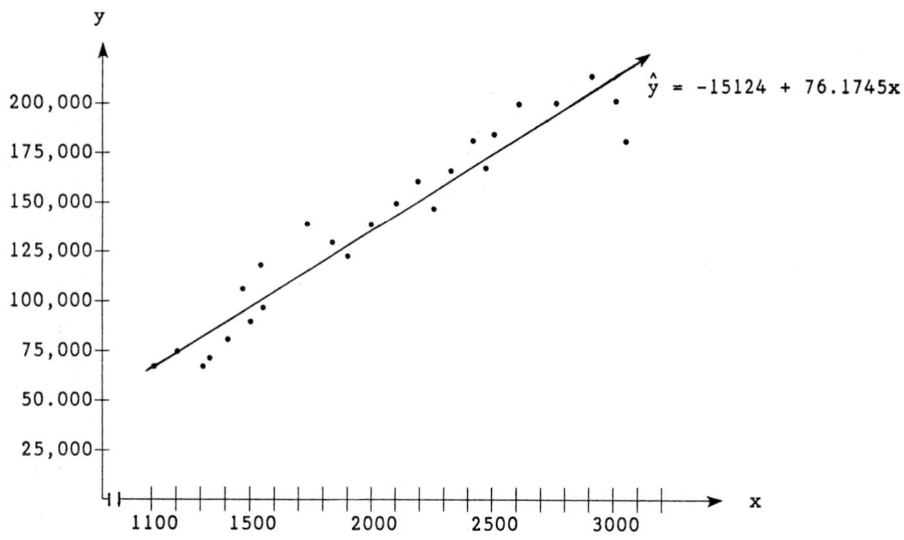


b. From the printout:

$\hat{\beta}_0$(INTERCEP) = -15124

$\hat{\beta}_1$(AREA) = 76.174547

The least squares line is $\hat{y} = -15124 + 76.1745x$.

c. $r^2$ = R-SQUARE = .9185

91.85% of the sample variability in price is explained by the linear relationship between price and area.

d. To determine if living area contributes information for predicting the price of a home, we test:

$H_0$: $\beta_1 = 0$
$H_a$: $\beta_1 \neq 0$

The test statistic is $t = 15.743$ (from printout)

The p-value is .0001.

Since the p-value is less than $\alpha = .05$, $H_0$ is rejected. There is sufficient evidence to indicate living area contributes information for predicting the price of a home at $\alpha = .05$.

e. For confidence coefficient .95, $\alpha = 1 - .95 = .05$ and $\alpha/2 = .05/2 = .025$. From Table VI, Appendix B, $t_{.025} = 2.074$ with df $= n - 2 = 24 - 2 = 22$. The confidence interval is

$$\hat{\beta}_1 \pm t_{\alpha/2}s_{\hat{\beta}_1} \Rightarrow 76.1745 \pm 2.074(4.8385)$$

$$\Rightarrow 76.1745 \pm 10.0350 \Rightarrow (66.1395,\ 86.2095)$$

Since 0 is not in the confidence interval, it is not a likely value for $\beta_1 \Rightarrow$ reject $H_0$. This corresponds to the conclusion in (d).

f. The observed significance level is .0001. Since this is less than $\alpha = .05$, $H_0$ is rejected in part (d).

g. From the 25 observations on the printout, the point estimate for price when $x_p = 2200$ is $\hat{y} = 152{,}460$. The 95% confidence interval is (146,713, 158,206).

11.83 Some preliminary calculations are:

$\sum x_i = 254.75 \qquad \sum x_i^2 = 2860.6875 \qquad \sum x_i y_i = 174.2575$

$\sum y_i = 16.52 \qquad \sum y_i^2 = 19.553$

$$SS_{xy} = \sum x_i y_i - \frac{\sum x_i \sum y_i}{n} = 174.2575 - \frac{254.75(16.52)}{23} = -8.7194565$$

$$SS_{xx} = \sum x_i^2 - \frac{(\sum x_i)^2}{n} = 2860.6875 - \frac{254.75^2}{23} = 39.054348$$

$$SS_{yy} = \sum y_i^2 - \frac{(\sum y_i)^2}{n} = 19.553 - \frac{16.52^2}{23} = 7.68733043$$

$$r = \frac{SS_{xy}}{\sqrt{SS_{xx}SS_{yy}}} = \frac{-8.7194565}{\sqrt{39.054348(7.68733043)}} = -.503$$

This correlation coefficient is not very close to 0, so it probably is not spurious. To check for sure, we could run a test of hypothesis.

| | | | | | | | | | | | | | | | | | | | | | | | | | | | | | | | | | | | | | |

# CHAPTER 12

## MULTIPLE REGRESSION

12.1 a. $\hat{\beta}_0$(INTERCEP) = 506.346 The estimated mean value of y when $x_1 = 0$ and $x_2 = 0$ is 506.346.

$\hat{\beta}_1$(X1) = -941.9 The mean value of y is estimated to decrease by 941.9 for each unit increase in $x_1$, with $x_2$ held constant.

$\hat{\beta}_2$(X2) = -429.06 The mean value of y is estimated to decrease by 429.06 for each unit increase in $x_2$, with $x_1$ held constant.

b. The least squares equation is $\hat{y} = 506.34 - 941.9x_1 - 429.06x_2$

c. SSE = SUM OF SQUARES for error

SSE = 151,015.72376

$$MSE = \frac{151,015.72376}{17} = 8883.27787$$

$$s = \sqrt{\frac{SSE}{n - 3}} = \sqrt{MSE} = \text{ROOT MSE} = 94.25114$$

About 95% of the observations will fall within 2(94.25114) = 188.50228 of the fitted regression surface.

d. $H_0$: $\beta_1 = 0$
$H_a$: $\beta_1 \neq 0$

The test statistic is t = -3.424 (from printout). The p-value = .0032. Since p-value $< \alpha = .05$, we reject $H_0$ and conclude $\beta_1$ is significantly different from zero.

e. A 95% confidence interval for $\beta_2$ is

$$\hat{\beta}_2 \pm t_{\alpha/2} s_{\hat{\beta}_2}$$

$s_{\hat{\beta}_2}$ is the standard error for $\hat{\beta}_2$ which is 379.82567.

For confidence coefficient .95, $\alpha = 1 - .95 = .05$ and $\alpha/2 = .05/2 = .025$. From Table VI, Appendix B, with $df = n - 3 = 20 - 3 = 17$, $t_{.025} = 2.110$. The confidence interval is:

$$-429.06 \pm 2.11(379.82567)$$

$$\Rightarrow -429.06 \pm 801.432$$

$$\Rightarrow (-1230.492, 372.372)$$

12.3 a. We are given, $\hat{\beta}_2 = .47$, $s_{\hat{\beta}_2} = .15$, $n = 25$

Test $H_0$: $E(y) = \beta_0 + \beta_1 x$ or $H_0$: $\beta_2 = 0$
$H_a$: $E(y) = \beta_0 + \beta_1 x_1 + \beta_2 x_2$ $H_a$: $\beta_2 \neq 0$

The test statistic is $t = \dfrac{\hat{\beta}_2}{s_{\hat{\beta}_2}} = \dfrac{.47}{.15} = 3.13$

The rejection region requires $\alpha/2 = .05/2 = .025$ in each tail of the t distribution with $df = n - (k + 1) = 25 - (2 + 1) = 22$. From Table VI, Appendix B, $t_{.025} = 2.074$. The rejection region is $t < -2.074$ or $t > 2.074$.

Since the observed value of the test statistic falls in the rejection region ($t = 3.13 > 2.074$), $H_0$ is rejected. There is sufficient evidence to indicate $\beta_2 \neq 0$ at $\alpha = .05$.

b. $H_0$: $\beta_2 = 0$
$H_a$: $\beta_2 > 0$

The test statistic is $t = \dfrac{.47}{.15} = 3.13$.

The rejection region requires $\alpha = .05$ in the upper tail of the t distribution with $df = n - (k + 1) = 25 - (2 + 1) = 22$. From Table VI, Appendix B, $t_{.05} = 1.717$. The rejection region is $t > 1.717$.

Since the observed value of the test statistic falls in the rejection region ($t = 3.13 > 1.717$), $H_0$ is rejected. There is sufficient evidence to indicate $\beta_2 > 0$ at $\alpha = .05$.

c. The F statistic is equivalent to $(t)^2$, i.e.,

$$F = t^2 = 3.13^2 = 9.82$$

d. No, since the F test is not appropriate for one-tailed tests.

12.5 a. The least squares prediction equation is:

$$\hat{y} = 1.4326 + .01x_1 + .379x_2$$

b. To determine if the mean food consumption increases with household income, we test:

$H_0$: $\beta_1 = 0$
$H_a$: $\beta_1 \neq 0$

The test statistic is $t = 3.15$.

The rejection region requires $\alpha/2 = .01/2 = .005$ in each tail of the t distribution with df = n - (k + 1) = 25 - (2 + 1) = 22. From Table VI, Appendix B, $t_{.005} = 2.819$. The rejection region is $t < -2.819$ or $t > 2.819$.

Since the observed value of the test statistic falls in the rejection region ($t = 3.15 > 2.819$), $H_0$ is rejected. There is sufficient evidence to indicate $\beta_1$ is not 0 at $\alpha = .01$.

c.

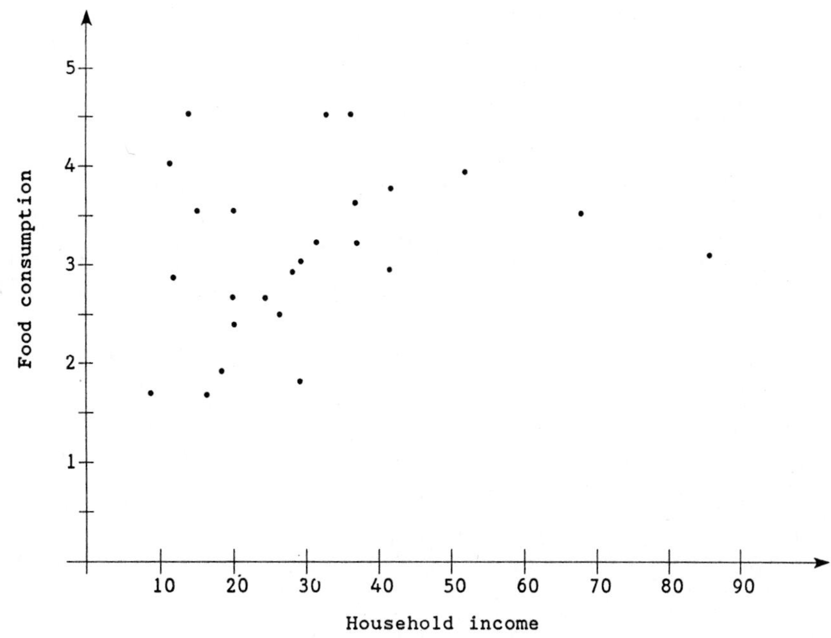


The plot supports the conclusion in part (b) since there is an increasing trend.

12.7 a. From the output, $\hat{\beta}_0 = 20.09$, $\hat{\beta}_1 = -.6705$ and $\hat{\beta}_2 = .0095$. Therefore, $\hat{y} = 20.09 - .6705x + .0095x^2$.

b.

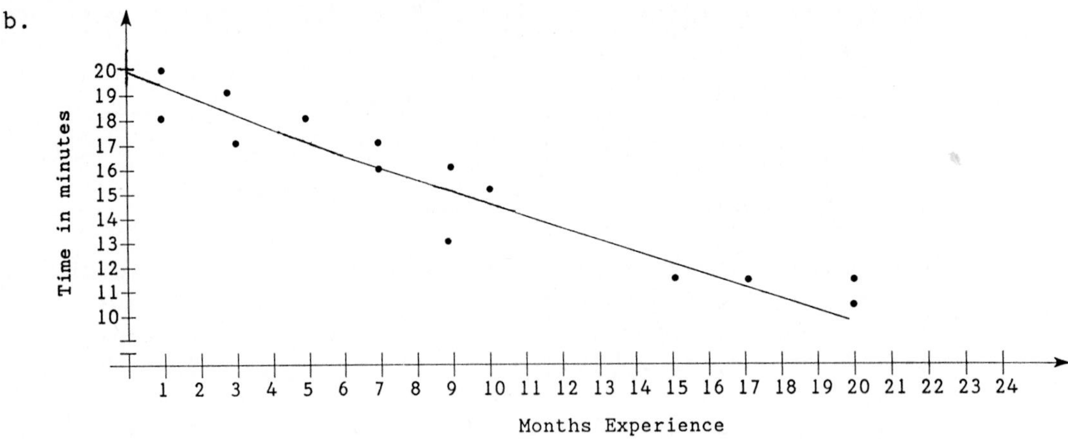


The data do not seem to support the equation, rather, only a linear trend.

c. Test $H_0$: $\beta_2 = 0$
$H_a$: $\beta_2 \neq 0$

The test statistic is $t = 1.51$.

The rejection region requires $\alpha/2 = .01/2 = .005$ in each tail of the t distribution with $df = n - (k + 1) = 15 - (2 + 1) = 12$. From Table VI, Appendix B, $t_{.005} = 3.055$. The rejection region is $t < -3.055$ or $t > 3.055$.

Since the observed value of the test statistic does not fall in the rejection region ($t = 1.51 \not> 3.05$), $H_0$ is not rejected. There is insufficient evidence to indicate $\beta_2$ is not 0 at $\alpha = .01$.

d. Some preliminary calculations are:

$\sum x = 151$ $\quad \sum x^2 = 2295$ $\quad \sum xy = 1890$

$\sum y = 222$ $\quad \sum y^2 = 3456$

$$SS_{xy} = \sum xy - \frac{\sum x \sum y}{n} = 1890 - \frac{151(222)}{15} = -344.8$$

$$SS_{xx} = \sum x^2 - \frac{(\sum x)^2}{n} = 2295 - \frac{151^2}{15} = 774.933333$$

$$SS_{yy} = \sum y^2 - \frac{(\sum y)^2}{n} = 3456 - \frac{222^2}{15} = 170.4$$

$$\hat{\beta}_1 = \frac{SS_{xy}}{SS_{xx}} = \frac{-344.8}{774.933333} = -.4449415$$

$\hat{\beta}_0 = \bar{y} - \hat{\beta}_1\bar{x} = \frac{222}{15} - (-.4449415)\left(\frac{151}{15}\right) = 19.2791$

The fitted "reduced model" is $\hat{y} = 19.2791 - .4449x$.

e. $\hat{\beta}_1$ is the estimate of the change in mean time to complete the task for each unit increase in months of experience.

$SSE = SS_{yy} - \hat{\beta}_1 SS_{xy} = 170.4 - (-.4449415)(-334.8) = 16.9841708$

$MSE = \frac{SSE}{n - 2} = \frac{16.9841708}{15 - 2} = 1.30647$

$s = \sqrt{1.30647} = 1.143$

For confidence coefficient .90, $\alpha = 1 - .90 = .10$ and $\alpha/2 = .10/2 = .05$. From Table VI, Appendix B, with $df = n - 2 = 15 - 2 = 13$, $t_{.05} = 1.771$. The confidence interval is

$$\hat{\beta}_1 \pm t_{.05}(s_{\hat{\beta}_1}) \Rightarrow -.4449 \pm 1.771\sqrt{\frac{MSE}{SS_{xx}}}$$

$$\Rightarrow -.4449 \pm 1.771\sqrt{\frac{1.30647}{774.9333}} \Rightarrow -.4449 \pm .0727$$

$$\Rightarrow (-.5176, -.3722)$$

12.9 $H_0$: $\beta_2 = 0$
$H_a$: $\beta_2 > 0$

The test statistic is $t = \frac{\hat{\beta}_2}{s_{\hat{\beta}_2}} = \frac{.0015}{.000712} = 2.11$

The rejection region requires $\alpha = .05$ in the upper tail of the t distribution with $df = n - (k + 1) = 50 - (2 + 1) = 47$. From Table VI, Appendix B, $t_{.05} \approx 1.645$. The rejection region is $t > 1.645$.

Since the observed value of the test statistic falls in the rejection region ($t = 2.11 > 1.645$), $H_0$ is rejected. There is sufficient evidence to indicate $\beta_1$ is greater than 0 at $\alpha = .05$.

12.11 The SAS output is:

```
DEP VARIABLE: PRICE
                              ANALYSIS OF VARIANCE

                         SUM OF           MEAN
SOURCE      DF          SQUARES         SQUARE        F VALUE        PROB>F

MODEL        5   1.05289E+12  210578940102        190.749        0.0001
ERROR       19   20975246806    1103960358
C TOTAL     24   1.07387E+12

       ROOT MSE       33225.9      R-SQUARE        0.9805
       DEP MEAN      290573.5      ADJ R-SQ        0.9753
       C.V.          11.43459

                              PARAMETER ESTIMATES

                      PARAMETER        STANDARD       T FOR HO:
VARIABLE    DF         ESTIMATE           ERROR     PARAMETER=0      PROB > |T|

INTERCEP     1      93073.85223     28720.89686           3.241          0.0043
APTUNITS     1       4152.20701      1491.62587           2.784          0.0118
AGE          1       -854.94161       298.44765          -2.865          0.0099
LOTSIZE      1       0.92424393      2.87673442           0.321          0.7515
PARKSPAC     1       2692.46175      1577.28623           1.707          0.1041
BLDGAREA     1      15.54276851      1.46287006          10.625          0.0001
```

a. The least squares equation is

$$\hat{y} = 93074 + 4152x_1 - 855x_2 + .92x_3 + 2692x_4 + 15.5x_5$$

b. The standard deviation is ROOT MSE = 33225.9. In predicting price, we would expect 95% of the observations to be ±2s or ±2(33225.9) dollars from the mean selling price.

c. To determine if the value increases with the number of units, we test:

$H_0$: $\beta_1 = 0$
$H_a$: $\beta_1 \neq 0$

The test statistic is $t = 2.784$ (from printout).

The rejection region requires $\alpha/2 = .05/2 = .025$ in the each tail of the t distribution with df = n - (k + 1) = 25 - (2 + 1) = 19. From Table VI, Appendix B, $t_{.025} = 2.093$. The rejection region is $t < -2.093$ or $t > 2.093$.

Since the observed value of the test statistic falls in the rejection region ($t = 2.784 > 2.093$), $H_0$ is rejected. There is sufficient evidence to indicate the value increases with the number of units at $\alpha = .05$.

p-value = .0118

d. We estimate the change in mean sale price to be 4152 for each additional unit, all other variables held constant.

e.

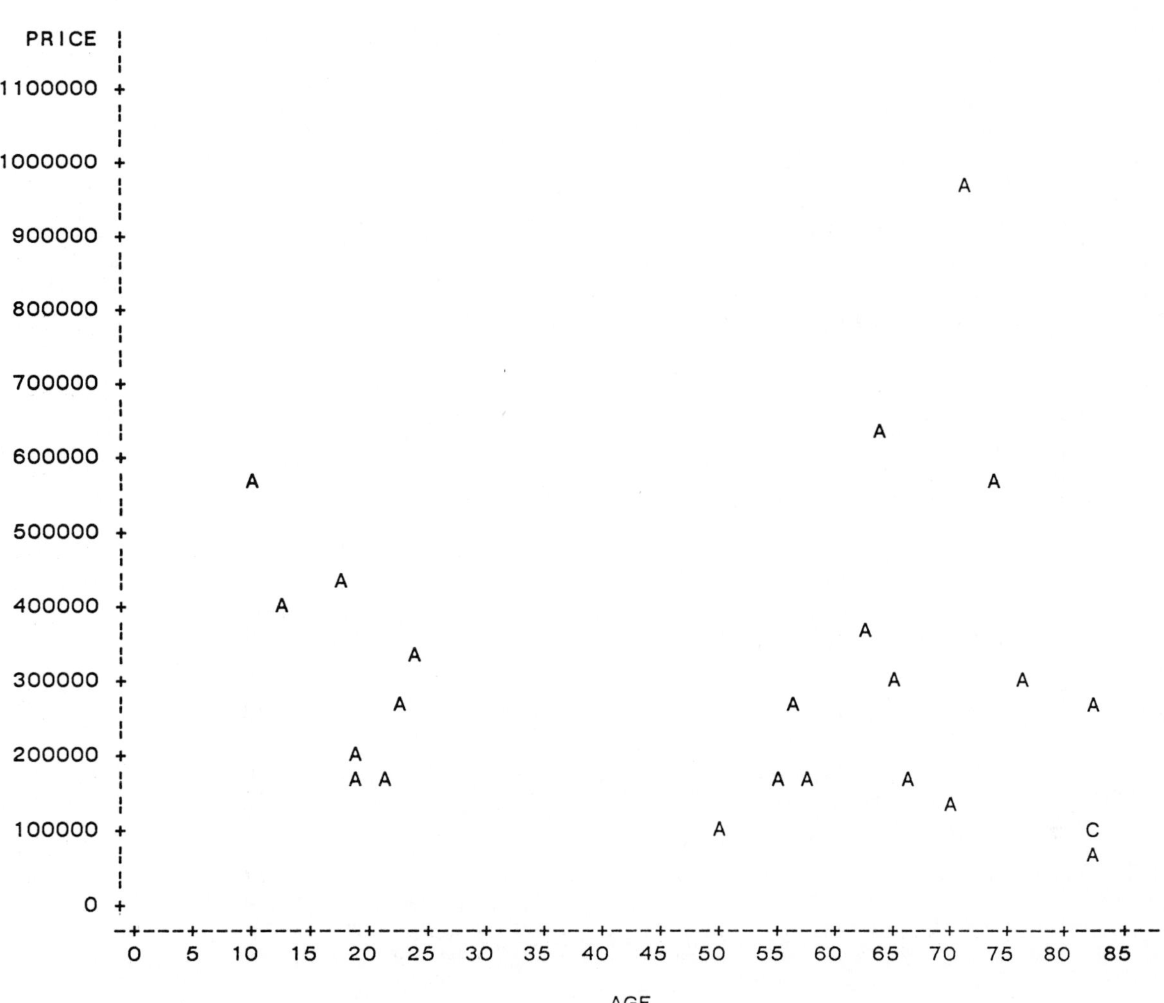


There does not appear to be much of a relationship between price and age without the other variables.

f. $H_0$: $\beta_2 = 0$
$H_a$: $\beta_2 < 0$

The test statistic is $t = \frac{\hat{\beta}_2}{s_{\hat{\beta}_2}} = -2.865$.

The rejection region requires $\alpha = .01$ in the lower tail of the t distribution with df = n - (k + 1) = 25 - (5 + 1) = 19. From Table VI, Appendix B, $t_{.01} = 2.539$. The rejection region is $t < -2.539$.

Since the observed value of the test statistic falls in the rejection region ($t = -2.865 < -2.539$), $H_0$ is rejected. There is sufficient evidence to indicate that sale price decreases as age increases adjusted for all other variables in the model at $\alpha = .01$.

g. The observed significance level is $P(t < -2.865)$. From Table VI, Appendix B, with df = 19,

$$P(t < -2.865) \approx .005.$$

12.13 a. The two statistics, SSE and $R^2$, seem to imply a good fit of the data since SSE is small and $R^2 > .9$.

b. $H_0$: $\beta_1 = \beta_2 = \beta_3 = \beta_4 = \beta_5 = 0$
$H_a$: At least 1 $\beta_i \neq 0$, for $i = 1, 2, \ldots, 5$

The test statistic is $F = \dfrac{R^2/k}{(1 - R^2)/(n - (k + 1)}$

$$F = \frac{.91/5}{(1 - .91)/(30 - (5 + 1))} = \frac{.182}{.00375} = 48.53$$

The rejection region requires $\alpha = .05$ in the upper tail of the F distribution with $\nu_1 = k = 5$ and $\nu_2 = n - (k + 1) = 30 - (5 + 1) = 24$. From Table VIII, Appendix B, $F_{.05} = 2.62$. The rejection region is $F > 2.62$.

Since the observed value of the test statistic falls in the rejection region ($F = 48.53 > 2.62$), $H_0$ is rejected. There is sufficient evidence to indicate the model is useful in predicting y at $\alpha = .05$.

12.15 No, the F test leads to the conclusion that at least one model parameter is nonzero. We do not know which ones are nonzero, but at least one $\beta_i \neq 0$. We cannot conclude that all parameters are nonzero. We can only conclude at least one parameter is nonzero.

12.17. Refer to the output in the solution to Exercise 12.11.

a. $R^2$ = R-SQUARE = .9805

98.05% of the variability in sale prices is explained by the relationship between sale prices and the five independent variables.

b. To determine the usefulness of the model, we test:

$H_0$: $\beta_1 = \beta_2 = \beta_3 = \beta_4 = \beta_5 = 0$
$H_a$: At least 1 $\beta_i \neq 0$ for $i = 1, 2, \ldots, 5$

The test statistic is $F = \frac{MSR}{MSE} = 190.749$

The rejection region requires $\alpha = .01$ in the upper tail of the F distribution with $\nu_1 = k = 5$ and $\nu_2 = n - (k + 1) = 25 - (5 + 1) = 19$. From Table X, Appendix B, $F_{.01} = 4.17$. The rejection region is $F > 4.17$.

Since the observed value of the test statistic falls in the rejection region ($F = 190.749 > 4.17$), $H_0$ is rejected. There is sufficient evidence to indicate the model is useful at $\alpha = .01$. There is a relationship between sale price and at least one of the independent variables.

c. The observed significance level is $P(F > 190.749) = .0001$ (from printout).

12.19 a. The least squares equation is:

$$\hat{y} = 131.924 + 2.726x_1 + .04721x_2 - 2.587x_3$$

b. To test the usefulness of the model, we test:

$H_0$: $\beta_1 = \beta_2 = \beta_3 = 0$
$H_a$: At least 1 $\beta_i \neq 0$ for $i = 1, 2, 3$

The test statistic is $F = \frac{MSR}{MSE} = \frac{1719.4379}{96.242886} = 17.87$

The rejection region requires $\alpha = .01$ in the upper tail of the F distribution with $\nu_1 = k = 3$ and $\nu_2 = n - (k + 1) = 20 - (3 + 1) = 16$. From Table X, Appendix B, $F_{.01} = 5.29$. The rejection region is $F > 5.29$.

Since the observed value of the test statistic falls in the rejection region ($F = 17.87 > 5.29$), $H_0$ is rejected. There is sufficient evidence to indicate a relationship exists between hours of labor and at least one of the independent variables at $\alpha = .01$.

c. $H_0$: $\beta_2 = 0$
$H_a$: $\beta_2 \neq 0$

The test statistic is $t = .51$. The p-value = .6199. We reject $H_0$ if p-value $< \alpha$. Since $.6199 > .05$, do not reject $H_0$. There is insufficient evidence to indicate a relationship exists between hours of labor and percentage of units shipped by truck at $\alpha = .05$.

d. $R^2$ is printed as R-SQUARE. $R^2 = .7701$. We conclude that 77% of the sample variation of the labor hours is explained by the regression model.

e. If the average number of pounds per shipment increases from 20 to 21, the estimated change in mean number of hours of labor is -2.587. Thus, it will cost 7.50(2.587) = 19.4025 less, if the variables $x_1$ and $x_2$ are constant.

f. Since s = 9.81, we can estimate approximately with ±2s precision or ±2(9.81) = 19.62 hours.

12.21 a. The value $R^2$ = .87. 87% of the sample variation in attitude is explained by the regression model.

b. $H_0$: $\beta_1 = \beta_2 = \beta_3 = \beta_4 = 0$
$H_a$: At least 1 $\beta_i \neq 0$ for i = 1, 2, ... , 4

The test statistic $F = \dfrac{R^2/k}{\dfrac{1 - R^2}{(n - (k + 1))}}$ where k = 4, n = 40

$$= \frac{.87/4}{(1 - .87)/(40 - (4 + 1))} = \frac{.2175}{.0037} = 58.56$$

The rejection region requires $\alpha$ = .01 in the upper tail of the F distribution with $\nu_1 = k = 4$ and $\nu_2 = n - (k + 1)$ = 40 - (4 + 1) = 35. From Table X, Appendix B, $F_{.01} \approx 3.93$. The rejection region is F > 3.93.

Since the observed value of the test statistic falls in the rejection region (F = 58.56 > 3.93), $H_0$ is rejected. There is sufficient evidence to indicate the model is useful in predicting attitude at $\alpha$ = .01. Attitude is related to at least one of the independent variables.

c. To determine if the interaction between sex and years of experience is useful in the prediction model, we test:

$H_0$: $\beta_4 = 0$
$H_a$: $\beta_4 \neq 0$

The test statistic is $t = \dfrac{\hat{\beta}_4}{s_{\hat{\beta}_4}} = \dfrac{-1}{.02} = -50$

The rejection region requires $\alpha/2$ = .05/2 = .025 in each tail of the t distribution with df = n - (k + 1) = 40 - (4 + 1) = 35. From Table VI, Appendix B, $t_{.025} \approx 1.96$. The rejection region is t < -1.96 or t > 1.96.

Since the observed value of the test statistic falls in the rejection region (t = -50 < -1.96), $H_0$ is rejected. There is sufficient evidence to indicate the interaction between sex and years of experience is useful in the prediction model at $\alpha$ = .05.

d. For $x_1 = 0$, $\hat{y} = 50 + 5(0) + 6x_2 - .2x_2^2 - 0(x_2)$
$= 50 + 6x_2 - .2x_2^2$

For $x_1 = 1$, $\hat{y} = 50 + 5(1) + 6x_2 - .2x_2^2 - x_2$
$= 55 + 5x_2 - .2x_2^2$

| $x_1 = 0$ | | $x_1 = 1$ | |
|---|---|---|---|
| $x_2$ | $\hat{y}$ | $x_2$ | $\hat{y}$ |
| 0 | 50 | 0 | 55 |
| 2 | 61.2 | 2 | 64.2 |
| 4 | 70.8 | 4 | 71.8 |
| 6 | 78.8 | 6 | 77.8 |
| 8 | 85.2 | 8 | 82.2 |
| 10 | 90 | 10 | 85 |

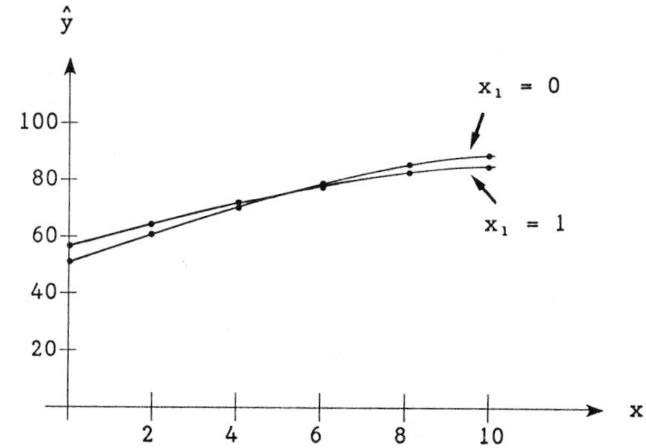


12.23 The SAS output is:

DEP VARIABLE: TIME

ANALYSIS OF VARIANCE

| SOURCE | DF | SUM OF SQUARES | MEAN SQUARE | F VALUE | PROB>F |
|---|---|---|---|---|---|
| MODEL | 2 | 251.60167 | 125.80083 | 54.807 | 0.0001 |
| ERROR | 7 | 16.06733367 | 2.29533338 | | |
| C TOTAL | 9 | 267.66900 | | | |

| | | | |
|---|---|---|---|
| ROOT MSE | 1.515036 | R-SQUARE | 0.9400 |
| DEP MEAN | 8.19 | ADJ R-SQ | 0.9228 |
| C.V. | 18.49861 | | |

PARAMETER ESTIMATES

| VARIABLE | DF | PARAMETER ESTIMATE | STANDARD ERROR | T FOR HO: PARAMETER=0 | PROB > ¦T¦ |
|---|---|---|---|---|---|
| INTERCEP | 1 | 2.40524442 | 1.24836624 | 1.927 | 0.0954 |
| MICRO | 1 | 1.42614858 | 0.14062909 | 10.141 | 0.0001 |
| EXPER | 1 | -0.36629552 | 0.13168833 | -2.782 | 0.0272 |

a. Fitting the model to the data, the least squares prediction equation is

$$\hat{y} = 2.41 + 1.43x_1 - .366x_2$$

b. To test if the model is useful, we test:

$H_0$: $\beta_1 = \beta_2 = 0$
$H_a$: At least 1 $\beta_i \neq 0 \quad i = 1, 2$

The test statistic is $F = \dfrac{MS(Model)}{MS(error)} = 54.807$

To see if this is significant, that is, if we can reject $H_0$, we compare the p-value to our $\alpha$ level. Since $\alpha = .1$ and the p-value $\leq .0001 < .1$, we reject $H_0$. We conclude that at least one variable is significant in predicting maintenance time at $\alpha = .1$.

c. $R^2$, which is printed next to R-SQUARE, is .9400. This tells us we can explain approximately 94% of the sample variation in maintenance time with this model.

d. The SAS output is:

DEP VARIABLE: TIME

ANALYSIS OF VARIANCE

| SOURCE | DF | SUM OF SQUARES | MEAN SQUARE | F VALUE | PROB>F |
|---|---|---|---|---|---|
| MODEL | 3 | 264.05135 | 88.01711754 | 145.980 | 0.0001 |
| ERROR | 6 | 3.61764738 | 0.60294123 | | |
| C TOTAL | 9 | 267.66900 | | | |

| | | | |
|---|---|---|---|
| ROOT MSE | 0.7764929 | R-SQUARE | 0.9865 |
| DEP MEAN | 8.19 | ADJ R-SQ | 0.9797 |
| C.V. | 9.480988 | | |

PARAMETER ESTIMATES

| VARIABLE | DF | PARAMETER ESTIMATE | STANDARD ERROR | T FOR HO: PARAMETER=0 | PROB > \|T\| |
|---|---|---|---|---|---|
| INTERCEP | 1 | -0.34875688 | 0.88129883 | -0.396 | 0.7060 |
| MICRO | 1 | 2.06539551 | 0.15806738 | 13.067 | 0.0001 |
| EXPER | 1 | 0.02152454 | 0.10880943 | 0.198 | 0.8497 |
| INTER | 1 | -0.09187342 | 0.02021846 | -4.544 | 0.0039 |

The least squares prediction equation is:

$$\hat{y} = -.349 + 2.07x_1 + .0215x_2 - .0919x_1x_2$$

e. $R^2$, which is printed next to R-SQUARE, is .9865. This tells us we can explain approximately 98.65% of the sample variation in maintenance time with this model.

f. In comparing $R^2$, we must realize that additional variables added to the existing model will always increase $R^2$. We need to determine if the increase is significant.

g. $H_0$: $\beta_3 = 0$
$H_a$: $\beta_3 \neq 0$

The test statistic is $t = -4.544$.

Since the p-value is $.0039 < .05$, reject $H_0$. We conclude the interaction is significant in predicting maintenance time at $\alpha = .05$.

h. No. We must test to make sure each term in the model contributes information.

12.25 In multiple regression, as in simple regression, the confidence interval for the mean value of y is narrower than the prediction interval of a particular value of y.

12.27 a. The least squares equation from the SPSS printout is

$$\hat{y} = 506.346 - 941.9x_1 - 429.06x_2$$

b. The standard deviation for the regression model is labeled STANDARD ERROR, which is 94.25114. We would expect about 95% of the observations to be within ±188.5 units of the mean.

c. The test statistic is:

$$F = \frac{\text{Mean Square (Regression)}}{\text{Mean Square (Error)}} = \frac{64164.63812}{8883.27787}$$

$$= 7.223$$

The p-value or $P(F > 7.223) = .0054$.

To determine if the model contributes information, we test:

$H_0$: $\beta_1 = \beta_2 = 0$
$H_a$: At least 1 $\beta_i \neq 0$ $i = 1, 2$

The test statistic is $F = 7.223$.

Since the p-value $= .0054$ is less than $\alpha = .05$, $H_0$ is rejected. There is sufficient evidence to indicate the model contributes information for the prediction of y at $\alpha = .05$.

d. The standard error of $\hat{\beta}_2$ is under the column SE B and is 379.82566. For confidence coefficient .90, $\alpha = 1 - .90 = .10$ and $\alpha/2 = .10/2$. From Table VI, Appendix B, with $df = n - (k + 1) = 20 - (2 + 1) = 17$, $t_{.05} = 1.74$. The confidence interval is:

$\hat{\beta}_2 \pm t_{\alpha/2} s_{\hat{\beta}_2}$

=> $-429.06 \pm 1.74(379.8)$

=> $-429.06 \pm 660.85$

=> $(-1089.912, 231.788)$

e. $R^2$ is labeled R-Square on the printout and is .459.

45.9% of the sample variation in the y's can be explained by the model.

12.29 Plot $\hat{\varepsilon}$ vs $x_1$.

There is no definite mound or bowl shape to the plot. This implies there is no need for a quadratic term in $x_1$. From Exercise 12.5, ROOT MSE is .277. Two standard deviations from the mean is $\pm 2(.277)$ => $-.554$ to $.554$. Three standard deviations from the mean is $\pm 3(.277)$ => $-.831$ to $.831$. There are two points more than two standard deviations from the mean, but none beyond three standard deviations. Thus, there is no evidence to indicate outliers are present.

Plot $\hat{\varepsilon}$ vs $x_2$.

There is a possible mound shape to the plot. We may want to try a model with size$^2$ added. Again, there are two data points more than 2 standard deviations from the mean, but none more than 3 standard deviations from the mean.

12.31 a. Neither plot, $\hat{\varepsilon}$ vs $x_1$ nor $\hat{\varepsilon}$ vs $x_2$, has a mound or bowl shape. This implies there is no need for quadratic terms to be added to the model. The standard deviation is $\sqrt{MSE} = \sqrt{.311} = .558$.

Two standard deviations form the mean is $\pm 2(.558)$ => $-1.116$ to $1.116$. Three standard deviations form the mean is $\pm 3(.558)$ => $-1.674$ to $1.674$.

On both plots, there is one point that is more than three standard deviations above the mean. This point is the 26th household. It appears the additional point is not typical compared to the others or there may be an error.

12.33 a. For the straight-line model, the standard deviation is $\sqrt{MSE} = \sqrt{1.30647} = 1.14301$. We would expect about 95% of the observations to fall within $\pm 2(1.14301)$ or $\pm 2.8602$ units of the fitted line.

For the quadratic model, the standard deviation is $\sqrt{MSE} = \sqrt{1.19004} = 1.0909$. We would expect about 95% of the observations to fall within $\pm 2(1.0909)$ or $\pm 2.1818$ units of the fitted line.

b. For the straight-line model, $R^2 = .90033$. About 90% of the sample variability in the completion times is explained by the linear model.

For the quadratic model, $R^2 = .91619$. About 91.6% of the sample variability in the completion times is explained by the quadratic model.

c. For the straight-line model, we test:

$H_0$: $\beta_1 = 0$
$H_a$: $\beta_1 \neq 0$

The test statistic is $F = \frac{MSR}{MSE} = 117.42733$

The p-value is .0000 which is less than $\alpha = .05$. Thus, reject $H_0$. There is sufficient evidence to indicate a linear relationship between completion time and months of experience.

For the quadratic model, we test

$H_0$: $\beta_1 = \beta_2 = 0$
$H_a$: At least 1 $\beta_i \neq 0$ $i = 1, 2$

The test statistic is $F = \frac{MSR}{MSE} = 65.59402$

The p-value is .0000 which is less than $\alpha = .05$. Thus, reject $H_0$. There is sufficient evidence to indicate that there is a relationship between completion time and at least one of the independent variables--months of experience or (months of experience)$^2$ at $\alpha = .05$.

d. To test the quadratic term, we test

$H_0$: $\beta_2 = 0$
$H_a$: $\beta_2 \neq 0$

The test statistic is $t = \frac{\hat{\beta}_2}{s_{\hat{\beta}_2}} = \frac{.0095347}{.0063258} = 1.507$

The p-value is .1576 which is greater than $\alpha = .05$. Thus, do not reject $H_0$. There is insufficient evidence to indicate adding $x^2$ to the model will improve the model at $\alpha = .05$.

12.35 a. The least squares equation is $\hat{y} = 90.1 - 1.836x_1 + .285x_2$.

b. $R^2 = .916$. About 91.6% of the sample variability in the y's is explained by the model $E(y) = \beta_0 + \beta_1 x_1 + \beta_2 x_2$.

c. To determine if the model is useful for predicting y, we test:

$H_0$: $\beta_1 = \beta_2 = 0$
$H_a$: At least 1 $\beta_i \neq 0$ $i = 1, 2$

The test statistic is $F = \frac{MSR}{MSE} = \frac{7400}{114} = 64.91$

The rejection region requires $\alpha = .05$ in the upper tail of the F distribution with $\nu_1 = k = 2$ and $\nu_2 = n - (k + 1) = 15 - (2 + 1) = 12$. From Table VIII, Appendix B, $F_{.05} = 3.89$. The rejection region is $F > 3.89$.

Since the observed value of the test statistic falls in the rejection region ($F = 64.91 > 3.89$), $H_0$ is rejected. There is sufficient evidence to indicate the model is useful for predicting y at $\alpha = .05$.

d. $H_0$: $\beta_1 = 0$
$H_a$: $\beta_1 \neq 0$

The test statistic is $t = \frac{\hat{\beta}_1}{s_{\hat{\beta}_1}} = \frac{-1.836}{.367} = -5.01$

The rejection region requires $\alpha/2 = .05/2 = .025$ in each tail of the t distribution with df $= n - (k + 1) = 15 - (2 + 1) = 12$. From Table VI, Appendix B, $t_{.025} = 2.179$. The rejection region is

$t < -2.179$ or $t > 2.179$.

Since the observed value of the test statistic falls in the rejection region ($t = -5.01 < -2.179$), $H_0$ is rejected. There is sufficient evidence to indicate $\beta_1$ is not 0 at $\alpha = .05$.

e. The standard deviation is $\sqrt{MSE} = \sqrt{114} = 10.677$. We would expect about 95% of the observations to fall within $2(10.677) = 21.354$ units of the fitted regression line.

12.37 a. The least squares prediction equation is

$$\hat{y} = .6013 + .595x_1 - 3.725x_2 - 16.232x_3 + .235x_1x_2 + .308x_1x_3$$

b. $R^2 = .928$ which tells us we can explain about 92.8% of the variation in test scores with the model

$$E(y) = \beta_0 + \beta_1x_1 + \beta_2x_2 + \beta_3x_3 + \beta_4x_1x_2 + \beta_5x_1x_3$$

To see whether this model is useful for predicting achievement test scores, we test:

$H_0$: $\beta_1 = \beta_2 = \beta_3 = \beta_4 = \beta_5 = 0$
$H_a$: At least 1 $\beta_i \neq 0$ for $i = 1, 2, \ldots, 5$

The test statistic is $F = \frac{MSR}{MSE} = 139.42$

The p-value is .0001. Since $.0001 < \alpha = .05$, reject $H_0$. We conclude the model is useful in predicting achievement test scores at $\alpha = .05$.

c. For $x_2 = 0$ and $x_3 = 0$ (SES low)

$$\hat{y} = .601 + .595x_1$$

For $x_2 = 1$ and $x_3 = 0$ (SES medium)

$$\hat{y} = .601 + .595x_1 - 3.725(1) + .235(1)x_1$$
$$= -3.124 + .83x_1$$

For $x_2 = 0$ and $x_3 = 1$ (SES high)

$$\hat{y} = .601 + .595x_1 - 16.232(1) + .308(1)x_1$$
$$= -15.631 + .903x_1$$

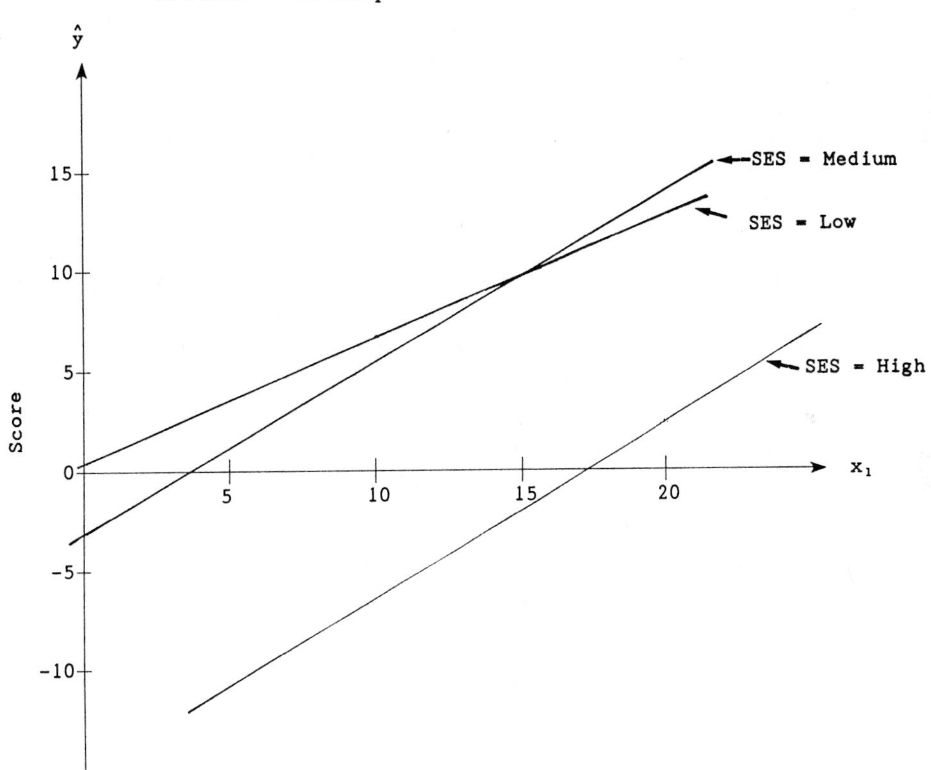


12.39 a. Some preliminary calculations are:

$\sum x_1 = 304$ $\qquad \sum x_1^2 = 7496$ $\qquad \sum x_1x_5 = 6,128,709$

$\sum x_5 = 285,585$ $\qquad \sum x_5^2 = 5,671,647,425$

$$SS_{x_1x_5} = \sum x_1x_5 - \frac{\sum x_1 \sum x_5}{n} = 6,128,709 - \frac{304(7496)}{25} = 2,655,995.4$$

$$SS_{x_1x_1} = \sum x_1^2 - \frac{(\sum x_1)^2}{n} = 7496 - \frac{304^2}{25} = 3799.36$$

$$SS_{x_5x_5} = \sum x_5^2 - \frac{(\sum x_5)^2}{n} = 5,671,647,425 - \frac{285,585^2}{25} = 2,409,295,736$$

$$r_{x_1x_5} = \frac{SS_{x_1x_5}}{\sqrt{SS_{x_1x_1} SS_{x_5x_5}}} = \frac{2,655,995.4}{\sqrt{3799.36(2,409,295,736)}} = .878$$

b. The SAS output is:

DEP VARIABLE: PRICE

ANALYSIS OF VARIANCE

| SOURCE | DF | SUM OF SQUARES | MEAN SQUARE | F VALUE | PROB>F |
|---|---|---|---|---|---|
| MODEL | 4 | 1.04434E+12 | 261085064760 | 176.829 | 0.0001 |
| ERROR | 20 | 29529688276 | 1476484414 | | |
| C TOTAL | 24 | 1.07387E+12 | | | |

| | | | |
|---|---|---|---|
| ROOT MSE | 38425.05 | R-SQUARE | 0.9725 |
| DEP MEAN | 290573.5 | ADJ R-SQ | 0.9670 |
| C.V. | 13.22386 | | |

PARAMETER ESTIMATES

| VARIABLE | DF | PARAMETER ESTIMATE | STANDARD ERROR | T FOR HO: PARAMETER=0 | PROB > \|T\| |
|---|---|---|---|---|---|
| INTERCEP | 1 | 52291.07539 | 28568.71613 | 1.830 | 0.0821 |
| AGE | 1 | -665.28140 | 336.03403 | -1.980 | 0.0617 |
| LOTSIZE | 1 | 5.80257605 | 2.63829961 | 2.199 | 0.0398 |
| PARKSPAC | 1 | 4172.00037 | 1717.41371 | 2.429 | 0.0247 |
| BLDGAREA | 1 | 18.67019411 | 1.08349581 | 17.231 | 0.0001 |

The standard deviation for the model fit in Exercise 12.11 is $\sqrt{MSE} = \sqrt{1103960358} = 33225.9$.

The standard deviation for the model fit above is $\sqrt{MSE} = \sqrt{147648441} = 38425.05$.

The standard deviation for the new model is larger than that for the old model.

The new fitted regression line is $\hat{y} = 52291 - 665x_2 + 5.80x_3 + 4172x_4 + 18.67x_5$.

c. To test the usefulness of this model, we test:

$H_0$: $\beta_2 = \beta_3 = \beta_4 = \beta_5 = 0$
$H_a$: At least 1 $\beta_i \neq 0$ for i = 2, 3, 4, or 5

The test statistic is $F = \frac{MSR}{MSE} = 176.829$.

The rejection region requires $\alpha = .05$ in the upper tail of the F distribution with $\nu_1 = k = 4$ and $\nu_2 = n - (k + 1) = 25 - (4 + 1) = 20$. From Table VIII, Appendix B, $t_{.05} = 2.87$. The rejection region is $F > 2.87$.

Since the observed value of the test statistic falls in the rejection region ($F = 176.829 > 2.87$), $H_0$ is rejected. There is sufficient evidence to indicate the model is useful for predicting the sale price at $\alpha = .05$.

d. For $x_2 = 50$, $x_3 = 15{,}000$, $x_4 = 10$, and $x_5 = 20{,}000$

$$\hat{y} = 52291.075 - 665.2814(50) + 5.802576(15{,}000) + 4172(10) + 18.67019(20{,}000) = 521189.5$$

The SAS output is:

GENERAL LINEAR MODELS PROCEDURE

DEPENDENT VARIABLE: Y

| OBSERVATION | OBSERVED | PREDICTED<br>RESIDUAL | LOWER 95% CLM<br>UPPER 95% CLM |
|---|---|---|---|
| 1 | 90300.00000000 | 104279.98907744<br>-13979.98907744 | 76544.11579713<br>132015.86235775 |
| 2 | 384000.00000000 | 415599.42932739<br>-31599.42932739 | 361910.19475511<br>469288.66389966 |
| 3 | 157500.00000000 | 166196.46956683<br>-8696.46956683 | 145349.29837715<br>187043.64075650 |
| 4 | 676200.00000000 | 717190.14048983<br>-40990.14048983 | 659990.94530217<br>774389.33567748 |
| 5 | 165000.00000000 | 159845.45329932<br>5154.54670068 | 137766.54375271<br>181924.36284594 |
| 6 | 300000.00000000 | 353303.46555332<br>-53303.46555332 | 325806.32898973<br>380800.60211691 |
| 7 | 108750.00000000 | 96041.83563149<br>12708.16436851 | 65861.38560960<br>126222.28565339 |
| 8 | 276538.00000000 | 213838.59249541<br>62699.40750459 | 178840.74092032<br>248836.44407051 |
| . | . | . | . |
| . | . | . | . |
| . | . | . | . |
| . | . | . | . |
| 23 | 573200.00000000 | 553138.97386946<br>20061.02613054 | 508008.55037116<br>598269.39736776 |
| 24 | 79300.00000000 | 113187.80056358<br>-33887.80056358 | 83564.36848821<br>142811.23263896 |
| 25 | 272000.00000000 | 219408.31360769<br>52591.68639231 | 194596.26914571<br>244220.35806967 |
| 26 * | . | 521189.53235852<br>. | 482786.10930348<br>559592.95541356 |

The 95% confidence interval for $E(y)$ is (482,786, 559,593).

12.41 To determine if there is interaction between temperature and pressure, we test:

$H_0$: $\beta_3 = 0$
$H_a$: $\beta_3 \neq 0$

The test statistic is $t = \frac{\hat{\beta}_3}{s_{\hat{\beta}_3}} = \frac{-.7}{.34} = -2.06$

The rejection region requires $\alpha/2 = .05/2 = .025$ in each tail of the t distribution with df = n - (k + 1) = 16 - (3 + 1) = 12. From Table VI, Appendix B, $t_{.025} = 2.179$. The rejection region is $t < -2.179$ or $t > 2.179$.

Since the observed value of the test statistic does not fall in the rejection region ($t = -2.06 \nless -2.179$), $H_0$ is not rejected. There is insufficient evidence to indicate there is interaction between temperature and pressure at $\alpha = .05$.

12.43 a. To determine if the relationship between the mean number of riders and gasoline price is different for the 2 types of bus routes, we test:

$H_0$: $\beta_2 = \beta_3 = 0$
$H_a$: At least 1 $\beta_i \neq 0$ for i = 1, 2

b. For $x_2 = 0$ (suburb-city route), $\hat{y} = 500 + 50x_1$

For $x_2 = 1$ (city route), $\hat{y} = 500 + 50x_1 + 5(1) - 10x_1(1)$
$= 505 + 40x_1$

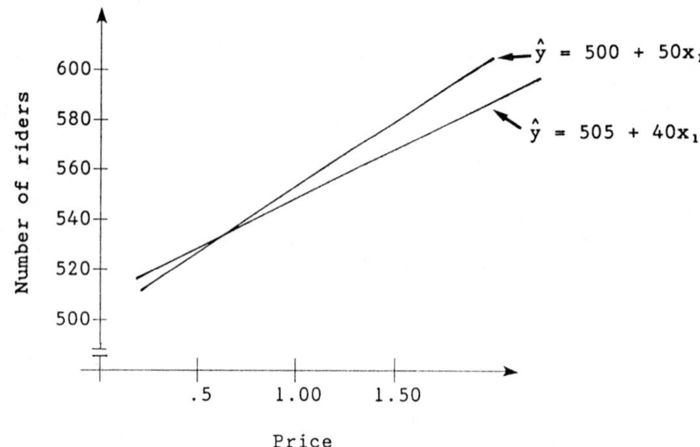


The estimated slope for the city route (40) is less than that for the suburb-city route (50).

c. To determine if interaction exists between route and gasoline price, we test:

$H_0$: $\beta_3 = 0$
$H_a$: $\beta_3 \neq 0$

The test statistic is $t = \frac{\hat{\beta}_3 - 0}{s_{\hat{\beta}_3}} = \frac{-10}{3} = -3.33$

The rejection region requires $\alpha/2 = .05/2 = .025$ in each tail of the t distribution with df = n - (k + 1) = 12 - (3 + 1) = 8. From Table VI, Appendix B, $t_{.025} = 2.306$. The rejection region is $t < -2.306$ or $t > 2.306$.

Since the observed value of the test statistic falls in the rejection region ($t = -3.33 < -2.306$), $H_0$ is rejected. There is sufficient evidence to indicate that gasoline price affects the number of riders differently for city and suburb-city buses at $\alpha = .05$.

12.45 The SAS printout is:

DEP VARIABLE: LIFE

ANALYSIS OF VARIANCE

| SOURCE | DF | SUM OF SQUARES | MEAN SQUARE | F VALUE | PROB>F |
|---|---|---|---|---|---|
| MODEL | 2 | 5.16263683 | 2.58131842 | 0.613 | 0.5857 |
| ERROR | 4 | 16.83736317 | 4.20934079 | | |
| C TOTAL | 6 | 22.00000000 | | | |

| | | | |
|---|---|---|---|
| ROOT MSE | 2.051668 | R-SQUARE | 0.2347 |
| DEP MEAN | 22.5 | ADJ R-SQ | -0.1480 |
| C.V. | 9.118524 | | |

PARAMETER ESTIMATES

| VARIABLE | DF | PARAMETER ESTIMATE | STANDARD ERROR | T FOR HO: PARAMETER=0 | PROB > \|T\| |
|---|---|---|---|---|---|
| INTERCEP | 1 | 53.62173702 | 44.51329691 | 1.205 | 0.2947 |
| GESTATE | 1 | -0.19761588 | 0.26608876 | -0.743 | 0.4989 |
| GESTSQ | 1 | 0.000304300 | 0.000387839 | 0.785 | 0.4765 |

a. From the printout, $\hat{y} = 53.622 - .1976x + .0003x^2$

To test for model adequacy, we test:

$H_0\colon \beta_1 = \beta_2 = 0$
$H_a\colon$ At least 1 $\beta_i \neq 0$ for i = 1, 2

The test statistic is $F = \frac{MSR}{MSE} = .613$

The rejection region requires $\alpha = .05$ in the upper tail of the F distribution with $\nu_1 = k = 2$ and $\nu_2 = n - (k + 1) = 7 - (2 + 1) = 4$. From Table VIII, Appendix B, $F_{.05} = 6.94$. The rejection region is $F > 6.94$.

Since the observed value of the test statistic does not fall in the rejection region ($F = .613 \not> 6.94$), $H_0$ is not rejected. There is insufficient evidence to indicate the model is adequate at $\alpha = .05$.

b. $H_0$: $\beta_2 = 0$
$H_a$: $\beta_2 \neq 0$

The test statistic is $t = \dfrac{\hat{\beta}_2 - 0}{s_{\hat{\beta}_2}} = .785$

The rejection region requires $\alpha/2 = .05/2 = .025$ in each tail of the t distribution with df = n - (k + 1) = 7 - (2 + 1) = 4. From Table VI, Appendix B, $t_{.025} = 2.776$. The rejection region is $t < -2.776$ or $t > 2.776$.

Since the observed value of the test statistic does not fall in the rejection region ($t = .785 \not> 2.776$), $H_0$ is not rejected. There is insufficient evidence to indicate the addition of the quadratic term contributed significant information for the prediction of a thoroughbred horse's lifetime at $\alpha = .05$.

c. The plot of the residuals vs x from the straight-line model is:

PLOT OF RESID1*GESTATE LEGEND: A = 1 OBS, B = 2 OBS, ETC.

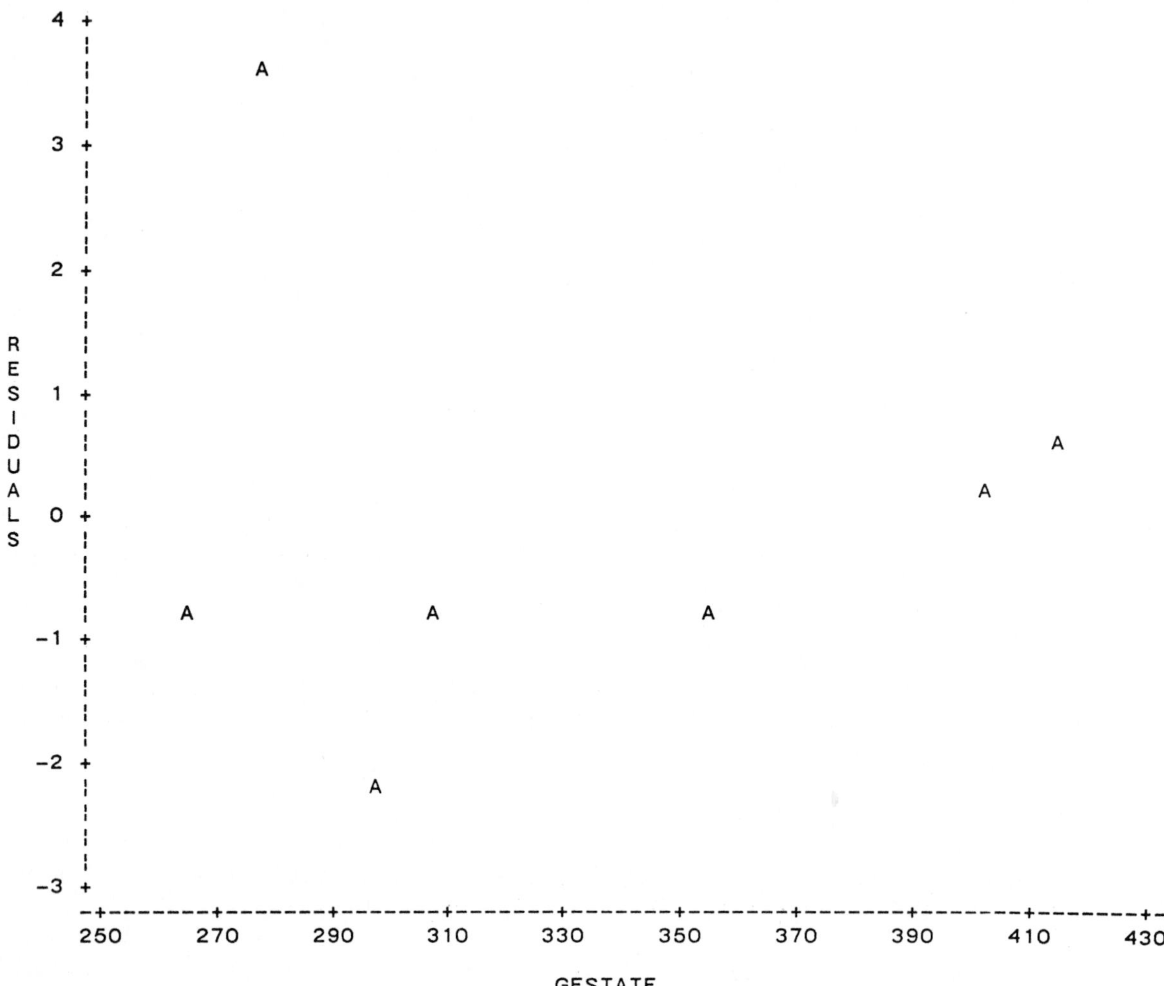

From this plot, there is no mound or bowl shaped trend which implies $x^2$ will not add to the model adequacy. Also, none of the observations are more than 2 standard deviations from the mean, indicating there are no outliers.

The plot of the residuals vs x from the quadratic model is:

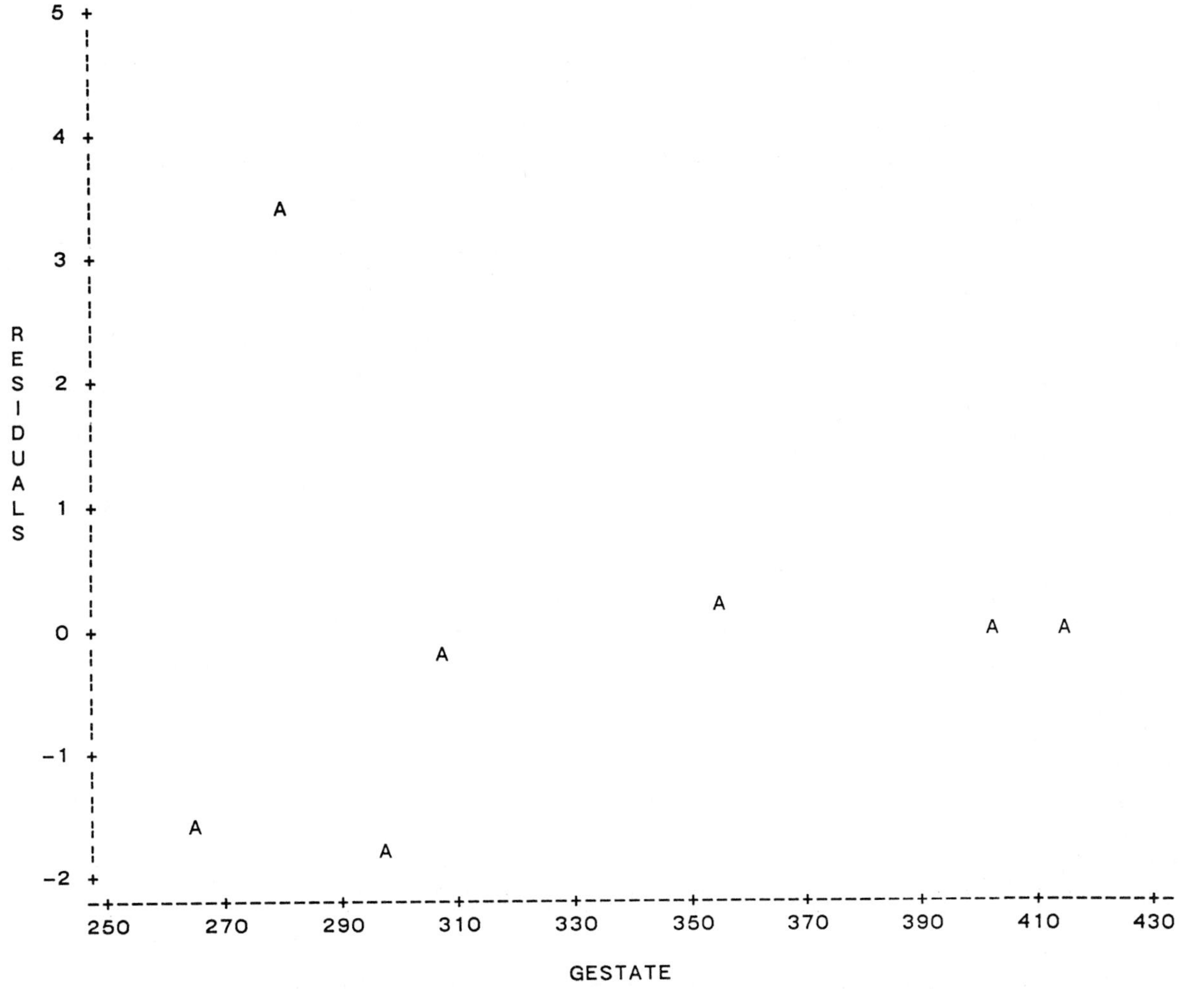


This plot looks almost exactly like that for the straight-line model. This implies adding $x^2$ had no effect. This agrees with the results in (b).

12.47 a. $\hat{y} = 12.3 + .25(6) - .0033(6^2) = 13.6812$

b. We are 95% confident the actual time lost after 6 hour of work is between 1.35 and 26.01.

Yes. This interval is so wide that it is virtually worthless.

12.49 To determine if plant A has a lower mean assembly time than plant B, we test:

$H_0$: $\beta_2 = 0$
$H_a$: $\beta_2 < 0$

The test statistic is $t = \dfrac{\hat{\beta}_2 - 0}{s_{\hat{\beta}_2}} = \dfrac{-.53}{.48} = -1.10$

The rejection region requires $\alpha = .01$ in the lower tail of the t distribution with df $= n - (k + 1) = 42 - (2 + 1) = 39$. From Table VI, Appendix B, $t_{.01} \approx 2.326$. The rejection region is $t < -2.326$ .

Since the observed value of the test statistic does not fall in the rejection region ($t = -1.10 \nless -2.326$), $H_0$ is not rejected. There is insufficient evidence to indicate plant A had a lower mean assembly time than plant B at $\alpha = .01$.

12.51 $\beta_0$ is defined as the mean proportion of customers who buy its product when price and years of experience are both 0. Since price cannot be 0, $\beta_0$ will not have a meaningful interpretation.

12.53 a. $\hat{\beta}_1 = 25$. It is estimated that the difference in mean attendance between weekend and non-weekend days is 25 people.

$\hat{\beta}_2 = 100$. It is estimated that the difference in mean attendance between sunny and overcast days is 100 people.

$\hat{\beta}_3 = 10$. It is estimated that the change in mean attendance for each additional degree is 10 people.

b. To determine if the model is useful in the prediction of daily attendance, we test:

$H_0$: $\beta_1 = \beta_2 = \beta_3 = 0$
$H_a$: At least 1 $\beta_i \neq 0$ for i = 1, 2, 3

The test statistic is $F = \dfrac{R^2/k}{(1 - R^2)/(n - (k + 1))}$

$$F = \frac{.65/3}{(1 - .65)/(30 - (3 + 1))} = \frac{.21667}{.01346} = 16.10$$

The rejection region requires $\alpha = .05$ in the upper tail of the F distribution with $\nu_1 = k = 3$ and $\nu_2 = n - (k + 1) = 30 - (3 + 1) = 26$. From Table VIII, Appendix B, $F_{.05} = 2.98$. The rejection region is $F > 2.98$.

Since the observed value of the test statistic falls in the rejection region ($F = 16.10 > 2.98$), $H_0$ is rejected. There is sufficient evidence to indicate the model is useful in the prediction of daily attendance.

c. To determine if the mean attendance increases on weekends, we test:

$H_0$: $\beta_1 = 0$
$H_a$: $\beta_1 > 0$

The test statistic is $t = \frac{\hat{\beta}_1 - 0}{s_{\hat{\beta}_1}} = \frac{25 - 0}{10} = 2.5$

The rejection region requires $\alpha = .10$ in the upper tail of the t distribution with df = n - (k + 1) = 30 - (3 + 1) = 26. From Table VI, Appendix B, $t_{.10} = 1.315$. The rejection region is $t > 1.315$.

Since the observed value of the test statistic falls in the rejection region ($t = 2.5 > 1.315$), $H_0$ is rejected. There is sufficient evidence to indicate the mean attendance increases on weekends at $\alpha = .10$.

d. For $x_1 = 0$, $x_2 = 1$, and $x_3 = 95$,

$$\hat{y} = -105 + 25(0) + 100(1) + 10(95) = 945$$

e. We are 90% confident the actual number of people attending the park will be between 645 and 1245 when the predicted temperature is 95° and the day is a sunny weekday.

12.55 Because of the interaction term, the true coefficient for $x_1$ is $(-700 + 15x_3)$. As long as the temperature, $x_3$, is more than 47°, $-700 + 15x_3$ will be a positive term.

12.57 a. To convert the data, we use

$$y_2 = \frac{y_1}{PPI} \times 100, \quad x_4 = \frac{x_2}{PPI} \times 100, \quad x_5 = \frac{x_3}{PPI} \times 100$$

The new data are:

| YEAR | $y_2$ | $x_4$ | $x_5$ |
|---|---|---|---|
| 1967 | 50.00 | 30.00 | 25.00 |
| 1968 | 117.07 | 29.27 | 25.37 |
| 1969 | 131.46 | 30.99 | 26.29 |
| 1970 | 122.28 | 30.80 | 27.17 |
| 1971 | 142.98 | 28.95 | 27.19 |
| 1972 | 195.63 | 30.23 | 28.55 |
| 1973 | 178.92 | 29.70 | 27.47 |
| 1974 | 159.28 | 28.11 | 26.23 |
| 1975 | 163.52 | 28.59 | 27.44 |
| 1976 | 180.33 | 28.96 | 29.51 |
| 1977 | 200.31 | 29.87 | 29.87 |
| 1978 | 203.06 | 28.67 | 29.14 |
| 1979 | 188.88 | 30.14 | 30.56 |
| 1980 | 175.60 | 29.76 | 30.13 |
| 1981 | 170.76 | 30.67 | 31.70 |

b. The SAS printout is:

```
DEP VARIABLE: Y2
                          ANALYSIS OF VARIANCE

                       SUM OF          MEAN
SOURCE       DF       SQUARES        SQUARE       F VALUE       PROB>F

MODEL         3   15140.33485    5046.77828         8.646       0.0017
ERROR        14    8171.79888     583.69992
C TOTAL      17   23312.13373

     ROOT MSE        24.15988      R-SQUARE        0.6495
     DEP MEAN        159.7152      ADJ R-SQ        0.5743
     C.V.            15.12685

                          PARAMETER ESTIMATES

                      PARAMETER       STANDARD      T FOR HO:
VARIABLE    DF         ESTIMATE          ERROR    PARAMETER=0     PROB > |T|

INTERCEP     1        238.42901      208.25299          1.145         0.2714
PEOPLE       1      -0.45718495     1.45936980         -0.313         0.7587
X4           1     -19.48214999     9.28088891         -2.099         0.0544
X5           1      18.03525887     8.88053110          2.031         0.0617
```

The fitted model is $\hat{y}_2 = 238.429 - .4572x_1 - 19.4821x_4 + 18.0353x_5$

The mean sales revenue (in constant dollars) is estimated to decrease by .46 (thousands of dollars) for each additional sales person, with mean price and mean competitor's price held constant.

The mean sales revenue (in constant dollars) is estimated to decrease by 19.48 (thousands of dollars) for each additional one constant dollar increase in mean price, with sales people and mean competitor's price held constant.

The mean sales revenue (in constant dollars) is estimated to increase by 18.04 (thousands of dollars) for each additional one constant dollar increase in the competitor's mean price, mean price and sales people held constant.

c. From the printout $R^2 = .6495$. About 65% of the sample variability in sales revenue (in constant dollars) is explained by the fitted model containing sales people, mean price (constant dollars), and mean competitor's price (constant dollar).

d. To investigate the usefulness of the model, we test:

$H_0$: $\beta_1 = \beta_2 = \beta_3 = 0$
$H_a$: At least 1 $\beta_i \neq 0 \quad i = 1, 2, 3$

e. The test statistic is $F = \frac{MSR}{MSE} = 8.646$.

The p-value is .0017 which is less than $\alpha = .05$. Thus, we reject $H_0$. There is sufficient evidence to indicate the model is useful for predicting sales revenue at $\alpha = .05$.

The p-value is .0017.

f. $H_0$: $\beta_2 = 0$
$H_a$: $\beta_2 < 0$

The test statistic is $t = \frac{\hat{\beta}_2 - 0}{s_{\hat{\beta}_2}} = -2.099$

The rejection region requires $\alpha = .05$ in the lower tail of the t distribution with $df = n - (k + 1) = 18 - (3 + 1) = 14$. From Table VI, Appendix B, $t_{.05} = 1.761$. The rejection region is $t < -1.761$.

Since the observed value of the test statistic falls in the rejection region ($t = -2.099 < -1.761$), $H_0$ is rejected. There is sufficient evidence to indicate that the mean sales price decreases as the mean price (constant dollars) increases, with the other variables held constant, at $\alpha = .05$.

g. For confidence coefficient .95, $\alpha = 1 - .95 = .05$ and $\alpha/2 = .05/2 = .025$. From Table VI, Appendix B, with df = 14, $t_{.025} = 2.145$. The confidence interval is:

$$\hat{\beta}_1 \pm t_{.025} s_{\hat{\beta}_1} = -.457 \pm 2.145(1.459)$$

$$\Rightarrow -.457 \pm 3.13 \Rightarrow (-3.587, 2.673)$$

We are 95% confident that the value of $\beta_1$ will fall between -3.587 and 2.673. Because the interval contains 0, there is insufficient evidence to conclude sales revenue and the number of sales people are related.

h. $x_4 = \frac{x_2}{PPI} \times 100 = \frac{90}{315} \times 100 = 28.57$

$$x_5 = \frac{x_3}{PPI} \times 100 = \frac{92}{315} \times 100 = 29.21$$

Thus, $\hat{y} = 238.429 - .457(35) - 19.482(28.57) + 18.035(29.21)$
$= 192.636$

12.59 a. $\hat{\beta}_1 = .02573$. The mean GPA is estimated to increase by .02573 for each 1 point increase in verbal score, mathematics score held constant.

$\hat{\beta}_2 = .03361$. The mean GPA is estimated to increase by .03361 for each 1 point increase in mathematics score, verbal score held constant.

b. The standard deviation is $\sqrt{MSE} = \sqrt{.16183} = .40228$. We would expect about 95% of the observations to fall within $2(.40228) = .80456$ of the predicted value.

$R^2 = .68106$. About 68% of the sample variability in GPA's is explained by the model containing verbal and mathematics scores.

c. To determine if the model is useful for predicting GPA, we test:

$H_0$: $\beta_1 = \beta_2 = 0$
$H_a$: At least 1 $\beta_i \neq 0$ $i = 1, 2$.

The test statistic is $F = \frac{MSR}{MSE} = \frac{6.39297}{.16183} = 39.505$

The p-value is .0000. Since $.0000 < \alpha = .05$, $H_0$ is rejected. There is sufficient evidence to indicate the model is useful for predicting GPA at $\alpha = .05$.

d. For $x_2 = 60$, $\hat{y} = -1.57 + .026x_1 + .034(60) = .47 + .026x_1$

For $x_2 = 75$, $\hat{y} = -1.57 + .026x_1 + .034(75) = .98 + .026x_1$

For $x_2 = 90$, $\hat{y} = -1.57 + .026x_1 + .034(90) = 1.49 + .026x_1$

The plot is:

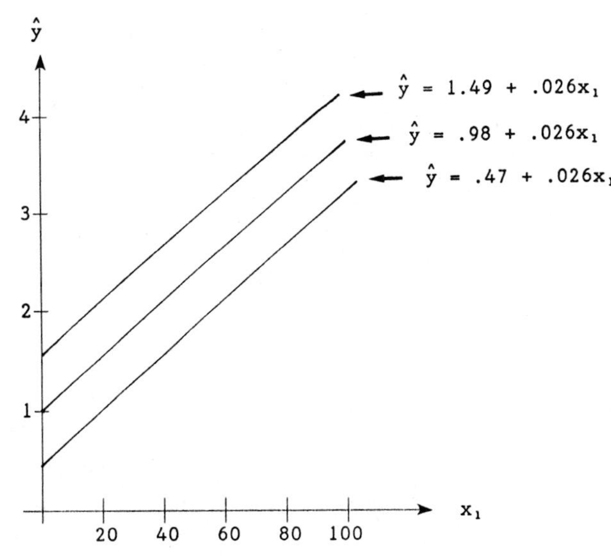


12.61 a. The standard deviation for the first-order model is

$$\sqrt{MSE} = \sqrt{.16183} = .4023$$

The standard deviation for the second-order model is

$$\sqrt{MSE} = \sqrt{.03502} = .1871$$

The relative precision for the first-order model is $\pm 2(.4023) \Rightarrow \pm .8046$.

The relative precision for the second-order model is $\pm 2(.1871 \Rightarrow \pm .3742$.

b. To determine if the model is useful, we test:

$H_0$: $\beta_1 = \beta_2 = \beta_3 = \beta_4 = \beta_5 = 0$
$H_a$: At least 1 $\beta_i \neq 0$ $i = 1, 2, \ldots, 5$

The test statistic is $F = \frac{MSR}{MSE} = \frac{3.51655}{.03502} = 100.409$

The p-value is .0000. Since the p-value is less than $\alpha = .05$, $H_0$ is rejected. There is sufficient evidence to indicate the model is useful for predicting GPA at $\alpha = .05$.

c. To determine if the interaction term is important, we test:

$H_0$: $\beta_5 = 0$
$H_a$: $\beta_5 \neq 0$

The test statistic is $t = 1.675$.

The p-value is .1032. Since the p-value is not less than $\alpha = .10$, $H_0$ is not rejected. There is insufficient evidence to indicate the interaction term is important for predicting GPA at $\alpha = .10$.

12.63 a. The yearly per capita motor fuel consumption is the average amount of fuel consumed per person per year.

b. First, compute $y_2 = \frac{y}{\text{population}}$ to get the per capita fuel consumption.

The model is $y_2 = \beta_0 + \beta_1 x_1 + \varepsilon_i$, where $x_1$ is the relative price of a gallon of gasoline. The SAS printout is:

DEP VARIABLE: PERCAP

ANALYSIS OF VARIANCE

| SOURCE | DF | SUM OF SQUARES | MEAN SQUARE | F VALUE | PROB>F |
|---|---|---|---|---|---|
| MODEL | 1 | 172.38330 | 172.38330 | 0.134 | 0.7185 |
| ERROR | 17 | 21808.64849 | 1282.86168 | | |
| C TOTAL | 18 | 21981.03179 | | | |

| | | | |
|---|---|---|---|
| ROOT MSE | 35.81706 | R-SQUARE | 0.0078 |
| DEP MEAN | 326.5969 | ADJ R-SQ | -0.0505 |
| C.V. | 10.96675 | | |

PARAMETER ESTIMATES

| VARIABLE | DF | PARAMETER ESTIMATE | STANDARD ERROR | T FOR HO: PARAMETER=0 | PROB > \|T\| |
|---|---|---|---|---|---|
| INTERCEP | 1 | 343.63428 | 47.19849286 | 7.281 | 0.0001 |
| RELPRICE | 1 | -15.77534131 | 43.03492828 | -0.367 | 0.7185 |

The estimated model is $\hat{y}_2 = 343.634 - 15.775x_1$

c. To determine if the model is useful, we test:

$H_0$: $\beta_1 = 0$
$H_a$: $\beta_1 \neq 0$

The test statistic is $F = \frac{MSR}{MSE} = .134$

The p-value is .7185. Since the p-value is not less than $\alpha = .05$, $H_0$ is not rejected. There is insufficient evidence to indicate the model is useful at $\alpha = .05$.

$R^2 = .0078$.

d. The SAS printout for fitting the model $y_2 = \beta_0 + \beta_1 x_1 + \beta_2 x_2 + \varepsilon$ where $x_2$ = average gross real weekly earnings is:

DEP VARIABLE: PERCAP

ANALYSIS OF VARIANCE

| SOURCE | DF | SUM OF SQUARES | MEAN SQUARE | F VALUE | PROB>F |
|---|---|---|---|---|---|
| MODEL | 2 | 8614.33837 | 4307.16919 | 5.156 | 0.0187 |
| ERROR | 16 | 13366.69341 | 835.41834 | | |
| C TOTAL | 18 | 21981.03179 | | | |

| | | | |
|---|---|---|---|
| ROOT MSE | 28.9036 | R-SQUARE | 0.3919 |
| DEP MEAN | 326.5969 | ADJ R-SQ | 0.3159 |
| C.V. | 8.849932 | | |

PARAMETER ESTIMATES

| VARIABLE | DF | PARAMETER ESTIMATE | STANDARD ERROR | T FOR HO: PARAMETER=0 | PROB > \|T\| |
|---|---|---|---|---|---|
| INTERCEP | 1 | -854.61187 | 378.86315 | -2.256 | 0.0384 |
| RELPRICE | 1 | 189.86600 | 73.42289466 | 2.586 | 0.0199 |
| REALEARN | 1 | 9.59538342 | 3.01851138 | 3.179 | 0.0058 |

The least squares estimated model is

$$\hat{y}_2 = -854.612 + 189.866x_1 + 9.595x_2$$

e. To determine the usefulness of the model, we test:

$H_0$: $\beta_1 = \beta_2 = 0$
$H_a$: At least 1 $\beta_i \neq 0$ for i = 1, 2

The test statistic is $F = \frac{MSR}{MSE} = 5.156$

The p-value is .0187. Since the p-value is less than $\alpha = .05$, $H_0$ is rejected. There is sufficient evidence to indicate the model is useful for predicting per capita consumption at $\alpha = .05$.

$R^2 = .3919$.

f. No. It seems like as the mean relative price of gasoline increases, the per capita consumption should go down which would mean $\beta_1 < 0$. Our estimate of $\beta_1$ is $> 0$.

g. For $x_1 = 1.521$ and $x_2 = 110.36$,

$$\hat{y}_2 = -854.612 + 189.866(1.521) + 9.595(110.36) = 493.078$$

Both $x_1 = 1.521$ and $x_2 = 110.36$ are outside the observed range for those values. Therefore, we must be very cautious using this prediction.

h. The plot of the residuals versus the relative price is:

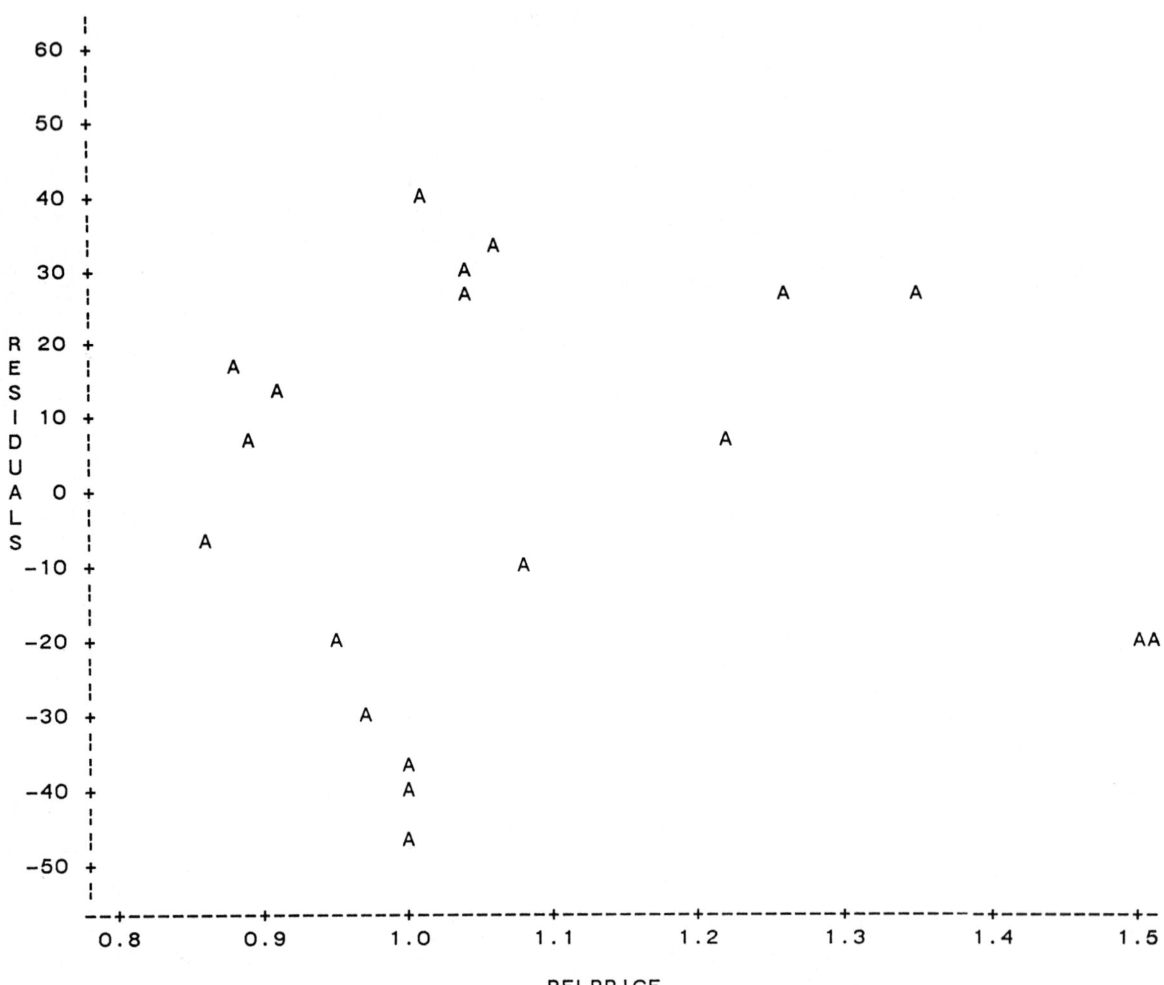


There is no apparent mound or bowl shaped trend. Thus, it appears that adding (relative price)$^2$ will not improve the model. The standard deviation is $\sqrt{MSE} = 28.90$. All residuals lie within $\pm 2(28.90) \Rightarrow \pm 57.80$. Thus, there is no evidence of any outliers.

The plot of the residuals versus real weekly earnings is:

PLOT OF RESID1*REALEARN     LEGEND:  A = 1 OBS, B = 2 OBS, ETC.

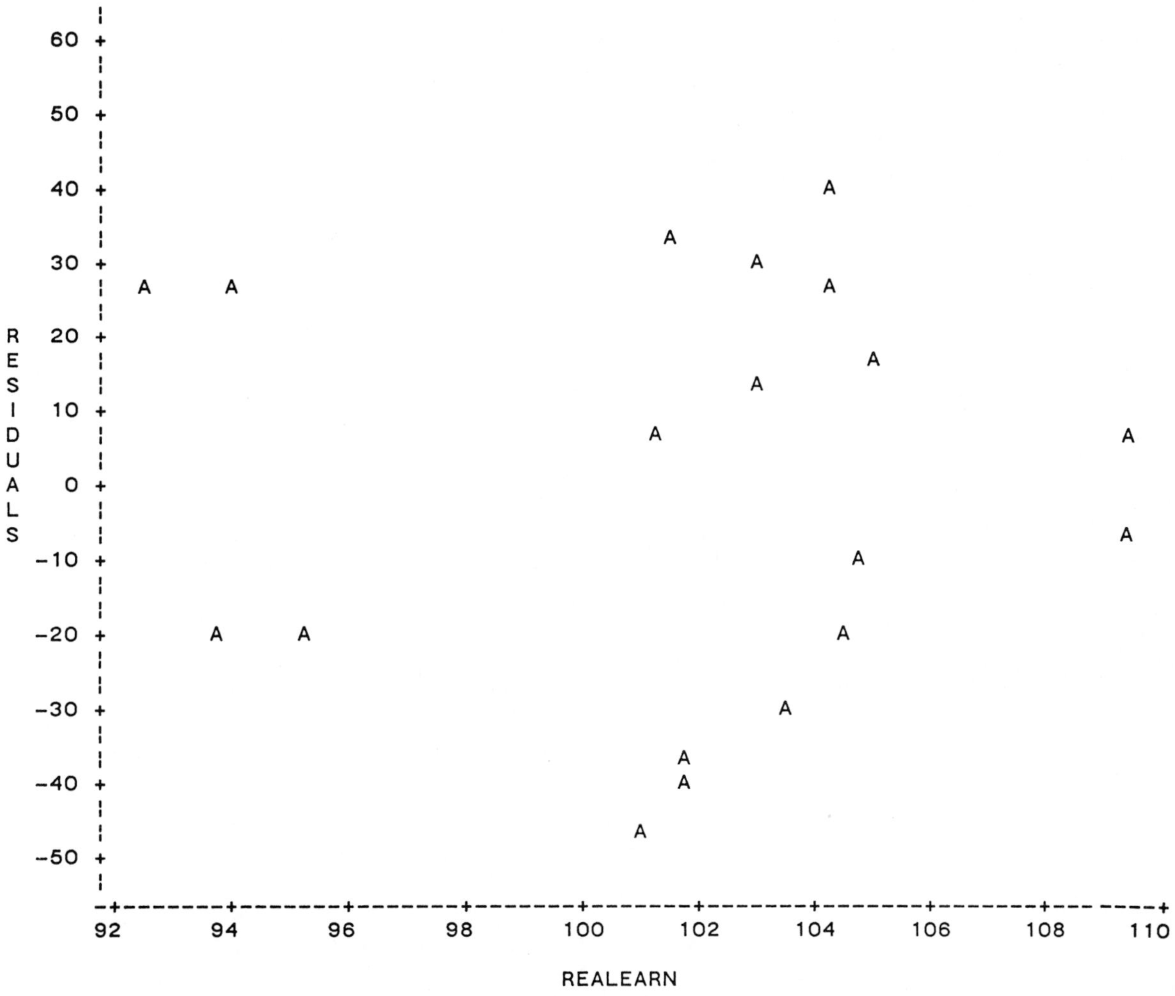

```
         |
      60 +
         |
         |
      50 +
         |
         |
      40 +                                                        A
         |
         |                                           A
      30 +                                                  A
         |   A     A                                              A
         |
R     20 +
E        |                                                           A
S        |                                                  A
I     10 +
D        |                                          A                                    A
U        |
A      0 +
L        |
S        |                                                                               A
     -10 +                                                          A
         |
         |
     -20 +        A      A                                         A
         |
         |
     -30 +                                                    A
         |
         |                                            A
     -40 +                                            A
         |
         |                                         A
     -50 +
         |
     -+--------+--------+--------+--------+--------+--------+--------+--------+--------+
     92       94       96       98      100      102      104      106      108      110

                                     REALEARN
```

Again, there is no bowl or mound shape trend in the plot. This indicates that adding (real weekly earnings)$^2$ will not improve the model. The standard deviation is 28.90. All observations fall within two standard deviations of the mean. Thus, there are no outliers.

# CHAPTER 13

## INTRODUCTION TO MODEL BUILDING

13.1 a. Weight would be quantitative. It could take on values greater than 0.

b. Color would be qualitative. Values color could take on are blue, red, green, etc.

c. Age would be quantitative. Age could take on values greater than 0.

d. Hardness would be quantitative. It could take on values greater than 0.

e. Package design would be qualitative. Values it could take on include design A, design B, etc.

13.3 a. Age is quantitative. Values could range from 18 to 70 years.

b. Years of experience is quantitative. Values could range from 0 to 50 years.

c. Highest education degree is qualitative. Possible levels include high school, bachelors degree, masters degree, Ph.D., etc.

d. Job classification is qualitative. Possible levels include maintenance, clerical, managerial, etc.

e. Marital status is qualitative. Possible levels include single, married, divorced, widowed, etc.

f. Religious preference is qualitative. Possible levels include Catholic, Jewish, Presbyterian, Methodist, Baptist, etc.

g. Salary is quantitative. Values could range from $10,000 to $150,000.

h. Sex is qualitative. Possible levels include male and female.

13.5 y: ocean transport rates - quantitative
$x_1$: shipment size - quantitative
$x_2$: distance to destination - quantitative
$x_3$: bunker fuel price - quantitative
$x_4$: type of flagship - qualitative

13.7 Since the lines graphed are both parabolas, the order of the polynomial in both cases is second order. In the graph (a), $\beta_0$ is 4 (value of y when x = 0) and $\beta_2$ is negative because the parabola opens downward. In graph (b), $\beta_0$ is 8 (value of y when x = 0) and $\beta_2$ is positive because the parabola opens upward.

13.9 $E(y) = \beta_0 + \beta_1 x + \beta_2 x^2$

13.11 a. Because the company suspects that new and old copiers require more service calls than those in the middle, the model would be

$$E(y) = \beta_0 + \beta_1 x + \beta_2 x^2$$

where y = number of service calls
x = age of copier

b. $\beta_0 > 0$ and $\beta_2 > 0$. Since the parabola will open upwards (number of service calls larger for young and old machines) both $\beta_0$ and $\beta_2$ will be greater than 0.

13.13 The model would be $E(y) = \beta_0 + \beta_1 x + \beta_2 x^2$. Since the value of y is expected to increase and then decrease as x gets larger, $\beta_2$ will be negative. A sketch of the model would be

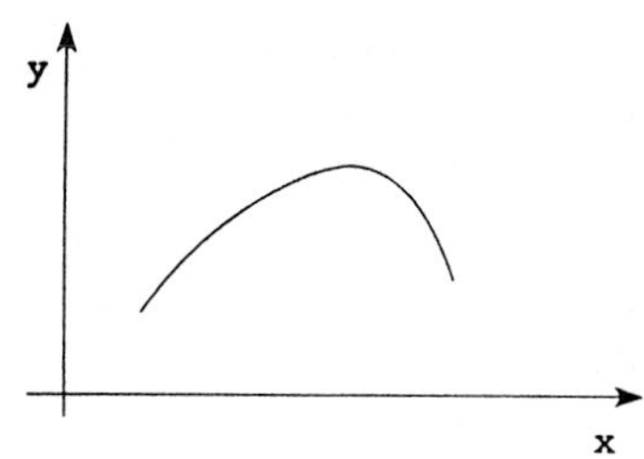


13.15 a. A model that would allow the assembly time to decrease and then increase would be

$$E(y) = \beta_0 + \beta_1 x + \beta_2 x^2$$

where y = assembly time
x = time since lunch
$\beta_0$ = y-intercept
$\beta_1$ = shifts parabola to right or left
$\beta_2$ = rate of curvature

b. The sketch of the model is:

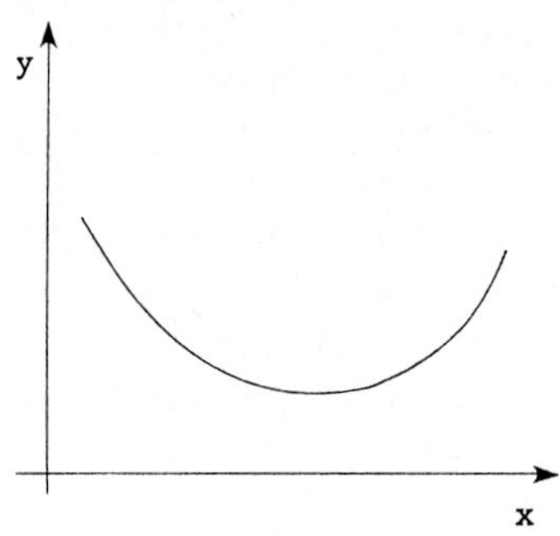


13.17 a. A scattergram for the data is:

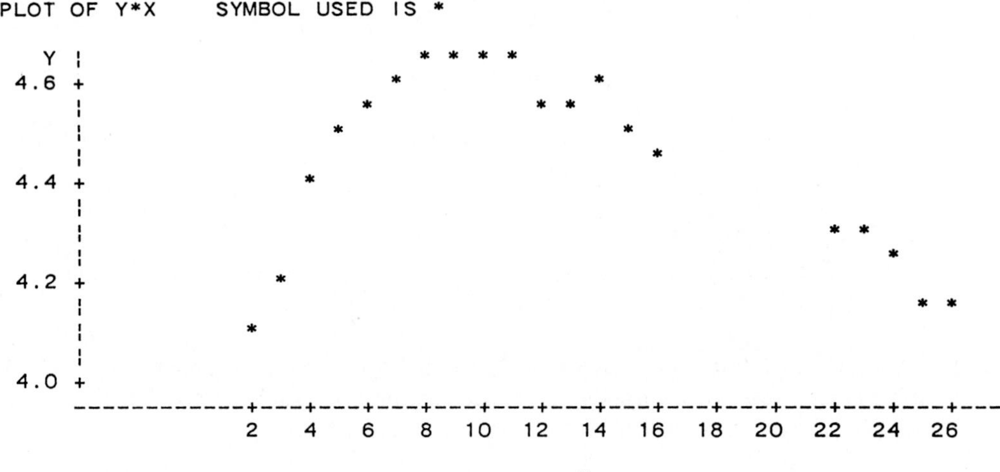


From the scattergram, it appears that as the age of the mill increases, the productivity increases for a while and then decreases.

b. $E(y) = \beta_0 + \beta_1 x + \beta_2 x^2$

c. The SAS computer printout for fitting the model to the data is shown below:

DEPENDENT VARIABLE: y

| SOURCE | DF | SUM OF SQUARES | MEAN SQUARE | F VALUE |
|---|---|---|---|---|
| MODEL | 2 | 0.60046005 | 0.30023002 | 42.61 |
| ERROR | 17 | 0.11979495 | 0.00704676 | PR > F |
| CORRECTED TOTAL | 19 | 0.72025500 | | 0.0001 |

| R-SQUARE | C.V. | ROOT MSE | Y MEAN |
|---|---|---|---|
| 0.833677 | 1.8921 | 0.08394499 | 4.43650000 |

| PARAMETER | ESTIMATE | T FOR HO: PARAMETER = 0 | PR > \|T\| | STD ERROR OF ESTIMATE |
|---|---|---|---|---|
| INTERCEPT | 4.07745257 | 61.22 | 0.0001 | 0.06659959 |
| X | 0.08399653 | 7.51 | 0.0001 | 0.01118441 |
| X*X | -0.00324702 | -8.52 | 0.0001 | 0.00038121 |

The least squares prediction equation is

$$\hat{y} = 4.077 + .084x - .0032x^2$$

d. To determine if the model in b provides information for the prediction of productivity, we test:

$H_0$: $\beta_1 = \beta_2 = 0$
$H_a$: At least one of the $\beta$'s is not 0

The test statistic is $F = 42.61$.

The rejection region requires $\alpha = .05$ in the upper tail of the F distribution with numerator df = k = 2 and denominator df = n - (k + 1) = 20 - (2 + 1) = 17. From Table VIII, Appendix B, $F_{.05} = 3.59$. The rejection region is $F > 3.59$.

Since the observed values of the test statistic falls in the rejection region ($F = 42.61 > 3.59$), $H_0$ is rejected. There is sufficient evidence to indicate the model provides information for the prediction of productivity at $\alpha = .05$.

13.19 a. The model for a straight line is $E(y) = \beta_0 + \beta_1 x$.

Some preliminary calculations are:

$\sum x_i = 16.52 \quad \sum x_i^2 = 19.553 \quad \sum x_i y_i = 174.2575$

$\sum y_i = 254.75 \quad \sum y_i^2 = 2860.6875$

$$SS_{xy} = \sum x_i y_i - \frac{\sum x_i \sum y_i}{n} = 174.2575 - \frac{16.52(254.75)}{23} = -8.7194565$$

$$SS_{xx} = \sum x_i^2 - \frac{(\sum x_i)^2}{n} = 19.553 - \frac{16.52^2}{23} = 7.68733043$$

$$SS_{yy} = \sum y_i^2 - \frac{(\sum y_i)^2}{n} = 2860.6875 - \frac{254.75^2}{23} = 39.054348$$

$$\hat{\beta}_1 = \frac{SS_{xy}}{SS_{xx}} = \frac{-8.7194565}{7.68733043} = -1.134263263 \approx -1.13$$

$$\hat{\beta}_0 = \bar{y} - \hat{\beta}_1 \bar{x} = \frac{254.75}{23} - (-1.134263263)\frac{16.52}{23} = 11.89078387 \approx 11.9$$

The fitted line is $\hat{y} = 11.9 - 1.13x$.

$$SSR = \frac{SS_{xy}^2}{SS_{xx}} = \frac{(-8.7194565)^2}{7.68733043} = 9.890159184$$

$$SS(\text{Total}) = SS_{yy} = 39.054348$$

$$R^2 = \frac{SSR}{SS(\text{Total})} = \frac{9.890159184}{39.054348} = .253$$

b. Based on the results of (a), it appears that as the rate of growth in money supply increases, the prime interest rate decreases (because $\hat{\beta}_1$ is negative).

c. The scatter plot, using SAS, is

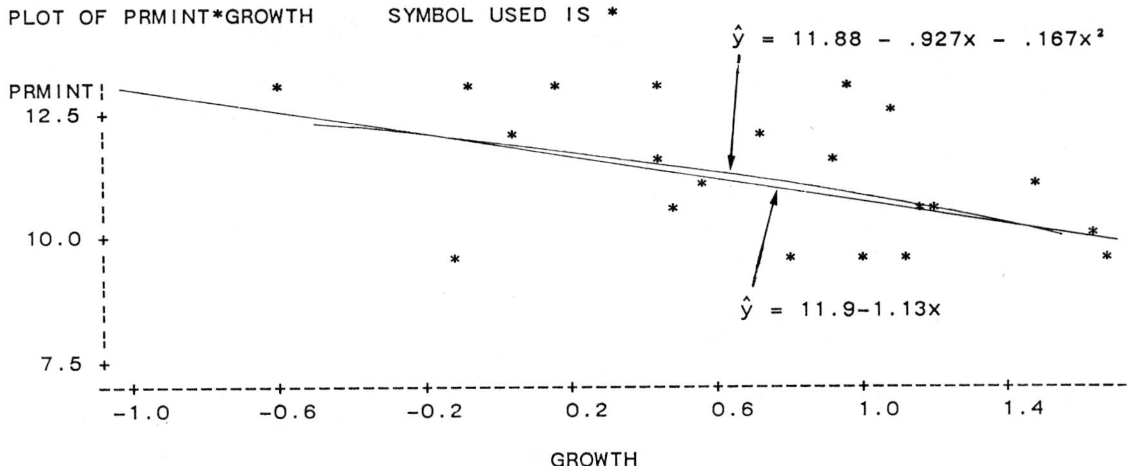


From the scattergram and the least squares line, there is no indication that a second-order model would better explain the variation in interest rates.

d. The SAS computer printout for fitting the model to the data is:

DEPENDENT VARIABLE: PRMINT

| SOURCE | DF | SUM OF SQUARES | MEAN SQUARE | F VALUE |
|---|---|---|---|---|
| MODEL | 2 | 9.99620762 | 4.99810381 | 3.44 |
| ERROR | 20 | 29.05814020 | 1.45290701 | PR > F |
| CORRECTED TOTAL | 22 | 39.05434783 | | 0.0520 |

| R-SQUARE | C.V. | ROOT MSE | PRMINT MEAN |
|---|---|---|---|
| 0.255956 | 10.8826 | 1.20536592 | 11.07608696 |

| PARAMETER | ESTIMATE | T FOR HO: PARAMETER = 0 | PR > ¦T¦ | STD ERROR OF ESTIMATE |
|---|---|---|---|---|
| INTERCEPT | 11.88419801 | 29.59 | 0.0001 | 0.40158319 |
| GROWTH | -0.92731426 | -1.05 | 0.3050 | 0.88077244 |
| GROWTH*GROWTH | -0.16710084 | -0.27 | 0.7898 | 0.61850824 |

The fitted model is

$$\hat{y} = 11.88 - .927x - .167x^2$$

$$R^2 = \frac{SSR}{SSTOT} = \frac{9.9962}{39.0543} = .256.$$

f. To determine if $\beta_2$ is equal to 0 or not, we test:

$H_0: \beta_2 = 0$
$H_a: \beta_2 \neq 0$

The test statistic is $t = \dfrac{\hat{\beta}_2 - 0}{s(\hat{\beta}_2)} = -.27$ from printout.

The rejection region requires $\alpha/2 = .05/2 = .025$ in each tail of the t distribution with df = n - (k + 1) = 23. From Table VI, Appendix B, $t_{.025} = 2.069$. The rejection region is $t < -2.069$ or $t > 2.069$.

Since the observed value of the test statistic does not fall in the rejection region ($t = -.27 \nless -2.069$ and $-.27 \ngtr 2.069$), $H_0$ is not rejected. There is insufficient evidence to indicate $\beta_2$ is not 0 at $\alpha = .05$. Thus, it appears the first order model is adequate for explaining the variation in interest rates.

13.21 a. $E(y) = \beta_0 + \beta_1 x_1 + \beta_2 x_2$

b. $E(y) = \beta_0 + \beta_1 x_1 + \beta_2 x_2 + \beta_3 x_1 x_2$

c. $E(y) = \beta_0 + \beta_1 x_1 + \beta_2 x_2 + \beta_3 x_1 x_2 + \beta_4 x_1^2 + \beta_5 x_2^2$

13.23 a. The order of the model is second order, because it has the term $x_1 x_2$ in it.

b. The response surface is a twisted plane.

c. The contour line when $x_1 = 0$ is

$E(y) = 4 - 0 + 2x_2 + 0(x_2) = 4 + 2x_2$

The contour line when $x_1 = 1$ is

$E(y) = 4 - 1 + 2x_2 + x_2 = 3 + 3x_2$

The contour line when $x_1 = 2$ is

$E(y) = 4 - 2 + 2x_2 + 2x_2 = 2 + 4x_2$

The plots are:

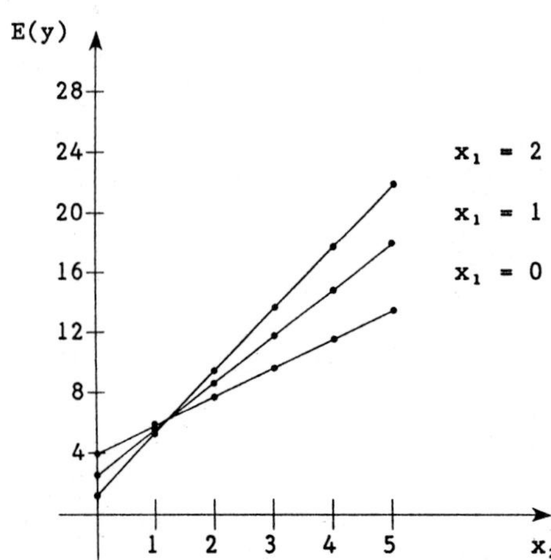

d. The interactive term $x_1x_2$ allows the contour lines to be non-parallel.

e. When $x_1 = 0$, the contour line is $E(y) = 4 + 2x_2$. For each unit change in $x_2$, $E(y)$ increases by 2 units.

When $x_1 = 1$, the contour line is $E(y) = 3 + 3x_2$. For each unit change in $x_2$, $E(y)$ increases by 3 units.

When $x_1 = 2$, the contour line is $E(y) = 2 + 4x_2$. For each unit change in $x_2$, $E(y)$ increases by 4 units.

f. When $x_1 = 2$ and $x_2 = 4$, $E(y) = 18$. When $x_1 = 0$ and $x_2 = 5$, $E(y) = 14$. Thus, the change in $E(y)$ is from 18 to 14 or -4.

13.25 a. The prediction equation is $\hat{y} = \hat{\beta}_0 + \hat{\beta}_1x_1 + \hat{\beta}_2x_2 + \hat{\beta}_3x_1x_2$ or $\hat{y} = -2.550 + 3.82x_1 + 2.63x_2 - 1.29x_1x_2$

b. The response surface is a twisted plane.

c. For $x_2 = 1$, $\hat{y} = -2.55 + 3.82x_1 + 2.63(1) - 1.29x_1(1)$
$= .08 + 2.53x_1$

For $x_2 = 3$, $\hat{y} = -2.55 + 3.82x_1 + 2.63(3) - 1.29\ x_1(3)$
$= 5.34 - .05x_1$

For $x_2 = 5$, $\hat{y} = -2.55 + 3.82x_1 + 2.63(5) - 1.29x_1(5)$
$= 10.6 - 2.63x_1$

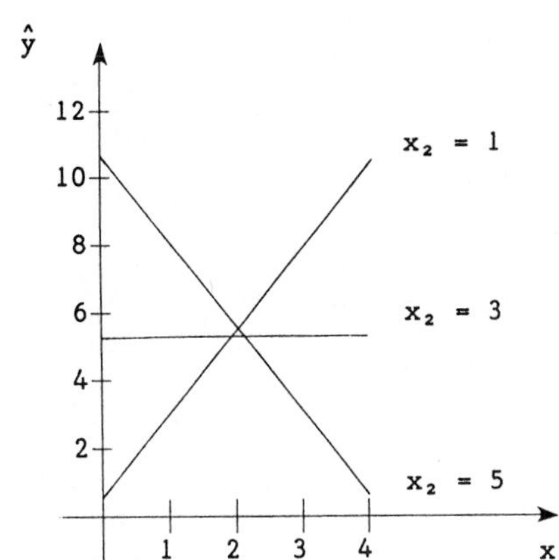


d. If $x_1$ and $x_2$ interact, the effect of $x_1$ on y is not the same at each level of $x_2$. When $x_2 = 1$, as $x_1$ increase from 0 to 4, $\hat{y}$ increases from .08 to 10.2. When $x_2 = 5$, as $x_1$ increases from 0 to 4, $\hat{y}$ decreases from 10.6 to .08.

e. $H_0: \beta_3 = 0$
$H_a: \beta_3 \neq 0$

f. The test statistic is $t = \frac{\hat{\beta}_3 - 0}{s(\hat{\beta}_3)} = \frac{-1.285 - 0}{.1594} = -8.06$

The rejection region requires $\alpha/2 = .01/2 = .005$ in each tail of the t distribution. From Table VI, Appendix B, $t_{.005} = 3.106$ with df = n - 4 = 15 - 4 = 11. The rejection region is $t > 3.106$ or $t < -3.106$.

Since the observed value of the test statistic falls in the rejection region ($t = -8.06 < -3.106$), $H_0$ is rejected. There is sufficient evidence to indicate that $x_1$ and $x_2$ interact at $\alpha = .01$.

13.27 a. Both independent variables are quantitative.

b. $E(y) = \beta_0 + \beta_1x_1 + \beta_2x_2$

c. $E(y) = \beta_0 + \beta_1x_1 + \beta_2x_2 + \beta_3x_1x_2$

If $x_1$ and $x_2$ interact, the plot of the contour lines may look like:

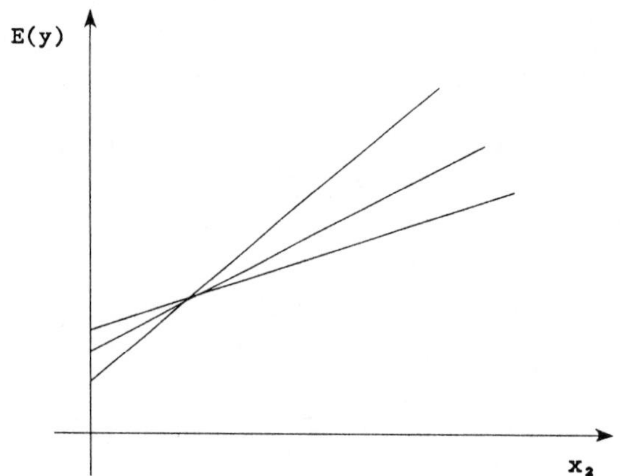


Each line corresponds to a different value of $x_1$.

d. $E(y) = \beta_0 + \beta_1x_1 + \beta_2x_2 + \beta_3x_1x_2 + \beta_4x_1^2 + \beta_5x_2^2$

13.29 a. The prediction equation is

$$\hat{y} = 149 + .472x_1 - .0993x_2 - .0005x_1^2 + .000015x_2^2$$

b. Since the signs of $x_1^2$ and $x_2^2$ differ, the response surface will be saddle-shaped.

c. To test to see if the model is useful for predicting quarterly sales, we test:

$H_0: \beta_1 = \beta_2 = \beta_3 = \beta_4 = 0$
$H_a$: At least 1 $\beta_i \neq 0$

The test statistic is $F = \frac{MSR}{MSE} = \frac{1500.52}{47.40} = 31.66$

The rejection region requires $\alpha = .01$ in the upper tail of the F distribution. From Table X, Appendix B, $F_{.01} = 5.67$ with numerator df = k = 4 and denominator df = n - (k + 1) = 16 - (4 + 1) = 11. The rejection region is $F > 5.67$.

Since the observed value of the test statistic falls in the rejection region ($F = 31.66 > 5.67$), $H_0$ is rejected. There is sufficient evidence to indicate the model is useful for predicting quarterly sales at $\alpha = .01$.

d. It appears the variation in air conditioner sales could be explained by a less complex model. The t-values associated with $\hat{\beta}_2$, $\hat{\beta}_3$, and $\hat{\beta}_4$ are all fairly small. This would indicate that the terms $x_2$, $x_1^2$, and $x_2^2$ may not be necessary.

13.31 a. $H_a$: At least one of the $\beta$'s ($\beta_3$, $\beta_4$, or $\beta_5$) is not 0.

b. To compute the test statistic, F, the following calculations are necessary. First the complete model with all terms is fit, and the sum of squares for error is computed, $SSE_2$. Then, the reduced model without the terms associated with $\beta_3$, $\beta_4$ and $\beta_5$ is fit, and the sum of squares for error is computed, $SSE_1$. The test statistic, then, is:

$$F = \frac{(SSE_1 - SSE_2)/(k - g)}{SSE_2/(n - (k + 1))}$$

where n = total sample size, k + 1 = number of $\beta$ parameters in the model, and k - g = number of $\beta$ parameters in $H_0$.

c. The numerator degrees of freedom is k - g = 3 and the denominator degrees of freedom is n - (k + 1) = 30 - (5 + 1) = 24.

13.33 By adding variables to the model, SSE will decrease or stay the same. Thus, $SSE_2 \leq SSE_1$. Therefore, the numerator of the F, $(SSE_1 - SSE_2)/(k - g)$, is always positive. The only time $H_0$ will be rejected is when the difference between $SSE_1$ and $SSE_2$ is large. Therefore, the F is only a one-tailed, upper-tailed test.

13.35 a. To determine whether the complete model contributes information for the prediction of y, we test:

$H_0: \beta_1 = \beta_2 = \beta_3 = \beta_4 = \beta_5 = 0$
$H_a$: At least one of the $\beta$'s is not 0

b. To determine whether a second-order model contributes more information than a first-order model for the prediction of y, we test:

$H_0$: $\beta_3 = \beta_4 = \beta_5 = 0$
$H_a$: At least one of the parameters $\beta_3$, $\beta_4$, or $\beta_5$, is not 0

c. The test statistic is $F = \frac{MSR}{MSE} = \frac{982.31}{53.84} = 18.24$

The rejection region requires $\alpha = .05$ in the upper tail of the F distribution with numerator df = k = 5 and denominator df = n - (k + 1) = 40 - (5 + 1) = 34. From Table VIII, Appendix B, $F_{.05} \approx 2.53$. The rejection region is F > 2.53.

Since the observed value of the test statistic falls in the rejection region (F = 18.24 > 2.53), $H_0$ is rejected. There is sufficient evidence to indicate that the complete model contributes information for the prediction of y at $\alpha = .05$.

d. The test statistic is $F = \frac{(SSE_1 - SSE_2)/(k - g)}{SSE_2/(n - (k + 1))}$

$$= \frac{(3197.16 - 1830.44)/(5 - 2)}{1830.44/(40 - (5 + 1))} = \frac{455.5733}{53.8365} = 8.4622$$

The rejection region requires $\alpha = .05$ in the upper tail of the F distribution with numerator df = k - g = 3 and denominator df = n - (k + 1) = 40 - (5 + 1) = 34. From Table VIII, Appendix B, $F_{.05} \approx 2.92$. The rejection region is F > 2.92.

Since the observed value of the test statistic falls in the rejection region (F = 8.4622 > 2.92), $H_0$ is rejected. There is sufficient evidence to indicate the second-order model contributes more information than a first-order model for the prediction of y at $\alpha = .05$.

13.37 To determine if the second-order model contributes more information for the prediction of y than a first-order model, we test:

$H_0$: $\beta_3 = \beta_4 = \beta_5 = 0$
$H_a$: At least one of the parameters, $\beta_3$, $\beta_4$, or $\beta_5$, is not 0

The test statistic is $F = \frac{(SSE_1 - SSE_2)/(k - g)}{SSE_2/(n - (k + 1))}$

$$= \frac{(2094.4 - 159.94)/(5 - 2)}{159.94/(12 - (5 + 1))} = \frac{644.82}{26.6567} = 24.19$$

The rejection region requires $\alpha = .05$ in the upper tail of the F distribution with numerator df = k - g = 5 - 2 = 3 and denominator df = n - (k + 1) = 12 - (5 + 1) = 6. From Table VIII, Appendix B, $F_{.05} = 4.76$. The rejection region is F > 4.76.

Since the observed value of the test statistic falls in the rejection region ($F = 24.19 > 4.76$), $H_0$ is rejected. There is sufficient evidence to conclude that a second-order model contributes more information for the prediction of y than a first-order model at $\alpha = .05$.

13.39 a. The SAS printout from fitting the model

$$E(y) = \beta_0 + \beta_1 x_1 + \beta_2 x_2 + \beta_3 x_1^2 + \beta_4 x_2^2 + \beta_5 x_1 x_2 \text{ is:}$$

DEPENDENT VARIABLE: y

| SOURCE | DF | SUM OF SQUARES | MEAN SQUARE | F VALUE |
|---|---|---|---|---|
| MODEL | 5 | 16.34407624 | 3.26881525 | 77.10 |
| ERROR | 19 | 0.80552376 | 0.04239599 | PR > F |
| CORRECTED TOTAL | 24 | 17.14960000 | | 0.0001 |

| R-SQUARE | C.V. | ROOT MSE | Y MEAN |
|---|---|---|---|
| 0.953030 | 6.6335 | 0.20590286 | 3.10400000 |

| PARAMETER | ESTIMATE | T FOR H0: PARAMETER = 0 | PR > \|T\| | STD ERROR OF ESTIMATE |
|---|---|---|---|---|
| INTERCEPT | 1.11899375 | 3.84 | 0.0011 | 0.29135795 |
| X1 | -0.00258029 | -0.15 | 0.8808 | 0.01697319 |
| X2 | 0.69999185 | 8.99 | 0.0001 | 0.07786716 |
| X1*X2 | 0.00017961 | 1.35 | 0.1929 | 0.00013306 |
| X2*X2 | -0.03025608 | -3.36 | 0.0033 | 0.00901297 |
| X1*X2 | -0.00148594 | -0.65 | 0.5248 | 0.00229363 |

The fitted model is

$$\hat{y} = 1.119 - .0026x_1 + .7x_2 + .00018x_1^2 - .03026x_2^2 - .00149x_1x_2$$

b. To determine if the complete second-order model is useful for explaining the variation in household food consumption, we test:

$H_0$: $\beta_1 = \beta_2 = \beta_3 = \beta_4 = \beta_5 = 0$
$H_a$: At least one of the $\beta$'s is not 0

The test statistic is $F = 77.10$ (from printout).

The rejection region requires $\alpha = .05$ in the upper tail of the F distribution with numerator df = k = 5 and denominator df = n - (k + 1) = 25 - (5 + 1) = 19. From Table VIII, Appendix B, $F_{.05} = 2.74$. The rejection region is $F > 2.74$.

Since the observed value of the test statistic falls in the rejection region ($F = 77.10 > 2.74$), $H_0$ is rejected. There is sufficient evidence to indicate the second-order model is useful for predicting household food consumption at $\alpha = .05$.

c. To determine if at least one of the β's associated with the second-order terms differ form 0, we test:

$H_0: \beta_3 = \beta_4 = \beta_5 = 0$
$H_a$: At least one of the β's is not 0

To compute the test statistic, the first order model, $E(y) = \beta_0 + \beta_1 x_1 + \beta_2 x_2$ must be fit. The SAS printout is shown on page 680. The test statistic is

$$F = \frac{(SSE_1 - SSE_2)/(k - g)}{SSE_2/[n - (k + 1)]} = \frac{(1.6873 - .8055)/(5 - 2)}{.8055/[25 - (5 + 1)]}$$

$$= \frac{.2939}{.0424} = 6.93$$

The rejection region requires $\alpha = .05$ in the upper tail of the F distribution with numerator df $= k - g = 5 - 2 = 3$ and denominator df $= n - (k + 1) = 25 - (5 + 1) = 19$. From Table VIII, Appendix B, $F_{.05} = 3.13$. The rejection region is $F > 3.13$.

Since the observed value of the test statistic falls in the rejection region ($F = 6.93 > 3.13$), $H_0$ is rejected. There is sufficient evidence to indicate at least one of the β's associated with the second-order terms is not 0 at $\alpha = .05$.

d. To determine if household income and size interact, we test:

$H_0: \beta_5 = 0$
$H_a: \beta_5 \neq 0$

The test statistic is $t = \dfrac{\hat{\beta}_5 - 0}{s(\hat{\beta}_5)} = -.65$

The rejection region requires $\alpha/2 = .05/2 = .025$ in the each tail of the t distribution with df $= n - (k + 1) = 25 - (5 + 1) = 19$. From Table VI, Appendix B, $t_{.025} = 2.093$. The rejection region is $t < -2.093$ or $t > 2.093$.

Since the observed value of the test statistic does not fall in the rejection region ($t = -.65 \nless -2.093$ and $-.65 \ngtr 2.093$), $H_0$ is not rejected. There is insufficient evidence to indicate household income and size interact at $\alpha = .05$.

e. The above tests are not independent because all the test statistics contain MSE. Thus, the overall α value has been inflated (α actually $> .05$). Thus, we may declare differences that do not exist.

13.41 a. The SAS printout from fitting the first-order model

$E(y) = \beta_0 + \beta_1 x_1 + \beta_2 x_2 + \beta_3 x_3 + \beta_4 x_4 + \beta_5 x_5$ is:

DEPENDENT VARIABLE: Y

| SOURCE | DF | SUM OF SQUARES | MEAN SQUARE | F VALUE |
|---|---|---|---|---|
| MODEL | 5 | 1052894700508.240 | 210578940101.648 | 190.75 |
| ERROR | 19 | 20975246806.001 | 1103960358.211 | PR > F |
| CORRECTED TOTAL | 24 | 1073869947314.240 | | 0.00001 |

| R-SQUARE | C.V. | ROOT MSE | Y MEAN |
|---|---|---|---|
| 0.980468 | 11.4346 | | |

| PARAMETER | ESTIMATE | T FOR HO: PARAMETER = 0 | PR > \|T\| | STD ERROR OF ESTIMATE |
|---|---|---|---|---|
| INTERCEPT | 93073.85223495 | 3.24 | 0.0043 | 28720.89686205 |
| X1 | 4152.20700875 | 2.78 | 0.0118 | 1491.62587008 |
| X2 | -854.94161450 | -2.86 | 0.0099 | 298.44765134 |
| X3 | 0.92424393 | 0.32 | 0.7515 | 2.87673442 |
| X4 | 2692.46175182 | 1.71 | 0.1041 | 1577.28622584 |
| X5 | 15.54276851 | 10.62 | 0.0001 | 1.46287006 |

The fitted model is $\hat{y} = 93073.85 + 4152.21x_1 - 854.94x_2 + .92x_3 + 2692.46x_4 + 15.5428x_5$.

b. To determine if the model in part a is useful for predicting sale price, we test:

$H_0: \beta_1 = \beta_2 = \beta_3 = \beta_4 = \beta_5 = 0$
$H_a$: At least one $\beta$ is not 0

The test statistic is $F = 190.75$ (from printout).

The rejection region requires $\alpha = .05$ to be in the upper tail of the $F$ distribution with numerator df $= k = 5$ and denominator df $= n - (k + 1) = 25 - (5 + 1) = 19$. From Table VIII, Appendix B, $F_{.05} = 2.74$. The rejection region is $F > 2.74$.

Since the observed value of the test statistic falls in the rejection region ($F = 190.75 > 2.74$), $H_0$ is rejected. There is sufficient evidence to indicate the model is useful for predicting sale price at $\alpha = .05$.

c. The SAS printout for fitting the model $E(y) = \beta_0 + \beta_1 x_1 + \beta_2 x_2 + \beta_5 x_5$ is:

DEPENDENT VARIABLE: Y

| SOURCE | DF | SUM OF SQUARES | MEAN SQUARE | F VALUE |
|---|---|---|---|---|
| MODEL | 3 | 1049676830368.870 | 349892276789.623 | 303.71 |
| ERROR | 21 | 24193116945.371 | 1152053187.875 | PR > F |
| CORRECTED TOTAL | 24 | 1073869947314.240 | | 0.0001 |

| R-SQUARE | C.V. | ROOT MSE | Y MEAN |
|---|---|---|---|
| 0.977471 | 11.6810 | 33941.909 | 290573.52000000 |

| PARAMETER | ESTIMATE | T FOR HO: PARAMETER = 0 | PR > ¦T¦ | STD ERROR OF ESTIMATE |
|---|---|---|---|---|
| INTERCEPT | 114368.60941436 | 6.56 | 0.0001 | 17421.00587457 |
| X1 | 5035.54287122 | 4.37 | 0.0003 | 1153.42438687 |
| X2 | -1057.00728279 | -3.94 | 0.0008 | 268.50633836 |
| X5 | 14.96135430 | 10.33 | 0.0001 | 1.44881935 |

The fitted model is

$$\hat{y} = 114368.61 + 5035.5429x_1 - 1057.01x_2 + 14.96x_5.$$

d. To determine if the reduced model is useful for predicting sale price, we test:

$H_0: \beta_1 = \beta_2 = \beta_5 = 0$
$H_a$: At least one of the $\beta$'s is not 0.

The test statistic is $F = 303.71$ from the printout.

The rejection region requires $\alpha = .05$ in the upper tail of the F distribution with numerator df = k = 3 and denominator df = n - (k + 1) = 25 - (3 + 1) = 21. From Table VIII, Appendix B, $F_{.05} = 3.07$. The rejection region is $F > 3.07$.

Since the observed value of the test statistic falls in the rejection region ($F = 303.71 > 3.07$), $H_0$ is rejected. There is sufficient evidence to indicate the model in part (c) is useful for predicting sale price at $\alpha = .05$.

13.43 $E(y) = \beta_0 + \beta_1 x_1 + \beta_2 x_2$

where $x_1 = \begin{cases} 1 & \text{if level of independent variable is 2} \\ 0 & \text{if not} \end{cases}$

$x_2 = \begin{cases} 1 & \text{if level of independent variable is 3} \\ 0 & \text{if not} \end{cases}$

13.45 a. The least squares prediction equation is

$$\hat{y} = 80 + 16.8x_1 + 40.4x_2$$

b. $\hat{\beta}_1$ is the estimate of the difference in the mean value of the dependent variable between level 2 and level 1 of the independent variable.

$\hat{\beta}_2$ is the estimate of the difference in the mean value of the dependent variable between level 3 and level 1 of the independent variable.

c. $H_0$: $\beta_1 = \beta_2 = 0$

means that the mean value of the dependent variable is the same for each level of the independent variable.

$H_a$: At least one of the parameters $\beta_1$ and $\beta_2$ differs from 0

means that the mean value of the dependent variable differs for levels 1 and 2 or differs for levels 1 and 3.

d. The test statistic is $F = \frac{MSR}{MSE} = \frac{2059.5}{83.3} = 24.72$.

The rejection region requires $\alpha = .05$ in the upper tail of the F distribution with numerator df = 2 and denominator df = 12. From Table VIII, Appendix B, $F_{.05} = 3.89$. The rejection region is $F > 3.89$.

Since the observed value of the test statistic falls in the rejection region ($F = 24.72 > 3.89$), $H_0$ is rejected. There is sufficient evidence to indicate the mean value of the dependent variable differs for either levels 1 and 2 or levels 1 and 3 at $\alpha = .05$.

13.47 a. The model would be $E(y) = \beta_0 + \beta_1 x_1 + \beta_2 x_2$

where

$$x_1 = \begin{cases} 1 & \text{if ASE} \\ 0 & \text{if not} \end{cases}$$

$$x_2 = \begin{cases} 1 & \text{if OTC} \\ 0 & \text{if not} \end{cases}$$

b. Using Minitab, the least squares prediction equation is

$$\hat{y} = 26.26 - 11.73x_1 - 10.6x_2$$

c. To determine if the mean prices differ, we test:

$H_0$: $\beta_1 = \beta_2 = 0$
$H_a$: At least one $\beta_i \neq 0$

The test statistic is $F = \frac{MSR}{MSE} = \frac{1377.431325}{335.2938707} = 4.11$ (from Minitab)

The rejection region requires $\alpha = .05$ in the upper tail of the F distribution with numerator df = k = 2 and denominator df = n - (k + 1) = 87 - (2 + 1) = 84. From Table VIII, Appendix B, $F_{.05} \approx 3.15$. The rejection region is $F > 3.15$.

Since the observed value of the test statistic falls in the rejection region ($F = 4.11 > 3.15$), $H_0$ is rejected. There is sufficient evidence to conclude the mean prices differ at $\alpha = .05$.

13.49 a. To determine if there is a difference in mean monthly sales among the three incentive plans, we test:

$H_0$: $\beta_1 = \beta_2 = 0$
$H_a$: At least one $\beta_i \neq 0$

The test statistic is $F = \frac{MSR}{MSE} = \frac{201.8}{42} = 4.80$

The rejection region requires $\alpha = .05$ in the upper tail of the F distribution with numerator df = k = 2 and denominator df = n - (k + 1) = 15 - (2 + 1) = 12. From Table VIII, Appendix B, $F_{.05} = 3.89$. The rejection region is $F > 3.89$.

Since the observed value of the test statistic falls in the rejection region ($F = 4.80 > 3.89$), $H_0$ is rejected. There is sufficient evidence to conclude that there is a difference in mean monthly sales among the three incentive plants at $\alpha = .05$.

b. The least squares prediction equation is

$$\hat{y} = 20.0 - 8.60x_1 - 3.80x_2.$$

$x_1 = 1$ if salesperson is paid a straight salary and $x_2 = 0$.

Thus, an estimate of the mean sales for those on a straight salary is

$$\hat{y} = 20.0 - 8.60(1) - 3.80(0) = 11.4$$

Thus, the mean sales is estimated to be $11,400.

c. For those on commission only, $x_1 = 0$ and $x_2 = 0$. The estimate of the mean sales for those on commission only is

$$\hat{y} = 20.0 -8.60(0) - 3.80(0) = 20.0$$

Thus, the mean sales is estimated to be $20,000.

13.51 a. Brand of beer is qualitative.

b. $E(y) = \beta_0 + \beta_1 x_1 + \beta_2 x_2$

where

$$x_1 = \begin{cases} 1 & \text{if brand } B_2 \\ 0 & \text{if not} \end{cases} \qquad x_2 = \begin{cases} 1 & \text{if brand } B_3 \\ 0 & \text{if not} \end{cases}$$

c. $\beta_0$ = mean sales for brand $B_1$

$\beta_1$ = difference in mean sales between brand $B_2$ and brand $B_1$

$\beta_2$ = difference in mean sales between brand $B_3$ and brand $B_1$

d. From part (c), $\beta_0 = \mu_{B_1}$, $\beta_1 = \mu_{B_2} - \mu_{B_1}$, and $\beta_2 = \mu_{B_3} - \mu_{B_1}$

Thus, $\mu_{B_2} = \beta_2 + \beta_0$

13.53 a. The model is $E(y) = \beta_0 + \beta_1 x_1 + \beta_2 x_2 + \beta_3 x_3 + \beta_4 x_4$

where

$$x_1 = \begin{cases} 1 & \text{if variety B} \\ 0 & \text{if not} \end{cases} \qquad x_3 = \begin{cases} 1 & \text{if variety D} \\ 0 & \text{if not} \end{cases}$$

$$x_2 = \begin{cases} 1 & \text{if variety C} \\ 0 & \text{if not} \end{cases} \qquad x_4 = \begin{cases} 1 & \text{if variety E} \\ 0 & \text{if not} \end{cases}$$

$\beta_0$ = mean yield for variety A
$\beta_1$ = difference in mean yield between varieties B and A.
$\beta_2$ = difference in mean yield between varieties C and A.
$\beta_3$ = difference in mean yield between varieties D and A.
$\beta_4$ = difference in mean yield between varieties E and A.

b. The least squares model is

$$\hat{y} = 20.35 + 4.75x_1 + 8.6x_2 + 11.3x_3 + 2.1x_4$$

c. The hypotheses are

$H_0$: $\beta_1 = \beta_2 = \beta_3 = \beta_4 = 0$
$H_a$: At least one $\beta_i \neq 0$

The null hypothesis says all $\beta_i$'s are 0 or that the mean yields of varieties B, C, D, and E are not different from the mean yield of variety A.

The alternative hypothesis says at least one $\beta_i \neq 0$ or that the mean yield of at least one of the varieties B, C, D, or E differs from the mean yield of variety A.

d. The test statistic is $F = \frac{MSR}{MSE} = \frac{85.51}{3.568} = 23.966$

The rejection region requires $\alpha = .05$ in the upper tail of the F distribution with numerator df = k = 4 and denominator df = n - (k + 1) = 20 - (4 + 1) = 15. From Table VIII, Appendix B, $F_{.05} = 3.06$. The rejection region is F > 3.06.

Since the observed value of the test statistic falls in the rejection region (F = 23.966 > 3.06), $H_0$ is rejected. There is sufficient evidence to indicate a difference in mean yields among the 5 varieties at $\alpha = .05$.

e. The sample mean yield for variety D is $\bar{y}_4 = \frac{\sum y_4}{n} = \frac{89.8}{4} = 22.45$

The sample mean yield for variety E is $\bar{y}_5 = \frac{\sum y_5}{n} = \frac{81.4}{4} = 20.35$

The form of the confidence interval for $\mu_4 - \mu_5$ is

$$(\bar{y}_4 - \bar{y}_5) \pm t_{\alpha/2} \sqrt{MSE(\frac{1}{n_4} + \frac{1}{n_5})}$$

where MSE is used to estimate the common variance.

For confidence coefficient .95, $\alpha = 1 - .95 = .05$ and $\alpha/2 = .05/2 = .025$. From Table VI, Appendix B, $t_{.025} = 2.131$ with df = n - (k + 1) = 20 - (4 + 1) = 15. The 95% confidence interval is

$$(22.45 - 20.35) \pm 2.131\sqrt{3.568(\frac{1}{4} + \frac{1}{4})}$$

$$\Rightarrow 2.1 \pm 2.846 \Rightarrow (-.746, 4.946)$$

13.55 a. $E(y) = \beta_0 + \beta_1 x_1$

b. $E(y) = \beta_0 + \beta_1 x_1 + \beta_2 x_2 + \beta_3 x_3$

where $x_2 = \begin{cases} 1 & \text{if qualitative variable at level 2} \\ 0 & \text{if not} \end{cases}$

$x_3 = \begin{cases} 1 & \text{if qualitative variable at level 3} \\ 0 & \text{if not} \end{cases}$

c. $E(y) = \beta_0 + \beta_1 x_1 + \beta_2 x_2 + \beta_3 x_3 + \beta_4 x_1 x_2 + \beta_5 x_1 x_3$

d. The response lines will be parallel if $\beta_4$ and $\beta_5$ are 0.

e. The model will have only one response line if $\beta_2$, $\beta_3$, $\beta_4$, and $\beta_5$ are all 0.

13.57 a. The type of juice extractor is qualitative.
The size of the orange is quantitative.

b. The model is $E(y) = \beta_0 + \beta_1 x_1 + \beta_2 x_2$

where

$x_1$ = diameter of orange

$$x_2 = \begin{cases} 1 & \text{if brand B} \\ 0 & \text{if not} \end{cases}$$

c. To allow the lines to differ, the interaction term is added:

$$E(y) = \beta_0 + \beta_1 x_1 + \beta_2 x_2 + \beta_3 x_1 x_2$$

d. For part b:

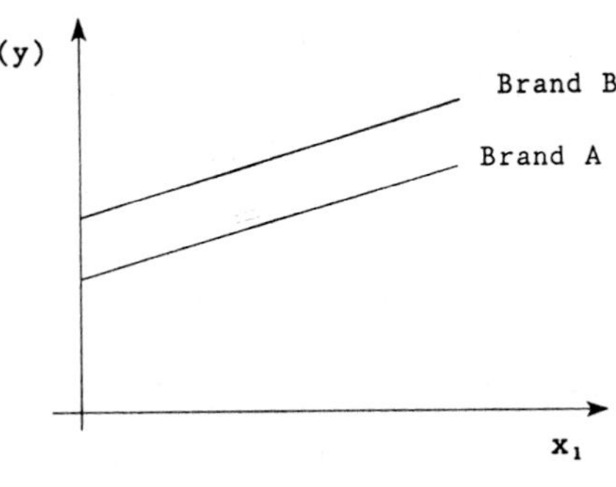


For part c:

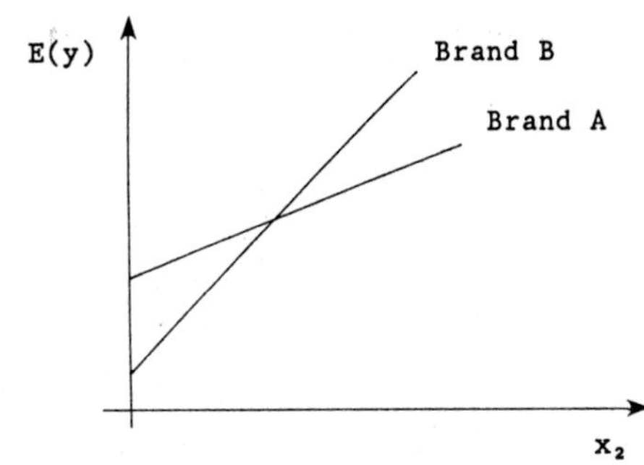


e. To determine whether the model in part (c) provides more information for predicting yield than does the model in part (b), we test:

$H_0$: $\beta_3 = 0$
$H_a$: $\beta_3 \neq 0$

f. The test statistic would be $F = \dfrac{(SSE_1 - SSE_2)/(k - g)}{SSE_2/(n - (k + 1))}$

To compute $SSE_1$: The model in part (b) is fit and $SSE_1$ is the sum of squares for error.

To compute $SSE_2$: The model in part (c) is fit and $SSE_2$ is the sum of squares for error.

$k - g$ = number of parameters in $H_0$ = 1
$n - (k + 1)$ = degrees of freedom for error in the complete model.

13.59 a. The model is $E(y) = \beta_0 + \beta_1 x_1 + \beta_2 x_2 + \beta_3 x_3$

where $x_1$ = number of apartment units

$$x_2 = \begin{cases} 1 & \text{if condition E} \\ 0 & \text{if not} \end{cases}$$

$$x_3 = \begin{cases} 1 & \text{if condition G} \\ 0 & \text{if not} \end{cases}$$

b.

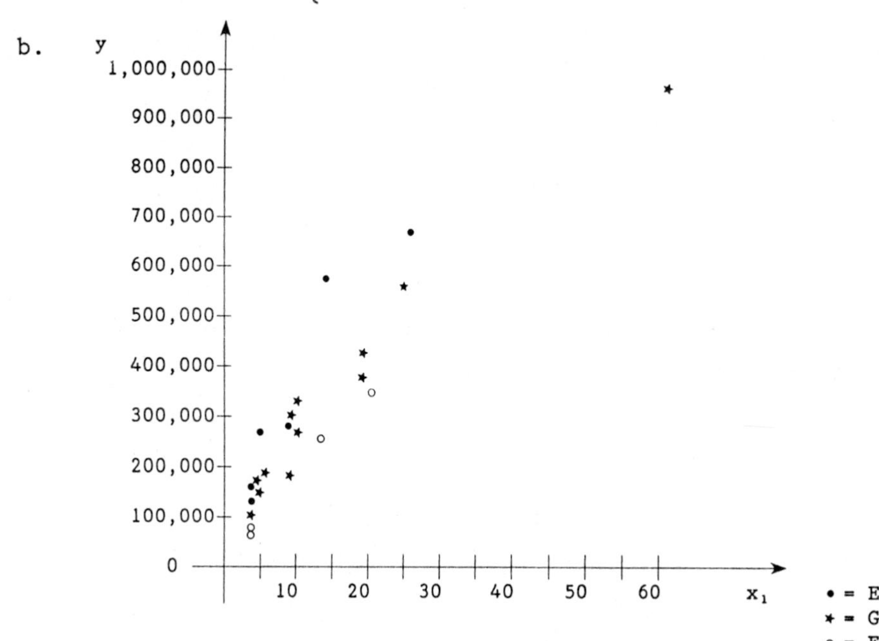


It does appear that the model in (a) is appropriate. The lines appear to be parallel.

c. The SAS printout is:

DEPENDENT VARIABLE: Y

| SOURCE | DF | SUM OF SQUARES | MEAN SQUARE | F VALUE |
|---|---|---|---|---|
| MODEL | 3 | 986169504463.134 | 328723168154.378 | 78.71 |
| ERROR | 21 | 87700442851.106 | 4176211564.338 | PR > F |
| CORRECTED TOTAL | 24 | 1073869947314.240 | | 0.0001 |

| R-SQUARE | C.V. | ROOT MSE | Y MEAN |
|---|---|---|---|
| 0.918332 | 22.2400 | 64623.615 | 290573.52000000 |

| PARAMETER | ESTIMATE | T FOR HO: PARAMETER = 0 | PR > ¦T¦ | STD ERROR OF ESTIMATE |
|---|---|---|---|---|
| INTERCEPT | 36387.63972373 | 1.19 | 0.2454 | 30450.08697797 |
| X1 | 15616.92891959 | 14.66 | 0.0001 | 1065.54040134 |
| X2 | 152487.42810722 | 3.89 | 0.0008 | 39157.32396921 |
| X3 | 49441.14619353 | 1.45 | 0.1619 | 34099.03698648 |

The least squares prediction equation is:

$$\hat{y} = 36,388 + 15,617x_1 + 152,487x_2 + 49,441x_3$$

The least squares prediction equation for condition E ($x_2 = 1$, $x_3 = 0$) is:

$$\hat{y} = 36,388 + 15,617x_1 + 152,487(1) = 188,875 + 15,617x_1$$

For condition G ($x_2 = 0$, $x_3 = 1$):

$$\hat{y} = 36,388 + 15,617x_1 + 49,441(1) = 85,829 + 15,617x_1$$

For condition F ($x_2 = x_3 = 0$):

$$\hat{y} = 36,388 + 15,617x_1$$

e. To determine if the relationship between the mean sale price and number of units differs depending on the physical condition of the apartments, we test:

$H_0$: $\beta_2 = \beta_3 = 0$
$H_a$: At least one $\beta_i \neq 0$

To calculate the test statistic, we must first fit the reduced model, $E(y) = \beta_0 + \beta_1 x_1$. The SAS printout is:

DEPENDENT VARIABLE: Y

| SOURCE | DF | SUM OF SQUARES | MEAN SQUARE | F VALUE |
|---|---|---|---|---|
| MODEL | 1 | 915775843108.351 | 915775843108.351 | 133.23 |
| ERROR | 23 | 158094104205.889 | 6873656704.604 | PR > F |
| CORRECTED TOTAL | 24 | 1073869947314.240 | | 0.0001 |

| R-SQUARE | C.V. | ROOT MSE | Y MEAN |
|---|---|---|---|
| 0.852781 | 28.5324 | 82907.519 | 290573.52000000 |

| PARAMETER | ESTIMATE | T FOR HO: PARAMETER = 0 | PR > \|T\| | STD ERROR OF ESTIMATE |
|---|---|---|---|---|
| INTERCEPT | 101786.14688790 | 4.37 | 0.0002 | 23290.75036701 |
| X1 | 15525.27739409 | 11.54 | 0.0001 | 1345.05082746 |

The test statistic is $F = \dfrac{(SSE_1 - SSE_2)/(k - g)}{SSE_2/[n - (k + 1)]}$

$$= \frac{(158,094,104,205.889 - 87,700,442,851.106)/(3 - 1)}{87,700,442,851.106/[25 - (3 + 1)]}$$

$$= \frac{35,196,830,680}{4,176,211,564} = 8.43$$

The rejection region requires $\alpha = .05$ in the upper tail of the F distribution with numerator df = k - g = 3 - 1 = 2 and denominator df = n - (k + 1) = 25 - (3 + 1) = 21. From Table VIII, Appendix B, $F_{.05} = 3.47$. The rejection region is F > 3.47.

Since the observed value of the test statistic falls in the rejection region (F = 8.43 > 3.47), $H_0$ is rejected. There is sufficient evidence to indicate the relationship between mean sale price and number of units differ depending on the physical condition of the apartments at $\alpha = .05$.

13.61 a. The model is $E(y) = \beta_0 + \beta_1 x_1$

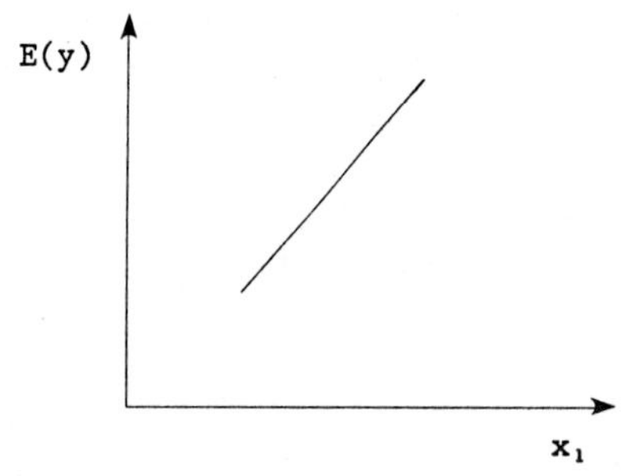


The response curve would be a straight line.

b. The model is $E(y) = \beta_0 + \beta_1 x_1 + \beta_2 x_2 + \beta_3 x_3$

where $x_2 = \begin{cases} 1 & \text{if brand B} \\ 0 & \text{if not} \end{cases}$ $x_3 = \begin{cases} 1 & \text{if brand C} \\ 0 & \text{if not} \end{cases}$

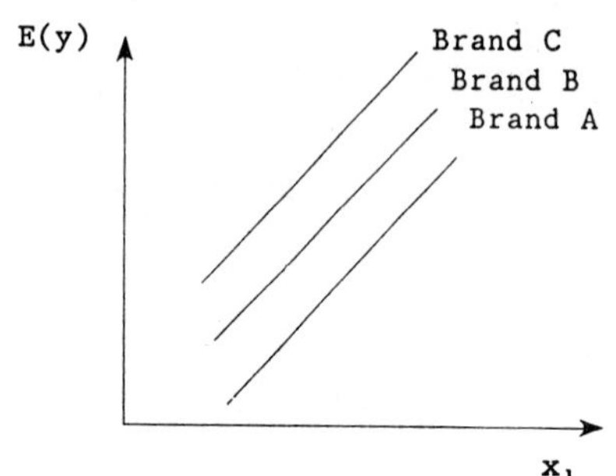


The typical response curves would look something like this.

c. The model is $E(y) + \beta_0 + \beta_1 x_1 + \beta_2 x_2 + \beta_3 x_3 + \beta_4 x_1 x_2 + \beta_5 x_1 x_3$

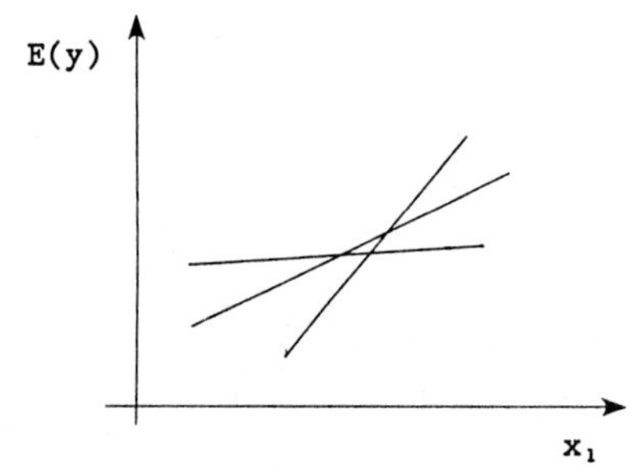


The typical response curves would look something like this.

13.63 To determine whether the mean work-hours lost differ for the 3 training programs, we test:

$H_0: \beta_2 = \beta_3 = 0$
$H_a$: At least one $\beta_i \neq 0$

The test statistic is $F = \dfrac{(SSE_1 - SSE_2)/(k - g)}{SSE_2/(n - (k + 1))}$

$$= \frac{(3113.14 - 1527.27)/(3 - 1)}{1527.27/(9 - (3 + 1))} = \frac{792.935}{305.454} = 2.60$$

The rejection region requires $\alpha = .05$ in the upper tail of the F distribution with numerator df = k - g = 3 - 1 = 2 and denominator df = n - (k + 1) = 9 - (3 + 1) = 5. From Table VIII, Appendix B, $F_{.05} = 5.79$. The rejection region is $F > 5.79$.

Since the observed value of the test statistic does not fall in the rejection region ($F = 2.60 \not> 5.79$), $H_0$ is not rejected. There is insufficient evidence to indicate the mean work-hours lost differ for the 3 training programs at $\alpha = .05$.

13.65 a. Remember that y is the per capita consumption, obtained by dividing total consumption (column 1) by population (column 2). Then the scattergram of the data is:

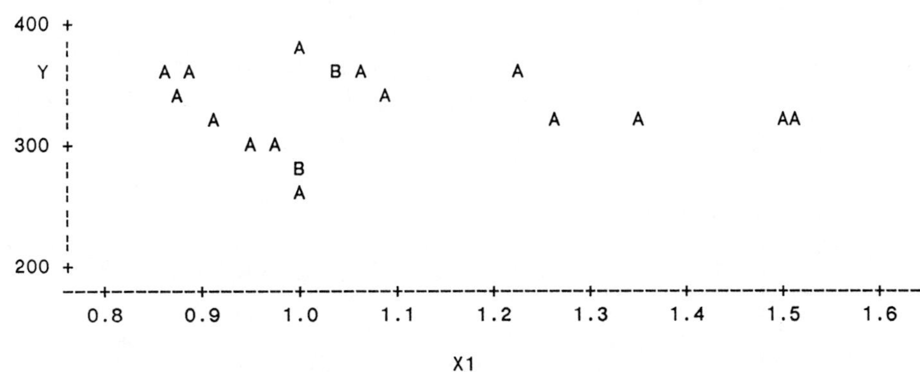


b. The model would be $E(y) = \beta_0 + \beta_1 x_1 + \beta_2 x_2 + \beta_3 x_1 x_2$

where $x_1$ = relative price of a gallon of gasoline

and $x_2 = \begin{cases} 1 \text{ if after 1973} \\ 0 \text{ otherwise} \end{cases}$

c. Using SAS, the output from fitting the model is:

Dep Variable: Y

Analysis of Variance

| Source | DF | Sum of Squares | Mean Square | F Value | Prob>F |
|---|---|---|---|---|---|
| Model | 3 | 19335.15329 | 6445.05110 | 36.538 | 0.0001 |
| Error | 15 | 2645.87850 | 176.39190 | | |
| C Total | 18 | 21981.03179 | | | |

| | | | |
|---|---|---|---|
| Root MSE | 13.28126 | R-Square | 0.8796 |
| Dep Mean | 326.59692 | Adj R-Sq | 0.8556 |
| C.V. | 4.06656 | | |

Parameter Estimates

| Variable | DF | Parameter Estimate | Standard Error | T for H0: Parameter=0 | Prob > \|T\| |
|---|---|---|---|---|---|
| INTERCEP | 1 | 884.841568 | 76.33041486 | 11.592 | 0.0001 |
| X1 | 1 | -612.577652 | 81.07545937 | -7.556 | 0.0001 |
| X2 | 1 | -409.361031 | 81.37043612 | -5.031 | 0.0001 |
| X1X2 | 1 | 502.201751 | 84.30593412 | 5.957 | 0.0001 |

The fitted model is

$$\hat{y} = 884.8416 - 612.5777x_1 - 409.3610x_2 + 502.2018x_1x_2$$

d. Using SAS, the plots of the fitted regression lines are:

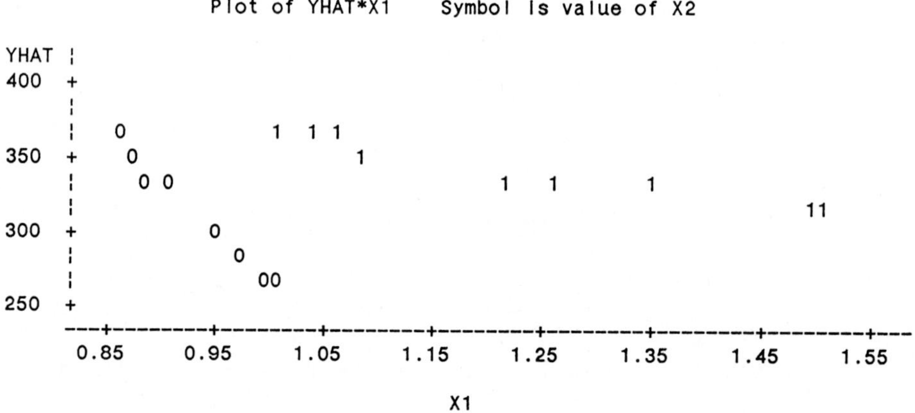


where the 1's correspond to the post-OPEC period, and the 0's correspond to the pre-OPEC period. The slope of the pre-OPEC line is much steeper than the slope of the post-OPEC line. It appears that OPEC had an effect on the consumption of gasoline.

e. To determine if the relationship between demand for motor fuel and the relative price of gasoline changed after 1973, we test:

$H_0$: $\beta_2 = \beta_3 = 0$
$H_a$: At least one of the $\beta$'s is not 0

To calculate the test statistic, we must first fit the reduced model, $E(y) = \beta_0 + \beta_1 x_1$.

Using SAS, the output from fitting the model is:

Dep Variable: Y

Analysis of Variance

| Source | DF | Sum of Squares | Mean Square | F Value | Prob>F |
|---|---|---|---|---|---|
| Model | 1 | 172.38330 | 172.38330 | 0.134 | 0.7185 |
| Error | 17 | 21808.64849 | 1282.86168 | | |
| C Total | 18 | 21981.03179 | | | |

| | | | |
|---|---|---|---|
| Root MSE | 35.81706 | R-Square | 0.0078 |
| Dep Mean | 326.59692 | Adj R-Sq | -0.0505 |
| C.V. | 10.96675 | | |

Parameter Estimates

| Variable | DF | Parameter Estimate | Standard Error | T for H0: Parameter=0 | Prob > \|T\| |
|---|---|---|---|---|---|
| INTERCEP | 1 | 343.634284 | 47.19849286 | 7.281 | 0.0001 |
| X1 | 1 | -15.775341 | 43.03492828 | -0.367 | 0.7185 |

The test statistic is $F = \dfrac{(SSE_1 - SSE_2)/(k - g)}{SSE_2/[n - (k + 1)]}$

$$= \frac{(21808.65 - 2645.88)/(3 - 1)}{2645.88/[19 - (3 + 1)]} = \frac{9581.385}{176.39} = 54.32$$

The rejection region requires $\alpha = .05$ in the upper tail of the F distribution with numerator df $= k - g = 3 - 1 = 2$ and denominator df $= n - (k + 1) = 19 - (3 + 1) = 15$. From Table VIII, Appendix B, $F_{.05} = 3.68$. The rejection region is $F > 3.68$.

Since the observed value of the test statistic falls in the rejection region ($F = 54.32 > 3.68$), $H_0$ is rejected. There is sufficient evidence to indicate the relationship between demand for motor fuel and the relative price of gasoline changed after 1973 at $\alpha = .05$.

f. To determine if the slopes differ, we test:

$H_0$: $\beta_3 = 0$
$H_a$: $\beta_3 \neq 0$

The test statistic is t = 5.957 (from the printout of fitting the complete model).

The rejection region requires $\alpha/2 = .05/2 = .025$ in each tail of the t distribution with df = n - (k + 1) = 19 - (3 + 1) = 15. From Table VI, Appendix B, $t_{.025} = 2.131$. The rejection region is t > 2.131 or t < -2.131.

Since the observed value of the test statistic falls in the rejection region (t = 5.957 > 2.131), $H_0$ is rejected. There is sufficient evidence to indicate the slopes differ at $\alpha = .05$.

13.67 a. Using the model $E(y) = \beta_0 + \beta_1x_1 + \beta_2x_1^2 + \beta_3x_2 + \beta_4x_3 + \beta_5x_1x_2 + \beta_6x_1x_3 + B_7x_1^2x_2 + \beta_8x_1^2x_3$

where $x_1$ = quantitative variable

$$x_2 = \begin{cases} 1 & \text{if level 2 of qualitative variable} \\ 0 & \text{if not} \end{cases}$$

$$x_3 = \begin{cases} 1 & \text{if level 3 of qualitative variable} \\ 0 & \text{if not} \end{cases}$$

The response curves will have the same slope but different y-intercepts if $\beta_5 = \beta_6 = \beta_7 = \beta_8 = 0$ and $\beta_3$ and $\beta_4$ are not 0.

b. In order for the response curves to be parallel lines, they must be straight lines. They will be parallel if $\beta_2 = \beta_5 = \beta_6 = \beta_7 = \beta_8 = 0$ and $\beta_3$ and $\beta_4$ are not 0.

c. The response curves will be identical if $\beta_3 = \beta_4 = \beta_5 = \beta_6 = \beta_7 = \beta_8 = 0$.

13.69 a. $\hat{y} = 48.8 - 3.36x_1 + .0749x_1^2 - 2.36x_2 - 7.6x_3 + 3.71x_1x_2 + 2.66x_1x_3 - .0183x_1^2x_2 - .0372x_1^2x_3$

b. When $x_2 = 0$ and $x_3 = 0$, $\hat{y} = 48.8 - 3.36x_1 + .0749x_1^2$

When $x_2 = 1$ and $x_3 = 0$, $\hat{y} = 48.8 - 3.36x_1 + .0749x_1^2 - 2.36(1) + 3.71x_1(1) - .0183x_1^2(1)$

$= 46.44 + .35x_1 + .0566x_1^2$

When $x_2 = 0$ and $x_3 = 1$, $\hat{y} = 48.8 - 3.36x_1 + .0749x_1^2 - 7.6(1) + 2.66x_1(1) - .0372x_1^2(1)$

$= 41.2 - .7x_1 + .0377x_1^2$

c.

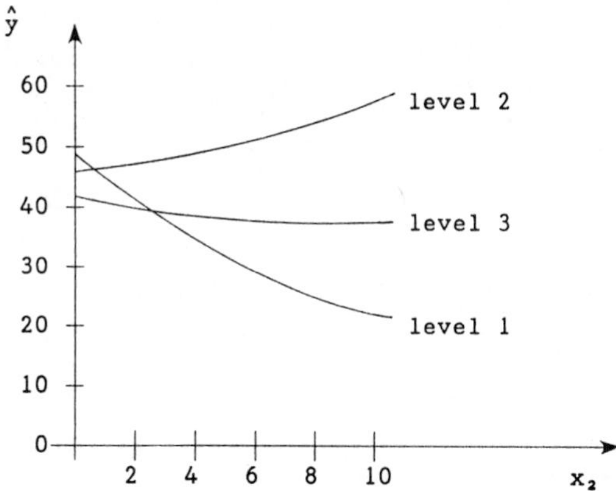


d. To determine whether the second-order response curves differ for the three levels, we test:

$H_0$: $\beta_3 = \beta_4 = \beta_5 = \beta_6 = \beta_7 = \beta_8 = 0$
$H_a$: At least one of the parameters, $\beta_3$, $\beta_4$, $\beta_5$, $\beta_6$, $\beta_7$, $\beta_8$, is not 0

e. The test statistic is $F = \dfrac{(SSE_1 - SSE_2)/(k - g)}{SSE_2/(n - (k + 1))}$

$$= \frac{(14986 - 162.9)/(8 - 2)}{162.9/(25 - (8 + 1))} = \frac{2470.5167}{10.18125} = 242.65$$

The rejection region requires $\alpha = .05$ in the upper tail of the F distribution with numerator df = k - g = 8 - 2 = 6 and denominator df = n - (k + 1) = 25 - (8 + 1) = 16. From Table VIII, Appendix B, $F_{.05} = 2.74$. The rejection region is $F > 2.74$.

Since the observed value of the test statistic falls in the rejection region ($F = 242.65 > 2.74$), $H_0$ is rejected. There is sufficient evidence to indicate the second-order response curves differ for the three levels at $\alpha = .05$.

13.71 To determine if the second-order term in the model proposed by the operations manager is necessary, we test:

$H_0$: $\beta_2 = 0$
$H_a$: $\beta_2 \neq 0$

The test statistic is $F = \dfrac{(SSE_1 - SSE_2)/(k - g)}{SSE_2/(n - (k + 1))}$

$$= \frac{(182.53 - 128.586)/(3 - 2)}{128.586/(20 - (3 + 1))} = \frac{53.944}{8.036625} = 6.71$$

The rejection region requires $\alpha = .05$ in the upper tail of the F distribution with numerator df = k - g = 3 - 2 = 1 and denominator df = n - (k + 1) = 20 - (3 + 1) = 16. From Table VIII, Appendix B, $F_{.05} = 4.49$. The rejection region is $F > 4.49$.

Since the observed value of the test statistic falls in the rejection region ($F = 6.71 > 4.49$), $H_0$ is rejected. There is sufficient evidence to indicate the second-order term in the model is necessary at $\alpha = .05$.

13.73 a. To determine whether the rate of increase of mean salary with experience is different for males and females, we test:

$H_0$: $\beta_4 = \beta_5 = 0$
$H_a$: At least one of the parameters $\beta_4$ and $\beta_5$ is not 0.

b. To determine whether there are differences in mean salaries that are attributable to sex, we test:

$H_0$: $\beta_3 = \beta_4 = \beta_5 = 0$
$H_a$: At least one of the parameters $\beta_3$, $\beta_4$, and $\beta_5$ is not 0.

13.75 To determine whether the speed limit contributes information for the prediction of the annual number of highway deaths, we test:

$H_0$: $\beta_3 = \beta_4 = \beta_5 = 0$
$H_a$: At least one of the parameters $\beta_3$, $\beta_4$ and $\beta_5$ is not 0.

The test statistic is $F = \dfrac{(SSE_1 - SSE_2)/(k - g)}{SSE_2/(n - (k + 1))}$

$$= \frac{(423.39322 - 215.67457)/(5 - 2)}{215.67457/(36 - (5 + 1))} = \frac{69.23955}{7.18915} = 9.63$$

The rejection region requires $\alpha = .05$ in the upper tail of the F distribution with numerator df $= k - g = 5 - 2 = 3$ and denominator df $= n - (k + 1) = 36 - (5 + 1) = 30$. From Table VIII, Appendix B, $F_{.05} = 2.92$. The rejection region is $F > 2.92$.

Since the observed value of the test statistic falls in the rejection region ($F = 9.63 > 2.92$), $H_0$ is rejected. There is sufficient evidence to indicate that the speed limit contributes information for the prediction of the annual number of highway deaths at $\alpha = .05$.

13.77 a. Using SAS, the scattergram of the data is:

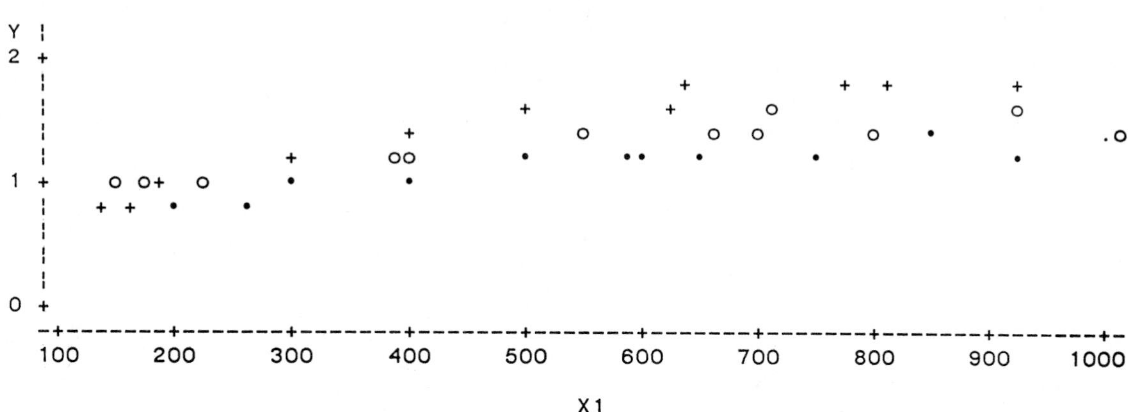


where • = north plant, o = south plant, and + = west plant.

b. It appears that the relationships between the productivity ratio and the number of units produced differ among the three plants. Also, there appears to be a slight curve to the relationships.

c. The model would be $E(y) = \beta_0 + \beta_1 x_1 + \beta_2 x_1^2 + \beta_3 x_2 + \beta_4 x_3 + \beta_5 x_1 x_2 + \beta_6 x_1 x_3 + \beta_7 x_1^2 x_2 + \beta_8 x_1^2 x_3$.

where $x_1$ = number of units produced and

$$x_2 = \begin{cases} 1 \text{ if North} \\ 0 \text{ otherwise} \end{cases} \qquad x_3 = \begin{cases} 1 \text{ if South} \\ 0 \text{ otherwise} \end{cases}$$

d. Using SAS, the output from fitting the proposed model is:

DEPENDENT VARIABLE: Y

| SOURCE | DF | SUM OF SQUARES | MEAN SQUARE | F VALUE |
|---|---|---|---|---|
| MODEL | 8 | 3.36610378 | 0.42076297 | 106.29 |
| ERROR | 27 | 0.10688511 | 0.00395871 | PR > F |
| CORRECTED TOTAL | 35 | 3.47298889 | | 0.0001 |

| R-SQUARE | C.V. | ROOT MSE | Y MEAN |
|---|---|---|---|
| 0.969224 | 5.0357 | 0.06291826 | 1.24944444 |

| PARAMETER | ESTIMATE | T FOR HO: PARAMETER = 0 | PR > ¦T¦ | STD ERROR OF ESTIMATE |
|---|---|---|---|---|
| INTERCEPT | 0.31115454 | 4.32 | 0.0002 | 0.07210798 |
| X1 | 0.00345608 | 9.96 | 0.0001 | 0.00034683 |
| X1*X1 | -0.0000019 | -5.80 | 0.0001 | 0.00000034 |
| X2 | 0.10524501 | 0.85 | 0.4032 | 0.12391154 |
| X3 | 0.36491296 | 3.55 | 0.0014 | 0.10288408 |
| X1*X2 | -0.00162938 | -3.18 | 0.0037 | 0.00051262 |
| X1*X3 | -0.00169600 | -3.69 | 0.0010 | 0.00045902 |
| X1*X1*X2 | 0.0000010 | 2.16 | 0.0395 | 0.00000046 |
| X1*X1*X3 | 0.0000010 | 2.27 | 0.0317 | 0.00000043 |

The fitted model is

$$\hat{y} = .311 + .0035x_1 - .000002x_1^2 + .10525x_2 + .36491x_3 - .0016x_1x_2 - .0017x_1x_3 + .000001x_1^2x_2 + .000001x_1^2x_3$$

e. To determine if the productivity response curves differ for the three plants, we test:

$H_0\colon \beta_3 = \beta_4 = \beta_5 = \beta_6 = \beta_7 = \beta_8 = 0$
$H_a\colon$ At least one $\beta$ is not 0

To compute the test statistic, we must first fit the reduced model $E(y) = \beta_0 + \beta_1 x_1 + \beta_2 x_1^2$. The SAS output is:

DEPENDENT VARIABLE: Y

| SOURCE | DF | SUM OF SQUARES | MEAN SQUARE | F VALUE |
|---|---|---|---|---|
| MODEL | 2 | 2.18467983 | 1.09233992 | 27.98 |
| ERROR | 33 | 1.28830906 | 0.03903967 | PR > F |
| CORRECTED TOTAL | 35 | 3.47298889 | | 0.0001 |

| R-SQUARE | C.V. | ROOT MSE | Y MEAN |
|---|---|---|---|
| 0.629049 | 15.8138 | 0.19758459 | 1.24944444 |

| PARAMETER | ESTIMATE | T FOR H0: PARAMETER = 0 | PR > ¦T¦ | STD ERROR OF ESTIMATE |
|---|---|---|---|---|
| INTERCEPT | 0.48177216 | 3.46 | 0.0015 | 0.13912917 |
| X1 | 0.00233100 | 4.01 | 0.0003 | 0.00058120 |
| X1*X1 | -0.0000013 | -2.60 | 0.0139 | 0.00000052 |

The test statistic is $F = \frac{(SSE_1 - SSE_2)/(k - g)}{SSE_2/[n - (k + 1)]}$

$$= \frac{(1.2883 - .1069)/(8 - 2)}{.1069/[36 - (8 + 1)]} = \frac{.1969}{.00396} = 49.73$$

The rejection region requires $\alpha = .05$ in the upper tail of the F distribution with numerator df $= k - g = 8 - 2 = 6$ and denominator df $= n - (k + 1) = 36 - (8 + 1) = 27$. From Table VIII, Appendix B, $F_{.05} = 2.46$. The rejection region is $F > 2.46$.

Since the observed value of the test statistic falls in the rejection region ($F = 49.73 > 2.46$), $H_0$ is rejected. There is sufficient evidence to indicate the productivity response curves differ for the three plants at $\alpha = .05$.

f. To determine if the second-order model contributes more information for the prediction of productivity than a first-order model, we test:

$H_0$: $\beta_2 = \beta_7 = \beta_8 = 0$
$H_a$: At least one $\beta$ is not 0

To compute the test statistic, we must first fit the reduced model, $E(y) = \beta_0 + \beta_1 x_1 + \beta_3 x_2 + \beta_4 x_3 + \beta_5 x_1 x_2 + \beta_6 x_1 x_3$.

The SAS output is:

DEPENDENT VARIABLE: Y

| SOURCE | DF | SUM OF SQUARES | MEAN SQUARE | F VALUE |
|---|---|---|---|---|
| MODEL | 5 | 3.14140031 | 0.62828006 | 56.84 |
| ERROR | 30 | 0.33158858 | 0.01105295 | PR > F |
| CORRECTED TOTAL | 35 | 3.47298889 | | 0.0001 |

| R-SQUARE | C.V. | ROOT MSE | Y MEAN |
|---|---|---|---|
| 0.904524 | 8.4144 | 0.10513302 | 1.24944444 |

| PARAMETER | ESTIMATE | T FOR HO: PARAMETER = 0 | PR > \|T\| | STD ERROR OF ESTIMATE |
|---|---|---|---|---|
| INTERCEPT | 0.66978856 | 10.81 | 0.0001 | 0.06195960 |
| X1 | 0.00148394 | 13.04 | 0.0001 | 0.00011380 |
| X2 | 0.02086737 | 0.21 | 0.8335 | 0.09842649 |
| | 0.23328955 | 2.54 | 0.0166 | 0.09192087 |
| X1*X2 | -0.00078937 | -4.78 | 0.0001 | 0.00016527 |
| | -0.00081433 | -5.17 | 0.0001 | 0.00015749 |

The test statistic is $F = \dfrac{(SSE_1 - SSE_2)/(k - g)}{SSE_2/[n - (k + 1)]}$

$$= \frac{(.3316 - .1069)/(8 - 5)}{.1069/[36 - (8 + 1)]} = \frac{.0749}{.00396} = 18.92$$

The rejection region requires $\alpha = .05$ in the upper tail of the F distribution with numerator df = k - g = 8 - 5 = 3 and denominator df = n - (k + 1) = 36 - (8 + 1) = 27. From Table VIII, Appendix B, $F_{.05} = 2.96$. The rejection region is F > 2.96.

Since the observed value of the test statistic falls in the rejection region (F = 18.92 > 2.96), $H_0$ is rejected. There is sufficient evidence to indicate the second-order model contributes more information for the prediction of productivity than a first order model at at $\alpha = .05$.

g. For the west plant, $x_2 = x_3 = 0$. With $x_1 = 890$,

$$\hat{y} = .311 + .0035(890) - .000002(890^2) = 1.84$$

13.81 a. $\sigma_{\hat{p}} = \sqrt{\frac{pq}{n}}$

b. p = .1 $\sigma_{\hat{p}} = \sqrt{\frac{.1(.9)}{100}} = .03$

p = .2 $\sigma_{\hat{p}} = \sqrt{\frac{.2(.8)}{100}} = .04$

p = .3 $\sigma_{\hat{p}} = \sqrt{\frac{.3(.7)}{100}} = .0458$

p = .4 $\sigma_{\hat{p}} = \sqrt{\frac{.4(.6)}{100}} = .0490$

p = .5 $\sigma_{\hat{p}} = \sqrt{\frac{.5(.5)}{100}} = .05$

p = .6 $\sigma_{\hat{p}} = \sqrt{\frac{6(.4)}{100}} = .0490$

p = .7 $\sigma_{\hat{p}} = \sqrt{\frac{.7(.3)}{100}} = .0458$

p = .8 $\sigma_{\hat{p}} = \sqrt{\frac{.8(.2)}{100}} = .04$

p = .9 $\sigma_{\hat{p}} = \sqrt{\frac{.9(.1)}{100}} = .03$

c.

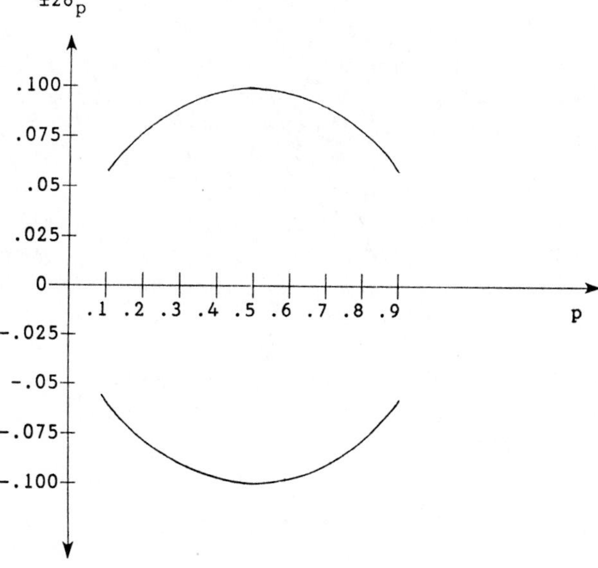


d. One assumption necessary is that we have uniform variance. From the plot in part (c), it is obvious that the variance of proportional data is not uniform.

13.83 a. The least squares estimate is $\log(\hat{y}) = 5.164 - .1138x_1$. Taking the antilog of this gives:

$$\hat{y} = \text{antilog}(5.164 - .1138x_1) = \text{antilog}(5.164)/\text{antilog}(.1138x_1)$$

$$= 174.8625/1.1205^{x_1} = 174.8625(.89244)^{x_1}$$

The second term indicates that each additional thousand tons is worth an estimated multiple of .89244 of the unit price.

The estimated standard deviation of log(y) is $\sqrt{MSE} = .13964$. To obtain a rough idea of the multiplicative model's predictive reliability, we look at the antilog of ±2s or ±2(.13964) = ±.27928.

Antilog(±.27928) = (.7563, 1.3222)

The interpretation is that the actual unit price will generally (with about 95% confidence) fall between 75.63% and 132.22% of the model's predicted value.

To evaluate the usefulness of the model for predicting unit price, we test:

$H_0: \beta_1 = 0$
$H_a: \beta_1 \neq 0$

The test statistic is $F = \frac{MSR}{MSE} = \frac{15.59165}{.0195} = 799.634$

The rejection region requires $\alpha = .05$ in the upper tail of the F distribution with numerator df = k = 1 and denominator df = n - (k + 1) = 30 - (1 + 1) = 28. From Table VIII, Appendix B, $F_{.05} = 2.89$. The rejection region is F > 2.89.

Since the observed value of the test statistic falls in the rejection region (F = 799.634 > 2.89), $H_0$ is rejected. There is sufficient evidence to indicate the model is useful for predicting unit price at $\alpha = .05$.

b. Since the residuals are evenly spread above and below the y-hat axis, we can assume the model has constant standard deviation.

13.85 a. The first order model is $E(y) = \beta_0 + \beta_1 x$. Using SAS, the output from fitting this model is:

DEPENDENT VARIABLE: Y

| SOURCE | DF | SUM OF SQUARES | MEAN SQUARE | F VALUE |
|---|---|---|---|---|
| MODEL | 1 | 1006466310905.950 | 1006466310905.950 | 343.43 |
| ERROR | 23 | 67403636408.295 | 2930592887.317 | PR > F |
| CORRECTED TOTAL | 24 | 1073869947314.240 | | 0.0001 |

| R-SQUARE | C.V. | ROOT MSE | Y MEAN |
|---|---|---|---|
| 0.937233 | 18.6304 | 54134.951 | 290573.52000000 |

| PARAMETER | ESTIMATE | T FOR HO: PARAMETER = 0 | PR > \|T\| | STD ERROR OF ESTIMATE |
|---|---|---|---|---|
| INTERCEPT | 57095.94483601 | 3.44 | 0.0022 | 16611.71804784 |
| X | 20.43867940 | 18.53 | 0.0001 | 1.10288684 |

The fitted first-order model is:

$$\hat{y} = 57096 + 20.4x$$

To determine if the model is useful in predicting the sales price, we test:

$$H_0: \beta_1 = 0$$
$$H_a: \beta_1 \neq 0$$

The test statistic is $F = 343.43$.

The rejection region requires $\alpha = .05$ in the upper tail of the F distribution with numerator df = k = 1 and denominator df = n - (k + 1) = 25 - (1 + 1) = 23. From Table VIII, Appendix B, $F_{.05} = 4.28$. The rejection region is $F > 4.28$.

Since the observed value of the test statistic falls in the rejection region ($F = 343.43 > 4.28$), $H_0$ is rejected. There is sufficient evidence to indicate the model is useful for predicting the sales price at $\alpha = .05$.

The estimate of the change in the mean sales price for each additional square foot of area is $20.40.

b. Using SAS, the plot of the residuals versus $\hat{y}$ is:

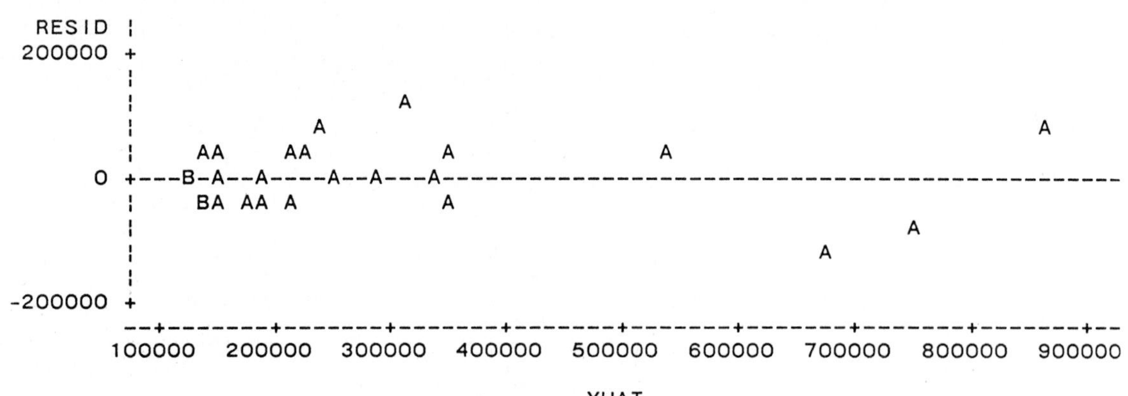


It appears that as $\hat{y}$ increases, the standard deviation also increases.

c. Using SAS, the output from fitting the transformed data is:

DEPENDENT VARIABLE: LOGY

| SOURCE | DF | SUM OF SQUARES | MEAN SQUARE | F VALUE |
|---|---|---|---|---|
| MODEL | 1 | 8.41933351 | 8.41933351 | 81.59 |
| ERROR | 23 | 2.37333026 | 0.10318827 | PR > F |
| CORRECTED TOTAL | 24 | 10.79266377 | | 0.0001 |

| R-SQUARE | C.V. | ROOT MSE | LOGY MEAN |
|---|---|---|---|
| 0.780098 | 2.5992 | 0.32122931 | 12.35890170 |

| PARAMETER | ESTIMATE | T FOR H0: PARAMETER = 0 | PR > \|T\| | STD ERROR OF ESTIMATE |
|---|---|---|---|---|
| INTERCEPT | 11.68362089 | 118.53 | 0.0001 | 0.09857164 |
| X | 0.0000591 | 9.03 | 0.0001 | 0.00000654 |

The fitted model is:

$$\log(\hat{y}) = 11.7 + .000059x$$

To determine if the model involving the transformed data is useful, we test:

$H_0$: $\beta_1 = 0$
$H_a$: $\beta_1 \neq 0$

The test statistic is $F = 81.59$.

The rejection region requires $\alpha = .05$ in the upper tail of the F distribution with numerator df = k = 1 and denominator df = n - (k + 1) = 25 - (1 + 1) = 23. From Table VIII, Appendix B, $F_{.05} = 4.28$. The rejection region is $F > 4.28$.

Since the observed value of the test statistic falls in the rejection region ($F = 81.59 > 4.28$), $H_0$ is rejected. There is sufficient evidence to indicate the model is useful for predicting the log of the sale price at $\alpha = .05$.

d. The plot of the residuals versus log (sales price) is:

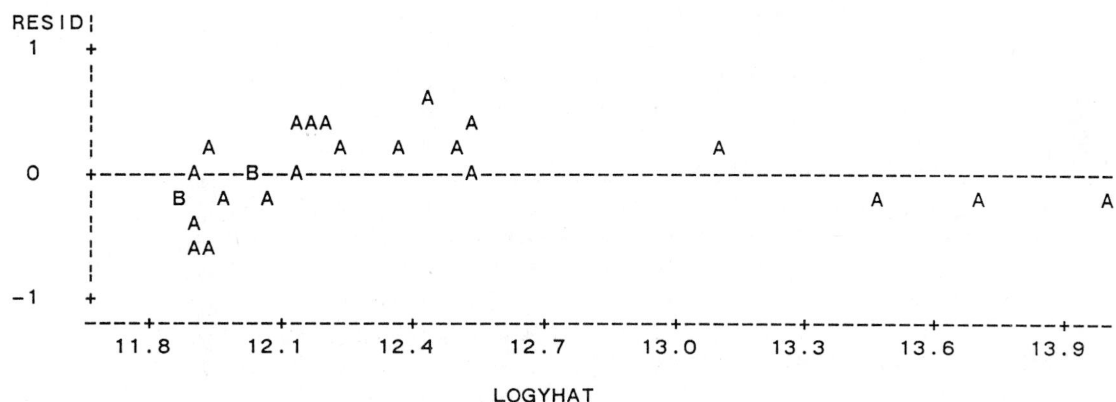


From the plot, it appears that the error component in the multiplicative model is constant.

12.87 a. The model is:

$$E(y) = \beta_0 + \beta_1 x_1 + \beta_2 x_2 + \beta_3 x_3$$

where $y$ = market share

$$x_1 = \begin{cases} 1 & \text{if VH} \\ 0 & \text{otherwise} \end{cases}$$

$$x_2 = \begin{cases} 1 & \text{if H} \\ 0 & \text{otherwise} \end{cases}$$

$$x_3 = \begin{cases} 1 & \text{if M} \\ 0 & \text{otherwise} \end{cases}$$

We assume that the error terms ($\varepsilon_i$) or y's are normally distributed at each exposure level, with a common variance. Also, we assume the $\varepsilon_i$'s have a mean of 0 and are independent.

b. No interaction terms were included because we have only one independent variable, exposure level. Even though we have 3 $x_i$'s in the model, they are dummy variables and correspond to different levels of the one independent variable.

c. The numerator df = k = 3 while the denominator df = n - (k + 1) = 24 - (3 + 1) = 20, where k = number of "dummy" variables in the model.

13.89 a. The quantitative variables are:

$x_1$ = number of people in household,
$x_2$ = miles to bank,
$x_3$ = number of cars in household,
$x_4$ = years of education,
$x_5$ = miles to work,
$x_6$ = total family income, and
$x_{11}$ = number of shopping trips

The qualitative variables are:

$x_7$, $x_8$, $x_9$, and $x_{10}$

b. The variable, kind of work, can assume 5 levels,. The number of dummy variables associated with a qualitative variable is equal to the number of levels of the qualitative variable minus 1.

c. $R^2 = .1836$. This implies that 18.36% of the sample variation in the number of trips to the bank is explained by the model containing the 11 variables.

d. To test the usefulness of the model, we test:

$H_0$: $\beta_1 = \beta_2 = \cdots = \beta_{11} = 0$
$H_a$: At least one of the $\beta$ parameters $\neq 0$

The test statistic is $F = \dfrac{R^2/k}{(1 - R^2)/[n - (k + 1)]}$

$$= \frac{.1836/11}{(1 - .1836)/[597 - (11 + 1)]} = \frac{.01669}{.0014} = 11.96.$$

The rejection region requires $\alpha = .01$ in the upper tail of the F distribution with numerator df = k = 11 and denominator df = n - (k + 1) = 597 - (11 + 1) = 585. From Table X, Appendix B, $F_{.01} \approx 2.32$. The rejection region is $F > 2.32$.

Since the observed value of the test statistic falls in the rejection region ($F = 11.96 > 2.32$), $H_0$ is rejected. There is sufficient evidence to indicate the model is useful in predicting the number of trips to the bank at $\alpha = .01$.

e. The hypotheses would be:

$H_0$: $\beta_7 = \beta_8 = \beta_9 = \beta_{10} = 0$
$H_a$: At least one of the $\beta$ parameters $\neq 0$

13.91 a. To determine whether the quadratic terms are useful, we test:

$H_0$: $\beta_2 = \beta_5 = 0$
$H_a$: At least one $\beta$ parameter $\neq 0$

b. To determine whether there is a difference in mean delivery time by rail and truck, we test:

$H_0$: $\beta_3 = \beta_4 = \beta_5 = 0$
$H_a$: At least one $\beta$ parameter $\neq 0$

13.93 a. Using SAS to fit the model $E(y) = \beta_0 + \beta_1 x_1 + \beta_2 x_2 + \beta_3 x_3$, we get:

DEPENDENT VARIABLE: Y

| SOURCE | DF | SUM OF SQUARES | MEAN SQUARE | F VALUE |
|---|---|---|---|---|
| MODEL | 3 | 13.34333333 | 4.44777778 | 63.09 |
| ERROR | 20 | 1.41000000 | 0.07050000 | PR > F |
| CORRECTED TOTAL | 23 | 14.75333333 | | 0.0001 |

| R-SQUARE | C.V. | ROOT MSE | Y MEAN |
|---|---|---|---|
| 0.904428 | 2.4065 | 0.26551836 | 11.03333333 |

| PARAMETER | | ESTIMATE | T FOR HO: PARAMETER = 0 | PR > \|T\| | STD ERROR OF ESTIMATE |
|---|---|---|---|---|---|
| INTERCEPT | | 10.23333333 | 94.41 | 0.0001 | 0.10839742 |
| X | VH | 0.50000000 | 3.26 | 0.0039 | 0.15329710 |
| | H | 2.01666667 | 13.16 | 0.0001 | 0.15329710 |
| | M | 0.68333333 | 4.46 | 0.0002 | 0.15329710 |

The fitted model is $\hat{y} = 10.2 + .5x_1 + 2.02x_2 + .683x_3$

where $x_1 = \begin{cases} 1 & \text{if VH} \\ 0 & \text{otherwise} \end{cases}$

$x_2 = \begin{cases} 1 & \text{if H} \\ 0 & \text{otherwise} \end{cases}$

$x_3 = \begin{cases} 1 & \text{if M} \\ 0 & \text{otherwise} \end{cases}$

To determine if the firm's expected market share differs for different levels of advertising exposure, we test:

$H_0: \beta_1 = \beta_2 = \beta_3 = 0$
$H_a$: At least one $\beta_i \neq 0$

The test statistic is $F = 63.09$.

The rejection region requires $\alpha = .05$ in the upper tail of the $F$ distribution with numerator df $= k = 3$ and denominator df $= n - (k + 1) = 24 - (3 + 1) = 20$. From Table VIII, Appendix B, $F_{.05} = 3.10$. The rejection region is $F > 3.10$.

Since the observed value of the test statistic falls in the rejection region ($F = 63.09 > 3.10$), $H_0$ is rejected. There is sufficient evidence to indicate the firm's expected market share differs for different levels of advertising exposure at $\alpha = .05$.

13.95 The model relating durability rating to bake time (second-order) and type of paint is:

$$E(y) = \beta_0 + \beta_1x_1 + \beta_2x_1^2 + \beta_3x_2 + \beta_4x_3 + \beta_5x_1x_2 + \beta_6x_1x_3 + \beta_7x_1^2x_2 + \beta_8x_1^2x_3$$

where

$x_1$ = bake time $\quad x_2 = \begin{cases} 1 & \text{if paint B} \\ 0 & \text{otherwise} \end{cases} \quad x_3 = \begin{cases} 1 & \text{if paint C} \\ 0 & \text{otherwise} \end{cases}$

13.97 When fitting models, we are trying to obtain a "general" relationship between the dependent and independent variables that can be used to estimate values of the dependent variable at different levels of the independent variables. By fitting a fourth-order model with 5 data points, we would have 0 degrees of freedom for error; thus, we could run no tests. Also, if a 6th observation is obtained, the model could change dramatically to fit all 6 variables instead of 5.

13.99 a. Using SAS, the output obtained by fitting the second-order model is:

DEP VARIABLE: Y

ANALYSIS OF VARIANCE

| SOURCE | DF | SUM OF SQUARES | MEAN SQUARE | F VALUE | PROB>F |
|---|---|---|---|---|---|
| MODEL | 5 | 1504.25099 | 300.85020 | 41.848 | 0.0001 |
| ERROR | 30 | 215.67457 | 7.18915219 | | |
| C TOTAL | 35 | 1719.92556 | | | |

| | | | |
|---|---|---|---|
| ROOT MSE | 2.681259 | R-SQUARE | 0.8746 |
| DEP MEAN | 45.86111 | ADJ R-SQ | 0.8537 |
| C.V. | 5.846477 | | |

PARAMETER ESTIMATES

| VARIABLE | DF | PARAMETER ESTIMATE | STANDARD ERROR | T FOR H0: PARAMETER=0 | DF | PROB > \|T\| |
|---|---|---|---|---|---|---|
| INTERCEP | 1 | 16.89448080 | 7.85600429 | 2.151 | 1 | 0.0397 |
| X1 | 1 | 0.35042735 | 0.18952193 | 1.849 | 1 | 0.0743 |
| X1SQ | 1 | -0.000175175 | 0.001079489 | -0.162 | 1 | 0.8722 |
| X2 | 1 | -361.16301 | 128.57354 | -2.809 | 1 | 0.0087 |
| X1X2 | 1 | 4.76208073 | 1.67614061 | 2.841 | 1 | 0.0080 |
| X1SQX2 | 1 | -0.01634485 | 0.005479575 | -2.983 | 1 | 0.0056 |

The fitted model is

$$\hat{y} = 16.894 + .3504x_1 - .00018x_1^2 - 361.1630x_2 + 4.7621x_1x_2 - .0163x_1^2x_2$$

where $x_1$ = number of licensed vehicles on the road

and $x_2 = \begin{cases} 1 & \text{if 55 mile-per hour speed limit} \\ 0 & \text{otherwise} \end{cases}$

The plot of the residuals versus $\hat{y}$ is:

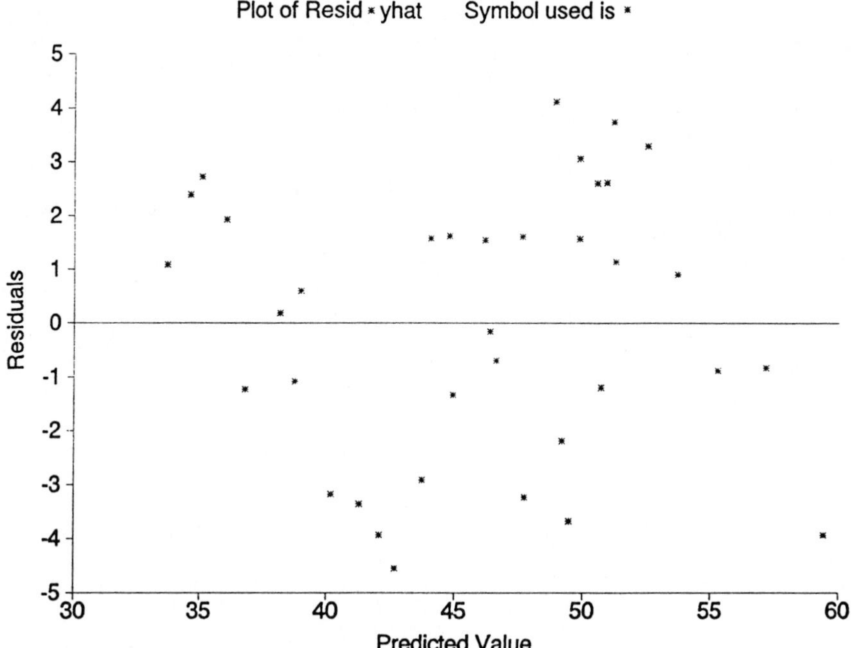


From this plot, there is not much indication that the standard deviation is not constant.

b. Using SAS to fit the model $E(\sqrt{y}) = \beta_0 + \beta_1 x_1 + \beta_2 x_1^2 + \beta_3 x_2 + \beta_4 x_1 x_2 + \beta_5 x_1^2 x_2$, the output is:

DEP VARIABLE: SQRTY

ANALYSIS OF VARIANCE

| SOURCE | DF | SUM OF SQUARES | MEAN SQUARE | F VALUE | PROB>F |
|---|---|---|---|---|---|
| MODEL | 5 | 8.32249868 | 1.66449974 | 42.859 | 0.0001 |
| ERROR | 30 | 1.16509350 | 0.03883645 | | |
| C TOTAL | 35 | 9.48759219 | | | |

| | | | |
|---|---|---|---|
| ROOT MSE | 0.1970697 | R-SQUARE | 0.8772 |
| DEP MEAN | 6.752597 | ADJ R-SQ | 0.8567 |
| C.V. | 2.918428 | | |

PARAMETER ESTIMATES

| VARIABLE | DF | PARAMETER ESTIMATE | STANDARD ERROR | T FOR H0: PARAMETER=0 | DF | PROB > ¦T¦ |
|---|---|---|---|---|---|---|
| INTERCEP | 1 | 4.47784490 | 0.57740779 | 7.755 | 1 | 0.0001 |
| X1 | 1 | 0.02899797 | 0.01392966 | 2.082 | 1 | 0.0460 |
| X1SQ | 1 | -0.000030418 | 0.000079341 | -0.383 | 1 | 0.7041 |
| X2 | 1 | -25.54462025 | 9.45001581 | -2.703 | 1 | 0.0112 |
| X1X2 | 1 | 0.33589781 | 0.12319452 | 2.727 | 1 | 0.0106 |
| X1SQX2 | 1 | -0.001148904 | 0.000402743 | -2.853 | 1 | 0.0078 |

The fitted model is

$$\sqrt{\hat{y}} = 4.478 + .029x_1 - .00003x_1^2 - 25.545x_2 + .336x_1x_2 - .0011x_1^2x_2$$

c. Using SAS to fit the first-order model

$$E(\sqrt{y}) = \beta_0 + \beta_1x_1 + \beta_3x_2 + \beta_4x_1x_2,$$

the output is:

DEP VARIABLE: SQRTY

ANALYSIS OF VARIANCE

| SOURCE | DF | SUM OF SQUARES | MEAN SQUARE | F VALUE | PROB>F |
|---|---|---|---|---|---|
| MODEL | 3 | 7.97034117 | 2.65678039 | 56.034 | 0.0001 |
| ERROR | 32 | 1.51725101 | 0.04741409 | | |
| C TOTAL | 35 | 9.48759219 | | | |

| | | | |
|---|---|---|---|
| ROOT MSE | 0.2177478 | R-SQUARE | 0.8401 |
| DEP MEAN | 6.752597 | ADJ R-SQ | 0.8251 |
| C.V. | 3.224652 | | |

PARAMETER ESTIMATES

| VARIABLE | DF | PARAMETER ESTIMATE | STANDARD ERROR | T FOR H0: PARAMETER=0 | DF | PROB > \|T\| |
|---|---|---|---|---|---|---|
| INTERCEP | 1 | 4.69169865 | 0.16482916 | 28.464 | 1 | 0.0001 |
| X1 | 1 | 0.02369928 | 0.001920136 | 12.342 | 1 | 0.0001 |
| X2 | 1 | 2.33665039 | 0.78770749 | 2.966 | 1 | 0.0057 |
| X1X2 | 1 | -0.02415756 | 0.005247750 | -4.603 | 1 | 0.0001 |

The fitted model is $\sqrt{\hat{y}} = 4.692 + .024x_1 + 2.337x_2 - .024x_1x_2$

To determine if the second-order model is useful for predicting the number of highway deaths, we test:

$H_0$: $\beta_2 = \beta_5 = 0$
$H_a$: At least one $\beta_i \neq 0$

The test statistic is $F = \dfrac{(SSE_1 - SSE_2)/(k - g)}{SSE_2/[n - (k + 1)]}$

$$= \frac{(1.51725 - 1.16509)/(5 - 3)}{1.16509/[36 - (5 + 1)]} = \frac{.17608}{.038836} = 4.53$$

The rejection region requires $\alpha = .05$ in the upper tail of the F distribution with numerator df = k - g = 5 - 3 = 2 and denominator df = n - (k + 1) = 36 - (5 + 1) = 30. From Table VIII, Appendix B, $F_{.05} = 3.32$. The rejection region is F > 3.32. Since the observed value of the test statistic falls in the rejection region (F = 4.53 > 3.32), $H_0$ is rejected.

There is sufficient evidence to indicate the second-order model is useful for predicting the number of highway deaths at $\alpha = .05$.

d. Using SAS to fit the model $E(\sqrt{y}) = \beta_0 + \beta_1 x_1 + \beta_2 x_1^2$, the output is:

DEP VARIABLE: SQRTY

ANALYSIS OF VARIANCE

| SOURCE | DF | SUM OF SQUARES | MEAN SQUARE | F VALUE | PROB>F |
|---|---|---|---|---|---|
| MODEL | 2 | 7.28901598 | 3.64450799 | 54.703 | 0.0001 |
| ERROR | 33 | 2.19857620 | 0.06662352 | | |
| C TOTAL | 35 | 9.48759219 | | | |

| | | | |
|---|---|---|---|
| ROOT MSE | 0.2581153 | R-SQUARE | 0.7683 |
| DEP MEAN | 6.752597 | ADJ R-SQ | 0.7542 |
| C.V. | 3.82246 | | |

PARAMETER ESTIMATES

| VARIABLE | DF | PARAMETER ESTIMATE | STANDARD ERROR | T FOR H0: PARAMETER=0 | DF | PROB > ¦T¦ |
|---|---|---|---|---|---|---|
| INTERCEP | 1 | 3.27397252 | 0.38840591 | 8.429 | 1 | 0.0001 |
| X1 | 1 | 0.06161806 | 0.007659347 | 8.045 | 1 | 0.0001 |
| X1SQ | 1 | -0.000238231 | 0.000033829 | -7.042 | 1 | 0.0001 |

The fitted model is $\sqrt{\hat{y}} = 3.274 + .0616x_1 - .0002x_1^2$.

To determine if the change in the speed-limit law is associated with a change in the number of highway deaths, we test:

$H_0: \beta_3 = \beta_4 = \beta_5 = 0$
$H_a$: At least one $\beta_i \neq 0$

The test statistic is $F = \dfrac{(SSE_1 - SSE_2)/(k - g)}{SSE_2/[n - (k + 1)]}$

$$= \frac{(2.19858 - 1.16509)/(5 - 2)}{1.16509/[36 - (5 + 1)]} = \frac{.34450}{.03884} = 8.87$$

The rejection region requires $\alpha = .05$ in the upper tail of the F distribution with numerator df = k - g = 5 - 2 = 3 and denominator df = n - (k + 1) = 36 - (5 + 1) = 30. From Table VIII, Appendix B, $F_{.05} = 2.92$. The rejection region is F > 2.92.

Since the observed value of the test statistic falls in the rejection region (F = 8.87 > 2.92), $H_0$ is rejected. There is sufficient evidence to indicate the change in the speed-limit law is associated with a change in the number of highway deaths at $\alpha = .05$.

e. Using SAS, the following are the 95% prediction intervals for the number of highway deaths for each of the observed data points plus a point with 10,000,000 licensed vehicles ($x_1$ = 100) before the 55 mph speed limit was put into effect ($x_2$ = 0). The model used corresponded to the original data:

| OBS | ID | ACTUAL | PREDICT VALUE | STD ERR PREDICT | LOWER95% PREDICT | UPPER95% PREDICT | RESIDUAL |
|---|---|---|---|---|---|---|---|
| 1 | 49.2 | 34.8000 | 33.7115 | 1.3525 | 27.5784 | 39.8445 | 1.0885 |
| 2 | 51.9 | 37.0000 | 34.6098 | 1.1716 | 28.6340 | 40.5856 | 2.3902 |
| 3 | 53.3 | 37.8000 | 35.0746 | 1.0875 | 29.1655 | 40.9837 | 2.7254 |
| 4 | 56.3 | 38.0000 | 36.0683 | 0.9317 | 30.2713 | 41.8653 | 1.9317 |
| 5 | 58.6 | 35.6000 | 36.8280 | 0.8366 | 31.0918 | 42.5642 | -1.2280 |
| 6 | 62.8 | 38.4000 | 38.2105 | 0.7222 | 32.5395 | 43.8814 | 0.1895 |
| 7 | 65.2 | 39.6000 | 38.9977 | 0.6905 | 33.3432 | 44.6521 | 0.6023 |
| 8 | 67.6 | 38.7000 | 39.7829 | 0.6799 | 34.1338 | 45.4320 | -1.0829 |
| 9 | 68.8 | 37.0000 | 40.1747 | 0.6810 | 34.5250 | 45.8244 | -3.1747 |
| 10 | 72.1 | 37.9000 | 41.2497 | 0.6995 | 35.5906 | 46.9088 | -3.3497 |
| 11 | 74.5 | 38.1000 | 42.0291 | 0.7213 | 36.3586 | 47.6996 | -3.9291 |
| 12 | 76.4 | 38.1000 | 42.6446 | 0.7404 | 36.9639 | 48.3254 | -4.5446 |
| 13 | 79.7 | 40.8000 | 43.7108 | 0.7725 | 38.0123 | 49.4094 | -2.9108 |
| 14 | 83.5 | 43.6000 | 44.9338 | 0.8019 | 39.2184 | 50.6493 | -1.3338 |
| 15 | 87.3 | 47.7000 | 46.1517 | 0.8192 | 40.4260 | 51.8774 | 1.5483 |
| 16 | 91.8 | 49.2000 | 47.5875 | 0.8233 | 41.8593 | 53.3156 | 1.6125 |
| 17 | 95.9 | 53.0000 | 48.8894 | 0.8147 | 43.1664 | 54.6125 | 4.1106 |
| 18 | 98.9 | 52.9000 | 49.8383 | 0.8055 | 44.1208 | 55.5559 | 3.0617 |
| 19 | 103.1 | 54.9000 | 51.1615 | 0.7984 | 45.4480 | 56.8750 | 3.7385 |
| 20 | 107.4 | 55.8000 | 52.5098 | 0.8158 | 46.7861 | 58.2335 | 3.2902 |
| 21 | 111.2 | 54.6000 | 53.6959 | 0.8692 | 47.9395 | 59.4523 | 0.9041 |
| 22 | 116.3 | 54.4000 | 55.2798 | 1.0174 | 49.4231 | 61.1366 | -0.8798 |
| 23 | 122.3 | 56.3000 | 57.1316 | 1.3125 | 51.0349 | 63.2283 | -0.8316 |
| 24 | 129.8 | 55.5000 | 59.4286 | 1.8481 | 52.7781 | 66.0791 | -3.9286 |
| 25 | 134.9 | 46.4000 | 44.7773 | 1.9776 | 37.9731 | 51.5814 | 1.6227 |
| 26 | 137.9 | 45.9000 | 46.5948 | 1.5322 | 40.2880 | 52.9016 | -0.6948 |
| 27 | 143.5 | 47.0000 | 49.1920 | 1.1513 | 43.2327 | 55.1512 | -2.1920 |
| 28 | 148.8 | 49.5000 | 50.6956 | 1.1703 | 44.7209 | 56.6703 | -1.1956 |
| 29 | 153.6 | 52.4000 | 51.2565 | 1.2133 | 45.2461 | 57.2669 | 1.1435 |
| 30 | 159.6 | 53.5000 | 50.8871 | 1.1222 | 44.9511 | 56.8232 | 2.6129 |
| 31 | 161.6 | 53.1000 | 50.4997 | 1.0619 | 44.6100 | 56.3893 | 2.6003 |
| 32 | 164.1 | 51.4000 | 49.8295 | 0.9932 | 43.9901 | 55.6689 | 1.5705 |
| 33 | 165.2 | 45.8000 | 49.4692 | 0.9759 | 43.6420 | 55.2964 | -3.6692 |
| 34 | 169.4 | 44.5000 | 47.7258 | 1.0876 | 41.8167 | 53.6350 | -3.2258 |
| 35 | 172 | 46.2000 | 46.3545 | 1.3484 | 40.2252 | 52.4838 | -0.1545 |
| 36 | 175.7 | 45.6000 | 44.0180 | 1.9532 | 37.2433 | 50.7927 | 1.5820 |
| 37 | 100 | . | 50.1855 | 0.8025 | 44.4697 | 55.9013 | . |

Thus, the 95% prediction interval for the point with $x_1$ = 100 and $x_2$ = 0 is (44.4697, 55.9013).

Again, using SAS, the following are the 95% prediction intervals for the transformed number of highway deaths for each of the observed data points plus the point with $x_1$ = 100 and $x_2$ = 0.

| OBS | ID | ACTUAL | PREDICT VALUE | STD ERR PREDICT | LOWER95% PREDICT | UPPER95% PREDICT | RESIDUAL |
|---|---|---|---|---|---|---|---|
| 1 | 49.2 | 5.8992 | 5.8309 | 0.0994 | 5.3801 | 6.2817 | 0.0682 |
| 2 | 51.9 | 6.0828 | 5.9009 | 0.0861 | 5.4617 | 6.3401 | 0.1819 |
| 3 | 53.3 | 6.1482 | 5.9370 | 0.0799 | 5.5027 | 6.3713 | 0.2111 |
| 4 | 56.3 | 6.1644 | 6.0140 | 0.0685 | 5.5879 | 6.4401 | 0.1504 |
| 5 | 58.6 | 5.9666 | 6.0727 | 0.0615 | 5.6511 | 6.4943 | -0.1061 |
| 6 | 62.8 | 6.1968 | 6.1790 | 0.0531 | 5.7621 | 6.5958 | 0.0178 |
| 7 | 65.2 | 6.2929 | 6.2392 | 0.0507 | 5.8236 | 6.6548 | 0.0536 |
| 8 | 67.6 | 6.2209 | 6.2991 | 0.0500 | 5.8839 | 6.7143 | -0.0782 |
| 9 | 68.8 | 6.0828 | 6.3289 | 0.0501 | 5.9137 | 6.7442 | -0.2462 |
| 10 | 72.1 | 6.1563 | 6.4105 | 0.0514 | 5.9945 | 6.8264 | -0.2542 |
| 11 | 74.5 | 6.1725 | 6.4694 | 0.0530 | 6.0526 | 6.8861 | -0.2968 |
| 12 | 76.4 | 6.1725 | 6.5157 | 0.0544 | 6.0982 | 6.9333 | -0.3432 |
| 13 | 79.7 | 6.3875 | 6.5958 | 0.0568 | 6.1769 | 7.0146 | -0.2083 |
| 14 | 83.5 | 6.6030 | 6.6871 | 0.0589 | 6.2670 | 7.1072 | -0.0841 |
| 15 | 87.3 | 6.9065 | 6.7775 | 0.0602 | 6.3567 | 7.1984 | 0.1290 |
| 16 | 91.8 | 7.0143 | 6.8835 | 0.0605 | 6.4625 | 7.3045 | 0.1308 |
| 17 | 95.9 | 7.2801 | 6.9790 | 0.0599 | 6.5584 | 7.3996 | 0.3011 |
| 18 | 98.9 | 7.2732 | 7.0482 | 0.0592 | 6.6280 | 7.4685 | 0.2250 |
| 19 | 103.1 | 7.4095 | 7.1442 | 0.0587 | 6.7243 | 7.5641 | 0.2653 |
| 20 | 107.4 | 7.4699 | 7.2414 | 0.0600 | 6.8207 | 7.6620 | 0.2286 |
| 21 | 111.2 | 7.3892 | 7.3263 | 0.0639 | 6.9032 | 7.7494 | 0.0629 |
| 22 | 116.3 | 7.3756 | 7.4389 | 0.0748 | 7.0084 | 7.8693 | -0.0632 |
| 23 | 122.3 | 7.5033 | 7.5693 | 0.0965 | 7.1212 | 8.0174 | -0.0660 |
| 24 | 129.8 | 7.4498 | 7.7293 | 0.1358 | 7.2405 | 8.2181 | -0.2795 |
| 25 | 134.9 | 6.8118 | 6.6963 | 0.1454 | 6.1963 | 7.1964 | 0.1154 |
| 26 | 137.9 | 6.7750 | 6.8259 | 0.1126 | 6.3623 | 7.2894 | -0.0509 |
| 27 | 143.5 | 6.8557 | 7.0109 | 0.0846 | 6.5729 | 7.4489 | -0.1552 |
| 28 | 148.8 | 7.0356 | 7.1178 | 0.0860 | 6.6787 | 7.5570 | -0.0822 |
| 29 | 153.6 | 7.2388 | 7.1575 | 0.0892 | 6.7158 | 7.5993 | 0.0813 |
| 30 | 159.6 | 7.3144 | 7.1307 | 0.0825 | 6.6944 | 7.5670 | 0.1837 |
| 31 | 161.6 | 7.2870 | 7.1029 | 0.0781 | 6.6700 | 7.5358 | 0.1841 |
| 32 | 164.1 | 7.1694 | 7.0549 | 0.0730 | 6.6257 | 7.4841 | 0.1145 |
| 33 | 165.2 | 6.7676 | 7.0291 | 0.0717 | 6.6008 | 7.4574 | -0.2615 |
| 34 | 169.4 | 6.6708 | 6.9043 | 0.0799 | 6.4700 | 7.3386 | -0.2335 |
| 35 | 172 | 6.7971 | 6.8062 | 0.0991 | 6.3557 | 7.2567 | -.009175 |
| 36 | 175.7 | 6.7528 | 6.6392 | 0.1436 | 6.1412 | 7.1371 | 0.1136 |
| 37 | 100 | . | 7.0735 | 0.0590 | 6.6534 | 7.4936 | . |

The 95% prediction interval for the point with $x_1 = 100$ and $x_2 = 0$ is (6.6534, 7.4936).

To compare the intervals, we must "untransform" the second interval by squaring the two end points. The "untransformed" prediction interval is

$$(6.6534^2, 7.4936^2) \Rightarrow (44.2677, 56.1540)$$

The width of this interval is 56.1540 - 44.2677 = 11.8863. The width of the first interval is 55.9013 - 44.4697 = 11.4316. Thus, the prediction interval using the original data is slightly smaller than that using the transformed data. This implies that estimations using the original data are made with more precision than with the transformed data.

f. The plot of the residuals from fitting the model in part (b) is:

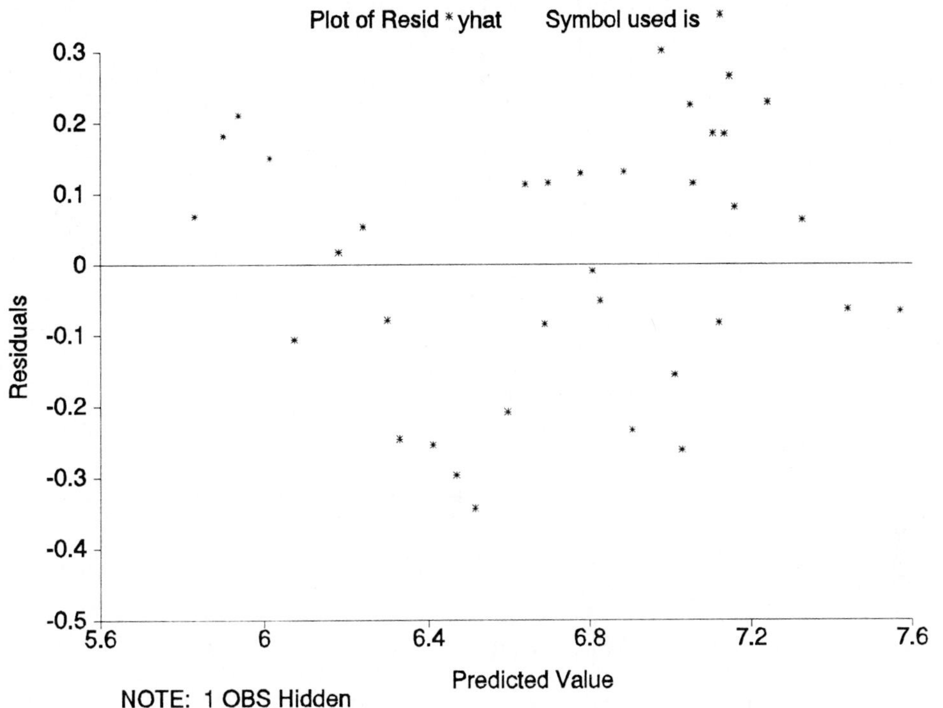


This plot is very similar to the plot in part (a). It does not appear the transformation is advisable in this case.

13.101 a. $E(y) = \beta_0 + \beta_1 x_1 + \beta_2 x_2$

where $x_1$ = total area of house

$$x_2 = \begin{cases} 1 & \text{if no central air conditioning} \\ 0 & \text{otherwise} \end{cases}$$

b. $E(y) = \beta_0 + \beta_1 x_1 + \beta_2 x_2 + \beta_3 x_1^2 + \beta_4 x_1 x_2 + \beta_5 x_1^2 x_2$

c. To determine whether the second-order terms are useful, we test:

$H_0$: $\beta_3 = \beta_4 = \beta_5 = 0$
$H_a$: At least one $\beta$ parameter $\neq 0$

d. The F would be

$$F = \frac{(SSE_1 - SSE_2)/(k - g)}{SSE_2/[n - (k + 1)]}$$

where $SSE_2$ is the sum of squares for error when the complete model is fit, while $SSE_1$ is the sum of squares for error when the reduced model is fit.

13.103 a. To determine if the second-order terms are important, we test:

$H_0$: $\beta_3 = \beta_4 = \beta_5 = 0$
$H_a$: At least one $\beta_i \neq 0$

The test statistic is $F = \dfrac{(SSE_1 - SSE_2)/(k - g)}{SSE_2/[n - (k + 1)]}$

$$= \frac{(8.548 - 6.133)/(5 - 2)}{6.133/[25 - (5 + 1)]} = \frac{.805}{.3228} = 2.49$$

The rejection region requires $\alpha = .05$ in the upper tail of the F distribution with numerator df = k - g = 5 - 2 = 3 and denominator df = n - (k + 1) = 25 - (5 + 1) = 19. From Table VIII, Appendix B, $F_{.05} = 3.13$. The rejection region is $F > 3.13$.

Since the observed value of the test statistic does not fall in the rejection region ($F = 2.49 \not> 3.13$), $H_0$ is not rejected. There is insufficient evidence to indicate the second-order terms are important for predicting the mean cost at $\alpha = .05$.

b. To determine if the main effects model is useful, we test

$H_0$: $\beta_1 = \beta_2 = 0$
$H_a$: At least one $\beta_i \neq 0$

The test statistic is: $F = \dfrac{R^2/k}{(1 - R^2)/[n - (k + 1)]}$

$$= \frac{.950/2}{(1 - .950)/[25 - (2 + 1)]} = \frac{.475}{.0023} = 209$$

The rejection region requires $\alpha = .05$ in the upper tail of the F distribution with numerator df = k = 2 and denominator df = n - (k + 1) = 25 - (2 + 1) = 22. From Table VIII, Appendix B, $F_{.05} = 3.44$. The rejection region is $F > 3.44$.

Since the observed value of the test statistic falls in the rejection region ($F = 209 > 3.44$), $H_0$ is rejected. There is sufficient evidence to indicate the main effects model is useful for predicting costs at $\alpha = .05$.

| | | | | | | | | | | | | | | | | | | | | | | | | | | | | | | | | | | | | | |

# C H A P T E R 14

# METHODS FOR QUALITY IMPROVEMENT

14.1 A control chart is a time series plot of individual measurements or means of a quality variable to which a centerline and two other horizontal lines called control limits have been added. The center line represents the mean of the process when the process is in a state of statistical control. The upper control limit and the lower control limit are positioned so that when the process is in control the probability of an individual measurement or mean falling outside the limits is very small. A control chart is used to determine if a process is in control (only common causes of variation present) or not (both common and special causes of variation present). This information helps us to determine when to take action to find and remove special causes of variation and when to leave the process alone.

14.3 When a control chart is first constructed, it is not known whether the process is in control or not. If the process is found not to be in control, then the centerline and control limits should not be used to monitor the process in the future.

14.5 Even if all the points of an $\bar{x}$-chart fall within the control limits, the process may be out of control. Nonrandom patterns may exist among the plotted points that are within the control limits, but are very unlikely if the process is in control. Examples include six points in a row steadily increasing or decreasing and fourteen points in a row alternating up and down.

14.7 Rule 1: One point beyond Zone A: No points are beyond Zone A.

Rule 2: Nine points in a row in Zone C or beyond: No sequence of 9 points are in Zone C (on one side of the centerline) or beyond.

Rule 3: Six points in a row steadily increasing or decreasing: No sequence of 6 points steadily increase or decrease.

Rule 4: Fourteen points in a row alternating up and down: This pattern does not exist.

Rule 5: Two out of three points in Zone A or beyond: There are no groups of three consecutive points that have two or more in Zone A or beyond.

Rule 6: Four out of five points in a row in Zone B or beyond: Points 18 thru 21 are all in Zone B or beyond. This indicates the process is out of control.

Thus, Rule 6 indicates this process is out of control.

14.9 Using Table XVII, Appendix B:

a. With $n = 3$, $A_2 = 1.023$

b. With $n = 10$, $A_2 = 0.308$

c. With $n = 22$, $A_2 = 0.167$

14.11 a. For each sample, we compute $\bar{x} = \frac{\sum x}{n}$ and R = range = largest measurement - smallest measurement. The results are listed in the table:

| Sample No. | $\bar{x}$ | R | Sample No. | $\bar{x}$ | R |
|---|---|---|---|---|---|
| 1 | 20.225 | 1.8 | 11 | 21.225 | 3.2 |
| 2 | 19.750 | 2.8 | 12 | 20.475 | 0.9 |
| 3 | 20.425 | 3.8 | 13 | 19.650 | 2.6 |
| 4 | 19.725 | 2.5 | 14 | 19.075 | 4.0 |
| 5 | 20.550 | 3.7 | 15 | 19.400 | 2.2 |
| 6 | 19.900 | 5.0 | 16 | 20.700 | 4.3 |
| 7 | 21.325 | 5.5 | 17 | 19.850 | 3.6 |
| 8 | 19.625 | 3.5 | 18 | 20.200 | 2.5 |
| 9 | 19.350 | 2.5 | 19 | 20.425 | 2.2 |
| 10 | 20.550 | 4.1 | 20 | 19.900 | 5.5 |

b. $\bar{\bar{x}} = \frac{\bar{x}_1 + \bar{x}_2 + \ldots + \bar{x}_{20}}{n} = \frac{402.325}{20} = 20.11625$

$\bar{R} = \frac{R_1 + R_2 + \ldots + R_{20}}{n} = \frac{66.2}{20} = 3.31$

c. Centerline $= \bar{\bar{x}} = 20.116$

From Table XVII, Appendix B, with $n = 4$, $A_2 = .729$.

Upper control limit $= \bar{\bar{x}} + A_2\bar{R} = 20.116 + .729(3.31) = 22.529$

Lower control limit $= \bar{\bar{x}} - A_2\bar{R} = 20.116 - .729(3.31) = 17.703$

d. Upper A-B Boundary $= \bar{x} + \frac{2}{3}(A_2\bar{R}) = 20.116 + \frac{2}{3}(.729)(3.31) = 21.725$

Lower A-B Boundary $= \bar{x} - \frac{2}{3}(A_2\bar{R}) = 20.116 - \frac{2}{3}(.729)(3.31) = 18.507$

Upper B-C Boundary $= \bar{x} + \frac{1}{3}(A_2\bar{R}) = 20.116 + \frac{1}{3}(.729)(3.31) = 20.920$

Lower B-C Boundary $= \bar{x} - \frac{1}{3}(A_2\bar{R}) = 20.116 - \frac{1}{3}(.729)(3.31) = 19.312$

e. The $\bar{x}$-chart is:

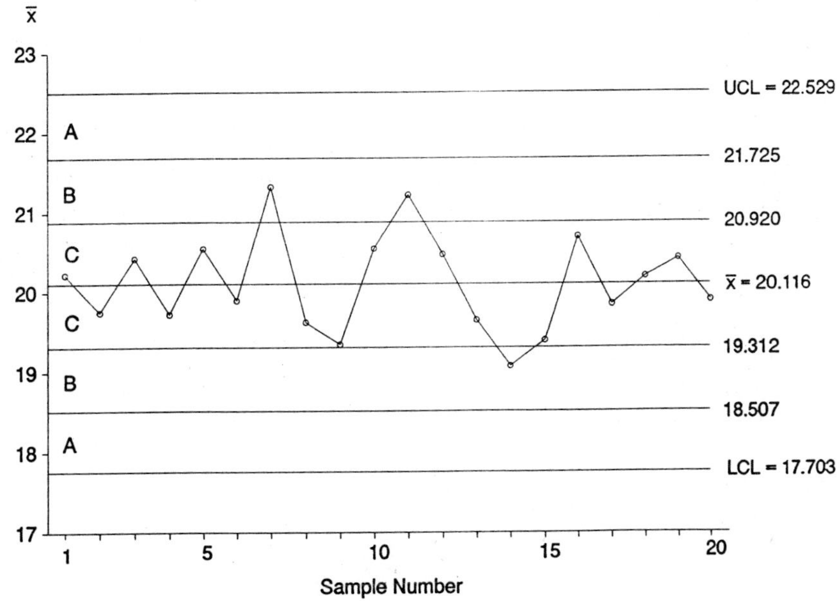


Rule 1: One point beyond Zone A: No points are beyond Zone A.

Rule 2: Nine points in a row in Zone C or beyond: No sequence of 9 points are in Zone C (on one side of the centerline) or beyond.

Rule 3: Six points in a row steadily increasing or decreasing: No sequence of 6 points steadily increase or decrease.

Rule 4: Fourteen points in a row alternating up and down: This pattern does not exist.

Rule 5: Two out of three points in Zone A or beyond: There are no groups of three consecutive points that have two or more in Zone A or beyond.

Rule 6: Four out of five points in a row in Zone B or beyond: No sequence of 5 points has 4 or more in Zone B or beyond.

The process appears to be in control.

14.13 a. The process of interest is the production of bolts used in military aircraft.

b. For each sample, we compute $\bar{x} = \frac{\sum x}{n}$ and R = range = largest measurement - smallest measurement. The results are listed in the table:

| Sample No. | $\bar{x}$ | R | Sample No. | $\bar{x}$ | R |
|---|---|---|---|---|---|
| 1 | 36.9725 | .20 | 14 | 37.0725 | .06 |
| 2 | 36.9575 | .19 | 15 | 36.9925 | .15 |
| 3 | 37.0675 | .17 | 16 | 36.9550 | .09 |
| 4 | 37.0650 | .22 | 17 | 37.0375 | .20 |
| 5 | 36.9475 | .29 | 18 | 37.0100 | .20 |
| 6 | 36.9975 | .24 | 19 | 36.9550 | .13 |
| 7 | 37.0000 | .13 | 20 | 37.0350 | .25 |
| 8 | 37.0050 | .21 | 21 | 36.9950 | .09 |
| 9 | 37.0275 | .27 | 22 | 37.0225 | .19 |
| 10 | 36.9700 | .24 | 23 | 37.0025 | .09 |
| 11 | 37.0200 | .22 | 24 | 36.9950 | .17 |
| 12 | 36.9825 | .16 | 25 | 37.0100 | .20 |
| 13 | 37.0700 | .31 | | | |

$$\bar{\bar{x}} = \frac{\bar{x}_1 + \bar{x}_2 + \ldots + \bar{x}_{25}}{n} = \frac{925.1650}{25} = 37.0066$$

$$\bar{R} = \frac{R_1 + R_2 + \ldots + R_{25}}{n} = \frac{4.67}{25} = .1868$$

Centerline = $\bar{\bar{x}}$ = 37.007

From Table XVII, Appendix B, with n = 4, $A_2$ = .729.

Upper control limit = $\bar{\bar{x}} + A_2\bar{R} = 37.007 + .729(.1868) = 37.143$

Lower control limit = $\bar{\bar{x}} - A_2\bar{R} = 37.007 - .729(.1868) = 36.871$

Upper A-B Boundary = $\bar{\bar{x}} + \frac{2}{3}(A_2\bar{R}) = 37.007 + \frac{2}{3}(.729)(.1868) = 37.098$

Lower A-B Boundary = $\bar{\bar{x}} - \frac{2}{3}(A_2\bar{R}) = 37.007 - \frac{2}{3}(.729)(.1868) = 36.916$

Upper B-C Boundary = $\bar{\bar{x}} + \frac{1}{3}(A_2\bar{R}) = 37.007 + \frac{1}{3}(.729)(.1868) = 37.052$

Lower B-C Boundary = $\bar{\bar{x}} - \frac{1}{3}(A_2\bar{R}) = 37.007 - \frac{1}{3}(.729)(.1868) = 36.962$

The $\bar{x}$-chart is:

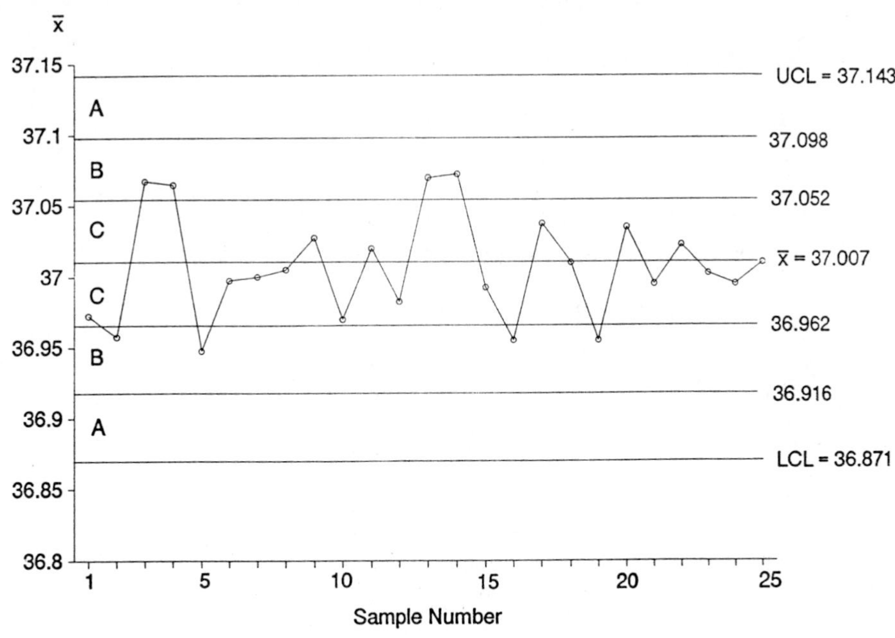


c. To determine if the process is in or out of control, we check the 6 rules:

Rule 1: One point beyond Zone A: No points are beyond Zone A.

Rule 2: Nine points in a row in Zone C or beyond: No sequence of 9 points are in Zone C (on one side of the centerline) or beyond.

Rule 3: Six points in a row steadily increasing or decreasing: No sequence of 6 points steadily increase or decrease.

Rule 4: Fourteen points in a row alternating up and down: This pattern does not exist.

Rule 5: Two out of three points in Zone A or beyond: There are no groups of three consecutive points that have two or more in Zone A or beyond.

Rule 6: Four out of five points in a row in Zone B or beyond: No sequence of 5 points has 4 or more in Zone B or beyond.

The process appears to be in control. No special causes of variation appear to be present.

d. An example of a special cause of variation would be if the machine used to produce the bolts slipped out of alignment and started producing bolts of a different length. An example of common cause variation would be the grade of the raw material used to make the bolts.

e. Since the process appears to be in control, it is appropriate to use these limits to monitor future process output.

14.15 The R-chart is designed to monitor the variation of the process.

14.17 Using Table XVII, Appendix B:

a. With $n = 4$, $D_3 = 0.000$ $D_4 = 2.282$

b. With $n = 12$, $D_3 = 0.283$ $D_4 = 1.717$

c. With $n = 24$, $D_3 = 0.451$ $D_4 = 1.548$

14.19 a. From Exercise 14.11, the R values are:

| Sample No. | R | Sample No. | R |
|---|---|---|---|
| 1 | 1.8 | 11 | 3.2 |
| 2 | 2.8 | 12 | 0.9 |
| 3 | 3.8 | 13 | 2.6 |
| 4 | 2.5 | 14 | 4.0 |
| 5 | 3.7 | 15 | 2.2 |
| 6 | 5.0 | 16 | 4.3 |
| 7 | 5.5 | 17 | 3.6 |
| 8 | 3.5 | 18 | 2.5 |
| 9 | 2.5 | 19 | 2.2 |
| 10 | 4.1 | 20 | 5.5 |

$$\bar{R} = \frac{R_1 + R_2 + \ldots + R_{20}}{n} = \frac{66.2}{20} = 3.31$$

Centerline $= \bar{R} = 3.31$

From Table XVII, Appendix B, with $n = 4$, $D_4 = 2.282$ and $D_3 = 0$.

Upper control limit $= \bar{R}D_4 = 3.31(2.282) = 7.553$

Since $D_3 = 0$, the lower control limit is negative and is not included on the chart.

b. From Table XVII, Appendix B, with n = 4, $d_2$ = 2.059 and $d_3$ = .880.

$$\text{Upper A-B Boundary} = \bar{R} + 2d_3 \frac{\bar{R}}{d_2} = 3.31 + 2(.880)\frac{3.31}{2.059} = 6.139$$

$$\text{Lower A-B Boundary} = \bar{R} - 2d_3 \frac{\bar{R}}{d_2} = 3.31 - 2(.880)\frac{3.31}{2.059} = 0.481$$

$$\text{Upper B-C Boundary} = \bar{R} + d_3 \frac{\bar{R}}{d_2} = 3.31 + (.880)\frac{3.31}{2.059} = 4.725$$

$$\text{Lower B-C Boundary} = \bar{R} - d_3 \frac{\bar{R}}{d_2} = 3.31 - (.880)\frac{3.31}{2.059} = 1.895$$

c. The R-chart is:

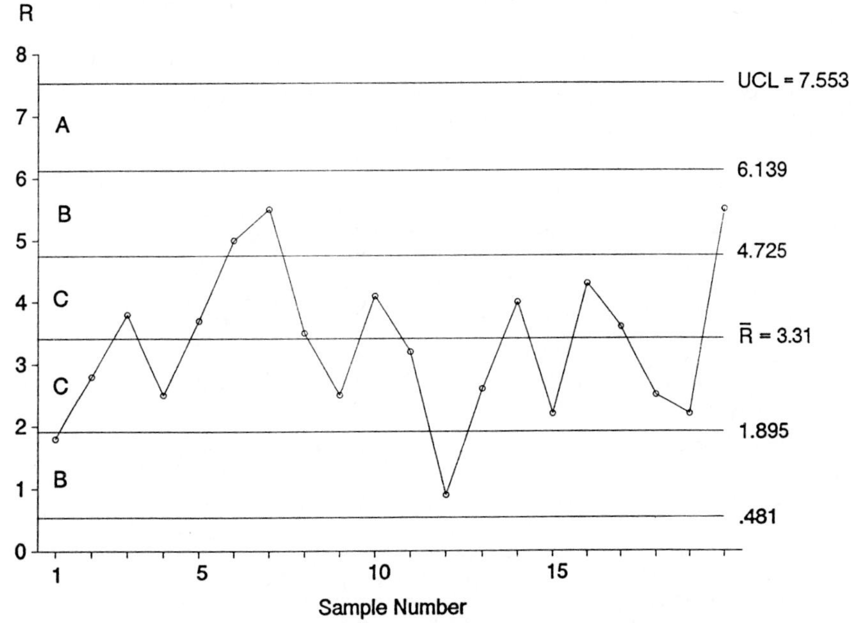


To determine if the process is in or out of control, we check the 6 rules:

Rule 1: One point beyond Zone A: No points are beyond Zone A.

Rule 2: Nine points in a row in Zone C or beyond: No sequence of 9 points are in Zone C (on one side of the centerline) or beyond.

Rule 3: Six points in a row steadily increasing or decreasing: No sequence of 6 points steadily increase or decrease.

Rule 4: Fourteen points in a row alternating up and down: This pattern does not exist.

Rule 5: Two out of three points in Zone A or beyond: There are no groups of three consecutive points that have two or more in Zone A or beyond.

Rule 6: Four out of five points in a row in Zone B or beyond: No sequence of 5 points has 4 or more in zone B or beyond.

The process appears to be in control.

14.21 a. Yes. Because all five observations in each sample were selected from the same dispenser, the rational subgrouping will enable the company to detect variation in fill caused by differences in the carbon dioxide dispensers.

b. For each sample, we compute the range = R = largest measurement - smallest measurement. The results are listed in the table:

| Sample No. | R | Sample No. | R |
|---|---|---|---|
| 1 | .05 | 13 | .05 |
| 2 | .06 | 14 | .04 |
| 3 | .06 | 15 | .05 |
| 4 | .05 | 16 | .05 |
| 5 | .07 | 17 | .06 |
| 6 | .07 | 18 | .06 |
| 7 | .09 | 19 | .05 |
| 8 | .08 | 20 | .08 |
| 9 | .08 | 21 | .08 |
| 10 | .11 | 22 | .12 |
| 11 | .14 | 23 | .12 |
| 12 | .14 | 24 | .15 |

$$\bar{R} = \frac{R_1 + R_2 + \ldots + R_{24}}{n} = \frac{1.91}{24} = .0796$$

Centerline = $\bar{R}$ = .0796

From Table XVII, Appendix B, with n = 5, $D_4$ = 2.114 and $D_3$ = 0.

Upper control limit = $\bar{R}D_4$ = .0796(2.114) = .168

Since $D_3$ = 0, the lower control limit is negative and is not included on the chart.

From Table XVII, Appendix B, with n = 5, $d_2$ = 2.326 and $d_3$ = .864.

$$\text{Upper A-B Boundary} = \bar{R} + 2d_3 \frac{\bar{R}}{d_2} = .0796 + 2(.864)\frac{.0796}{2.326} = .139$$

$$\text{Lower A-B Boundary} = \bar{R} - 2d_3 \frac{\bar{R}}{d_2} = .0796 - 2(.864)\frac{.0796}{2.326} = .020$$

$$\text{Upper B-C Boundary} = \bar{R} + d_3 \frac{\bar{R}}{d_2} = .0796 + (.864) \frac{.0796}{2.326} = .109$$

$$\text{Lower B-C Boundary} = \bar{R} - d_3 \frac{\bar{R}}{d_2} = .0796 - (.864) \frac{.0796}{2.326} = .050$$

The R-chart is:

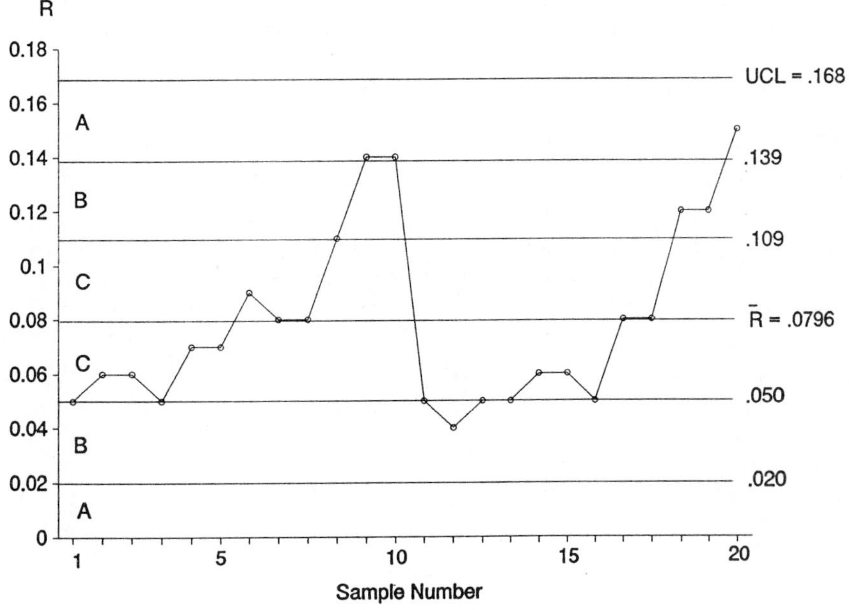


c. To determine if the process is in or out of control, we check the 6 rules:

Rule 1: One point beyond Zone A: No points are beyond Zone A.

Rule 2: Nine points in a row in Zone C or beyond: No sequence of 9 points are in Zone C (on one side of the centerline) or beyond.

Rule 3: Six points in a row steadily increasing or decreasing: No sequence of 6 points steadily increase or decrease.

Rule 4: Fourteen points in a row alternating up and down: This pattern does not exist.

$$\text{Upper A-B Boundary} = \bar{R} + 2d_3 \frac{\bar{R}}{d_2} = .1868 + 2(.880)\frac{.1868}{2.059} = .346$$

$$\text{Lower A-B Boundary} = \bar{R} - 2d_3 \frac{\bar{R}}{d_2} = .1868 - 2(.880)\frac{.1868}{2.059} = .027$$

$$\text{Upper B-C Boundary} = \bar{R} + d_3 \frac{\bar{R}}{d_2} = .1868 + (.880)\frac{.1868}{2.059} = .267$$

$$\text{Lower B-C Boundary} = \bar{R} - d_3 \frac{\bar{R}}{d_2} = .1868 - (.880)\frac{.1868}{2.059} = .107$$

The R-chart is:

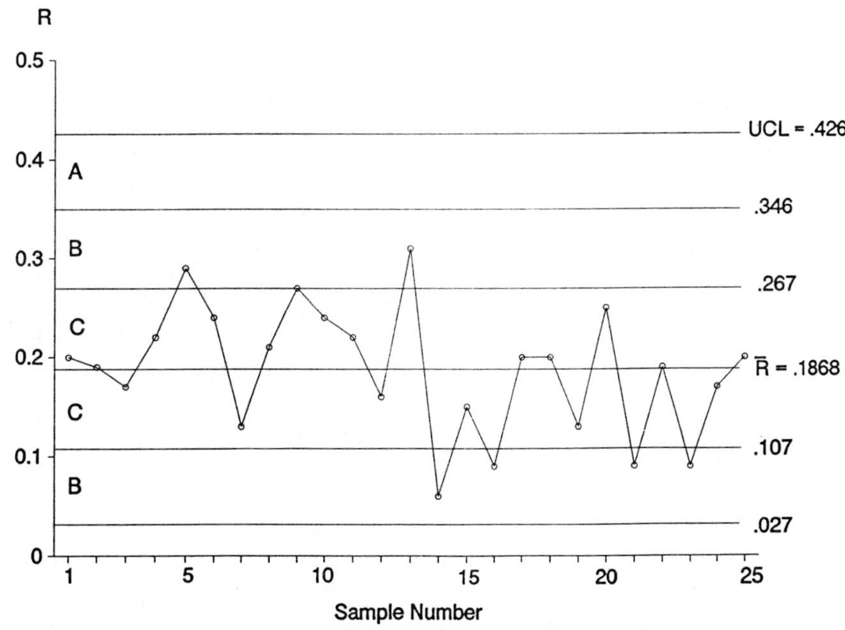


b. To determine if the process is in or out of control, we check the 6 rules:

Rule 1: One point beyond Zone A: No points are beyond Zone A.

Rule 2: Nine points in a row in Zone C or beyond: No sequence of 9 points are in Zone C (on one side of the centerline) or beyond.

Rule 3: Six points in a row steadily increasing or decreasing: No sequence of 6 points steadily increase or decrease.

Rule 4: Fourteen points in a row alternating up and down: This pattern does not exist.

Rule 5: Two out of three points in Zone A or beyond: No group of three consecutive points have two or more in Zone A or beyond.

Rule 6: Four out of five points in a row in Zone B or beyond: No sequence of 5 points has 4 or more in zone B or beyond.

The process appears to be in control. There do not appear to be any special causes of variation during the time the data were collected.

c. Since the process appears to be in control, it is appropriate to use these limits to monitor future process output.

14.25. The sample size is determined as follows:

$$n > \frac{9(1 - p_0)}{p_0} = \frac{9(1 - .08)}{.08} = 103.5 \approx 104$$

14.27 a. We must first calculate $\bar{p}$. To do this, it is necessary to find the total number of defectives in all the samples. To find the number of defectives per sample, we multiple the proportion by the sample size, 150. The number of defectives per sample are shown in the table:

| Sample No. | p | No. defectives | Sample No. | p | No. defectives |
|---|---|---|---|---|---|
| 1 | .03 | 4.5 | 11 | .07 | 10.5 |
| 2 | .05 | 7.5 | 12 | .04 | 6.0 |
| 3 | .10 | 15.0 | 13 | .06 | 9.0 |
| 4 | .02 | 3.0 | 14 | .05 | 7.5 |
| 5 | .08 | 12.0 | 15 | .07 | 10.5 |
| 6 | .09 | 13.5 | 16 | .06 | 9.0 |
| 7 | .08 | 12.0 | 17 | .07 | 10.5 |
| 8 | .05 | 7.5 | 18 | .02 | 3.0 |
| 9 | .07 | 10.5 | 19 | .05 | 7.5 |
| 10 | .06 | 9.0 | 20 | .03 | 4.5 |

Note: There cannot be a fraction of a defective. The proportions presented in the exercise have been rounded off. I have used the fractions to minimize the roundoff error.

To get the total number of defectives, sum the number of defectives for all 20 samples. The sum is 172.5. To get the total number of units sampled, multiply the sample size by the number of samples:

$$150(20) = 3000$$

$$\bar{p} = \frac{\text{Total defective in all samples}}{\text{Total units sampled}} = \frac{172.5}{3000} = .0575$$

Centerline = $\bar{p}$ = .0575

$$\text{Upper control limit} = \bar{p} + 3\sqrt{\frac{\bar{p}(1 - \bar{p})}{n}} = .0575 + 3\sqrt{\frac{.0575(.9425)}{150}}$$
$$= .1145$$

$$\text{Lower control limit} = \bar{p} - 3\sqrt{\frac{\bar{p}(1 - \bar{p})}{n}} = .0575 - 3\sqrt{\frac{.0575(.9425)}{150}}$$
$$= .0005$$

b. $$\text{Upper A-B boundary} = \bar{p} + 2\sqrt{\frac{\bar{p}(1 - \bar{p})}{n}} = .0575 + 2\sqrt{\frac{.0575(.9425)}{150}}$$
$$= .0955$$

$$\text{Lower A-B boundary} = \bar{p} - 2\sqrt{\frac{\bar{p}(1 - \bar{p})}{n}} = .0575 - 2\sqrt{\frac{.0575(.9425)}{150}}$$
$$= .0195$$

$$\text{Upper B-C boundary} = \bar{p} + \sqrt{\frac{\bar{p}(1 - \bar{p})}{n}} = .0575 + \sqrt{\frac{.0575(.9425)}{150}}$$
$$= .0765$$

$$\text{Lower B-C boundary} = \bar{p} - \sqrt{\frac{\bar{p}(1 - \bar{p})}{n}} = .0575 - \sqrt{\frac{.0575(.9425)}{150}}$$
$$= .0385$$

c. The p-chart is:

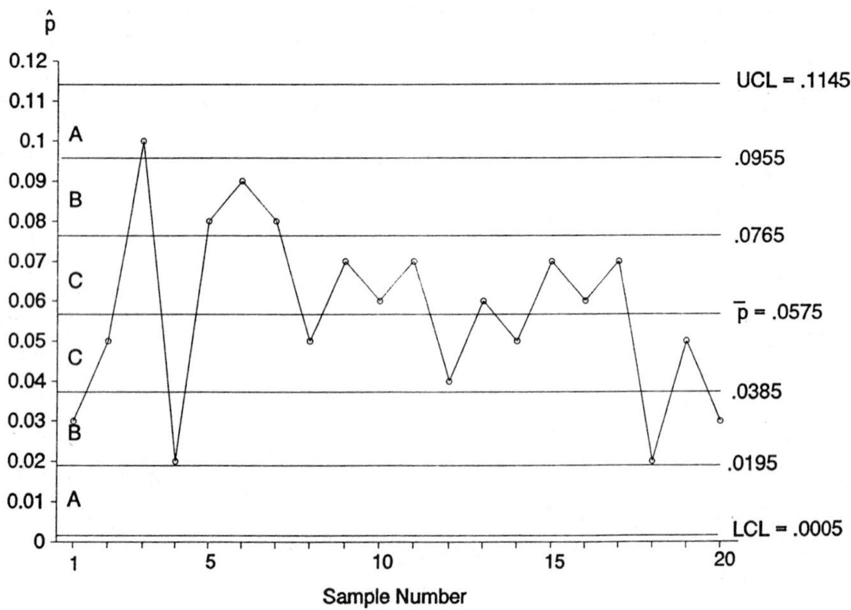


d. To determine if the process is in or out of control, we check the 6 rules:

Rule 1: One point beyond Zone A: No points are beyond Zone A.

Rule 2: Nine points in a row in Zone C or beyond: No sequence of 9 points are in Zone C (on one side of the centerline) or beyond.

Rule 3: Six points in a row steadily increasing or decreasing: No sequence of 6 points steadily increase or decrease.

Rule 4: Fourteen points in a row alternating up and down: Points 7 thru 20 alternate up and down. This indicates the process is out of control.

Rule 5: Two out of three points in Zone A or beyond: No group of three consecutive points have two or more in Zone A or beyond.

Rule 6: Four out of five points in a row in Zone B or beyond: Points 3, 5, 6, and 7 are in Zone B or beyond. This indicates the process is out of control.

Rules 4 and 6 indicate that the process is out of control.

e. Since the process is out of control, the centerline and control limits should not be used to monitor future process output. The centerline and control limits are intended to represent the behavior of the process when it is under control.

14.29 a. The sample size is determined as follows:

$$n > \frac{9(1 - p_0)}{p_0} = \frac{9(1 - .07)}{.07} = 119.6 \approx 120$$

The minimum sample size is 120.

b. To compute the proportion of defectives in each sample, divide the number of defectives by the number in the sample, 120:

$$\hat{p} = \frac{\text{No. defectives}}{\text{No. in sample}}$$

The sample proportions are listed in the table:

| Sample No. | $\hat{p}$ | Sample No. | $\hat{p}$ |
|---|---|---|---|
| 1 | .092 | 11 | .083 |
| 2 | .042 | 12 | .100 |
| 3 | .033 | 13 | .067 |
| 4 | .067 | 14 | .050 |
| 5 | .083 | 15 | .083 |
| 6 | .108 | 16 | .042 |
| 7 | .075 | 17 | .083 |
| 8 | .067 | 18 | .083 |
| 9 | .083 | 19 | .025 |
| 10 | .092 | 20 | .067 |

To get the total number of defectives, sum the number of defectives for all 20 samples. The sum is 171. To get the total number of units sampled, multiply the sample size by the number of samples:

$$120(20) = 2400.$$

$$\bar{p} = \frac{\text{Total defective in all samples}}{\text{Total units sampled}} = \frac{171}{2400} = .071$$

Centerline = $\bar{p}$ = .071

$$\text{Upper control limit} = \bar{p} + 3\sqrt{\frac{\bar{p}(1 - \bar{p})}{n}} = .071 + 3\sqrt{\frac{.071(.929)}{120}}$$

$$= .141$$

$$\text{Lower control limit} = \bar{p} - 3\sqrt{\frac{\bar{p}(1-\bar{p})}{n}} = .071 - 3\sqrt{\frac{.071(.929)}{120}} = .001$$

$$\text{Upper A-B boundary} = \bar{p} + 2\sqrt{\frac{\bar{p}(1-\bar{p})}{n}} = .071 + 2\sqrt{\frac{.071(.929)}{120}} = .118$$

$$\text{Lower A-B boundary} = \bar{p} - 2\sqrt{\frac{\bar{p}(1-\bar{p})}{n}} = .071 - 2\sqrt{\frac{.071(.929)}{120}} = .024$$

$$\text{Upper B-C boundary} = \bar{p} + \sqrt{\frac{\bar{p}(1-\bar{p})}{n}} = .071 + \sqrt{\frac{.071(.929)}{120}} = .094$$

$$\text{Lower B-C boundary} = \bar{p} - \sqrt{\frac{\bar{p}(1-\bar{p})}{n}} = .071 - \sqrt{\frac{.071(.929)}{120}} = .048$$

The p-chart is:

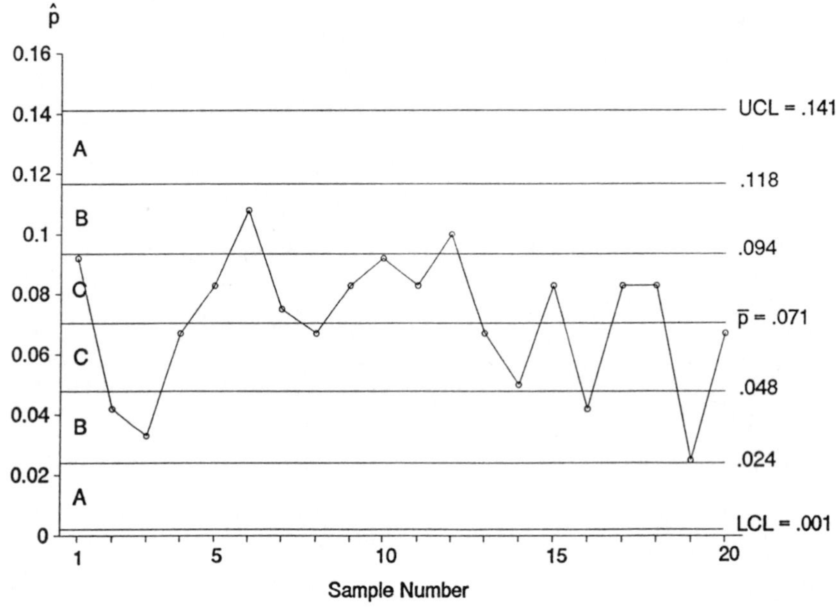


c. To determine if the process is in or out of control, we check the 6 rules:

Rule 1: One point beyond Zone A: No points are beyond Zone A.

Rule 2: Nine points in a row in Zone C or beyond: No sequence of 9 points are in Zone C (on one side of the centerline) or beyond.

Rule 3: Six points in a row steadily increasing or decreasing: No sequence of 6 points steadily increase or decrease.

Rule 4: Fourteen points in a row alternating up and down: This pattern does not exist.

Rule 5: Two out of three points in Zone A or beyond: No group of three consecutive points have two or more in Zone A or beyond.

Rule 6: Four out of five points in a row in Zone B or beyond: No sequence of 5 points has 4 or more in Zone B or beyond.

The process appears to be in control.

d. Since the process is in control, it is appropriate to use the control limits to monitor future process output.

e. No. The number of defectives recorded was per day, not per hour. Therefore, the p-chart is not capable of signaling hour-to-hour changes in p.

14.31 a. The sample size is determined as follows:

$$n > \frac{9(1 - p_0)}{p_0} = \frac{9(1 - .03)}{.03} = 291$$

The minimum sample size needed is 291. The sample size of 300 is large enough.

b. To compute the proportion of defectives in each sample, divide the number of defectives by the number in the sample, 300:

$$\hat{p} = \frac{\text{No. of defectives}}{\text{No. in sample}}$$

The sample proportions are listed in the table:

| Sample No. | $\hat{p}$ | Sample No. | $\hat{p}$ |
|---|---|---|---|
| 1 | .027 | 11 | .040 |
| 2 | .020 | 12 | .037 |
| 3 | .037 | 13 | .047 |
| 4 | .050 | 14 | .027 |
| 5 | .040 | 15 | .023 |
| 6 | .037 | 16 | .010 |
| 7 | .030 | 17 | .030 |
| 8 | .020 | 18 | .037 |
| 9 | .017 | 19 | .033 |
| 10 | .013 | 20 | .020 |

To get the total number of defectives, sum the number of defectives for all 20 samples. The sum is 178. To get the total number of units sampled, multiply the sample size by the number of samples:

$$300(20) = 6000$$

$$\bar{p} = \frac{\text{Total defective in all samples}}{\text{Total units sampled}} = \frac{178}{6000} = .0297$$

Centerline = $\bar{p}$ = .0297

$$\text{Upper control limit} = \bar{p} + 3\sqrt{\frac{\bar{p}(1 - \bar{p})}{n}} = .0297 + 3\sqrt{\frac{.0297(.9703)}{300}}$$
$$= .0591$$

$$\text{Lower control limit} = \bar{p} - 3\sqrt{\frac{\bar{p}(1 - \bar{p})}{n}} = .0297 - 3\sqrt{\frac{.0297(.9703)}{300}}$$
$$= .0003$$

b. $$\text{Upper A-B boundary} = \bar{p} + 2\sqrt{\frac{\bar{p}(1 - \bar{p})}{n}} = .0297 + 2\sqrt{\frac{.0297(.9703)}{300}}$$
$$= .0493$$

$$\text{Lower A-B boundary} = \bar{p} - 2\sqrt{\frac{\bar{p}(1 - \bar{p})}{n}} = .0297 - 2\sqrt{\frac{.0297(.9703)}{300}}$$
$$= .0101$$

$$\text{Upper B-C boundary} = \bar{p} + \sqrt{\frac{\bar{p}(1 - \bar{p})}{n}} = .0297 + \sqrt{\frac{.0297(.9703)}{300}}$$
$$= .0395$$

$$\text{Lower B-C boundary} = \bar{p} - \sqrt{\frac{\bar{p}(1 - \bar{p})}{n}} = .0297 - \sqrt{\frac{.0297(.9703)}{300}}$$
$$= .0199$$

The p-chart is:

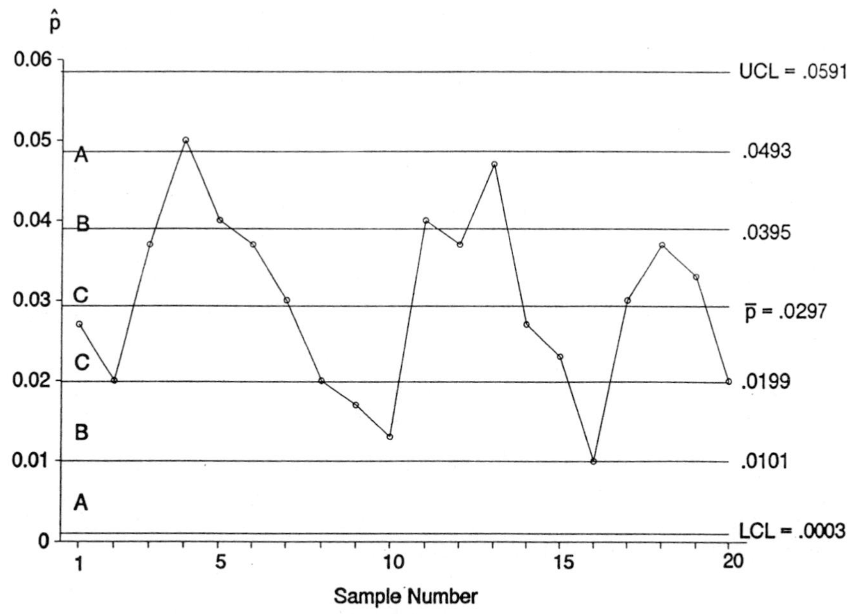


c. To determine if the process is in or out of control, we check the 6 rules:

Rule 1: One point beyond Zone A: No points are beyond Zone A.

Rule 2: Nine points in a row in Zone C or beyond: No sequence of 9 points are in Zone C (on one side of the centerline) or beyond.

Rule 3: Six points in a row steadily increasing or decreasing: Points 4 thru 10 are steadily decreasing. This indicates the process is out of control.

Rule 4: Fourteen points in a row alternating up and down: This pattern does not exist.

Rule 5: Two out of three points in Zone A or beyond: No group of three consecutive points have two or more in Zone A or beyond.

Rule 6: Four out of five points in a row in Zone B or beyond: No sequence of 5 points has 4 or more in Zone B or beyond.

Rule 3 indicates that the process is out of control. A special cause of variation appears to be present.

If we want to find the number of standard deviations from the mean the control limits should be set so the probability of the chart falsely indicating the presence of a special cause of variation is .10, we must find the z score such that:

$P(z > z_0) + P(z < -z_0) = .1000$ or $P(z > z_0) = .0500$.

Using Table IV, Appendix B, $z_0 = 1.645$. Thus the control limits should be set 1.645 standard deviations from the mean.

14.45 a. The centerline $= \bar{x} = \frac{\sum x}{n} = \frac{150.58}{20} = 7.529$

The time series plot is:

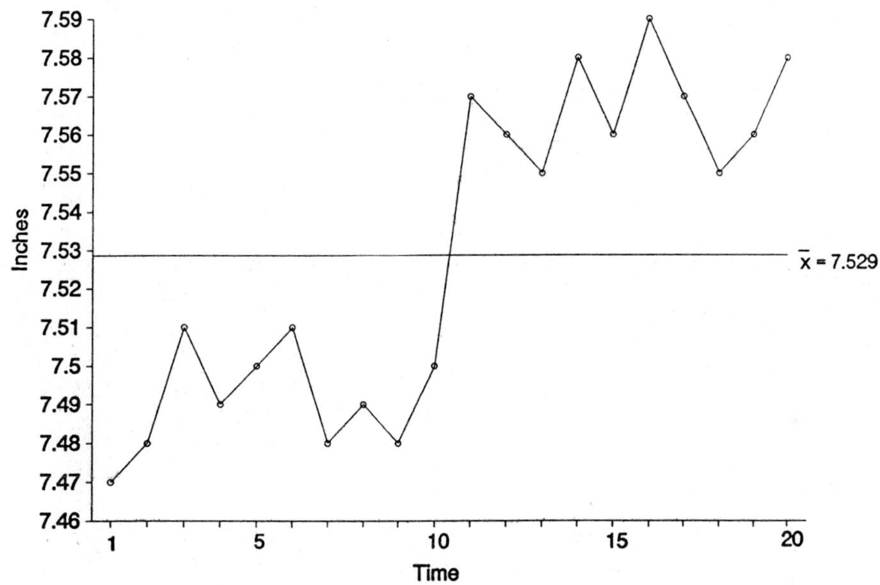


b. The variation pattern that best describes the pattern in this time series is the level shift. Points 1 through 10 all have fairly low values, while points 11 through 20 all have fairly high values.

14.47 a. In order for the $\bar{x}$-chart to be meaningful, we must assume the variation in the process is constant (i.e., stable).

For each sample, we compute $\bar{x} = \frac{\sum \bar{x}}{n}$ and R = range = largest measurement - smallest measurement. The results are listed in the table:

| Sample No. | $\bar{x}$ | R | Sample No. | $\bar{x}$ | R |
|---|---|---|---|---|---|
| 1 | 32.325 | 11.6 | 13 | 31.050 | 13.3 |
| 2 | 30.825 | 12.4 | 14 | 34.400 | 9.6 |
| 3 | 30.450 | 7.8 | 15 | 31.350 | 7.3 |
| 4 | 34.525 | 10.2 | 16 | 28.150 | 8.6 |
| 5 | 31.725 | 9.1 | 17 | 30.950 | 7.6 |
| 6 | 33.850 | 10.4 | 18 | 32.225 | 5.6 |
| 7 | 32.100 | 10.1 | 19 | 29.050 | 10.0 |
| 8 | 28.250 | 6.8 | 20 | 31.400 | 8.7 |
| 9 | 32.375 | 8.7 | 21 | 30.350 | 8.9 |
| 10 | 30.125 | 6.3 | 22 | 34.175 | 10.5 |
| 11 | 32.200 | 7.1 | 23 | 33.275 | 13.0 |
| 12 | 29.150 | 9.3 | 24 | 30.950 | 8.9 |

$$\bar{\bar{x}} = \frac{\bar{x}_1 + \bar{x}_2 + \ldots + \bar{x}_{24}}{n} = \frac{755.225}{24} = 31.4677$$

$$\bar{R} = \frac{R_1 + R_2 + \ldots + R_{24}}{n} = \frac{221.8}{24} = 9.242$$

Centerline = $\bar{\bar{x}}$ = 31.468

From Table XVII, Appendix B, with $n = 4$, $A_2 = .729$.

Upper control limit = $\bar{\bar{x}} + A_2\bar{R} = 31.468 + .729(9.242) = 38.205$

Lower control limit = $\bar{\bar{x}} - A_2\bar{R} = 31.468 - .729(9.242) = 24.731$

Upper A-B Boundary = $\bar{\bar{x}} + \frac{2}{3}(A_2\bar{R}) = 31.468 + \frac{2}{3}(.729)(9.242) = 35.960$

Lower A-B Boundary = $\bar{\bar{x}} - \frac{2}{3}(A_2\bar{R}) = 31.468 - \frac{2}{3}(.729)(9.242) = 26.976$

Upper B-C Boundary = $\bar{\bar{x}} + \frac{1}{3}(A_2\bar{R}) = 31.468 + \frac{1}{3}(.729)(9.242) = 33.714$

Lower B-C Boundary = $\bar{\bar{x}} - \frac{1}{3}(A_2\bar{R}) = 31.468 - \frac{1}{3}(.729)(9.242) = 29.222$

The $\bar{x}$-chart is:

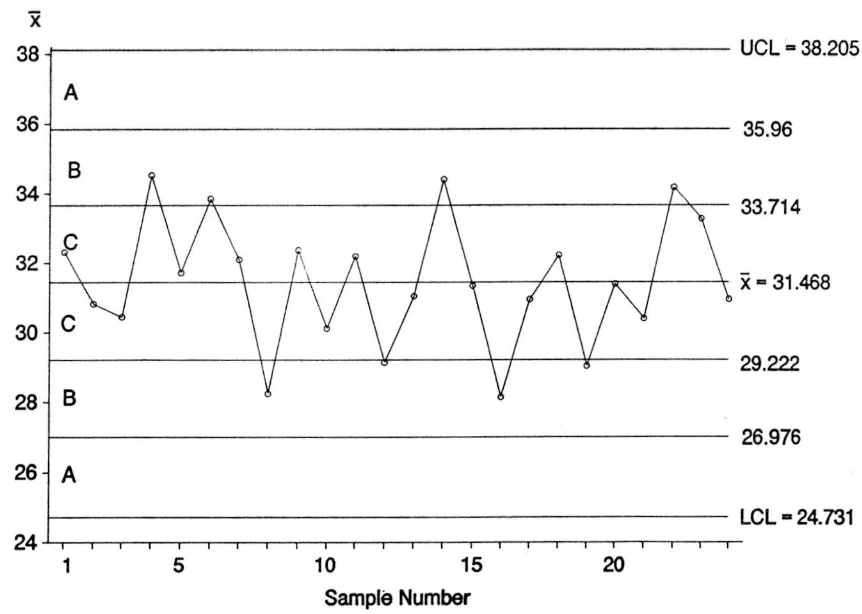


b. To determine if the process is in or out of control, we check the 6 rules:

Rule 1: One point beyond Zone A: No points are beyond Zone A.

Rule 2: Nine points in a row in Zone C or beyond: No sequence of 9 points are in Zone C (on one side of the centerline) or beyond.

Rule 3: Six points in a row steadily increasing or decreasing: No sequence of 6 points steadily increase or decrease.

Rule 4: Fourteen points in a row alternating up and down: This pattern does not exist.

Rule 5: Two out of three points in Zone A or beyond: There are no groups of three consecutive points that have two or more in Zone A or beyond.

Rule 6: Four out of five points in a row in Zone B or beyond: No sequence of 5 points has 4 or more in Zone B or beyond.

The process appears to be in control. There are no indications that special causes of variation are affecting the process.

c. Since the process appears to be in control, these limits should be used to monitor future process output.

14.49 a. The sample size is determined by the following:

$$n > \frac{9(1 - p_0)}{p_0} = \frac{9(1 - .06)}{.06} = 141$$

The minimum sample size is 141. Since the sample size of 150 was used, it is large enough.

b. To compute the proportion of defectives in each sample, divide the number of defectives by the number in the sample, 150:

$$\hat{p} = \frac{\text{No. of defectives}}{\text{No. in sample}}$$

The sample proportions are listed in the table:

| Sample No. | $\hat{p}$ | Sample No. | $\hat{p}$ |
|---|---|---|---|
| 1 | .060 | 11 | .047 |
| 2 | .073 | 12 | .040 |
| 3 | .080 | 13 | .080 |
| 4 | .053 | 14 | .067 |
| 5 | .067 | 15 | .073 |
| 6 | .040 | 16 | .047 |
| 7 | .087 | 17 | .040 |
| 8 | .060 | 18 | .080 |
| 9 | .073 | 19 | .093 |
| 10 | .033 | 20 | .067 |

To get the total number of defectives, sum the number of defectives for all 20 samples. The sum is 189. To get the total number of units sampled, multiply the sample size by the number of samples:

$$150(20) = 3000.$$

$$\bar{p} = \frac{\text{Total defective in all samples}}{\text{Total units sampled}} = \frac{189}{3000} = .063$$

Centerline $= \bar{p} = .063$

$$\text{Upper control limit} = \bar{p} + 3\sqrt{\frac{\bar{p}(1 - \bar{p})}{n}} = .063 + 3\sqrt{\frac{.063(.937)}{150}}$$
$$= .123$$

$$\text{Lower control limit} = \bar{p} - 3\sqrt{\frac{\bar{p}(1 - \bar{p})}{n}} = .063 - 3\sqrt{\frac{.063(.937)}{150}}$$
$$= .003$$

$$\text{Upper A-B boundary} = \bar{p} + 2\sqrt{\frac{\bar{p}(1 - \bar{p})}{n}} = .063 + 2\sqrt{\frac{.063(.937)}{150}} = .103$$

$$\text{Lower A-B boundary} = \bar{p} - 2\sqrt{\frac{\bar{p}(1 - \bar{p})}{n}} = .063 - 2\sqrt{\frac{.063(.937)}{150}} = .023$$

$$\text{Upper B-C boundary} = \bar{p} + \sqrt{\frac{\bar{p}(1 - \bar{p})}{n}} = .063 + \sqrt{\frac{.063(.937)}{150}} = .083$$

$$\text{Lower B-C boundary} = \bar{p} - \sqrt{\frac{\bar{p}(1 - \bar{p})}{n}} = .063 - \sqrt{\frac{.063(.937)}{150}} = .043$$

The p-chart is:

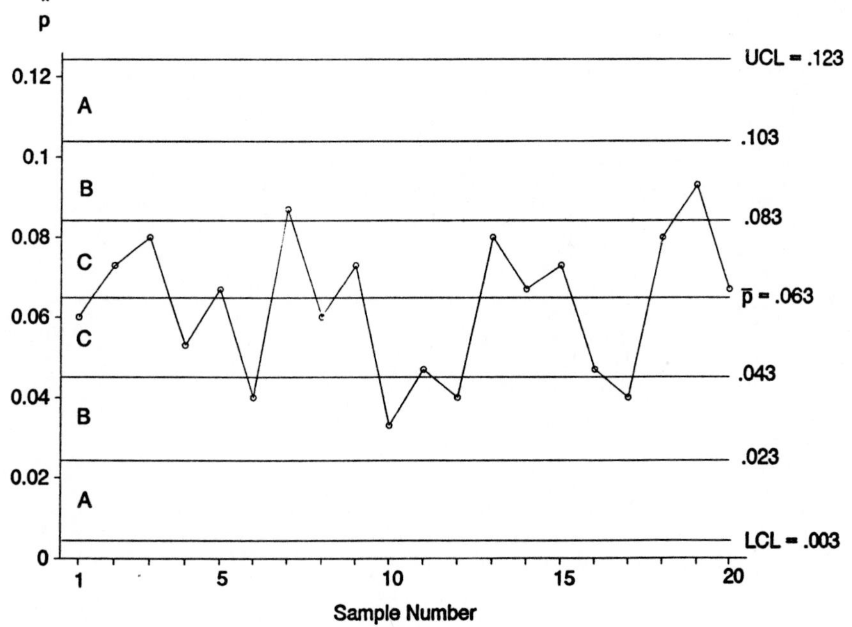


c. To determine if the process is in or out of control, we check the 6 rules:

Rule 1: One point beyond Zone A: No points are beyond Zone A.

Rule 2: Nine points in a row in Zone C or beyond: No sequence of 9 points are in Zone C (on one side of the centerline) or beyond.

Rule 3: Six points in a row steadily increasing or decreasing: No sequence of 6 points steadily increase or decrease.

Rule 4: Fourteen points in a row alternating up and down: Points 2 thru 16 alternate up and down. This indicates the process is out of control.

Rule 5: Two out of three points in Zone A or beyond: No group of three consecutive points have two or more in Zone A or beyond.

Rule 6: Four out of five points in a row in Zone B or beyond: No sequence of 5 points has 4 or more in Zone B or beyond.

Rule 4 indicates that the process is out of control. Special causes of variation appear to be present.

e. Since the process is out of control, the control limits should not be used to monitor future process output. It would not be appropriate to evaluate whether the process is in control using control limits determined during a period when the process was out of control.

Rule 5: Two out of three points in Zone A or beyond: Points 11 and 12 are in Zone A or beyond. This indicates the process is out of control.

Rule 6: Four out of five points in a row in Zone B or beyond: No sequence of 5 points has 4 or more in Zone B or beyond.

Rule 5 indicates that the process is out of control. The process is unstable.

d. Since the process variation is out of control, the R-chart should not be used to monitor future process output.

e. The $\bar{x}$-chart should not be constructed. The control limits of the $\bar{x}$-chart depend on the variation of the process. (In particular, they are constructed using $\bar{R}$.) If the variation of the process is out of control, the control limits of the $\bar{x}$-chart are meaningless.

14.23. a. From Exercise 14.13, we get the following data:

| Sample No. | R | Sample No. | R |
|---|---|---|---|
| 1 | .20 | 14 | .06 |
| 2 | .19 | 15 | .15 |
| 3 | .17 | 16 | .09 |
| 4 | .22 | 17 | .20 |
| 5 | .29 | 18 | .20 |
| 6 | .24 | 19 | .13 |
| 7 | .13 | 20 | .25 |
| 8 | .21 | 21 | .09 |
| 9 | .27 | 22 | .19 |
| 10 | .24 | 23 | .09 |
| 11 | .22 | 24 | .17 |
| 12 | .16 | 25 | .20 |
| 13 | .31 | | |

$$\bar{R} = \frac{R_1 + R_2 + \ldots + R_{25}}{n} = \frac{4.67}{25} = .1868$$

Centerline $= \bar{R} = .1868$

From Table XVII, Appendix B, with $n = 4$, $D_4 = 2.282$ and $D_3 = 0$.

Upper control limit $= \bar{R}D_4 = .1868(2.282) = .426$

Since $D_3 = 0$, the lower control limit is negative and is not included on the chart.

From Table XVII, Appendix B, with $n = 4$, $d_2 = 2.059$ and $d_3 = .880$.

# CHAPTER 15

## TIME SERIES: INDEX NUMBERS AND DESCRIPTIVE ANALYSES

15.1 To calculate a simple index number, first obtain the prices or quantities over a time period and select a base year. For each time period, the index number is the number at that time period divided by the values at the base period multiplied by 100.

15.3 To compute the simple index, divide each U.S. Beer Production value by the 1977 value, 170.5, and then multiply by 100.

| YEAR | SIMPLE INDEX | YEAR | SIMPLE INDEX |
|---|---|---|---|
| 1970 | (133.1/170.5) x 100 = 78.06 | 1978 | (179.1/170.5) x 100 = 105.04 |
| 1971 | (137.4/170.5) x 100 = 80.59 | 1979 | (184.2/170.5) x 100 = 108.04 |
| 1972 | (141.3/170.5) x 100 = 82.87 | 1980 | (194.1/170.5) x 100 = 113.84 |
| 1973 | (148.6/170.5) x 100 = 87.16 | 1981 | (193.7/170.5) x 100 = 113.61 |
| 1974 | (156.2/170.5) x 100 = 91.61 | 1982 | (196.2/170.5) x 100 = 115.07 |
| 1975 | (160.6/170.5) x 100 = 94.19 | 1983 | (195.38/170.5) x 100 = 114.59 |
| 1976 | (163.7/170.5) x 100 = 96.01 | 1984 | (192.23/170.5) x 100 = 112.74 |
| 1977 | (170.5/170.5) x 100 = 100 | | |

15.5 Using 1980 as the base period, the simple index is found by dividing each entry by 194.1 and then multiplying by 100.

| YEAR | SIMPLE INDEX | YEAR | SIMPLE INDEX |
|---|---|---|---|
| 1970 | (133.1/194.1) x 100 = 68.57 | 1978 | (179.1/194.1) x 100 = 92.97 |
| 1971 | (137.4/194.1) x 100 = 70.79 | 1979 | (184.2/194.1) x 100 = 94.90 |
| 1972 | (141.3/194.1) x 100 = 72.80 | 1980 | (194.1/194.1) x 100 = 100 |
| 1973 | (148.6/194.1) x 100 = 76.56 | 1981 | (193.7/194.1) x 100 = 99.79 |
| 1974 | (156.2/194.1) x 100 = 80.47 | 1982 | (196.2/194.1) x 100 = 101.08 |
| 1975 | (160.6/194.1) x 100 = 82.74 | 1983 | (195.38/194.1) x 100 = 100.66 |
| 1976 | (163.7/194.1) x 100 = 84.34 | 1984 | (192.23/194.1) x 100 = 99.04 |
| 1977 | (170.5/194.1) x 100 = 87.84 | | |

15.7 a. The simple index is computed by dividing the gasoline prices for each month by the price in January 1980, $111.0, and then multiplying by 100. The simple indexes are:

| YEAR | JAN | FEB | MAR | APR | MAY | JUN | JUL | AUG | SEP | OCT | NOV | DEC |
|---|---|---|---|---|---|---|---|---|---|---|---|---|
| 1980 | 100.0 | 106.8 | 110.8 | 111.9 | 112.1 | 112.3 | 112.3 | 112.0 | 110.9 | 110.2 | 110.1 | 110.9 |
| 1981 | 114.3 | 121.9 | 125.0 | 124.4 | 123.4 | 122.7 | 121.9 | 121.4 | 122.3 | 121.9 | 121.7 | 121.4 |
| 1982 | 120.8 | 118.7 | 114.2 | 109.0 | 110.3 | 116.8 | 118.7 | 118.0 | 116.7 | 115.3 | 114.2 | 112.1 |
| 1983 | 109.3 | 105.4 | 102.3 | 107.9 | 112.0 | 113.6 | 114.6 | 114.3 | 113.2 | 111.6 | 110.3 | 109.5 |
| 1984 | 108.1 | 107.5 | 107.6 | 109.1 | 110.0 | 109.4 | 107.8 | 106.7 | 107.1 | 107.7 | 107.5 | 106.2 |
| 1985 | 103.2 | 101.6 | 104.1 | 108.0 | 110.2 | 111.1 | 111.1 | 110.1 | 108.9 | 107.9 | 108.2 | 108.4 |
| 1986 | 107.2 | 100.8 | 88.6 | 80.6 | 83.5 | 86.3 | 80.6 | 76.4 | 78.1 | | | |

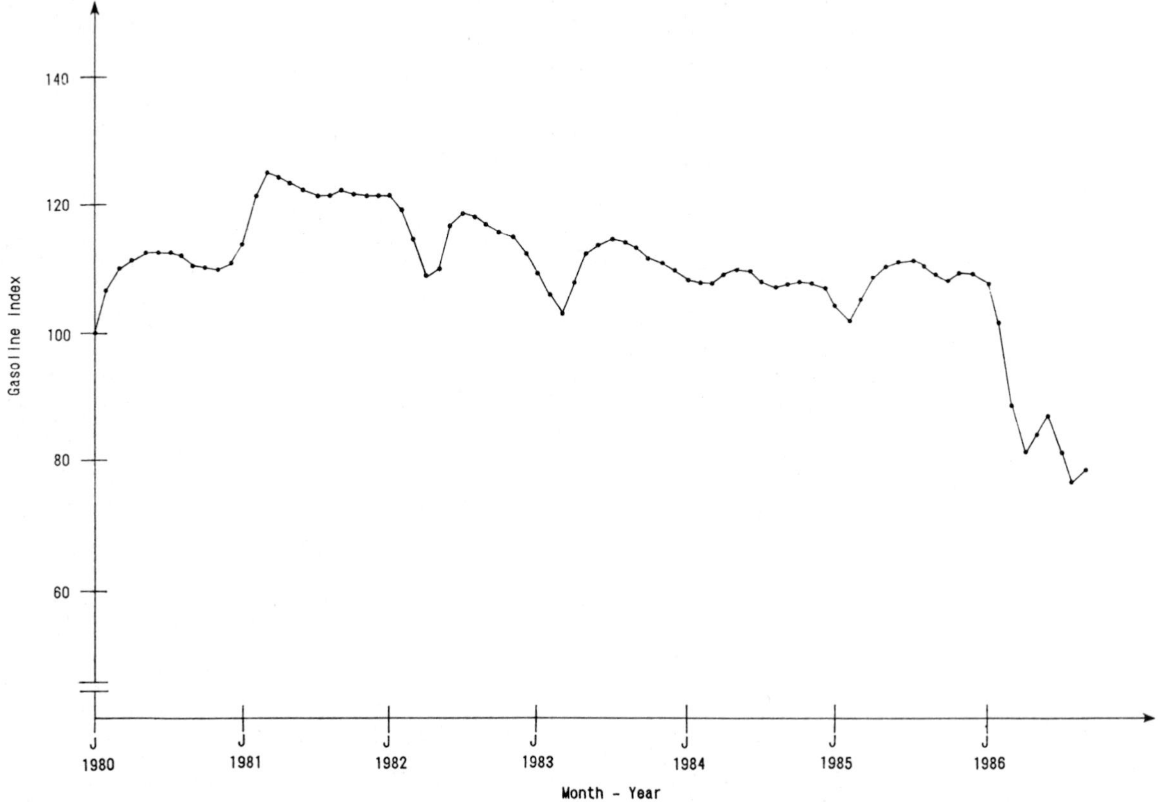


b. The index for March 1983 is 102.3. The gas price increased 102.3 - 100 = 2.3% from January 1980 until March 1983. The index for August 1986 is 76.4. The gas price decreased 100 - 76.4 = 23.6% from January 1980 until August 1986.

c. The simple index for March 1981 is 125.0 and for August 1986 is 76.4. Using the simple index in March 1981 as the base, the new simple index for August 1986 is (76.4/125.0) x 100 = 61.1. Thus, gasoline prices have decreased 100 - 61.1 = 38.9% from March 1981 until August 1986.

d. The index is a price index because it is based on gasoline prices, not quantities.

15.9 a. The simple composite index is calculated as follows:

First, sum the observations for all the series of interest at each time period. Select the base time period. Divide each sum by the sum in the base time period and multiply by 100.

b. To calculate a weighted composite index, we follow the following steps:

First, multiply the observations in each time series by its appropriate weight. Then sum the weighted observations across all times series for each time period. Select the base time period. Divide each weighted sum by the weighted sum in the base time period and multiply by 100.

c. The steps necessary to compute a Laspeyres Index are:

1. Collect data for each of k price series.
2. Select a base time period and collect purchase quantity information for each of the k series at the base time period.
3. Using the purchase quantity values at the base period as weights, multiply each value in the kth series by its corresponding weight.
4. Sum the products for each time period.
5. Divide each sum by the sum corresponding to the base period and multiply by 100.

d. The steps necessary to compute a Paasche index are:

1. Collect data for each of k price series.
2. Select a base period.
3. Collect purchase quantity information for each series at each time period.
4. For each time period, multiply the value in each price series by its corresponding purchase quantity for that time period. Sum the products for each time period.
5. To find the value of the Paasche index at a particular time period, multiply the purchase quantity values (weights) for that time period by the corresponding price values of the base time period. Sum the results for the base period. The Paasche Index is then found by dividing the sum found in (4) by the sum found in (5).

15.11 A Laspeyres index uses the purchase quantity at the base period as the weights for all other time periods. A Paasche index uses the purchase quantity at each time period as the weight for that time period. The weights at the specified time period are also used with the base period to find the index.

15.13 First, we need to get the personal consumption totals for each year by summing the 3 series:

| YEAR | TOTAL | INDEX(67) | INDEX(74) | YEAR | TOTAL | INDEX(67) | INDEX(74) |
|---|---|---|---|---|---|---|---|
| 1961 | 335 | 68.3 | 37.8 | 1973 | 808.6 | 164.9 | 91.3 |
| 1962 | 355.3 | 72.5 | 40.1 | 1974 | 885.9 | 180.7 | 100 |
| 1963 | 374.6 | 76.4 | 42.3 | 1975 | 976.5 | 199.2 | 110.2 |
| 1964 | 400.3 | 81.6 | 45.2 | 1976 | 1079.7 | 220.2 | 121.9 |
| 1965 | 430.1 | 87.7 | 48.5 | 1977 | 1204.4 | 245.6 | 136.0 |
| 1966 | 464.8 | 94.8 | 52.5 | 1978 | 1346.4 | 274.6 | 152.0 |
| 1967 | 490.3 | 100 | 55.3 | 1979 | 1507.1 | 307.4 | 170.1 |
| 1968 | 536 | 109.3 | 60.5 | 1980 | 1668 | 340.2 | 188.3 |
| 1969 | 579.7 | 118.2 | 65.4 | 1981 | 1849.1 | 377.1 | 208.7 |
| 1970 | 621.7 | 126.8 | 70.2 | 1982 | 1984.8 | 404.8 | 224.0 |
| 1971 | 668.2 | 136.3 | 75.4 | 1983 | 2155.9 | 439.7 | 243.4 |
| 1972 | 732.9 | 149.5 | 82.7 | 1984 | 2341.9 | 477.6 | 264.4 |

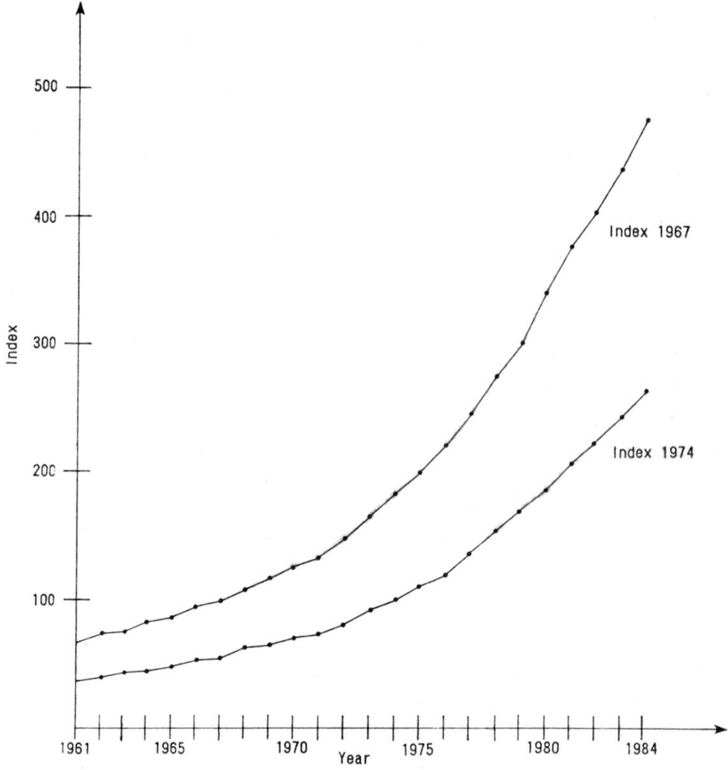


The graph for base year 1987 is above the graph for base year 1974. The index using 1967 as the base year has a denominator of 490.3 while the index using 1974 as the base year has a denominator of 885.9.

15.15 To find Laspeyres index, we multiply the durable goods by 8.5, the nondurable goods by 120.1, and the services by 30.7. The index is found by dividing the weighted sum at each time period by the weighted sum of 1967 and then multiplying by 100. Laspeyres index.

| YEAR | DURABLE GOODS x 8.5 | NONDURABLE GOODS x 120.1 | SERVICES x 30.7 | SUM | LASPEYRES INDEX |
|---|---|---|---|---|---|
| 1961 | 353.60 | 18651.53 | 4239.67 | 23244.80 | 71.49 |
| 1962 | 396.95 | 19408.16 | 4512.90 | 24318.01 | 74.79 |
| 1963 | 436.90 | 20068.71 | 4792.27 | 25297.88 | 77.81 |
| 1964 | 478.55 | 21245.69 | 5129.97 | 26854.21 | 82.59 |
| 1965 | 533.80 | 22650.86 | 5486.09 | 28670.75 | 88.18 |
| 1966 | 575.45 | 24584.47 | 5906.68 | 31066.60 | 95.55 |
| 1967 | 591.60 | 25533.26 | 6388.67 | 32513.53 | 100.00 |
| 1968 | 680.00 | 27671.04 | 6925.92 | 35276.96 | 108.50 |
| 1969 | 726.75 | 29664.70 | 7589.04 | 37980.49 | 116.81 |
| 1970 | 724.20 | 31910.57 | 8313.56 | 40948.33 | 125.94 |
| 1971 | 825.35 | 33351.77 | 9007.38 | 43184.50 | 132.82 |
| 1972 | 945.20 | 35945.93 | 9897.68 | 46788.81 | 143.91 |
| 1973 | 1044.65 | 40161.44 | 10784.91 | 51991.00 | 159.91 |
| 1974 | 1036.15 | 45121.57 | 11920.81 | 58078.53 | 178.63 |
| 1975 | 1123.70 | 48916.73 | 13415.90 | 63456.33 | 195.17 |
| 1976 | 1330.25 | 52892.04 | 14821.96 | 69044.25 | 212.36 |
| 1977 | 1514.70 | 57503.88 | 16805.18 | 75823.76 | 233.21 |
| 1978 | 1701.70 | 63436.82 | 18972.60 | 84111.12 | 258.70 |
| 1979 | 1813.90 | 72060.00 | 21296.59 | 95170.49 | 292.71 |
| 1980 | 1824.95 | 80322.88 | 24084.15 | 106231.98 | 326.73 |
| 1981 | 2000.90 | 87757.07 | 27108.10 | 116866.07 | 359.44 |
| 1982 | 2083.35 | 90975.75 | 30153.54 | 123212.64 | 378.96 |
| 1983 | 2378.30 | 96284.17 | 32984.08 | 131646.55 | 404.90 |
| 1984 | 2709.80 | 102913.69 | 35802.34 | 141425.83 | 434.98 |

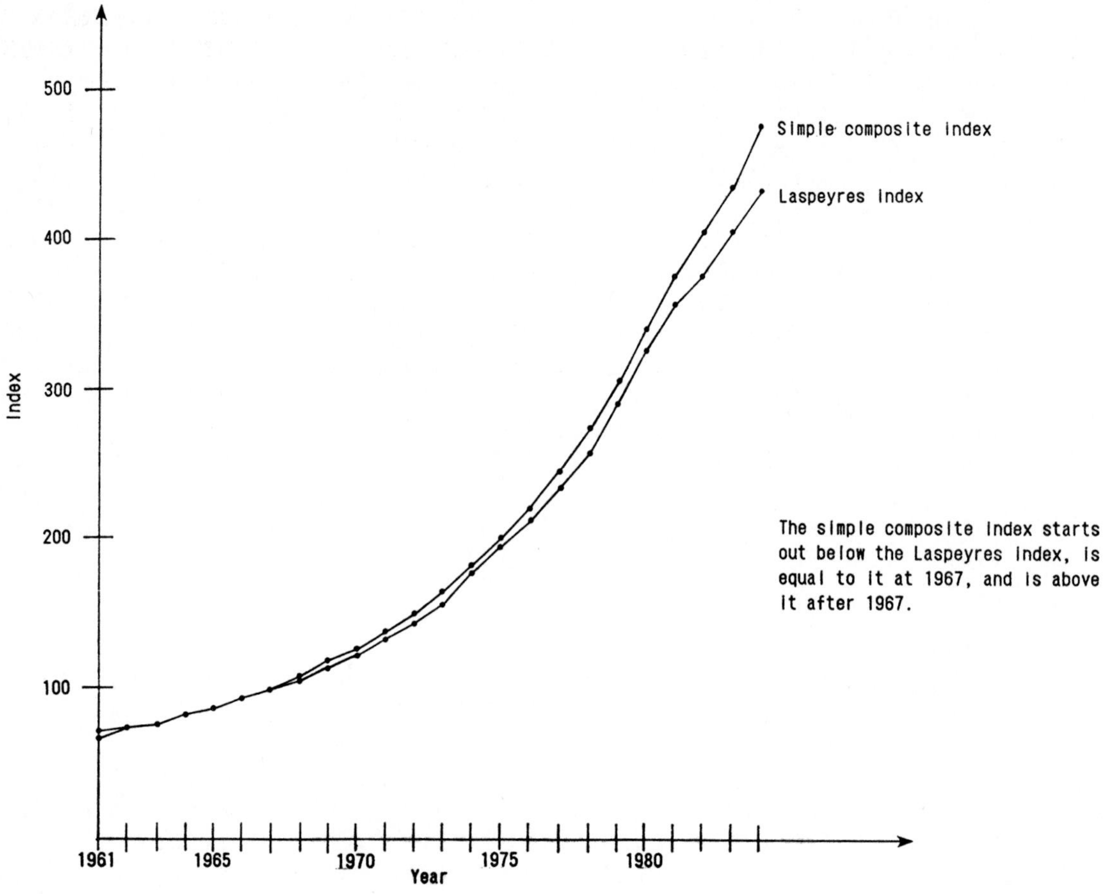


15.17 a. The following steps are used to compute the Paasche index.

1. First, multiply the price x production for copper, pig iron, and lead for each month. The numerator of the index is the sum of these 3 quantities at each month.
2. Next, multiply the production values of copper by 1361.6, the production of pig iron by 213, and the production of lead by 530. The denominator of the index is the sum of these 3 quantities at each month.
3. The values of the Paasche index is the ratio of these two values times 100.

The Laspeyres index is computed by dividing the numerator of the Paasche index by 1079789.12 times 100.

| MONTH | NUMERATOR | DENOMINATOR | PAASCHE INDEX | LASPEYRES INDEX |
|---|---|---|---|---|
| Jan | 1079789.12 | 1079789.12 | 100.0 | 100.0 |
| Feb | 1115345.90 | 1112259.16 | 100.3 | 100.3 |
| Mar | 1263952.40 | 1251315.40 | 101.0 | 101.1 |
| Apr | 1240241.96 | 1223759.96 | 101.3 | 101.6 |
| May | 1262272.46 | 1255056.28 | 100.6 | 100.7 |
| June | 1128103.22 | 1125055.04 | 100.3 | 100.4 |
| July | 1066929.84 | 1067176.44 | 100.0 | 100.2 |
| Aug | 1008183.04 | 1009481.72 | 99.9 | 100.0 |
| Sept | 875434.26 | 880919.12 | 99.4 | 99.4 |
| Oct | 922140.12 | 930763.56 | 99.1 | 99.0 |
| Nov | 960478.70 | 961256.80 | 99.9 | 99.9 |
| Dec | 926191.26 | 933548.04 | 99.2 | 99.2 |

b.

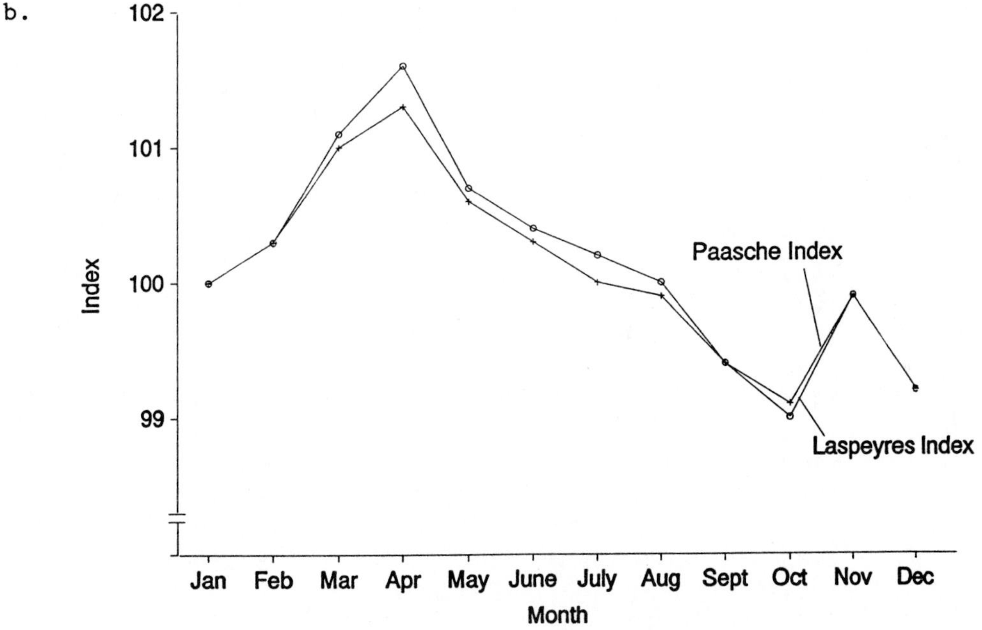


c. The Laspeyres index values for September and December are 99.4 and 99.2 The Paasche index values for the same months are 99.4 and 99.2.

The problem states that the price and production of metals is a measure of the strength of the industrial economy. Since the Paasche index takes into account the production values at each time period, it seems like it may be a more appropriate measure for describing the change in this 4-month period. The change is from 99.4 to 99.2--a very minor change.

15.19 To compute the 3-point moving averages, we find the average of 3 values: the previous time period, the time period of interest, and the following time period. The 3-point moving average for the 3rd time period is the average of 41, 59, and 98 or

$$\frac{41 + 59 + 98}{3} = 66$$

The 5-point moving average is found in a similar fashion: the average of the previous 2 time periods, the time period of interest, and the following 2 time periods. The 5-point moving average for the 3rd time period is the average of 36, 41, 59, 98, and 160, or

$$\frac{36 + 41 + 59 + 98 + 160}{5} = 78.8$$

The rest of the moving averages are found in the same way and are shown below:

| YEAR | PRICE OF GOLD | 3-POINT MOVING AVERAGE | 5-POINT MOVING AVERAGE |
|---|---|---|---|
| 1970 | 36 | | |
| 1971 | 41 | 45.33 | |
| 1972 | 59 | 66.00 | 78.80 |
| 1973 | 98 | 105.67 | 103.80 |
| 1974 | 160 | 139.67 | 120.60 |
| 1975 | 161 | 148.67 | 138.40 |
| 1976 | 125 | 144.67 | 157.60 |
| 1977 | 148 | 155.67 | 187.20 |
| 1978 | 194 | 216.67 | 277.60 |
| 1979 | 308 | 371.67 | 344.60 |
| 1980 | 613 | 460.33 | 390.20 |
| 1981 | 460 | 483.00 | 436.20 |
| 1982 | 376 | 420.00 | 446.80 |
| 1983 | 424 | 387.00 | 387.80 |
| 1984 | 361 | 367.67 | |
| 1985 | 318 | | |

15.21 To compute a 3-point moving average, we find the average of 3 values: the previous time period, the time period of interest, and the following time period. The 3-point moving average for the 2nd time period is

$$\frac{133.1 + 137.4 + 141.3}{3} = 137.27$$

To compute a 5-point moving average, we find the average of 5 values: the previous two time periods, the time period of interest, and the following two time periods. The 5-point moving average for the 3rd time period is

$$\frac{133.1 + 137.4 + 141.3 + 148.6 + 156.2}{5} = 143.32$$

The rest of the moving averages are found in the same way and are shown below:

| YEAR | PRICE OF GOLD | 3-POINT MOVING AVERAGE | 5-POINT MOVING AVERAGE |
|---|---|---|---|
| 1970 | 133.1 | | |
| 1971 | 137.4 | 137.27 | |
| 1972 | 141.3 | 142.43 | 143.32 |
| 1973 | 148.6 | 148.70 | 148.82 |
| 1974 | 156.2 | 155.13 | 154.08 |
| 1975 | 160.6 | 160.17 | 159.92 |
| 1976 | 163.7 | 164.93 | 166.02 |
| 1977 | 170.5 | 171.10 | 171.62 |
| 1978 | 179.1 | 177.93 | 178.32 |
| 1979 | 184.2 | 185.80 | 184.32 |
| 1980 | 194.1 | 190.67 | 189.46 |
| 1981 | 193.7 | 194.67 | 192.72 |
| 1982 | 196.2 | 195.09 | 194.32 |
| 1983 | 195.38 | 194.60 | |
| 1984 | 192.23 | | |

15.23 To compute a 3-point moving average, we find the average of 3 values: the previous time period, the time period of interest, and the following time period. The 3-point moving average for the second time period is

$$\frac{5.308 + 7.779 + 7.791}{3} = 7.0$$

To compute a 7-point moving average, we find the average of 7 values: the previous 3 time periods, the time period of interest, and the following 3 time periods. The 7-point moving average for the fourth time period is

$$\frac{5.308 + 7.779 + 7.791 + 8.684 + 6.690 + 6.629 + 8.568}{7} = 7.3$$

The rest of the moving averages are found in the same way and are shown below.

| YEAR | SALES | 3-POINT MOVING AVERAGE | 7-POINT MOVING AVERAGE |
|---|---|---|---|
| 1970 | 5.308 | | |
| 1971 | 7.779 | 7.0 | |
| 1972 | 7.791 | 8.1 | |
| 1973 | 8.684 | 7.7 | 7.3 |
| 1974 | 6.690 | 7.3 | 7.9 |
| 1975 | 6.629 | 7.3 | 8.1 |
| 1976 | 8.568 | 8.1 | 8.3 |
| 1977 | 9.068 | 9.0 | 8.1 |
| 1978 | 9.482 | 9.2 | 8.1 |
| 1979 | 8.993 | 8.5 | 8.0 |
| 1980 | 7.101 | 7.6 | 7.9 |
| 1981 | 6.762 | 6.7 | 7.8 |
| 1982 | 6.244 | 6.9 | 7.8 |
| 1983 | 7.769 | 7.4 | |
| 1984 | 8.256 | 8.4 | |
| 1985 | 9.305 | | |

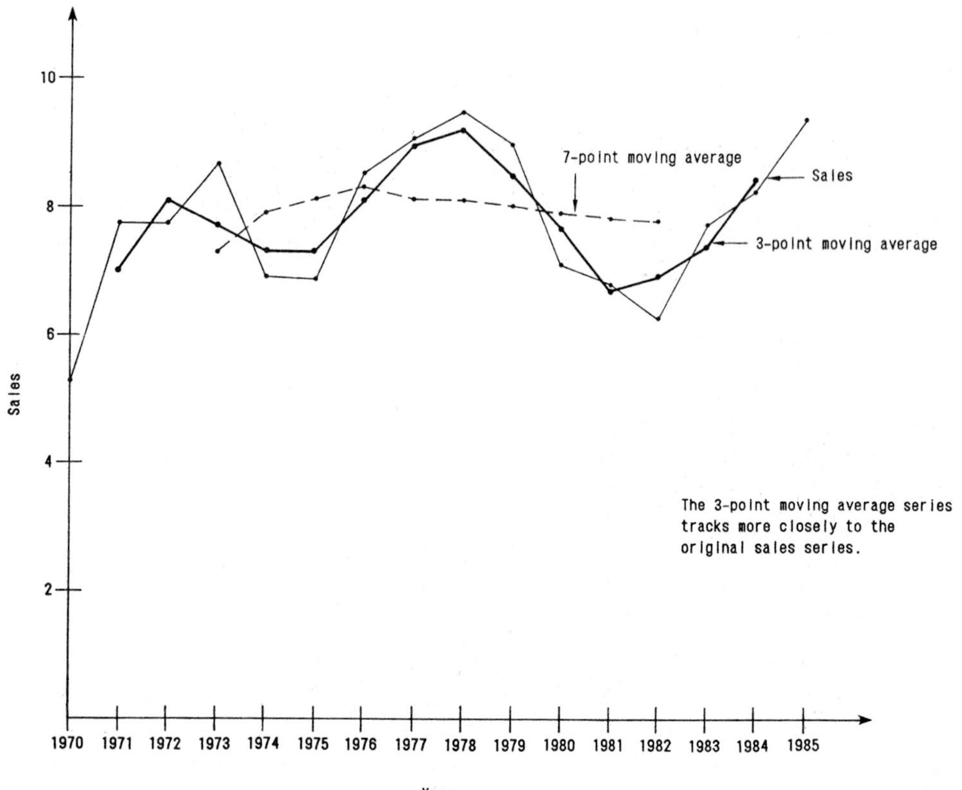

15.25 To compute the 5-point moving average, we find the average of five values: 2 periods previous, the time period of interest, and 2 periods following. The 5-point moving average for March 1988 is

$$\frac{111.0 + 118.6 + 123.0 + 124.2 + 124.4}{5} = 120.2$$

The rest of the moving averages are found in the same way and are shown below:

| YEAR | MONTH | PRICE | 5-POINT MOVING AVERAGE |
|---|---|---|---|
| 1980 | Jan | 111.0 | |
| 1980 | Feb | 118.6 | |
| 1980 | Mar | 123.0 | 120.2 |
| 1980 | Apr | 124.2 | 123.0 |
| 1980 | May | 124.4 | 124.2 |
| 1980 | June | 124.6 | 124.4 |
| 1980 | July | 124.7 | 124.2 |
| 1980 | Aug | 124.3 | 123.8 |
| 1980 | Sept | 123.1 | 123.3 |
| 1980 | Oct | 122.3 | 123.0 |
| 1980 | Nov | 122.2 | 123.5 |
| 1980 | Dec | 123.1 | 126.0 |
| 1981 | Jan | 126.9 | 129.3 |
| 1981 | Feb | 135.3 | 132.4 |
| 1981 | Mar | 138.8 | 135.2 |
| 1981 | Apr | 138.1 | 137.1 |
| 1981 | May | 137.0 | 137.1 |
| 1981 | June | 136.2 | 136.3 |
| 1981 | July | 135.3 | 135.8 |
| 1981 | Aug | 134.8 | 135.5 |
| 1981 | Sept | 135.8 | 135.3 |
| 1981 | Oct | 135.3 | 135.2 |
| 1981 | Nov | 135.1 | 135.0 |
| 1981 | Dec | 134.8 | 134.2 |
| 1982 | Jan | 134.1 | 132.5 |
| 1982 | Feb | 131.8 | 129.7 |
| 1982 | Mar | 126.8 | 127.2 |
| 1982 | Apr | 121.0 | 126.3 |
| 1982 | May | 122.4 | 126.3 |
| 1982 | June | 129.6 | 127.2 |
| 1982 | July | 131.8 | 128.9 |
| 1982 | Aug | 131.0 | 130.0 |
| 1982 | Sept | 129.5 | 129.4 |
| 1982 | Oct | 128.0 | 127.9 |
| 1982 | Nov | 126.8 | 126.0 |
| 1982 | Dec | 124.4 | 123.5 |
| 1983 | Jan | 121.3 | 120.6 |
| 1983 | Feb | 117.0 | 119.2 |
| 1983 | Mar | 113.5 | 119.2 |
| 1983 | Apr | 119.8 | 120.1 |
| 1983 | May | 124.3 | 122.2 |
| 1983 | June | 126.1 | 124.9 |
| 1983 | July | 127.2 | 126.0 |
| 1983 | Aug | 126.9 | 126.0 |
| 1983 | Sept | 125.7 | 125.2 |
| 1983 | Oct | 123.9 | 124.1 |
| 1983 | Nov | 122.4 | 122.7 |
| 1983 | Dec | 121.5 | 121.4 |
| 1984 | Jan | 120.0 | 120.5 |
| 1984 | Feb | 119.3 | 120.3 |
| 1984 | Mar | 119.4 | 120.4 |
| 1984 | Apr | 121.1 | 120.7 |
| 1984 | May | 122.1 | 120.7 |
| 1984 | June | 121.4 | 120.5 |
| 1984 | July | 119.7 | 120.1 |
| 1984 | Aug | 118.4 | 119.6 |
| 1984 | Sept | 118.9 | 119.2 |
| 1984 | Oct | 119.5 | 118.8 |
| 1984 | Nov | 119.3 | 118.0 |
| 1984 | Dec | 117.9 | 116.8 |
| 1985 | Jan | 114.5 | 116.0 |
| 1985 | Feb | 112.8 | 116.1 |
| 1985 | Mar | 115.5 | 117.0 |
| 1985 | Apr | 119.9 | 118.8 |
| 1985 | May | 122.3 | 120.9 |
| 1985 | June | 123.3 | 122.2 |
| 1985 | July | 123.3 | 122.4 |
| 1985 | Aug | 122.2 | 121.9 |
| 1985 | Sept | 120.9 | 121.3 |
| 1985 | Oct | 119.8 | 120.7 |
| 1985 | Nov | 120.1 | 120.0 |
| 1985 | Dec | 120.3 | 118.2 |
| 1986 | Jan | 119.0 | 113.9 |
| 1986 | Feb | 111.9 | 107.8 |
| 1986 | Mar | 98.3 | 102.3 |
| 1986 | Apr | 89.5 | 97.6 |
| 1986 | May | 92.7 | 93.2 |
| 1986 | June | 95.8 | 90.5 |
| 1986 | July | 89.5 | 89.9 |
| 1986 | Aug | 84.8 | |
| 1986 | Sept | 86.7 | |

| YEAR | BEER PRODUCTION | w = .2 EXPONENTIALLY SMOOTHED PRODUCTION | w = .8 EXPONENTIALLY SMOOTHED PRODUCTION |
|---|---|---|---|
| 1970 | 133.1 | 133.10 | 133.10 |
| 1971 | 137.4 | 133.96 | 136.54 |
| 1972 | 141.3 | 135.43 | 140.35 |
| 1973 | 148.6 | 138.06 | 146.95 |
| 1974 | 156.2 | 141.69 | 154.35 |
| 1975 | 160.6 | 145.47 | 159.35 |
| 1976 | 163.7 | 149.12 | 162.83 |
| 1977 | 170.5 | 153.39 | 168.97 |
| 1978 | 179.1 | 158.54 | 177.07 |
| 1979 | 184.2 | 163.67 | 182.77 |
| 1980 | 194.1 | 169.75 | 191.83 |
| 1981 | 193.7 | 174.54 | 193.33 |
| 1982 | 196.2 | 178.87 | 195.63 |
| 1983 | 195.38 | 182.18 | 195.43 |
| 1984 | 192.23 | 184.19 | 192.87 |

b. The above procedure is repeated with w = .8 instead of .2. The exponentially smoothed value for the second period is .8(137.4) + (1 - .8)(133.10) = 136.54. The rest of the values are shown in the table in part (a).

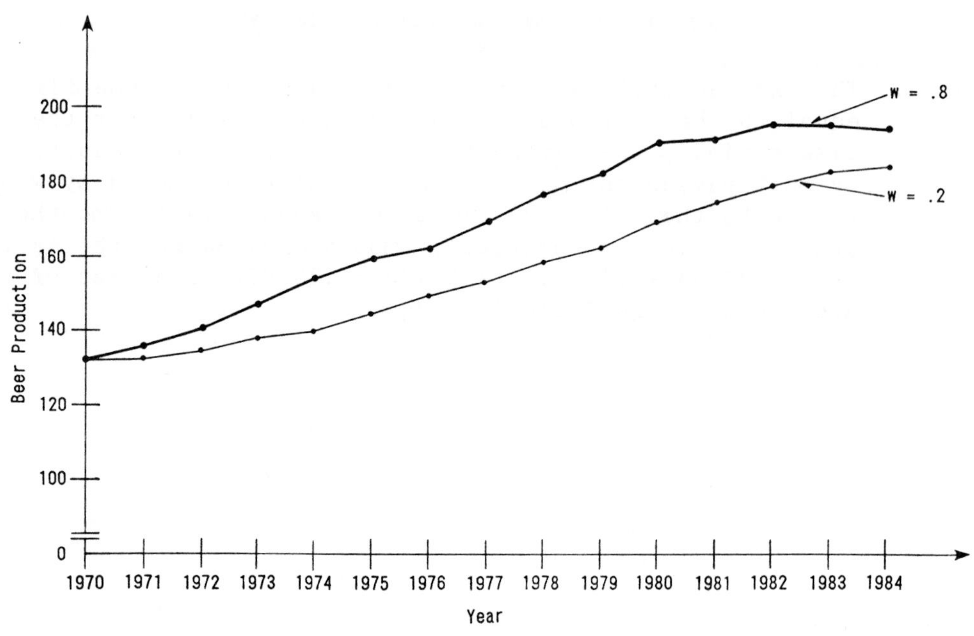

15.31 The exponentially smoothed gold price for the first time period is equal to the gold price for that period. For the rest of the time periods, the exponentially smoothed gold prices are found by multiplying the gold price for the time period by w = .5 and adding to that (1 - .5) times the exponentially smoothed value above it. The exponentially smoothed value for the year 1971 is .5(41) + (1 - .5)(36.0) = 38.5. The rest of the values appear in the table below:

| YEAR | PRICE OF GOLD | w = .5 EXPONENTIALLY SMOOTHED PRICE |
|---|---|---|
| 1970 | 36 | 36.0 |
| 1971 | 41 | 38.5 |
| 1972 | 59 | 48.8 |
| 1973 | 98 | 73.4 |
| 1974 | 160 | 116.7 |
| 1975 | 161 | 138.8 |
| 1976 | 125 | 131.9 |
| 1977 | 148 | 140.0 |
| 1978 | 194 | 167.0 |
| 1979 | 308 | 237.5 |
| 1980 | 613 | 425.2 |
| 1981 | 460 | 442.6 |
| 1982 | 376 | 409.3 |
| 1983 | 424 | 416.7 |
| 1984 | 361 | 388.8 |
| 1985 | 318 | 353.4 |

15.33 a. The exponentially smoothed expenditure for the first time period is equal to the expenditure for that period. For the rest of the time periods, the exponentially smoothed expenditures are found by multiplying the expenditures for the time period by w = .2 and adding to that (1 - .2) times the exponentially smoothed value above it. The exponentially smoothed values for the year 1961 is .2(44.8) + (1 - .2)(42.4) = 42.9. The rest of the values appear in the table. The process is repeated with w = .8.

| YEAR | EXPENDITURE | w = .2 EXP. SMOOTHED VALUE | w = .8 EXP. SMOOTHED VALUE | YEAR | EXPENDITURE | w = .2 EXP. SMOOTHED VALUE | w = .8 EXP. SMOOTHED VALUE |
|---|---|---|---|---|---|---|---|
| 1960 | 42.4 | 42.4 | 42.4 | 1973 | 114.6 | 84.7 | 112.1 |
| 1961 | 44.8 | 42.9 | 44.3 | 1974 | 117.9 | 91.3 | 116.7 |
| 1962 | 47.4 | 43.8 | 46.8 | 1975 | 129.4 | 98.9 | 126.9 |
| 1963 | 49.5 | 44.9 | 49.0 | 1976 | 155.2 | 110.2 | 149.5 |
| 1964 | 54.3 | 46.8 | 53.2 | 1977 | 179.3 | 124.0 | 173.3 |
| 1965 | 58.4 | 49.1 | 57.4 | 1978 | 198.1 | 138.8 | 193.1 |
| 1966 | 60.4 | 51.4 | 59.8 | 1979 | 219.4 | 154.9 | 214.1 |
| 1967 | 63.3 | 53.8 | 62.6 | 1980 | 236.6 | 171.3 | 232.1 |
| 1968 | 69.3 | 56.9 | 68.0 | 1981 | 261.5 | 189.3 | 255.6 |
| 1969 | 75.7 | 60.6 | 74.2 | 1982 | 267.3 | 204.9 | 265.0 |
| 1970 | 80.6 | 64.6 | 79.3 | 1983 | 291.9 | 222.3 | 286.5 |
| 1971 | 92.3 | 70.2 | 89.7 | 1984 | 319.5 | 241.8 | 312.9 |
| 1972 | 105.4 | 77.2 | 102.3 | | | | |

b.

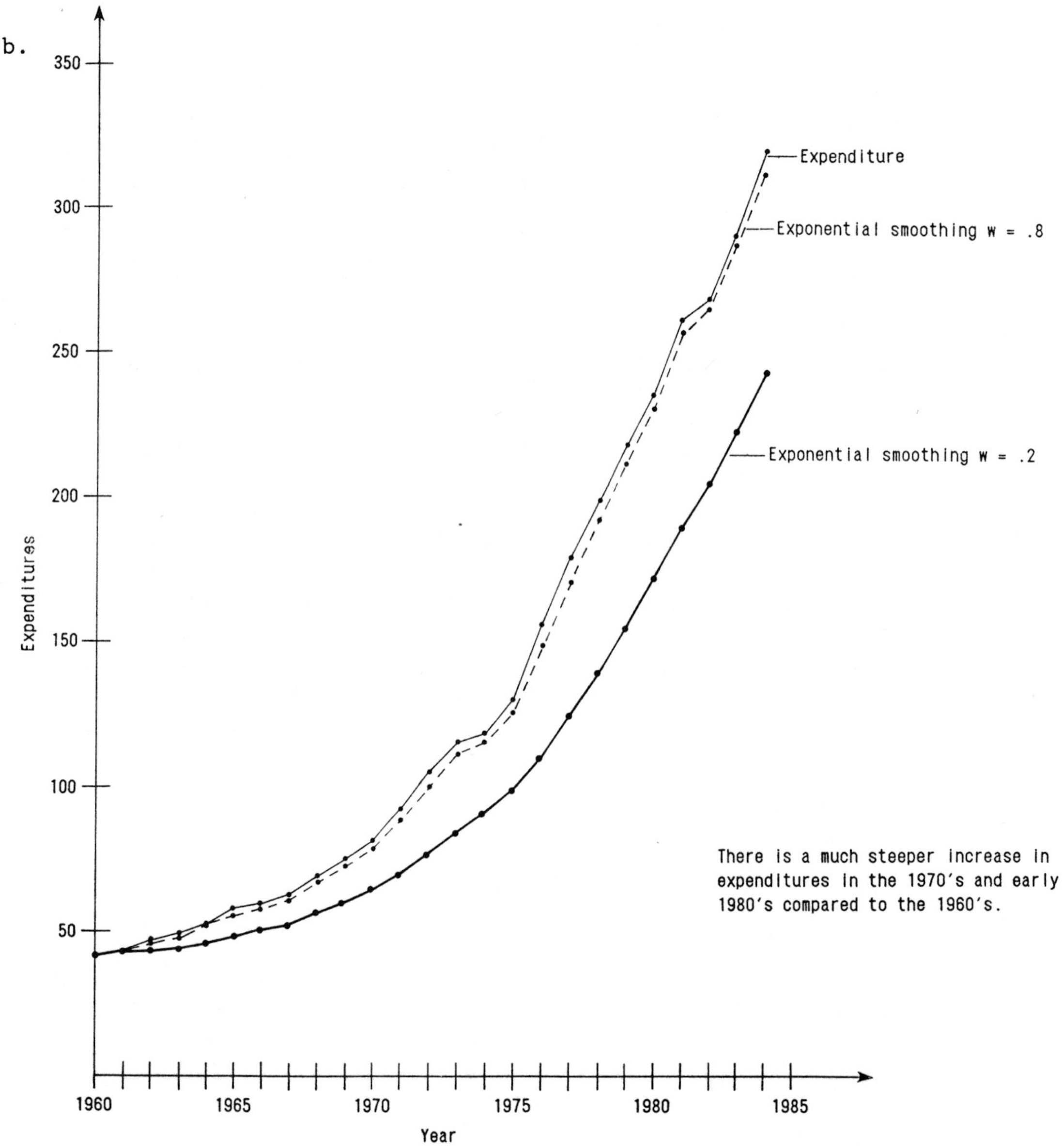

15.35 a. The exponentially smoothed price for the first time period is equal to the price for that period. For the rest of the time periods, the exponentially smoothed prices are found by multiplying the price for the time period by w = .5 and adding to that (1 - .5) times the exponentially smoothed value for the time period above it. We do this for each of the different kinds of steel.

The exponentially smoothed values for 1972 are:

Cold rolled steel: .5(10.77) + (1 - .5)(10.00) = 10.39
Hot rolled steel: .5(8.40) + (1 - .5)(7.48) = 7.94
Galvanized steel: .5(10.88) + (1 - .5)(9.61) = 10.25

The rest of the values are computed in a similar way and are displayed in the table:

| YEAR | COLD ROLLED STEEL PRICE | EXP. SMOOTHED VALUE, w=.5 | HOT ROLLED STEEL PRICE | EXP. SMOOTHED VALUE, w=.5 | GALVANIZED STEEL PRICE | EXP. SMOOTHED VALUE, w=.5 |
|---|---|---|---|---|---|---|
| 1971 | 10.00 | 10.00 | 7.48 | 7.48 | 9.61 | 9.61 |
| 1972 | 10.77 | 10.39 | 8.40 | 7.94 | 10.88 | 10.25 |
| 1973 | 11.08 | 10.73 | 8.40 | 8.17 | 10.59 | 10.42 |
| 1974 | 12.78 | 11.76 | 9.10 | 8.64 | 12.39 | 11.40 |
| 1975 | 16.03 | 13.89 | 11.13 | 9.88 | 14.80 | 13.10 |
| 1976 | 18.16 | 16.03 | 12.20 | 11.04 | 16.07 | 14.59 |
| 1977 | 20.39 | 18.21 | 13.79 | 12.42 | 18.10 | 16.34 |
| 1978 | 23.11 | 20.66 | 15.53 | 13.97 | 20.47 | 18.41 |
| 1979 | 25.55 | 23.10 | 17.05 | 15.51 | 22.32 | 20.36 |
| 1980 | 26.50 | 24.80 | 18.46 | 16.99 | 23.88 | 22.12 |
| 1981 | 31.50 | 28.15 | 20.15 | 18.57 | 26.88 | 24.50 |
| 1982 | 33.25 | 30.70 | 20.80 | 19.68 | 26.75 | 25.63 |
| 1983 | 36.17 | 33.44 | 22.23 | 20.96 | 28.43 | 27.03 |
| 1984 | 28.15 | 30.79 | 23.75 | 22.35 | 30.30 | 28.66 |

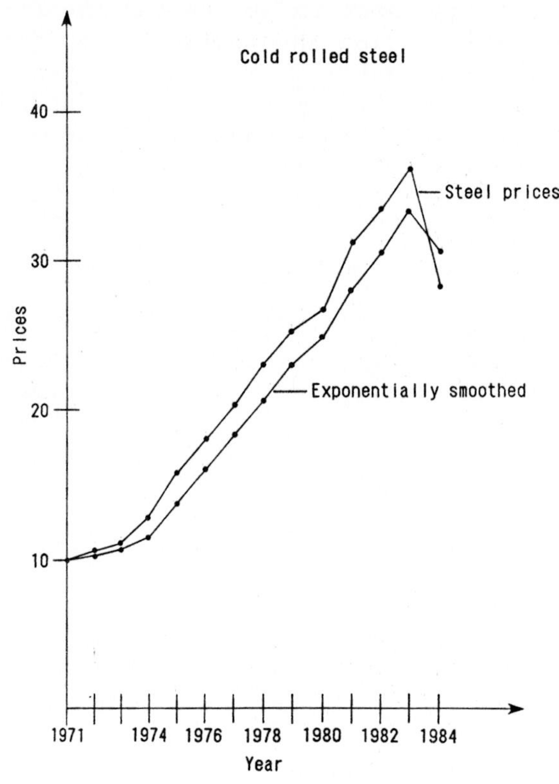
Cold rolled steel
40
30
20
10
Prices
Steel prices
Exponentially smoothed
1971
1974
1976
1978
1980
1982
1984
Year

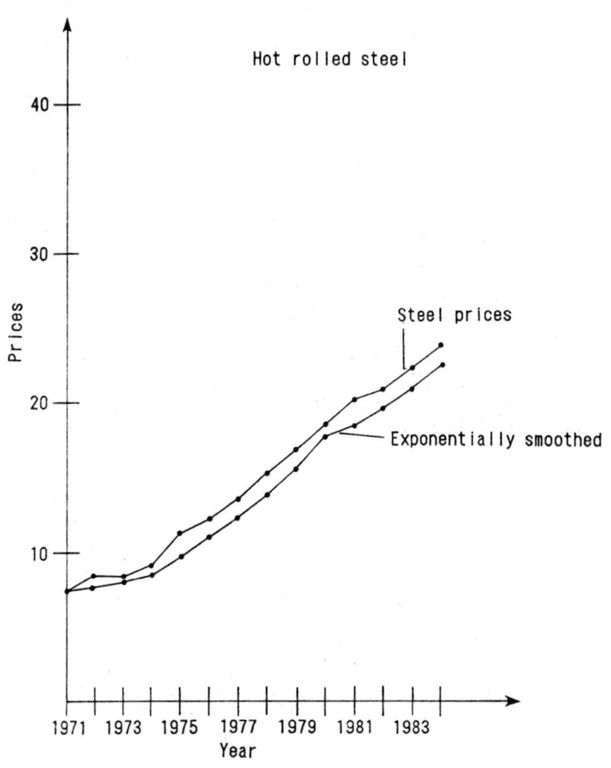
Hot rolled steel
40
30
20
10
Prices
Steel prices
Exponentially smoothed
1971
1973
1975
1977
1979
1981
1983
Year

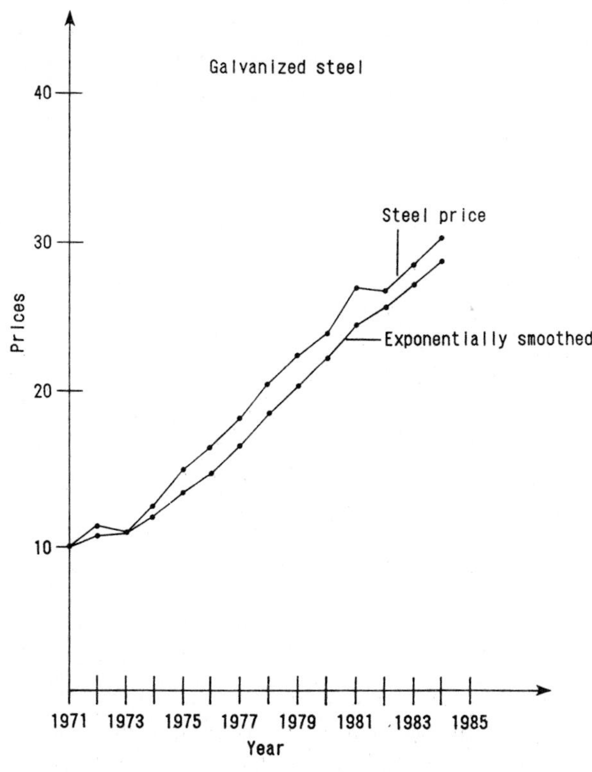


c. The main advantage associated with exponential smoothing is that we have values associated with every time period. Moving averages cannot be computed for the first and last time periods for a 3-point moving average. When the number of values to be averaged increases, the number of time periods where no moving averages can be computed increases.

15.37 a. The simple index is found by dividing each value in the series by the value in the base time period, January 1984, which is 1.41 and then multiplying by 100. The simple index for February 1984 is

$$\frac{1.44}{1.41} \times 100 = 102.1$$

The other values are computed in a similar way and are listed in the table.

| YEAR | MONTH | EXCHANGE RATE | SIMPLE INDEX |
|---|---|---|---|
| 1984 | Jan | 1.41 | 100.0 |
| 1984 | Feb | 1.44 | 102.1 |
| 1984 | Mar | 1.45 | 102.8 |
| 1984 | Apr | 1.43 | 101.4 |
| 1984 | May | 1.39 | 98.6 |
| 1984 | June | 1.37 | 97.2 |
| 1984 | July | 1.32 | 93.6 |
| 1984 | Aug | 1.31 | 92.9 |
| 1984 | Sept | 1.26 | 89.4 |
| 1984 | Oct | 1.23 | 87.2 |
| 1984 | Nov | 1.24 | 87.9 |
| 1984 | Dec | 1.18 | 83.7 |
| 1985 | Jan | 1.13 | 80.1 |
| 1985 | Feb | 1.10 | 78.0 |
| 1985 | Mar | 1.13 | 80.1 |
| 1985 | Apr | 1.23 | 87.2 |
| 1985 | May | 1.25 | 88.7 |
| 1985 | June | 1.28 | 90.8 |
| 1985 | July | 1.38 | 97.9 |
| 1985 | Aug | 1.39 | 98.6 |
| 1985 | Sept | 1.36 | 96.5 |
| 1985 | Oct | 1.42 | 100.7 |
| 1985 | Nov | 1.44 | 102.1 |
| 1985 | Dec | 1.44 | 102.1 |

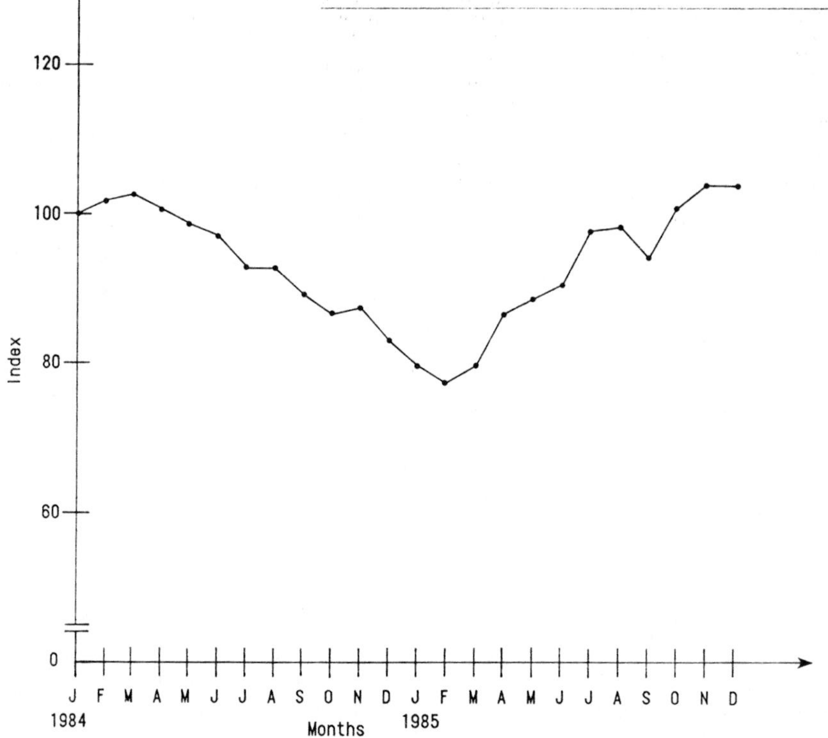


Based on the plot, the best time for a U.S. traveler would be January through March 1985. The index is dollars per pound. The Americans would be interested in pounds per dollar. Thus, low values for dollars per pound give high values for pounds per dollar.

15.39 a. The simple composite index is computed by first summing the 3 observations for each year. Using 1974 as the base period, the simple composite index is the sum for each time period divided by the sum for 1974 times 100.

The index number for 1975 is $\frac{57.2 + 14.4 + 15.0}{54.3 + 14.6 + 13.7} \times 100 = 104.8$

The rest of the numbers in the series are computed in a similar way and are shown in the table.

| YEAR | AUTOMOBILE | MOBILE HOME | REVOLVING CREDIT | SUM | SIMPLE INDEX BASE=1974 | SIMPLE INDEX BASE=1980 |
|---|---|---|---|---|---|---|
| 1974 | 54.3 | 14.6 | 13.7 | 82.6 | 100.0 | 43.6 |
| 1975 | 57.2 | 14.4 | 15.0 | 86.6 | 104.8 | 45.7 |
| 1976 | 67.7 | 14.6 | 17.2 | 99.5 | 120.5 | 52.5 |
| 1977 | 82.9 | 15.0 | 39.3 | 137.2 | 166.1 | 72.4 |
| 1978 | 101.6 | 15.2 | 48.3 | 165.1 | 199.9 | 87.1 |
| 1979 | 116.4 | 16.8 | 57.0 | 190.2 | 230.3 | 100.4 |
| 1980 | 112.2 | 18.8 | 58.5 | 189.5 | 229.4 | 100.0 |
| 1981 | 119.8 | 19.9 | 64.5 | 204.2 | 247.2 | 107.8 |
| 1982 | 126.3 | 22.4 | 69.6 | 218.3 | 264.3 | 115.2 |
| 1983 | 143.1 | 23.9 | 82.0 | 249.0 | 301.5 | 131.4 |
| 1984 | 172.6 | 24.6 | 101.6 | 298.8 | 361.7 | 157.7 |

b. The above procedure is repeated except the sum of the 3 observations for 1980 is used as the denominator rather than the sum of the 3 observations for 1974.

The index number for 1975 is $\frac{57.2 + 14.4 + 15.0}{112.2 + 18.8 + 58.5} \times 100 = 45.7$

c. The indexes in (a) and (b) are price indexes since they are based on dollars, not amounts.

d. To compute the simple index for automobile loans, we divide each number by the number in the base year, 1980, which is 112.2 and then multiplying by 100. The simple index value for 1974 is

$$\frac{54.3}{112.2} \times 100 = 48.4$$

The rest of the values are computed in a similar way and are shown in the table:

| YEAR | AUTOMOBILE | SIMPLE INDEX BASE=1980 |
|---|---|---|
| 1974 | 54.3 | 48.4 |
| 1975 | 57.2 | 51.0 |
| 1976 | 67.7 | 60.3 |
| 1977 | 82.9 | 73.9 |
| 1978 | 101.6 | 90.6 |
| 1979 | 116.4 | 103.7 |
| 1980 | 112.2 | 100.0 |
| 1981 | 119.8 | 106.8 |
| 1982 | 126.3 | 112.6 |
| 1983 | 143.1 | 127.5 |
| 1984 | 172.6 | 153.8 |

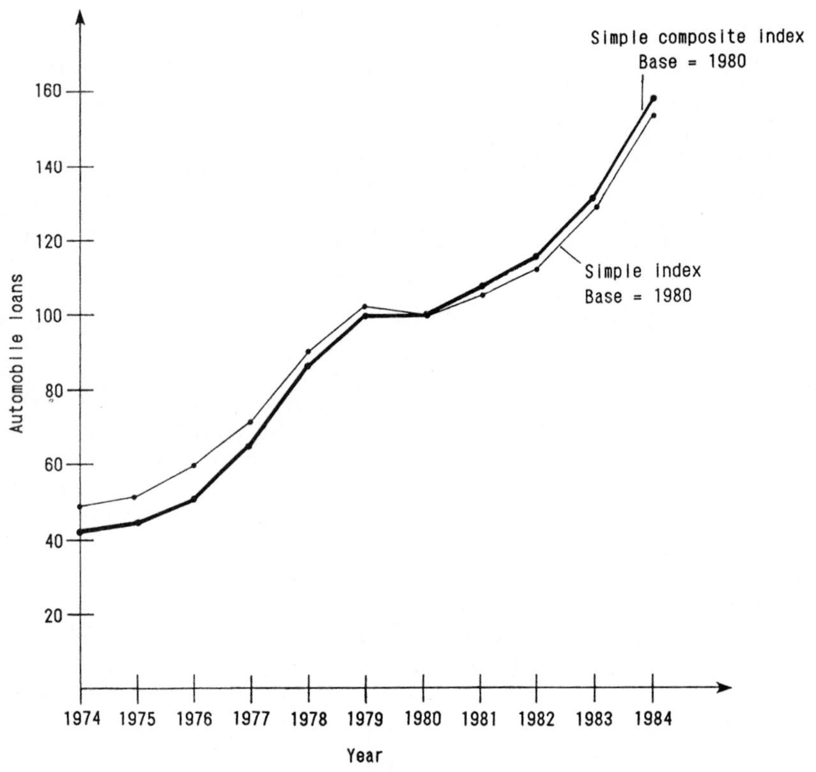


15.41 a. To compute Laspeyres index, first multiply everything in the automobile column by 40,000, everything in the mobile home column by 10,000 and everything in the revolving credit column by 100,000. Then, sum these for each year, divide by the sum for 1980 and multiply by 100. For year 1984, the index value is

$$\frac{172.6 \times 40{,}000 + 24.6 \times 10{,}000 + 101.6 \times 100{,}000}{112.2 \times 40{,}000 + 18.8 \times 10{,}000 + 58.5 \times 100{,}000} \times 100 = 164.45$$

The rest of the values are shown in the table for 1980 through 1984:

| YEAR | AUTOMOBILE | MOBILE HOME | REVOLVING CREDIT | WEIGHTED SUM | LASPEYRES INDEX |
|---|---|---|---|---|---|
| 1980 | 112.2 | 18.8 | 58.5 | 10526000 | 100.00 |
| 1981 | 119.8 | 19.9 | 64.5 | 11441000 | 108.69 |
| 1982 | 126.3 | 22.4 | 69.6 | 12236000 | 116.25 |
| 1983 | 143.1 | 23.9 | 82.0 | 14163000 | 134.55 |
| 1984 | 172.6 | 24.6 | 101.6 | 17310000 | 164.45 |

b. Revolving credit, with a weight of 100,000, is given the most weight.

15.43 a. The simple composite index is found by first summing the indexes at each time period. The sums are then divided by the sum for the base period, 1970, and multiplied by 100. The simple composite index value for 1971 is

$$\frac{108.5 + 109.6 + 158.8}{106.4 + 107.8 + 111.0} \times 100 = 115.90$$

The rest of the values are computed in a similar way and are listed below:

| YEAR | INDEX OF NET BUSINESS FORMATION | INDEX OF INDUSTRIAL PRODUCTION | INDEX OF HOUSING UNITS AUTHORIZED | SUM OF 3 INDEXES | COMPOSITE INDEX |
|---|---|---|---|---|---|
| 1970 | 106.4 | 107.8 | 111.0 | 325.2 | 100.00 |
| 1971 | 108.5 | 109.6 | 158.8 | 376.9 | 115.90 |
| 1972 | 115.9 | 119.7 | 182.4 | 418.0 | 128.54 |
| 1973 | 114.9 | 129.8 | 158.4 | 403.1 | 123.95 |
| 1974 | 109.2 | 129.3 | 103.6 | 342.1 | 105.20 |
| 1975 | 107.0 | 117.8 | 89.8 | 314.6 | 96.74 |
| 1976 | 115.6 | 130.5 | 119.0 | 365.1 | 112.27 |
| 1977 | 123.2 | 138.2 | 153.8 | 415.2 | 127.68 |
| 1978 | 128.2 | 144.1 | 156.3 | 428.6 | 131.80 |
| 1979 | 128.3 | 152.5 | 135.1 | 415.9 | 127.89 |
| 1980 | 122.4 | 147.0 | 100.0 | 369.4 | 113.59 |
| 1981 | 118.6 | 151.0 | 83.9 | 353.5 | 108.70 |
| 1982 | 113.2 | 138.6 | 82.2 | 334.0 | 102.71 |
| 1983 | 114.8 | 147.6 | 131.8 | 394.2 | 121.22 |
| 1984 | 117.1 | 163.3 | 135.4 | 415.8 | 127.86 |

b. The simple index for each series is computed by dividing each value in the series by the value in the base period and then multiplying by 100. The simple index for the net business formation is found by dividing each value by 106.4 and then multiplying by 100. The simple index for the industrial production is found by dividing each value by 107.8 and then multiplying by 100. The simple index for the new private housing units is found by dividing each value by 111 and then multiplying by 100. The values are found in the table below:

| YEAR | NET BUSINESS FORMATION | SIMPLE INDEX | INDUSTRIAL PRODUCTION | SIMPLE INDEX | HOUSING UNITS AUTHORIZED | SIMPLE INDEX |
|---|---|---|---|---|---|---|
| 1970 | 106.4 | 100.00 | 107.8 | 100.00 | 111.0 | 100.00 |
| 1971 | 108.5 | 101.97 | 109.6 | 101.67 | 158.8 | 143.06 |
| 1972 | 115.9 | 108.93 | 119.7 | 111.04 | 182.4 | 164.32 |
| 1973 | 114.9 | 107.99 | 129.8 | 120.41 | 158.4 | 142.70 |
| 1974 | 109.2 | 102.63 | 129.3 | 119.94 | 103.6 | 93.33 |
| 1975 | 107.0 | 100.56 | 117.8 | 109.28 | 89.8 | 80.90 |
| 1976 | 115.6 | 108.65 | 130.5 | 121.06 | 119.0 | 107.21 |
| 1977 | 123.2 | 115.79 | 138.2 | 128.20 | 153.8 | 138.56 |
| 1978 | 128.2 | 120.49 | 144.1 | 133.67 | 156.3 | 140.81 |
| 1979 | 128.3 | 120.58 | 152.5 | 141.47 | 135.1 | 121.71 |
| 1980 | 122.4 | 115.04 | 147.0 | 136.36 | 100.0 | 90.09 |
| 1981 | 118.6 | 111.47 | 151.0 | 140.07 | 83.9 | 75.59 |
| 1982 | 113.2 | 106.39 | 138.6 | 128.57 | 82.2 | 74.05 |
| 1983 | 114.8 | 107.89 | 147.6 | 136.92 | 131.8 | 118.74 |
| 1984 | 117.1 | 110.06 | 163.3 | 151.48 | 135.4 | 121.98 |

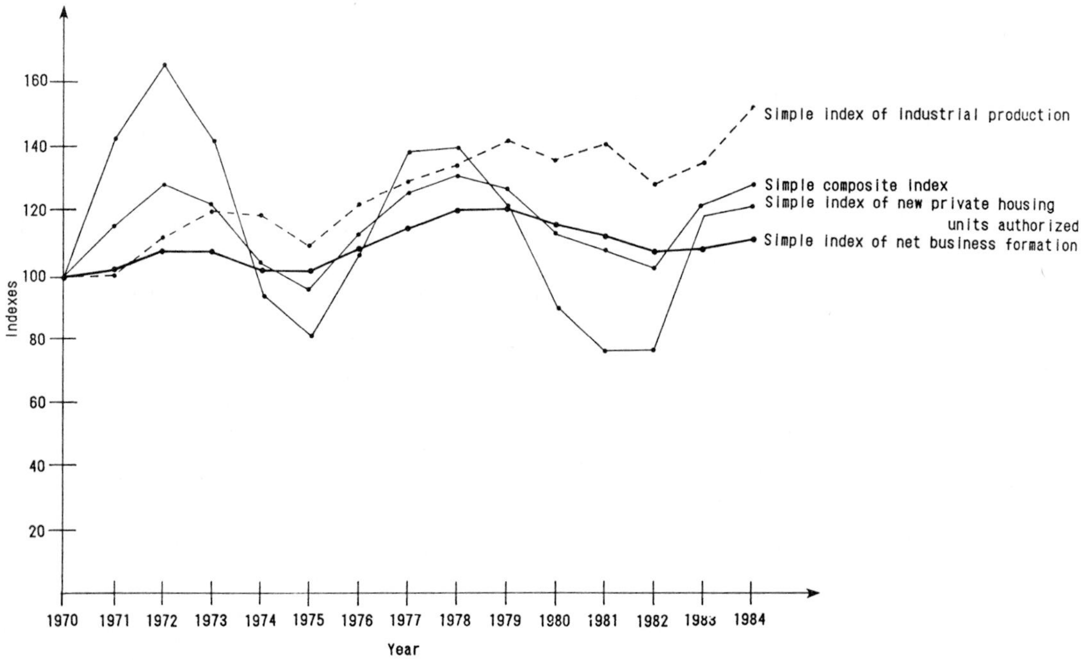

15.45 a. Real income 1970 = $\frac{\$20,000}{116.3} \times 100 = \$17,196.91$

Real income 1985 = $\frac{\$46,000}{322.2} \times 100 = \$14,276.85$

The real income for 1985 was less than that for 1970.

b. Let x = monetary income in 1985.

Then

$$\frac{x}{322.2} = \frac{\$20,000}{116.3}$$

Solving for x, we get x = \$55,408.43.

# CHAPTER 16

## TIME SERIES: MODELS AND FORECASTING

16.1 Two measures of forecasting accuracy are:

a. Mean absolute deviation (MAD) - mean absolute difference between the forecast and actual values of the time series.

b. Root mean squared error (RMSE) - square root of the mean squared difference between the forecast and actual values of the time series.

16.3 a. We first compute the exponentially smoothed values $E_1$, $E_2$, $E_t$ for years 1970 - 1981.

$$E_1 = Y_1 = 133.1$$

For $w = .3$, $E_2 = wY_2 + (1 - w)E_1 = .3(137.4) + (1 - .3)(133.1) = 134.39.$

$$E_3 = wY_3 + (1 - w)E_2 = .3(141.3) + (1 - .3)(134.39) = 136.46.$$

The rest of the values appear in the table.

For $= .7$, $E_2 = wY_2 + (1 - w)E_1 = .7(137.4) + (1 - .7)(133.1) = 136.11$

$$E_3 = wY_3 + (1 - w)E_2 = .7(141.3) + (1 - .7)(136.11) = 139.74$$

The rest of the values appear in the table.

| YEAR | BEER PRODUCTION | EXPONENTIALLY SMOOTHED VALUE w = .3 | EXPONENTIALLY SMOOTHED VALUE w = .7 |
|---|---|---|---|
| 1970 | 133.1 | 133.10 | 133.10 |
| 1971 | 137.4 | 134.39 | 136.11 |
| 1972 | 141.3 | 136.46 | 139.74 |
| 1973 | 148.6 | 140.10 | 145.94 |
| 1974 | 156.2 | 144.93 | 153.12 |
| 1975 | 160.6 | 149.63 | 158.36 |
| 1976 | 163.7 | 153.85 | 162.10 |
| 1977 | 170.5 | 158.85 | 167.98 |
| 1978 | 179.1 | 164.92 | 175.76 |
| 1979 | 184.2 | 170.71 | 181.67 |
| 1980 | 194.1 | 177.72 | 190.37 |
| 1981 | 193.7 | 182.52 | 192.70 |

To forecast using exponentially smoothed values, we use the following:

For w = .3:

$F_{1982} = F_{t+1} = E_t = 182.52$ Forecast error $= 196.2 - 182.52 = 13.68$

$F_{1983} = F_{t+2} = F_{t+1} = 182.52$ Forecast error $= 195.38 - 182.52 = 12.86$

$F_{1984} = F_{t+3} = F_{t+1} = 182.52$ Forecast error $= 192.23 - 182.52 = 9.71$

For w = .7:

$F_{1982} = F_{t+1} = E_t = 192.70$ Forecast error $= 196.2 - 192.70 = 3.5$

$F_{1983} = F_{t+2} = F_{t+1} = 192.70$ Forecast error $= 195.38 - 192.70 = 2.68$

$F_{1984} = F_{t+3} = F_{t+1} = 192.70$ Forecast error $= 192.23 - 192.70 = -.47$

b. We first compute the Holt-Winters values for years 1970 - 1981.

With w = .7 and v = .3,

$$E_2 = Y_2 = 137.40$$
$$E_3 = wY_3 + (1 - w)(E_2 + T_2)$$
$$= .7(141.3) + (1 - .7)(137.4 + 4.3)$$
$$= 141.42$$

e. Since the process is out of control, the centerline and control limits should not be used to monitor future process output. The special cause(s) of variation should be identified and eliminated. Any sample data that were influenced by the special cause(s) of variation should be dropped from the data set, and the centerline and control limits should be recalculated. This process should be repeated until the control chart indicates the process is in control. Alternatively, after eliminating the special cause(s) of variation, additional samples could be taken and a new p-chart constructed. If the process is then judged to be in control, the new control limits should be used to monitor future process output.

14.33 A system is a collection or arrangement of interacting components that has an on-going purpose or mission. A system receives inputs from its environment, transforms those inputs to outputs, and delivers those outputs to its environment.

14.35 The five major sources of process variation are: people, machines, materials, methods, and environment.

14.37 The use of a hierarchical systems model to facilitate and guide the description, exploration, analysis, and/or understanding of organizations and their problems is called systems thinking. It has many benefits, but one of the most important is that it focuses attention on the processes through which things get done rather than on final outcomes. Thus, it facilitates the prevention of problems rather than after-the-fact correction of problems.

14.39 If a process is in control and remains in control, its future will be like its past. It is predictable in that its output will stay within certain limits. If a process is out of control, there is no way of knowing what the future pattern of output from the process may look like.

14.41 The upper control limit and the lower control limit are positioned so that when the process is in control, the probability of an individual value falling outside the control limits is very small. Most practitioners position the control limits a distance of three standard deviations from the centerline. If the process is in control and follows a normal distribution, the probability of an individual measurement falling outside the control limits is .0026.

14.43 The probability of observing a value of $\bar{x}$ more than 3 standard deviations from its mean is:

$$P(\bar{x} > \mu + 3\sigma_{\bar{x}}) + P(\bar{x} < \mu - 3\sigma_{\bar{x}}) = P(z > 3) + P(z < 3)$$
$$= .5000 - .4987 + .5000 - .4987 = .0026$$

$$T_2 = Y_2 - Y_1 = 137.4 - 133.1 = 4.3$$
$$T_3 = v(E_3 - E_2) + (1 - v)T_2$$
$$= .3(141.42 - 137.40) + (1 - .3)(4.3)$$
$$= 4.22$$

The rest of the $E_t$'s and $T_t$'s appear in the table below.

With w = .3 and v = .7,

$$E_2 = Y_2 = 137.40$$
$$E_3 = .3(141.3) + (1 - .3)(137.4 + 4.3)$$
$$= 141.58$$

$$T_2 = Y_2 - Y_1 = 137.4 - 133.1 = 4.3$$
$$T_3 = .7(141.58 - 137.40) + (1 - .7)(4.3)$$
$$= 4.22$$

The rest of the $E_t$'s and $T_t$'s appear in the table below.

| YEAR | $E_t$ w = .7 v = .3 | $T_t$ w = .7 v = .3 | $E_t$ w = .3 v = .7 | $T_t$ w = .3 v = .7 |
|---|---|---|---|---|
| 1970 | | | | |
| 1971 | 137.40 | 4.30 | 137.40 | 4.30 |
| 1972 | 141.42 | 4.22 | 141.58 | 4.22 |
| 1973 | 147.71 | 4.84 | 146.64 | 4.80 |
| 1974 | 155.10 | 5.61 | 152.87 | 5.80 |
| 1975 | 160.63 | 5.58 | 159.25 | 6.21 |
| 1976 | 164.45 | 5.05 | 164.93 | 5.84 |
| 1977 | 170.20 | 5.26 | 170.69 | 5.78 |
| 1978 | 178.01 | 6.03 | 177.26 | 6.33 |
| 1979 | 184.15 | 6.06 | 183.78 | 6.46 |
| 1980 | 192.93 | 6.88 | 191.40 | 7.27 |
| 1981 | 195.53 | 5.59 | 197.18 | 6.23 |

To forecast using the Holt-Winters Model:

For w = .7 and v = .3,

$$F_{1982} = F_{t+1} = E_t + T_t = 195.53 + 5.59 = 201.12$$

Forecast error = 196.2 - 201.12 = -4.92

$$F_{1983} = F_{t+2} = E_t + 2T_t = 195.53 + 2(5.59) = 206.71$$

Forecast error = 195.38 - 206.71 = -11.33

$$F_{1984} = F_{t+3} = E_t + 3T_t = 195.53 + 3(5.59) = 212.3$$

Forecast error $\doteq$ 192.23 - 212.3 = -20.07

For $w = .3$ and $v = .7$,

$$F_{1982} = F_{t+1} = E_t + T_t = 197.18 + 6.23 = 203.41$$

Forecast error = 196.2 - 203.41 = -7.21

$$F_{1983} = F_{t+2} = E_t + 2T_t = 197.18 + 2(6.23) = 209.64$$

Forecast error = 195.38 - 209.64 = -14.26

$$F_{1984} = F_{t+3} = E_t + 3T_t = 197.18 + 3(6.23) = 215.87$$

Forecast error = 192.23 - 215.87 = -23.64

c. For the exponential smoothed forecasts,

$w = .3$,

$$MAD = \frac{\sum_{t=1}^{n} |F_t - Y_t|}{N} = \frac{|182.52 - 196.2| + |182.52 - 195.38| + |182.52 - 192.23|}{3}$$

$$= \frac{36.25}{3} = 12.083$$

$$RMSE = \sqrt{\frac{\sum_{t=1}^{n} (F_t - Y_t)^2}{N}} = \sqrt{\frac{(-13.68)^2 + (-12.86)^2 + (-9.71)^2}{3}} = 12.204$$

$w = .7$,

$$MAD = \frac{\sum |F_t - Y_t|}{N} = \frac{|192.70 - 196.2| + |192.70 - 195.38| + |192.70 - 192.23|}{3}$$

$$= \frac{6.65}{3} = 2.217$$

$$RMSE = \sqrt{\frac{\sum (F_t - Y_t)^2}{N}} = \sqrt{\frac{(-3.5)^2 + (-2.68)^2 + (.47)^2}{3}} = 2.560$$

For the Holt-Winters forecasts,

$w = .7$ and $v = .3$,

$$MAD = \frac{\sum |F_t - Y_t|}{N} = \frac{|201.12 - 196.2| + |206.71 - 195.38| + |212.3 - 192.23|}{3}$$

$$= \frac{36.32}{3} = 12.107$$

$$\text{RMSE} = \sqrt{\frac{\sum(F_t - Y_t)^2}{N}} = \sqrt{\frac{(4.92)^2 + (11.33)^2 + (20.07)^2}{3}} = 13.606$$

$w = .3$ and $v = .7$,

$$\text{MAD} = \frac{\sum|F_t - Y_t|}{N} = \frac{|203.41 - 196.2| + |209.64 - 195.38| + |215.87 - 192.23|}{3}$$

$$= \frac{45.11}{3} = 15.037$$

$$\text{RMSE} = \sqrt{\frac{\sum(F_t - Y_t)^2}{N}} = \sqrt{\frac{(7.21)^2 + (14.26)^2 + (23.64)^2}{3}} = 16.474$$

Both the MAD measures for the exponentially smoothed forecasts (12.083 and 2.217) are smaller than the MAD measures for the Holt-Winters forecasts (12.107 and 15.037). Similarly, the RMSE measures for the exponentially smoothed forecasts (12.204 and 2.560) are smaller than the RMSE measures for the Holt-Winters forecasts (13.606 and 16.474).

Even though the MAD and RMSE measures for the Holt-Winters forecasts are larger than those of the exponentially smoothed forecasts, there does appear to be a trend in the beer production time series. The series increases for every year from 1970 to 1980 and then begins to decline. Thus, we are basing our forecasts on a series that is increasing, but trying to estimate values that are actually decreasing. This explains why the MAD and RMSE values are larger for the Holt-Winters forecasts.

16.5 a. We first compute the exponentially smoothed values $E_1$, $E_2$, ... , $E_t$ for 1971 through 1984.

$$E_1 = Y_1 = 100.31$$

For $w = .7$,

$$E_2 = wY_2 + (1 - w)E_1 = .7(99.20) + (1 - .7)(100.31) = 99.533$$
$$E_3 = wY_3 + (1 - w)E_2 = .7(98.34) + (1 - .7)(99.533) = 98.697$$

The rest of the values appear in the table:

| YEAR | S&P 500 | EXPONENTIALLY SMOOTHED VALUE (w=.7) | YEAR | S&P 500 | EXPONENTIALLY SMOOTHED VALUE (w=.7) |
|---|---|---|---|---|---|
| 1971 | 100.31 | 100.31 | 1978 | 89.21 | 91.22 |
| 1971 | 99.20 | 99.53 | 1978 | 95.53 | 94.24 |
| 1971 | 98.34 | 98.70 | 1978 | 102.54 | 100.05 |
| 1971 | 102.09 | 101.07 | 1978 | 96.11 | 97.29 |
| 1972 | 107.20 | 105.36 | 1979 | 101.59 | 100.30 |
| 1972 | 107.14 | 106.61 | 1979 | 102.91 | 102.13 |
| 1972 | 110.55 | 109.37 | 1979 | 109.32 | 107.16 |
| 1972 | 118.06 | 115.45 | 1979 | 107.94 | 107.71 |
| 1973 | 111.52 | 112.70 | 1980 | 105.36 | 106.06 |
| 1973 | 104.26 | 106.79 | 1980 | 113.72 | 111.42 |
| 1973 | 108.43 | 107.94 | 1980 | 127.14 | 122.42 |
| 1973 | 97.55 | 100.67 | 1980 | 131.44 | 128.74 |
| 1974 | 93.98 | 95.99 | 1981 | 134.94 | 133.08 |
| 1974 | 86.00 | 89.00 | 1981 | 129.06 | 130.27 |
| 1974 | 63.54 | 71.18 | 1981 | 118.77 | 122.22 |
| 1974 | 68.56 | 69.35 | 1981 | 119.13 | 120.06 |
| 1975 | 83.36 | 79.16 | 1982 | 117.09 | 117.98 |
| 1975 | 95.19 | 90.38 | 1982 | 109.82 | 112.27 |
| 1975 | 83.87 | 85.82 | 1982 | 121.79 | 118.93 |
| 1975 | 98.19 | 94.48 | 1982 | 138.91 | 132.92 |
| 1976 | 102.77 | 100.28 | 1983 | 152.96 | 146.95 |
| 1976 | 104.28 | 103.08 | 1983 | 168.11 | 161.76 |
| 1976 | 105.24 | 104.59 | 1983 | 166.07 | 164.78 |
| 1976 | 107.46 | 106.60 | 1983 | 164.93 | 164.88 |
| 1977 | 98.42 | 100.87 | 1984 | 159.18 | 160.89 |
| 1977 | 100.48 | 100.60 | 1984 | 153.18 | 155.49 |
| 1977 | 96.53 | 97.75 | 1984 | 166.10 | 162.92 |
| 1977 | 95.10 | 95.90 | 1984 | 167.24 | 165.94 |

The forecasts for the 4 quarters of 1985 based on 1971 - 1984 data are:

$$F_{1985,I} = F_{t+1} = E_t = 165.94$$

$$F_{1985,II} = F_{t+2} = F_{t+1} = 165.94$$

$$F_{1985,III} = F_{t+3} = F_{t+1} = 165.94$$

$$F_{1985,IV} = F_{t+4} = F_{t+1} = 165.94$$

b. The forecast errors are:

1985, I   180.66 - 165.94 = 14.72
1985, II  191.85 - 165.94 = 25.91
1985, III 182.08 - 165.94 = 16.14
1986, IV  211.28 - 165.94 = 45.34

c. We first compute the exponentially smoothed values $E_1$, $E_2$, ..., $E_t$ for 1971 - 1984.

For w = .3,

$$E_1 = Y_1 = 100.31$$
$$E_2 = wY_2 + (1 - w)E_1 = .3(99.20) + (1 - .3)(100.31) = 99.977$$
$$E_3 = wY_3 + (1 - w)E_2 = .3(98.34) + (1 - .3)(99.977) = 99.4859$$

The rest of the values appear in the table.

| YEAR | S&P 500 | EXPONENTIALLY SMOOTHED VALUE (w=.7) | YEAR | S&P 500 | EXPONENTIALLY SMOOTHED VALUE (w=.7) |
|---|---|---|---|---|---|
| 1971 | 100.31 | 100.31 | 1978 | 89.21 | 95.44 |
| 1971 | 99.20 | 99.98 | 1978 | 95.53 | 95.47 |
| 1971 | 98.34 | 99.49 | 1978 | 102.54 | 97.59 |
| 1971 | 102.09 | 100.27 | 1978 | 96.11 | 97.14 |
| 1972 | 107.20 | 102.35 | 1979 | 101.59 | 98.48 |
| 1972 | 107.14 | 103.78 | 1979 | 102.91 | 99.81 |
| 1972 | 110.55 | 105.81 | 1979 | 109.32 | 102.66 |
| 1972 | 118.06 | 109.49 | 1979 | 107.94 | 104.25 |
| 1973 | 111.52 | 110.10 | 1980 | 105.36 | 104.58 |
| 1973 | 104.26 | 108.35 | 1980 | 113.72 | 107.32 |
| 1973 | 108.43 | 108.37 | 1980 | 127.14 | 113.27 |
| 1973 | 97.55 | 105.13 | 1980 | 131.44 | 118.72 |
| 1974 | 93.98 | 101.78 | 1981 | 134.94 | 123.59 |
| 1974 | 86.00 | 97.05 | 1981 | 129.06 | 125.23 |
| 1974 | 63.54 | 86.99 | 1981 | 118.77 | 123.29 |
| 1974 | 68.56 | 81.46 | 1981 | 119.13 | 122.04 |
| 1975 | 83.36 | 82.03 | 1982 | 117.09 | 120.56 |
| 1975 | 95.19 | 85.98 | 1982 | 109.82 | 117.34 |
| 1975 | 83.87 | 85.35 | 1982 | 121.79 | 118.67 |
| 1975 | 98.19 | 89.20 | 1982 | 138.91 | 124.74 |
| 1976 | 102.77 | 93.27 | 1983 | 152.96 | 133.21 |
| 1976 | 104.28 | 96.57 | 1983 | 168.11 | 143.68 |
| 1976 | 105.24 | 99.17 | 1983 | 166.07 | 150.40 |
| 1976 | 107.46 | 101.66 | 1983 | 164.93 | 154.76 |
| 1977 | 98.42 | 100.69 | 1984 | 159.18 | 156.08 |
| 1977 | 100.48 | 100.63 | 1984 | 153.18 | 155.21 |
| 1977 | 96.53 | 99.40 | 1984 | 166.10 | 158.48 |
| 1977 | 95.10 | 98.11 | 1984 | 167.24 | 161.11 |

The forecasts for the 4 quarters of 1985 based on 1971 - 1984 data are:

$F_{1985,I} = F_{t+1} = E_t = 161.11$

Forecast error = 180.66 - 161.11 = 19.55

$F_{1985,II} = F_{t+2} = F_{t+1} = 161.11$

Forecast error = 191.85 - 161.11 = 30.74

$F_{1985,III} = F_{t+3} = F_{t+1} = 161.11$

Forecast error = 182.08 - 161.11 = 20.97

$F_{1985,IV} = F_{t+4} = F_{t+1} = 161.11$

Forecast error = 211.28 - 161.11 = 50.17

d. We first compute the Holt-Winters values for years 1971 - 1984.

With w = .7 and v = .5,

$$\begin{aligned} E_2 &= Y_2 = 99.20 \\ E_3 &= wY_3 + (1 - w)(E_2 + T_2) \\ &= .7(98.34) + (1 - .7)(99.20 - 1.11) \\ &= 98.265 \end{aligned}$$

$$\begin{aligned} T_2 &= Y_2 - Y_1 = 99.20 - 100.31 = -1.11 \\ T_3 &= v(E_3 - E_2) + (1 - v)T_2 \\ &= .5(98.265 - 99.20) + (1 - .5)(-1.11) \\ &= -1.0225 \end{aligned}$$

The rest of the $E_t$'s and $T_t$'s appear in the table below.

With w = .3 and v = .5,

$$\begin{aligned} E_2 &= Y_2 = 99.20 \\ E_3 &= wY_3 + (1 - w)(E_2 + T_2) \\ &= .3(98.34) + (1 - .3)(99.20 - 1.11) \\ &= 98.165 \end{aligned}$$

$$\begin{aligned} T_2 &= Y_2 - Y_1 = 99.20 - 100.31 = -1.11 \\ T_3 &= v(E_3 - E_2) + (1 - v)T_2 \\ &= .5(98.165 - 99.20) + (1 - .5)(-1.11) \\ &= -1.0725 \end{aligned}$$

The rest of the $E_t$'s and $T_t$'s appear in the table.

| YEAR | S&P 500 | HOLT-WINTERS MODEL 1 E(w = .7) | T(v = .5) | HOLT-WINTERS MODEL 2 E(w = .3) | T(v = .5) |
|---|---|---|---|---|---|
| 1971 | 100.31 | | | | |
| 1971 | 99.20 | 99.20 | -1.11 | 99.20 | -1.11 |
| 1971 | 98.34 | 98.27 | -1.02 | 98.17 | -1.07 |
| 1971 | 102.09 | 100.64 | 0.67 | 98.59 | -0.32 |
| 1972 | 107.20 | 105.43 | 2.74 | 100.95 | 1.02 |
| 1972 | 107.14 | 107.45 | 2.38 | 103.52 | 1.79 |
| 1972 | 110.55 | 110.33 | 2.63 | 106.88 | 2.58 |
| 1972 | 118.06 | 116.53 | 4.41 | 112.04 | 3.87 |
| 1973 | 111.52 | 114.35 | 1.12 | 114.59 | 3.21 |
| 1973 | 104.26 | 107.62 | -2.81 | 113.74 | 1.18 |
| 1973 | 108.43 | 107.35 | -1.54 | 112.97 | 0.21 |
| 1973 | 97.55 | 100.03 | -4.43 | 108.49 | -2.14 |
| 1974 | 93.98 | 94.47 | -5.00 | 102.64 | -3.99 |
| 1974 | 86.00 | 87.04 | -6.21 | 94.85 | -5.89 |
| 1974 | 63.54 | 68.73 | -12.26 | 81.33 | -9.70 |
| 1974 | 68.56 | 64.93 | -8.03 | 70.71 | -10.16 |
| 1975 | 83.36 | 75.42 | 1.23 | 67.39 | -6.74 |
| 1975 | 95.19 | 89.63 | 7.72 | 71.01 | -1.56 |
| 1975 | 83.87 | 87.91 | 3.00 | 73.78 | 0.60 |
| 1975 | 98.19 | 96.01 | 5.55 | 81.52 | 4.17 |
| 1976 | 102.77 | 102.41 | 5.97 | 90.82 | 6.74 |
| 1976 | 104.28 | 105.51 | 4.54 | 99.57 | 7.74 |
| 1976 | 105.24 | 106.68 | 2.86 | 106.69 | 7.43 |
| 1976 | 107.46 | 108.08 | 2.13 | 112.13 | 6.43 |
| 1977 | 98.42 | 101.96 | -2.00 | 112.52 | 3.41 |
| 1977 | 100.48 | 100.32 | -1.82 | 111.29 | 1.09 |
| 1977 | 96.53 | 97.12 | -2.51 | 107.63 | -1.28 |
| 1977 | 95.10 | 94.95 | -2.34 | 102.97 | -2.97 |
| 1978 | 89.21 | 90.23 | -3.53 | 96.76 | -4.59 |
| 1978 | 95.53 | 92.88 | -0.44 | 93.18 | -4.09 |
| 1978 | 102.54 | 99.51 | 3.09 | 93.13 | -2.07 |
| 1978 | 96.11 | 98.06 | 0.82 | 92.57 | -1.31 |
| 1979 | 101.59 | 100.78 | 1.77 | 94.36 | 0.24 |
| 1979 | 102.91 | 102.80 | 1.90 | 97.09 | 1.48 |
| 1979 | 109.32 | 107.93 | 3.51 | 101.80 | 3.10 |
| 1979 | 107.94 | 108.99 | 2.29 | 105.81 | 3.55 |
| 1980 | 105.36 | 107.14 | 0.22 | 108.16 | 2.95 |
| 1980 | 113.72 | 111.81 | 2.44 | 111.90 | 3.34 |
| 1980 | 127.14 | 123.27 | 6.95 | 118.81 | 5.13 |
| 1980 | 131.44 | 131.08 | 7.38 | 126.19 | 6.25 |
| 1981 | 134.94 | 135.99 | 6.15 | 133.19 | 6.63 |
| 1981 | 129.06 | 132.98 | 1.57 | 136.59 | 5.01 |
| 1981 | 118.77 | 123.51 | -3.96 | 134.76 | 1.59 |
| 1981 | 119.13 | 119.26 | -4.10 | 131.18 | -0.99 |
| 1982 | 117.09 | 116.51 | -3.42 | 126.26 | -2.96 |
| 1982 | 109.82 | 110.80 | -4.57 | 119.26 | -4.98 |
| 1982 | 121.79 | 117.12 | 0.88 | 116.53 | -3.85 |
| 1982 | 138.91 | 132.64 | 8.20 | 120.55 | 0.08 |
| 1983 | 152.96 | 149.32 | 12.44 | 130.33 | 4.93 |
| 1983 | 168.11 | 166.21 | 14.66 | 145.12 | 9.86 |
| 1983 | 166.07 | 170.51 | 9.48 | 158.30 | 11.52 |
| 1983 | 164.93 | 169.45 | 4.21 | 168.36 | 10.79 |
| 1984 | 159.18 | 163.52 | -0.86 | 173.16 | 7.79 |
| 1984 | 153.18 | 156.03 | -4.18 | 172.62 | 3.63 |
| 1984 | 166.10 | 161.82 | 0.81 | 173.20 | 2.11 |
| 1984 | 167.24 | 165.86 | 2.42 | 172.89 | 0.90 |

The forecasts using the Holt-Winters model are:

Model 1

$F_{1985,I} = F_{t+1} = E_t + T_t = 165.86 + 2.42 = 168.28$

$F_{1985,II} = F_{t+2} = E_t + 2T_t = 165.86 + 2(2.42) = 170.70$

$F_{1985,III} = F_{t+3} = E_t + 3T_t = 165.86 + 3(2.42) = 173.12$

$F_{1985,IV} = F_{t+4} = E_t + 4T_t = 165.86 + 4(2.42) = 175.54$

Model 2

$F_{1985,I} = F_{t+1} = E_t + T_t + 172.89 + .90 = 173.79$

$F_{1985,II} = F_{t+2} = E_t + 2T_t = 172.89 + 2(.90) = 174.69$

$F_{1985,III} = F_{t+3} = E_t + 3T_t = 172.89 + 3(.90) = 175.59$

$F_{1985,IV} = F_{t+4} = E_t + 4T_t = 172.89 + 4(.90) = 176.49$

The forecast errors are:

| | Model 1 | Model 2 |
|---|---|---|
| 1985, I | 180.66 - 168.28 = 12.38 | 180.66 - 173.79 = 6.87 |
| 1985, II | 191.85 - 170.70 = 21.15 | 191.85 - 174.69 = 17.16 |
| 1985, III | 182.08 - 173.12 = 8.96 | 182.08 - 175.59 = 6.49 |
| 1985, IV | 211.28 - 175.54 = 35.74 | 211.28 - 176.49 = 34.79 |

16.7 a. We first compute the exponentially smoothed values $E_1, E_2, \ldots, E_t$ for 1980 - 1985.

For w = .3,

$E_1 = Y_1 = 105.36$
$E_2 = wY_2 + (1 - w)E_1 = .3(113.72) + (1 - .3)(105.36) = 107.868$
$E_3 = wY_3 + (1 - w)E_2 = .3(127.14) + (1 - .3)(107.868) = 113.6496$

The rest of the values appear in the table.

For w = .7,

$E_1 = Y = 105.36$
$E_2 = wY_2 = (1 - w)E_1 = .7(113.72 + (1 - .7)(105.36) = 111.212$
$E_3 = wY_3 + (1 - w)E_2 = .7(127.14) + (1 - .7)(111.212) = 122.3616$

The rest of the values appear in the table.

| YEAR | S&P 500 | EXPONENTIALLY SMOOTHED VALUE w = .3 | EXPONENTIALLY SMOOTHED VALUE w = .7 |
|---|---|---|---|
| 1980 | 105.36 | 105.36 | 105.36 |
| 1980 | 113.72 | 107.87 | 111.21 |
| 1980 | 127.14 | 113.65 | 122.36 |
| 1980 | 131.44 | 118.99 | 128.72 |
| 1981 | 134.94 | 123.77 | 133.07 |
| 1981 | 129.06 | 125.36 | 130.26 |
| 1981 | 118.77 | 123.38 | 122.22 |
| 1981 | 119.13 | 122.11 | 120.06 |
| 1982 | 117.09 | 120.60 | 117.98 |
| 1982 | 109.82 | 117.37 | 112.27 |
| 1982 | 121.79 | 118.69 | 118.93 |
| 1982 | 138.91 | 124.76 | 132.92 |
| 1983 | 152.96 | 133.22 | 146.95 |
| 1983 | 168.11 | 143.69 | 161.76 |
| 1983 | 166.07 | 150.40 | 164.78 |
| 1983 | 164.93 | 154.76 | 164.88 |
| 1984 | 159.18 | 156.09 | 160.89 |
| 1984 | 153.18 | 155.21 | 155.49 |
| 1984 | 166.10 | 158.48 | 162.92 |
| 1984 | 167.24 | 161.11 | 165.94 |
| 1985 | 180.66 | 166.97 | 176.25 |
| 1985 | 191.85 | 174.44 | 187.17 |
| 1985 | 182.08 | 176.73 | 183.61 |
| 1985 | 211.28 | 187.09 | 202.98 |

The forecasts for the 4 quarters of 1986 based on 1980 - 1985 data are:

$w = .3$, 

$F_{1986,I} = F_{t+1} = E_t = 187.09$

$F_{1986,II} = F_{t+2} = F_{t+1} = 187.09$

$F_{1986,III} = F_{t+3} = F_{t+1} = 187.09$

$F_{1986,IV} = F_{t+4} = F_{t+1} = 187.09$

$w = .7$,

$F_{t+1} = E_t = 202.98$

$F_{t+2} = F_{t+1} = 202.98$

$F_{t+3} = F_{t+1} = 202.98$

$F_{t+4} = F_{t+1} = 202.98$

b. We first compute the Holt-Winters values for the year 1980 - 1985.

With $w = .3$ and $v = .5$,

$$\begin{aligned} E_2 &= Y_2 = 113.72 \\ E_3 &= wY_3 + (1 - w)(E_2 + T_2) \\ &= .3(127.14) + (1 - .3)(113.72 + 8.36) \\ &= 123.598 \end{aligned}$$

$$T_2 = Y_2 - Y_1 = 113.72 - 105.36 = 8.36$$
$$T_3 = v(E_3 - E_2) + (1 - v)T_2$$
$$= .5(123.598 - 113.72) + (1 - .5)(8.36)$$
$$= 9.119$$

The rest of the $E_t$'s and $T_t$'s appear in the table.

With $w = .7$ and $v = .5$,

$$E_2 = Y_2 = 113.72$$
$$E_3 = .7(127.14) + (1 - .7)(113.72 + 8.36)$$
$$= 125.622$$

$$T_2 = Y_2 - Y_1 = 113.72 - 105.36 = 8.36$$
$$T_3 = .5(125.622 - 113.72) + (1 - .5)(8.36)$$
$$= 10.131$$

The rest of the $E_t$'s and $T_t$'s appear in the table.

| | | HOLT-WINTERS MODEL 1 | | HOLT-WINTERS MODEL 2 | |
|---|---|---|---|---|---|
| YEAR | S&P 500 | E(w = .3) | T(v = .5) | E(w = .7) | T(v = .5) |
| 1980 | 105.36 | | | | |
| 1980 | 113.72 | 113.72 | 8.36 | 113.72 | 8.36 |
| 1980 | 127.14 | 123.60 | 9.12 | 125.62 | 10.13 |
| 1980 | 131.44 | 132/33 | 8.93 | 132.73 | 8.62 |
| 1981 | 134.94 | 139.36 | 7.98 | 136.86 | 6.38 |
| 1981 | 129.06 | 141.86 | 5.24 | 133.31 | 1.41 |
| 1981 | 118.77 | 138.60 | 0.99 | 123.56 | -4.17 |
| 1981 | 119.13 | 133.45 | -2.08 | 119.21 | -4.26 |
| 1982 | 117.09 | 127.08 | -4.22 | 116.45 | -3.51 |
| 1982 | 109.82 | 118.95 | -6.18 | 110.75 | -4.60 |
| 1982 | 121.79 | 115.48 | -4.83 | 117.10 | 0.87 |
| 1982 | 138.91 | 119.13 | -0.59 | 132.63 | 8.20 |
| 1983 | 152.96 | 128.87 | 4.58 | 149.32 | 12.45 |
| 1983 | 168.11 | 143.84 | 9.78 | 166.21 | 14.67 |
| 1983 | 166.07 | 157.35 | 11.64 | 170.51 | 9.49 |
| 1983 | 164.93 | 167.78 | 11.03 | 169.45 | 4.21 |
| 1984 | 159.18 | 172.92 | 8.09 | 163.52 | -0.86 |
| 1984 | 153.18 | 172.66 | 3.91 | 156.03 | -4.18 |
| 1984 | 166.10 | 173.43 | 2.34 | 161.82 | 0.81 |
| 1984 | 167.24 | 173.21 | 1.06 | 165.86 | 2.42 |
| 1985 | 180.66 | 176.19 | 2.02 | 176.95 | 6.75 |
| 1985 | 191.85 | 182.30 | 4.07 | 189.41 | 9.61 |
| 1985 | 182.08 | 185.08 | 3.42 | 187.16 | 3.68 |
| 1985 | 211.28 | 195.34 | 6.84 | 205.15 | 10.83 |

The forecasts using the Holt-Winters model are:

Model 1

$$F_{1986,I} = F_{t+1} = E_t + T_t = 195.34 + 6.84 = 202.18$$

$$F_{1986,II} = F_{t+2} = E_t + 2T_t = 195.34 + 2(6.84) = 209.02$$

$$F_{1986,III} = F_{t+3} = E_t + 3T_t = 195.34 + 3(6.84) = 215.86$$

$$F_{1986,IV} = F_{t+4} = E_t + 4T_t = 195.34 + 4(6.84) = 222.70$$

Model 2

$$F_{1986,I} = F_{t+1} = E_t + T_t + 205.15 + 10.83 = 215.98$$

$$F_{1986,II} = F_{t+2} = E_t + 2T_t = 205.15 + 2(10.83) = 226.81$$

$$F_{1986,III} = F_{t+3} = E_t + 3T_t = 205.15 + 3(10.83) = 237.64$$

$$F_{1986,IV} = F_{t+4} = E_t + 4T_t = 205.15 + 4(10.38) = 248.47$$

c. Since we do not know the S&P 500 values for 1986, there is no way to know which set of forecasts is best. In Exercise 16.6, the MAD and RMSE were computed for all four models. The values of MAD and RMSE for the Holt-Winters model with w = .3 and v = .5 are the smallest. Thus, we would choose this model to forecast 1986 values.

16.9 a. Using just the 1979 - 1984 data, the forecasts using the exponentially smoothed model with w = .5 and the differences between the forecasts and the actual values, $F_t - Y_t$, are listed in the table:

| YEAR | MONTH | GOLD PRICE, $Y_t$ | FORECAST $F_t$ | DIFFERENCE $F_t - Y_t$ |
|---|---|---|---|---|
| 1985 | Jan | 302.7 | 331.3 | 28.6 |
| 1985 | Feb | 299.2 | 331.3 | 32.1 |
| 1985 | Mar | 304.4 | 331.3 | 26.9 |
| 1985 | Apr | 325.3 | 331.3 | 6.0 |
| 1985 | May | 316.5 | 331.3 | 14.8 |
| 1985 | June | 316.8 | 331.3 | 14.5 |
| 1985 | July | 318.2 | 331.3 | 13.1 |
| 1985 | Aug | 330.4 | 331.3 | 0.9 |
| 1985 | Sept | 322.9 | 331.3 | 8.4 |
| 1985 | Oct | 326.2 | 331.3 | 5.1 |
| 1985 | Nov | 325.7 | 331.3 | 5.6 |
| 1985 | Dec | 322.8 | 331.3 | 8.5 |

$$\text{MAD} = \frac{\sum|F_t - Y_t|}{N} = \frac{|28.6| + |32.1| + \ldots + |8.5|}{12} = \frac{164.5}{12}$$

$$= 13.708$$

$$\text{RMSE} = \sqrt{\frac{\sum(F_t - Y_t)^2}{N}} = \sqrt{\frac{(28.6)^2 + (32.1)^2 + \ldots + (8.5)^2}{12}}$$

$$= \sqrt{\frac{3409.87}{12}} = 16.857$$

Using just the 1979 - 1984 data, the forecasts using the Holt-Winters model with w = .5 and v = .5 and the differences between the forecasts and the actual values, $F_t - Y_t$, are listed in the table:

| YEAR | MONTH | GOLD PRICE, $Y_t$ | FORECAST $F_t$ | DIFFERENCE $F_t - Y_t$ |
|---|---|---|---|---|
| 1985 | Jan | 302.7 | 317.9 | 15.2 |
| 1985 | Feb | 299.2 | 310.9 | 11.7 |
| 1985 | Mar | 304.4 | 303.9 | -0.5 |
| 1985 | Apr | 325.3 | 296.9 | -28.4 |
| 1985 | May | 316.5 | 289.8 | -26.7 |
| 1985 | June | 316.8 | 282.8 | -34.0 |
| 1985 | July | 318.2 | 275.8 | -42.4 |
| 1985 | Aug | 330.4 | 268.8 | -61.6 |
| 1985 | Sept | 322.9 | 261.8 | -61.1 |
| 1985 | Oct | 326.2 | 254.7 | -71.5 |
| 1985 | Nov | 325.7 | 247.7 | -78.0 |
| 1985 | Dec | 322.8 | 240.7 | -82.1 |

$$\text{MAD} = \frac{\sum|F_t - Y_t|}{N} = \frac{|15.2| + |11.7| + \ldots + |-82.1|}{12} = \frac{513.2}{12}$$

$$= 42.767$$

$$\text{RMSE} = \sqrt{\frac{\sum(F_t - Y_t)^2}{N}} = \sqrt{\frac{15.2^2 + 11.7^2 + \ldots + (-82.1)^2}{12}}$$

$$= \sqrt{\frac{30305.82}{12}} = 50.254$$

Using both the MAD and RMSE, forecasts based on the exponentially smoothed model appear to be better than those based on the Holt-Winters model. The MAD and RMSE for the exponentially smoothed forecasts are less than those for the Holt-Winters forecasts.

b. The one-step ahead forecasts based on the exponentially smoothed model with w = .5 and the differences between the forecasts and the actual values, $F_t - Y_t$, are listed in the table.

| YEAR | MONTH | GOLD PRICE, $Y_t$ | FORECAST $F_t$ | DIFFERENCE $F_t - Y_t$ |
|---|---|---|---|---|
| 1985 | Jan | 302.7 | 331.3 | 28.6 |
| 1985 | Feb | 299.2 | 317.0 | 17.8 |
| 1985 | Mar | 304.4 | 308.1 | 3.7 |
| 1985 | Apr | 325.3 | 306.2 | -19.1 |
| 1985 | May | 316.5 | 315.8 | -0.7 |
| 1985 | June | 316.8 | 316.1 | -0.7 |
| 1985 | July | 318.2 | 316.5 | -1.7 |
| 1985 | Aug | 330.4 | 317.3 | -13.1 |
| 1985 | Sept | 322.9 | 323.9 | 1.0 |
| 1985 | Oct | 326.2 | 323.4 | -2.8 |
| 1985 | Nov | 325.7 | 324.8 | -0.9 |
| 1985 | Dec | 322.8 | 325.2 | 2.4 |

$$\text{MAD} = \frac{\sum|F_t - Y_t|}{N} = \frac{|28.6| + |17.8| + \ldots + |2.4|}{12} = \frac{92.5}{12}$$

$$= 7.708$$

$$\text{RMSE} = \sqrt{\frac{\sum(F_t - Y_t)^2}{N}} = \sqrt{\frac{(28.6)^2 + (17.8)^2 + \ldots + (2.4)^2}{12}}$$

$$= \sqrt{\frac{1704.19}{12}} = 11.917$$

The one-step ahead forecasts based on the Holt-Winters model with w = .5 and v = .5 and the differences between the forecasts and the actual values, $F_t - Y_t$ are listed in the table:

| YEAR | MONTH | GOLD PRICE, $Y_t$ | FORECAST $F_t$ | DIFFERENCE $F_t - Y_t$ |
|---|---|---|---|---|
| 1985 | Jan | 302.7 | 317.9 | 15.2 |
| 1985 | Feb | 299.2 | 299.5 | 0.3 |
| 1985 | Mar | 304.4 | 288.4 | -16.0 |
| 1985 | Apr | 325.3 | 289.5 | -35.8 |
| 1985 | May | 316.5 | 309.4 | -7.1 |
| 1985 | June | 316.8 | 316.8 | .0 |
| 1985 | July | 318.2 | 320.6 | 2.4 |
| 1985 | Aug | 330.4 | 322.6 | -7.8 |
| 1985 | Sept | 322.9 | 331.7 | 8.8 |
| 1985 | Oct | 326.2 | 330.2 | 4.0 |
| 1985 | Nov | 325.7 | 330.2 | 4.5 |
| 1985 | Dec | 322.8 | 328.8 | 6.0 |

$$\text{MAD} = \frac{\sum|F_t - Y_t|}{N} = \frac{|15.2| + |.3| + \ldots + |6.0|}{12} = \frac{107.9}{12}$$

$$= 8.992$$

$$\text{RMSE} = \sqrt{\frac{\sum(F_t - Y_t)^2}{N}} = \sqrt{\frac{(15.2)^2 + (.3)^2 + \ldots + (6.0)^2}{12}}$$

$$= \sqrt{\frac{2035.47}{12}} = 13.024$$

Again, using both MAD and RMSE, the forecasts based on the exponentially smoothed model appear to be better than those based on the Holt-Winters model. The MAD and RMSE for the exponentially smoothed forecasts are less than those for the Holt-Winters forecasts.

16.11 a. The estimates of the parameters in the model, $E(Y_t) = \beta_0 + \beta_1 t$, are

$\hat{\beta}_0 = 6.609231$ and $\hat{\beta}_1 = 1.704198$.

b. The forecast for 1985 is:

Using $t = 15$, $\hat{Y}_{1985} = 6.609231 + 1.704198(15) = 32.1723$

The forecast for 1986 is:

Using $t = 16$, $\hat{Y}_{1986} = 6.609231 + 1.704198(16) = 33.8764$

c. From the printout, the 95% forecast intervals are:

1985 (30.0704, 34.2740)
1986 (31.7193, 36.0335)

16.13 a. The SAS printout for this problem is:

DEP VARIABLE: Y
ANALYSIS OF VARIANCE

| SOURCE | DF | SUM OF SQUARES | MEAN SQUARE | F VALUE | PROB>F |
|---|---|---|---|---|---|
| MODEL | 1 | 167208.30 | 167208.30 | 217.274 | 0.0001 |
| ERROR | 23 | 17700.17827 | 769.57297 | | |
| C TOTAL | 24 | 184908.48 | | | |

| | | | |
|---|---|---|---|
| ROOT MSE | 27.74118 | R-SQUARE | 0.9043 |
| DEP MEAN | 133.38 | ADJ R-SQ | 0.9001 |
| C.V. | 20.7986 | | |

PARAMETER ESTIMATES

| VARIABLE | DF | PARAMETER ESTIMATE | STANDARD ERROR | T FOR HO: PARAMETER =0 | PROB > \|T\| |
|---|---|---|---|---|---|
| INTERCEP | 1 | -2.71384615 | 10.77162590 | -0.252 | 0.8033 |
| T | 1 | 11.34115385 | 0.76940185 | 14.740 | 0.0001 |

| OBS | ACTUAL | PREDICT VALUE | STD ERR PREDICT | LOWER95% PREDICT | UPPER95% PREDICT | RESIDUAL |
|---|---|---|---|---|---|---|
| 1 | 42.4000 | -2.7138 | 10.7716 | -64.2746 | 58.8469 | 45.1138 |
| 2 | 44.8000 | 8.6273 | 10.1199 | -52.4584 | 69.7130 | 36.1727 |
| 3 | 47.4000 | 19.9685 | 9.4858 | -40.6803 | 80.6172 | 27.4315 |
| 4 | 49.5000 | 31.3096 | 8.8732 | -28.9410 | 91.5602 | 18.1904 |
| 5 | 54.3000 | 42.6508 | 8.2867 | -17.2414 | 102.5 | 11.6492 |
| 6 | 58.4000 | 53.9919 | 7.7324 | -5.5822 | 113.6 | 4.4081 |
| 7 | 60.4000 | 65.3331 | 7.2176 | 6.0360 | 124.6 | -4.9331 |
| 8 | 63.3000 | 76.6742 | 6.7515 | 17.6126 | 135.7 | -13.3742 |
| 9 | 69.3000 | 88.0154 | 6.3447 | 29.1471 | 146.9 | -18.7154 |
| 10 | 75.7000 | 99.3565 | 6.0092 | 40.6391 | 158.1 | -23.6565 |
| 11 | 80.6000 | 110.7 | 5.7577 | 52.0882 | 169.3 | -30.0977 |
| 12 | 92.3000 | 122.0 | 5.6013 | 63.4942 | 180.6 | -29.7388 |
| 13 | 105.4 | 133.4 | 5.5482 | 74.8570 | 191.9 | -27.9800 |
| 14 | 114.6 | 144.7 | 5.6013 | 86.1765 | 203.3 | -30.1212 |
| 15 | 117.9 | 156.1 | 5.7577 | 97.4528 | 214.7 | -38.1623 |
| 16 | 129.4 | 167.4 | 6.0092 | 108.7 | 226.1 | -38.0035 |
| 17 | 155.2 | 178.7 | 6.3447 | 119.9 | 237.6 | -23.5446 |
| 18 | 179.3 | 190.1 | 6.7515 | 131.0 | 249.1 | -10.7858 |
| 19 | 198.1 | 201.4 | 7.2176 | 142.1 | 260.7 | -3.3269 |
| 20 | 219.4 | 212.8 | 7.7324 | 153.2 | 272.3 | 6.6319 |
| 21 | 236.6 | 224.1 | 8.2867 | 164.2 | 284.0 | 12.4908 |
| 22 | 261.5 | 235.5 | 8.8732 | 175.2 | 295.7 | 26.0496 |
| 23 | 267.3 | 246.8 | 9.4858 | 186.1 | 307.4 | 20.5085 |
| 24 | 291.9 | 258.1 | 10.1199 | 197.0 | 319.2 | 33.7673 |
| 25 | 319.5 | 269.5 | 10.7716 | 207.9 | 331.0 | 50.0262 |
| 26 | . | 280.8 | 11.4380 | 218.7 | 342.9 | . |
| 27 | . | 292.2 | 12.1166 | 229.5 | 354.8 | . |
| 28 | . | 303.5 | 12.8054 | 240.3 | 366.7 | . |

The fitted model is $\hat{Y}_t = -2.7138 + 11.3412t$

b. The forecasts for 1985 to 1987 are:

1985 $\hat{Y}_{1985} = -2.7138 + 11.3412(25) = 280.8162$

1986 $\hat{Y}_{1986} = -2.7138 + 11.3412(26) = 292.1574$

1987 $\hat{Y}_{1987} = -2.7138 + 11.3412(27) = 303.4986$

The formula for the prediction interval is:

$$\hat{Y}_t \pm t_{\alpha/2} \sqrt{MSE\left[1 + \frac{1}{n} + \frac{(t - \bar{t})^2}{SS_{tt}}\right]}$$

where $\bar{t} = \frac{0 + 1 + 2 + \ldots + 24}{25} = \frac{300}{25} = 12$,

$$SS_{tt} = \sum t^2 - \frac{(\sum t)^2}{n} = 4900 - \frac{300^2}{25} = 1300$$

For confidence coefficient .95, $\alpha = 1 - .95 = 05$ and $\alpha/2 = .05/2 = .025$. From Table VI, Appendix B, $t_{.025} = 2.069$ with df $= n - 2 = 25 - 2 = 23$.

The prediction intervals are:

1985 $280.8162 \pm 2.069 \sqrt{769.57297\left[1 + \frac{1}{25} + \frac{(25 - 12)^2}{1300}\right]}$

$\Rightarrow 280.8162 \pm 62.0838 \Rightarrow (218.7324, 342.9000)$

1986 $292.1574 \pm 2.069 \sqrt{769.57297\left[1 + \frac{1}{25} + \frac{(26 - 12)^2}{1300}\right]}$

$\Rightarrow 292.1574 \pm 62.6324 \Rightarrow (229.5250, 354.7898)$

1987 $303.4986 \pm 2.069 \sqrt{769.57297\left[1 + \frac{1}{25} + \frac{(27 - 12)^2}{1300}\right]}$

$\Rightarrow 303.4986 \pm 63.2164 \Rightarrow (240.2822, 366.7150)$

16.15 a. The SAS printout for this problem is shown on the following page:

DEP VARIABLE: Y
ANALYSIS OF VARIANCE

| SOURCE | DF | SUM OF SQUARES | MEAN SQUARE | F VALUE | PROB>F |
|---|---|---|---|---|---|
| MODEL | 1 | 1454425898 | 1454425898 | 2206.066 | 0.0001 |
| ERROR | 13 | 8570702.51 | 659284.81 | | |
| C TOTAL | 14 | 1462996600 | | | |

| | | | |
|---|---|---|---|
| ROOT MSE | 811.9636 | R-SQUARE | 0.9941 |
| DEP MEAN | 100569.8 | ADJ R-SQ | 0.9937 |
| C.V. | 0.8073632 | | |

PARAMETER ESTIMATES

| VARIABLE | DF | PARAMETER ESTIMATE | STANDARD ERROR | T FOR HO: PARAMETER =0 | PROB > \|T\| |
|---|---|---|---|---|---|
| INTERCEP | 1 | 82336.85714 | 441.18703 | 186.626 | 0.0001 |
| T | 1 | 2279.11786 | 48.52410331 | 46.969 | 0.0001 |

| OBS | ACTUAL | PREDICT VALUE | STD ERR PREDICT | LOWER95% PREDICT | UPPER95% PREDICT | RESIDUAL |
|---|---|---|---|---|---|---|
| 1 | 84889.0 | 84616.0 | 399.2 | 82661.3 | 86570.6 | 273.0 |
| 2 | 86355.0 | 86895.1 | 358.8 | 84977.3 | 88812.8 | -540.1 |
| 3 | 88847.0 | 89174.2 | 320.7 | 87288.2 | 91060.2 | -327.2 |
| 4 | 91203.0 | 91453.3 | 285.7 | 89593.8 | 93312.9 | -250.3 |
| 5 | 93670.0 | 93732.4 | 255.2 | 91893.7 | 95571.2 | -62.4464 |
| 6 | 95453.0 | 96011.6 | 231.0 | 94187.8 | 97835.3 | -558.6 |
| 7 | 97826.0 | 98290.7 | 215.2 | 96476.0 | 100105 | -464.7 |
| 8 | 100665 | 100570 | 209.6 | 98758.1 | 102381 | 95.2000 |
| 9 | 103882 | 102849 | 215.2 | 101034 | 104664 | 1033.1 |
| 10 | 106559 | 105128 | 231.0 | 103304 | 106952 | 1431.0 |
| 11 | 108544 | 107407 | 255.2 | 105568 | 109246 | 1136.8 |
| 12 | 110315 | 109686 | 285.7 | 107827 | 111546 | 628.7 |
| 13 | 111872 | 111965 | 320.7 | 110079 | 113851 | -93.3893 |
| 14 | 113226 | 114245 | 358.8 | 112327 | 116162 | -1018.5 |
| 15 | 115241 | 116524 | 399.2 | 114569 | 118478 | -1282.6 |
| 16 | . | 118803 | 441.2 | 116806 | 120799 | . |
| 17 | . | 121082 | 484.4 | 119039 | 123124 | . |

The fitted regression model is $\hat{Y}_t = 82336.9 + 2279.1t$

b. The forecasts for 1985 and 1986 are:

$$\hat{Y}_{1985} = 82336.9 + 2279.1(16) = 118802.5$$

$$\hat{Y}_{1986} = 82336.9 + 2279.1(17) = 121081.6$$

c. The formula for the prediction interval is:

$$\hat{Y}_t \pm t_{\alpha/2}\sqrt{MSE\left[1 + \frac{1}{n} + \frac{(t - \bar{t})^2}{SS_{tt}}\right]}$$

where $\bar{t} = \dfrac{1 + 2 + \ldots + 15}{15} = 8,$

$$SS_{tt} = \sum t^2 - \frac{(\sum t)^2}{n} = 1240 - \frac{120^2}{15} = 280$$

For confidence coefficient .95, $\alpha = 1 - .95 = .05$ and $\alpha/2 = .05/2 = .025$. From Table VI, Appendix B, $t_{.025} = 2.160$ with $df = n - 2 = 15 - 2 = 13$.

The prediction intervals are:

1985 $\quad 118802.5 \pm 2.160 \sqrt{659284.81\left(1 + \frac{1}{15} + \frac{(16 - 8)^2}{280}\right)}$

$\Rightarrow 118802.5 \pm 1996.02 \Rightarrow (116806.48,\ 120798.52)$

1986 $\quad 121081.6 \pm 2.160 \sqrt{659284.81\left(1 + \frac{1}{15} + \frac{(17 - 8)^2}{280}\right)}$

$\Rightarrow 121081.6 \pm 2042.27 \Rightarrow (119039.3,\ 123123.87)$

16.17 a. $d = 3.9$ indicates the residuals are very strongly negatively autocorrelated.

b. $d = .2$ indicates the residuals are very strongly positively autocorrelated.

c. $d = 1.99$ indicates the residuals are probably uncorrelated.

16.19 a. The fitted model is $\hat{Y}_t = 1.1495 - .04195t$

The residuals are calculated using $\hat{R}_t = Y_t - \hat{Y}_t$, and appear in the table:

| | ACTUAL | PREDICT VALUE | RESIDUAL |
|---|---|---|---|
| 1 | 1.0760 | 1.1076 | -0.0316 |
| 2 | 1.0580 | 1.0656 | -0.0076 |
| 3 | 1.0290 | 1.0237 | 0.0053 |
| 4 | 1.0000 | 0.9817 | 0.0183 |
| 5 | 0.9600 | 0.9398 | 0.0202 |
| 6 | 0.9110 | 0.8978 | 0.0132 |
| 7 | 0.8600 | 0.8559 | 0.0041 |
| 8 | 0.8240 | 0.8139 | 0.0101 |
| 9 | 0.7990 | 0.7720 | 0.0270 |
| 10 | 0.7510 | 0.7300 | 0.0210 |
| 11 | 0.6770 | 0.6880 | -0.0110 |
| 12 | 0.6200 | 0.6461 | -0.0261 |
| 13 | 0.5870 | 0.6041 | -0.0171 |
| 14 | 0.5510 | 0.5622 | -0.0112 |
| 15 | 0.5120 | 0.5202 | -0.0082 |
| 16 | 0.4600 | 0.4783 | -0.0183 |
| 17 | 0.4050 | 0.4363 | -0.0313 |
| 18 | 0.3670 | 0.3944 | -0.0274 |
| 19 | 0.3460 | 0.3524 | -0.0064 |
| 20 | 0.3350 | 0.3105 | 0.0245 |
| 21 | 0.3210 | 0.2685 | 0.0525 |

The plot of the residuals versus time is:

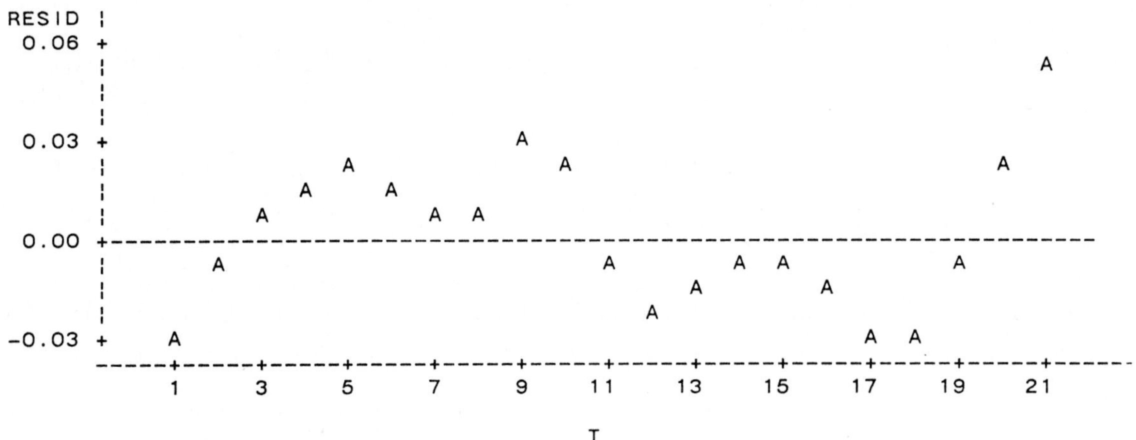


There is a tendency for the residuals to have long positive runs and negative runs. Residuals 3 through 10 are positive, while residuals 11 through 19 are negative. This indicates the error terms are correlated.

b. $d = \dfrac{\sum_{t=2}^{n} (\hat{R}_t - \hat{R}_{t-1})^2}{\sum_{t=1}^{n} \hat{R}_t^2}$ where $\hat{R}_t$ = residual for time t

$$= \frac{(-.0076-(-.0316))^2+(.0053-(-.0076))^2+(.0183-.0053)^2+\ldots+(.0525-.0245)^2}{(-.0316)^2 + (-.0076)^2 + (.0053)^2 + \ldots + (.0525)^2}$$

$$= \frac{.00525}{.01004} = .523$$

To determine if the time series residuals are autocorrelated, we test:

$H_0$: No first-order autocorrelation of residuals
$H_a$: Positive or negative first-order autocorrelation of residuals

The test statistics is d = .523.

For $\alpha = .10$, the rejection region is $d < d_{L,\alpha/2} = d_{L,.05} = 1.22$ or $(4 - d) < d_{L,.05} = 1.22$. The value $d_{L,.05}$ is found in Table XIV, Appendix B, with k = 1, n = 21, and $\alpha = .10$.

Since the observed value of the test statistic falls in the rejection region ($d = .523 < 1.22$), $H_0$ is rejected. There is sufficient evidence to indicate the time series residuals are autocorrelated at $\alpha = .10$.

16.21 The regression-autoregression pair of models if only a secular trend were being postulated are:

$$Y_t = \beta_0 + \beta_1 t + R_t$$

$$R_t = \phi R_{t-1} + \varepsilon_t$$

where $\phi$ is the first-order autocorrelation between residuals $R_t$ and $R_{t-1}$, $\beta_0$ is the value of the time series at time 0, and $\beta_1$ is the slope of the line for the secular trend.

16.23 First note that the coefficient estimates change from $\hat{\beta}_0 = 753.4038$ and $\hat{\beta}_1 = 10.4287$ to $\hat{\beta}_0 = 743.4372$ and $\hat{\beta}_1 = 11.5297$ when the autoregressive model is added. The mean increase in the Dow Jones Industrial Average is estimated to be 11.5297 (as compared to 10.4287). The estimate of the standard deviation ($\sqrt{MSE}$) changes from 105.0354 to 102.0986. We expect the prediction error associated with the pair of models to be approximately $\pm 2(102.986) \Rightarrow \pm 205.972$. This represents a reduction of about

$$\frac{2(105.0354) - 205.972}{2(105.0354)} = \frac{4.0988}{210.0708} = .0195$$

or 1.95% when compared with the error associated with the regression model. Because this is a very small reduction, it appears the regression model by itself is adequate.

16.25 The approximate 95% forecast bounds for 1984 - 1986 are:

1984 $\hat{Y}_{24} \pm 2\sqrt{MSE} \Rightarrow 1082.18 \pm 2(102.986) \Rightarrow 1082.18 \pm 205.972$
$\Rightarrow (876.208, 1288.152)$

This interval contains the actual value of 1211.57.

1985 $\hat{Y}_{25} \pm 2\sqrt{MSE(1 + \hat{\phi}^2)} \Rightarrow 1047.06 \pm 2(102.986)\sqrt{1 + .248^2}$
$\Rightarrow 1047.06 \pm 212.212$
$\Rightarrow (834.848, 1259.272)$

This interval does not contain the actual value of 1546.67.

1986 $\hat{Y}_{26} \pm 2\sqrt{MSE(1 + \hat{\phi}^2 + \hat{\phi}^4)} \Rightarrow 1047.02 \pm 2(102.986)\sqrt{1 + .248^2 + .248^4}$
$\Rightarrow 1047.02 \pm 212.589$
$\Rightarrow (834.431, 1259.609)$

This interval does not contain the actual value of 1895.95.

16.27. a. We first compute the exponentially smoothed values for the years 1974 - 1984 for both series.

For the agricultural data with w = .5,

$$E_1 = Y_1 = 3515$$
$$E_2 = .5Y_2 + (1 - .5)E_1 = .5(3408) + .5(3515) = 3461.5$$
$$E_3 = .5Y_3 + (1 - .5)E_2 = .5(3331) + .5(3461.5) = 3396.25$$

The rest of the values appear in the table.

Similarly, we compute the values for the nonagricultural data:

$$E_1 = Y_1 = 83{,}279$$
$$E_2 = .5Y_2 + (1 - .5)E_1 = .5(82{,}438) + .5(83{,}279) = 82{,}858.5$$
$$E_3 = .5Y_3 + (1 - .5)E_2 = .5(85{,}421) + .5(82{,}858.5) = 84{,}139.75$$

| YEAR | AGRICULTURAL | EXPONENTIALLY SMOOTHED VALUES (w=.5) | NON-AGRICULTURAL | EXPONENTIALLY SMOOTHED VALUES (w=.5) |
|---|---|---|---|---|
| 1974 | 3515 | 3515.0 | 83279 | 83279.0 |
| 1975 | 3408 | 3461.5 | 82438 | 82858.5 |
| 1976 | 3331 | 3396.3 | 85421 | 84139.8 |
| 1977 | 3283 | 3339.6 | 88734 | 86436.9 |
| 1978 | 3387 | 3363.3 | 92661 | 89548.9 |
| 1979 | 3347 | 3355.2 | 95477 | 92513.0 |
| 1980 | 3364 | 3359.6 | 95938 | 94225.5 |
| 1981 | 3368 | 3363.8 | 97030 | 95627.7 |
| 1982 | 3401 | 3382.4 | 96125 | 95876.4 |
| 1983 | 3383 | 3382.7 | 97450 | 96663.2 |
| 1984 | 3321 | 3351.8 | 101685 | 99174.1 |

The forecasts for 1985 are:

Agricultural $F_{1985} = F_{t+1} = E_t = 3351.8$

Nonagricultural $F_{1985} = F_{t+1} = E_t = 99174.1$

b. We first compute the Holt-Winters values for years 1974 - 1984.

For the agricultural data with w = .5 and v = .5,

$$E_2 = Y_2 = 3408$$
$$E_3 = .5Y_3 + (1 - .5)(E_2 + T_2)$$
$$= .5(3331) + .5(3408 - 107)$$
$$= 3316$$

$$T_2 = Y_2 - Y_1 = 3408 - 3515 = -107$$
$$T_3 = .5(E_3 - E_2) + (1 - .5)(T_2)$$
$$= .5(3316 - 3408) + .5(-107)$$
$$= -99.5$$

The rest of the values appear in the table.

For the nonagricultural data with w = .5 and v = .5,

$$E_2 = Y_2 = 82,438$$
$$E_3 = .5Y_3 + (1 - .5)(E_2 + T_2)$$
$$= .5(85,421) + .5(85,438 - 841)$$
$$= 83509$$

$$T_2 = Y_2 - Y_1 = 82,438 - 83,279 = -841$$
$$T_3 = .5(E_3 - E_2) + (1 - .5)T_2$$
$$= .5(83509 - 82438) + .5(-841)$$
$$= 115$$

The rest of the values appear in the table.

| YEAR | AGRICULTURAL | $E_t$ w=.5 v=.5 | $T_t$ w=.5 v=.5 | NON AGRICULTURAL | $E_t$ w=.5 v=.5 | $T_t$ w=.5 v=.5 |
|---|---|---|---|---|---|---|
| 1974 | 3515 | | | 83279 | | |
| 1975 | 3408 | 3408.0 | -107.0 | 82438 | 82438.0 | -841.0 |
| 1976 | 3331 | 3316.0 | -99.5 | 85421 | 83509.0 | 115.0 |
| 1977 | 3283 | 3249.8 | -82.9 | 88734 | 86179.0 | 1392.5 |
| 1978 | 3387 | 3276.9 | -27.8 | 92661 | 90116.3 | 2664.9 |
| 1979 | 3347 | 3298.0 | -3.4 | 95477 | 94129.1 | 3338.8 |
| 1980 | 3364 | 3329.3 | 14.0 | 95938 | 96703.0 | 2956.4 |
| 1981 | 3368 | 3355.7 | 20.1 | 97030 | 98344.7 | 2299.0 |
| 1982 | 3401 | 3388.4 | 26.4 | 96125 | 98384.3 | 1169.4 |
| 1983 | 3383 | 3398.9 | 18.5 | 97450 | 98501.9 | 643.4 |
| 1984 | 3321 | 3369.2 | -5.6 | 101685 | 100415.1 | 1278.4 |

The forecasts for 1985 are:

Agricultural $F_{1985} = F_{t+1} = E_t + T_t = 3369.2 - 5.6 = 3363.6$

Nonagricultural $F_{1985} = F_{t+1} = E_t + T_t = 100415.1 + 1278.4$
$= 101693.5$

16.29 a. We first calculate the exponentially smoothed values for 1973 -1986.

$$E_1 = Y_1 = 49.875$$
$$E_2 = .8Y_1 + (1 - .8)E_1 = .8(50.750) + .2(49.875) = 50.575$$
$$E_3 = .8Y_2 + (1 - .8)E_2 = .8(41.250) + .2(50.575) = 43.115$$

The rest of the values appear in the table.

| YEAR | CLOSING PRICE | EXPONENTIALLY SMOOTHED VALUE (w=.8) |
|---|---|---|
| 1973 | 49.875 | 49.875 |
| 1974 | 50.750 | 50.575 |
| 1975 | 41.250 | 43.115 |
| 1976 | 49.125 | 47.923 |
| 1977 | 56.500 | 54.785 |
| 1978 | 33.750 | 37.957 |
| 1979 | 41.125 | 40.491 |
| 1980 | 56.500 | 53.298 |
| 1981 | 27.000 | 32.260 |
| 1982 | 38.750 | 37.452 |
| 1983 | 45.250 | 43.690 |
| 1984 | 41.750 | 42.138 |
| 1985 | 68.375 | 63.128 |
| 1986 | 45.625 | 49.126 |

The forecasts for 1987 and 1988 are:

$$F_{1987} = F_{t+1} = E_t = 49.126$$

$$F_{1988} = F_{t+2} = F_{t+1} = 49.126$$

The expected gain is $F_{1988} - Y_{1986} = 49.126 - 45.625 = 3.501$

b. We first calculate the Holt-Winters values for 1973 - 1986.

For w = .8 and v = .5,

$$E_2 = Y_2 = 50.750$$
$$E_3 = .8Y_3 + (1 - .8)(E_2 + T_2)$$
$$= .8(41.25) + .2(50.750 + .875)$$
$$= 43.325$$

$$T_2 = Y_2 - Y_1 = 50.750 - 49.875 = .875$$
$$T_3 = .5(E_3 - E_2) + (1 - .5)(T_2)$$
$$= .5(43.325 - 50.750) + .5(.875)$$
$$= -3.275$$

The rest of the values appear in the table.

| YEAR | CLOSING PRICE | $E_t$ w=.8 v=.5 | $T_t$ w=.8 v=.5 |
|---|---|---|---|
| 1973 | 49.875 | | |
| 1974 | 50.750 | 50.750 | 0.875 |
| 1975 | 41.250 | 43.325 | -3.275 |
| 1976 | 49.125 | 47.310 | 0.355 |
| 1977 | 56.500 | 54.733 | 3.889 |
| 1978 | 33.750 | 38.724 | -6.060 |
| 1979 | 41.125 | 39.433 | -2.676 |
| 1980 | 56.500 | 52.551 | 5.221 |
| 1981 | 27.000 | 33.155 | -7.088 |
| 1982 | 38.750 | 36.213 | -2.014 |
| 1983 | 45.250 | 43.040 | 2.406 |
| 1984 | 41.750 | 42.489 | 0.928 |
| 1985 | 68.375 | 63.383 | 10.911 |
| 1986 | 45.625 | 51.359 | -0.557 |

The forecasts for 1987 and 1988 are:

$$F_{1987} = F_{t+1} = E_t + T_t = 51.359 - .557 = 50.802$$

$$F_{1988} = F_{t+2} = E_t + 2T_t = 51.359 + 2(-.557) = 50.245$$

The expected gain is $F_{1988} - Y_{1986} = 50.245 - 45.625 = 4.62$

16.31 The fitted regression model is

$$\hat{Y} = 45.7473 + .0492t$$

The residuals are:

| | ACTUAL | PREDICT VALUE | RESIDUAL |
|---|---|---|---|
| 1 | 49.8750 | 45.7964 | 4.0786 |
| 2 | 50.7500 | 45.8456 | 4.9044 |
| 3 | 41.2500 | 45.8948 | -4.6448 |
| 4 | 49.1250 | 45.9440 | 3.1810 |
| 5 | 56.5000 | 45.9931 | 10.5069 |
| 6 | 33.7500 | 46.0423 | -12.2923 |
| 7 | 41.1250 | 46.0915 | -4.9665 |
| 8 | 56.5000 | 46.1407 | 10.3593 |
| 9 | 27.0000 | 46.1898 | -19.1898 |
| 10 | 38.7500 | 46.2390 | -7.4890 |
| 11 | 45.2500 | 46.2882 | -1.0382 |
| 12 | 41.7500 | 46.3374 | -4.5874 |
| 13 | 68.3750 | 46.3865 | 21.9885 |
| 14 | 45.6250 | 46.4357 | -0.8107 |

The Durbin-Watson statistic is

$$d = \frac{\sum_{t=2}^{n} (\hat{R}_t - \hat{R}_{t-1})^2}{\sum \hat{R}_t^2}$$

$$= \frac{(4.9044 - 4.0786)^2 + (-4.6448 - 4.9044)^2 + \ldots + (-.8107 - 21.9855)^2}{4.0786^2 + 4.9044^2 + \ldots + (-.8107)^2}$$

$$= \frac{3305.482}{1396.469} = 2.367$$

To determine if the time series residuals are autocorrelated, we test:

$H_0$: No first-order autocorrelation of residuals
$H_a$: Positive or negative first-order autocorrelation of residuals

The test statistic is $d = 2.367$.

For $\alpha = .10$, the rejection region is $d < d_{L,\alpha/2} = d_{L,.05} \approx 1.08$ or $(4 - d) < d_{L,.05} \approx 1.08$. The value $d_{L,.05}$ is found in Table XIV, Appendix B, with $k = 1$, $n = 14$ and $\alpha = .10$. Since $n = 14$ is not in the table, we will use $n = 15$.

Since the observed value of the test statistic does not fall in the rejection region ($d = 2.367 \nless 1.08$ and $4 - d = 4 - 2.367 = 1.633 \nless 1.08$), $H_0$ is not rejected. There is insufficient evidence to indicate positive or negative first-order autocorrelation of the residuals at $\alpha = .10$.

16.33 a. The following model is fit: $E(Y_t) = \beta_0 + \beta_1 t$. The SAS output is:

```
DEP VARIABLE: Y
ANALYSIS OF VARIANCE

                       SUM OF          MEAN
SOURCE      DF        SQUARES        SQUARE       F VALUE         PROB>F

MODEL        1    48772947.24   48772947.24      2609.096         0.0001
ERROR       58     1084219.00   18693.43101
C TOTAL     59    49857166.24

    ROOT MSE        136.7239      R-SQUARE         0.9783
    DEP MEAN        2294.763      ADJ R-SQ         0.9779
    C.V.            5.958084

PARAMETER ESTIMATES

                        PARAMETER          STANDARD       T FOR HO:
VARIABLE   DF            ESTIMATE             ERROR    PARAMETER =0    PROB > |T|

INTERCEP    1           706.89893       35.74790225          19.775        0.0001
T           1         52.06112809        1.01922152          51.079        0.0001
```

| OBS | ACTUAL | PREDICT VALUE | STD ERR PREDICT | LOWER95% PREDICT | UPPER95% PREDICT | RESIDUAL |
|---|---|---|---|---|---|---|
| 1 | 1049.3 | 759.0 | 34.8652 | 476.5 | 1041.4 | 290.3 |
| 2 | 1068.9 | 811.0 | 33.9902 | 529.0 | 1093.0 | 257.9 |
| 3 | 1086.6 | 863.1 | 33.1234 | 581.5 | 1144.7 | 223.5 |
| 4 | 1105.8 | 915.1 | 32.2655 | 633.9 | 1196.3 | 190.7 |
| 5 | 1142.4 | 967.2 | 31.4173 | 686.4 | 1248.0 | 175.2 |
| 6 | 1171.7 | 1019.3 | 30.5795 | 738.8 | 1299.7 | 152.4 |
| . | . | . | . | . | . | . |
| . | . | . | . | . | . | . |
| . | . | . | . | . | . | . |
| 49 | 3171.5 | 3257.9 | 25.8281 | 2979.4 | 3536.4 | -86.3942 |
| 50 | 3272.0 | 3310.0 | 26.5813 | 3031.1 | 3588.8 | -37.9553 |
| 51 | 3362.2 | 3362.0 | 27.3517 | 3082.9 | 3641.1 | 0.1835 |
| 52 | 3436.2 | 3414.1 | 28.1380 | 3134.7 | 3693.5 | 22.1224 |
| 53 | 3553.3 | 3466.1 | 28.9388 | 3186.4 | 3745.9 | 87.1613 |
| 54 | 3644.7 | 3518.2 | 29.7530 | 3238.1 | 3798.3 | 126.5 |
| 55 | 3694.6 | 3570.3 | 30.5795 | 3289.8 | 3850.7 | 124.3 |
| 56 | 3758.7 | 3622.3 | 31.4173 | 3341.5 | 3903.1 | 136.4 |
| 57 | 3909.3 | 3674.4 | 32.2655 | 3393.2 | 3955.6 | 234.9 |
| 58 | 3965.0 | 3726.4 | 33.1234 | 3444.8 | 4008.0 | 238.6 |
| 59 | 4030.5 | 3778.5 | 33.9902 | 3496.5 | 4060.5 | 252.0 |
| 60 | 4087.7 | 3830.6 | 34.8652 | 3548.1 | 4113.0 | 257.1 |
| 61 | . | 3882.6 | 35.7479 | 3599.7 | 4165.5 | . |
| 62 | . | 3934.7 | 36.6377 | 3651.4 | 4218.0 | . |
| 63 | . | 3986.7 | 37.5340 | 3702.9 | 4270.6 | . |
| 64 | . | 4038.8 | 38.4365 | 3754.5 | 4323.1 | . |

The estimated regression line is $\hat{Y}_t = 706.8989 + 52.0611t$.

From the printout, the 1986 quarterly GNP forecasts are:

| | | FORECAST | 95% LOWER LIMIT | 95% UPPER LIMIT |
|---|---|---|---|---|
| 1986 | Q1 | 3882.6 | 3599.7 | 4165.5 |
| | Q2 | 3934.7 | 3651.4 | 4218.0 |
| | Q3 | 3986.7 | 3702.9 | 4270.6 |
| | Q4 | 4038.8 | 3754.5 | 4323.1 |

b. The following model is fit: $E(Y_t) = \beta_0 + \beta_1 t + \beta_2 Q_1 + \beta_3 Q_2 + \beta_4 Q_3$

where $Q_1 = \begin{cases} 1 & \text{if quarter 1} \\ 0 & \text{otherwise} \end{cases}$ $\quad Q_2 = \begin{cases} 1 & \text{if quarter 2} \\ 0 & \text{otherwise} \end{cases}$

$Q_3 = \begin{cases} 1 & \text{if quarter 3} \\ 0 & \text{otherwise} \end{cases}$

The SAS printout is:

```
DEPENDENT VARIABLE: Y

SOURCE              DF       SUM OF SQUARES        MEAN SQUARE    F VALUE

MODEL                4    48773586.86428570  12193396.71607140     618.91

ERROR               55     1083579.37504790     19701.44318269     PR > F

CORRECTED TOTAL     59    49857166.23933360                        0.0001


R-SQUARE          C.V.            ROOT MSE             Y MEAN

0.978266        6.1166        140.36182951      2294.76333333


                                  T FOR HO:      PR > |T|    STD ERROR OF
PARAMETER             ESTIMATE   PARAMETER = 0                  ESTIMATE

INTERCEPT         701.52857143          14.20      0.0001     49.38852396
T                  52.07285714          49.66      0.0001      1.04852796
Q          1        9.13857143           0.18      0.8594     51.34933095
           2        5.81904762           0.11      0.9101     51.29577697
           3        5.09285714           0.10      0.9212     51.26361772

OBSERVATION           OBSERVED           PREDICTED          LOWER 95% CLI
                                          RESIDUAL          UPPER 95% CLI

      57         3909.30000000       3678.82000000          3382.40574750
                                      230.48000000          3975.23425250
      58         3965.00000000       3727.57333333          3431.15908083
                                      237.42666667          4023.98758583
      59         4030.50000000       3778.92000000          3482.50574750
                                      251.58000000          4075.33425250
      60         4087.70000000       3825.90000000          3529.48574750
                                      261.80000000          4122.31425250
      61 *                   .       3887.11142857          3588.91499135
                                                 .          4185.30786579
      62 *                   .       3935.86476190          3637.66832468
                                                 .          4234.06119913
      63 *                   .       3987.21142857          3689.01499135
                                                 .          4285.40786579
      64 *                   .       4034.19142857          3735.99499135
                                                 .          4332.38786579
```

The fitted model is

$$\hat{Y} = 701.5286 + 52.0729t + 9.1386Q_1 + 5.8190Q_2 + 5.0929Q_3$$

To determine whether the data indicate a significant seasonal component, we test:

$H_0$: $\beta_2 = \beta_3 = \beta_4 = 0$
$H_a$: At least one $\beta_i \neq 0$

The test statistic is $F = \dfrac{(SSE_1 - SSE_2)/(k - g)}{SSE_2/[n - (k + 1)]}$

$$= \frac{1084219.00 - 1083579.375)/(4 - 1)}{1083579.375/[60 - (4 + 1)]} = \frac{213.2083}{19701.443} = .011$$

The rejection region requires $\alpha = .05$ in the upper tail of the F distribution with numerator df = k - g = 4 - 1 = 3 and denominator df = n - (k + 1) = 60 - (4 + 1) = 55. From Table VIII, Appendix B, $F_{.05} \approx 3.23$. The rejection region is $F > 3.23$.

Since the observed value of the test statistic does not fall in the rejection region ( $F = .011 \not> 3.23$), $H_0$ is not rejected. There is insufficient evidence to indicate a seasonal component at $\alpha = .05$. This supports the assertion that the data has been seasonally adjusted.

c. Using the printout, the 1986 quarterly GNP forecasts are:

| | | FORECAST |
|---|---|---|
| 1986 | $Q_1$ | 3887.11 |
| | $Q_2$ | 3935.86 |
| | $Q_3$ | 3987.21 |
| | $Q_4$ | 4034.19 |

16.35 a. The following model is fit: $E(\log Y_t) = \beta_0 + \beta_1 t$. The SAS output is:

DEP VARIABLE: LOGY
ANALYSIS OF VARIANCE

| SOURCE | DF | SUM OF SQUARES | MEAN SQUARE | F VALUE | PROB>F |
|---|---|---|---|---|---|
| MODEL | 1 | 10.13644957 | 10.13644957 | 15297.614 | 0.0001 |
| ERROR | 58 | 0.03843175 | 0.000662616 | | |
| C TOTAL | 59 | 10.17488132 | | | |

| | | | |
|---|---|---|---|
| ROOT MSE | 0.02574134 | R-SQUARE | 0.9962 |
| DEP MEAN | 7.655946 | ADJ R-SQ | 0.9962 |
| C.V. | 0.3362267 | | |

PARAMETER ESTIMATES

| VARIABLE | DF | PARAMETER ESTIMATE | STANDARD ERROR | T FOR HO: PARAMETER =0 | PROB > \|T\| |
|---|---|---|---|---|---|
| INTERCEP | 1 | 6.93206580 | 0.006730342 | 1029.972 | 0.0001 |
| T | 1 | 0.02373379 | 0.000191891 | 123.684 | 0.0001 |

| OBS | ACTUAL | PREDICT VALUE | STD ERR PREDICT | LOWER95% PREDICT | UPPER95% PREDICT | RESIDUAL |
|---|---|---|---|---|---|---|
| 1 | 6.9559 | 6.9558 | .0065642 | 6.9026 | 7.0090 | 7.9E-05 |
| 2 | 6.9744 | 6.9795 | .0063994 | 6.9264 | 7.0326 | -.005148 |
| 3 | 6.9908 | 7.0033 | .0062362 | 6.9502 | 7.0563 | -0.0125 |
| 4 | 7.0083 | 7.0270 | .0060747 | 6.9741 | 7.0799 | -0.0187 |
| 5 | 7.0409 | 7.0507 | 0.005915 | 6.9979 | 7.1036 | -.009848 |
| 6 | 7.0662 | 7.0745 | .0057573 | 7.0217 | 7.1273 | -.008258 |
| . | . | . | . | . | . | . |
| . | . | . | . | . | . | . |
| . | . | . | . | . | . | . |
| 49 | 8.0620 | 8.0950 | .0048627 | 8.0426 | 8.1475 | -0.0331 |
| 50 | 8.0932 | 8.1188 | .0050045 | 8.0663 | 8.1712 | -0.0256 |
| 51 | 8.1204 | 8.1425 | .0051496 | 8.0899 | 8.1950 | -0.0221 |
| 52 | 8.1421 | 8.1662 | .0052976 | 8.1136 | 8.2188 | -0.0241 |
| 53 | 8.1756 | 8.1900 | .0054484 | 8.1373 | 8.2426 | -0.0143 |
| 54 | 8.2010 | 8.2137 | .0056017 | 8.1610 | 8.2664 | -0.0127 |
| 55 | 8.2146 | 8.2374 | .0057573 | 8.1846 | 8.2902 | -0.0228 |
| 56 | 8.2318 | 8.2612 | 0.005915 | 8.2083 | 8.3140 | -0.0293 |
| 57 | 8.2711 | 8.2849 | .0060747 | 8.2319 | 8.3378 | -0.0138 |
| 58 | 8.2853 | 8.3086 | .0062362 | 8.2556 | 8.3616 | -0.0234 |
| 59 | 8.3016 | 8.3324 | .0063994 | 8.2793 | 8.3855 | -0.0307 |
| 60 | 8.3157 | 8.3561 | .0065642 | 8.3029 | 8.4093 | -0.0404 |
| 61 | . | 8.3798 | .0067303 | 8.3266 | 8.4331 | . |
| 62 | . | 8.4036 | .0068979 | 8.3502 | 8.4569 | . |
| 63 | . | 8.4273 | .0070666 | 8.3739 | 8.4807 | . |
| 64 | . | 8.4510 | .0072365 | 8.3975 | 8.5046 | . |

The fitted model is $\widehat{\log Y_t} = 6.932 + .0237t$

The following model is fit:

$$E(\log Y_t) = \beta_0 + \beta_1 t + \beta_2 Q_1 + \beta_3 Q_2 + \beta_4 Q_3$$

where $Q_1$, $Q_2$, and $Q_3$ are defined in Exercise 16.33(b). The SAS output is:

DEPENDENT VARIABLE: LOGY

| SOURCE | DF | SUM OF SQUARES | MEAN SQUARE | F VALUE |
|---|---|---|---|---|
| MODEL | 4 | 10.13659892 | 2.53414973 | 3640.79 |
| ERROR | 55 | 0.03828240 | 0.00069604 | PR > F |
| CORRECTED TOTAL | 59 | 10.17488132 | | 0.0001 |

| R-SQUARE | C.V. | ROOT MSE | Y MEAN |
|---|---|---|---|
| 0.996238 | 0.3446 | 0.02638264 | 7.65594625 |

| PARAMETER | | ESTIMATE | | T FOR HO: PARAMETER = 0 | PR > \|T\| | STD ERROR OF ESTIMATE |
|---|---|---|---|---|---|---|
| INTERCEPT | | 6.92945728 | B | 746.46 | 0.0001 | 0.00928315 |
| T | | 0.02373951 | | 120.45 | 0.0001 | 0.00019708 |
| Q | 1 | 0.00437049 | B | 0.45 | 0.6525 | 0.00965170 |
| | 2 | 0.00299739 | B | 0.31 | 0.7571 | 0.00964164 |
| | 3 | 0.00236751 | B | 0.25 | 0.8068 | 0.00963559 |

| OBSERVATION | OBSERVED | PREDICTED<br>RESIDUAL | LOWER 95% CLI<br>UPPER 95% CLI |
|---|---|---|---|
| 57 | 8.27111361 | 8.28697997<br>-0.01586636 | 8.23126546<br>8.34269448 |
| 58 | 8.28526113 | 8.30934638<br>-0.02408525 | 8.25363188<br>8.36506089 |
| 59 | 8.30164572 | 8.33245602<br>-0.03081030 | 8.27674151<br>8.38817052 |
| 60 | 8.31573774 | 8.35382801<br>-0.03809027 | 8.29811351<br>8.40954252 |
| 61 * | . | 8.38193802<br>. | 8.32588853<br>8.43798751 |
| 62 * | . | 8.40430443<br>. | 8.34825494<br>8.46035392 |
| 63 * | . | 8.42741406<br>. | 8.37136458<br>8.48346355 |
| 64 * | . | 8.44878606<br>. | 8.39273658<br>8.50483555 |

The fitted model is

$$\widehat{\log Y_t} = 6.929 + .0237t + .00437Q_1 \quad .00300Q_2 + .00237Q_3$$

b. From the outputs, the forecasts and limits for the transformed data are listed in the table. The antilogs are taken to obtain the forecasts in the original units.

| MODEL | QUARTER | LOG FORECAST | 95% LOWER LIMIT | 95% UPPER LIMIT | FORECAST | 95% LOWER LIMIT | 95% UPPER LIMIT |
|---|---|---|---|---|---|---|---|
| Simple | 1 | 8.3798 | 8.3266 | 8.4331 | 4358.14 | 4132.34 | 4596.73 |
| | 2 | 8.4036 | 8.3502 | 8.4569 | 4463.11 | 4231.03 | 4707.44 |
| | 3 | 8.4273 | 8.3739 | 8.4807 | 4570.14 | 4332.50 | 4820.82 |
| | 4 | 8.4510 | 8.3975 | 8.5046 | 4679.75 | 4435.96 | 4937.43 |
| Seasonal | 1 | 8.3819 | 8.3259 | 8.4380 | 4367.30 | 4129.45 | 4619.31 |
| | 2 | 8.4043 | 8.3483 | 8.4604 | 4466.23 | 4223.00 | 4723.95 |
| | 3 | 8.4274 | 8.3714 | 8.4835 | 4570.60 | 4321.68 | 4834.34 |
| | 4 | 8.4488 | 8.3927 | 8.5048 | 4669.47 | 4414.72 | 4938.42 |

16.37 a. The following model is fit: $E(Y_t) = \beta_0 + \beta_1 t$,

where t = 0 corresponds to 1945,
t = 5 corresponds to 1950, etc.

The SAS printout is:

```
DEP VARIABLE: YP
ANALYSIS OF VARIANCE

                      SUM OF         MEAN
SOURCE     DF        SQUARES       SQUARE      F VALUE        PROB>F

MODEL       1      326.56177    326.56177      136.393        0.0001
ERROR       8    19.15422711   2.39427839
C TOTAL     9      345.71600

      ROOT MSE      1.547346     R-SQUARE      0.9446
      DEP MEAN         48.08     ADJ R-SQ      0.9377
      C.V.          3.218273

PARAMETER ESTIMATES

                      PARAMETER          STANDARD       T FOR HO:
VARIABLE   DF          ESTIMATE             ERROR    PARAMETER =0    PROB > |T|

INTERCEP    1       36.66659341        1.09293555          33.549        0.0001
T           1        0.69172161        0.05922922          11.679        0.0001

                        PREDICT     STD ERR     LOWER95%     UPPER95%
OBS        ACTUAL         VALUE     PREDICT      PREDICT      PREDICT     RESIDUAL

  1       34.3000       36.6666      1.0929      32.2980      41.0352      -2.3666
  2       43.4000       40.1252      0.8387      36.0666      44.1838       3.2748
  3       42.5000       43.5838      0.6226      39.7376      47.4301      -1.0838
  4       48.1000       47.0424      0.4973      43.2944      50.7904       1.0576
  5       50.9000       50.5010      0.5314      46.7282      54.2738       0.3990
  6       51.0000       51.1927      0.5572      47.4002      54.9853      -0.1927
  7       51.5000       51.8845      0.5878      48.0674      55.7015      -0.3845
  8       52.4000       52.5762      0.6226      48.7299      56.4224      -0.1762
  9       52.9000       53.2679      0.6609      49.3879      57.1480      -0.3679
 10       53.8000       53.9596      0.7021      50.0413      57.8780      -0.1596
 11             .       54.6514      0.7457      50.6904      58.6123            .
 12             .       55.3431      0.7913      51.3353      59.3508            .
 13             .       56.0348      0.8387      51.9762      60.0934            .
 14             .       56.7265      0.8875      52.6131      60.8399            .
 15             .       57.4182      0.9374      53.2463      61.5902            .
```

The fitted model is $\hat{Y}_t = 36.67 + .692t$.

b. The plot of the data and fitted regression line is shown using SAS.

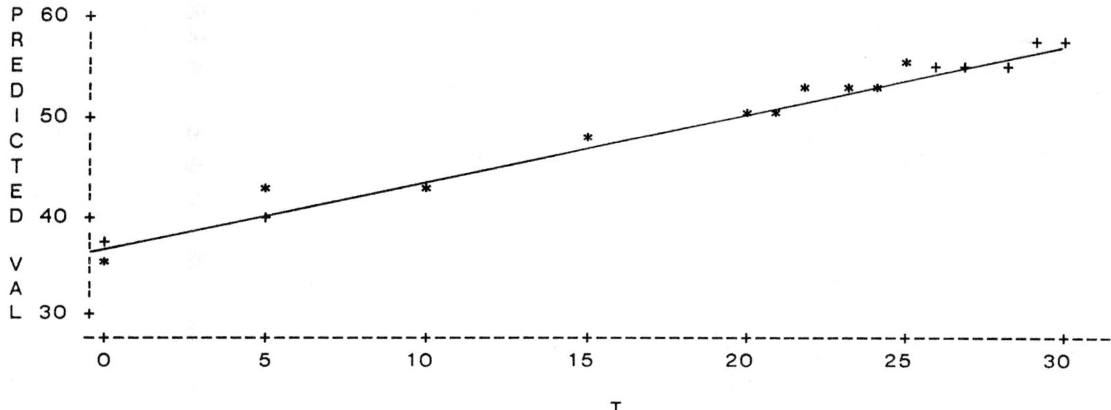


NOTE: 5 OBS HAD MISSING VALUES 8 OBS HIDDEN

c. Using the printout, the forecasts for 1971 - 1975 are:

| | FORECASTS |
|---|---|
| 1971 | 54.6514 |
| 1972 | 55.3431 |
| 1973 | 56.0348 |
| 1974 | 56.7265 |
| 1975 | 57.4182 |

d. The following model is fit: $E(Y_t) = \beta_0 + \beta_1 t$ where $Y_t$ is the market share of secondary lenders. The SAS output is:

DEP VARIABLE: YS
ANALYSIS OF VARIANCE

| SOURCE | DF | SUM OF SQUARES | MEAN SQUARE | F VALUE | PROB>F |
|---|---|---|---|---|---|
| MODEL | 1 | 351.65130 | 351.65130 | 145.245 | 0.0001 |
| ERROR | 8 | 19.36870330 | 2.42108791 | | |
| C TOTAL | 9 | 371.02000 | | | |

| | | | |
|---|---|---|---|
| ROOT MSE | 1.555985 | R-SQUARE | 0.9478 |
| DEP MEAN | 50.6 | ADJ R-SQ | 0.9413 |
| C.V. | 3.075068 | | |

PARAMETER ESTIMATES

| VARIABLE | DF | PARAMETER ESTIMATE | STANDARD ERROR | T FOR HO: PARAMETER =0 | PROB > \|T\| |
|---|---|---|---|---|---|
| INTERCEP | 1 | 62.44373626 | 1.09903750 | 56.817 | 0.0001 |
| T | 1 | -0.71780220 | 0.05955990 | -12.052 | 0.0001 |

The fitted model is $\hat{Y}_t = 62.444 - .718t$

The forecast for market share of secondary lenders for 1975 is

$$\hat{Y}_{1975} = 62.444 - .718(30) = 40.904$$

The forecasts are:

| YEAR | PRIMARY | SECONDARY |
|---|---|---|
| 1955 (actual) | 42.5 | 56.4 |
| 1975 (forecast) | 57.42 | 40.90 |

The projections yield the same conclusions.

16.39 b. The forecasts are:

$$Y_{1987,J} = F_{t+1} = E_t = 124.383$$

$$Y_{1987,F} = F_{t+2} = F_{t+1} = 124.383$$

$$Y_{1987,M} = F_{t+3} = F_{t+1} = 124.383$$

16.41 a. The estimated average increase in load per month is .6367 (compared with .8611 in original model). The estimate of the standard deviation is $\sqrt{MSE} = 6.7944$ (compared with 10.6093 in original model).

b. $\hat{R}_t = Y_t - (\hat{\beta}_0 + \hat{\beta}_1 t) = 120.000 - (116.1446 + .6367(36)) = -19.0658$

$\hat{R}_{t+1} = \hat{\phi}\hat{R}_t = .7164(-19.0658) = -13.6587$

1987-Jan $\hat{Y}_{t+1} = 116.1446 + .6367(37) + (-13.6587) = 126.0438$

$\hat{R}_{t+2} = \hat{\phi}R_{t+1} = .7164(-13.6587) = -9.7851$

1987-Feb $\hat{Y}_{t+2} = 116.1446 + .6367(38) + (-9.7851) = 130.55$

$\hat{R}_{t+3} = \hat{\phi}R_{t+2} = .7164(-9.7851) = -7.0100$

1987-Mar $\hat{Y}_{t+3} = 116.1446 + .6367(39) + (-7.0100) = 133.97$

The 95% forecast intervals are:

1987-Jan $\hat{Y}_{t+1} \pm 2\sqrt{MSE}$ => $126.0438 \pm 2\sqrt{46.164}$ => $126.0438 \pm 13.5888$
=> (112.4550, 139.6326)

1987-Feb $\hat{Y}_{t+2} \pm 2\sqrt{MSE(1 + \hat{\phi}^2)}$ => $130.55 \pm 2\sqrt{46.164(1 + .7164^2)}$
=> $130.55 \pm 16.7161$ => (113.8339, 147.2661)

1987-Mar $\hat{Y}_{t+3} \pm 2\sqrt{MSE(1 + \hat{\phi}^2 + \hat{\phi}^4)}$ => $133.97 \pm 2\sqrt{46.164(1 + .7164^2 + .7164^4)}$
=> $133.97 \pm 18.1126$ => (115.8574, 152.0826)

# CHAPTER 17

# DESIGN OF EXPERIMENTS AND ANALYSIS OF VARIANCE

17.1 The treatments are the factor levels A, B, C, and D.

17.3 a. College GPA's are measured on college students. The experimental units are college students.

b. Unemployment rate is measured by counting the number of unemployed workers and dividing by the total number of workers. The experimental units are the workers of the state.

c. Gasoline mileage is measured on automobiles. The experimental units are the automobiles of a particular model.

d. The experimental units are the sectors on a computer diskette.

17.5 a. The response is the debt-to-equity ratio measured on each company.

b. The factor is the type of company, which is qualitative.

c. The treatments are the 4 types of companies: insurance, publishing, electric utility, and banking.

d. The experimental units are the companies.

17.7 a. The response is the quality of a steel ingot on a scale from 0 to 10.

b. There are two factors--temperature and pressure. Both factors are quantitative.

c. There are $3 \times 5 = 15$ treatments. Each treatment is a combination of a temperature and a pressure. One example is temperature 1100 and pressure 500.

d. The experimental units are the steel ingots.

17.9 a. From Table VIII with $\nu_1 = 2$ and $\nu_2 = 2$, $F_{.05} = 19.00$.

b. From Table X with $\nu_1 = 2$ and $\nu_2 = 2$, $F_{.01} = 99.00$.

c. From Table VII with $\nu_1 = 20$ and $\nu_2 = 40$, $F_{.10} = 1.61$.

d. From Table IX with $\nu = 12$, and $\nu_2 = 9$, $F_{.025} = 3.87$.

17.11 In dot diagram b, the difference between the sample means is small relative to the variability within the sample observations. The observations for Sample 1 overlap those of Sample 2. In diagram a, no observations from Sample 1 overlap any observations from Sample 2, implying the variation within the sample observations is small relative to the difference between the sample means.

17.13 Some preliminary calculations are:

For diagram a:

$$\bar{y}_1 = \frac{\sum y_1}{n_1} = \frac{54}{6} = 9 \qquad s_1^2 = \frac{\sum y_1^2 - \frac{(\sum y_1)^2}{n_1}}{n_1 - 1} = \frac{496 - \frac{54^2}{6}}{6 - 1} = \frac{10}{5} = 2$$

$$\bar{y}_2 = \frac{\sum y^2}{n_2} = \frac{84}{6} = 14 \qquad s_2^2 = \frac{\sum y_2^2 - \frac{(\sum y_2)^2}{n_2}}{n_2 - 1} = \frac{1186 - \frac{84^2}{6}}{6 - 1} = \frac{10}{5} = 2$$

$$s_p^2 = \frac{(n_1 - 1)s_1^2 + (n_2 - 1)s_2^2}{n_1 + n_2 - 2} = \frac{(6 - 1)2 + (6 - 1)2}{6 + 6 - 2} = \frac{20}{10} = 2$$

From Exercise 17.12, $MSE = \frac{20}{10} = 2$.

To determine if the two treatment means are different, we test:

$H_0$: $\mu_1 - \mu_2 = 0$
$H_a$: $\mu_1 - \mu_2 \neq 0$

The test statistic is

$$t = \frac{(\bar{y}_1 - \bar{y}_2) - 0}{\sqrt{s_p^2\left(\frac{1}{n_1} + \frac{1}{n_2}\right)}} = \frac{9 - 14 - 0}{\sqrt{2\left(\frac{1}{6} + \frac{1}{6}\right)}} = \frac{-5}{.8165} = -6.12$$

From Exercise 17.12, $F = 37.5$, $t^2 = (-6.12)^2 = 37.5$.

The rejection region requires $\alpha/2 = .05/2 = .025$ in each tail of the $t$ distribution with $df = n_1 + n_2 - 2 = 6 + 6 - 2 = 10$. From Table VI, Appendix B, $t_{.025} = 2.228$. The rejection region is $t > 2.228$ or $t < -2.228$. The critical value from Exercise 17.12 is $F_{.05} = 4.96$, $t^2 = 2.228^2 = 4.96$.

Since the observed value of the test statistic falls in the rejection region ($t = -6.12 < -2.228$), $H_0$ is rejected. There is sufficient evidence to indicate the population means are different at $\alpha = .05$. The conclusion in Exercise 17.12 is reject $H_0$ at $\alpha = .05$.

The assumptions necessary for the t test are:

1. Both populations are normal.
2. Samples are independent.
3. The population variances are equal.

These are the same assumptions necessary for the F test.

For diagram b.

$$\bar{y}_1 = \frac{\sum y_1}{n_1} = \frac{54}{6} = 9 \qquad s_1^2 = \frac{\sum y_1^2 - \frac{(\sum y_1)^2}{n_1}}{n_1 - 1} = \frac{558 - \frac{54^2}{6}}{6 - 1} = \frac{72}{5} = 14.4$$

$$\bar{y}_2 = \frac{\sum y^2}{n_2} = \frac{84}{6} = 14 \qquad s_2^2 = \frac{\sum y_2^2 - \frac{(\sum y_2)^2}{n_2}}{n_2 - 1} = \frac{1248 - \frac{84^2}{6}}{6 - 1} = \frac{72}{5} = 14.4$$

$$s_p^2 = \frac{(n_1 - 1)s_1^2 + (n_2 - 1)s_2^2}{n_1 + n_2 - 2} = \frac{(6 - 1)14.4 + (6 - 1)14.4}{6 + 6 - 2} = \frac{144}{10} = 14.4$$

From Exercise 17.12, $MSE = \frac{144}{10} = 14.4$.

To determine if the two treatment means are different, we test:

$H_0: \mu_1 - \mu_2 = 0$
$H_a: \mu_1 - \mu_2 \neq 0$

The test statistic is

$$t = \frac{(\bar{y}_1 - \bar{y}_2) - 0}{\sqrt{s_p^2\left(\frac{1}{n_1} + \frac{1}{n_2}\right)}} = \frac{9 - 14 - 0}{\sqrt{14.4\left(\frac{1}{6} + \frac{1}{6}\right)}} = \frac{-5}{2.1909} = -2.282$$

From Exercise 17.12, $F = 5.21$, $t^2 = (-2.282)^2 = 5.21$.

The rejection region requires $\alpha/2 = .05/2 = .025$ in each tail of the t distribution with $df = n_1 + n_2 - 2 = 6 + 6 - 2 = 10$. From Table VI, Appendix B, $t_{.025} = 2.228$. The rejection region is $t > 2.228$ or $t < -2.228$. The critical value from Exercise 17.12 is $F_{.05} = 4.96$, $t^2 = 2.228^2 = 4.96$.

Since the observed value of the test statistic falls in the rejection region ($t = -2.282 < -2.228$), $H_0$ is rejected. There is sufficient evidence to indicate the population means are different at $\alpha = .05$. The conclusion in Exercise 17.12 is reject $H_0$ at $\alpha = .05$.

The assumptions for both tests are the same as those stated in diagram a.

17.15 For all parts, the hypotheses are:

$H_0$: $\mu_1 = \mu_2 = \mu_3 = \mu_4 = \mu_5 = \mu_6$
$H_a$: At least two treatment means differ

The rejection region for all parts is the same.

The rejection region requires $\alpha = .10$ in the upper tail of the F distribution with $\nu_1 = p - 1 = 6 - 1 = 5$ and $\nu_2 = n - p = 36 - 6 = 30$. From Table VII, Appendix B, $F_{.10} = 2.05$. The rejection region is $F > 2.05$.

a. SST = .2(500) = 100 SSE = SS(Total) - SST = 500 - 100 = 400

$$MST = \frac{SST}{p - 1} = \frac{100}{6 - 1} = 20 \qquad MSE = \frac{SSE}{n - p} = \frac{400}{36 - 6} = 13.333$$

$$F = \frac{MST}{MSE} = \frac{20}{13.333} = 1.5$$

Since the observed value of the test statistic does not fall in the rejection region ($F = 1.5 \not> 2.05$), $H_0$ is not rejected. There is insufficient evidence to indicate differences among the treatment means at $\alpha = .10$.

b. SST = .5(500) = 250 SSE = SS(Total) - SST = 500 - 250 = 250

$$MST = \frac{SST}{p - 1} = \frac{250}{6 - 1} = 50 \qquad MSE = \frac{SSE}{n - p} = \frac{250}{36 - 6} = 8.333$$

$$F = \frac{MST}{MSE} = \frac{50}{8.333} = 6$$

Since the observed value of the test statistic falls in the rejection region ($F = 6 > 2.05$), $H_0$ is rejected. There is sufficient evidence to indicate differences among the treatment means at $\alpha = .10$.

c. SST = .8(500) = 400 SSE = SS(Total) - SST = 500 - 400 = 100

$$MST = \frac{SST}{p - 1} = \frac{400}{6 - 1} = 80 \qquad MSE = \frac{SSE}{n - p} = \frac{100}{36 - 6} = 3.333$$

$$F = \frac{MST}{MSE} = \frac{80}{3.333} = 24$$

Since the observed value of the test statistic falls in the rejection region, ($F = 24 > 2.05$), $H_0$ is rejected. There is sufficient evidence to indicate differences among the treatment means at $\alpha = .10$.

d. The F ratio increases as the treatment sum of squares increases.

17.17 a. The number of treatments is 3 + 1 = 4. The total sample size is 37 + 1 = 38.

b. To determine if the treatment means differ, we test:

$H_0$: $\mu_1 = \mu_2 = \mu_3 = \mu_4$
$H_a$: At least two treatment means differ

The test statistic is F = 14.80.

The rejection region requires $\alpha = .01$ in the upper tail of the F distribution with $\nu_1 = p - 1 = 4 - 1 = 3$ and $\nu_2 = n - p = 38 - 4 = 34$. From Table X, Appendix B, $F_{.01} \approx 4.51$. The rejection region is $F > 4.51$.

Since the observed value of the test statistic falls in the rejection region ($F = 14.80 > 4.51$), $H_0$ is rejected. There is sufficient evidence to indicate differences among the treatment means at $\alpha = .01$.

c. We need the sample means to compare specific pairs of treatment means.

17.19 a. Some preliminary calculations are:

$$CM = \frac{(\sum y_i)^2}{n} = \frac{37.1^2}{12} = 114.701$$

$$SS(Total) = \sum y_i^2 - CM = 145.89 - 114.701 = 31.189.$$

$$SST = \sum \frac{T_i^2}{n_i} - CM = \frac{16.9^2}{5} + \frac{16.0^2}{4} + \frac{4.2^2}{3} - 114.701$$

$$= 127.002 - 114.701 = 12.301$$

$$SSE = SS(Total) - SST = 31.189 - 12.301 = 18.888$$

$$MST = \frac{SST}{p - 1} = \frac{12.301}{3 - 1} = 6.1505 \qquad MSE = \frac{SSE}{n - p} = \frac{18.888}{12 - 3} = 2.0987$$

$$F = \frac{MST}{MSE} = \frac{6.1505}{2.0987} = 2.931$$

| Source | df | SS | MS | F |
|---|---|---|---|---|
| Treatments | 2 | 12.301 | 6.1505 | 2.931 |
| Error | 9 | 18.888 | 2.0987 | |
| Total | 11 | 31.189 | | |

b. $H_0$: $\mu_1 = \mu_2 = \mu_3$
$H_a$: At least two treatment means differ

The test statistic is F = 2.931.

The rejection region requires $\alpha = .01$ in the upper tail of the F distribution with $\nu_1 = p - 1 = 3 - 1 = 2$ and $\nu_2 = n - p = 12 - 3 = 9$. From Table X, Appendix B, $F_{.01} = 8.02$. The rejection region is $F > 8.02$.

Since the observed value of the test statistic does not fall in the rejection region ($F = 2.931 \not> 8.02$), $H_0$ is not rejected. There is insufficient evidence to indicate a difference in the treatment means at $\alpha = .01$.

c. There are 3 pairs of treatments to compare, implying c = 3. For $\alpha/2c = .05/2(3) = .0083 \approx .005$ and df $= n - p = 12 - 3 = 9$, $t_{.005} = 3.250$ from Table VI, Appendix B.

We now form confidence intervals for the difference between each pair of treatments using the formula.

$$(\bar{y}_i - \bar{y}_j) \pm t_{\alpha/2c} s\sqrt{\frac{1}{n_i} + \frac{1}{n_j}} \quad \text{where } s = \sqrt{MSE} = \sqrt{2.0987} = 1.4487$$

$$\bar{y}_1 = \frac{\sum y_1}{n_1} = \frac{16.9}{5} = 3.38,\ \bar{y}_2 = \frac{\sum y_2}{n_2} = \frac{16.0}{4} = 4,\ \bar{y}_3 = \frac{\sum y_3}{n_3} = \frac{4.2}{3} = 1.4$$

<u>Pair</u>

1-2 $\quad (3.38 - 4) \pm 3.25(1.4487)\sqrt{\frac{1}{5} + \frac{1}{4}} \Rightarrow -.62 \pm 3.158$

$\Rightarrow (-3.778, 2.538)$

1-3 $\quad (3.38 - 1.4) \pm 3.25(1.4487)\sqrt{\frac{1}{5} + \frac{1}{3}} \Rightarrow 1.98 \pm 3.438$

$\Rightarrow (-1.458, 5.418)$

2-3 $\quad (4 - 1.4) \pm 3.25(1.4487)\sqrt{\frac{1}{4} + \frac{1}{3}} \Rightarrow 2.6 \pm 3.596$

$\Rightarrow (-.996, 6.196)$

All the intervals contain 0. This indicates there is insufficient evidence to say any two treatment means are different.

17.21 a. SS(Total) = SST + SSE = 509.87 + 12259.96 = 12769.83

$$MST = \frac{SST}{p - 1} = \frac{509.87}{3 - 1} = 254.935$$

$$MSE = \frac{SSE}{n - p} = \frac{12259.96}{93 - 3} = 136.222$$

$$F = \frac{MST}{MSE} = \frac{254.935}{136.222} = 1.871$$

| Source | df | SS | MS | F |
|---|---|---|---|---|
| Treatments | 2 | 509.87 | 254.935 | 1.871 |
| Error | 90 | 12,259.96 | 136.222 | |
| Total | 92 | 12,769.83 | | |

b. To determine if differences in mean risk-taking propensities exist among the three groups, we test:

$H_0$: $\mu_1 = \mu_2 = \mu_3$
$H_a$: At least two treatment means differ

The test statistic is $F = 1.871$.

The rejection region requires $\alpha = .05$ in the upper tail of the F distribution with $\nu_1 = p - 1 = 3 - 1 = 2$ and $\nu_2 = n - p = 93 - 3 = 90$. From Table VIII, Appendix B, $F_{.05} \approx 3.15$. The rejection region is $F > 3.15$.

Since the observed value of the test statistic does not fall in the rejection region ($F = 1.871 \not> 3.15$), $H_0$ is not rejected. There is insufficient evidence to indicate differences in the mean risk-raking propensities among the three groups at $\alpha = .05$.

c. We must assume:

1. All 3 population probability distributions are normal.
2. The 3 population variances are equal.
3. Samples are selected randomly and independently from the 3 populations.

d. No. No differences were found using ANOVA.

e. The experiment is observational. The experimenter "observed" from which group the individuals came.

17.23 a. Some preliminary calculations are:

$$CM = \frac{(\sum y_i)^2}{n} = \frac{5369^2}{12} = 2,402,180.083$$

$$SS(Total) = \sum y_i^2 - CM = 2,419,553 - 2,402,180.083 = 17,372.917$$

$$SST = \sum \frac{T_i^2}{n_i} - CM = \frac{1693^2}{4} + \frac{1695^2}{4} + \frac{1981^2}{4} - 2,402,180.083$$

$$= 2,415,908.75 - 2,402,180.083 = 13,728.667$$

$SSE = SS(Total) - SST = 17,372.917 - 13,728.667 = 3644.25$

$MST = \frac{SST}{p - 1} = \frac{13728.667}{3 - 1} = 6864.3335 \quad MSE = \frac{SSE}{n - p} = \frac{3644.25}{12 - 3} = 404.9167$

$F = \frac{MST}{MSE} = \frac{6864.3335}{404.9167} = 16.952$

| Source | df | SS | MS | F |
|---|---|---|---|---|
| Treatments | 2 | 13,728.667 | 6864.3335 | 16.952 |
| Error | 9 | 3,664.25 | 404.9167 | |
| Total | 11 | 17,372.917 | | |

To determine whether there is a difference among the mean sales at the three locations, we test:

$H_0$: $\mu_1 = \mu_2 = \mu_3$
$H_a$: At least two treatment means differ

The test statistic is $F = 16.952$.

The rejection region requires $\alpha = .05$ in the upper tail of the F distribution with $\nu_1 = p - 1 = 3 - 1 = 2$ and $\nu_2 = n - p = 12 - 3 = 9$. From Table VIII, Appendix B, $F_{.05} = 4.26$. The rejection region is $F > 4.26$.

Since the observed value of the test statistic falls in the rejection region ($F = 16.952 > 4.26$), $H_0$ is rejected. There is sufficient evidence to indicate a difference among the mean sales at the three locations at $\alpha = .05$.

b. The confidence interval for $\mu_1 - \mu_3$ is:

$(\bar{y}_1 - \bar{y}_3) \pm t_{\alpha/2}\, s\sqrt{\frac{1}{n_1} + \frac{1}{n_2}}$ where $s = \sqrt{MSE} = \sqrt{404.9167} = 20.1225$

For confidence coefficient .90, $\alpha = 1 - .90 = .10$ and $\alpha/2 = .10/2 = .05$. From Table VI, Appendix B, $t_{.05} = 1.833$ with $df = n - p = 12 - 3 = 9$.

$\bar{y}_1 = \frac{\sum y_1}{n_1} = \frac{1693}{4} = 423.25, \qquad \bar{y}_3 = \frac{\sum y_3}{n_3} = \frac{1981}{4} = 495.25$

The 90% confidence interval is

$$(423.25 - 495.25) \pm 1.833(20.1225)\sqrt{\frac{1}{4} + \frac{1}{4}}$$

$$\Rightarrow (-72) \pm 26.081 \Rightarrow (-98.081, -45.919)$$

17.25 a. Let o = commissioned, □ = Fixed Salary, and Δ = Commission plus salary. The dot diagram is:

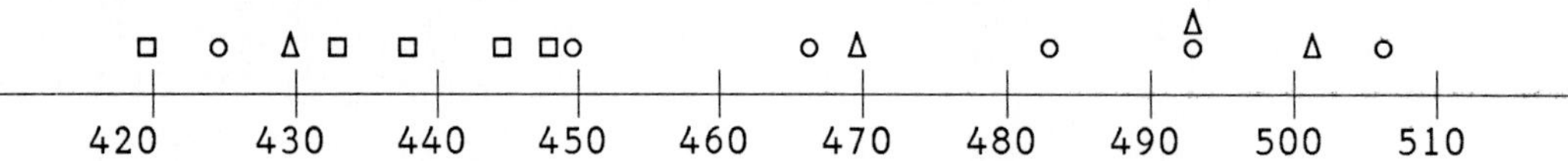


b. To determine if the mean sales differ among the three types of compensation, we test:

$H_0$: $\mu_1 = \mu_2 = \mu_3$
$H_a$: At least two treatment means differ

The test statistic is F = 3.17.

The rejection region requires $\alpha = .05$ in the upper tail of the F distribution with $\nu_1 = p - 1 = 3 - 1 = 2$ and $\nu_1 = n - p = 15 - 3 = 12$. From Table VIII, Appendix B, $F_{.05} = 3.89$. The rejection region is F > 3.89.

Since the observed value of the test statistic does not fall in the rejection region ($F = 3.17 \not> 3.89$), $H_0$ is not rejected. There is insufficient evidence to indicate the mean sales differ among the three types of compensation at $\alpha = .05$.

c. The form of the confidence interval for $\mu_3$ is

$$\bar{y}_3 \pm t_{\alpha/2}\, s\sqrt{\frac{1}{n_3}} \quad \text{where } s = \sqrt{MSE} = \sqrt{662} = 25.7294$$

$$\bar{y}_3 = \frac{\sum y_3}{n_3} = \frac{1893}{4} = 473.25$$

For confidence coefficient .90, $\alpha = 1 - .90 = .10$ and $\alpha/2 = .10/2 = .05$. From Table VI, Appendix B, $t_{.05} = 1.782$ with df = n - p = 15 - 3 = 12.

The 90% confidence interval is

$$473.25 \pm 1.782(25.7294)\sqrt{\frac{1}{4}} \Rightarrow 473.25 \pm 22.925$$

$$\Rightarrow (450.325, 496.175)$$

17.27 a. Some preliminary calculations:

SS(Total) = SST + SSE = .023015 + .486047 = .509062

$$MST = \frac{SST}{p - 1} = \frac{.023015}{5 - 1} = .005754$$

$$MSE = \frac{SSE}{n - p} = \frac{.486047}{96 - 5} = .005341$$

$F = \frac{MST}{MSE} = \frac{.005754}{.005341} = 1.08$

| Source | df | SS | MS | F |
|---|---|---|---|---|
| Treatments | 4 | .023015 | .005754 | 1.08 |
| Error | 91 | .486047 | .005341 | |
| Total | 95 | .509062 | | |

b. To determine if differences among the mean bond price changes for the five underwriters, we test:

$H_0$: $\mu_1 = \mu_2 = \mu_3 = \mu_4 = \mu_5$
$H_a$: At least two treatment means differ

The test statistic is F = 1.08.

The rejection region requires $\alpha = .05$ in the upper tail of the F distribution with $\nu_1 = p - 1 = 5 - 1 = 4$ and $\nu_2 = n - p = 96 - 5 = 91$. From Table VIII, Appendix B, $F_{.05} \approx 2.53$. The rejection region is $F > 2.53$.

Since the observed value of the test statistic does not fall in the rejection region ($F = 1.08 \not> 2.53$), $H_0$ is not rejected. There is insufficient evidence to indicate differences among the mean bond price changes for the five underwriters at $\alpha = .05$.

c. No. No differences among the five means were found using ANOVA.

17.29 a. The number of blocks = 2 + 1 = 3, and the number of treatments = 4 + 1 = 5.

b. The number of observations is 14 + 1 = 15.

c. $H_0$: $\mu_1 = \mu_2 = \mu_3 = \mu_4 = \mu_5$
$H_a$: At least two treatment means differ

d. $F = \frac{MST}{MSE} = 9.109$

e. The rejection region requires $\alpha = .01$ in the upper tail of the F distribution with $\nu_1 = p - 1 = 5 - 1 = 4$ and $\nu_2 = n - b - p + 1 = 15 - 5 - 3 + 1 = 8$. From Table X, Appendix B, $F_{.01} = 7.01$. The rejection region is $F > 7.01$.

f. Since the observed value of the test statistic falls in the rejection region ($F = 9.109 > 7.01$), $H_0$ is rejected. There is sufficient evidence to indicate differences among the treatment means at $\alpha = .01$.

g. The necessary assumptions are:

1. The probability distributions of observations corresponding to all block-treatment combinations are normal.
2. The variances of all probability distributions are equal.

17.31 a.

| Source | df | SS | MS | F |
|---|---|---|---|---|
| Treatments | 2 | 12.032 | 6.016 | 50.98 |
| Blocks | 3 | 71.749 | 23.916 | 202.68 |
| Error | 6 | 0.708 | 0.118 | |
| Total | 11 | 84.489 | | |

b. To determine if the treatment means differ, we test:

$H_0$: $\mu_A = \mu_B = \mu_C$
$H_a$: At least two treatment means differ

The test statistic is F = 50.98.

The rejection region requires $\alpha = .05$ in the upper tail of the F distribution with $\nu_1 = p - 1 = 3 - 1 = 2$ and $\nu_2 = n - p - b + 1 = 12 - 3 - 4 + 1 = 6$. From Table VIII, Appendix B, $F_{.05} = 5.14$. The rejection region is F > 5.14.

Since the observed value of the test statistic falls in the rejection region (F = 50.98 > 5.14), $H_0$ is rejected. There is sufficient evidence to indicate differences among the treatment means at $\alpha = .05$.

c. To determine if the blocking was effective in reducing the experimental error, we test:

$H_0$: $\mu_1 = \mu_2 = \mu_3 = \mu_4$
$H_a$: At least two block means differ

The test statistic is F = 202.68.

The rejection region requires $\alpha = .05$ in the upper tail of the F distribution with $\nu_1 = b - 1 = 4 - 1 = 3$ and $\nu_2 = n - p - b + 1 = 12 - 3 - 4 + 1 = 6$. From Table VIII, Appendix B, $F_{.05} = 4.76$. The rejection region is F > 4.76.

Since the observed value of the test statistic falls in the rejection region (F = 202.68 > 4.76), $H_0$ is rejected. There is sufficient evidence to indicate the blocking was effective in reducing the experimental error at $\alpha = .05$.

d. There are 3 pairs of treatment means to compare, implying c = 3. For $\alpha/2c = .10/2(3) = .0167 \approx .01$ and df = n - p - b + 1 = 12 - 3 - 4 + 1 = 6, $t_{.01} = 3.143$ from Table VI, Appendix B. We now form confidence intervals for the difference between each pair of treatments using the formula:

$$(\bar{y}_i - \bar{y}_j) \pm t_{\alpha/2c} s \sqrt{\frac{1}{n_i} + \frac{1}{n_j}} \quad \text{where } s = \sqrt{MSE} = \sqrt{.118} = .3435.$$

$$\bar{y}_1 = \frac{\sum y_1}{n_1} = \frac{18.1}{4} = 4.525, \qquad \bar{y}_2 = \frac{\sum y_2}{n_2} = \frac{22.6}{4} = 5.65,$$

$$\bar{y}_3 = \frac{\sum y_3}{n_3} = \frac{12.8}{4} = 3.2$$

<u>Pair</u>

A-B $(4.525 - 5.65) \pm 3.143(.3435)\sqrt{\frac{1}{4} + \frac{1}{4}} \Rightarrow -1.125 \pm .763$

$\Rightarrow (-1.888, -.362)$

A-C $(4.525 - 3.2) \pm 3.143(.3435)\sqrt{\frac{1}{4} + \frac{1}{4}} \Rightarrow -1.325 \pm .763$

$\Rightarrow (.562, 2.088)$

B-C $(5.65 - 3.2) \pm 3.143(.3435)\sqrt{\frac{1}{4} + \frac{1}{4}} \Rightarrow 2.45 \pm .763$

$\Rightarrow (1.687, 3.213)$

None of the intervals contain 0. This indicates all means are different from each other.

The equal sample sizes cause the value that is added to and subtracted from the difference in means to be the same for each interval.

e. The necessary assumptions are:

1. The probability distributions of observations corresponding to all block-treatment combinations are normal.
2. The variances of all probability distributions are equal.

17.33 a. SST = .2(500) = 100 SSB = .3(500) = 150

SSE = SS(Total) - SST - SSB = 500 - 100 - 150 = 250

$$MST = \frac{SST}{p - 1} = \frac{100}{4 - 1} = 33.3333 \qquad MSB = \frac{SSB}{b - 1} = \frac{150}{9 - 1} = 18.75$$

$$MSE = \frac{SSE}{n - p - b + 1} = \frac{250}{36 - 4 - 9 + 1} = \frac{250}{24} = 10.4167$$

$$F_T = \frac{MST}{MSE} = \frac{33.3333}{10.4167} = 3.20 \qquad F_B = \frac{MSB}{MSE} = \frac{18.75}{10.4167} = 1.80$$

To determine if differences exist among the treatment means, we test:

$H_0$: $\mu_1 = \mu_2 = \mu_3 = \mu_4$
$H_a$: At least two treatment means differ

The test statistic is F = 3.20.

The rejection region requires $\alpha = .05$ in the upper tail of the F distribution with $\nu_1 = p - 1 = 4 - 1 = 3$ and $\nu_2 = n - p - b + 1 = 36 - 4 - 9 + 1 = 24$. From Table VIII, Appendix B, $F_{.05} = 3.01$. The rejection region is F > 3.01.

Since the observed value of the test statistic falls in the rejection region (F = 3.20 > 3.01), $H_0$ is rejected. There is sufficient evidence to indicate differences among the treatment means at $\alpha = .05$.

To determine if differences exist among the block means, we test:

$H_0$: $\mu_1 = \mu_2 = \ldots = \mu_9$
$H_a$: At least two block means differ

The test statistic is F = 1.80.

The rejection region requires $\alpha = .05$ in the upper tail of the F distribution with $\nu_1 = b - 1 = 9 - 1 = 8$ and $\nu_2 = n - b - p + 1 = 36 - 9 - 4 + 1 = 24$. From Table VIII, Appendix B, $F_{.05} = 2.36$. The rejection region is F > 2.36.

Since the observed value of the test statistic does not fall in the rejection region ($F = 1.80 \not> 2.36$), $H_0$ is not rejected. There is insufficient evidence to indicate differences among the treatment means at $\alpha = .05$.

b. SST = .5(500) = 250 SSB = .2(500) = 100

SSE = SS(Total) - SST - SSB = 500 - 250 - 100 = 150

$$MST = \frac{SST}{p - 1} = \frac{250}{4 - 1} = 83.3333 \qquad MSB = \frac{SSB}{b - 1} = \frac{100}{9 - 1} = 12.5$$

$$MSE = \frac{SSE}{n - p - b + 1} = \frac{150}{36 - 4 - 9 + 1} = 6.25$$

$$F_T = \frac{MST}{MSE} = \frac{83.3333}{6.25} = 13.33 \qquad F_B = \frac{MSB}{MSE} = \frac{12.5}{6.25} = 2$$

To determine if differences exist among the treatment means, we test:

$H_0$: $\mu_1 = \mu_2 = \mu_3 = \mu_4$
$H_a$: At least two treatment means differ

The test statistic is F = 13.33.

The rejection region is F > 3.01 (same as above).

Since the observed value of the test statistic falls in the rejection region (F = 13.33 > 3.01), $H_0$ is rejected. There is sufficient evidence to indicate differences exist among the treatment means at $\alpha = .05$.

To determine if differences exist among the block means, we test:

$H_0$: $\mu_1 = \mu_2 = \ldots = \mu_9$
$H_a$: At least two block means differ

The test statistic is F = 2.00.

The rejection region is F > 2.36 (same as above).

Since the observed value of the test statistic does not fall in the rejection region (F = 2.00 $\not>$ 2.36), $H_0$ is not rejected. There is insufficient evidence to indicate differences exist among the block means at $\alpha = .05$.

c. $SST = .2(500) = 100$ $\qquad$ $SSB = .5(500) = 250$

$SSE = SS(Total) - SST - SSB = 500 - 100 - 250 = 150$

$$MST = \frac{SST}{p - 1} = \frac{100}{4 - 1} = 33.3333 \qquad MSB = \frac{SSB}{b - 1} = \frac{250}{9 - 1} = 31.25$$

$$MSE = \frac{SSE}{n - p - b + 1} = \frac{150}{36 - 4 - 9 + 1} = 6.25$$

$$F_T = \frac{MST}{MSE} = \frac{33.3333}{6.25} = 5.33 \qquad F_B = \frac{MSB}{MSE} = \frac{31.25}{6.25} = 5.00$$

To determine if differences exist among the treatment means, we test:

$H_0$: $\mu_1 = \mu_2 = \mu_3 = \mu_4$
$H_a$: At least two treatment means differ

The test statistic is F = 5.33.

The rejection region is F > 3.01 (same as above).

Since the observed value of the test statistic falls in the rejection region ($F = 5.33 > 3.01$), $H_0$ is rejected. There is sufficient evidence to indicate differences exist among the treatment means at $\alpha = .05$.

To determine if differences exist among the block means, we test:

$H_0$: $\mu_1 = \mu_2 = \ldots = \mu_9$
$H_a$: At least two block means differ

The test statistic is $F = 5.00$.

The rejection region is $F > 2.36$ (same as above).

Since the observed value of the test statistic falls in the rejection region ($F = 5.00 > 2.36$), $H_0$ is rejected. There is sufficient evidence to indicate differences exist among the block means at $\alpha = .05$.

d. $SST = .4(500) = 200$ $\qquad$ $SSB = .4(500) = 200$

$SSE = SS(\text{Total}) - SST - SSB = 500 - 200 - 200 = 100$

$$MST = \frac{SST}{p - 1} = \frac{200}{4 - 1} = 66.6667 \qquad MSB = \frac{SSB}{b - 1} = \frac{200}{9 - 1} = 25$$

$$MSE = \frac{SSE}{n - p - b + 1} = \frac{100}{36 - 4 - 9 + 1} = 4.1667$$

$$F_T = \frac{MST}{MSE} = \frac{66.6667}{4.1667} = 16.0 \qquad F_B = \frac{MSB}{MSE} = \frac{25}{4.1667} = 6.00$$

To determine if differences exist among the treatment means, we test:

$H_0$: $\mu_1 = \mu_2 = \mu_3 = \mu_4$
$H_a$: At least two treatment means differ

The test statistic is $F = 16.0$.

The rejection region is $F > 3.01$ (same as above).

Since the observed value of the test statistic falls in the rejection region ($F = 16.0 > 3.01$), $H_0$ is rejected. There is sufficient evidence to indicate differences among the treatment means at $\alpha = .05$.

To determine if differences exist among the block means, we test:

$H_0$: $\mu_1 = \mu_2 = \ldots = \mu_9$
$H_a$: At least two block means differ

The test statistic is $F = 6.00$.

The rejection region is $F > 2.36$ (same as above).

Since the observed value of the test statistic falls in the rejection region ($F = 6.00 > 2.36$), $H_0$ is rejected. There is sufficient evidence to indicate differences exist among the block means at $\alpha = .05$.

e. $SST = .2(500) = 100$ $SSB = .2(500) = 100$

$SSE = SS(Total) - SST - SSB = 500 - 100 - 100 = 300$

$$MST = \frac{SST}{p - 1} = \frac{100}{4 - 1} = 33.3333 \qquad MSB = \frac{SSB}{b - 1} = \frac{100}{9 - 1} = 12.5$$

$$MSE = \frac{SSE}{n - p - b + 1} = \frac{300}{36 - 4 - 9 + 1} = 12.5$$

$$F_T = \frac{MST}{MSE} = \frac{33.3333}{12.5} = 2.67 \qquad F_B = \frac{MSB}{MSE} = \frac{12.5}{12.5} = 1.00$$

To determine if differences exist among the treatment means, we test:

$H_0$: $\mu_1 = \mu_2 = \mu_3 = \mu_4$
$H_a$: At least two treatment means differ

The test statistic is $F = 2.67$.

The rejection region is $F > 3.01$ (same as above).

Since the observed value of the test statistic does not fall in the rejection region ($F = 2.67 \not> 3.01$), $H_0$ is not rejected. There is insufficient evidence to indicate differences exist among the treatment means at $\alpha = .05$.

To determine if differences exist among the block means, we test:

$H_0$: $\mu_1 = \mu_2 = \dots = \mu_9$
$H_a$: At least two block means differ

The test statistic is $F = 1.00$.

The rejection region is $F > 2.36$ (same as above).

Since the observed value of the test statistic does not fall in the rejection region ($F = 1.00 \not> 2.36$), $H_0$ is not rejected. There is insufficient evidence to indicate differences among the block means at $\alpha = .05$.

17.35 a. Randomized block design. The manufacturer suspected large variations among the experimental units (company employees) due to length of time with the company.

b. To determine whether the mean productivity levels differ among the four pay programs, we test:

$H_0$: $\mu_1 = \mu_2 = \mu_3 = \mu_4$
$H_a$: At least two treatment means differ.

The test statistic is F = 8.452.

The rejection region requires $\alpha = .05$ in the upper tail of the F distribution with $\nu_1 = p - 1 = 4 - 1 = 3$ and $\nu_2 = n - p - b + 1 = 12 - 4 - 3 + 1 = 6$. From Table VIII, Appendix B, $F_{.05} = 4.76$. The rejection region is $F > 4.76$.

Since the observed value of the test statistic falls in the rejection region ($F = 8.452 > 4.76$), $H_0$ is rejected. There is sufficient evidence to indicate the mean productivity levels differ among the 4 pay programs at $\alpha = .05$.

c. From the printout, the level of significance is .014.

d. There are 6 pairs of treatments to compare, implying c = 6. For $\alpha/2c = .10/2(6) = .0083 \approx .005$ and $df = n - p - b + 1 = 12 - 4 - 3 + 1 = 6$, $t_{.005} = 3.707$ from Table VI, Appendix B. We now form confidence intervals for the difference between each pair of treatment means using the formula:

$$(\bar{y}_i - \bar{y}_j) \pm t_{\alpha/2c}s\sqrt{\frac{1}{n_i} + \frac{1}{n_j}} \quad \text{where } s = \sqrt{MSE} = \sqrt{.148} = .3847$$

$$\bar{y}_1 = \frac{\sum y_1}{n_1} = \frac{12.3}{3} = 4.1 \qquad \bar{y}_2 = \frac{\sum y_2}{n_2} = \frac{16.1}{3} = 5.37$$

$$\bar{y}_3 = \frac{\sum y_3}{n_3} = \frac{16.2}{3} = 5.4 \qquad \bar{y}_4 = \frac{\sum y_4}{n_4} = \frac{16.2}{3} = 5.4$$

Pair

1-2 $(4.1 - 5.37) \pm 3.707(.3847)\sqrt{\frac{1}{3} + \frac{1}{3}} \Rightarrow (-1.27) \pm 1.164$
$\Rightarrow (-2.434, -.106)$

1-3 $(4.1 - 5.4) \pm 1.164 \Rightarrow -1.3 \pm 1.164 \Rightarrow (-2.464, -.136)$

1-4 $(4.1 - 5.4) \pm 1.164 \Rightarrow -1.3 \pm 1.164 \Rightarrow (-2.464, -.136)$

2-3 $(5.37 - 5.4) \pm 1.164 \Rightarrow -.03 \pm 1.164 \Rightarrow (-1.194, 1.134)$

2-4 $(5.37 - 5.4) \pm 1.164 \Rightarrow -.03 \pm 1.164 \Rightarrow (-1.194, 1.134)$

3-4 $(5.4 - 5.4) \pm 1.164 \Rightarrow 0 \pm 1.164 \Rightarrow (-1.164, 1.164)$

Treatments 1 and 2, 1 and 3, and 1 and 4 are significantly different from each other because 0 is not in the confidence intervals. Treatments 2 and 3, 2 and 4, and 3 and 4 are not significantly different from each other because 0 is in the confidence intervals.

17.37 Some preliminary calculations are:

$$CM = \frac{(\sum y_i)^2}{n} = \frac{49.9^2}{10} = 249.001$$

$$SS(Total) = \sum y_i^2 - CM = 253.19 - 249.001 = 4.189$$

$$SST = \sum \frac{T_i^2}{b} - CM = \frac{25.3^2}{5} + \frac{24.6^2}{5} - 249.001$$

$$= 249.05 - 249.001 = .049$$

$$SST = \sum \frac{B_i^2}{p} - CM = \frac{8.0^2}{2} + \frac{10.3^2}{2} + \frac{10.0^2}{2} + \frac{9.6^2}{2} + \frac{12.0^2}{2} - 249.001$$

$$= 253.125 - 249.001 = 4.124$$

$$SSE = SS(Total) - SST - SSB = 4.189 - .049 - 4.124 = .016$$

$$MST = \frac{SST}{p - 1} = \frac{.049}{2 - 1} = .049$$

$$MSE = \frac{SSE}{n - p - b + 1} = \frac{.016}{10 - 2 - 5 + 1} = .004$$

$$MSB = \frac{SSB}{b - 1} = \frac{4.124}{5 - 1} = 1.031$$

$$F_T = \frac{MST}{MSE} = \frac{.049}{.004} = 12.25 \qquad F_T = \frac{MSB}{MSE} = \frac{1.031}{.004} = 257.75$$

| Source | df | SS | MS | F |
|---|---|---|---|---|
| Treatments | 1 | .049 | .049 | 12.25 |
| Blocks | 4 | 4.124 | 1.031 | 257.75 |
| Error | 4 | .016 | .004 | |
| Total | 9 | 4.189 | | |

a. To determine if there is a difference in mean turn times for the two economy brands, we test:

$H_0$: $\mu_1 = \mu_2$
$H_a$: $\mu_1 \neq \mu_2$

The test statistic is F = 12.25.

The rejection region requires $\alpha = .05$ in the upper tail of the F distribution with $\nu_1 = p - 1 = 2 - 1 = 1$ and $\nu_2 = 10 - 2 - 5 + 1 = 4$. From Table VIII, Appendix B, $F_{.05} = 7.71$. The rejection region is $F > 7.71$.

Since the observed value of the test statistic falls in the rejection region ($F = 12.25 > 7.71$), $H_0$ is rejected. There is sufficient evidence to indicate a difference in mean turn times for the two economy brands at $\alpha = .05$.

b. The purpose of the blocks is to eliminate store-to-store differences. The mean square for blocks is so large because there are large differences among the stores.

c.

| ECONOMY BRAND 1 | 2 | DIFFERENCE (1 - 2) |
|---|---|---|
| 4.1 | 3.9 | .2 |
| 5.2 | 5.1 | .1 |
| 5.0 | 5.0 | 0 |
| 4.9 | 4.7 | .2 |
| 6.1 | 5.9 | .2 |

$$\bar{x}_D = \frac{\sum x_{D_i}}{n_D} = \frac{.7}{5} = .14$$

$$s_D^2 = \frac{\sum x_{D_i}^2 - \frac{(\sum x_{D_i})^2}{n}}{n_D - 1}$$

$$= \frac{.13 - \frac{.7^2}{5}}{5 - 1} = \frac{.032}{4} = .008$$

$$s_D = \sqrt{.008} = .0894$$

To determine if there is a difference in mean turn times for the two economy brands, we test:

$H_0$: $\mu_1 - \mu_2 = 0$
$H_a$: $\mu_1 - \mu_2 \neq 0$

The test statistic is $t = \dfrac{\bar{x}_D - 0}{s_D/\sqrt{n_D}} = \dfrac{.14 - 0}{.0894/\sqrt{5}} = \dfrac{.14}{.04} = 3.5$

The rejection region requires $\alpha/2 = .05/2 = .025$ in each tail of the t distribution with $df = n_D - 1 = 5 - 1 = 4$. From Table VI, Appendix B, $t_{.025} = 2.776$. The rejection region is $t > 2.776$ or $t < -2.776$.

Since the observed value of the test statistic falls in the rejection region ($F = 3.5 > 2.776$), $H_0$ is rejected. There is sufficient evidence to indicate a difference in mean turn times for the two economy brands at $\alpha = .05$.

d. $t^2 = 3.5^2 = 12.25 = F$

$t^2_{.025} = 2.776^2 = 7.71 = F_{.05}$

17.39 a. Some preliminary calculations are:

$$MST = \frac{SST}{p - 1} = \frac{.941}{3 - 1} = .4705 \qquad MSB = \frac{SSB}{b - 1} = \frac{10239.969}{6 - 1} = 2047.9938$$

$$MSE = \frac{SSE}{n - p - b + 1} = \frac{13.919}{18 - 3 - 6 + 1} = 1.3919$$

$$F_T = \frac{MST}{MSE} = \frac{.4705}{1.3919} = .338 \qquad F_B = \frac{MSB}{MSE} = \frac{2047.9938}{1.3919} = 1471.37$$

To determine whether the means for at least two of the estimators differ, we test:

$H_0$: $\mu_1 = \mu_2 = \mu_3$
$H_a$: At least two estimator means differ

The test statistic is $F = \frac{MST}{MSE} = .338$

The rejection region requires $\alpha = .05$ in the upper tail of the F distribution with $\nu_1 = p - 1 = 3 - 1 = 2$ and $\nu_2 = n - p - b + 1 = 18 - 3 - 6 + 1 = 10$. From Table VIII, Appendix B, $F_{.05} = 4.10$. The rejection region is $F > 4.10$.

Since the observed value of the test statistic does not fall in the rejection region ($F = .338 \not> 4.10$), $H_0$ is not rejected. There is insufficient evidence to indicate that the means for at least two of the estimators differ at $\alpha = .05$.

b. The observed significance level is $P(F \geq .34) > .10$ from Table VII, Appendix B, where $\nu_1 = 2$ and $\nu_2 = 10$.

c. SS(Total) = SST + SSB + SSE = .941 + 10239.969 + 13.919 = 10254.892.

The ANOVA table is:

| Source | df | SS | MS | F |
|---|---|---|---|---|
| Treatments | 2 | .941 | .4705 | .338 |
| Blocks | 5 | 10239.969 | 2047.9938 | 1471.37 |
| Error | 10 | 13.919 | 1.3919 | |
| Total | 17 | 10254.892 | | |

d. No. Since no differences were found among the estimator means, there is no reason to make pairwise comparisons. There will not be any pairwise differences.

17.41 a. Some preliminary calculations are:

$$SS(Total) = SST + SSB + SSE = .1858 + 5.0607 + .0778 = 5.3243$$

$$MST = \frac{SST}{p - 1} = \frac{.1858}{4 - 1} = .06193 \qquad MSB = \frac{SSB}{b - 1} = \frac{5.0607}{10 - 1} = .5623$$

$$MSE = \frac{SSE}{n - p - b + 1} = \frac{.0778}{40 - 4 - 10 + 1} = .00288$$

The ANOVA table is:

| Source | df | SS | MS | F |
|---|---|---|---|---|
| Treatments | 3 | .1858 | .06193 | 21.50 |
| Blocks | 9 | 5.0607 | .56230 | 195.24 |
| Error | 27 | .0778 | .00288 | |
| Total | 39 | 5.3243 | | |

b. To determine if the mean prices of items differ among the four supermarkets, we test:

$H_0$: $\mu_1 = \mu_2 = \mu_3 = \mu_4$
$H_a$: At least two supermarket means differ

The test statistic is $F = 21.50$.

The rejection region requires $\alpha = .05$ in the upper tail of the F distribution with $\nu_1 = p - 1 = 4 - 1 = 3$ and $\nu_2 = n - p - b + 1 = 40 - 4 - 10 + 1 = 27$. From Table VIII, Appendix B, $F_{.05} = 2.96$. The rejection region is $F > 2.96$.

Since the observed value of the test statistic falls in the rejection region ($F = 21.50 > 2.96$), $H_0$ is rejected. There is sufficient evidence to indicate the mean prices of items differ among the four supermarkets at $\alpha = .05$.

c. There are 6 pairs of treatments to compare, implying $c = 6$. For $\alpha/2c = .05/2(6) = .0042 \approx .005$ and $df = n - p - b + 1 = 40 - 4 - 10 + 1 = 27$, $t_{.005} = 2.771$ from Table VI, Appendix B. We now form confidence intervals for the difference between each pair of means using the formula:

$$(\bar{y}_i - \bar{y}_j) \pm t_{\alpha/2c} s\sqrt{\frac{1}{n_i} + \frac{1}{n_j}} \quad \text{where } s = \sqrt{MSE} = \sqrt{.00288} = .0537$$

$$\bar{y}_1 = \frac{\sum y_1}{n_1} = \frac{6.63}{10} = .663 \qquad \bar{y}_2 = \frac{\sum y_2}{n_2} = \frac{7.07}{10} = .707$$

$$\bar{y}_3 = \frac{\sum y_3}{n_3} = \frac{8.41}{10} = .841 \qquad \bar{y}_4 = \frac{\sum y_4}{n_4} = \frac{6.94}{10} = .694$$

<u>Pair</u>

A-B $\quad (.663 - .707) \pm 2.771(.0537)\sqrt{\frac{1}{10} + \frac{1}{10}} \Rightarrow (-.044) \pm .0665$

$\Rightarrow (-.1105, .0225)$

A-C $\quad (.663 - .841) \pm .0665 \Rightarrow -.178 \pm .0665 \Rightarrow (-.2445, -.1115)$

A-D $\quad (.663 - .694) \pm .0665 \Rightarrow -.031 \pm .0665 \Rightarrow (-.0975, .0975)$

B-C $\quad (.707 - .841) \pm .0665 \Rightarrow -.134 \pm .0665 \Rightarrow (-.2005, -.0675)$

B-D $\quad (.707 - .694) \pm .0665 \Rightarrow .013 \pm .0665 \Rightarrow (-.0535, .0795)$

C-D $\quad (.841 - .694) \pm .0665 \Rightarrow .147 \pm .0665 \Rightarrow (.0805, .2135)$

Supermarkets A and C, B and C, and C and D are significantly different from each other because 0 is not in the confidence intervals. Supermarkets A and B, A and D, and B and D are not significantly different from each other because 0 is in the confidence intervals.

d. The mean price at supermarket A is significantly lower than the mean price at supermarket C. However, the mean price at supermarket A is not significantly different from the mean prices at supermarkets B and D. Thus, we are not convinced that we would save money by shopping at supermarket A.

17.43 a. The ANOVA table is:

| Source | df | SS | MS | F |
|---|---|---|---|---|
| A | 2 | .8 | .4000 | 3.69 |
| B | 3 | 5.3 | 1.7667 | 16.31 |
| AB | 6 | 9.6 | 1.6000 | 14.77 |
| Error | 12 | 1.3 | .1083 | |
| Total | 23 | 17.0 | | |

df for A is $a - 1 = 3 - 1 = 2$
df for B is $b - 1 = 4 - 1 = 3$
df for AB is $(a - 1)(b - 1) = 2(3) = 6$
df for Error is $n - ab = 24 - 3(4) = 12$
df for Total is $n - 1 = 24 - 1 = 23$

$SSE = SS(Total) - SSA - SSB - SSAB = 17.0 - .8 - 5.3 - 9.6 = 1.3$

$$MSA = \frac{SSA}{a - 1} = \frac{.8}{3 - 1} = .40 \qquad MSB = \frac{SSB}{b - 1} = \frac{5.3}{4 - 1} = 1.7667$$

$$MSAB = \frac{SSAB}{(a - 1)(b - 1)} = \frac{9.6}{(3 - 1)(4 - 1)} = 1.60$$

$$MSE = \frac{MSE}{n - ab} = \frac{1.3}{24 - 3(4)} = .1083$$

$$F_A = \frac{MSA}{MSE} = \frac{.4000}{.1083} = 3.69 \qquad F_B = \frac{MSB}{MSE} = \frac{1.7667}{.1083} = 16.31$$

$$F_{AB} = \frac{MSAB}{MSE} = \frac{1.6000}{.1083} = 14.77$$

b. Sum of Squares for Treatment = SSA + SSB + SSAB = .8 = 5.3 + 2.6 = 15.7.

$$MST = \frac{SST}{ab - 1} = \frac{15.7}{3(4) - 1} = 1.4273$$

$$F_T = \frac{MST}{MSE} = \frac{1.4273}{.1083} = 13.18$$

To determine if the treatment means differ, we test:

$H_0$: $\mu_1 = \mu_2 = \ldots = \mu_{12}$
$H_a$: At least two treatment means differ

The test statistic is F = 13.18.

The rejection region requires $\alpha = .05$ in the upper tail of the F distribution with $\nu_1 = ab - 1 = 3(4) - 1 = 11$ and $\nu_2 = n - ab = 24 - 3(4) = 12$. From Table VIII, Appendix B, $F_{.05} \approx 2.75$. The rejection region is $F > 2.75$.

Since the observed value of the test statistic falls in the rejection region ($F = 13.18 > 2.75$), $H_0$ is rejected. There is sufficient evidence to indicate the treatment means differ at $\alpha = .05$.

c. Yes. We need to partition the Treatment Sum of Squares into the Main Effects and Interaction Sum of Squares. Then we test whether factors A and B interact. Depending on the conclusion of the test for interaction, we either test for main effects or compare the treatment means.

d. Two factors are said to interact if the effects of one factor on the dependent variable are not the same at different levels of the second factor. If the factors interact, then tests for main effects are not necessary. We need to compare the treatment means for one factor at each level of the second.

e. To determine if the factors interact, we test:

$H_0$: Factors A and B do not interact to affect the response mean

$H_a$: Factors A and B do interact to affect the response mean

The test statistic is $F = \frac{MSAB}{MSE} = 14.77$

The rejection region requires $\alpha = .05$ in the upper tail of the F distribution with $\nu_1 = (a - 1)(b - 1) = (3 - 1)(4 - 1) = 6$ and $\nu_2 = n - ab = 24 - 3(4) = 12$. From Table VIII, Appendix B, $F_{.05} = 3.00$. The rejection region is $F > 3.00$.

Since the observed value of the test statistic falls in the rejection region ($F = 14.77 > 3.00$), $H_0$ is rejected. There is sufficient evidence to indicate the two factors interact to affect the response mean at $\alpha = .05$.

f. No. Testing for main effects is not warranted. Instead, we compare the treatment means of one factor at each level of the second factor.

17.45 a. The treatments for this experiment consist of a level for factor A and a level for factor B. There are 6 treatments--(1, 1), (1, 2), (1, 3), (2, 1), (2, 2), and (2, 3) where the first number represents the level of factor A and the second number represents the level of factor B.

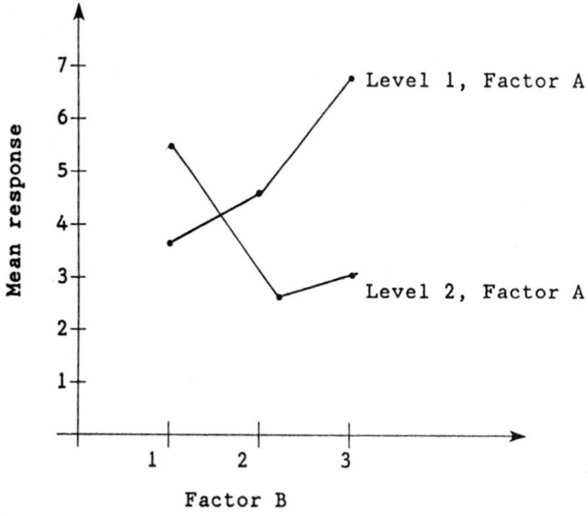


The treatment means appear to be different because the sample means are quite different. The factors appear to interact because the lines are not parallel.

b. $SST = SSA + SSB + SSAB = 4.441 + 4.127 + 18.007 = 26.575$

$MST = \frac{SST}{ab - 1} = \frac{26.575}{2(3) - 1} = 5.315 \qquad F_T = \frac{MST}{MSE} = \frac{5.315}{.246} = 21.61$

To determine whether the treatment means differ, we test:

$H_0$: $\mu_1 = \mu_2 = \mu_3 = \mu_4 = \mu_5 = \mu_6$
$H_a$: At least two treatment means differ

The test statistic is $F = \frac{MST}{MSE} = 21.61$

The rejection region requires $\alpha = .05$ in the upper tail of the F distribution with $\nu_1 = ab - 1 = 2(3) - 1 = 5$ and $\nu_2 = n - ab = 12 - 2(3) = 6$. From Table VIII, Appendix B, $F_{.05} = 4.39$. The rejection region is $F > 4.39$.

Since the observed value of the test statistic falls in the rejection region ($F = 21.61 > 4.39$), $H_0$ is rejected. There is sufficient evidence to indicate that the treatment means differ at $\alpha = .05$. This supports the plot in (a).

c. Yes. Since there are differences among the treatment means, we test for interaction. To determine whether the factors A and B interact, we test:

$H_0$: Factors A and B do not interact to affect the mean response
$H_a$: Factors A and B do interact to affect the mean response

The test statistic is $F = \frac{MSAB}{MSE} = \frac{9.003}{.246} = 36.60$

The rejection region requires $\alpha = .05$ in the upper tail of the F distribution with $\nu_1 = (a - 1)(b - 1) = (2 - 1)(3 - 1) = 2$ and $\nu_2 = n - ab = 12 - 2(3) = 6$. From Table VIII, Appendix B, $F_{.05} = 5.14$. The rejection region is $F > 5.14$.

Since the observed value of the test statistic falls in the rejection region ($F = 36.60 > 5.14$), $H_0$ is rejected. There is sufficient evidence to indicate that factors A and B interact to affect the response mean at $\alpha = .05$.

d. No. Because interaction is present, the tests for main effects are not warranted.

e. The results of the tests in parts b and c support the visual interpretation in part (a).

f. There are 15 pairs of treatment means to compare, implying $c = 15$. For $\alpha/2c = .10/2(15) = .0033 \approx .005$ and $df = n - ab = 12 - 2(3) = 6$, $t_{.005} = 3.707$ from Table VI, Appendix B. We now form confidence intervals for the difference between each pair of means using the formula:

$(\bar{y}_i - \bar{y}_j) \pm t_{\alpha/2c} s \sqrt{\frac{1}{n_i} + \frac{1}{n_j}}$ where $s = \sqrt{MSE} = \sqrt{.246} = .4959$

$\bar{y}_{11} = \frac{7.1}{2} = 3.55$ $\quad\bar{y}_{12} = \frac{8.8}{2} = 4.4$ $\quad\bar{y}_{13} = \frac{13.5}{2} = 6.75$

$\bar{y}_{21} = \frac{11.2}{2} = 5.6$ $\quad\bar{y}_{22} = \frac{5.1}{2} = 2.55$ $\quad\bar{y}_{23} = \frac{5.8}{2} = 2.9$

<u>Pair</u>

$A_1B_1 - A_1B_2$ $\quad(3.55 - 4.4) \pm 3.707(.4959) \sqrt{\frac{1}{2} + \frac{1}{2}}$

=> -.85 ± 1.838 => (-2.688, .988)

$A_1B_1 - A_1B_3$ $\quad$(3.55 - 6.75) ± 1.838 => -3.2 ± 1.838
=> (-5.038, -1.362)

$A_1B_1 - A_2B_1$ $\quad$(3.55 - 5.6) ± 1.838 => -2.05 ± 1.838
=> (-3.888, -.212)

$A_1B_1 - A_2B_2$ $\quad$(3.55 - 2.55) ± 1.838 => 1.00 ± 1.838
=> (-.838, 2.838)

$A_1B_1 - A_2B_3$ $\quad$(3.55 - 2.9) ± 1.838 => .65 ± 1.838
=> (-1.188, 2.488)

$A_1B_2 - A_1B_3$ $\quad$(4.4 - 6.75) ± 1.838 => -2.35 ± 1.838
=> (-4.188, -.512)

$A_1B_2 - A_2B_1$ $\quad$(4.4 - 5.6) ± 1.838 => -1.2 ± 1.838
=> (-3.038, .638)

$A_1B_2 - A_2B_2$ $\quad$(4.4 - 2.55) ± 1.838 => 1.85 ± 1.838
=> (.012, 3.638)

$A_1B_2 - A_2B_3$ $\quad$(4.4 - 2.9) ± 1.838 => 1.5 ± 1.838
=> (-.338, 3.338)

$A_1B_3 - A_2B_1$ $\quad$(6.75 - 5.6) ± 1.838 => 1.15 ± 1.838
=> (-.688, 2.988)

$A_1B_3 - A_2B_2$ $\quad$(6.75 - 2.55) ± 1.838 => 4.2 ± 1.838
=> (2.362, 6.038)

$A_1B_3 - A_2B_3$ $\quad$(6.75 - 2.9) ± 1.838 => 3.85 ± 1.838
=> (2.012, 5.688)

$A_2B_1 - A_2B_2$ $\quad$(5.6 - 2.55) ± 1.838 => 3.05 ± 1.838
=> (1.212, 4.888)

$A_2B_1 - A_2B_3$ $(5.6 - 2.9) \pm 1.838 \Rightarrow 2.7 \pm 1.838$
$\Rightarrow (.862, 4.538)$

$A_2B_2 - A_2B_3$ $(2.55 - 2.9) \pm 1.838 \Rightarrow -.35 \pm 1.838$
$\Rightarrow (-2.188, 1.488)$

The pairs that are significantly different are those that do not have 0 within their confidence interval. They are: $A_1B_1$ and $A_1B_3$, $A_1B_1$ and $A_2B_1$, $A_1B_2$ and $A_1B_3$, $A_1B_2$ and $A_2B_2$, $A_1B_3$ and $A_2B_2$, $A_1B_3$ and $A_2B_3$, $A_2B_1$ and $A_2B_2$, and $A_2B_1$ and $A_2B_3$.

17.47 a. SSA = .2(1000) = 200, SSB = .1(1000) = 100, SSAB = .1(1000) = 100

SSE = SS(Total) - SSA - SSB - SSAB = 1000 - 200 - 100 - 100 = 600

SST = SSA + SSB + SSAB = 200 + 100 + 100 = 400

$$MSA = \frac{SSA}{a - 1} = \frac{200}{3 - 1} = 100 \qquad MSB = \frac{SSB}{b - 1} = \frac{100}{3 - 1} = 50$$

$$MSAB = \frac{SSAB}{(a - 1)(b - 1)} = \frac{100}{(3 - 1)(3 - 1)} = 25$$

$$MSE = \frac{SSE}{n - ab} = \frac{600}{27 - 3(3)} = 33.333$$

$$MST = \frac{SST}{ab - 1} = \frac{400}{3(3) - 1} = 50$$

$$F_A = \frac{MSA}{MSE} = \frac{100}{33.333} = 3.00 \qquad F_B = \frac{MSB}{MSE} = \frac{50}{33.333} = 1.50$$

$$F_{AB} = \frac{MSAB}{MSE} = \frac{25}{33.333} = .75 \qquad F_T = \frac{MST}{MSE} = \frac{50}{33.333} = 1.50$$

| Source | df | SS | MS | F |
|---|---|---|---|---|
| A | 2 | 200 | 100 | 3.00 |
| B | 2 | 100 | 50 | 1.50 |
| AB | 4 | 100 | 25 | .75 |
| Error | 18 | 600 | 33.333 | |
| Total | 26 | 1000 | | |

To determine whether the treatment means differ, we test:

$H_0$: $\mu_1 = \mu_2 = \ldots = \mu_9$
$H_a$: At least two treatment means differ

The test statistic is $F = \frac{MST}{MSE} = 1.50$.

The rejection region requires $\alpha = .05$ in the upper tail of the F distribution with $\nu_1 = ab - 1 = 3(3) - 1 = 8$ and $\nu_2 = n - ab = 27 - 3(3) = 18$. From Table VIII, Appendix B, $F_{.05} = 2.51$. The rejection region is $F > 2.51$.

Since the observed value of the test statistic does not fall in the rejection region ($F = 1.50 \not> 2.51$), $H_0$ is not rejected. There is insufficient evidence to indicate the treatment means differ at $\alpha = .05$. Since there are no treatment mean differences, we have nothing more to do.

b. SSA = .1(1000) = 100, SSB = .1(1000) = 100, SSAB = .5(1000) = 500

SSE = SS(Total) - SSA - SSB - SSAB = 1000 - 100 - 100 - 500 = 300

SST = SSA + SSB + SSAB = 100 + 100 + 500 = 700

$$MSA = \frac{SSA}{a - 1} = \frac{100}{3 - 1} = 50 \qquad MSB = \frac{SSB}{b - 1} = \frac{100}{3 - 1} = 50$$

$$MSAB = \frac{SSAB}{(a - 1)(b - 1)} = \frac{500}{(3 - 1)(3 - 1)} = 125$$

$$MSE = \frac{SSE}{n - ab} = \frac{300}{27 - 3(3)} = 16.667$$

$$MST = \frac{SST}{ab - 1} = \frac{700}{9 - 1} = 87.5$$

$$F_A = \frac{MSA}{MSE} = \frac{50}{16.667} = 3.00 \qquad F_B = \frac{MSB}{MSE} = \frac{50}{16.667} = 3.00$$

$$F_{AB} = \frac{MSAB}{MSE} = \frac{125}{16.667} = 7.50 \qquad F_T = \frac{MST}{MSE} = \frac{87.5}{16.667} = 5.25$$

| Source | df | SS | MS | F |
|---|---|---|---|---|
| A | 2 | 100 | 50 | 3.00 |
| B | 2 | 100 | 50 | 3.00 |
| AB | 4 | 500 | 125 | 7.50 |
| Error | 18 | 300 | 16.667 | |
| Total | 26 | 1000 | | |

To determine if the treatment means differ, we test:

$H_0$: $\mu_1 = \mu_2 = \ldots = \mu_9$
$H_a$: At least two treatment means differ

The test statistic is $F = \frac{MST}{MSE} = 5.25$.

The rejection region requires $\alpha = .05$ in the upper tail of the F distribution with $\nu_1 = ab - 1 = 3(3) - 1 = 8$ and $\nu_2 = n - ab = 27 - 3(3) = 18$. From Table VIII, Appendix B, $F_{.05} = 2.51$. The rejection region is $F > 2.51$.

Since the observed value of the test statistic falls in the rejection region ($F = 5.25 > 2.51$), $H_0$ is rejected. There is sufficient evidence to indicate the treatment means differ at $\alpha = .05$.

Since the treatment means differ, we next test for interaction between factors A and B. To determine if factors A and B interact, we test:

$H_0$: Factors A and B do not interact to affect the mean response
$H_a$: Factors A and B do interact to affect the mean response

The test statistic is $F = \dfrac{MSAB}{MSE} = 7.50$.

The rejection region requires $\alpha = .05$ in the upper tail of the F distribution with $\nu_1 = (a - 1)(b - 1) = (3 - 1)(3 - 1) = 4$ and $\nu_2 = n - ab = 27 - 3(3) = 18$. From Table VIII, Appendix B, $F_{.05} = 2.93$. The rejection region is $F > 2.93$.

Since the observed value of the test statistic falls in the rejection region ($F = 7.50 > 2.93$), $H_0$ is rejected. There is sufficient evidence to indicate the Factors A and B interact at $\alpha = .05$. Since interaction is present, no tests for main effects are necessary.

c. $SSA = .4(1000) = 400$, $SSB = .1(1000) = 100$, $SSAB = .2(1000) = 200$

$$SSE = SS(Total) - SSA - SSB - SSAB = 1000 - 400 - 100 - 200 = 300$$

$$SST = SSA + SSB + SSAB = 400 + 100 + 200 = 700$$

$$MSA = \frac{SSA}{a - 1} = \frac{400}{3 - 1} = 50 \qquad MSB = \frac{SSB}{b - 1} = \frac{100}{3 - 1} = 50$$

$$MSAB = \frac{SSAB}{(a - 1)(b - 1)} = \frac{200}{(3 - 1)(3 - 1)} = 50$$

$$MSE = \frac{SSE}{n - ab} = \frac{300}{27 - 3(3)} = 16.667$$

$$MST = \frac{SST}{ab - 1} = \frac{700}{3(3) - 1} = 87.5$$

$$F_A = \frac{MSA}{MSE} = \frac{200}{16.667} = 12.00 \qquad F_B = \frac{MSB}{MSE} = \frac{50}{16.667} = 3.00$$

$$F_{AB} = \frac{MSAB}{MSE} = \frac{50}{16.667} = 3.00 \qquad F_T = \frac{MST}{MSE} = \frac{87.5}{16.667} = 5.25$$

| Source | df | SS | MS | F |
|---|---|---|---|---|
| A | 2 | 400 | 200 | 12.00 |
| B | 2 | 100 | 50 | 3.00 |
| AB | 4 | 200 | 50 | 3.00 |
| Error | 18 | 300 | 16.667 | |
| Total | 26 | 1000 | | |

To determine if the treatment means differ, we test:

$H_0$: $\mu_1 = \mu_2 = \ldots = \mu_9$
$H_a$: At least two treatment means differ

The test statistic is $F = \frac{MST}{MSE} = 5.25$.

The rejection region requires $\alpha = .05$ in the upper tail of the F distribution with $\nu_1 = ab - 1 = 3(3) - 1 = 8$ and $\nu_2 = n - ab = 27 - 3(3) = 18$. From Table VIII, Appendix B, $F_{.05} = 2.51$. The rejection region is $F > 2.51$.

Since the observed value of the test statistic falls in the rejection region ($F = 5.25 > 2.51$), $H_0$ is rejected. There is sufficient evidence to indicate the treatment means differ at $\alpha = .05$.

Since the treatment means differ, we next test for interaction between factors A and B. To determine if factors A and B interact, we test:

$H_0$: Factors A and B do not interact to affect the mean response
$H_a$: Factors A and B do interact to affect the mean response

The test statistic is $F = \frac{MSAB}{MSE} = 3.00$.

The rejection region requires $\alpha = .05$ in the upper tail of the F distribution with $\nu_1 = (a - 1)(b - 1) = (3 - 1)(3 - 1) = 4$ and $\nu_2 = n - ab = 27 - 3(3) = 18$. From Table VIII, Appendix B, $F_{.05} = 2.93$. The rejection region is $F > 2.93$.

Since the observed value of the test statistic falls in the rejection region ($F = 3.00 > 2.93$), $H_0$ is rejected. There is sufficient evidence to indicate the factors A and B interact at $\alpha = .05$. Since interaction is present, no tests for main effects are necessary.

d. $SSA = .4(1000) = 400$, $SSB = .4(1000) = 400$, $SSAB = .1(1000) = 100$

$SSE = SS(\text{Total}) - SSA - SSB - SSAB = 1000 - 400 - 400 - 100 = 100$

$SST = SSA + SSB + SSAB = 400 + 400 + 100 = 900$

$$MSA = \frac{SSA}{a - 1} = \frac{400}{3 - 1} = 200 \qquad MSB = \frac{SSB}{b - 1} = \frac{400}{3 - 1} = 200$$

$$MSAB = \frac{SSAB}{(a - 1)(b - 1)} = \frac{100}{(3 - 1)(3 - 1)} = 25$$

$$MSE = \frac{SSE}{n - ab} = \frac{100}{27 - 3(3)} = 5.556$$

$$MST = \frac{SST}{ab - 1} = \frac{900}{3(3) - 1} = 112.5$$

$$F_A = \frac{MSA}{MSE} = \frac{200}{5.556} = 36.00 \qquad F_B = \frac{MSB}{MSE} = \frac{200}{5.556} = 36.00$$

$$F_{AB} = \frac{MSAB}{MSE} = \frac{25}{5.556} = 4.50 \qquad F_T = \frac{MST}{MSE} = \frac{112.5}{5.556} = 20.25$$

| Source | df | SS | MS | F |
|---|---|---|---|---|
| A | 2 | 400 | 200 | 36.00 |
| B | 2 | 400 | 200 | 36.00 |
| AB | 4 | 100 | 25 | 4.50 |
| Error | 18 | 100 | 5.556 | |
| Total | 26 | 1000 | | |

To determine if the treatment means differ, we test:

$H_0$: $\mu_1 = \mu_2 = \ldots = \mu_9$
$H_a$: At least two treatment means differ

The test statistic is $F = \frac{MST}{MSE} = 20.25$.

The rejection region requires $\alpha = .05$ in the upper tail of the F distribution with $\nu_1 = ab - 1 = 3(3) - 1 = 8$ and $\nu_2 = n - ab = 27 - 3(3) = 18$. From Table VIII, Appendix B, $F_{.05} = 2.51$. The rejection region is $F > 2.51$.

Since the observed value of the test statistic falls in the rejection region ($F = 20.25 > 2.51$), $H_0$ is rejected. There is sufficient evidence to indicate the treatment means differ at $\alpha = .05$.

Since the treatment means differ, we next test for interaction between factors A and B. To determine if factors A and B interact, we test:

$H_0$: Factors A and B do not interact to affect the mean response

$H_a$: Factors A and B do interact to affect the mean response

The test statistic is $F = \frac{MSAB}{MSE} = 4.50$.

The rejection region requires $\alpha = .05$ in the upper tail of the F distribution with $\nu_1 = (a - 1)(b - 1) = (3 - 1)(3 - 1) = 4$ and $\nu_2 = n - ab = 27 - 3(3) = 18$. From Table VIII, Appendix B, $F_{.05} = 2.93$. The rejection region is $F > 2.93$.

Since the observed value of the test statistic falls in the rejection region ($F = 4.50 > 2.93$), $H_0$ is rejected. There is sufficient evidence to indicate the factors A and B interact at $\alpha = .05$. Since interaction is present, no tests for main effects are necessary.

17.49 a. The response variable is the dollar increases in sales per advertising dollar. There are two factors: advertising medium at 3 levels, and agency at 2 levels. Both factors are qualitative--the levels of each are not measured on a numerical scale. The treatments are the combinations of levels of the 2 factors. There are 2 x 3 = 6 treatments consisting of an agency type and an advertising medium. The experimental units are the twelve small towns. The experiment is a complete factorial experiment and is completely randomized.

b. $SST = SSA + SSB + SSAB = 39.967 + 198.332 + 77.345 = 315.644$

$$MST = \frac{SST}{ab - 1} = \frac{315.644}{3(2) - 1} = 63.1288$$

$$F_T = \frac{MST}{MSE} = \frac{63.1288}{5.701} = 11.073$$

To determine if there is a difference among the treatment means, we test:

$H_0$: $\mu_1 = \mu_2 = \mu_3 = \mu_4 = \mu_5 = \mu_6$

$H_a$: At least two treatment means differ

The test statistic is $F = \frac{MST}{MSE} = 11.073$

The rejection region requires $\alpha = .10$ in the upper tail of the F distribution with $\nu_1 = ab - 1 = 3(2) - 1 = 5$ and $\nu_2 = n - ab = 12 - 3(2) = 6$. From Table VII, Appendix B, $F_{.10} = 3.11$. The rejection region is $F > 3.11$.

Since the observed value of the test statistic falls in the rejection region ($F = 11.073 > 3.11$), $H_0$ is rejected. There is sufficient evidence to indicate a difference among the treatment means at $\alpha = .10$.

Since differences exist among the treatment means, we continue to test. To determine if an interaction between agency and advertising medium exist, we test:

$H_0$: Factors A and B do not interact to affect the response means

$H_a$: Factors A and B do interact to affect the response means

The test statistic is $F = \dfrac{MSAB}{MSE} = 6.789$.

The rejection region requires $\alpha = .10$ in the upper tail of the F distribution with $\nu_1 = (a - 1)(b - 1) = (2 - 1)(3 - 1) = 2$ and $\nu_2 = n - ab = 12 - 3(2) = 6$. From Table VII, Appendix B, $F_{.10} = 3.46$. The rejection region is $F > 3.46$.

Since the observed value of the test statistic falls in the rejection region ($F = 6.789 > 3.46$), $H_0$ is rejected. There is sufficient evidence to indicate interaction between the two factors is present at $\alpha = .10$.

Since interaction is present, we use the Bonferroni multiple comparisons procedure to compare all pairs of treatment means. There are 15 pairs of treatments, so $c = 15$. For $\alpha/2c = .10/2(15) = .0033 \approx .005$ and $df = n - ab = 12 - 3(2) = 6$, $t_{.005} = 3.707$ from Table V, Appendix B. We now form confidence intervals for the difference between each pair of means using the formula:

$$(\bar{y}_i - \bar{y}_j) \pm t_{\alpha/2c}\, s\sqrt{\frac{1}{n_i} + \frac{1}{n_j}} \quad \text{where } s = \sqrt{MSE} = \sqrt{5.701} = 2.3877$$

$$\bar{y}_{1N} = \frac{28.0}{2} = 14.0 \qquad \bar{y}_{1R} = \frac{37.5}{2} = 18.75 \qquad \bar{y}_{1T} = \frac{28.9}{2} = 14.45$$

$$\bar{y}_{2N} = \frac{41.3}{2} = 20.65 \qquad \bar{y}_{2R} = \frac{53.1}{2} = 26.55 \qquad y_{2T} = \frac{21.9}{2} = 10.95$$

Pair

| | |
|---|---|
| $A_1N - A_1R$ | $(14 - 18.75) \pm 3.707(2.3877)\sqrt{\frac{1}{2} + \frac{1}{2}} \Rightarrow -4.75 \pm 8.85 \Rightarrow (-13.6, 4.1)$ |
| $A_1N - A_1T$ | $(14 - 14.45) \pm 8.85 \Rightarrow -.45 \pm 8.85 \Rightarrow (-8.4, 9.3)$ |
| $A_1N - A_2N$ | $(14 - 20.65) \pm 8.85 \Rightarrow -6.65 \pm 8.85 \Rightarrow (-15.5, 2.2)$ |
| $A_1N - A_2R$ | $(14 - 26.55) \pm 8.85 \Rightarrow -12.55 \pm 8.85 \Rightarrow (-21.4, -3.7)$ |
| $A_1N - A_2T$ | $(14 - 10.95) \pm 8.85 \Rightarrow 3.05 \pm 8.85 \Rightarrow (-5.8, 11.9)$ |
| $A_1R - A_1T$ | $(18.75 - 14.45) \pm 8.85 \Rightarrow 4.3 \pm 8.85 \Rightarrow (-4.55, 13.15)$ |
| $A_1R - A_2N$ | $(18.75 - 20.65) \pm 8.85 \Rightarrow -1.9 \pm 8.85 \Rightarrow (-10.75, 6.95)$ |
| $A_1R - A_2R$ | $(18.75 - 26.55) \pm 8.85 \Rightarrow -7.8 \pm 8.85 \Rightarrow (-16.65, 1.05)$ |
| $A_1R - A_2T$ | $(18.75 - 10.95) \pm 8.85 \Rightarrow 7.8 \pm 8.85 \Rightarrow (-1.05, 16.65)$ |
| $A_1T - A_2N$ | $(14.45 - 20.65) \pm 8.85 \Rightarrow -6.2 \pm 8.85 \Rightarrow (-15.05, 2.65)$ |
| $A_1T - A_2R$ | $(14.45 - 26.55) \pm 8.85 \Rightarrow -12.1 \pm 8.85 \Rightarrow (-20.95, -3.25)$ |
| $A_1T - A_2T$ | $(14.45 - 10.95) \pm 8.85 \Rightarrow 3.5 \pm 8.85 \Rightarrow (-5.35, 12.35)$ |
| $A_2N - A_2R$ | $(20.65 - 26.55) \pm 8.85 \Rightarrow -5.9 \pm 8.85 \Rightarrow (-14.75, 2.95)$ |
| $A_2N - A_2T$ | $(20.65 - 10.95) \pm 8.85 \Rightarrow 9.7 \pm 8.85 \Rightarrow (.85, 18.55)$ |
| $A_2R - A_2T$ | $(26.55 - 10.95) \pm 8.85 \Rightarrow 15.6 \pm 8.85 \Rightarrow (6.75, 24.45)$ |

The following treatment pairs are significantly different because 0 is not in the confidence interval:

$A_1N$ and $A_2R$, $A_1T$ and $A_2R$, $A_2N$ and $A_2T$, and $A_2R$ and $A_2T$.

There are no significant differences among the other pairs.

c.

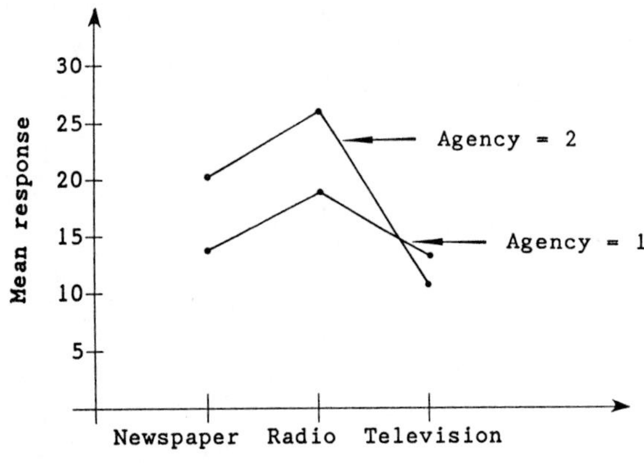


The lines are not parallel which implies interaction is present. Also, because the sample mean responses appear quite different, it appears that there are differences among the treatment means.

17.51 a. We first calculate the total of n = 10 pulling force measurements for each of the four categories by multiplying the means in each category by 10.

| | Light | Heavy | Totals |
|---|---|---|---|
| Females | 462.6 | 627.2 | 1089.8 |
| Males | 880.7 | 862.9 | 1743.6 |
| Totals | 1343.3 | 1490.1 | |

$$\sum x_i = 462.6 + 627.2 + 880.7 + 862.9 = 2833.4$$

$$CM = \frac{(\sum x_i)^2}{n} = \frac{2833.4^2}{40} = 200703.889$$

$$SS(Sex) = \frac{\sum A_i^2}{br} - CM = \frac{1089.8^2}{2(10)} + \frac{1743.6^2}{2(10)} - 200703.889$$

$$= 211390.25 - 200703.889 = 10686.361$$

$$SS(Weight) = \frac{\sum B_i^2}{ar} - CM = \frac{1343.3^2}{2(10)} + \frac{1490.1^2}{2(10)} - 200703.889$$

$$= 201242.645 - 200703.889 = 538.756$$

$$SS(Sex \times Weight) = \frac{\sum\sum AB_{ij}^2}{r} - SS(Sex) - SS(Weight) - CM$$

$$= \frac{462.6^2}{10} + \frac{627.2^2}{10} + \frac{880.7^2}{10} + \frac{862.9^2}{10} - 10686.361$$

$$- 538.756 - 200703.889$$

$$= 212760.75 - 211929.006 = 831.744$$

The sum of squares of deviations within each sample are found by multiplying the variance by n - 1.

| | STANDARD DEVIIATION | VARIANCE | SS |
|---|---|---|---|
| Female, Light | 14.23 | 202.4929 | 1822.4361 |
| Female, Heavy | 13.97 | 195.1609 | 1756.4481 |
| Male, Light | 8.32 | 69.2224 | 623.0016 |
| Male, Heavy | 12.45 | 155.0025 | 1395.0225 |
| | | | 5596.9083 |

SSE = 5596.9083

$$\begin{aligned} \text{SS(Total)} &= \text{SS(Sex)} + \text{SS(Weight)} + \text{SS(Sex} \times \text{Weight)} + \text{SSE} \\ &= 10686.361 + 538.756 + 831.744 + 5596.9083 \\ &= 17653.7693 \end{aligned}$$

| Source | df | SS | MS | F |
|---|---|---|---|---|
| Sex | 1 | 10686.361 | 10686.361 | 68.74 |
| Weight | 1 | 538.756 | 538.756 | 3.47 |
| Sex × Weight | 1 | 831.744 | 831.744 | 5.35 |
| Error | 36 | 5596.9083 | 155.4697 | |
| Total | 39 | 17653.7693 | | |

b. $$\begin{aligned} \text{SST} &= \text{SS(Sex)} + \text{SS(Weight)} + \text{SS(Sex} \times \text{Weight)} \\ &= 10686.361 + 538.756 + 831.744 \\ &= 12056.861 \end{aligned}$$

$$\text{MST} = \frac{\text{SST}}{ab - 1} = \frac{12056.861}{2(2) - 1} = 4018.954$$

$$F_T = \frac{\text{MST}}{\text{MSE}} = \frac{4018.954}{155.4697} = 25.85$$

To determine if differences exist among the treatment means, we test:

$H_0$: $\mu_1 = \mu_2 = \mu_3 = \mu_4$
$H_a$: At least one treatment mean is different

The test statistic is $F = \frac{\text{MST}}{\text{MSE}} = 25.85$

The rejection region requires $\alpha = .05$ in the upper tail of the F distribution with $\nu_1 = ab - 1 = 2(2) - 1 = 3$ and $\nu_2 = n - ab = 40 - 2(2) = 36$. From Table VIII, Appendix B, $F_{.05} \approx 2.92$. The rejection region is $F > 2.92$.

Since the observed value of the test statistic falls in the rejection region ($F = 25.85 > 2.92$), $H_0$ is rejected. There is sufficient evidence to indicate the treatment means differ at $\alpha = .05$.

To determine if sex and weight interact, we test:

$H_0$: Sex and weight do not interact to affect the response mean

$H_a$: Sex and weight do interact to affect the response mean

The test statistic is $F = \dfrac{MS(\text{Sex} \times \text{Weight})}{MSE} = 5.35$

The rejection region requires $\alpha = .05$ in the upper tail of the F distribution with $\nu_1 = (a - 1)(b - 1) = (2 - 1)(2 - 1) = 1$ and $\nu_2 = n - ab = 40 - 2(2) = 36$. From Table VIII, Appendix B, $F_{.05} \approx 4.17$. The rejection region is $F > 4.17$.

Since the observed value of the test statistic falls in the rejection region ($F = 5.35 > 4.17$), $H_0$ is rejected. There is sufficient evidence to indicate sex and weight interact at $\alpha = .05$.

Since interaction is present, we use the Bonferroni multiple comparisons procedure to compare all pairs of treatment means. There are 6 pairs of treatments, so $c = 6$. For $\alpha/2c = .05/2(6) = .004 \approx .005$ and $df = n - ab = 40 - 2(2) = 36$, $t_{.005} \approx 2.756$ from Table VI, Appendix B. We now form confidence intervals for the difference between each pair of means using the formula:

$$(\bar{y}_i - \bar{y}_j) \pm t_{\alpha/2c}\, s\sqrt{\frac{1}{n_i} + \frac{1}{n_j}} \quad \text{where } s = \sqrt{MSE} = \sqrt{155.4697} = 12.4687$$

F, L - F, H $\quad (46.26 - 62.72) \pm 2.756(12.4687)\sqrt{\frac{1}{10} + \frac{1}{10}}$

$\Rightarrow -16.46 \pm 15.368 \Rightarrow (-31.828, -1.092)$

F, L - M, L $\quad (46.26 - 88.07) \pm 15.368 \Rightarrow$

$\Rightarrow -41.81 \pm 15.368 \Rightarrow (-57.178, -26.442)$

F, L - M, H $\quad (46.26 - 86.29) \pm 15.368 \Rightarrow$

$\Rightarrow -40.03 \pm 15.368 \Rightarrow (-55.398, -26.662)$

F, H - M, L (62.72 - 88.07) ± 15.368 =>
=> -25.35 ± 15.368 => (-40.718, -9.982)

F, H - M, H (62.72 - 86.29) ± 15.368 =>
=> -23.57 ± 15.368 => (-38.938, -8.202)

M, L - M, H (88.07 - 86.29) ± 15.368 =>
=> 1.78 ± 15.368 => (-13.588, 17.148)

All pairs are significantly different except M, L and M, H.

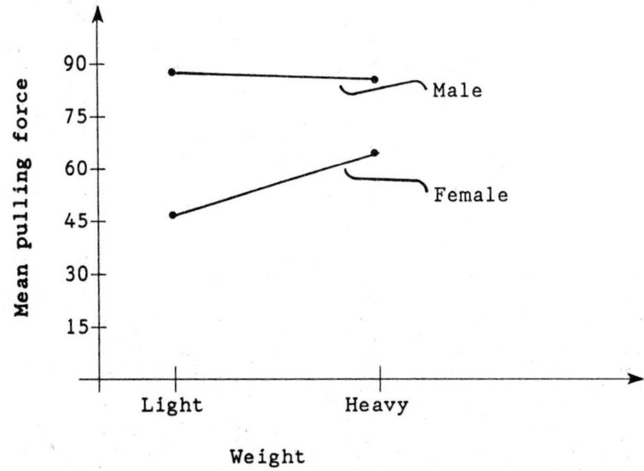


c. These standard deviations are sample standard deviations. Even though the sample standard deviations are different, it is not necessarily true that the population standard deviations are different. We would need to run a test to determine if the sample standard deviations are different enough to infer the population standard deviations are different.

17.53 a. Randomized block design.

b. $\beta_0$ = mean value for treatment C, block 2.
$\beta_1$ = difference in mean values between treatment A and treatment C
$\beta_2$ = difference in mean values between treatment B and treatment C
$\beta_3$ = difference in mean values between block 1 and block 2, treatment C

c. To determine if the treatment means differ, we test:

$H_0$: $\beta_1 = \beta_2 = 0$
$H_a$: At least one $\beta_i \neq 0$

The test statistic is $F = \frac{(\text{SSE(Reduced)} - \text{SSE(Complete)})/2}{\text{SSE(Complete)}/2}$

where SSE(Reduced) is the sum of squares for errors found using the model $y_i = \beta_0 + \beta_3 x_{i3}$ and SSE(Complete) is the sum of squares for errors found using the model $y_i = \beta_0 + \beta_1 x_{i1} + \beta_2 x_{i2} + \beta_3 x_{i3}$.

The rejection region requires $\alpha$ in the upper tail of the F distribution with $\nu_1 = 2$ and $\nu_2 = n - 4 = 6 - 4 = 2$. The rejection region is $F > F_\alpha$.

17.55 a. To determine if the mean costs differ among the three groups, we test:

$H_0$: $\beta_1 = \beta_2 = 0$
$H_a$: At least one $\beta_i \neq 0$

The test statistic is $F = 8.438$.

The rejection region requires $\alpha = .05$ in the upper tail of the F distribution with $\nu_1 = 2$ and $\nu_2 = 27$. From Table VIII, Appendix B, $F_{.05} = 3.35$. The rejection region is $F > 3.35$.

Since the observed value of the test statistic falls in the rejection region ($F = 8.438 > 3.35$), $H_0$ is rejected. There is sufficient evidence to indicate a difference in the treatment means among the 3 groups at $\alpha = .05$. This is the same result as found in Exercise 17.20.

b. The observed significance level for this problem is .0014, while the observed significance level for Exercise 17.20 is .0014.

c. SST = 318861.66667 for this problem and SST = 318861.667 for Exercise 17.20. SSE = 510163 for this problem and SSE = 510163 for Exercise 17.20.

d. $R^2 = .3846$. 38.46% of the simple variation in costs incurred in audits is explained by the three groups.

$\beta_0$ = mean costs incurred in audits for group C.
$\beta_1$ = difference in mean costs incurred for audits between groups A and C
$\beta_2$ = difference in mean costs incurred in audits between groups B and C

c. $H_0$: $\mu_A = \mu_B$
$H_a$: $\mu_A \neq \mu_B$

The test statistic is $F = \frac{MST}{MSE} = .21$.

The rejection region requires $\alpha = .05$ in the upper tail of the F distribution with $\nu_1 = p - 1 = 2 - 1 = 1$ and $\nu_2 = n - p = 16 - 2 = 14$. From Table VIII, Appendix B, $F_{.05} = 4.60$. The rejection region is $F > 4.60$.

Since the observed value of the test statistic does not fall in the rejection region ($F = .21 \not> 4.60$), $H_0$ is not rejected. There is insufficient evidence to indicate the average home value is different in the two communities at $\alpha = .05$.

d. The test statistics in parts (a) and (b) are the same except for the sign, and the rejection regions are identical. We can also see that $t^2 = .46^2 = .21 = F$ in part (c). Also, $t^2_{.025} = 2.145^2 = 4.60 = F$ in part (c).

17.77 a. This is an observational experiment and is completely randomized.

b. SSE = SS(Total) - SST = 30,935.513 - 2,759.905 = 28,175.608

$$MST = \frac{SST}{p - 1} = \frac{2759.905}{3 - 1} = 1379.9525$$

$$MSE = \frac{SST}{n - p} = \frac{28175.608}{87 - 3} = 335.4239$$

$$F = \frac{MST}{MSE} = \frac{1379.9525}{335.4239} = 4.11$$

| Source | df | SS | MS | F |
|---|---|---|---|---|
| Treatment | 2 | 2759.905 | 1379.9525 | 4.11 |
| Error | 84 | 28175.608 | 335.4239 | |
| Total | 86 | 30935.513 | | |

c. To determine if the mean closing price differed among the three markets, we test:

$H_0$: $\mu_1 = \mu_2 = \mu_3$
$H_a$: At least two treatment means differ

The test statistic is $F = \frac{MST}{MSE} = 4.11$.

The rejection region requires $\alpha = .10$ in the upper tail of the F distribution with $\nu_1 = p - 1 = 3 - 1 = 2$ and $\nu_2 = n - p = 87 - 3 = 84$. From Table VII, Appendix B, $F_{.10} \approx 2.39$. The rejection region is $F > 2.39$.

Since the observed value of the test statistic falls in the rejection region ($F = 4.11 > 2.39$), $H_0$ is rejected. There is sufficient evidence to indicate the mean closing price differed among the three markets at $\alpha = .10$.

d. There are 3 pairs of means, so $c = 6$. For $\alpha/2c = .10/2(3) = .0167$, and $df = n - p = 87 - 3 = 84$, we use the z table, Table IV, instead of the t table. From Table IV, Appendix B, $z_{.0167} = 2.13$. We form confidence intervals for the difference between each pair of means using:

$$(\bar{y}_i - \bar{y}_j) \pm z_{.0167}\, s\sqrt{\frac{1}{n_i} + \frac{1}{n_j}} \quad \text{where } s = \sqrt{MSE} = \sqrt{335.4239} = 18.3146$$

$$\bar{y}_1 = \frac{\sum y_1}{n_1} = \frac{941.75}{36} = 26.16 \qquad \bar{y}_2 = \frac{\sum y_2}{n_2} = \frac{518.99}{36} = 14.42$$

$$\bar{y}_3 = \frac{\sum y_3}{n_3} = \frac{233.375}{15} = 15.56$$

<u>Pairs</u>

NYSE - ASE $\quad (26.16 - 14.42) \pm 2.13(18.3146)\sqrt{\frac{1}{36} + \frac{1}{36}}$

$$\Rightarrow 11.74 \pm 9.195 \Rightarrow (2.545,\ 20.935)$$

NYSE - OTC $\quad (26.16 - 15.56) \pm 2.13(18.3146)\sqrt{\frac{1}{36} + \frac{1}{15}}$

$$\Rightarrow 10.60 \pm 11.989 \Rightarrow (-1.389,\ 22.589)$$

ASE - OTC $\quad (14.42 - 15.56) \pm 2.13(18.3146)\sqrt{\frac{1}{36} + \frac{1}{15}}$

$$\Rightarrow -1.14 \pm 11.989 \Rightarrow (-13.129,\ 10.849)$$

The mean closing prices for the NYSE and ASE are significantly different.

17.79 Some preliminary calculations are:

$$CM = \frac{(\sum x_i)^2}{n} = \frac{2132^2}{19} = 239{,}232.8421$$

$$SS(\text{Total}) = \sum x_i^2 - CM = 250{,}048 - 239{,}232.8421 = 10815.1579$$

$$SST = \sum \frac{T_i^2}{n_1} - CM = \frac{732^2}{8} + \frac{825^2}{7} + \frac{575^2}{4} - 239{,}232.8421$$

$$= 246{,}866.3929 - 239{,}232.8421 = 7633.5508$$

$$SSE = SS(\text{Total}) - SST = 10815.1579 - 7633.5508 = 3181.6071$$

$$MST = \frac{SST}{p - 1} = \frac{7633.5508}{3 - 1} = 3816.7754$$

$$MSE = \frac{SSE}{n - p} = \frac{3181.6071}{19 - 3} = 198.8504$$

$$F = \frac{MST}{MSE} = \frac{3816.7754}{198.8504} = 19.19$$

| Source | df | SS | MS | F |
|---|---|---|---|---|
| Treatments | 2 | 7633.5508 | 3816.7754 | 19.19 |
| Error | 16 | 3181.6071 | 195.8504 | |
| Total | 18 | 10815.1579 | | |

The analysis of variance table is the same as that in Figure 17.4.

The form of the confidence interval for the difference in two means is:

$$(\bar{y}_i - \bar{y}_j) \pm t_{\alpha/2}\, s\sqrt{\frac{1}{n_i} + \frac{1}{n_j}} \quad \text{where } s = \sqrt{MSE} = \sqrt{198.8504} = 14.1014$$

For confidence coefficient .95, $\alpha = 1 - .95 = .05$ and $\alpha/2 = .05/2 = .025$. From Table VI, Appendix B, $t_{.025} = 2.120$ with df $= n - p = 19 - 3 = 16$.

The 95% confidence interval for the difference in the mean score for expertises 1 and 2 is:

$$(117.9 - 91.5) \pm 2.12(14.1014)\sqrt{\frac{1}{8} + \frac{1}{7}} \Rightarrow 26.4 \pm 15.47$$

$$\Rightarrow (10.93, 41.87)$$

The 95% confidence interval for the difference in the mean score for expertises 2 and 3 is:

$$(1438 - 117.9) \pm 2.12(14.1014)\sqrt{\frac{1}{4} + \frac{1}{7}} \Rightarrow 25.9 \pm 18.74$$

$$\Rightarrow (7.16, 44.64)$$

Again, these intervals are the same as those shown in Figure 17.11.

17.81 a. The model is $E(y) = \beta_0 + \beta_1 x_1 + \beta_2 x_2 + \beta_3 x_3 + \beta_4 x_1 x_2 + \beta_5 x_1 x_3$

where

$$x_1 = \begin{cases} 1 & \text{if Union} \\ 0 & \text{otherwise} \end{cases}$$

$$x_2 = \begin{cases} 1 & \text{if 20¢/casting} \\ 0 & \text{otherwise} \end{cases}$$

$$x_3 = \begin{cases} 1 & \text{if 30¢/casting} \\ 0 & \text{otherwise} \end{cases}$$

b. Using SAS, the printout is:

DEPENDENT VARIABLE: Y

| SOURCE | DF | SUM OF SQUARES | MEAN SQUARE | F VALUE |
|---|---|---|---|---|
| MODEL | 5 | 62779.61111111 | 12555.92222222 | 8.42 |
| ERROR | 12 | 17902.00000000 | 1491.83333333 | PR > F |
| CORRECTED TOTAL | 17 | 80681.61111112 | | 0.0013 |

| R-SQUARE | C.V. | ROOT MSE | Y MEAN |
|---|---|---|---|
| 0.778115 | 2.4497 | 38.62425835 | 1576.72222222 |

| PARAMETER | ESTIMATE | T FOR HO: PARAMETER = 0 | PR > ¦T¦ | STD ERROR OF ESTIMATE |
|---|---|---|---|---|
| INTERCEPT | 1650.00000000 | 73.99 | 0.0001 | 22.29972596 |
| PLANT | -46.33333333 | -1.47 | 0.1675 | 31.53657489 |
| INCENT | -125.00000000 | -3.96 | 0.0019 | 31.53657489 |
| | -21.66666667 | -0.69 | 0.5051 | 31.53657489 |
| PLANT*INCENT | 0.66666667 | 0.01 | 0.9883 | 44.59945191 |
| | -8.00000000 | -0.18 | 0.8606 | 44.59945191 |

The fitted model is $\hat{y} = 1650 - 46.3x_1 - 125x_2 - 21.7x_3 + .67x_1x_2 - 8x_1x_3$.

SSE = 17902 which is the same as SSE in Exercise 17.80.

c. The reduced model is $E(y) = \beta_0 + \beta_1 x_1 + \beta_2 x_2 + \beta_3 x_3$. The printout using SAS is:

DEPENDENT VARIABLE: Y

| SOURCE | DF | SUM OF SQUARES | MEAN SQUARE | F VALUE |
|---|---|---|---|---|
| MODEL | 3 | 62709.83333333 | 20903.277777778 | 16.28 |
| ERROR | 14 | 17971.77777778 | 1283.69841270 | PR > F |
| CORRECTED TOTAL | 17 | 80681.61111112 | | 0.0001 |

| R-SQUARE | C.V. | ROOT MSE | Y MEAN |
|---|---|---|---|
| 0.777251 | 2.2724 | 35.82873725 | 1576.72222222 |

| PARAMETER | ESTIMATE | T FOR H0: PARAMETER = 0 | PR > \|T\| | STD ERROR OF ESTIMATE |
|---|---|---|---|---|
| INTERCEPT | 1651.22222222 | 97.76 | 0.0001 | 16.88982871 |
| PLANT | -48.77777778 | -2.89 | 0.0119 | 16.88982871 |
| INCENT | -124.66666667 | -6.03 | 0.0001 | 20.68573109 |
| | -25.66666667 | -1.24 | 0.2351 | 20.68573109 |

The fitted model is $\hat{y} = 1651.2 - 48.8x_1 - 124.7x_2 - 25.7x_3$.

To determine if the interaction terms contribute to the model, we test:

$H_0$: $\beta_4 = \beta_5 = 0$
$H_a$: At least one $\beta_i \neq 0$

The test statistic is $F = \dfrac{(\text{SSE(Reduced)} - \text{SSE(Complete)})/(k - g)}{\text{SSE(Complete)}/[n - (k + 1)]}$

$$= \frac{(17971.7778 - 17902)/(5 - 3)}{17902/[18 - (5 + 1)]} = \frac{34.8889}{1491.8333} = .023$$

The rejection region requires $\alpha = .05$ in the upper tail of the F distribution with $\nu_1 = k - g = 5 - 3 = 2$ and $\nu_2 = n - (k + 1) = 18 - (5 + 1) = 12$. From Table VIII, Appendix B, $F_{.05} = 3.89$. The rejection region is $F > 3.89$.

Since the observed value of the test statistic does not fall in the rejection region ($F = .023 \not> 3.89$), $H_0$ is not rejected. There is insufficient evidence to indicate the interaction terms contribute to the model at $\alpha = .05$.

# CHAPTER 18

## NONPARAMETRIC STATISTICS

18.1 The sign test is preferred to the t-test when the population from which the sample is selected is not normal.

18.3 a. $P(x \geq 6) = 1 - P(x \leq 5) = 1 - .937 = .063$

b. $P(x \geq 5) = 1 - P(x \leq 4) = 1 - .500 = .500$

c. $P(x \geq 8) = 1 - P(x \leq 7) = 1 - .996 = .004$

d. $P(x \geq 10) = 1 - P(x \leq 9) = 1 - .849 = .151$

$\mu = np = 15(.5) = 7.5$ and $\sigma = \sqrt{npq} = \sqrt{15(.5)(.5)} = 1.9365$

$$P(x \geq 10) \approx P(z \geq \frac{(10 - .5) - 7.5}{1.9365}) = P(z \geq 1.03) = .5 - .3485$$
$$= .1515$$

e. $P(x \geq 15) = 1 - P(x \leq 14) = 1 - .788 = .212$

$\mu = np = 25(.5) = 12.5$ and $\sigma = \sqrt{npq} = \sqrt{25(.5)(.5)} = 2.5$

$$P(x \geq 15) \approx P(z \geq \frac{(15 - .5) - 12.5}{2.5}) = P(z \geq .80) = .5 - .2881$$
$$= .2119$$

18.5 To determine if the median is greater than 75, we test:

$H_0$: $M = 75$
$H_a$: $M > 75$

The test statistic is S = number of measurements greater than 75 = 16.

The p-value = $P(x \geq 16)$ where x is a binomial random variable with $n = 25$ and $p = .5$. From Table II,

p-value = $P(x \geq 16) = 1 - P(x \leq 15) = 1 - .885 = .115$

Since the p-value = $.115 > \alpha = .10$, $H_0$ is not rejected. There is insufficient evidence to indicate the median is greater than 75 at $\alpha = .10$.

We must assume the sample was randomly selected from a continuous probability distribution.

Note: Since $n \geq 10$, we could use the large-sample approximation.

18.7 a. I would recommend the sign test because 5 of the sample measurements are of similar magnitude, but the 6th is about three times as large as the others. It would be very unlikely to observe this sample if the population were normal.

b. To determine if the airline is meeting the requirement, we test:

$H_0$: $M = 30$
$H_a$: $M < 30$

c. The test statistic is S = number of measurements less than 30 = 5.

$H_0$ will be rejected if the p-value $< \alpha = .01$.

d. The test statistic is $S = 5$.

The p-value = $P(x \geq 5)$ where x is a binomial random variable with $n = 6$ and $p = .5$. From Table II,

$$\text{p-value} = P(x \geq 5) = 1 - P(x \leq 4) = 1 - .891 = .109$$

Since the p-value = .109 is not less than $\alpha = .01$, $H_0$ is not rejected. There is insufficient evidence to indicate the airline is meeting the maintenance requirement at $\alpha = .01$.

18.9 a. The test statistic is $T_B$, the rank sum of population B (because $n_B < n_A$).

The rejection region is $T_B \leq 32$ or $T_B \geq 58$, from Table XI, Appendix B, with $n_A = 8$, $n_B = 6$, and $\alpha = .10$.

b. The test statistic is $T_A$, the rank sum of population A (because $n_A < n_B$).

The rejection region is $T_A \geq 40$, from Table XI, Appendix B, with $n_A = 5$, $n_B = 6$, and $\alpha = .05$.

c. The test statistic is $T_B$, the rank sum of population B (because $n_B < n_A$).

The rejection region is $T_B \geq 98$.

d. Since $n_A = n_B = 20$, the test statistic is

$$z = \frac{T_A - \frac{n_1(n_1 + n_2 + 1)}{2}}{\sqrt{\frac{n_1 n_2(n_1 + n_2 + 1)}{12}}}$$

The rejection region is $z < -z_{\alpha/2}$ or $z > z_{\alpha/2}$. For $\alpha = .05$ and $\alpha/2 = .05/2 = .025$, $z_{.025} = 1.96$ from Table IV, Appendix B. The rejection region is $z < -1.96$ or $z > 1.96$.

18.11 The alternative hypotheses differ for one- and two-tailed versions of the Wilcoxon rank sum test. For a two-tailed test, the alternative hypothesis is $H_a$: The probability distribution for one population is shifted to the right or left of the other distribution. For a one-tailed test, the alternative hypothesis is $H_a$: The probability distribution for one population is shifted to the right (left) of the other distribution.

The rejection regions are also different. For a two-tailed test, the rejection region is $T \leq T_L$ or $T \geq T_U$ where T is the rank sum of the sample with the smallest sample size. For a one-tailed test, the rejection region is $T \geq T_U$ (or $T \leq T_L$).

18.13 a. We first rank all observations:

| NEIGHBORHOOD A OBSERVATION | RANK | NEIGHBORHOOD B OBSERVATION | RANK |
|---|---|---|---|
| .850 | 11 | .911 | 16 |
| 1.060 | 18 | .770 | 3 |
| .910 | 15 | .815 | 8 |
| .813 | 7 | .748 | 2 |
| .787 | 1 | .835 | 9 |
| .880 | 13 | .800 | 6 |
| .895 | 14 | .793 | 4 |
| .844 | 10 | .769 | 5 |
| .965 | 17 | | |
| .875 | 12 | | |
| | $T_A = 118$ | | $T_B = 53$ |

To determine the fairness of the assessments between the two neighborhoods, we test:

$H_0$: Two sampled populations have identical probability distributions

$H_a$: The probability distribution for Neighborhood A is shifted to the right or left of that for Neighborhood B

18.17 a. Some preliminary calculations are:

$$\bar{x}_A = \frac{\sum x_A}{n_A} = \frac{279}{6} = 46.5 \qquad \bar{x}_B = \frac{\sum x_B}{n_B} = \frac{442}{8} = 55.25$$

$$s_A^2 = \frac{\sum x_A^2 - \frac{(\sum x_A)^2}{n_A}}{n_A - 1} = \frac{13247 - \frac{279^2}{6}}{6 - 1} = \frac{273.5}{5} = 54.7$$

$$s_B^2 = \frac{\sum x_B^2 - \frac{(\sum x_B)^2}{n_B}}{n_B - 1} = \frac{26136 - \frac{442^2}{8}}{8 - 1} = \frac{1715.5}{7} = 245.0714$$

$$s_p^2 = \frac{(n_A - 1)s_A^2 + (n_B - 1)s_B^2}{n_A + n_B - 2}$$

$$= \frac{(6 - 1)(54.7) + (8 - 1)(245.0714)}{6 + 8 - 2} = \frac{1989}{12} = 165.75$$

To determine whether the mean prices per house differ in the two subdivisions, we test:

$H_0$: $\mu_1 = \mu_2$
$H_a$: $\mu_1 \neq \mu_2$

The test statistic is

$$t = \frac{(\bar{x}_A - \bar{x}_B) - 0}{\sqrt{s_p^2\left(\frac{1}{n_A} + \frac{1}{n_B}\right)}} = \frac{46.5 - 55.25}{\sqrt{165.75\left(\frac{1}{6} + \frac{1}{8}\right)}} = \frac{-8.75}{6.9530} = -1.26$$

The rejection region requires $\alpha/2 = .05/2 = .025$ in each tail of the t distribution with df $= n_A + n_B - 2 = 6 + 8 - 2 = 12$. From Table VI, Appendix B, $t_{.025} = 2.179$. The rejection region is $t < -2.179$ or $t > 2.179$.

Since the observed value of the test statistic does not fall in the rejection region ($t = -1.26 \nless -2.179$), $H_0$ is not rejected. There is insufficient evidence to indicate the mean prices differ for the two subdivisions at $\alpha = .05$.

We must assume:

1. Both populations are normal
2. The samples are independent
3. $\sigma_1^2 = \sigma_2^2$

Because $s_A^2 = 54.7$ and $s_B^2 = 245.0714$, it appears the assumption $\sigma_1^2 = \sigma_2^2$ may not be reasonable.

b. The data and their ranks are:

| A | Rank | B | Rank |
|---|---|---|---|
| 43 | 5 | 57 | 11 |
| 48 | 8 | 39 | 1.5 |
| 42 | 4 | 55 | 10 |
| 60 | 12 | 52 | 9 |
| 39 | 1.5 | 88 | 14 |
| 47 | 7 | 46 | 6 |
| | | 41 | 3 |
| | | 64 | 13 |
| | $T_A = 37.5$ | | $T_B = 67.5$ |

To determine whether there is a shift in the locations of the probability distributions of house prices in the two subdivisions, we test:

$H_0$: The 2 sampled populations have identical probability distributions

$H_a$: The probability distribution for subdivision A is shifted to the right or left of that for subdivision B

The test statistic is $T_A = 37.5$.

The rejection region is $T_A \leq 29$ or $T_A \geq 61$ from Table XI, Appendix B, with $n_A = 6$, $n_B = 8$, and $\alpha = .05$.

Since the observed value of the test statistic does not fall in the rejection region ($T_A = 37.5 \nleq 29$ and $\ngeq 61$), $H_0$ is not rejected. There is insufficient evidence to indicate a shift in the locations of the distributions of house prices in the two subdivisions.

18.19 a. We first rank all the data:

| FIRMS WITH SUCCESSFUL MIS (A) | | | | FIRMS WITH UNSUCCESSFUL MIS (B) | | | |
|---|---|---|---|---|---|---|---|
| SCORE | RANK | SCORE | RANK | SCORE | RANK | SCORE | RANK |
| 52 | 5 | 90 | 25.5 | 60 | 10.5 | 65 | 12.5 |
| 70 | 15 | 75 | 17 | 50 | 4 | 55 | 7 |
| 40 | 1.5 | 80 | 19 | 55 | 7 | 70 | 15 |
| 80 | 19 | 95 | 30 | 70 | 15 | 90 | 25.5 |
| 82 | 21 | 90 | 25.5 | 41 | 3 | 85 | 22 |
| 65 | 12.5 | 86 | 23 | 40 | 1.5 | 80 | 19 |
| 59 | 9 | 95 | 29 | 55 | 7 | 90 | 25.5 |
| 60 | 10.5 | 93 | 28 | | | | |
| $T_A = 290.5$ | | | | $T_B = 174.5$ | | | |

To determine whether the distribution of quality scores for successfully implemented systems lies above that for unsuccessfully implemented systems, we test:

$H_0$: The two sampled populations have identical probability distributions

$H_a$: The probability distribution for successful MIS is shifted to the right of that for the unsuccessful MIS

The test statistic is

$$z = \frac{T_A - \frac{n_1(n_1 + n_2 + 1)}{2}}{\sqrt{\frac{n_1 n_2(n_1 + n_2 + 1)}{12}}} = \frac{290.5 - \frac{16(16 + 14 + 1)}{2}}{\sqrt{\frac{16(14)(16 + 14 + 1)}{12}}}$$

$$= \frac{42.5}{24.0555} = 1.77$$

The rejection region requires $\alpha = .05$ in the upper tail of the z distribution. From Table IV, Appendix B, $z_{.05} = 1.645$. The rejection region is $z > 1.645$.

Since the observed value of the test statistic falls in the rejection region ($z = 1.77 > 1.645$), $H_0$ is rejected. There is sufficient evidence to indicate the distribution of quality scores for successfully implemented systems lies above that for the unsuccessfully implemented systems at $\alpha = .05$.

b. We could use the two-sample t test if

1. Both populations are normal.
2. The variances of the two populations are the same.

18.21 a. The hypotheses are:

$H_0$: The two sampled populations have identical probability distributions

$H_a$: The probability distributions for population A is shifted to the right of that for population B

b. Some preliminary calculations are:

| TREATMENT A | TREATMENT B | DIFFERENCE A - B | RANK OF ABSOLUTE DIFFERENCE |
|---|---|---|---|
| 56 | 42 | 14 | 8.5 |
| 62 | 45 | 17 | 10 |
| 98 | 87 | 11 | 6 |
| 45 | 31 | 14 | 8.5 |
| 82 | 71 | 11 | 6 |
| 76 | 75 | 1 | 1.5 |
| 74 | 63 | 11 | 6 |
| 29 | 30 | -1 | 1.5 |
| 63 | 59 | 4 | 4 |
| 80 | 82 | -2 | 3 |
| | | | $T_- =$ 4.5 |

The test statistic is $T_- = 4.5$

The rejection region is $T_- \leqq 8$, from Table XII, Appendix B, with $n = 10$ and $\alpha = .025$.

Since the observed value of the test statistic falls in the rejection region ($T_- = 4.5 \leqq 8$), $H_0$ is rejected. There is sufficient evidence to indicate the responses for A tend to be larger than those for B at $\alpha = .025$.

18.23 We assume that the probability distribution of differences is continuous so that the absolute differences will have unique ranks. Although tied (absolute) differences can be assigned average ranks, the number of ties should be small relative to the number of observations to assure validity.

18.25 a. This is a paired difference experimental design.

b. The hypotheses are:

$H_0$: The two sampled populations have identical probability distributions

$H_a$: The probability distribution for the teleconferencing groups is shifted to the right of that for the face-to-face group

c. Some preliminary calculations are:

| GROUP | FACE-TO-FACE | VIDEO TELECONFERENCING | DIFFERENCE F - VT | RANK OF ABSOLUTE DIFFERENCES |
|---|---|---|---|---|
| 1 | 65 | 75 | -10 | 7.5 |
| 2 | 82 | 80 | 2 | 1 |
| 3 | 54 | 60 | -6 | 6 |
| 4 | 69 | 65 | 4 | 2.5 |
| 5 | 40 | 55 | -15 | 9 |
| 6 | 85 | 90 | -5 | 4.5 |
| 7 | 98 | 98 | 0 | (Eliminated) |
| 8 | 35 | 40 | -5 | 4.5 |
| 9 | 85 | 89 | -4 | 2.5 |
| 10 | 70 | 80 | -10 | 7.5 |
| | | | | $T_+ = 3.5$ |

The test statistic is $T_+ = 3.5$

The rejection region is $T_+ \leq 8$ from Table XII, Appendix B, with $n = 9$ and $\alpha = .05$.

Since the observed value of the test statistic falls in the rejection region ($T_+ = 3.5 \leq 8$), $H_0$ is rejected. There is sufficient evidence to indicate the problem-solving performance of video teleconferencing groups is superior to that of groups that interact face-to-face at $\alpha = .05$.

d. The p-value for the test is $P(T_+ \leq 3.5)$. From Table XII, Appendix B, and $n = 9$, $.01 \leq P(T_+ \leq 3.5) \leq .025$.

18.27 Some preliminary calculations are:

| EMPLOYEE | BEFORE FLEXTIME | AFTER FLEXTIME | DIFFERENCE (B - A) | RANK OF ABSOLUTE DIFFERENCE |
|---|---|---|---|---|
| 1 | 54 | 68 | -14 | 7 |
| 2 | 25 | 42 | -17 | 9 |
| 3 | 80 | 80 | 0 | (Eliminated) |
| 4 | 76 | 91 | -15 | 8 |
| 5 | 63 | 70 | -7 | 5 |
| 6 | 82 | 88 | -6 | 3.5 |
| 7 | 94 | 90 | 4 | 2 |
| 8 | 72 | 81 | -9 | 6 |
| 9 | 33 | 39 | -6 | 3.5 |
| 10 | 90 | 93 | -3 | 1 |
| | | | | $T_+ = 2$ |

To determine if the pilot flextime program is a success, we test:

$H_0$: The two probability distributions are identical
$H_a$: The probability distribution before is shifted to the left of that after

The test statistic is $T_+ = 2$.

The rejection region is $T_+ \leq 8$, from Table XII, Appendix B, with n = 9 and $\alpha = .05$.

Since the observed value of the test statistic falls in the rejection region ($T_+ = 2 \leq 8$), $H_0$ is rejected. There is sufficient evidence to indicate the pilot flextime program has been a success at $\alpha = .05$.

18.29 Some preliminary calculations are:

| FIRM | NUMBER OF LITIGATIONS 1960's | 1970's | DIFFERENCE (1960's-1970's) | RANK OF ABSOLUTE DIFFERENCE |
|---|---|---|---|---|
| 1 | 10 | 10 | 0 | (Eliminate) |
| 2 | 8 | 12 | -4 | 5 |
| 3 | 9 | 8 | 1 | 1.5 |
| 4 | 7 | 16 | -9 | 9 |
| 5 | 8 | 14 | -6 | 8 |
| 6 | 7 | 6 | 1 | 1.5 |
| 7 | 6 | 11 | -5 | 6.5 |
| 8 | 9 | 12 | -3 | 3.5 |
| 9 | 8 | 11 | -3 | 3.5 |
| 10 | 7 | 12 | -5 | 6.5 |
| | | | | $T_+ = 3$ |

To determine whether companies faced more antitrust litigations in the 1970's than in the 1960's, we test:

$H_0$: The two sampled population probability distributions are identical
$H_a$: The probability distribution for the 1960's is shifted to the left of that for the 1970's

The test statistic is $T_+ = 3$.

The rejection region is $T_+ \leq 8$ from Table XII, Appendix B, with $n = 9$ and $\alpha = .05$.

Since the observed value of the test statistic falls in the rejection region ($T_+ = 3 \leq 8$), $H_0$ is rejected. There is sufficient evidence to indicate that the companies faced more antitrust litigations in the 1970's than in the 1960's at $\alpha = .05$.

18.31 Some preliminary calculations are:

| WEEK | MACHINE TYPE A | MACHINE TYPE B | DIFFERENCE (A - B) | RANK OF ABSOLUTE DIFFERENCE |
|---|---|---|---|---|
| 1 | 14 | 12 | 2 | 2.5 |
| 2 | 17 | 13 | 4 | 5.5 |
| 3 | 10 | 14 | -4 | 5.5 |
| 4 | 15 | 12 | 3 | 4 |
| 5 | 14 | 9 | 5 | 7 |
| 6 | 9 | 11 | -2 | 2.5 |
| 7 | 12 | 11 | 1 | 1 |
| | | | | $T_- = 8$ |

To determine if the distribution of the number of breakdowns for machine A is shifted to the left or right of that for machine B, we test:

$H_0$: The two population probability distributions are identical
$H_a$: The probability distribution of the number of breakdowns for machine A is shifted to the right or left of that for machine B

The test statistic is $T_- = 8$.

The rejection region is $T_- \leq 2$, from Table XII, Appendix B, with $n = 7$ and $\alpha = .05$.

Since the observed value of the test statistic does not fall in the rejection region ($T_- = 8 \not\leq 2$), $H_0$ is not rejected. There is insufficient evidence to indicate the distribution of the number of breakdowns for machine A is shifted to the right or left of that for machine B at $\alpha = .05$.

18.33 a. For df = 20, $\chi^2_{.05} = 31.4104$

b. For df = 15, $\chi^2_{.025} = 27.4884$

c. For df = 36, $\chi^2_{.01} \approx \chi^2_{.01,30} + \frac{6}{10}(\chi^2_{.01,40} - \chi^2_{.01,30})$

$$= 50.8922 + (63.6907 - 50.8922)\frac{6}{10}$$

$$= 58.5713 \quad \text{(by interpolation)}$$

d. For df = 80, $\chi^2_{.10} = 96.5782$

e. For df = 2, $\chi^2_{.05} = 5.99147$

f. For df = 10, $\chi^2_{.005} = 25.1882$

18.35 a. The hypotheses are:

$H_0$: The three probability distributions are identical
$H_a$: At least two of the three probability distributions differ in location

b. The test statistic is

$$H = \frac{12}{n(n+1)} \sum \frac{R_j^2}{n_j} - 3(n+1)$$

$$= \frac{12}{45(46)}\left[\frac{235^2}{15} + \frac{439^2}{15} + \frac{361^2}{15}\right] - 3(46)$$

$$= 146.1901 - 138 = 8.190$$

The rejection region requires $\alpha = .05$ in the upper tail of the $\chi^2$ distribution with df = p - 1 = 3 - 1 = 2. From Table XIII, Appendix B, $\chi^2_{.05} = 5.99147$. The rejection region is $H > 5.99147$.

Since the observed value of the test statistic falls in the rejection region ($H = 8.190 > 5.99147$), $H_0$ is rejected. There is sufficient evidence to indicate that the probability distributions of populations A, B, and C differ in location at $\alpha = .05$.

c. The approximate p-value is $P(\chi^2 \geq 8.190)$. From Table XIII, Appendix B, with df = 2, $.01 \leq P(\chi^2 \leq 8.190) \leq .025$.

d. $\bar{R}_A = \frac{R_A}{15} = \frac{235}{15} = 15.667$ $\bar{R}_B = \frac{R_B}{15} = \frac{439}{15} = 29.267$

$\bar{R}_C = \frac{R_C}{15} = \frac{361}{15} = 24.067$ $\bar{R} = \frac{n + 1}{2} = \frac{45 + 1}{2} = 23$

$$H = \frac{12}{n(n + 1)} \sum n_j(\bar{R}_j - \bar{R})^2$$

$$= \frac{12}{45(46)}\left[15(15.667 - 23)^2 + 15(29.267 - 23)^2 + 15(24.067 - 23)^2\right]$$

$$= .0058(1412.8005) = 8.19.$$

18.37 The $\chi^2$ distribution provides an appropriate characterization of the sampling distribution of H if the p sample sizes exceed 5.

18.39 a. The F test would be appropriate if

1. All p populations sampled from are normal
2. The variances of the p populations are equal
3. The p samples are independent

b. The variances for the 3 populations are probably not the same.

c. To determine whether the salary distributions differ among the three cities, we test:

$H_0$: The three probability distributions are identical
$H_a$: At least two of the three probability distributions differ in location

Some preliminary calculations are:

| A<br>ATLANTA | RANK | B<br>LOS ANGELES | RANK | C<br>WASHINGTON, D.C. | RANK |
|---|---|---|---|---|---|
| 45,500 | 12 | 52,000 | 17.5 | 41,500 | 7 |
| 47,900 | 13 | 72,000 | 21 | 40,100 | 5 |
| 43,100 | 10 | 41,000 | 6 | 39,000 | 3.5 |
| 42,000 | 8.5 | 54,000 | 19 | 56,500 | 20 |
| 49,000 | 14.5 | 33,000 | 1 | 37,000 | 2 |
| 52,000 | 17.5 | 42,000 | 8.5 | 49,000 | 14.5 |
| 39,000 | 3.5 | 50,000 | 16 | 43,500 | 11 |
| | $R_A = 79$ | | $R_B = 89$ | | $R_C = 63$ |

The test statistic is $H = \frac{12}{n(n + 1)} \sum \frac{R_j^2}{n_j} - 3(n + 1)$

$$= \frac{12}{21(22)}\left(\frac{79^2}{7} + \frac{89^2}{7} + \frac{63^2}{7}\right) - 3(22) = 67.2764 - 66 = 1.2764$$

The rejection region requires $\alpha = .05$ in the upper tail of the $\chi^2$ distribution with df = p - 1 = 3 - 1 = 2. From Table XIII, Appendix B, $\chi^2_{.05} = 5.99147$. The rejection region is $H > 5.99147$.

Since the observed value of the test statistic does not fall in the rejection region ($H = 1.2764 \not> 5.99147$), $H_0$ is not rejected. There is insufficient evidence to indicate the salary distributions differ among the three cities at $\alpha = .05$.

18.41 Some preliminary calculations are:

| URBAN | RANK | SUBURBAN | RANK | RURAL | RANK |
|---|---|---|---|---|---|
| 4.3 | 4.5 | 5.9 | 14 | 5.1 | 9 |
| 5.2 | 10.5 | 6.7 | 17 | 4.8 | 7 |
| 6.2 | 15.5 | 7.6 | 19 | 3.9 | 2 |
| 5.6 | 12 | 4.9 | 8 | 6.2 | 15.5 |
| 3.8 | 1 | 5.2 | 10.5 | 4.2 | 3 |
| 5.8 | 13 | 6.8 | 18 | 4.3 | 4.5 |
| 4.7 | 6 | | | | |
| | $R_A$ = 62.5 | | $R_B$ = 86.5 | | $R_C$ = 41 |

To determine if the level of property taxes among the three types of school districts, we test:

$H_0$: The three probability distributions are identical
$H_a$: At least two of the three probability distributions differ in location

The test statistic is $H = \frac{12}{n(n + 1)} \sum \frac{R_j^2}{n_j} - 3(n + 1)$

$$= \frac{12}{19(20)}\left[\frac{62.5^2}{7} + \frac{86.5^2}{6} + \frac{41^2}{6}\right] - 3(20)$$

$$= 65.8498 - 60 = 5.8498$$

The rejection region requires $\alpha = .05$ in the upper tail of the $\chi^2$ distribution with df = p - 1 = 3 - 1 = 2. From Table XIII, Appendix B, $\chi^2_{.05} = 5.99147$. The rejection region is $H > 5.99147$.

Since the observed value of the test statistic does not fall in the rejection region ($H = 5.8498 \not> 5.99147$), $H_0$ is not rejected. There is insufficient evidence to indicate the level of property taxes differ among the three types of school districts at $\alpha = .05$.

18.43 a. The assumptions for the F test are:

1. All p population probability distributions are normal.
2. The p population variances are equal.
3. Samples are selected randomly and independently from the respective populations.

The assumptions for the Kruskal-Wallis H test are:

1. The k samples are random and independent.
2. There are 5 or more measurements in each sample.
3. The observations can be ranked.

The assumptions for the Kruskal-Wallis H test are less restrictive than those for the F test.

b. Some preliminary calculations are:

| INSURANCE | RANK | PUBLISHING | RANK | ELECTRIC UTILITIES | RANK | BANKING | RANK |
|---|---|---|---|---|---|---|---|
| .24 | 9 | .03 | 2 | .84 | 19 | .54 | 14 |
| .09 | 4.5 | .32 | 11 | 1.00 | 20 | .29 | 10 |
| .12 | 6 | .51 | 13 | 1.03 | 21 | .82 | 17 |
| .09 | 4.5 | .15 | 8 | 1.11 | 22 | .13 | 7 |
| .00 | 1 | .73 | 16 | .83 | 18 | .41 | 12 |
| .07 | 3 | | | 1.16 | 23 | | |
| | | | | .70 | 15 | | |
| $R_A$ = | 28 | $R_B$ = | 50 | $R_C$ = | 138 | $R_D$ = | 60 |

To determine whether debt-to-equity ratios differ among the four industries, we test:

$H_0$: The four probability distributions are identical
$H_a$: At least two of the four probability distributions differ in location

The test statistic is $H = \frac{12}{n(n+1)} \sum \frac{R_j^2}{n_j} - 3(n+1)$

$$= \frac{12}{23(24)}\left[\frac{23^2}{6} + \frac{50^2}{5} + \frac{138^2}{7} + \frac{60^2}{5}\right] - 3(24)$$

$$= 88.5052 - 72 = 16.5052$$

The rejection region requires $\alpha = .05$ in the upper tail of the $\chi^2$ distribution with df = p - 1 = 4 - 1 = 3. From Table XIII, Appendix B, $\chi^2_{.05} = 7.81473$. The rejection region is H > 7.81473.

Since the observed value of the test statistic falls in the rejection region (H = 16.5052 > 7.81473), $H_0$ is rejected. There is sufficient evidence to indicate the debt-to-equity ratios differ among the four industries at $\alpha = .05$.

c. The distributions of debt-to-ratios for the electric utility and banking industries could be compared using the Wilcoxon rank sum test.

18.45 a. For df = 10, $P(\chi^2 \geq 18.3070) = .05$

b. For df = 18, $P(\chi^2 < 25.9894) = 1 - .10 = .90$

c. For df = 20, $P(\chi^2 \geq 39.9968) = .005$

18.47 a. The hypotheses are:

$H_0$: The probability distributions for p treatments are identical

$H_a$: At least two of the probability distributions differ in location

b. The rejection region requires $\alpha = .10$ in the upper tail of the $\chi^2$ distribution with df = p - 1 = 3 - 1 = 2. From Table XIII, Appendix B, $\chi^2_{.10} = 4.60517$. The rejection region is $F_r > 4.60517$.

c. Some preliminary calculations are:

| BLOCK | A | RANK | B | RANK | C | RANK |
|---|---|---|---|---|---|---|
| 1 | 9 | 1 | 11 | 2 | 18 | 3 |
| 2 | 13 | 2 | 13 | 2 | 13 | 2 |
| 3 | 11 | 1 | 12 | 2.5 | 12 | 2.5 |
| 4 | 10 | 1 | 15 | 2 | 16 | 3 |
| 5 | 9 | 2 | 8 | 1 | 10 | 3 |
| 6 | 14 | 2 | 12 | 1 | 16 | 3 |
| 7 | 10 | 1 | 12 | 2 | 15 | 3 |
| | $R_A =$ | 10 | $R_B =$ | 12.5 | $R_C =$ | 19.5 |

The test statistic is $F_r = \frac{12}{bp(p + 1)} \sum R_j^2 - 3b(p + 1)$

$= \frac{12}{7(3)(4)}[10^2 + 12.5^2 + 19.5^2] - 3(7)(4)$

$= 90.9286 - 84 = 6.9286$

For all comparisons except A with E, T = 0. Since the observed value of the test statistic falls in the rejection region ($T = 0 \leq 1$), $H_0$ is rejected. For pairs A and B, A and C, A and D, B and C, B and D, B and E, C and D, C and E, and D and E, the distributions have different locations at $\alpha = .05$.

For A and E, since the observed value of the test statistic does not fall in the rejection region, ($T = 3 \nleq 1$), $H_0$ is not rejected. There is insufficient evidence to indicate the locations of A and E differ at $\alpha = .05$.

18.51 To determine whether a difference in the abilities of the sealers to prevent corrosion exist, we test:

$H_0$: The three populations have identical probability distributions
$H_a$: At least two of the probability distributions differ in location

Some preliminary calculations are:

| PANEL MEMBER | RANK SEALER 1 | RANK SEALER 2 | RANK SEALER 3 |
|---|---|---|---|
| 1 | 2 | 1 | 3 |
| 2 | 3 | 1 | 2 |
| 3 | 1.5 | 3 | 1.5 |
| 4 | 3 | 1 | 2 |
| 5 | 3 | 1 | 2 |
| 6 | 2 | 1 | 3 |
| 7 | 1.5 | 1.5 | 3 |
| 8 | 1 | 2 | 3 |
| 9 | 3 | 1 | 2 |
| 10 | 3 | 1 | 2 |
| | $R_1 = 23$ | $R_2 = 13.5$ | $R_3 = 23.5$ |

The test statistic is $F_r = \frac{12}{bp(p + 1)} \sum R_j^2 - 3b(p + 1)$

$= \frac{12}{10(3)(4)}[23^2 + 13.5^2 + 23.5^2] - 3(10)(4)$

$= 126.35 - 120 = 6.35$

The rejection region requires $\alpha = .05$ in the upper tail of the $\chi^2$ distribution with df = p - 1 = 3 - 1 = 2. From Table XIII, Appendix B, $\chi^2_{.05} = 5.99147$. The rejection region is $F_r = 5.99147$.

Since the observed value of the test statistic falls in the rejection region ($F_r = 6.35 > 5.99147$), $H_0$ is rejected. There is sufficient evidence to indicate a difference in location in the abilities of the sealers to prevent corrosion among the three sealers at $\alpha = .05$.

18.53 a. Some preliminary calculations are:

| EAR | RANK SPRAY A | RANK SPRAY B | RANK SPRAY C |
|---|---|---|---|
| 1 | 2 | 3 | 1 |
| 2 | 2 | 3 | 1 |
| 3 | 1 | 3 | 2 |
| 4 | 3 | 2 | 1 |
| 5 | 2 | 1 | 3 |
| 6 | 1 | 3 | 2 |
| 7 | 2.5 | 2.5 | 1 |
| 8 | 2 | 3 | 1 |
| 9 | 2 | 3 | 1 |
| 10 | 2 | 3 | 1 |
| | $R_1 = 19.5$ | $R_2 = 26.5$ | $R_3 = 14$ |

To determine whether the distributions of the levels of aflatoxins in corn differ for at least two of the three sprays, we test:

$H_0$: The three populations have probability distributions that are identical

$H_a$: At least two of the populations have probability distributions that differ in location

The test statistic is $F_r = \frac{12}{bp(p + 1)} \sum R_j^2 - 3b(p + 1)$

$= \frac{12}{10(3)(4)}[19.5^2 + 26.5^2 + 14^2] - 3(10)(4)$

$= 127.85 - 120 = 7.85$

The rejection region requires $\alpha = .05$ in the upper tail of the $\chi^2$ distribution with df $= p - 1 = 3 - 1 = 2$. From Table XIII, Appendix B, $\chi^2_{.05} = 5.99147$. The rejection region is $F_r > 5.99147$.

Since the observed value of the test statistic falls in the rejection region ($F_r = 7.85 > 5.99147$), $H_0$ is rejected. There is sufficient evidence to indicate that the distributions of the levels of aflatoxin in corn differ for at least 2 of the 3 sprays at $\alpha = .05$.

b. Yes, because $H_0$ was rejected.

Some preliminary calculations:

| DIFFERENCE (A - B) | RANK OF ABSOLUTE DIFFERENCE | DIFFERENCE (A - C) | RANK OF ABSOLUTE DIFFERENCE | DIFFERENCE (B - C) | RANK OF ABSOLUTE DIFFERENCE |
|---|---|---|---|---|---|
| -2 | 3 | 6 | 7.5 | 8 | 6.5 |
| -1 | 1.5 | 8 | 9.5 | 9 | 8 |
| -3 | 5 | -2 | 4 | 1 | 1.5 |
| 1 | 1.5 | 2 | 4 | 1 | 1.5 |
| 3 | 5 | -1 | 1.5 | -4 | 3 |
| -7 | 9 | -1 | 1.5 | 6 | 4.5 |
| 0 | (Eliminated) | 6 | 7.5 | 6 | 4.5 |
| -6 | 7.5 | 5 | 6 | 11 | 9.5 |
| -3 | 5 | 8 | 9.5 | 11 | 9.5 |
| -6 | 7.5 | 2 | 4 | 8 | 6.5 |
| | $T_+ = 6.5$ | | $T_- = 7$ | | $T_- = 3$ |

When comparing A and C, and B and C, the rejection region is $T \leq 3$, from Table XII, Appendix B, with $n = 10$ and $\alpha = .01$.

When comparing A and B, the rejection region is $T \leq 2$, from Table XII, Appendix B, with $n = 9$ and $\alpha = .01$.

The comparisons are:

$H_0$: Populations A and B have identical probability distributions

$H_a$: The probability distribution for population A is shifted to the right or left of that for population B

The test statistic is $T_+ = 6.5$.

The rejection region is $T \leq 2$.

Since the observed value of the test statistic does not fall in the rejection region ($T_+ = 6.5 \nleq 2$), $H_0$ is not rejected. There is insufficient evidence to indicate the probability distributions for populations A and B differ in location.

$H_0$: Populations A and C have identical probability distributions

$H_a$: The probability distribution for population A is shifted to the right or left of that for population C

The test statistic is $T_- = 7$.

The test statistic is $T_B = 53$ because $n_B < n_A$.

The rejection region is $T_B \leq 54$ or $T_B \geq 98$ from Table XI, Appendix B, with $n_A = 10$, $n_B = 5$, and $\alpha = .05$.

Since the observed value of the test statistic falls in the rejection region ($T = 53 \leq 54$), $H_0$ is rejected. There is sufficient evidence to indicate the fairness of the assessments are not the same for the two neighborhoods at $\alpha = .05$.

b. In order to use the two-sample t-test, we have to have normal distributions for both neighborhoods A and B, the samples must be independent, and the population variances must be equal.

c. We must assume the two samples are random and independent, and the two probability distributions are continuous.

18.15 We first rank all data:

| BEFORE RIGHT-TURN LAW | RANK | AFTER RIGHT-TURN LAW | RANK |
|---|---|---|---|
| 150 | 3 | 145 | 2 |
| 500 | 11 | 390 | 8 |
| 250 | 5 | 680 | 13 |
| 301 | 7 | 560 | 12 |
| 242 | 4 | 899 | 14 |
| 435 | 10 | 1250 | 16 |
| 100 | 1 | 290 | 6 |
| 402 | 9 | 963 | 15 |
| | 50 | | 86 |

To determine whether the damages tended to increase after the enactment of the law, we test:

$H_0$: The distributions before and after the right-turn law are identical

$H_a$: The distribution after the right-turn law is shifted to the right of that before the right-turn law

The test statistic is $T_{After} = 86$.

The rejection region is $T \geq 84$ from Table XI, Appendix B, with $n_A = n_B = 8$ and $\alpha = .05$.

Since the observed value of the test statistic falls in the rejection region ($T = 86 \geq 84$), $H_0$ is rejected. There is sufficient evidence to indicate the damages tended to increase after the enactment of the law at $\alpha = .05$.

The rejection region is $T \leq 3$.

Since the observed value of the test statistic does not fall in the rejection region ($T_- = 7 \nleq 3$), $H_0$ is not rejected. There is insufficient evidence to indicate the probability distributions for populations A and B differ in location.

$H_0$: Populations B and C have identical probability distributions

$H_a$: The probability distribution for population B is shifted to the right or left of that for population C

The test statistic is $T_- = 3$.

The rejection region is $T \leq 3$.

Since the observed value of the test statistic falls in the rejection region ($T_- = 3 \leq 3$), $H_0$ is rejected. There is sufficient evidence to indicate the probability distributions for populations B and C differ in location.

From the above, we know that Spray C is better than Spray B in controlling aflatoxin. However, there is no difference between Spray A and C. Therefore, either Spray A or C should be used.

c. The assumptions for the Friedman test are:

1. The treatments are randomly assigned to experimental units within the blocks.
2. Either the number of blocks (10) or the number of treatments (3) should exceed 5.
3. The 3 probability distributions from which the samples within each block are drawn are continuous.

The assumptions necessary for the Wilcoxon signed rank test are:

1. The sample of differences is randomly selected from the population of differences.
2. The probability distribution from which the sample of paired differences is drawn is continuous.

18.55 a. For $n = 23$, $P(r_s > .496) = .01$

b. For $n = 28$, $P(r_s > .496) = .005$

c. For $n = 9$, $P(r_s \leq .600) = 1 - .05 = .95$

d. For $n = 20$, $P(r_s < -.377 \text{ or } r_s > .377) = 2(.05) = .10$

18.57 a. $H_0: \rho_s = 0$
$H_a: \rho_s \neq 0$

b. Some preliminary calculations are

| X RANK ($u_i$) | Y RANK ($v_i$) |
|---|---|
| 2.5 | 2 |
| 5 | 4 |
| 1 | 1 |
| 2.5 | 4 |
| 6 | 7 |
| 4 | 4 |
| 7 | 6 |
| 28 | 28 |

$$SS_{uv} = \sum u_i v_i - \frac{\sum u_i \sum v_i}{n} = 136 - \frac{28(28)}{7} = 24$$

$$SS_{uu} = \sum u_i^2 - \frac{(\sum u_i)^2}{n} = 139.5 - \frac{28^2}{7} = 27.5$$

$$SS_{vv} = \sum v_i^2 - \frac{(\sum v_i)^2}{n} = 138 - \frac{28^2}{7} = 26$$

$$r_s = \frac{SS_{uv}}{\sqrt{SS_{uu}SS_{vv}}} = \frac{24}{\sqrt{27.5(26)}} = \frac{24}{26.7395} = .898$$

The test statistic is $r_s = .898$.

From Table XVI, Appendix B, $r_{s,.05/2} = r_{s,.025} = .786$ for $n = 7$. The rejection region is $r_s < -.786$ or $r_s > .786$.

Since the observed value of the test statistic falls in the rejection region ($r_s = .898 > .786$), $H_0$ is rejected. There is sufficient evidence to indicate x and y are correlated.

c. The p-value is $P(r_s \leq -.898) + P(r_s \geq .898)$. From Table XVI, Appendix B, with $n = 7$,

$$2(.01) \leq P(r_s \leq -.898) + P(r_s \geq .898) \leq 2(.025)$$
$$.02 \leq P(r_s \leq -.898) + P(r_s \geq .898) \leq .05$$

d. The necessary assumptions are:

1. The sample of experimental units on which the two variables are measured is randomly selected.
2. The probability distributions of the two variables are continuous.

18.59 a. Since there are no ties, we can use the formula

$$r_s = 1 - \frac{6\sum d_i^2}{n(n^2 - 1)}$$

| DIFFERENCES $d_i = u_i - v_i$ | $d_i^2$ |
|---|---|
| 0 | 0 |
| 0 | 0 |
| 0 | 0 |
| 0 | 0 |
| -1 | 1 |
| 1 | 1 |
| -2 | 4 |
| -3 | 9 |
| 1 | 1 |
| 0 | 0 |
| -3 | 9 |
| 0 | 0 |
| 6 | 36 |
| 1 | 1 |
| | 62 |

$$r_s = 1 - \frac{6(62)}{14(14^2 - 1)}$$

$$= 1 - .136264$$

$$= .863736$$

$H_0$: $\rho_s = 0$
$H_a$: $\rho_s > 0$

The test statistic is $r_s = .863736$

From Table XVI, Appendix B, $r_{s,.05} = .457$ for $n = 14$. The rejection region is $r_s > .457$.

Since the observed value of the test statistic falls in the rejection region ($r_s = .863736 > .457$), $H_0$ is rejected. There is sufficient evidence to indicate the magnitude of brake pressure and the electrodermal response are positively correlated at $\alpha = .05$. This supports Helander's finding.

b. Type I error = concluding the variables are positively related when in fact they are not.

Type II error = concluding the variables are not related when in fact they are positively related.

c. p-value = $P(r_s \geq .863736) < .005$ from Table XVI, Appendix B, with $n = 14$.

To determine if the new drug is more effective than aspirin in reducing pain, we test:

$H_0$: The two sampled populations have identical probability distributions
$H_a$: The probability distribution for the new drug is shifted to the left of that for aspirin

The test statistic is $T_- = 3$.

The rejection region is $T_- \leq 4$ from Table XII, Appendix B, with $n = 7$ and $\alpha = .05$.

Since the observed value of the test statistic falls in the rejection region ($T_- = 3 \leq 4$), $H_0$ is rejected. There is sufficient evidence to indicate the new drug is more effective than aspirin in reducing pain at $\alpha = .05$.

18.73 a. A randomized complete block design was used. The response is the response to certain items on a questionnaire; the factor is the items which are qualitative; the treatments are the 4 items; and the experimental units are the people.

b. To determine if the probability distributions of ratings differ for at least two of the four items, we test:

$H_0$: The probability distributions for the 4 treatments are identical
$H_a$: At least two of the probability distributions for the items differ in location

The test statistic is $F_r = \frac{12}{bp(p + 1)} \sum R_j^2 - 3b(p + 1)$

$$= \frac{12}{10(4)(4 + 1)}[19^2 + 21.5^2 + 27.5^2 + 32^2] - 3(10)(4 + 1)$$

$$= 156.21 - 150 = 6.21$$

The rejection region requires $\alpha = .05$ in the upper tail of the $\chi^2$ distribution with df $= p - 1 = 4 - 1 = 3$. From Table XIII, Appendix B, $\chi^2_{.05} = 7.81473$. The rejection region is $F_r > 7.81473$.

Since the observed value of the test statistic does not fall in the rejection region ($F_r = 6.21 \not> 7.81473$), $H_0$ is not rejected. There is insufficient evidence to indicate the probability distributions of ratings differ for at least two of the four items at $\alpha = .05$.

c. The necessary assumptions are:

1. The treatments are randomly assigned to experimental units within the blocks.
2. Either the number of blocks (10) or the number of treatments (4) should exceed 5.
3. The 4 probability distributions from which the samples within each block are drawn are continuous.

d. No further comparisons are necessary because no differences are found in part (b).

18.75 Some preliminary calculations are:

| FAMILY | CLAIMS ($u_i$) | ANNUAL INCOME ($v_i$) | $u_iv_i$ |
|---|---|---|---|
| 1 | 7 | 5 | 35 |
| 2 | 3 | 2 | 6 |
| 3 | 10 | 10 | 100 |
| 4 | 1.5 | 9 | 13.5 |
| 5 | 6 | 3 | 18 |
| 6 | 9 | 6 | 54 |
| 7 | 1.5 | 1 | 1.5 |
| 8 | 4 | 8 | 32 |
| 9 | 8 | 7 | 56 |
| 10 | 5 | 4 | 20 |
| | 55 | 55 | 336 |

$$SS_{uv} = \sum u_iv_i - \frac{\sum u_i \sum v_i}{n} = 336 - \frac{55(55)}{10} = 33.5$$

$$SS_{uu} = \sum u_i^2 - \frac{(\sum u_i)^2}{n} = 384.5 - \frac{55^2}{10} = 82$$

$$SS_{vv} = \sum v_i^2 - \frac{(\sum v_i)^2}{n} = 385 - \frac{55^2}{10} = 82.5$$

$$r_s = \frac{SS_{uv}}{\sqrt{SS_{uu}SS_{vv}}} = \frac{33.5}{\sqrt{82(82.5)}} = .4073$$

To determine if a correlation exists between the number of claims per policy and the annual income of the policyholder, we test:

$H_0$: $\rho_s = 0$
$H_a$: $\rho_s \neq 0$

The test statistic is $r_s = .4073$.

From Table XVI, Appendix B, $r_{s,.05} = .564$ with $n = 10$. The rejection region is $r_s < -.564$ or $r_s > .564$.

Since the observed value of the test statistic does not fall in the rejection region ($r_s = .4073 \not> .564$), $H_0$ is not rejected. There is insufficient evidence to indicate a correlation exists between the number of claims per policy and the annual income of the policyholder at $\alpha = .10$.

18.77 a. Some preliminary calculations are:

| DAY | DIFFERENCE HIGHWAY 1 - HIGHWAY 2 |
|---|---|
| 1 | -25 |
| 2 | 4 |
| 3 | -23 |
| 4 | -16 |
| 5 | -16 |

$$\bar{d} = \frac{\sum d_i}{n} = \frac{-76}{5} = -15.2$$

$$s_d^2 = \frac{\sum d_i^2 - \frac{(\sum d_i)^2}{n}}{n - 1} = \frac{1682 - \frac{(-76)^2}{5}}{5 - 1} = 131.7$$

$$s_d = \sqrt{131.7} = 11.4761$$

To determine if the mean number of speeders per 100 cars differ for the two highways, we test:

$H_0$: $\mu_1 = \mu_2$
$H_a$: $\mu_1 \neq \mu_2$

The test statistic is $t = \dfrac{\bar{d} - 0}{s_d/\sqrt{n}} = \dfrac{-15.2}{\frac{11.4761}{\sqrt{5}}} = -2.96$

The rejection region requires $\alpha/2 = .05/2 = .025$ in each tail of the t distribution with $df = n - 1 = 5 - 1 = 4$. From Table VI, Appendix B, $t_{.025} = 2.776$. The rejection region is $t > 2.776$ and $t < -2.776$. Since the observed value of the test statistic falls in the rejection region ($t = -2.96 < -2.776$), $H_0$ is rejected. There is sufficient evidence to indicate the mean number of speeders per 100 cars differ for the 2 highways at $\alpha = .05$.

b. Some preliminary calculations are:

| DIFFERENCE HIGHWAY 1 - HIGHWAY 2 | RANK OF ABSOLUTE DIFFERENCES |
|---|---|
| -25 | 5 |
| 4 | 1 |
| -23 | 4 |
| -16 | 2.5 |
| -16 | 2.5 |
| | $T_+ = 1$ |

The hypotheses are:

$H_0$: The two sampled populations have identical probability distributions

$H_a$: The probability distribution for highway 1 is shifted to the right or left of that for highway 2

The test statistic is $T_+ = 1$.

The rejection region is $T_+ \leq 1$ from Table XII, Appendix B, with $n = 5$ and $\alpha = .10$.

Since the observed value of the test statistic falls in the rejection region ($T_+ = 1 \leq 1$), $H_0$ is rejected. There is sufficient evidence to indicate the probability distribution for highway 1 is shifted to the right or left of that for highway 2 at $\alpha = .10$.

18.79 Some preliminary calculations are:

| DIFFERENCE A - B | RANK OF ABSOLUTE DIFFERENCE |
|---|---|
| 4 | 6 |
| -2 | 3.5 |
| 2 | 3.5 |
| 0 | (Eliminated) |
| 5 | 7 |
| 1 | 1.5 |
| 1 | 1.5 |
| 0 | (Eliminated) |
| 3 | 5 |
| 6 | 8 |
| | $T_- = 3.5$ |

To determine if the households tend to subscribe to fewer magazines, we test:

$H_0$: The two sampled population probability distributions are identical

$H_a$: The probability distribution of 3 years ago is shifted to the right of that of now

The test statistic is $T_- = 3.5$.

The rejection region is $T_- \leq 6$ from Table XII, Appendix B, with $n = 8$ and $\alpha = .05$.

Since the observed value of the test statistic falls in the rejection region ($T_- = 3.5 \leq 6$), $H_0$ is rejected. There is sufficient evidence to indicate the probability distribution of 3 years ago is shifted to the right of that for now at $\alpha = .05$.

18.81 a. The design utilized was a completely randomized design.

b. Some preliminary calculations are:

| SITE 1 | RANK | SITE 2 | RANK | SITE 3 | RANK |
|---|---|---|---|---|---|
| 14.3 | 6 | 19.3 | 17 | 14.5 | 7 |
| 15.5 | 11 | 25.5 | 25 | 9.3 | 2 |
| 12.1 | 3 | 30.2 | 28 | 17.2 | 14 |
| 8.3 | 1 | 52.1 | 29 | 13.2 | 5 |
| 20.5 | 19 | 28.6 | 27 | 12.6 | 4 |
| 16.2 | 12 | 22.2 | 21 | 18.3 | 16 |
| 23.5 | 23 | 83.5 | 30 | 23.3 | 22 |
| 14.7 | 8 | 27.9 | 26 | 16.7 | 13 |
| 18.0 | 15 | 21.2 | 20 | 20.0 | 18 |
| 15.1 | 9 | 24.0 | 24 | 15.2 | 10 |
| | $R_A = 107$ | | $R_B = 247$ | | $R_C = 111$ |

To determine if the probability distributions for the three sites differ, we test:

$H_0$: The three sampled population probability distributions are identical

$H_a$: At least two of the three sampled population probability distributions differ in location

The test statistic is $H = \frac{12}{n(n + 1)} \sum \frac{R_j^2}{n_j} - 3(n + 1)$

$$= \frac{12}{30(31)}\left[\frac{107^2}{10} + \frac{247^2}{10} + \frac{111^2}{10}\right] - 3(31)$$

$$= 109.3923 - 93 = 16.3923$$

The rejection region requires $\alpha = .05$ in the upper tail of the $\chi^2$ distribution with df = p - 1 = 3 - 1 = 2. From Table XIII, Appendix B, $\chi^2_{.05} = 5.99147$. The rejection region is $H > 5.99147$.

Since the observed value of the test statistic falls in the rejection region ($H = 16.3923 > 5.99147$), $H_0$ is rejected. There is sufficient evidence to indicate the probability distributions for at least two of the three sites differ at $\alpha = .05$.

Since $H_0$ was rejected, we need to compare all pairs of sites.

c. Some preliminary calculations are:

| SITE 1 | RANK | SITE 2 | RANK |
|---|---|---|---|
| 14.3 | 3 | 19.3 | 9 |
| 15.5 | 6 | 25.5 | 15 |
| 12.1 | 2 | 30.2 | 18 |
| 8.3 | 1 | 52.1 | 19 |
| 20.5 | 10 | 28.6 | 17 |
| 16.2 | 7 | 22.2 | 12 |
| 23.5 | 13 | 83.5 | 20 |
| 14.7 | 4 | 27.9 | 16 |
| 18.0 | 8 | 21.2 | 11 |
| 15.1 | 5 | 24.0 | 14 |
| | $T_A = 59$ | | $T_B = 151$ |

| SITE 1 | RANK | SITE 3 | RANK |
|---|---|---|---|
| 14.3 | 6 | 14.3 | 7 |
| 15.5 | 11 | 9.3 | 2 |
| 12.1 | 3 | 17.2 | 14 |
| 8.3 | 1 | 13.2 | 5 |
| 20.5 | 18 | 12.6 | 4 |
| 16.2 | 12 | 18.3 | 16 |
| 23.5 | 20 | 23.3 | 19 |
| 14.7 | 8 | 16.7 | 13 |
| 18.0 | 15 | 20.0 | 17 |
| 15.1 | 9 | 15.2 | 10 |
| | $T_A = 103$ | | $T_C = 107$ |

| SITE 2 | RANK | SITE 3 | RANK |
|---|---|---|---|
| 19.3 | 9 | 14.5 | 4 |
| 25.5 | 15 | 9.3 | 1 |
| 30.2 | 18 | 17.2 | 7 |
| 52.1 | 19 | 13.2 | 3 |
| 28.6 | 17 | 12.6 | 2 |
| 22.2 | 12 | 18.3 | 8 |
| 83.5 | 20 | 23.3 | 13 |
| 27.9 | 16 | 16.7 | 6 |
| 21.2 | 11 | 20.0 | 10 |
| 24.0 | 14 | 15.2 | 5 |
| | $T_B = 151$ | | $T_C = 59$ |

For each pair, we test:

$H_0$: The two sampled population probability distributions are identical
$H_a$: The probability distribution for one site is shifted to the right or left of the other.

The rejection region for each pair is $T \leq 79$ or $T \geq 131$ from Table XI, Appendix B, with $n_1 = n_2 = 10$ and $\alpha = .05$.

For sites 1 and 2:

The test statistic is $T_A = 59$.

Since the observed value of the test statistic falls in the rejection region, ($T_A = 59 \leq 79$), $H_0$ is rejected. There is sufficient evidence to indicate the probability distribution for site 1 is shifted to the left of that for site 2 at $\alpha = .05$.

For sites 1 and 3:

The test statistic is $T_A = 103$.

Since the observed value of the test statistic does not fall in the rejection region ($T_A = 103 \nleq 79$ and $103 \ngeq 131$), $H_0$ is not rejected. There is insufficient evidence to indicate the probability distribution for site 1 is shifted to the right or left of that for site 3 at $\alpha = .05$.

For sites 2 and 3:

The test statistic is $T_B = 151$.

Since the observed value of the test statistic falls in the rejection region ($T_B = 151 \geq 131$), $H_0$ is rejected. There is sufficient evidence to indicate the probability distribution for site 2 is shifted to the right of that for site 3 at $\alpha = .05$.

d. The necessary assumptions are:

1) The 3 samples are random and independent.
2) There are 5 or more measurements in each sample.
3) The 3 probability distributions from which the samples are drawn are continuous.

For parametric tests, the assumptions are:

1) The 3 populations are normal.
2) The samples are random and independent
3) The 3 population variances are equal.

18.83 a. To determine if the median hourly fraction defective exceeds .05, we test:

$H_0$: $M = .05$
$H_a$: $M > .05$

The test statistic is S = number of measurements greater than .05 = 5.

The p-value = $P(x \geq 5)$ where x is a binomial random variable with $n = 8$ and $p = .5$. From Table II,

$$\text{p-value} = P(x \geq 5) = 1 - P(x \leq 4) = 1 - .637 = .363.$$

Since the p-value = $.363 > \alpha = .10$, $H_0$ is not rejected. There is insufficient evidence to indicate the median hourly fraction defective exceeds .05 at $\alpha = .10$.

b. The manufacturer might want to use a relatively high level of significance so that it is easier to reject $H_0$. The manufacturer would rather reject $H_0$ when it is true (conclude the median fraction of defective exceeds .05 when it does not) than not reject $H_0$ when it is false (conclude the median fraction defective is .05 when it exceeds .05). The manufacturer would rather be conservative and declare too many defectives, shut down the process and correct it, than say the process is working correctly and let too many defectives be produced.

c. We must assume the sample was randomly selected from a continuous distribution of defective rates. In order to conduct a t-test, we must also assume the population of defective rates is normally distributed.

18.85 Some preliminary calculations are:

| COST ($u_i$) | MONTHS OF WEAR ($v_i$) | $d_i = u_i - v_i$ | $d_i^2$ |
|---|---|---|---|
| 3 | 10 | -7 | 49 |
| 1 | 3 | -2 | 4 |
| 7 | 5 | 2 | 4 |
| 4 | 1 | 3 | 9 |
| 10 | 7 | 3 | 9 |
| 12 | 2 | 10 | 100 |
| 5 | 4 | 1 | 1 |
| 11 | 12 | -1 | 1 |
| 8 | 11 | -3 | 9 |
| 6 | 8 | -2 | 4 |
| 9 | 9 | 0 | 0 |
| 2 | 6 | -4 | 16 |
| | | Total = | 206 |

$$r_s = 1 - \frac{6\sum d_i^2}{n(n^2 - 1)} = 1 - \frac{6(206)}{12(12^2 - 1)} = .2797$$

To determine if the wearability increases as the price increases, we test:

$H_0$: $\rho_s = 0$
$H_a$: $\rho_s > 0$

The test statistic is $r_s = .2797$.

From Table XVI, Appendix B, $r_{s,.05} = .497$ with $n = 12$. The rejection region is $r_s > .497$.

Since the observed value of the test statistic does not fall in the rejection region ($r_s = .2797 \not> .497$), $H_0$ is not rejected. There is insufficient evidence to indicate the wearability increases as the price increases at $\alpha = .05$.

18.87 Some preliminary calculations are:

| DOOR-TO-DOOR OBSERVATION | RANK | GROCERY STORE STAND OBSERVATION | RANK |
|---|---|---|---|
| 47 | 4 | 113 | 11 |
| 93 | 10 | 50 | 5 |
| 58 | 6 | 68 | 8 |
| 37 | 1.5 | 37 | 1.5 |
| 62 | 7 | 39 | 3 |
| | | 77 | 9 |
| | $T_A$ = 28.5 | | $T_B$ = 37.5 |

To determine if the probability distributions of the number of sales for the door-to-door and grocery store stand techniques differ in location, we test:

$H_0$: The two sampled probability distributions are identical
$H_a$: The probability distribution for the sales for the door-to-door technique is shifted to the right or left of that for the grocery store stand technique

The test statistic is $T_A = 28.5$.

The rejection region is $T_A \leq 19$ from Table XI, Appendix B, with $n_A = 5$, $n_B = 6$, $\alpha = .05$, and two tailed.

Since the observed value of the test statistic does not fall in the rejection region ($T_A = 28.5 \nleq 19$), $H_0$ is not rejected. There is insufficient evidence to indicate the probability distributions of the number of sales for the door-to-door and grocery store stand techniques differ in location at $\alpha = .05$.

18.89 Some preliminary calculations are:

| PERSON | A | B | C |
|---|---|---|---|
| 1 | 2 | 3 | 1 |
| 2 | 2.5 | 2.5 | 1 |
| 3 | 1 | 2.5 | 2.5 |
| 4 | 3 | 1 | 2 |
| 5 | 3 | 2 | 1 |
| 6 | 3 | 2 | 1 |
| 7 | 1 | 3 | 2 |
| 8 | 2.5 | 2.5 | 1 |
| 9 | 2 | 3 | 1 |
| 10 | 3 | 2 | 1 |
| | $R_A$ = 23 | $R_B$ = 23.5 | $R_C$ = 13.5 |

To determine if one brand of beer is preferred to the others, we test:

$H_0$: The probability distributions for the 3 treatments are identical

$H_a$: At least two of the probability distributions of the brands differ in location

The test statistic is $F_r = \frac{12}{bp(p + 1)} \sum R_j^2 - 3b(p + 1)$

$$= \frac{12}{10(3)(3 + 1)}[23^2 + 23.5^2 + 13.5^2] - 3(10)(3 + 1)$$

$$= 126.35 - 120 = 6.35$$

The rejection region requires $\alpha = .05$ in the upper tail of the $\chi^2$ distribution with df = p - 1 = 3 - 1 = 2. From Table XIII, Appendix B, $\chi^2_{.05} = 5.99147$. The rejection region is $F_r > 5.99147$.

Since the observed value of the test statistic falls in the rejection region ($F_r = 6.35 > 5.99147$), $H_0$ is rejected. There is sufficient evidence to indicate at least one brand of beer is preferred to the others at $\alpha = .05$.

To compare all pairs, we use the following calculations:

| BRANDS A AND B | | BRANDS A AND C | | BRANDS B AND C | |
|---|---|---|---|---|---|
| $d_i$ | RANK OF ABSOLUTE DIFFERENCES | $d_i$ | RANK OF ABSOLUTE DIFFERENCES | $d_i$ | RANK OF ABSOLUTE DIFFERENCES |
| -2 | 6 | 2 | 6 | 4 | 9 |
| 0 | (Eliminate) | 3 | 8.5 | 3 | 7 |
| -1 | 2.5 | -1 | 2.5 | 0 | (Eliminate) |
| 3 | 8 | 2 | 6 | -1 | 2.5 |
| 1 | 2.5 | 4 | 10 | 3 | 7 |
| 1 | 2.5 | 2 | 6 | 1 | 2.5 |
| -2 | 6 | -1 | 2.5 | 1 | 2.5 |
| 0 | (Eliminate) | 1 | 2.5 | 1 | 2.5 |
| -2 | 6 | 1 | 2.5 | 3 | 7 |
| 1 | 2.5 | 3 | 8.5 | 2 | 5 |
| | $T_+ = 15.5$ | | $T_- = 5$ | | $T_- = 2.5$ |

$H_0$: The probability distributions for Brands A and B are identical

$H_a$: The probability distribution for Brand A is shifted to the right or left of that for Brand B

The test statistic is $T_+ = 15.5$.

The rejection region is $T_+ \leq 4$ from Table XII, Appendix B, with $n = 8$, $\alpha = .05$, and two-tailed.

Since the observed value of the test statistic does not fall in the rejection region ($T_+ = 15.5 \nleq 4$), $H_0$ is not rejected. There is insufficient evidence to indicate the probability distributions for Brands A and B differ in location at $\alpha = .05$.

$H_0$: The probability distributions for Brands A and C are identical

$H_a$: The probability distribution for Brand A is shifted to the right or left of that for Brand C

The test statistic is $T_- = 5$.

The rejection region is $T_- \leq 8$ from Table XII, Appendix B, with $n = 10$, $\alpha = .05$, and two-tailed.

Since the observed value of the test statistic falls in the rejection region ($T_- = 5 \leq 8$), $H_0$ is rejected. There is sufficient evidence to indicate a difference in location for the probability distributions for Brands A and C at $\alpha = .05$.

$H_0$: The probability distributions for Brands B and C are identical

$H_a$: The probability distribution for Brand B is shifted to the right or left of that for Brand C

The test statistic is $T_- = 2.5$.

The rejection region is $T_- \leq 6$ from Table XII, Appendix B, with $n = 9$, $\alpha = .05$, and two-tailed.

Since the observed value of the test statistic falls in the rejection region ($T_- = 2.5 \leq 6$), $H_0$ is rejected. There is sufficient evidence to indicate a difference in location for the distributions for Brands B and C at $\alpha = .05$.

Thus, Brands A and B are preferred over Brand C.

18.91 $$SS_{uv} = \sum u_i v_i - \frac{\sum u_i \sum v_i}{n} = 2774.75 - \frac{210(210)}{20} = 569.75$$

$$SS_{uu} = \sum u_i^2 - \frac{(\sum u_i)^2}{n} = 2869.5 - \frac{210^2}{20} = 664.5$$

$$SS_{vv} = \sum v_i^2 - \frac{(\sum v_i)^2}{n} = 2869.5 - \frac{210^2}{20} = 664.5$$

$$r_s = \frac{SS_{uv}}{\sqrt{SS_{uu}SS_{vv}}} = \frac{569.75}{\sqrt{664.5(664.5)}} = .8574$$

Since $r_s = .8574$ is greater than 0, the relationship between current importance and ideal importance is positive. The relationship is fairly strong since $r_s$ is close to 1. This implies the views on current importance and ideal importance are very similar.

18.93 a. To determine if the median level differs from the target, we test:

$H_0$: $M = .75$
$H_a$: $M \neq .75$

b. $S_1$ = number of observations less than .75 and $S_2$ = number of observations greater than .75.

The test statistic is $S$ = larger of $S_1$ and $S_2$.

The p-value = $2P(x \geq S)$ where x is a binomial random variable with $n = 25$ and $p = .5$. If the p-value is less than $\alpha = .10$, reject $H_0$.

c. A Type I error would be concluding the median level is not .75 when it is. If a Type I error were committed, the supervisor would correct the fluoridation process when it was not necessary. A Type II error would be concluding the median level is .75 when it is not. If a Type II error were committed, the supervisor would not correct the fluoridation process when it was necessary.

d. $S_1$ = number of observations less than .75 = 7 and $S_2$ = number of observations greater than .75 = 18.

The test statistic is S = larger of $S_1$ and $S_2$ = 18.

The p-value = $2P(x \geq 18)$ where x is a binomial random variable with n = 25 and p = .5. From Table II,

$$\text{p-value} = 2P(x \geq 18) = 2(1 - P(x \leq 17)) = 2(1 - .978)$$

$$= 2(.022) = .044$$

Since the p-value = $.044 < \alpha = .10$, $H_0$ is rejected. There is sufficient evidence to indicate the median level of fluoridation differs from the target of .75 at $\alpha = .10$.

e. A distribution heavily skewed to the right might look something like the following:

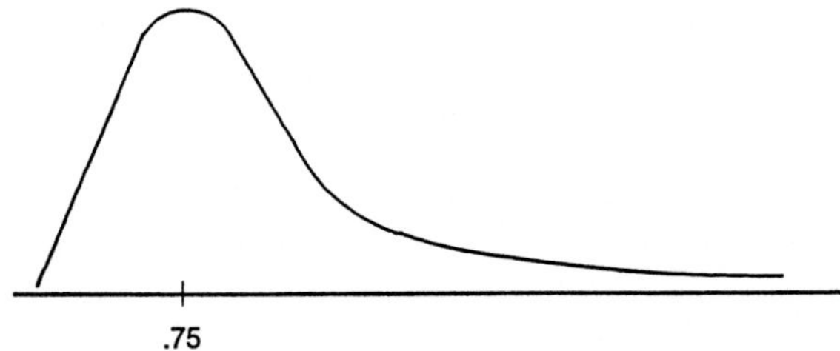


One assumption necessary for the t-test is that the distribution from which the sample is drawn is normal. A distribution which is heavily skewed in one direction is not normal. Thus, the sign test would be preferred.

# CHAPTER 19

# THE CHI-SQUARE TEST AND THE ANALYSIS OF CONTINGENCY TABLES

19.1 a. For df = 15, $\chi^2_{.05} = 24.9958$

b. For df = 100, $\chi^2_{.990} = 70.0648$

c. For df = 12, $\chi^2_{.10} = 18.5494$

d. For df = 2, $\chi^2_{.005} = 10.5966$

19.3 a. The rejection region requires $\alpha = .10$ in the upper tail of the $\chi^2$ distribution with df = k - 1 = 3 - 1 = 2. From Table XIII, Appendix B, $\chi^2_{.10} = 4.60517$. The rejection region is $\chi^2 > 4.60517$.

b. The rejection region requires $\alpha = .01$ in the upper tail of the $\chi^2$ distribution with df = k - 1 = 5 - 1 = 4. From Table XIII, Appendix B, $\chi^2_{.01} = 13.2767$. The rejection region is $\chi^2 > 13.2767$.

c. The rejection region requires $\alpha = .05$ in the upper tail of the $\chi^2$ distribution with df = k - 1 = 4 - 1 = 3. From Table XIII, Appendix B, $\chi^2_{.05} = 7.81473$. The rejection region is $\chi^2 > 7.81473$.

19.5 The sample size n will be large enough so that, for every cell, the expected cell count, $E(n_i)$, will be equal to 5 or more.

19.7 a. If all probabilities are equal, $p_1 = p_2 = p_3 = p_4 = .25$

Some preliminary calculations are:

$$E(n_1) = np_{1,0} = 206(.25) = 51.5$$

$$E(n_2) = E(n_3) = E(n_4) = np_{i,0} = 206(.25) = 51.5$$

To determine if the probabilities differ, we test:

$H_0$: $p_1 = p_2 = p_3 = p_4 = .25$
$H_a$: At least one of the multinomial probabilities does not equal .25

The test statistic is $\chi^2 = \dfrac{\sum[n_i - E(n_i)]^2}{E(n_i)}$

$$= \frac{(45 - 51.5)^2}{51.5} + \frac{(54 - 51.5)^2}{51.5} + \frac{(60 - 51.5)^2}{51.5} + \frac{(47 - 51.5)^2}{51.5}$$

$$= 2.7379$$

The rejection region requires $\alpha = .05$ in the upper tail of the $\chi^2$ distribution with df = k - 1 = 4 - 1 = 3. From Table XIII, Appendix B, $\chi^2_{.05} = 7.81473$. The rejection region is $\chi^2 > 7.81473$.

Since the observed value of the test statistic does not fall in the rejection region ($\chi^2 = 2.7379 \not> 7.81473$), $H_0$ is not rejected. There is insufficient evidence to indicate the probabilities differ at $\alpha = .05$.

b. The Type I error is concluding the multinomial probabilities differ when, in fact, they don't.

The Type II error is concluding the multinomial probabilities do not differ when, in fact, they do.

19.9 a. To determine if a difference in the preference of entrepreneurs for the cars, we test:

$H_0$: $p_1 = p_2 = p_3 = 1/3$
$H_a$: At least one of the multinomial probabilities does not equal 1/3

Where $p_1$ = proportion who prefer U.S. cars
$p_2$ = proportion who prefer European cars
$p_3$ = proportion who prefer Japanese cars

$$E(n_1) = np_{1,0} = 100(\tfrac{1}{3}) = 33\tfrac{1}{3}$$

$$E(n_2) = np_{2,0} = 100(\tfrac{1}{3}) = 33\tfrac{1}{3}$$

$$E(n_3) = np_{3,0} = 100(\tfrac{1}{3}) = 33\tfrac{1}{3}$$

The test statistic is $\chi^2 = \sum \dfrac{[n_i - E(n_i)]^2}{E(n_i)} = \dfrac{\left(45 - 33\frac{1}{3}\right)^2}{33\frac{1}{3}}$

$$+ \frac{(46 - 33\frac{1}{3})^2}{33\frac{1}{3}} + \frac{\left(9 - 33\frac{1}{3}\right)^2}{33\frac{1}{3}} = 26.66$$

The rejection region requires $\alpha = .05$ in the upper tail of the $\chi^2$ distribution with df = k - 1 = 3 - 1 = 2. From Table XIII, Appendix B, $\chi^2_{.05} = 5.99147$. The rejection region is $\chi^2 > 5.99147$.

Since the observed value of the test statistic falls in the rejection region ($\chi^2 = 26.66 > 5.99147$), $H_0$ is rejected. There is sufficient evidence to indicate a difference in the preference of entrepreneurs for the cars at $\alpha = .05$.

b. To determine if there is a difference in the preference of entrepreneurs for domestic versus foreign cars, we test:

$H_0$: $p_1 = p_2 = .5$
$H_a$: At least one probability differs from .5

Where $p_1$ = proportion who prefer U.S. cars
$p_2$ = proportion who prefer foreign cars

$E(n_1) = np_{1,0} = 100(.5) = 50$
$E(n_2) = np_{2,0} = 100(.5) = 50$

The test statistic is $\chi^2 = \sum \frac{[n_i - E(n_i)]^2}{E(n_i)} = \frac{(45 - 50)^2}{50}$

$+ \frac{(55 - 50)^2}{50} = 1$

The rejection region requires $\alpha = .05$ in the upper tail of the $\chi^2$ distribution with df = k - 1 = 2 - 1 = 1. From Table XIII, Appendix B, $\chi^2_{.05} = 3.84146$. The rejection region is $\chi^2 > 3.84146$.

Since the observed value of the test statistic does not fall in the rejection region ($\chi^2 = 1 \not> 3.84146$), $H_0$ is not rejected. There is insufficient evidence to indicate a difference in the preference of entrepreneurs for domestic and foreign cars at $\alpha = .05$.

c. We must assume the sample size n is large enough so that the expected cell count, $E(n_i)$, will be equal to 5 or more for every cell.

19.11 a. To determine if the number of overweight trucks per week is distributed over the 7 days of the week in direct proportion to the volume of truck traffic, we test:

$H_0$: $p_1 = .191$, $p_2 = .198$, $p_3 = .187$, $p_4 = .180$, $p_5 = .155$, $p_6 = .043$, and $p_7 = .046$
$H_a$: At least one of the probabilities differs from the hypothesized value

$$E(n_1) = np_{1,0} = 414(.191) = 79.074$$
$$E(n_2) = np_{2,0} = 414(.198) = 81.972$$
$$E(n_3) = np_{3,0} = 414(.187) = 77.418$$
$$E(n_4) = np_{4,0} = 414(.180) = 74.520$$
$$E(n_5) = np_{5,0} = 414(.155) = 64.170$$
$$E(n_6) = np_{6,0} = 414(.043) = 17.802$$
$$E(n_7) = np_{7,0} = 414(.046) = 19.044$$

The test statistic is $\chi^2 = \sum \frac{(n_i - E(n_i))^2}{E(n_i)}$

$$= \frac{(90 - 79.074)^2}{79.074} + \frac{(82 - 81.972)^2}{81.972} + \frac{(72 - 77.418)^2}{77.418}$$
$$+ \frac{(70 - 74.520)^2}{74.520} + \frac{(51 - 64.170)^2}{64.170} + \frac{(18 - 17.802)^2}{17.802}$$
$$+ \frac{(31 - 19.044)^2}{19.044} = 12.374$$

The rejection region requires $\alpha = .05$ in the upper tail of the $\chi^2$ distribution with df = k - 1 = 7 - 1 = 6. From Table XIII, Appendix B, $\chi^2_{.05} = 12.5916$. The rejection region is $\chi^2 > 12.5916$.

Since the observed value of the test statistic does not fall in the rejection region ($\chi^2 = 12.374 \not> 12.5916$), $H_0$ is not rejected. There is insufficient evidence to indicate the number of overweight trucks per week is distributed over the 7 days of the week is not in direct proportion to the volume of truck traffic at $\alpha = .05$.

b. The p-value is $P(\chi^2 \geq 12.374)$. From Table XIII, Appendix B, with df = k - 1 = 7 - 1 = 6, $.05 < P(\chi^2 \geq 12.374) = .10$.

19.13 a. Some preliminary calculations are:

$$E(n_1) = np_{1,0} = 300(.90) = 270$$
$$E(n_2) = np_{2,1} = 300(.04) = 36$$
$$E(n_3) = np_{3,0} = 300(.03) = 9$$
$$E(n_4) = np_{4,0} = 300(.02) = 6$$
$$E(n_5) = np_{5,0} = 300(.005) = 1.5$$
$$E(n_6) = np_{6,0} = 300(.005) = 1.5$$

To determine if the proportions of printed invoices in the six error categories differ from the proportions using the previous format, we test:

$H_0$: $p_1 = .9$, $p_2 = .04$, $p_3 = .03$, $p_4 = .02$, $p_5 = .005$, and $p_6 = .005$

$H_a$: At least one of the proportions differs from the hypothesized value

The test statistic is $\chi^2 = \sum\frac{(n_i - E(n_i))^2}{E(n_i)} = \frac{(150 - 270)^2}{270}$

$$+ \frac{(120 - 36)^2}{36} + \frac{(15 - 9)^2}{9} + \frac{(7 - 6)^2}{6} + \frac{(4 - 1.5)^2}{1.5}$$

$$+ \frac{(4 - 1.5)^2}{1.5} = 1038$$

The rejection region requires $\alpha = .05$ in the upper tail of the $\chi^2$ distribution with df = k - 1 = 6 - 1 = 5. From Table XIII, Appendix B, $\chi^2_{.05} = 11.0705$. The rejection region is $\chi^2 > 11.0705$.

Since the observed value of the test statistic falls in the rejection region ($\chi^2 = 1038 > 11.0705$), $H_0$ is rejected. There is sufficient evidence to indicate the proportions of printed invoices in the six error categories differ from the proportions using the previous format at $\alpha = .05$.

b. The observed significance level is $P(\chi^2 > 1038)$. From Table XIII, Appendix B, with df = 5, $P(\chi^2 > 1038) < .005$. Since $P(\chi^2 > 16.7496) = .005$, we know $P(\chi^2 > 1038)$ is much smaller than .005 or approximately 0.

19.15 Some preliminary calculations are:

$$E(n_1) = np_{1,0} = 200(.25) = 50$$
$$E(n_2) = np_{2,0} = 200(.25) = 50$$
$$E(n_3) = np_{3,0} = 200(.25) = 50$$
$$E(n_4) = np_{4,0} = 200(.25) = 50$$

To determine if there are differences in the proportions of businesses preferring each technique, we test:

$H_0$: $p_1 = p_2 = p_3 = p_4 = .25$
$H_a$: At least one of the proportions differs from the hypothesized value

The test statistic is $\chi^2 = \sum\frac{(n_i - E(n_i))^2}{E(n_i)} = \frac{(48 - 50)^2}{50} + \frac{(68 - 50)^2}{50}$

$$+ \frac{(45 - 50)^2}{50} + \frac{(39 - 50)^2}{50} = 9.48$$

The rejection region requires $\alpha = .05$ in the upper tail of the $\chi^2$ distribution with df = k - 1 = 4 - 1 = 3. From Table XIII, Appendix B, $\chi^2_{.05} = 7.81473$. The rejection region is $\chi^2 > 7.81473$.

Since the observed value of the test statistic falls in the rejection region ($\chi^2 = 9.48 > 7.81473$), $H_0$ is rejected. There is sufficient evidence to indicate differences in the proportions of businesses preferring each technique at $\alpha = .05$.

19.17 a. df = (r - 1)(c - 1) = (5 - 1)(5 - 1) = 16. From Table XIII, Appendix B, $\chi^2_{.05}$ = 26.2962. The rejection region is $\chi^2 > 26.2962$.

b. df = (r - 1)(c - 1) = (3 - 1)(6 - 1) = 10. From Table XIII, Appendix B, $\chi^2_{.10}$ = 15.9871. The rejection region is $\chi^2 > 15.9871$.

c. df = (r - 1)(c - 1) = (2 - 1)(3 - 1) = 2. From Table XIII, Appendix B, $\chi^2_{.01}$ = 9.21034. The rejection region is $\chi^2 > 9.21034$.

19.19 a. To convert the frequencies to percentages, divide the numbers in each column by the column total and multiply by 100. Also, divide the row totals by the overall total and multiply by 100. The column totals are 25, 62, and 78, while the row totals are 95 and 70. The overall sample size is 165. The table of percentages are:

| | | Column 1 | Column 2 | Column 3 | |
|---|---|---|---|---|---|
| Row | 1 | $\frac{10}{25} \cdot 100 = 40\%$ | $\frac{32}{62} \cdot 100 = 51.6\%$ | $\frac{53}{78} \cdot 100 = 67.9\%$ | $\frac{95}{165} \cdot 100 = 57.6\%$ |
| | 2 | $\frac{15}{25} \cdot 100 = 60\%$ | $\frac{30}{62} \cdot 100 = 48.4\%$ | $\frac{25}{78} \cdot 100 = 32.1\%$ | $\frac{70}{165} \cdot 100 = 42.4\%$ |

b.

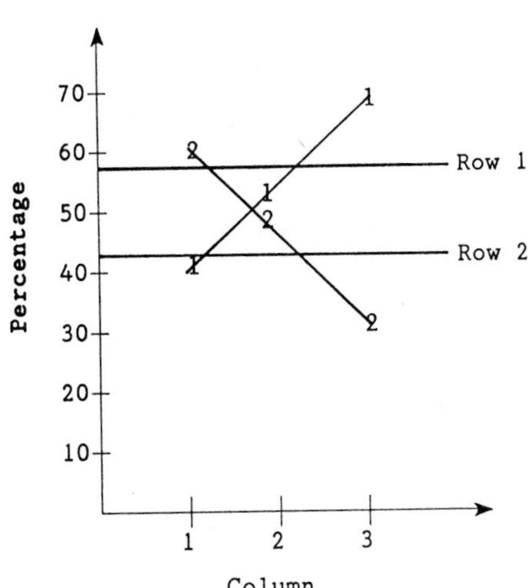


c. If the rows and columns are independent, the row percentages in each column would be close to the row total percentages. This pattern is not evident in the plot, implying the rows and columns are not independent.

19.21 To convert the frequencies to percentages, divide the numbers in each column by the column total and multiply by 100. Also, divide the row totals by the overall total and multiply by 100.

| | | B: $B_1$ | $B_2$ | $B_3$ | |
|---|---|---|---|---|---|
| Row | $A_1$ | $\frac{39}{132} \cdot 100 = 29.5\%$ | $\frac{75}{164} \cdot 100 = 45.7\%$ | $\frac{42}{141} \cdot 100 = 29.8\%$ | $\frac{156}{437} \cdot 100 = 35.7\%$ |
| | $A_2$ | $\frac{63}{132} \cdot 100 = 47.7\%$ | $\frac{51}{164} \cdot 100 = 31.1\%$ | $\frac{70}{141} \cdot 100 = 49.6\%$ | $\frac{184}{437} \cdot 100 = 42.1\%$ |
| | $A_3$ | $\frac{30}{132} \cdot 100 = 22.7\%$ | $\frac{38}{164} \cdot 100 = 23.2\%$ | $\frac{29}{141} \cdot 100 = 20.6\%$ | $\frac{97}{437} \cdot 100 = 22.2\%$ |

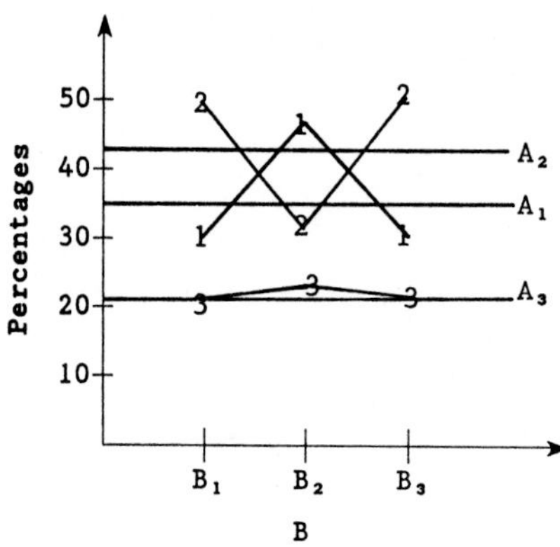


The graph supports the conclusion that the rows and columns are not independent. The percentages of category A at $B_2$ are switched for $A_1$ and $A_2$ from what is expected.

19.23 For each table, divide the numbers in each column by the column total and multiply by 100. Also, divide the row totals by the overall total and multiply by 100.

a.

| | | B: $B_1$ | $B_2$ | |
|---|---|---|---|---|
| A | $A_1$ | $\frac{50}{60} \cdot 100 = 83.3\ \%$ | $\frac{10}{50} \cdot 100 = 20\%$ | $\frac{60}{110} \cdot 100 = 54.5\%$ |
| | $A_2$ | $\frac{10}{60} \cdot 100 = 16.7\%$ | $\frac{40}{50} \cdot 100 = 80\%$ | $\frac{50}{110} \cdot 100 = 45.5\%$ |

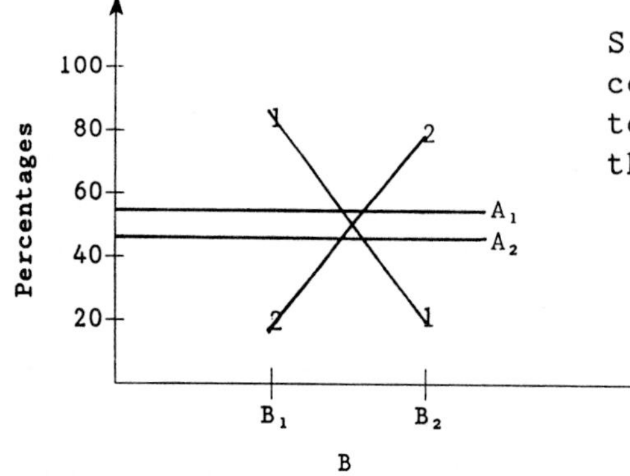


Since the row percentages in each column are not similar to the row total percentages, the graph implies the variables are dependent.

b.

| | | D | | |
|---|---|---|---|---|
| | | $D_1$ | $D_2$ | |
| C | $C_1$ | $\frac{15}{95} \cdot 100 = 15.8\%$ | $\frac{70}{85} \cdot 100 = 82.4\%$ | $\frac{85}{180} \cdot 100 = 47.2\%$ |
| | $C_2$ | $\frac{80}{95} \cdot 100 = 84.2\%$ | $\frac{15}{85} \cdot 100 = 17.6\%$ | $\frac{95}{180} \cdot 100 = 52.8\%$ |

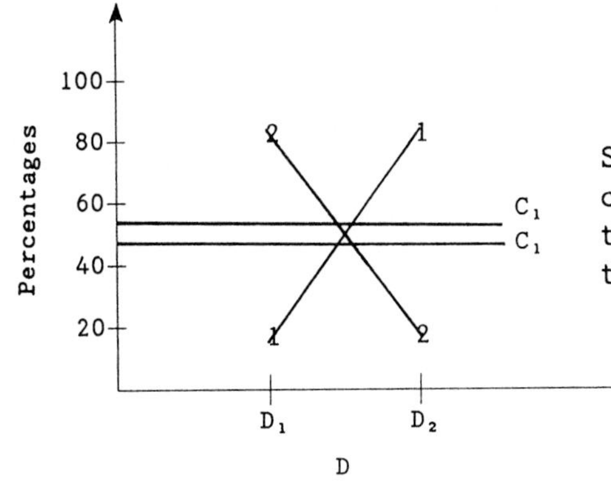


Since the row percentages in each column are not similar to the row total percentages, the graph implies the variables are dependent.

c.

| | | F | | | |
|---|---|---|---|---|---|
| | | $F_1$ | $F_2$ | $F_3$ | |
| E | $E_1$ | $\frac{10}{40} \cdot 100 = 25\%$ | $\frac{30}{40} \cdot 100 = 75\%$ | $\frac{15}{30} \cdot 100 = 50\%$ | $\frac{55}{110} \cdot 100 = 50\%$ |
| | $E_2$ | $\frac{30}{40} \cdot 100 = 75\%$ | $\frac{10}{40} \cdot 100 = 25\%$ | $\frac{15}{30} \cdot 100 = 50\%$ | $\frac{55}{110} \cdot 100 = 50\%$ |

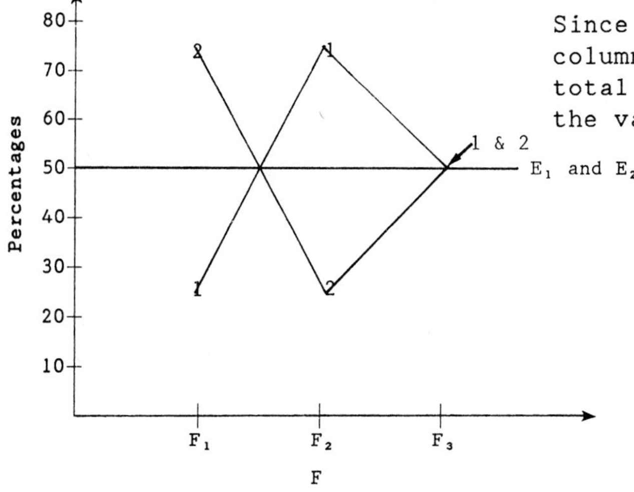


Since the row percentages in each column are not similar to the row total percentages, the graph implies the variables are dependent.

The rejection region requires $\alpha = .05$ in the upper tail of the $\chi^2$ distribution with df = k - 1 = 3 - 1 = 2. From Table XIII, Appendix B, $\chi^2_{.05} = 5.99147$. The rejection region is $\chi^2 > 5.99147$.

Since the observed value of the test statistic falls in the rejection region ($\chi^2 = 87.38 > 5.99147$), $H_0$ is rejected. There is sufficient evidence to indicate the consumer attitudes toward warranties have changed at $\alpha = .05$.

b. Post-Magnuson-Moss Warranty Act

Yes $\quad \dfrac{156}{237} \cdot 100\% = 65.8\%$

Uncertain $\quad \dfrac{61}{237} \cdot 100\% = 25.7\%$

No $\quad \dfrac{20}{237} \cdot 100\% = 8.4\%$

The percentages that said "no" prior to the Warranty Act and after are about the same, 9.7% and 8.4%. However, the percentage that said "yes" increased from 37.0% to 65.8%.

19.37 a. Some preliminary calculations are:

$E(n_1) = np_{1,0} = 200(.65) = 130 \qquad n_1 = np_1 = 200(.78) = 156$
$E(n_2) = np_{2,0} = 200(.15) = 30 \qquad n_2 = np_2 = 200(.12) = 24$
$E(n_3) = np_{3,0} = 200(.10) = 20 \qquad n_3 = np_3 = 200(.05) = 10$
$E(n_4) = np_{4,0} = 200(.07) = 14 \qquad n_4 = np_4 = 200(.02) = 4$
$E(n_5) = np_{5,0} = 200(.03) = 6 \qquad n_5 = np_5 = 200(.03) = 6$

To determine if the increase in interest rates affected the timing of buyers' payments, we test:

$H_0$: $p_1 = .65$, $p_2 = .15$, $p_3 = .10$, $p_4 = .07$, and $p_5 = .03$
$H_a$: At least one proportion differs from its hypothesized value

The test statistic is $\chi^2 = \sum \dfrac{(n_i - E(n_i))^2}{E(n_i)}$

$$= \frac{(156 - 130)^2}{130} + \frac{(24 - 30)^2}{30} + \frac{(10 - 20)^2}{20} + \frac{(4 - 14)^2}{14} + \frac{(6 - 6)^2}{6} = 18.54$$

The rejection region requires $\alpha = .10$ in the upper tail of the $\chi^2$ distribution with df = k - 1 = 5 - 1 = 4. From Table XIII, Appendix B, $\chi^2_{.10} = 7.77944$. The rejection region is $\chi^2 > 7.77944$.

$$\chi^2 = \sum\sum \frac{(n_{ij} - \hat{E}(n_{ij}))^2}{\hat{E}(n_{ij})} = \frac{(12 - 19.765)^2}{19.765} + \frac{(37 - 29.235)^2}{29.235}$$

$$+ \frac{(36 - 28.235)^2}{28.235} + \frac{(34 - 41.765)^2}{41.765} = 8.692$$

b. The hypotheses are:

$H_0$: Refusal rate and previous exposure to false surveys are independent
$H_a$: Refusal rate and previous exposure to false surveys are dependent

The test statistic is $\chi^2 = 8.692$.

The rejection region requires $\alpha = .05$ in the upper tail of the $\chi^2$ distribution with df = $(r - 1)(c - 1) = (2 - 1)(2 - 1) = 1$. From Table XIII, Appendix B, $\chi^2_{.05} = 3.84146$. The rejection region is $\chi^2 > 3.84146$.

Since the observed value of the statistic falls in the rejection region ($\chi^2 = 8.692 > 3.84146$), $H_0$ is rejected. There is sufficient evidence to indicate refusal rate and previous exposure to false surveys are dependent at $\alpha = .05$.

c. The p-value is $P(\chi^2 > 8.692)$. From Table XIII, Appendix B, with df = 1, $P(\chi^2 > 8.692) < .005$.

d. Type I error is concluding the refusal rate and previous exposure to false surveys are dependent when, in fact, they are independent.

Type II error is concluding the two variables are independent when, in fact, they are dependent.

19.45 a. To construct a contingency table, multiply the percentages in the first row by 1980 and divide by 100 and multiply the percentages in the second row by 3961 and divide by 100.

| | PERFORMANCE | | | | | |
|---|---|---|---|---|---|---|
| | 1 | 2 | 3 | 4 | Quit or Fired A | Totals |
| Job-matched | 178 | 792 | 634 | 277 | 99 | 1980 |
| Not job-matched | 79 | 673 | 990 | 1228 | 991 | 3961 |
| | 257 | 1465 | 1624 | 1505 | 1090 | 5941 |

(There is some round off error.)

b. Some preliminary calculations are:

$\hat{E}(n_{11}) = \frac{r_1c_1}{n} = \frac{1980(257)}{5941} = 85.65$ $\hat{E}(n_{12}) = \frac{1980(1465)}{5941} = 488.25$

$\hat{E}(n_{21}) = \frac{3961(257)}{5941} = 171.35$ $\hat{E}(n_{22}) = \frac{3961(1465)}{5941} = 976.75$

$\hat{E}(n_{13}) = \frac{1980(1624)}{5941} = 541.24$ $\hat{E}(n_{15}) = \frac{1980(1090)}{5941} = 363.27$

$\hat{E}(n_{23}) = \frac{3961(1624)}{5941} = 1082.76$ $\hat{E}(n_{25}) = \frac{3961(1090)}{5941} = 726.73$

$\hat{E}(n_{14}) = \frac{1980(1505)}{5941} = 501.58$ $\hat{E}(n_{24}) = \frac{3961(1505)}{5941} = 1003.42$

$H_0$: Proportion of sales personnel falling in performance categories and job-matched categories are independent
$H_a$: Proportion of sales personnel falling in performance categories and job-matched categories are dependent

The test statistic is $\chi^2 = \sum\sum \frac{(n_{ij} - \hat{E}(n_{ij}))^2}{\hat{E}(n_{ij})}$

$$= \frac{(178 - 85.65)^2}{85.65} + \frac{(79 - 171.35)^2}{171.35} + \frac{(792 - 488.25)^2}{488.25} + \frac{(673 - 976.75)^2}{976.75}$$

$$+ \frac{(634 - 541.24)^2}{541.24} + \frac{(990 - 1082.76)^2}{1082.76} + \frac{(277 - 501.58)^2}{501.58}$$

$$+ \frac{(1228 - 1003.42)^2}{1003.42} + \frac{(99 - 363.27)^2}{363.27} + \frac{(991 - 726.73)^2}{9726.73} = 875.79$$

The rejection region requires $\alpha = .05$ in the upper tail of the $\chi^2$ distribution with $df = (r - 1)(c - 1) = (2 - 1)(5 - 1) = 4$. From Table XIII, Appendix B, $\chi^2_{.05} = 9.48773$. The rejection region is $\chi^2 > 9.48773$.

Since the observed value of the test statistic falls in the rejection region ($\chi^2 = 895.79 > 9.48773$), $H_0$ is rejected. There is sufficient evidence to indicate the proportions of sales personnel falling in the performance categories depend on whether the people are job-matched at $\alpha = .025$.

c. To determine if the proportion of sales personnel receiving the highest rating is larger if job-matched, we test:

$H_0$: $p_1 - p_2 = 0$
$H_a$: $p_1 - p_2 > 0$

$\hat{p}_1 = .09$, $\hat{p}_2 = .02$, $\hat{p} = \frac{178 - 79}{5941} = .043$

The test statistic is $z = \frac{\hat{p}_1 - \hat{p}_2 - 0}{\sqrt{\frac{\hat{p}\hat{q}}{n_1} + \frac{\hat{p}\hat{q}}{n_2}}} = \frac{.09 - .02 - 0}{\sqrt{\frac{.043(.957)}{1980} + \frac{.043(.957)}{3961}}}$

$$= \frac{.07}{.0056} = 12.53$$

The rejection region requires $\alpha = .05$ in the upper tail of the z distribution. From Table IV, Appendix B, $z_{.05} = 1.645$. The rejection region is $z > 1.645$.

Since the observed value of the test statistic falls in the rejection region ($z = 12.53 > 1.645$), $H_0$ is rejected. There is sufficient evidence to indicate the proportion of sales personnel receiving the highest rating is larger if job-matched at $\alpha = .05$.

19.47 Some preliminary calculations are:

$\hat{E}(n_{11}) = \frac{r_1c_1}{n} = \frac{202(432)}{1000} = 87.264$

$\hat{E}(n_{21}) = \frac{247(432)}{1000} = 106.704$

$\hat{E}(n_{31}) = \frac{234(432)}{1000} = 101.088$

$\hat{E}(n_{41}) = \frac{198(432)}{1000} = 85.536$

$\hat{E}(n_{51}) = \frac{119(432)}{1000} = 51.408$

$\hat{E}(n_{12}) = \frac{202(457)}{1000} = 92.314$

$\hat{E}(n_{22}) = \frac{247(457)}{1000} = 112.879$

$\hat{E}(n_{32}) = \frac{234(457)}{1000} = 106.938$

$\hat{E}(n_{42}) = \frac{198(457)}{1000} = 90.486$

$\hat{E}(n_{52}) = \frac{119(457)}{1000} = 54.383$

$\hat{E}(n_{13}) = \frac{202(111)}{1000} = 22.422$

$\hat{E}(n_{23}) = \frac{247(111)}{1000} = 27.417$

$\hat{E}(n_{33}) = \frac{234(111)}{1000} = 25.974$

$\hat{E}(n_{43}) = \frac{198(111)}{1000} = 21.978$

$\hat{E}(n_{53}) = \frac{119(111)}{1000} = 13.209$

To determine if a relationship exists between age and number of games attended per year, we test:

$H_0$: Age and number of games attended are independent
$H_a$: Age and number of games attended are dependent

The test statistic is $\chi^2 = \sum\sum \frac{(n_{ij} - \hat{E}(n_{ij}))^2}{\hat{E}(n_{ij})}$

$$= \frac{(78 - 87.264)^2}{87.264} + \frac{(147 - 106.704)^2}{106.704} + \frac{(129 - 101.088)^2}{101.088} + \cdots$$

$$+ \frac{(22 - 13.209)^2}{13.209} = 103.08$$

The rejection region requires $\alpha = .05$ in the upper tail of the $\chi^2$ distribution with df = $(r - 1)(c - 1) = (5 - 1)(3 - 1) = 8$. From Table XIII, Appendix B, $\chi^2_{.05} = 15.5073$. The rejection region is $\chi^2 > 15.5073$.

Since the observed value of the test statistic falls in the rejection region ($\chi^2 = 103.08 > 15.5073$), $H_0$ is rejected. There is sufficient evidence to indicate age and number of games attended are related at $\alpha = .05$.

19.49 a. Some preliminary calculations are:

The contingency table is:

| | | Defectives | Non-Defectives | |
|---|---|---|---|---|
| | 1 | 25 | 175 | 200 |
| Shift | 2 | 35 | 165 | 200 |
| | 3 | 80 | 120 | 200 |
| | | 140 | 460 | 600 |

$$\hat{E}(n_{11}) = \frac{r_1 c_1}{n} = \frac{200(140)}{600} = 46.667$$

$$\hat{E}(n_{21}) = \hat{E}(n_{31}) = \frac{200(140)}{600} = 46.667$$

$$\hat{E}(n_{12}) = \hat{E}(n_{22}) = \hat{E}(n_{32}) = \frac{200(460)}{600} = 153.333$$

To determine if quality of the filters are related to shift, we test:

$H_0$: Quality of filters and shift are independent
$H_a$: Quality of filters and shift are dependent

The test statistic is $\chi^2 = \sum\sum \dfrac{(n_{ij} - \hat{E}(n_{ij}))^2}{\hat{E}(n_{ij})}$

$$= \frac{(35 - 46.667)^2}{46.667} + \frac{(35 - 46.667)^2}{46.667} + \frac{(80 - 46.667)^2}{46.667}$$

$$+ \frac{(175 - 153.333)^2}{153.333} + \frac{(165 - 153.333)^2}{153.333} + \frac{(120 - 153.333)^2}{153.333}$$

$= 47.98$

The rejection region requires $\alpha = .05$ in the upper tail of the $\chi^2$ distribution with df $= (r - 1)(c - 1) = (3 - 1)(2 - 1) = 2$. From Table XIII, Appendix B, $\chi^2_{.05} = 5.99147$. The rejection region is $\chi^2 > 5.99147$.

Since the observed value of the test statistic falls in the rejection region ($\chi^2 = 47.98 > 5.99147$), $H_0$ is rejected. There is sufficient evidence to indicate quality of filters and shift are related at $\alpha = .05$.

b. The form of the confidence interval for p is

$$\hat{p} \pm z_{\alpha/2}\sqrt{\frac{\hat{p}\hat{q}}{n}} \quad \text{where } \hat{p} = \frac{25}{200} = .125$$

For confidence coefficient .95, $\alpha = 1 - .95 = .05$ and $\alpha/2 = .05/2 = .025$. From Table IV, Appendix B, $z_{.025} = 1.96$. The 95% confidence interval is:

$$.125 \pm 1.96\sqrt{\frac{.125(.875)}{200}} \Rightarrow .125 \pm .046 \Rightarrow (.079, .171)$$

19.51 Some preliminary calculations are:

$E(n_1) = np_{1,0} = 169(.25) = 42.25$
$E(n_2) = np_{2,0} = 169(.25) = 42.25$
$E(n_3) = np_{3,0} = 169(.25) = 42.25$
$E(n_4) = np_{4,0} = 169(.25) = 42.25$

To determine if the proportions of customers who learned about the sale differ for the four modes, we test:

$H_0$: $p_1 = p_2 = p_3 = p_4 = .25$
$H_a$: At least one proportion differs from its hypothesized value

The test statistic is $\chi^2 = \sum\sum \dfrac{(n_i - E(n_i))^2}{E(n_i)}$

$$= \frac{(53 - 42.25)^2}{42.25} + \frac{(32 - 42.25)^2}{42.25} + \frac{(36 - 42.25)^2}{42.25} + \frac{(48 - 42.25)^2}{42.25} = 6.93$$

The rejection region requires $\alpha = .05$ in the upper tail of the $\chi^2$ distribution with df = k - 1 = 4 - 1 = 3. From Table XIII, Appendix B, $\chi^2_{.05} = 7.81473$. The rejection region is $\chi^2 > 7.81473$.

Since the observed value of the test statistic does not fall in the rejection region ($\chi^2 = 6.93 \not> 7.81473$), $H_0$ is not rejected. There is insufficient evidence to indicate the proportions of customers who learned about the sale differ for the four modes at $\alpha = .05$.

19.53 a. Some preliminary calculations are:

$$\hat{E}(n_{11}) = \frac{r_1 c_1}{n_1} = \frac{107(129)}{400} = 34.5075 \qquad \hat{E}(n_{13}) = \frac{107(103)}{400} = 27.5525$$

$$\hat{E}(n_{21}) = \frac{237(129)}{400} = 76.4325 \qquad \hat{E}(n_{23}) = \frac{237(103)}{400} = 61.0275$$

$$\hat{E}(n_{31}) = \frac{56(129)}{400} = 18.06 \qquad \hat{E}(n_{33}) = \frac{56(103)}{400} = 14.42$$

$$\hat{E}(n_{12}) = \frac{107(132)}{400} = 35.31 \qquad \hat{E}(n_{14}) = \frac{107(36)}{400} = 9.63$$

$$\hat{E}(n_{22}) = \frac{237(132)}{400} = 78.21 \qquad \hat{E}(n_{24}) = \frac{237(36)}{400} = 21.33$$

$$\hat{E}(n_{32}) = \frac{56(132)}{400} = 18.48 \qquad \hat{E}(n_{34}) = \frac{56(36)}{400} = 5.04$$

To determine if a relationship exists between employee income and amount stolen, we test:

$H_0$: Employee income and amount stolen are independent
$H_a$: Employee income and amount stolen are dependent

The test statistic is $\chi^2 = \sum\sum \dfrac{(n_{ij} - \hat{E}(n_{ij}))^2}{\hat{E}(n_{ij})}$

$$= \frac{(46 - 34.5075)^2}{34.5075} + \frac{(78 - 76.4325)^2}{76.4325} + \frac{(5 - 18.06)^2}{18.06} + \cdots + \frac{(12 - 5.04)^2}{5.04} = 38.68$$

The rejection region requires $\alpha = .05$ in the upper tail of the $\chi^2$ distribution with df = (r - 1)(c - 1) = (3 - 1)(4 - 1) = 6. From Table XIII, Appendix B, $\chi^2_{.05} = 12.5916$. The rejection region is $\chi^2 > 12.5916$.

Since the observed value of the test statistic falls in the rejection region ($\chi^2 = 38.68 > 12.5916$), $H_0$ is rejected. There is sufficient evidence to indicate a relationship exists between employee income and amount stolen at $\alpha = .05$.

b. To convert the responses to percentages, divide the numbers in each column by the column total and multiply by 100. The percentages in each income category are found by dividing the row totals by the total sample size and multiplying by 100.

| | | AMOUNT STOLEN | | | | |
|---|---|---|---|---|---|---|
| | | Under 5,000 | 5000- 9,999 | 10,000- 19,999 | 20,000 or more | |
| Income of Employee | Under 15 | $\frac{46}{129} \cdot 100$ = 35.7% | $\frac{39}{132} \cdot 100$ = 29.5% | $\frac{17}{103} \cdot 100$ = 16.5% | $\frac{5}{36} \cdot 100$ = 13.9% | $\frac{107}{400} \cdot 100 = 26.75\%$ |
| | 15 - 25 | $\frac{78}{129} \cdot 100$ = 60.5% | $\frac{79}{132} \cdot 100$ = 59.8% | $\frac{61}{103} \cdot 100$ = 59.2% | $\frac{19}{36} \cdot 100$ = 52.8% | $\frac{237}{400} \cdot 100 = 59.25\%$ |
| | Over 25 | $\frac{5}{129} \cdot 100$ = 3.9% | $\frac{14}{132} \cdot 100$ = 10.6% | $\frac{25}{103} \cdot 100$ = 24.3% | $\frac{12}{36} \cdot 100$ = 33.3% | $\frac{56}{400} \cdot 100 = 14\%$ |

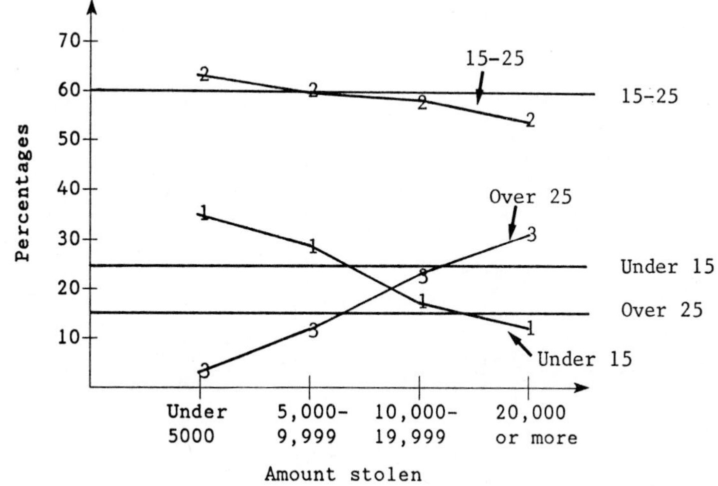


Since the lines are not close to the horizontal lines representing the row percentages, there is evidence to support the conclusion in part (a).

19.55 Some preliminary calculations are:

$$\hat{E}(n_{11}) = \frac{r_1c_1}{n} = \frac{117(155)}{300} = 60.45 \qquad \hat{E}(n_{13}) = \frac{117(31)}{300} = 12.09$$

$$\hat{E}(n_{21}) = \frac{120(155)}{300} = 62 \qquad \hat{E}(n_{23}) = \frac{120(31)}{300} = 12.4$$

$$\hat{E}(n_{31}) = \frac{63(155)}{300} = 32.55 \qquad \hat{E}(n_{33}) = \frac{63(31)}{300} = 6.51$$

$$\hat{E}(n_{12}) = \frac{117(114)}{300} = 44.46$$

$$\hat{E}(n_{22}) = \frac{120(114)}{300} = 45.6$$

$$\hat{E}(n_{32}) = \frac{63(114)}{300} = 23.94$$

To determine if time and size of purchase are related, we test:

$H_0$: Time and size of purchase are independent
$H_a$: Time and size of purchase are dependent

The test statistic is $\chi^2 = \sum\sum \frac{(n_{ij} - \hat{E}(n_{ij}))^2}{\hat{E}(n_{ij})}$

$$= \frac{(65 - 60.45)^2}{60.45} + \frac{(61 - 62)^2}{62} + \frac{(29 - 32.55)^2}{32.55} + \cdots + \frac{(7 - 6.51)^2}{6.51} = 3.13$$

The rejection region requires $\alpha = .05$ in the upper tail of the $\chi^2$ distribution with df $= (r - 1)(c - 1) = (3 - 1)(3 - 1) = 4$. From Table XIII, Appendix B, $\chi^2_{.05} = 9.48773$. The rejection region is $\chi^2 > 9.48773$.

Since the observed value of the test statistic does not fall in the rejection region ($\chi^2 = 3.13 \not> 9.48773$), $H_0$ is not rejected. There is insufficient evidence to indicate time and size of purchase are related at $\alpha = .05$.

19.57 a. Some preliminary calculations are:

$E(n_1) = np_{1,0} = 2000(.2) = 400$ $\qquad E(n_4) = np_{4,0} = 2000(.2) = 400$
$E(n_2) = np_{2,0} = 2000(.2) = 400$ $\qquad E(n_5) = np_{5,0} = 2000(.2) = 400$
$E(n_3) = np_{3,0} = 2000(.2) = 400$

To determine if a difference in preference for the five candidates exists, we test:

$H_0$: $p_1 = p_2 = p_3 = p_4 = p_5 = .2$
$H_a$: At least one of the proportions differs from its hypothesized value

The test statistic is $\chi^2 = \sum \frac{(n_i - E(n_i))^2}{E(n_i)}$

$$= \frac{(385 - 400)^2}{400} + \frac{(493 - 400)^2}{400} + \frac{(628 - 400)^2}{400} + \frac{(235 - 400)^2}{400}$$
$$+ \frac{(259 - 400)^2}{400} = 269.91$$

The rejection region requires $\alpha = .01$ in the upper tail of the $\chi^2$ distribution with df = k - 1 = 5 - 1 = 4. From Table XIII, Appendix B, $\chi^2_{.01} = 13.2767$. The rejection region is $\chi^2 > 13.2767$.

Since the observed value of the test statistic falls in the rejection region ($\chi^2 = 269.91 > 13.2767$), $H_0$ is rejected. There is sufficient evidence to indicate a difference in preference for the five candidates exists at $\alpha = .01$.

b. The observed significance is $P(\chi^2 > 269.91)$. From Table XIII, Appendix B, with df = 4, $P(\chi^2 > 269.91) < .005$.

19.59 a. Some preliminary calculations are:

$\hat{E}(n_{11}) = \frac{r_1c_1}{n} = \frac{819(331)}{1600} = 169.4306$ $\hat{E}(n_{22}) = \frac{781(60)}{1600} = 29.2875$

$\hat{E}(n_{12}) = \frac{781(331)}{1600} = 161.5694$ $\hat{E}(n_{31}) = \frac{819(1209)}{1600} = 618.8569$

$\hat{E}(n_{21}) = \frac{819(60)}{1600} = 30.7125$ $\hat{E}(n_{32}) = \frac{78(1209)}{1600} = 590.1431$

To determine if life insurance preference of students depends on their sex, we test:

$H_0$: Life insurance preference of students and students' sex are independent
$H_a$: Life insurance preference of students and students' sex are dependent

The test statistic is $\sum\sum \frac{(n_{ij} - \hat{E}(n_{ij}))^2}{\hat{E}(n_{ij})}$

$$= \frac{(116 - 169.4306)^2}{169.4306} + \frac{(215 - 161.5694)^2}{161.5694} + \cdots$$

$$+ \frac{(533 - 590.1431)^2}{590.1431} = 46.25$$

The rejection region requires $\alpha = .05$ in the upper tail of the $\chi^2$ distribution with df = (r - 1)(c - 1) = (2 - 1)(3 - 1) = 2. From Table XIII, Appendix B, $t^2_{.05} = 5.99147$. The rejection region is $\chi^2 > 5.99147$.

Since the observed value of the test statistic falls in the rejection region ($\chi^2 = 46.25 > 5.99147$), $H_0$ is rejected. There is sufficient evidence to indicate life insurance preference of students depends on their sex at $\alpha = .05$.

b. The observed significance level is $P(\chi^2 > 46.25)$. From Table XIII, Appendix B, with df = 2, $P(\chi^2 > 46.25) < .005$.

c. To calculate the appropriate percentages, divide the numbers in each column by the total for that column and multiply by 100. Divide each row total by the total sample size and multiply by 100.

| | Preferred a Term Policy | Preferred Whole Life | No Preference | |
|---|---|---|---|---|
| Females | $\frac{116}{331} \cdot 100 = 35.0\%$ | $\frac{27}{60} \cdot 100 = 45\%$ | $\frac{676}{1209} \cdot 100 = 55.9\%$ | $\frac{819}{1600} \cdot 100 = 51.2\%$ |
| Males | $\frac{215}{331} \cdot 100 = 65\%$ | $\frac{33}{60} \cdot 100 = 55\%$ | $\frac{533}{1209} \cdot 100 = 44.1\%$ | $\frac{781}{1600} \cdot 100 = 48.8\%$ |

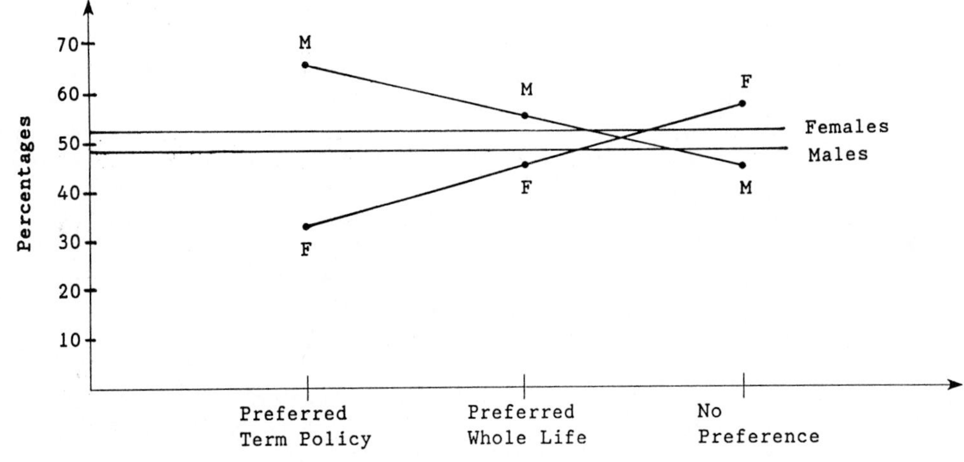

19.61 a. $$\chi^2 = \frac{\sum(\text{Observed} - \text{Expected})^2}{\text{Expected}}$$

$$= \frac{(26 - 23)^2}{23} + \frac{(146 - 136)^2}{136} + \frac{(361 - 341)^2}{341} + \frac{(311 - 341)^2}{341}$$

$$+ \frac{(143 - 136)^2}{136} + \frac{(13 - 23)^2}{23} = 9.647$$

b. From Table XIII, Appendix B, with df = 5, $\chi^2_{.05} = 11.0705$.

c. $H_0$: The distribution is normal with mean \$1200 and $\sigma = 200$
$H_a$: The distribution is nonnormal

The test statistic is $\chi^2 = 9.647$.

The rejection region is $\chi^2 > 11.0705$.

Since the observed value of the test statistic does not fall in the rejection region ($\chi^2 = 9.647 \not> 11.0705$), $H_0$ is not rejected. There is insufficient evidence to indicate the distribution is nonnormal at $\alpha = .05$.

d. The observed significance level is $P(\chi^2 > 9.647)$. From Table XIII, Appendix B, with df = 5, $.05 < P(\chi^2 > 9.647) < .10$.

19.63 The contingency table is:

| | Agreed with Action | Disagreed with Action | No Opinion | |
|---|---|---|---|---|
| Consumers | 89 | 3 | 8 | 100 |
| Managers | 37 | 54 | 9 | 100 |
| | 126 | 57 | 17 | 200 |

Some preliminary calculations are:

$$\hat{E}(n_{11}) = \frac{r_1c_1}{n} = \frac{100(126)}{200} = 63 \qquad \hat{E}(n_{22}) = \frac{100(57)}{200} = 28.5$$

$$\hat{E}(n_{21}) = \frac{100(126)}{200} = 63 \qquad \hat{E}(n_{31}) = \frac{100(17)}{200} = 8.5$$

$$\hat{E}(n_{12}) = \frac{100(57)}{200} = 28.5 \qquad \hat{E}(n_{32}) = \frac{100(17)}{200} = 8.5$$

To determine if differences exist between retailers' and consumers' perceptions, we test:

$H_0$: Retailers' and consumers' perceptions are the same
$H_a$: Retailers' and consumers' perceptions are not the same

The test statistic is $\sum\sum\frac{(n_{ij} - \hat{E}(n_{ij}))^2}{\hat{E}(n_{ij})}$

$$= \frac{(89 - 63)^2}{63} + \frac{(37 - 63)^2}{63} + \frac{(3 - 28.5)^2}{28.5} + \frac{(54 - 28.5)^2}{28.5}$$

$$+ \frac{(8 - 8.5)^2}{28.5} + \frac{(9 - 8.5)^2}{8.5} = 67.15.$$

The rejection region requires $\alpha = .01$ in the upper tail of the $\chi^2$ distribution with df = (r - 1)(c - 1) = (2 - 1)(3 - 1) = 2. From Table XIII, Appendix B, $t^2_{.01} = 9.21034$. The rejection region is $\chi^2 > 9.21034$.

Since the observed value of the test statistic falls in the rejection region ($\chi^2 = 67.15 > 9.21034$), $H_0$ is rejected. There is sufficient evidence to indicate retailers and consumers' perceptions are not the same at $\alpha = .01$.

The necessary assumption is:

> The sample size will be large enough so that, for every cell, the expected cell count, $E(n_{ij})$ will be 5 or more.

# CHAPTER 20

## DECISION ANALYSIS

20.3 a. This problem is decision-making under uncertainty. The management does not know whether the applicant will default on the loan or not.

b. This problem is decision-making under conflict. The manufacturer is "playing against" his competitors.

c. This problem is decision-making under certainty. The company knows the outcomes of the possible decisions.

20.5 1. Actions: The set of two or more alternatives the decision-maker has chosen to consider. The decision-maker's problem is to choose one action from this set.
2. States of Nature: The set of two or more mutually exclusive and collectively exhaustive chance events upon which the outcome of the decision-maker's chosen action depends.
3. Outcomes: The set of consequences resulting from all possible action/state of nature combinations.
4. Objective variables: The quantity used to measure and express the outcomes of a decision problem.

20.9 ACTIONS

$a_1$: Add a new building to existing facilities.
$a_2$: Do not add a new building.

STATES OF NATURE

$S_1$: Economy continues to expand.
$S_2$: Economy remains stable or experiences a downward trend.

OUTCOMES [The outcome is indicated for each action-state combination $(a_i, S_j)$.]

$(a_1, S_1)$: $650,000
$(a_1, S_2)$: -$475,000
$(a_2, S_1)$: $550,000
$(a_2, S_2)$: $550,000

OBJECTIVE VARIABLE

Profit per year

20.13 Action $a_3$ is inadmissable because it is dominated by action $a_2$. That is, for each state of nature, the payoff for $a_2$ is greater than or equal to the payoff for $a_3$.

The opportunity losses are calculated as shown in the table below.

| | | STATE OF NATURE | | | |
|---|---|---|---|---|---|
| | | $S_1$ | $S_2$ | $S_3$ | $S_4$ |
| ACTION | $a_2$ | 0 | 0 | 40 - 0 = 40 | 80 - 45 = 35 |
| | $a_3$ | -60 - (-65) = 5 | -5 - (-10) = 5 | 0 | 80 - 75 = 5 |
| | $a_4$ | -60 - (-80) = 20 | -5 - (-40) = 35 | 40 - (-10) = 50 | 0 |

20.15 a. Action $a_4$ is dominated by action $a_2$ and thus is inadmissible.

b. For each action-state combination ($a_i$, $S_j$), the opportunity loss table displays the difference between the payoff received for action a and the maximum payoff attainable for state $S_j$. From this information, it is not possible to determine the original payoffs.

20.17 The payoff is $15 million if the minicomputer is not marketed in Europe. If it is marketed in Europe, and a 3% market share is attained, the company profits $3 million (or $18 million for the company), 2% market share gives $1 million profit ($16 million), 1% market share gives $1 million loss ($14 million). The payoff table is:

| | | STATE OF NATURE | | |
|---|---|---|---|---|
| | | 1% | 2% | 3% |
| ACTION | Market | 14 | 16 | 18 |
| | Do not market | 15 | 15 | 15 |

The opportunity losses are calculated as shown in the following table.

| | | STATE OF NATURE 1% | 2% | 3% |
|---|---|---|---|---|
| ACTION | Market | 15 - 14 = 1 | 0 | 0 |
| | Do not market | 0 | 16 - 15 = 1 | 18 - 15 = 3 |

20.19 a. The increase in sales will be $200,000 if advertising is not increased. If it is increased by $1 million, sales will increase by $1.6 million, a profit of $600,000, if campaign is successful. If advertising is increased by $1 million, and the campaign fails, sales will increase by only $400,000, a loss of $600,000. The payoff table is as shown below.

| | | STATE OF NATURE Successful | Unsuccessful |
|---|---|---|---|
| ACTION | Increase advertising | $600,000 | $-600,000 |
| | Do not increase advertising | $200,000 | $200,000 |

b. Neither action is inadmissable. Depending on the state of nature, one action is more profitable than the other.

c.

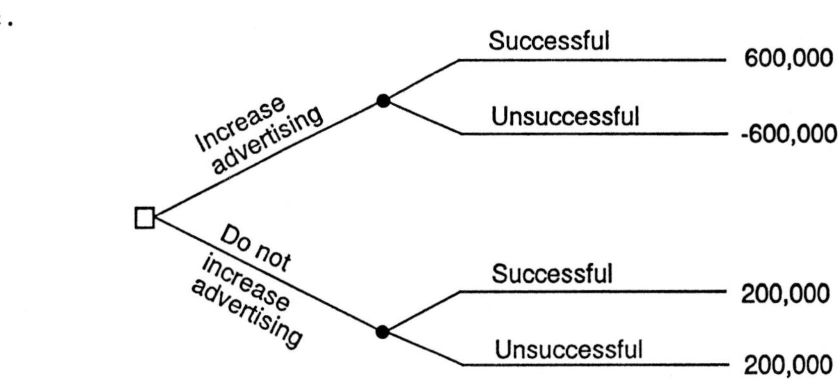


20.21 a. If the company settles out of court, they will lose $50 million. If they go to court and win, they will lose $1 million in court costs. If they go to court and lose, they will lose $100 million plus the $1 million in court fees. The payoff table is shown:

| | | STATE OF NATURE Win | Lose |
|---|---|---|---|
| ACTION | Go to court | -\$1 million | -\$101 million |
| | Settle out of court | -\$50 million | -\$50 million |

b.

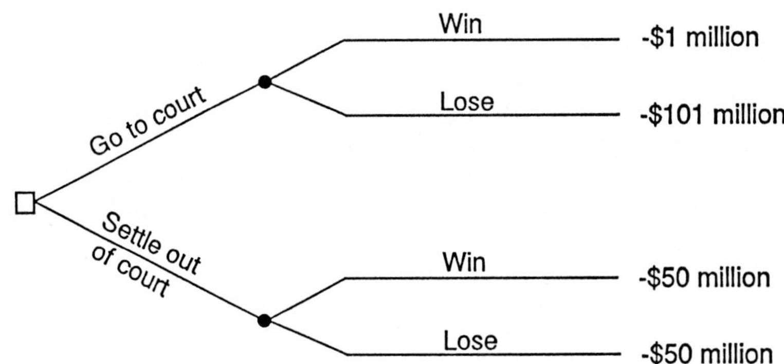


20.23 $E(x) = \sum_{\text{all } x} xp(x)$

$EP(a_1) = (-250)(.1) + (-400)(.3) + (0)(.4) + (300)(.2) = -85$
$EP(a_2) = (-300)(.1) + (-100)(.3) + (300)(.4) + (100)(.2) = 80$
$EP(a_3) = (-100)(.1) + (-40)(.3) + (-10)(.4) + (85)(.2) = -9$

We would choose $a_2$, the action that produced the largest expected payoff.

20.25

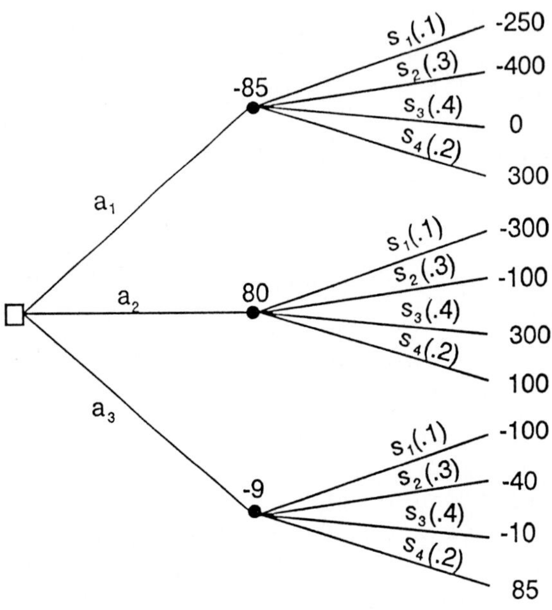

20.27 $EOL(a_1) = (56)(.6) + (0)(.4) = 33.6$
$EOL(a_2) = (0)(.6) + (70)(.4) = 28.0$

We would choose $a_2$, since it produces the smallest expected opportunity loss.

20.29 a. $EP(a_1) = .5(800,000) + .5(-200,000) = 300,000$
$EP(a_2) = .5(660,000) + .5(10,000) = 335,000$

We would choose action $a_2$: Design B, because the expected payoff is larger.

b. $EP(a_1) = 2/3(800,000) + 1/3(-200,000) = 466,666.67$
$EP(a_2) = 2/3(660,000) + 1/3(10,000) = 443,333.33$

We would choose action $a_1$: Design A, because the expected payoff is larger.

20.31 The payoff table, with state of nature probabilities shown in parentheses is given below.

| | | | STATE (Percent Defective) | | |
|---|---|---|---|---|---|
| | | | 5% (.55) | 10% (.24) | 50% (.21) |
| ACTION | $a_1$: | Purchase the guarantee | -1250 | -1500 | -1500 |
| | $a_2$: | Don't purchase the guarantee | -250 | -500 | -2500 |

$EP(a_1) = -1250(.55) - 1500(.24) - 1500(.21) = -1362.5$
$EP(a_2) = -250(.55) - 500(.24) - 2500(.21) = -782.5$

The greater expected payoff is associated with action $a_2$: Do not purchase the guarantee.

20.33 a. The payoff table for this decision problem is shown below.

| | | | STATE | |
|---|---|---|---|---|
| | | | Successful (2/3) | Unsuccessful (1/3) |
| ACTION | $a_1$: | Increase advertising budget | 1,600,000 - 1,000,000 = 600,000 | 400,000 - 1,000,000 = -600,000 |
| | $a_2$: | Do not increase budget | 200,000 | 200,000 |

$EP(a_1) = 600,000(2/3) - 600,000(1/3) = 200,000$
$EP(a_2) = 200,000(2/3) + 200,000(1/3) = 200,000$

Thus, both actions have the same expected payoff and neither is preferred over the other.

b.

| | | STATE | |
|---|---|---|---|
| | | Successful (2/3) | Unsuccessful (1/3) |
| ACTION | $a_1$: Increase advertising budget | 0 | 800,000 |
| | $a_2$: Do not increase budget | 400,000 | 0 |

c. $EOL(a_1) = 0(2/3) + 800,000(1/3) = 266,667$
$EOL(a_2) = 400,000(2/3) + 0(1/3) = 266,667$

Both actions have the same expected outcome.

20.35 a. Utilities were computed using the function $U(x) = x^2$, and are shown in the following table.

| | | STATE OF NATURE | | |
|---|---|---|---|---|
| | | $S_1$ (.25) | $s_2$ (.30) | $s_3$ (.45) |
| ACTION | $a_1$ | 5625 | 2500 | 900 |
| | $a_2$ | 3600 | 6400 | 0 |

b. $EU(a_1) = 5626(.25) + 2500(.30) + 900(.45) = 2561.25$
$EU(a_2) = 3600(.25) + 6400(.30) + 0(.45) = 2820.00$

Therefore, the expected utility criterion selects action $a_2$.

20.37 a. Utilities were computed using the function $U(x) = -1 + .01x$, and are shown in the following table.

| | | STATE OF NATURE | | | |
|---|---|---|---|---|---|
| | | $S_1$ (.20) | $s_2$ (.15) | $s_3$ (.40) | $s_4$ (.25) |
| ACTION | $a_1$ | .20 | .80 | 0 | 0 |
| | $a_2$ | .05 | .65 | .90 | .50 |
| | $a_2$ | 0 | .20 | .60 | 1.00 |

b. $EU(a_1) = (.20)(.20) + (.80)(.15) + (0)(.40) = (0)(.25) = .16$
$EU(a_2) = (.05)(.20) + (.65)(.15) + (.90)(.40) + (.50)(.25) = .5925$
$EU(a_3) = (0)(.20) + (.20)(.15) + (.60)(.40) + (1.00)(.25) = .52$

The expected utility criterion selects action $a_2$.

20.39 a.

| | | STATE OF NATURE | | |
|---|---|---|---|---|
| | | Dry (.5) | Moderate (.3) | Gusher (.2) |
| ACTION | Invest | -500,000 | 600,000 | 1,500,000 |
| | Do not invest | 0 | 0 | 0 |

b. EP(Invest) = (-500,000)(.5) + (600,000)(.3) + (1,500,000)(.2)
= 230,000
EP(Do not invest) = (0)(.5) + (0)(.3) + (0)(.2) = 0

Using the expected payoff criterion, we would choose to invest in the oil well.

c. First, from Exercise 20.38, we compute the utility values for the table.

The maximum payoff is 1,500,000. The utility of 1,500,000 is U(1,500,000) = 1

The minimum payoff is -500,000. The utility of -500,000 is U(-500,000) = 0.

From part (a), Exercise 20.38, U(600,000) = .9 and U(0) = .8.

The utility table is:

| | | STATE OF NATURE | | |
|---|---|---|---|---|
| | | Dry (.5) | Moderate (.3) | Gusher (.2) |
| ACTION | Invest | 0 | .9 | 1.0 |
| | Do not invest | .8 | .8 | .8 |

EU(Invest) = 0(.5) + .9(.3) + 1(.2) = .47
EU(Do not invest) = .8(.5) + .8(.3) + .8(.2) = .8

The expected utility criterion prescribes action: Do not invest.

20.41 a.

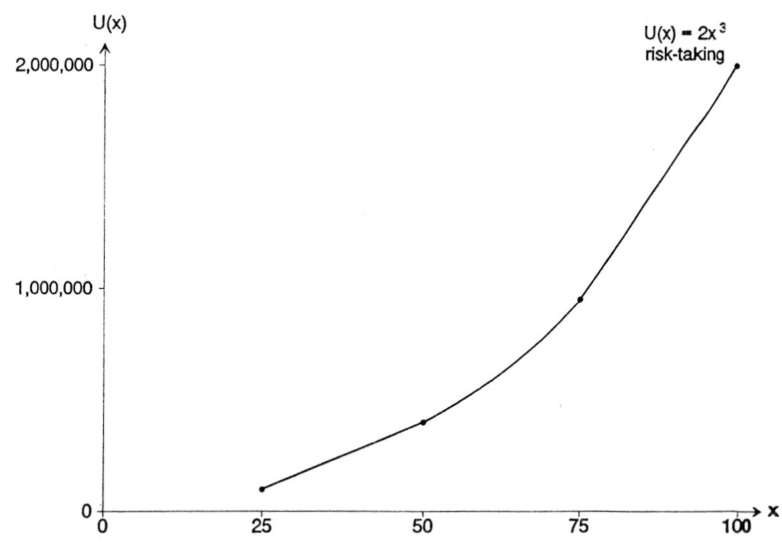


b.

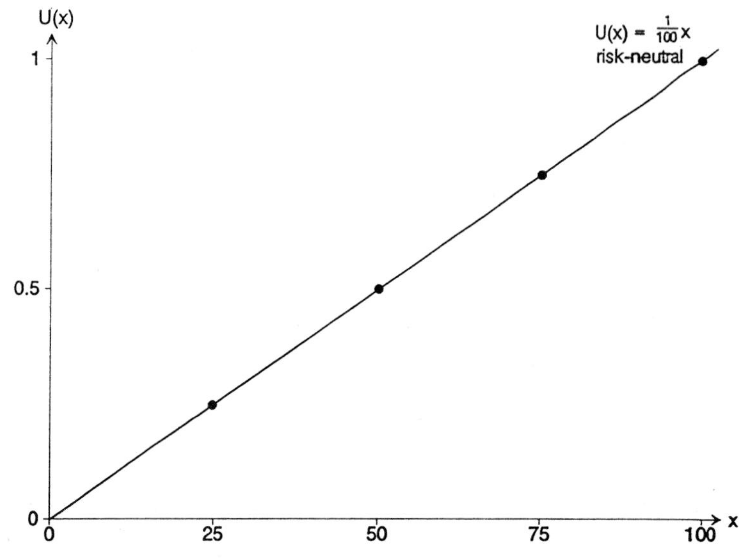

c.

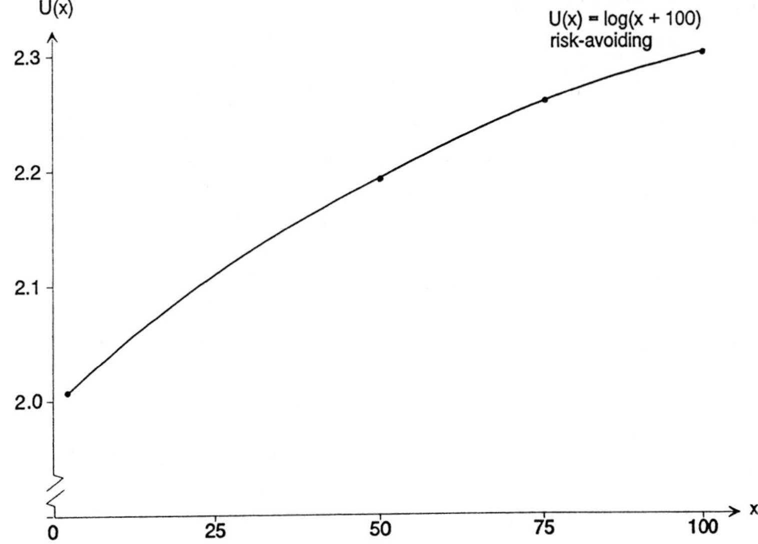
U(x)
U(x) = log(x + 100)
risk-avoiding
2.3
2.2
2.1
2.0
0
25
50
75
100
x

d.

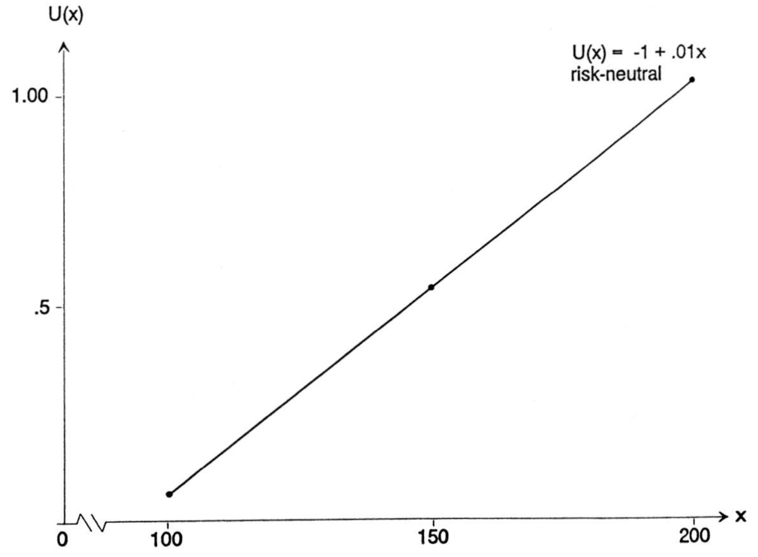
U(x)
U(x) = -1 + .01x
risk-neutral
1.00
.5
0
100
150
200
x

20.43 a.

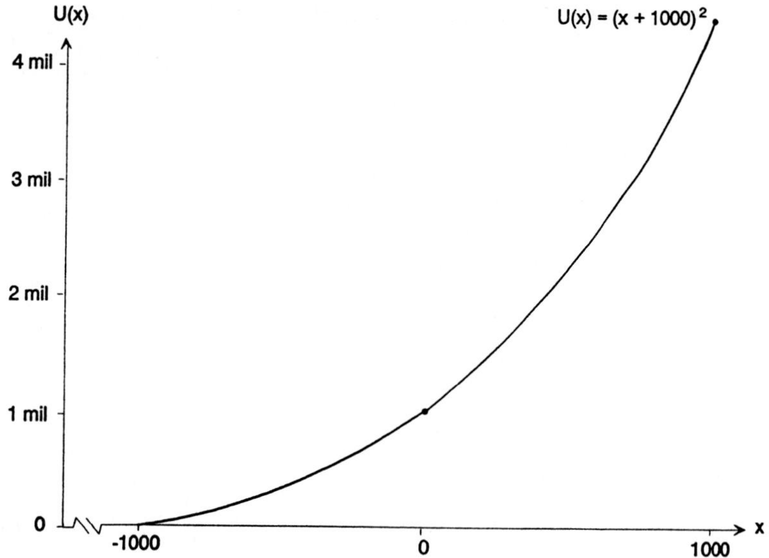


b. The graph of the utility function is convex and, thus, represents a risk-taking attitude.

c. The utilities were computed using the utility function

$$U(x) = (x + 1000)^2,$$

and are shown in the table.

| | | STATE OF NATURE | | |
|---|---|---|---|---|
| | | $S_1$ (.2) | $S_2$ (.6) | $S_3$ (.2) |
| ACTION | $a_1$ | 250,000 | 4,000,000 | 1,562,500 |
| | $a_2$ | 62,500 | 3,610,000 | 3,276,100 |
| | $a_2$ | 1,092,025 | 810,000 | 2,722,500 |

$$EU(a_1) = (250{,}000)(.2) + (4{,}000{,}000)(.6) + (1{,}562{,}500)(.2) = 2{,}762{,}500$$

$$EU(a_2) = (62{,}500)(.2) + (3{,}610{,}000)(.6) + (3{,}276{,}100(.2) = 2{,}833{,}720$$

$$EU(a_3) = (1{,}092{,}025)(.2) + (810{,}000)(.6) + (2{,}722{,}500)(.2) = 1{,}248{,}905$$

The expected utility criterion identifies action $a_2$ as the optimal action.

20.45 a. The plot of the utility function is:

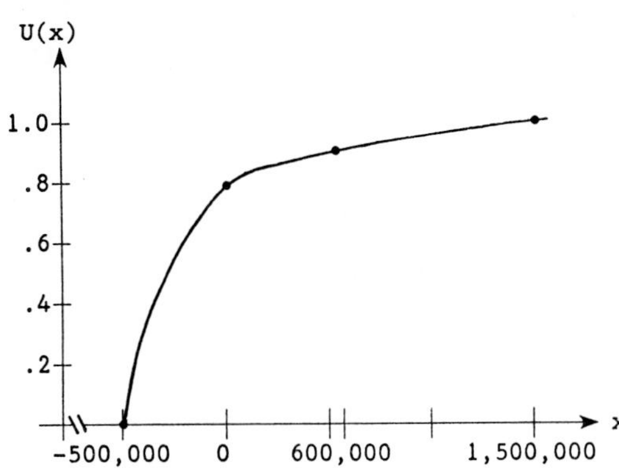


b. Since the graph is concave, the investor is a risk-avoider.

20.49

| (1) STATE OF NATURE | (2) PRIOR PROBABILITY | (3) CONDITIONAL PROBABILITY OF SAMPLE INFORMATION | (4) (2) × (3) | (5) POSTERIOR PROBABILITY (4) ÷ TOTAL OF (4) |
|---|---|---|---|---|
| $S_1$ | .35 | .90 | .315 | .538 |
| $S_2$ | .15 | .10 | .015 | .026 |
| $S_3$ | .30 | .65 | .195 | .333 |
| $S_4$ | .20 | .30 | .060 | .103 |
| | 1.00 | | .585 | 1.000 |

20.53 a. $\mu = E(x) = \sum xp(x) = .09(.40) + .10(.25) + .11(.15) + .12(.10) + .13(.10) = .1025$

$$\sigma^2 = E(x - \mu)^2 = E(x^2) - \mu^2 = .09^2(.4) + .1^2(.25) + .11^2(.15) + .12^2(.10) + .13^2(.10) - .1025^2 = .010685 - .010506 = .000179$$

b. $P(3|S_1) = \binom{25}{3}.09^3.91^{22} = .2106$

$P(3|S_2) = \binom{25}{3}.1^3.9^{22} = .2265$

$P(3|S_3) = \binom{25}{3}.11^3.89^{22} = .2358$

$P(3|S_4) = \binom{25}{3}.12^3.88^{22} = .2387$

$P(3|S_5) = \binom{25}{3}.13^3.87^{22} = .2360$

| (1) STATE OF NATURE | (2) PRIOR PROBABILITY | (3) CONDITIONAL PROBABILITY | (4) PROBABILITY OF INTERSECTION (2) × (3) | (5) POSTERIOR PROBABILITY (4) ÷ TOTAL OF (4) |
|---|---|---|---|---|
| .09 | .40 | .2106 | .08424 | .377 |
| .10 | .25 | .2265 | .05663 | .253 |
| .11 | .15 | .2358 | .03537 | .158 |
| .12 | .10 | .2387 | .02387 | .107 |
| .13 | .10 | .2360 | .02360 | .105 |
| | 1.00 | | .22371 | 1.000 |

c. $\mu = E(x) = .09(.377) + .10(.253) + .11(.158) + .12(.107) + .13(.105) = .1031$

$$\sigma^2 = E(x^2) - \mu^2 = .09^2(.377) + .1^2(.253) + .11^2(.158) + .12^2(.107) + .13^2(.105) - .1031^2$$
$$= .010811 - .010630$$
$$= .000181$$

d. The probability of observing .09 errors is .40 in the prior distribution and .377 in the posterior distribution. All other probabilities are larger in the posterior distribution than the corresponding values in the prior distribution. The sample information has indicated that the proportion of errors is actually higher than the prior distribution indicated.

20.55 Using the posterior probabilities from Exercise 20.54 as the prior probabilities, we get the following:

| (1) STATE | (2) PRIOR PROBABILITY | (3) CONDITIONAL PROBABILITY | (4) PROBABILITY OF INTERSECTION (2) × (3) | (5) POSTERIOR PROBABILITY (4) ÷ TOTAL OF (4) |
|---|---|---|---|---|
| $S_1$: Correctly adjusted | .474 | .05 | .0237 | .0827 |
| $S_2$: Incorrectly adjusted | .526 | .50 | .2630 | .9173 |
| | 1.000 | | .2867 | 1.0000 |

20.57 a. $P(x = 4|\lambda = 2) = \frac{2^4 e^{-2}}{4!} = .0902$

$P(x = 4|\lambda = 3) = \frac{3^4 e^{-3}}{4!} = .1680$

$P(x = 4|\lambda = 4) = \frac{4^4 e^{-4}}{4!} = .1954$

| (1) STATE | (2) PRIOR PROBABILITY | (3) CONDITIONAL PROBABILITY | (4) PROBABILITY OF INTERSECTION (2) × (3) | (5) POSTERIOR PROBABILITY (4) ÷ TOTAL OF (4) |
|---|---|---|---|---|
| 2 | .25 | .0902 | .0226 | .1454 |
| 3 | .50 | .1680 | .0840 | .5405 |
| 4 | .25 | .1954 | .0488 | .3140 |
| | 1.00 | | .1554 | .9999 |

b. $P(2|\lambda = 2) = \frac{2^2 e^{-2}}{2!} = .2707$

$P(2|\lambda = 3) = \frac{3^2 e^{-3}}{2!} = .2240$

$P(2|\lambda = 4) = \frac{4^2 e^{-4}}{2!} = .1465$

Using the posterior distribution from part (a) as the prior distribution, we get:

| (1) STATE | (2) PRIOR PROBABILITY | (3) CONDITIONAL PROBABILITY | (4) PROBABILITY OF INTERSECTION (2) × (3) | (5) POSTERIOR PROBABILITY (4) ÷ TOTAL OF (4) |
|---|---|---|---|---|
| 2 | .1454 | .2707 | .0394 | .191 |
| 3 | .5405 | .2240 | .1211 | .586 |
| 4 | .3140 | .1465 | .0460 | .223 |
| | .9999 | | .2065 | 1.000 |

c. Each time new information is available, we can update our prior information to better reflect what we know.

20.59 a. $EP(a_1) = 10(.6) + 20(.1) + (-14)(.3) = 3.8$
$EP(a_2) = -16(.6) + 18(.1) + 15(.3) = -3.3$
$EP(a_3) = 21(.6) + 12(.1) + 9(.3) = 16.5$
$EP(a_4) = 8(.6) + 25(.1) + (-20)(.3) = 1.3$

The expected payoff criterion selects action $a_3$.

b.

| (1) STATE | (2) PRIOR PROBABILITY | (3) CONDITIONAL PROBABILITY | (4) PROBABILITY OF INTERSECTION (2) × (3) | (5) POSTERIOR PROBABILITY (4) ÷ TOTAL OF (4) |
|---|---|---|---|---|
| $S_1$ | .6 | .8 | .48 | .889 |
| $S_2$ | .1 | .3 | .03 | .056 |
| $S_3$ | .3 | .1 | .03 | .056 |
| | 1.0 | | .54 | 1.001 |

c. $EP(a_1) = 10(.889) + 20(.056) - 14(.056) = 9.226$
$EP(a_2) = -16(.889) + 18(.056) + 15(.056) = -12.376$
$EP(a_3) = 21(.889) + 12(.056) + 9(.056) = 19.845$
$EP(a_4) = 8(.889) + 25(.056) - 20(.056) = 7.392$

d. The expected payoff criterion selects action $a_3$. This is the same action chosen using just the prior probabilities.

20.61 a.

| | | STATE OF NATURE .00(.4) | .05(.3) | .10(.1) | .15(.1) | .20(.1) |
|---|---|---|---|---|---|---|
| ACTION | Agreement 1 | -46,000 | -46,000 | -46,000 | -46,000 | -46,000 |
| | Agreement 2 | -40,000 | -42,000 | -44,000 | -46,000 | -48,000 |

b. $EP(a_1) = -46{,}000(.4) - 46{,}000(.3) - 46{,}000(.1) - 46{,}000(.1) - 46{,}000(.1) = -46{,}000$

$EP(a_2) = -40{,}000(.4) - 42{,}000(.3) - 44{,}000(.1) - 46{,}000(.1) - 48{,}000(.1) = -42{,}400$

The expected payoff criterion selects agreement 2.

c. $P(1 \mid .00) = 0$ $\quad$ $P(0 \mid .00) = 1$
$P(1 \mid .05) = .05$ $\quad$ $P(0 \mid .05) = .95$
$P(1 \mid .10) = .10$ $\quad$ $P(0 \mid .10) = .90$
$P(1 \mid .15) = .15$ $\quad$ $P(0 \mid .15) = .85$
$P(1 \mid .20) = .20$ $\quad$ $P(0 \mid .20) = .80$

If the sampled set was defective the posterior distribution is:

| (1) STATE | (2) PRIOR PROBABILITY | (3) CONDITIONAL PROBABILITY | (4) PROBABILITY OF INTERSECTION (2) × (3) | (5) POSTERIOR PROBABILITY (4) ÷ TOTAL OF (4) |
|---|---|---|---|---|
| .00 | .4 | 0 | .000 | 0.000 |
| .05 | .3 | .05 | .015 | .250 |
| .10 | .1 | .10 | .010 | .167 |
| .15 | .1 | .15 | .015 | .250 |
| .20 | .1 | .20 | .020 | .333 |
| | 1.0 | | .060 | 1.000 |

$$EP(a_1) = -46{,}000(0) - 46{,}000(.25) - 46{,}000(.167) - 46{,}000(.25) - 46{,}000(.333) = -46{,}000$$

$$EP(a_2) = -40{,}000(0) - 42{,}000(.25) - 44{,}000(.167) - 46{,}000(.25) - 48{,}000(.333) = -45{,}332$$

The expected payoff criterion selects agreement 2.

If the sampled set is not defective, the posterior distribution is:

| (1) STATE | (2) PRIOR PROBABILITY | (3) CONDITIONAL PROBABILITY | (4) PROBABILITY OF INTERSECTION (2) × (3) | (5) POSTERIOR PROBABILITY (4) ÷ TOTAL OF (4) |
|---|---|---|---|---|
| .00 | .4 | 1 | .400 | .426 |
| .05 | .3 | .95 | .285 | .303 |
| .10 | .1 | .90 | .090 | .096 |
| .15 | .1 | .85 | .085 | .090 |
| .20 | .1 | .80 | .080 | .085 |
| | 1.0 | | .94 | 1.000 |

$$EP(a_1) = -46{,}000(.426) - 46{,}000(.303) - 46{,}000(.096) - 46{,}000(.09) - 46{,}000(.085) = -46{,}000$$

$$EP(a_2) = -40{,}000(.426) - 42{,}000(.303) - 44{,}000(.096) - 46{,}000(.09) - 48{,}000(.085) = -42{,}210$$

The expected payoff criterion selects agreement 2.

20.63 a. To compute the opportunity loss, subtract the payoffs from the maximum payoff in each state.

| | | STATE OF NATURE $S_1$ (.65) | $S_2$ (.20) | $S_3$ (.15) |
|---|---|---|---|---|
| ACTION | $a_1$ | 40 | 250 | 0 |
| | $a_2$ | 115 | 0 | 125 |
| | $a_3$ | 0 | 210 | 20 |

b. $EOL(a_1) = 40(.65) + 250(.20) + 0(.15) = 76$
$EOL(a_2) = 115(.65) + 0(.20) + 125(.15) = 134.4$
$EOL(a_3) = 0(.65) + 210(.20) + 20(.15) = 45$

The expected opportunity loss criterion selects action $a_3$. Thus, $EVPI = EOL(a_3) = 45$.

20.65 a. First, we must find the opportunity loss table. To find the opportunity loss, subtract the payoff from the largest payoff for each state of nature.

| | | STATE OF NATURE $S_1$ (.15) | $s_2$ (.85) |
|---|---|---|---|
| ACTION | $a_1$ | 0 | 23,000 |
| | $a_2$ | 12,000 | 0 |

$EOL(a_1) = 0(.15) + 23,000(.85) = 19,550$
$EOL(a_2) = 12,000(.15) + 0(.85) = 1,800$

The $EVPI = EOL(a_2) = 1,800$.

b.

| (1) STATE | (2) PRIOR PROBABILITY | (3) CONDITIONAL PROBABILITY | (4) PROBABILITY OF INTERSECTION (2) × (3) | (5) POSTERIOR PROBABILITY (4) ÷ TOTAL OF (4) |
|---|---|---|---|---|
| $S_1$ | .15 | .7 | .105 | .382 |
| $S_2$ | .85 | .2 | .170 | .618 |
| | | | .275 | 1.000 |

$EOL(a_1) = 0(.382) + 23,000(.618) = 14,214$
$EOL(a_2) = 12,000(.382) + 0(.618) = 4,584$

The EVPI = $EOL(a_2)$ = 4,584. The EVPI has increased because the posterior probabilities for the two states of nature are closer to .5 than the prior probabilities. Thus, we need more information to be able to determine the correct state of nature.

c.

| STATE (1) | PRIOR PROBABILITY (2) | CONDITIONAL PROBABILITY (3) | PROBABILITY OF INTERSECTION (2) × (3) (4) | POSTERIOR PROBABILITY (4) ÷ TOTAL OF (4) (5) |
|---|---|---|---|---|
| $S_1$ | .15 | .3 | .045 | .062 |
| $S_2$ | .85 | .8 | .680 | .938 |
| | | | .725 | 1.000 |

$EOL(a_1)$ = 0(.062) + 23,000(.938) = 21,574
$EOL(a_2)$ = 12,000(.062) + 0(.938) = 744

The EVPI = $EOL(a_2)$ = 744. The EVPI has decreased because the posterior probabilities for the two states of nature are further from .5 than the prior probabilities. Thus, we need less information to be able to determine the correct state of nature.

d. The closer the state probabilities are to each other, the greater the expected value of perfect information. The further the state probabilities are from each other, the less the expected value of perfect information.

20.67 a.

| | | STATE OF NATURE Errors ($S_1$) | No Error($S_2$) |
|---|---|---|---|
| ACTION | $a_1$: Certify | -10 | 0 |
| | $a_2$: Do not certify | 0 | -2 |

(Amounts in millions of dollars)

b. One could sample previous audits to see what proportion contained errors and what proportion did not.

c. $P(S_1) = .1$ $P(S_2) = .9$
$EP(a_1)$ = -10(.1) + 0(.9) = -1 million
$EP(a_2)$ = 0(.1) + -2(.9) = -1.8 million

The expected payoff criterion would select action $a_1$, certify the account.

d. The opportunity loss table is:

| | | STATE OF NATURE Errors | No Error |
|---|---|---|---|
| ACTION | Certify | 0 | 2 |
| | Do not certify | 10 | 0 |

$EOL(a_1) = 0(.1) + 2(.9) = 1.8$ million
$EOL(a_2) = 10(.1) = 0(.9) = 1$ million

Thus, EVPI = $EOL(a_2)$ = \$1 million

20.69 First we must find the opportunity loss table. Refer to Exercise 19.17 for the payoff table. To find the opportunity loss, subtract the payoffs from the largest payoff in each state of nature.

| | | STATE OF NATURE Pass bill (.6) | Do not pass bill(.4) |
|---|---|---|---|
| ACTION | $a_1$: Stay in business | 0 | 2 |
| | $a_2$: Lease facility | 2 | 0 |

$EOL(a_1) = 0(.6) + 2(.4) = .8$
$EOL(a_2) = 2(.6) + 0(.4) = 1.2$

The expected opportunity loss criterion selects action $a_1$, stay in business.

The EVPI = $EOL(a_1)$ = \$.8 million.

20.71 a. First we construct the probability revision tables to derive posterior probabilities for each of the two sample outcomes:

| (1) STATE | (2) PRIOR PROBABILITY | (3) CONDITIONAL PROBABILITY | (4) PROBABILITY OF INTERSECTION (2) × (3) | (5) POSTERIOR PROBABILITY (4) ÷ TOTAL OF (4) |
|---|---|---|---|---|
| | | Sample Outcome: $S_1$ True | | |
| $S_1$ | .3 | .6 | .18 | .391 |
| $S_2$ | .7 | .4 | .28 | .609 |
| | | | .46 | 1.000 |
| | | Sample Outcome: $S_2$ True | | |
| $S_1$ | .3 | .4 | .12 | .222 |
| $S_2$ | .7 | .6 | .42 | .778 |
| | | | .54 | 1.000 |

From the upper portion of the previous table,

$$EP(a_1 | \text{Sample information indicates } S_1 \text{ True}) = 500(.391) + (-50)(.609) = 165.05$$
$$EP(a_2 | \text{Sample information indicates } S_1 \text{ True}) = -100(.391) + 250(.609) = 113.15$$

The expected payoff criterion selects action $a_1$, when the sample information indicates $S_1$ is the true state of nature.

From the lower portion of the table,

$$EP(a_1 | \text{Sample information indicates } S_2 \text{ True}) = 500(.222) + (-50)(.778) = 72.1$$
$$EP(a_2 | \text{Sample information indicates } S_2 \text{ True}) = -100(.222) + 250(.778) = 172.3$$

The expected payoff criterion selects action $a_2$ when the sample information indicates $S_2$ is the true state of nature.

The expected payoff of sampling (EPS) is computed as follows:

$$EPS = 165.05(.46) + 172.3(.54) = 168.965$$

$$EVSI = EPS - EPNS = 168.965 - 145 = 23.965$$
(EPNS = 145 is from Exercise 20.70)

$$ENGS = EVSI - CS = 23.965 - 10 = 13.965$$

b. Since the ENGS for the second source is smaller than for the first source, the decision maker should choose the first source.

20.73 a. To find EVPI, we first find the opportunity loss table:

| | | STATE OF NATURE | | |
|---|---|---|---|---|
| | | Failure(.6) | Successful(.3) | Very Successful(.1) |
| ACTION | $a_1$: Market | 200,000 | 0 | 0 |
| | $a_2$: Do not market | 0 | 300,000 | 600,000 |

$EOL(a_1) = .6(200,000) + .3(0) + .1(0) = 120,000$
$EOL(a_2) = .6(0) + .3(300,000) + .1(600,000) = 150,000$

The expected opportunity loss criterion selects action $a_1$.

The EVPI = $EOL(a_1)$ = \$120,000.

The most the company should pay for perfect information is \$120,000.

b. We now construct probability revision tables to derive posterior probabilities for each of the four possible sample outcomes.

| (1) STATE | (2) PRIOR PROBABILITY | (3) CONDITIONAL PROBABILITY | (4) PROBABILITY OF INTERSECTION (2) × (3) | (5) POSTERIOR PROBABILITY (4) ÷ TOTAL OF (4) |
|---|---|---|---|---|
| | Sample Outcome: Product is "Very Successful" | | | |
| Failure | .6 | .1 | .06 | .333 |
| Successful | .3 | .2 | .06 | .333 |
| Very Successful | .1 | .6 | .06 | .333 |
| | | | .18 | 0.999 |
| | Sample Outcome: Product is "Successful" | | | |
| Failure | .6 | .1 | .06 | .300 |
| Successful | .3 | .4 | .12 | .600 |
| Very Successful | .1 | .2 | .02 | .100 |
| | | | .20 | 1.000 |
| | Sample Outcome: Product is "Failure" | | | |
| Failure | .6 | .5 | .30 | .811 |
| Successful | .3 | .2 | .06 | .162 |
| Very Successful | .1 | .1 | .01 | .027 |
| | | | .37 | 1.000 |
| | Sample Outcome: Product is "Uncertain" | | | |
| Failure | .6 | .3 | .18 | .72 |
| Successful | .3 | .2 | .06 | .24 |
| Very Successful | .1 | .1 | .01 | .04 |
| | | | .25 | 1.00 |

From the first portion of the table, Product is "Very Successful,"

$$EP(a_1) = -200{,}000(.333) + 300{,}000(.333) + 600{,}000(.333) = 233{,}100$$

$$EP(a_2) = 0(.333) + 0(.333) + 0(.333) = 0$$

The expected payoff criterion selects action $a_1$.

From the second portion of the table, Product is " Successful,"

$$EP(a_1) = -200{,}000(.3) + 300{,}000(.6) + 600{,}000(.1) = 180{,}000$$

$$EP(a_2) = 0(.3) + 0(.6) + 0(.1) = 0$$

The expected payoff criterion selects action $a_1$.

From the third portion of the table, Product is "Failure,"

$$EP(a_1) = -200,000(.811) + 300,000(.162) + 600,000(.027) = -97,400$$
$$EP(a_2) = 0(.811) + 0(.162) + 0(.027) = 0$$

The expected payoff criterion selects action $a_2$.

From the fourth portion of the table, Product is "Uncertain,"

$$EP(a_1) = -200,000(.72) + 300,000(.24) + 600,000(.04) = -48,000$$
$$EP(a_2) = 0(.72) + 0(.24) + 0(.04) = 0$$

The expected payoff criterion selects action $a_2$.

The expected payoff of sampling is

$$EPS = 233,100(.18) + 180,000(.20) + 0(.37) + 0(.25) = 77,958$$

The expected payoff with no sampling is:

$$EP(a_1) = -200,000(.6) + 300,000(.3) + 600,000(.1) = 30,000$$
$$EP(a_2) = 0(.6) + 0(.3) + 0(.1) = 0$$

The EPNS = 30,000

Thus, EVSI = EPS - EPNS = 77,958 - 30,000 = 47,958

The most the company should pay for sampling information is $47,958.

c. ENGS = EVSI - CS(Cost of Sampling) = 47,958 - 30,000 = 17,958.

Since this is a positive, the company should undertake the proposed market survey.

20.75 We will calculate a payoff table for marketing the athletic shoes using the formula

$\pi = 100p - 2.5$, where p = market share.

| | STATE OF NATURE (Prior Probabilities in Parentheses) | | | | | |
|---|---|---|---|---|---|---|
| ACTION | 0 (.10) | .01 (.22) | .02 (.30) | .03 (.24) | .04 (.13) | .05 (.01) |
| Market Shoes | -2.5 | -1.5 | -.5 | .5 | 1.5 | 2.5 |
| Do not market shoes | 0 | 0 | 0 | 0 | 0 | 0 |

To find the amount the show company should spend for information, EVPI, we need to calculate the opportunity loss table.

| ACTION | STATE OF NATURE (Prior Probabilities in Parentheses) 0 (.10) | .01 (.22) | .02 (.30) | .03 (.24) | .04 (.13) | .05 (.01) |
|---|---|---|---|---|---|---|
| Market Shoes | 2.5 | 1.5 | .5 | 0 | 0 | 0 |
| Do not market shoes | 0 | 0 | 0 | .5 | 1.5 | 2.5 |

EOL(Market shoes) = (2.5)(.10) + (1.5)(.22) + (.5)(.30) = .73
EOL(Do not market shoes) = (.5)(.24) + (1.5)(.13) + (2.5)(.01) = .34
EVPI = EOL(Do not market shoes) = .34

20.77 a. OBJECTIVE VARIABLE

Profit next year (in millions of dollars)

ACTIONS

$a_1$: Stay in business (do not lease).
$a_2$: Lease the facility to Japanese firm.

STATES OF NATURE

$S_1$: Bill passes in Congress.
$S_2$: Bill does not pass in Congress.

b.

| | | STATE Bill Passes (.6) | Bill Does Not Pass (.4) |
|---|---|---|---|
| ACTION | $a_1$: Don't lease | 2.5 | -1.5 |
| | $a_2$: Lease | .5 | .5 |

c.

| | | STATE | |
|---|---|---|---|
| | | Bill Passes (.6) | Bill Does Not Pass (.4) |
| ACTION | $a_1$: Don't lease | 2.5 - 2.5 = 0 | .5 - (-1.5) = 2 |
| | $a_2$: Lease | 2.5 - .5 = 2 | .5 - .5 = 0 |

d. $EP(a_1) = 2.5(.6) - 1.5(.4) = .9$
$EP(a_2) = .5(.6) + .5(.4) = .5$

The expected payoff criterion selects action $a_1$: Stay in business (do not lease the plant).

$EOL(a_1) = 0(.6) + 2(.4) = .8$
$EOL(a_2) = 2(.6) + 0(.4) = 1.2$

The expected opportunity loss criterion also prescribes action $a_1$.

20.79 a. Action $a_2$ is inadmissible because it is dominated by action $a_4$.

b.

| | | STATE | | |
|---|---|---|---|---|
| | | $S_1$ (.5) | $S_2$ (.3) | $S_3$ (.2) |
| ACTION | $a_1$ | 28 | 0 | 107 |
| | $a_3$ | 60 | 36 | 0 |
| | $a_4$ | 15 | 72 | 10 |
| | $a_5$ | 0 | 27 | 70 |

c. $EP(a_1) = 12(.5) + 77(.3) - 27(.2) = 23.7$
$EP(a_3) = -20(.5) + 41(.3) + 80(.2) = 18.3$
$EP(a_4) = 25(.5) + 5(.3) + 70(.2) = 28$
$EP(a_5) = 40(.5) + 50(.3) + 10(.2) = 37$

The expected payoff criterion selects action $a_5$.

$EOL(a_1) = 28(.5) + 0(.3) + 107(.2) = 35.4$
$EOL(a_3) = 60(.5) + 36(.3) + 0(.2) = 40.8$
$EOL(a_4) = 15(.5) + 72(.3) + 10(.2) = 31.1$
$EOL(a_5) = 0(.5) + 27(.3) + 70(.2) = 22.1$

The expected opportunity loss criterion chooses the same action as that selected by the expected payoff criterion, namely action $a_5$.

d.

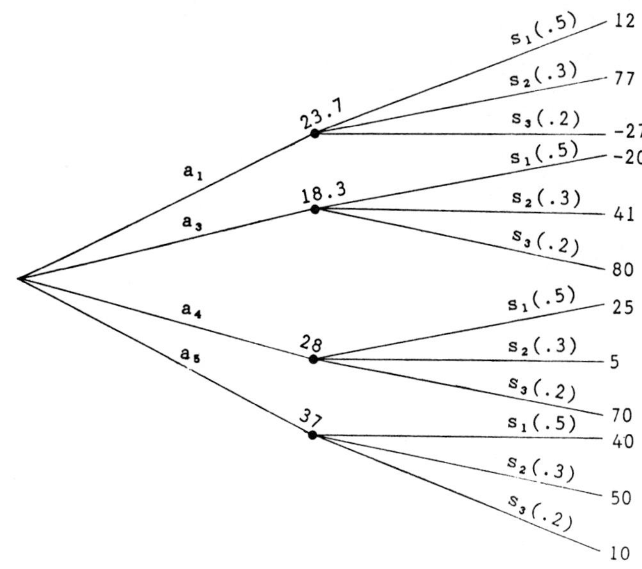


20.81 a.

| | | STATE | |
|---|---|---|---|
| | Outcome 1 | Outcome 2 | Outcome 3 |
| ACTION Make loan | 7,500 | 6,500 | -30,000 |
| ACTION Do not make loan | 6,000 | 6,000 | 6,000 |

b.

| | | STATE | |
|---|---|---|---|
| | Outcome 1 | Outcome 2 | Outcome 3 |
| ACTION Make loan | 0 | 0 | 36,000 |
| ACTION Do not make loan | 1,500 | 500 | 0 |

c.

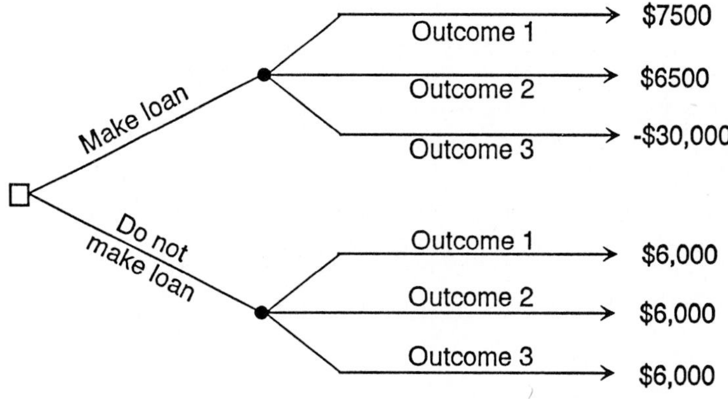

20.83 a.

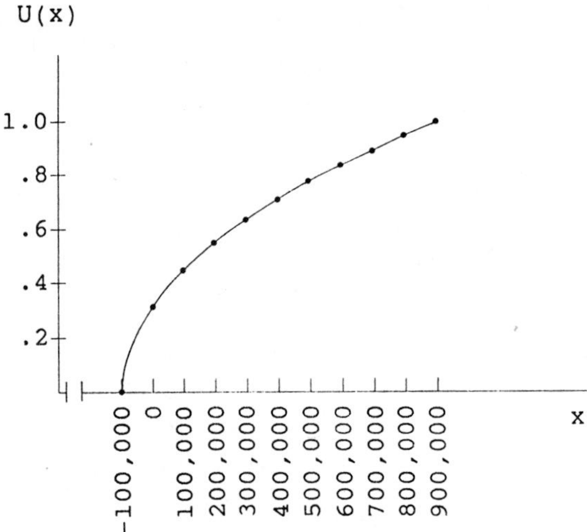


The utility function is concave implying the decision-maker is a risk-avoider.

b.

| | | STATE OF NATURE Repaid | Repaid with difficulty | Defaulted |
|---|---|---|---|---|
| ACTION | Make loan | .3279 | .3263 | .2646 |
| | Do not make loan | .3256 | .3256 | .3256 |

EU(Make loan) = .8625(.3279) + .09375(.3263) + .04375(.2646)
= .3250
EU(Do not make loan) = .8625(.3256) + .09375(.3256)
+ .04375(.3256) = .3256

The expected utility criterion selects action do not make loan.

20.85 a. The payoff table is (in thousands of dollars):

| | | STATE OF NATURE Loses (.8) | Wins (.2) |
|---|---|---|---|
| ACTION | $a_1$: Goes to court | -1,000 | 0 |
| | $a_2$: Out of court | -250 | -250 |

b.

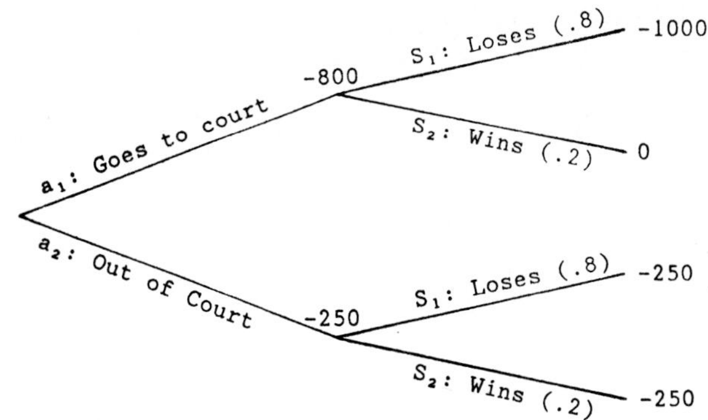


c. $EP(a_1) = .8(-1000) + .2(0) = -800$
$EP(a_2) = .8(-250) + .2(-250) = -250$

The expected payoff criterion selects action $a_2$, settle out of court.

20.87 a.

| | | STATE | |
|---|---|---|---|
| | | Use System (.05) | Do Not Use System (.95) |
| ACTION | $a_1$: Install system | 2.75 | -1 |
| | $a_2$: Do not install system | 0 | 0 |

The payoffs (in millions of dollars) are computed as illustrated by the following example: Suppose that the company installs and uses the system. Then over the next five-year period, the net savings to the company will be:

Savings over 5-year period - Cost to build and operate

$$= 5(.75) - 1$$
$$= 3.75 - 1$$
$$= 2.75 \text{ (million dollars)}$$

b.

| | | STATE | |
|---|---|---|---|
| | | Use System (.05) | Do Not Use System (.95) |
| ACTION | $a_1$: Install system | 0 | 1 |
| | $a_2$: Do not install system | 2.75 | 0 |

c. $EOL(a_1) = 0(.05) + 1(.95) = .95$
$EOL(a_2) = 2.75(.05) + 0(.95) = .1375$

The expected opportunity loss criterion prescribes action $a_2$: Do not install the MIS.

20.89 a. From the information given, we obtain the following values of the utility function:

$U(-20) = 0$, $U(0) = .15$, $U(20) = .3$, $U(40) = .55$, $U(60) = .8$, $U(80) = 1.0$

The utility function is plotted on the following graph:

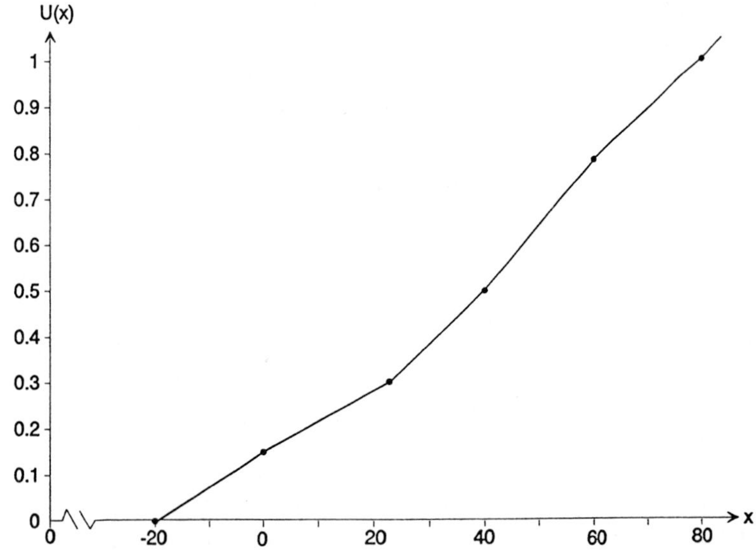


b. The utility function of part a is used to assign utility values to all payoffs in the table.

| | | STATE | | |
|---|---|---|---|---|
| | | $s_1$ (.4) | $s_2$ (.35) | $s_3$ (.25) |
| ACTION | $a_1$ | .24 | .95 | .09 |
| | $a_2$ | 0 | .55 | 1.00 |
| | $a_3$ | .35 | .19 | .90 |
| | $a_4$ | .55 | .66 | .22 |

c. The expected utilities and expected payoffs are computed for each action, as follows:

$EU(a_1) = .24(.4) + .95(.35) + .09(.25) = .451$
$EU(a_2) = 0(.4) + .55(.35) + 1.00(.25) + .4425$
$EU(a_3) = .35(.4) + .19(.35) + .90(.25) = .4315$
$EU(a_4) = .55(.4) + .66(.35) + .22(.25) = .506$
$EP(a_1) = 12(.4) + 77(.35) - 10(.25) = 29.25$
$EP(a_2) = -20(.4) + 41(.35) + 80(.25) = 26.35$
$EP(a_3) = 25(.4) + 5(.35) + 70(.25) = 29.25$
$EP(a_4) = 40(.4) + 50(.35) + 10(.25) + 36.00$

Thus, the expected utility criterion and the expected payoff criterion both prescribe the same optimal action, namely action $a_4$.

20.91 a. Expected profit = $25,000 × 5 years × E(x)
= 25,000(5)[0(.01) + 10(.04) + .. + 90(.05)]
= 125,000(47.9) = $5,987,500

b. The payoff table for this problem would be:

| | | STATE OF NATURE Use (.2) | Not use (.8) |
|---|---|---|---|
| ACTION | $a_1$: Purchase | 4,487,500 | -1,500,000 |
| | $a_2$: Do not purchase | 0 | 0 |

$EP(a_1) = .2(4,487,500) - .8(1,500,000) = -302,500$
$EP(a_2) = .2(0) + .8(0) = 0$

The expected payoff criterion selects action $a_2$, do not purchase.

c. We will construct probability tables to derive posterior probabilities for each of the 2 possible outcomes.

| (1)<br>STATE | (2)<br>PRIOR PROBABILITY | (3)<br>CONDITIONAL PROBABILITY | (4)<br>PROBABILITY OF INTERSECTION (2) x (3) | (5)<br>POSTERIOR PROBABILITY (4) ÷ TOTAL OF (4) |
|---|---|---|---|---|
| | | Sample Outcome: Will use system | | |
| Use | .2 | .7 | .14 | .636 |
| Do not use | .8 | .1 | .08 | .364 |
| | | | .22 | 1.000 |
| | | Sample Outcome: Will not use system | | |
| Use | .2 | .3 | .06 | .077 |
| Do not use | .8 | .9 | .72 | .923 |
| | | | .78 | 1.000 |

$EP(a_1|\text{will use system}) = 4{,}487{,}500(.636) - 1{,}500{,}000(.364)$
$= 2{,}308.050$
$EP(a_2|\text{will use system}) = 0(.636)$ to $(.364) = 0$

The expected payoff criterion selects action $a_1$, purchase.

$EP(a_1|\text{will not use system}) = 4{,}487{,}500(.077) - 1{,}500{,}000(.923)$
$= -1038962.5$
$EP(a_2|\text{will not use system}) = 0(.077) + 0(.923) = 0$

The expected payoff criterion selects action $a_2$, do not purchase system.

The expected payoff for sampling is

$$EPS = .22(2{,}308{,}050) + .78(0) = 507{,}771$$

The EVSI = EPS - EPNS
= 507,771 - 0 = 507,771

ENGS = EVSI - CS = 507,771 - 50,000 = 457,771.

Since this is a positive number, the bank should purchase the survey.

20.93 a. First we will construct probability tables to derive posterior probabilities for each of the 4 possible outcomes.

| (1) STATE | (2) PRIOR PROBABILITY | (3) CONDITIONAL PROBABILITY | (4) PROBABILITY OF INTERSECTION (2) × (3) | (5) POSTERIOR PROBABILITY (4) ÷ TOTAL OF (4) |
|---|---|---|---|---|
| | | Sample Outcome: x = 0 defectives | | |
| $S_1$ | .8 | .8574 | .6859 | .8247 |
| $S_2$ | .2 | .7290 | .1458 | .1753 |
| | | | .8317 | 1.0000 |
| | | Sample Outcome: x = 1 defective | | |
| $S_1$ | .8 | .1354 | .1083 | .6902 |
| $S_2$ | .2 | .2430 | .0486 | .3098 |
| | | | .1569 | 1.0000 |
| | | Sample Outcome: x = 2 defectives | | |
| $S_1$ | .8 | .0071 | .0057 | .5135 |
| $S_2$ | .2 | .0270 | .0054 | .4865 |
| | | | .0111 | 1.0000 |
| | | Sample Outcome: x = 3 defectives | | |
| $S_1$ | .8 | .0001 | .00008 | .2857 |
| $S_2$ | .2 | .0010 | .00020 | .7143 |
| | | | .00028 | 1.0000 |

$$P(x = 0|p = .05) = \binom{3}{0}.05^0.95^3 = .8574$$

$$P(x = 0|p = .10) = \binom{3}{0}.10^0.90^3 = .729$$

$$P(x = 1|p = .05) = \binom{3}{1}.05^1.95^2 = .1354$$

$$P(x = 1|p = .10) = \binom{3}{1}.10^1.90^2 = .243$$

$$P(x = 2|p = .05) = \binom{3}{2}.05^2.95 = .0071$$

$$P(x = 2|p = .10) = \binom{3}{2}.10^2.90 = .027$$

$$P(x = 3|p = .05) = \binom{3}{3}.05^3.95^0 = .0001$$

$$P(x = 3|p = .10) = \binom{3}{3}.10^3.90^0 = .001$$

$EP(a_1|x = 0) = .8247(-1000) + .1753(0) = -824.7$
$EP(a_2|x = 0) = .8247(0) + .1753(-4100) = -718.73$

The expected payoff criterion selects action $a_2$.

$EP(a_1|x = 1) = .6902(-1000) + .3098(0) = -690.2$
$EP(a_2|x = 1) = .6902(0) + .3098(-4100) = -1270.18$

The expected payoff criterion selects action $a_1$.

$EP(a_1|x = 2) = .5135(-1000) + .4865(0) = -513.5$
$EP(a_2|x = 2) = .5135(0) + .4865(-4100) = -1994.65$

The expected payoff criterion selects action $a_1$.

$EP(a_1|x = 3) = .2857(-1000) + .7143(0) = -285.7$
$EP(a_2|x = 3) = .2857(0) + .7143(-4100) = -2928.63$

The expected payoff criterion selects action $a_1$.

$$\begin{aligned} EPS &= .8317(-718.73) + .1569(-690.2) + .0111(-513.5) \\ &\quad + .00028(-285.7) \\ &= -711.84 \end{aligned}$$

$EVSI = EPS - EPNS = -711.84 - (-800) = 88.16$

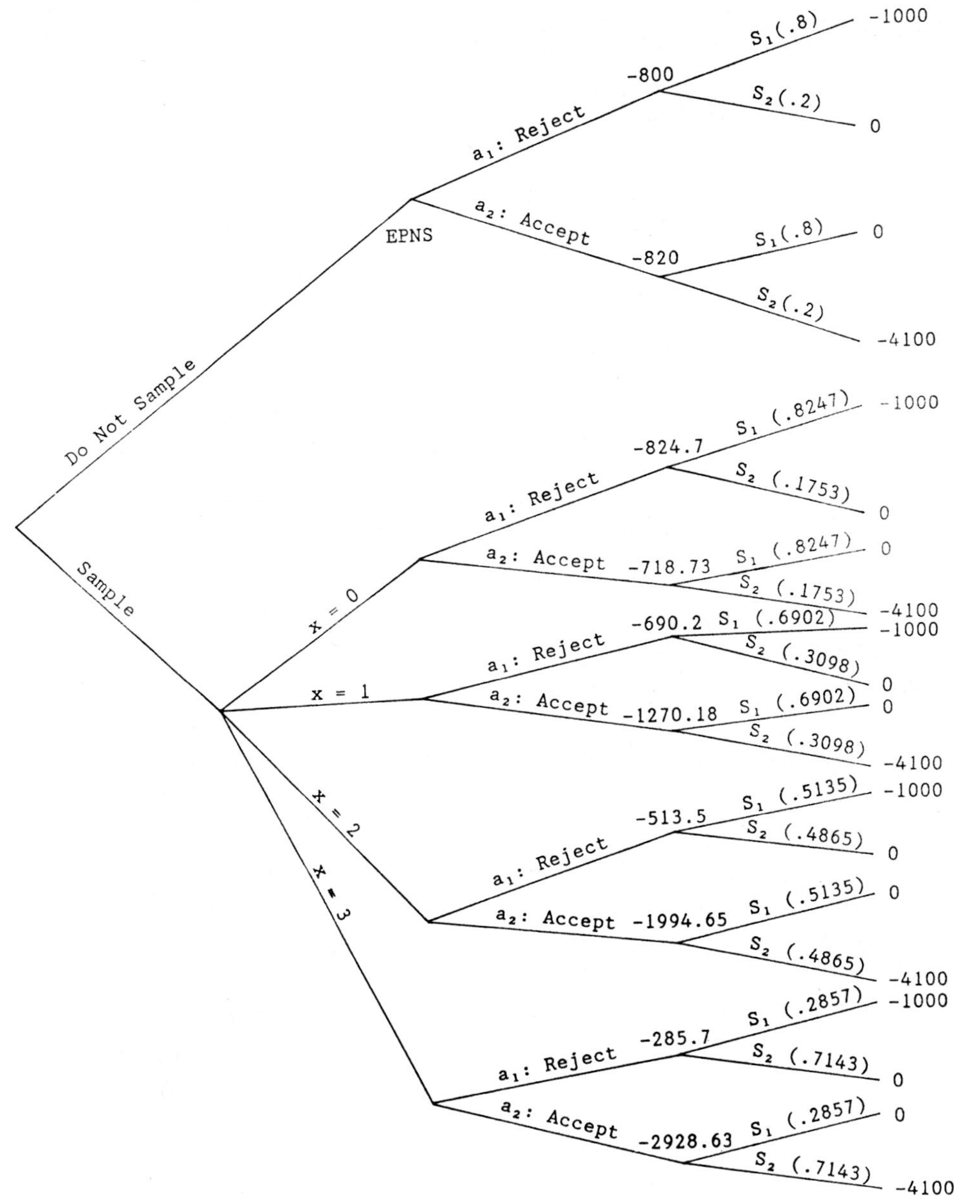


b. Efficiency $= \frac{\text{EVSI}}{\text{EVPI}} \times 100\% = \frac{88.16}{800} \times 100\% = 11.02\%$

c. ENGS = EVSI - CS = 88.16 - (10 + 3(10)) = \$48.16

20.95 To find EVPI, we need to calculate the opportunity loss table as shown below.

| | | STATE OF NATURE | | |
|---|---|---|---|---|
| | | $S_1$ (.3) | $S_2$ (.5) | $S_3$ (.2) |
| ACTION | $a_1$ | 7000 - 5000 = 2000 | 0 | 8000 - 6000 = 2000 |
| | $a_2$ | 0 | 2000 - 0 = 2000 | 0 |

$EOL(a_1) = (2000)(.3) + (0)(.5) + (2000(.2) = 1000$
$EOL(a_2) = (0)(.3) + (2000)(.5) + (0)(.2) = 1000$

The expected opportunity loss criterion would select either action $a_1$ or $a_2$. Thus, $EVPI = EOL(a_1) = EOL(a_2) = 1000$.

20.97 a. Using the midpoints as states of nature, 55,000 trees might need to be cut. Since the forester's staff can cut 15,000 trees, 40,000 might need to be cut down by private contractors. Since each contractor can cut 6,000 trees, between one and seven contractors might be needed. Thus, there are eight actions possible—$a_0$-$a_7$—corresponding to the number of contractors to hire, that is, between 0 and seven. If no contractors are hired, there is no loss for the first three states of nature: $2500, $7500, or $15,000. After that, the loss is $300 per tree. If contractors are hired, the loss for the first three states of nature is $2000 per contractor. If one contractor is hired, then $2000 is the loss for the first three states of nature, since the foresters can handle these. The next state of nature is 25,000 trees. This leaves 10,000 trees that the forester's staff cannot cut. One contractor can cut 6,000 of these ($2,000 for the contract and $250 per tree). This leaves 4,000 trees for which the city will be fined $300 each. Thus, for $S_4a_2$, the payoff is:

$$-2000 + (-250)(6000) + (-300)(4000) = -2,702,000.$$

The other payoffs are calculated similarly. The payoff table then is (in thousands of dollars):

| | | STATE OF NATURE | | | | | |
|---|---|---|---|---|---|---|---|
| | (.05) | (.20) | (.30) | (.20) | (.10) | (.08) | (.07) |
| | $S_1$ | $S_2$ | $S_3$ | $S_4$ | $S_5$ | $S_6$ | $S_7$ |
| | (2500) | (7500) | (15,000) | (25,000) | (35,000) | (45,000) | (55,000) |
| ACTION 0 = $a_1$ | 0 | 0 | 0 | -3000 | -6000 | -9000 | -12,000 |
| 1 - $a_2$ | -2 | -2 | -2 | -2702 | -5702 | -8702 | -11,702 |
| 2 = $a_3$ | -4 | -4 | -4 | -2504 | -5404 | -8404 | -11,404 |
| 3 = $a_4$ | -6 | -6 | -6 | -2506 | -5106 | -8106 | -11,106 |
| 4 = $a_5$ | -8 | -8 | -8 | -2508 | -5008 | -7808 | -10,808 |
| 5 = $a_6$ | -10 | -10 | -10 | -2510 | -5010 | -7510 | -10,510 |
| 6 = $a_7$ | -12 | -12 | -12 | -2512 | -5012 | -7512 | -10,212 |
| 7 = $a_8$ | -14 | -14 | -14 | -2514 | -5014 | -7514 | -10,014 |

c. $EP(a_0) = (0)(.05) + (0)(.20) + (0)(.30) + (-3000)(.20) + (-6000)(.10) + (-9000)(.08) + (-12,000)(.07) = -2760$

$EP(a_1) = (-2)(.05) + (-2)(.20) + (-2)(.30) + (-2702)(.20) + (-5702)(.10) + (-8702)(.08) + (11,702)(.07) = -2627$

Similarly,

$EP(a_2) = -2514$ $\quad$ $EP(a_5) = -2345$
$EP(a_3) = -2441$ $\quad$ $EP(a_6) = -2326$
$EP(a_4) = -2388$ $\quad$ $EP(a_7) = -2314$

The expected payoff criterion selects $a_7$, that is, seven contractors.

d. To find EVPI, we need to construct the opportunity loss table as shown below:

| ACTION | STATE OF NATURE (.05) $S_1$ | (.20) $S_2$ | (.30) $S_3$ | (.20) $S_4$ | (.10) $S_5$ | (.08) $S_6$ | (.07) $S_7$ |
|---|---|---|---|---|---|---|---|
| $a_0$ | 0 | 0 | 0 | 496 | 992 | 1496 | 1986 |
| $a_1$ | 2 | 2 | 2 | 198 | 694 | 1192 | 1688 |
| $a_2$ | 4 | 4 | 4 | 0 | 396 | 894 | 1390 |
| $a_3$ | 6 | 6 | 6 | 2 | 98 | 596 | 1092 |
| $a_4$ | 8 | 8 | 8 | 4 | 0 | 298 | 794 |
| $a_5$ | 10 | 10 | 10 | 6 | 2 | 0 | 496 |
| $a_6$ | 12 | 12 | 12 | 8 | 4 | 2 | 198 |
| $a_7$ | 14 | 14 | 14 | 10 | 6 | 4 | 0 |

e. $EOL(a_0) = 0(.05) + 0(.20) + 0(.30) + 496(.20) + 992(.10) + 1490(.08) + 1986(.07) = 456.62$

Similarly,

$EOL(a_1) = 323.62$ $EOL(a_5) = 41.62$
$EOL(a_2) = 210.62$ $EOL(a_6) = 22.62$
$EOL(a_3) = 137.62$ $EOL(a_7) = 10.62$
$EOL(a_4) = 84.62$

Thus, EVPI = $EOL(a_7)$ = \$10,620.

20.99 To find EVPI, calculate the opportunity loss table.

| ACTION | STATE OF NATURE $S_1$ (.5) | $S_2$ (.3) | $S_3$ (.2) |
|---|---|---|---|
| $a_1$ | 20 - 12 = 8 | 50 - 40 = 10 | 20 - (-5) = 25 |
| $a_2$ | 20 - 5 = 15 | 0 | 20 - (-10) = 30 |
| $a_3$ | 0 | 50 - 20 = 30 | 0 |

$EOL(a_1) = (8)(.5) + (10)(.3) + (25)(.2) = 12$
$EOL(a_2) = (15)(.5) + (0)(.3) + (30)(.2) = 13.5$
$EOL(a_3) = (0)(.5) + (30)(.3) + (0)(.2) = 9$

EVPI = $EOL(a_3) = 9$

# CHAPTER 21

## SURVEY SAMPLING

21.1 An object upon which a measurement is made is called an element; a sampling unit is a collection of elements; and a sample is a collection of sampling units selected from a list of sampling units.

21.3 The frame was constructed from sources such as telephone directories, club membership lists, magazine subscriber lists, and lists of car owners. The sample was probably not representative of the whole population of voters in 1936; it was biased in favor of Republican voters. Also, it seemed to be affected by nonresponse bias. Only the proportion of the population with intense interest answered the questionnaire.

21.5 a. Percentage sampled $= \frac{n}{N}(100\%) = \frac{1000}{2500}(100\%) = 40\%$

Finite population correction factor:

$$\sqrt{\frac{N - n}{N}} = \sqrt{\frac{2500 - 1000}{2500}} = \sqrt{.6} = .7746$$

b. Percentage sampled $= \frac{n}{N}(100\%) = \frac{1000}{5000}(100\%) = 20\%$

Finite population correction factor:

$$\sqrt{\frac{N - n}{N}} = \sqrt{\frac{5000 - 1000}{5000}} = \sqrt{.8} = .8944$$

c. Percentage sampled $= \frac{n}{N}(100\%) = \frac{1000}{10,000}(100\%) = 10\%$

Finite population correction factor:

$$\sqrt{\frac{N - n}{N}} = \sqrt{\frac{10,000 - 1000}{10,000}} = \sqrt{.9} = .9487$$

d. Percentage sampled $= \frac{n}{N}(100\%) = \frac{1000}{100,000}(100\%) = 1\%$

Finite population correction factor:

$$\sqrt{\frac{N - n}{N}} = \sqrt{\frac{100,000 - 1000}{100,000}} = \sqrt{.99} = .995$$

21.7 a. For n = 36,

with the finite population correction factor:

$$\hat{\sigma}_{\bar{x}} = s/\sqrt{n}\left(\sqrt{\frac{N - n}{N}}\right) = \frac{12}{\sqrt{36}}\left(\sqrt{\frac{5000 - 36}{5000}}\right)$$

$$= 2\sqrt{.9928} = 1.9928$$

without the finite population correction factor:

$$\hat{\sigma}_{\bar{x}} = s/\sqrt{n} = \frac{12}{\sqrt{36}} = 2$$

$\hat{\sigma}_{\bar{x}}$ without the finite population correction factor is slightly larger.

b. For n = 500,

with the finite population correction factor:

$$\hat{\sigma}_{\bar{x}} = s/\sqrt{n}\left(\sqrt{\frac{N - n}{N}}\right) = \frac{12}{\sqrt{500}}\left(\sqrt{\frac{5000 - 500}{5000}}\right)$$

$$= .5367\sqrt{.9} = .5091$$

without the finite population correction factor:

$$\hat{\sigma}_{\bar{x}} = s/\sqrt{n} = 12/\sqrt{500} = .5367$$

c. In part (a), n is smaller relative to N than in part (b). Therefore, the finite population correction factor did not make as much difference in the answer in part (a) as in part (b).

21.9 An approximate 95% confidence interval for $\mu$ is:

$$\bar{x} \pm 2\hat{\sigma}_{\bar{x}}$$

$$\Rightarrow \bar{x} \pm 2\frac{s}{\sqrt{n}}\sqrt{\frac{N - n}{N}}$$

$$\Rightarrow 375 \pm 2\frac{11}{\sqrt{30}}\sqrt{\frac{305 - 30}{305}}$$

$$\Rightarrow 375 \pm 3.814$$

21.11 An approximate 95% confidence interval for $\tau$ is:

$$\hat{\tau} \pm 2\hat{\sigma}_{\hat{\tau}}$$

$$\Rightarrow N\bar{x} \pm 2\sqrt{N^2 \frac{s^2}{n}\left(\frac{N - n}{N}\right)}$$

$$\Rightarrow 3500(39.4) \pm 2\sqrt{3500^2 \frac{4^2}{100}\left(\frac{3500 - 100}{3500}\right)}$$

$$\Rightarrow 137,900 \pm 2759.7101$$

21.13 a. An approximate 95% confidence interval for $\mu$ is:

$$\bar{x} \pm 2\hat{\sigma}_{\bar{x}}$$

$$\Rightarrow \bar{x} \pm 2 \frac{s}{\sqrt{n}} \sqrt{\frac{N - n}{N}}$$

$$\Rightarrow 779,030 \pm 2 \frac{1,083,162}{\sqrt{32}} \sqrt{\frac{1500 - 32}{1500}}$$

$$\Rightarrow 779,030 \pm 378,848.7165$$

b. An approximate 95% confidence interval for $\tau$ is:

$$\hat{\tau} \pm 2\hat{\sigma}_{\hat{\tau}}$$

$$\Rightarrow N\bar{x} \pm 2\sqrt{N^2 \frac{s^2}{n}\left(\frac{N - n}{N}\right)}$$

$$\Rightarrow 1500(779,030) \pm 2\sqrt{1500^2 \frac{1,083,162^2}{32}\left(\frac{1500 - 32}{1500}\right)}$$

$$\Rightarrow 1,168,545,000 \pm 568,273,074.8$$

c. Approximately 95% confident the total amount spent by all firms in the population on external audits in 1981 is between \$600,271,925 and \$1,736,818,075.

d. The necessary assumption is:

1. Sample size is sufficiently large.

21.15 a. p is the proportion of corn-related products having EDB residues above the safe level in a particular state.

b. The estimated bound on the error of estimation:

$$2\hat{\sigma}_{\hat{p}} = 2\sqrt{\frac{\hat{p}(1 - \hat{p})}{n}\left(\frac{N - n}{N}\right)}$$

$$= 2\sqrt{\frac{.086(1 - .086)}{175}\left(\frac{3000 - 175}{3000}\right)}$$

$$= .041$$

c. An approximate 95% confidence interval for p is:

$\hat{p} \pm 2\hat{\sigma}_{\hat{p}}$

$\Rightarrow .086 \pm .041$

d. $H_0$: $p = .07$
$H_a$: $p > .07$

The test statistic is $z = \dfrac{\hat{p} - p_0}{\sigma_{\hat{p}}}$

$$= \frac{\hat{p} - p_0}{\sqrt{\dfrac{p_0(1 - p_0)}{n}\left(\dfrac{N - n}{N}\right)}} = \frac{.080 - .07}{\sqrt{\dfrac{.07(.93)}{175}\left(\dfrac{3000 - 175}{3000}\right)}} = .85$$

The rejection region requires $\alpha = .05$ in the upper tail of the z distribution. From Table IV, Appendix B, $z_{.05} = 1.645$. The rejection region is $z > 1.645$.

Since the observed value of the test statistic does not fall in the rejection region ($z = .85 \not> 1.645$), $H_0$ is not rejected. There is insufficient evidence to indicate that more than 7% of the corn-related products in this state would have to be removed from shelves and warehouses at $\alpha = .05$.

21.17 a. An approximate 95% confidence interval for $\mu$ is:

$\bar{x} \pm 2\hat{\sigma}_{\bar{x}}$

$$\Rightarrow \bar{x} \pm 2 \frac{s}{\sqrt{n}} \sqrt{\frac{N - n}{N}}$$

$$\Rightarrow 330 \pm 2 \frac{546}{\sqrt{60}} \sqrt{\frac{410 - 60}{410}}$$

$\Rightarrow 330 \pm 130.25$

b. An approximate 95% confidence interval for $\tau$ is:

$\hat{\tau} \pm 2\hat{\sigma}_{\hat{\tau}}$

$$\Rightarrow N\bar{x} \pm 2 \sqrt{N^2 \frac{s^2}{n}\left(\frac{N - n}{N}\right)}$$

$$\Rightarrow 410(330) \pm 2\sqrt{410^2 \frac{546^2}{60}\left(\frac{410 - 60}{410}\right)}$$

$\Rightarrow 135{,}300 \pm 53{,}403.8987$

21.19 $\hat{p} = \frac{x}{n} = \frac{572}{6150} = .093$

The estimated bound on the error of estimation:

$$2\hat{\sigma}_{\hat{p}} = 2\sqrt{\frac{\hat{p}(1 - \hat{p})}{n}\left(\frac{N - n}{N}\right)}$$

$$= 2\sqrt{\frac{.093(1 - .093)}{6150}\left(\frac{70,500 - 6150}{70,500}\right)}$$

$$= .0071$$

21.21 First summarize the data for each stratum:

$\underline{N_1 = 4000}$

$$\bar{x}_1 = \frac{\sum x_i}{n_i} = \frac{10 + 15 + \ldots + 28}{10} = \frac{237}{10} = 23.7$$

$$s^2 = \frac{\sum x_i^2 - \frac{(\sum x_1)^2}{n_1}}{n_1 - 1} = \frac{7379 - \frac{(237)^2}{10}}{9} = 195.79$$

$\underline{N_2 = 6000}$

$$\bar{x}_2 = \frac{5 + 33 + \ldots + 45 + 68}{15} = \frac{530}{15} = 35.33$$

$$s_2^2 = \frac{22,710 - \frac{(530)^2}{15}}{14} = 284.52$$

$\underline{N_3 = 10,000}$

$$\bar{x}_3 = \frac{28 + 75 + \ldots + 62 + 40}{20} = \frac{840}{20} = 42$$

$$s_3^2 = \frac{42,576 - \frac{(840)^2}{20}}{19} = 384$$

$\underline{N_4 = 15,000}$

$$\bar{x}_4 = \frac{45 + 43 + \ldots + 41 + 50}{25} = \frac{1246}{25} = 49.84$$

$$s_4^2 = \frac{76,498 - \frac{(1246)^2}{25}}{24} = 599.89$$

a. Estimator of $\mu$: $\bar{x}_{st} = \frac{1}{N}(N_1\bar{x}_1 + N_2\bar{x}_2 + N_3\bar{x}_3 + N_4\bar{x}_4)$

$$= \frac{1}{35,000}(4000(23.7) + 6000(35.33) + 10,000(42) + 15,000(49.84))$$

$$= 42.13$$

Estimated bound on the error of estimation:

$$2\hat{\sigma}_{\bar{x}_{st}} = 2\sqrt{\frac{1}{N^2}\sum N_i^2\left(\frac{N_i - n_i}{N_i}\frac{s_i^2}{n_i}\right)}$$

$$= 2\sqrt{\frac{1}{35{,}000^2}\left[4000^2\left(\frac{4000 - 10}{4000}\right)\left(\frac{195.79}{10}\right) + 6000^2\left(\frac{6000 - 15}{6000}\right)\left(\frac{284.52}{15}\right) + 10{,}000^2\left(\frac{10{,}000 - 20}{10{,}000}\right)\left(\frac{384}{20}\right) + 15{,}000^2\left(\frac{15{,}000 - 25}{15{,}000}\right)\left(\frac{599.89}{25}\right)\right]}$$

$$= 2\sqrt{\frac{1}{3500^2}(8{,}299{,}793{,}372)}$$

$$= 5.206$$

b. $\hat{\tau} = N\bar{x}_{st} = (35{,}000)(42.13) = 1{,}474{,}550$

Estimated bound on the error of estimation:

$$2\hat{\sigma}_{\hat{\tau}} = 2\sqrt{\sum N_i^2\left(\frac{N_i - n_i}{N_i}\right)\frac{s_i^2}{n_i}} = 2\sqrt{8{,}299{,}793{,}372} = 182{,}206.4$$

c. $\hat{p}_i$ = the proportion of measurements between 35 and 55, inclusive, in stratum i

Estimator of p: $\hat{p}_{st} = \frac{1}{N}(N_1\hat{p}_1 + N_2\hat{p}_2 + N_3\hat{p}_3 + N_4\hat{p}_4)$

$$= \frac{1}{35{,}000}\left[4000\left(\frac{2}{10}\right) + 6000\left(\frac{5}{15}\right) + 10{,}000\left(\frac{8}{20}\right) + 15{,}000\left(\frac{15}{25}\right)\right]$$

$$= .45$$

Estimated bound on the error of estimation:

$$2\hat{\sigma}_{\hat{p}_{st}} = 2\sqrt{\frac{1}{N^2}\sum_{i=1}^{k} N_i^2\left(\frac{N_i - n_i}{N_i}\right)\frac{\hat{p}_i(1 - \hat{p}_i)}{n_i - 1}}$$

$$= 2\sqrt{\frac{1}{35000^2}\left[4000^2\left(\frac{4000 - 10}{4000}\right)\left(\frac{\frac{2}{10}\left(1 - \frac{2}{10}\right)}{10 - 1}\right) + 6000^2\left(\frac{6000 - 15}{6000}\right)\left(\frac{\frac{5}{15}\left(1 - \frac{5}{15}\right)}{15 - 1}\right) + 10{,}000^2\left(\frac{10{,}000 - 20}{10{,}000}\right)\left(\frac{\frac{8}{20}\left(1 - \frac{8}{20}\right)}{20 - 1}\right) + 15{,}000^2\left(\frac{15{,}000 - 25}{15{,}000}\right)\left(\frac{\frac{15}{25}\left(1 - \frac{15}{25}\right)}{25 - 1}\right)\right]}$$

$$= 2\sqrt{\frac{1}{35{,}000^2}(4{,}360{,}614.912)}$$

$$= .119$$

21.23 a. The data represent the usable responses that were received by Training Magazine. There may be a nonresponse bias in the results. Also, the proportion of usable responses in the largest stratum is quite small and may not be representative.

b. An approximate 95% confidence interval for $\mu$ is:

$$\bar{x}_{st} \pm 2\hat{\sigma}_{\bar{x}_{st}}$$

where

$$\bar{x}_{st} = \frac{1}{N}(N_1\bar{x}_1 + N_2\bar{x}_2 + N_3\bar{x}_3 + N_4\bar{x}_4 + N_5\bar{x}_5 + N_6\bar{x}_6)$$

$$= \frac{1}{229,386}(114,464(11.7) + 91,754(26.6) + 11,011(42.3) + 7340(89.6) + 3670(142.5) + 1147(604.5))$$

$$= \frac{1}{229,386}(1,339,228.8 + 2,440,656.4 + 465,765.3 + 657,664 + 522,975 + 693,361.5)$$

$$= 26.6784$$

$$2\hat{\sigma}_{\bar{x}_{st}} = 2\sqrt{\frac{1}{N^2}\sum_{i=1}^{6} N_i^2\left(\frac{N_i - n_i}{N_i}\right)\frac{s_i^2}{n_i}}$$

$$= 2\sqrt{\frac{1}{229,386^2}\left[114,464^2\left(\frac{114,464 - 87}{114,464}\right)\frac{2^2}{87} + 91,754^2\left(\frac{91,754 - 444}{91,754}\right)\frac{4.3^2}{444} + 11,011^2\left(\frac{11,011 - 357}{11,011}\right)\frac{7.1^2}{357} + 7,340^2\left(\frac{7340 - 533}{7340}\right)\frac{10.8^2}{533} + 3670^2\left(\frac{3670 - 575}{3670}\right)\frac{15.3^2}{575} + 1147^2\left(\frac{1147 - 534}{1147}\right)\frac{100.5^2}{534}\right]}$$

$$= 2\sqrt{\frac{1}{229,386^2}(601,933,284 + 348,897,044.2 + 16.564,866.36 + 10,933,824.85 + 4,624,254.571 + 13,298,870.56)}$$

$$= 2\sqrt{\frac{1}{229,386^2}(996,252,144.5)}$$

$$= .2752$$

Therefore, the approximate 95% confidence interval for $\mu$ is:

$$\bar{x}_{st} \pm 2\hat{\sigma}_{\bar{x}_{st}}$$

$$\Rightarrow 26.6784 \pm .2752$$

c. An approximate 95% confidence interval for $\tau$ is:

$$\hat{\tau}_{st} \pm 2\hat{\sigma}_{\hat{\tau}_{st}}$$

where

$$\hat{\tau}_{st} = N\bar{x}_{st} = 229,386(26.6784) = 6,119,651.462$$

$$2\hat{\sigma}_{\hat{\tau}_{st}} = 2\sqrt{\sum_{i=1}^{6} N_i^2\left(\frac{N_i - n_i}{N_i}\right)\frac{s_i^2}{n_i}}$$

$$= 2\sqrt{996,456,978.1}$$

$$= 63,133.414$$

Therefore, the approximate 95% confidence interval for $\tau$ is:

$$\hat{\tau} \pm 2\hat{\sigma}_{\hat{\tau}_{st}}$$

$$\Rightarrow 6,119,651.462 \pm 63,133.414$$

e. Yes, it would change since the last 3 strata do have a large sample size in proportion to the total size of the population. It would not make much difference for the first 3 strata, however, since n is small relative to N.

21.25 a. Estimator of $\tau$:

$$\hat{\tau}_{st} = N_1\bar{x}_1 + N_2\bar{x}_2 + N_3\bar{x}_3 + N_4\bar{x}_4$$

$$\bar{x}_1 = \frac{\sum x_1}{n_1} = \frac{10 + 0 + 0 - 15 + 25 + 20}{6} = 6.6667$$

$$\bar{x}_2 = \frac{\sum x_2}{n_2} = \frac{0 + 0 + 100 + 0 - 50 + 0 + 550 + 0}{8} = 75$$

$$\bar{x}_3 = \frac{\sum x_3}{n_3} = \frac{750 + 0 + 0 + 1000 + 0 + 0 + 0 + 1500 + 0 + 2000}{10} = 525$$

$$\bar{x}_4 = \frac{\sum x_4}{n_4} = \frac{0 + 0 + 5000 + 0 + 0 + 0 + 1800 + 0 + 0 + 0 + 0 + 0 + 0 + 0 + 500}{15}$$

$$= 486.6667$$

Therefore,

$$\hat{\tau}_{st} = 100(6.6667) + 400(75) + 300(525) + 200(48.6667)$$

$$= \$285,500$$

b. Estimated bound on the error of estimation:

$$2\hat{\sigma}_{\hat{\tau}_{st}} = 2\sqrt{\sum N_i^2\left(\frac{N_i - n_i}{N_i}\right)\frac{s_i^2}{n_i}} \qquad s_i^2 = \frac{\sum x_i^2 - \frac{(\sum x_i)^2}{n_i}}{n_i - 1}$$

$$s_1^2 = \frac{1350 - \frac{(40)^2}{6}}{5} = 216.67 \qquad s_2^2 = \frac{315{,}000 - \frac{(600)^2}{8}}{7} = 38{,}571.43$$

$$s_3^2 = \frac{7{,}812{,}500 - \frac{(5250)^2}{10}}{9} = 561{,}805.56$$

$$s_4^2 = \frac{28{,}490{,}000 - \frac{(7300)^2}{15}}{14} = 1{,}781{,}238.10$$

$$2\hat{\sigma}_{\hat{\tau}_{st}} = 2\sqrt{100^2\left(\frac{100 - 6}{100}\right)\frac{216.67}{6} + 400^2\left(\frac{400 - 8}{400}\right)\frac{38{,}571.43}{8} + 300^2\left(\frac{300 - 10}{300}\right)\frac{561{,}805.56}{10} + 200^2\left(\frac{200 - 15}{200}\right)\frac{1{,}781{,}238.10}{15}}$$

$$= \$200{,}377.33$$

c. Approximate 95% confidence interval for $\tau$ is:

$$\hat{\tau}_{st} \pm 2\hat{\sigma}_{\hat{\tau}_{st}}$$

$$\Rightarrow 285{,}500 \pm 200{,}377.33$$

21.27 Estimator of p:

$$\hat{p}_{st} = \frac{1}{N}(N_1\hat{p}_1 + N_2\hat{p}_2 + N_3\hat{p}_3 + N_4\hat{p}_4)$$

$$= \frac{1}{9929}(1572(.28) + 2369(.31) + 3007(.35) + 2981(.10)) = .2543$$

Estimated bound on the error of estimation:

$$2\hat{\sigma}_{\hat{\tau}_{st}} = 2\sqrt{\frac{1}{N^2}\sum N_i^2\left(\frac{N_i - n_i}{N_i}\right)\frac{\hat{p}_i(1 - \hat{p}_i)}{n_i - 1}}$$

$$= 2\sqrt{\frac{1}{9929^2}\left[1572^2\left(\frac{1572 - 100}{1572}\right)\frac{.28(.72)}{99} + 2369^2\left(\frac{2369 - 100}{2369}\right)\frac{.31(.69)}{99} + 3007^2\left(\frac{3007 - 120}{3007}\right)\frac{.35(.65)}{119} + 2981^2\left(\frac{2981 - 120}{2981}\right)\frac{.10(.90)}{119}\right]}$$

$$= 2\sqrt{\frac{1}{9929^2}(39{,}372.59602)}$$

$$= .03997$$

21.29 a. $M = 5000,\ N = 300,\ n = 4$

$m_1 = 8,\ m_2 = 9,\ m_3 = 12,\ m_4 = 6$

b. $\bar{m} = \dfrac{\sum m_i}{n} = \dfrac{8 + 9 + 12 + 6}{4} = 8.75$

$\bar{M} = \dfrac{M}{N} = \dfrac{5000}{300} = 16.6667$

c. $x_1 = 6 + 10 + 5 + 4 + 11 + 9 + 6 + 11 = 62$

$x_2 = 21 + 15 + 9 + 12 + 18 + 17 + 17 + 23 + 29 = 161$

$x_3 = 30 + 28 + 36 + 20 + 31 + 29 + 30 + 16 + 20 + 40 + 31 + 10 = 321$

$x_4 = 2 + 40 + 29 + 18 + 15 + 11 = 115$

d. Some preliminary calculations:

$\sum x_i = 62 + 161 + 321 + 115 = 659$

$\sum m_i = 8 + 9 + 12 + 6 = 35$

$\sum x_i^2 = 62^2 + 161^2 + 321^2 + 115^2 = 146{,}031$

$\sum m_i^2 = 8^2 + 9^2 + 12^2 + 6^2 = 325$

$\sum x_i m_i = 62(8) + 161(9) + 321(12) + 115(6) = 6487$

$\bar{x} = \dfrac{\sum x_i}{\sum m_i} = \dfrac{659}{35} = 18.8286$

$$\begin{aligned}\sum(x_i - \bar{x}m_i)^2 &= \sum x_i^2 - 2\bar{x}\sum x_i m_i + \bar{x}^2\sum m_i^2 \\ &= 146{,}031 - 2(18.8286)(6487) + 18.8286^2(325) \\ &= 16{,}966.50143\end{aligned}$$

$$\hat{\sigma}_{\bar{x}} = \sqrt{\left(\frac{N - n}{Nn\bar{M}^2}\right)\frac{\sum(x_i - \bar{x}m_i)^2}{n - 1}}$$

$$= \sqrt{\left(\frac{300 - 4}{300(4)(16.6667)^2}\right)\frac{16966.50143}{4 - 1}}$$

$= 2.241$

e. Estimator of $\mu$: $\bar{x} = \dfrac{\sum x_i}{\sum m_i} = 18.8286$

Estimated bound on the error of estimation:

$\bar{x} \pm 2\hat{\sigma}_{\bar{x}} \Rightarrow 18.8286 \pm 2(2.241) \Rightarrow 18.8286 \pm 4.482$

f. $\hat{\sigma}_{\hat{\tau}} = \sqrt{N^2 \frac{(N - n)}{Nn} \frac{\sum(x_i - \bar{x}m_i)^2}{n - 1}}$

$= \sqrt{300^2\left(\frac{300 - 4}{300(4)}\right)\frac{16,966.50143}{4 - 1}}$ (refer to part (d))

$= 11205$

g. Estimator of $\tau$: $\hat{\tau} = M\bar{x} = 5000(18.8286) = 94,143$

Estimated bound on the error of estimation:

$\hat{\tau} \pm 2\hat{\sigma}_{\hat{\tau}} \Rightarrow 94,143 \pm 2(11,205) \Rightarrow 94,143 \pm 22,410$

21.31 Some preliminary calculations:

$N = 200,\ n = 6,\ M = 2000,$

$m_1 = 10,\ m_2 = 7,\ m_3 = 6,\ m_4 = 10,\ m_5 = 7,\ m_6 = 12$

$x_1 = 5 + 18 + 33 + 22 + 19 + 18 + 20 + 8 + 9 + 25 = 177$

$x_2 = 2 + 25 + 16 + 38 + 11 + 14 + 17 = 123$

$x_3 = 22 + 18 + 33 + 50 + 35 + 40 = 198$

$x_4 = 28 + 24 + 19 + 31 + 27 + 26 + 26 + 24 + 24 + 26 = 255$

$x_5 = 13 + 21 + 19 + 15 + 26 + 41 + 12 = 147$

$x_6 = 41 + 28 + 30 + 15 + 31 + 29 + 29 + 40 + 21 + 25 + 18 + 50 = 357$

$\sum x_i = 177 + 123 + 198 + 255 + 147 + 357 = 1257$

$\sum m_i = 10 + 7 + 6 + 10 + 7 + 12 = 52$

$\sum x_i^2 = 177^2 + 123^2 + 198^2 + 255^2 + 147^2 + 357^2 = 299,745$

$\sum m_i^2 = 10^2 + 7^2 + 6^2 + 10^2 + 7^2 + 12^2 = 478$

$\sum x_i m_i = 177(10) + 123(7) + 198(6) + 255(10) + 147(7) + 357(12)$
$= 11,682$

a. Estimator of $\mu$:

$$\bar{x} = \frac{\sum x_i}{\sum m_i} = \frac{1257}{52} = 24.1731$$

Estimated bound on the error of estimation:

$$2\hat{\sigma}_{\bar{x}} = \sqrt{\left(\frac{N - n}{Nn\bar{M}^2}\right)\frac{\sum(x_i - \bar{x}m_i)^2}{n - 1}}$$

where $\bar{M} = \frac{M}{N} = \frac{2000}{200} = 10$

$$\sum(x_i - \bar{x}m_i)^2 = \sum x_i^2 - 2\bar{x}\sum x_i m_i + \bar{x}^2\sum m_i^2$$
$$= 299{,}745 - 2(24.1731)(11{,}682) + 24.1731^2(478)$$
$$= 14{,}278.6206$$

$$2\hat{\sigma}_{\bar{x}} = 2\sqrt{\frac{200 - 6}{200(6)(10)^2}\ \frac{14278.6206}{6 - 1}} = 4.297$$

b. Estimator of $\tau$: $\hat{\tau} = M\bar{x} = 2000\left(\frac{1257}{52}\right) = 48{,}346.15$

Estimated bound on the error of estimation:

$$2\hat{\sigma}_{\hat{\tau}} = \sqrt{N^2\left(\frac{N - n}{Nn}\right)\frac{\sum(x_i - \bar{x}m_i)^2}{n - 1}}$$

$$= \sqrt{200^2\left(\frac{200 - 6}{200(6)}\right)\frac{14{,}278.6206}{6 - 1}} \quad \text{(refer to part (a))}$$

$$= 8594.6532$$

c. Some preliminary calculations:

$a_i$ is the number of elements in cluster i that are less than 30.

$\sum a_i = 9 + 6 + 2 + 9 + 6 + 7 = 39$

$\sum a_i^2 = 9^2 + 6^2 + 2^2 + 9^2 + 6^2 + 7^2 = 287$

$\sum a_i m_i = 9(10) + 6(7) + 2(6) + 9(10) + 6(7) + 7(12) = 360$

Estimator of p: $\hat{p} = \frac{\sum a_i}{\sum m_i} = \frac{39}{52} = .75$

Estimated bound on the error estimation:

$$2\hat{\sigma}_{\hat{p}} = 2\sqrt{\left(\frac{N - n}{Nn\bar{M}^2}\right)\frac{\sum(a_i - \hat{p}m_i)^2}{n - 1}}$$

where $\sum(a_i - \hat{p}m_i)^2 = \sum a_i^2 - 2\hat{p}\sum a_i m_i + \hat{p}^2\sum m_i^2$

$$= 287 - 2(.75)(360) + (.75)^2 478$$
$$= 15.875$$

$$2\hat{\sigma}_{\hat{p}} = 2\sqrt{\left(\frac{200 - 6}{200(6)10^2}\right)\frac{15.875}{6 - 1}} = .1433$$

21.33 Some preliminary calculations:

$N = 100,\ M = 12{,}968,\ n = 12$

$\sum m_i = 25 + 101 + \ldots + 33 = 1621$

$\sum x_i = 1.2 + 4.0 + \ldots + .9 = 34.2$

$\sum m_i^2 = 25^2 + 101^2 + \ldots + 33^2 = 480{,}251$

$\sum x_i^2 = 1.2^2 + 4.0^2 + \ldots + .9^2 = 203.18$

$\sum x_i m_i = (25)(1.2) + (101)(4.0) + \ldots + (33)(.9) = 9370.4$

$$\bar{x} = \frac{\sum x_i}{\sum m_i} = \frac{34.2}{1621} = .0211$$

a. Estimator of $\tau$:

$$\hat{\tau} = M\left(\frac{\sum x_i}{\sum m_i}\right) = (12{,}968)\left(\frac{34.2}{1621}\right) = 273.60 \quad \text{(in thousands)}$$

Thus, $\hat{\tau} = \$273{,}600$

To calculate the estimated bound on the error of estimation:

$$\begin{aligned}\sum(x_i - \bar{x}m_i)^2 &= \sum x_i^2 - 2\bar{x}\sum x_i m_i + \bar{x}^2\sum m_i^2 \\ &= 203.18 - 2(.0211)(9370.4) + (.0211)^2(480251) \\ &= 21.5617\end{aligned}$$

The estimated bound on the error of estimation:

$$2\hat{\sigma}_{\hat{\tau}} = \sqrt{N^2\left(\frac{(N - n)}{Nn}\right)\frac{\sum(x_i - \bar{x}m_i)^2}{n - 1}}$$

$$= 2\sqrt{100^2\left(\frac{100 - 12}{100(12)}\right)\left(\frac{21.5617}{11}\right)} = 75.827 \text{ (in thousands)}$$

$$2\hat{\sigma}_{\hat{\tau}} = \$75{,}827$$

b. Since the total value of the inventory is estimated as \$273,600 and the bound on the error of the estimate is \$75,827, we can be approximately 95% confident the actual inventory is between \$197,773 and \$349,427.

c. The value \$280,000 is contained in the approximate 95% confidence interval found in (b). Therefore, this seems very reasonable.

21.35 Some preliminary calculations:

$N = 70, \; n = 10$

$\sum m_i = 550 + 163 + \ldots + 47 = 3867$

$\sum a_i = 401 + 80 + \ldots + 38 = 2939$

$\sum m_i^2 = 550^2 + 163^2 + \ldots + 47^2 = 2{,}389{,}707$

$\sum a_i^2 = 401^2 + 80^2 + \ldots + 39^2 = 1{,}297{,}643$

$\sum a_i m_i = (401)(500) + (80)(163) + \ldots + (38)(47) = 1{,}752{,}592$

Approximate $\bar{M}$ with $\bar{m} = \dfrac{\sum m_i}{n} = \dfrac{3867}{10} = 386.7$

Estimator of p: $\hat{p} = \dfrac{\sum a_i}{\sum m_i} = \dfrac{2939}{3867} = .76$

To calculate the bound on the error of estimation,

where $\sum(a_i - \hat{p}m_i)^2 = \sum a_i^2 - 2\hat{p}\sum a_i m_i + \hat{p}^2 \sum m_i^2$

$$= 1{,}297{,}643 - 2(.76)(1{,}752{,}592) + (.76)^2(2{,}389{,}707)$$

$$= 1{,}297{,}643 - 2{,}663{,}939.84 + 1{,}380{,}294.76$$

$$= 13{,}997.92$$

The estimated bound on the error of estimation is:

$$2\hat{\sigma}_{\hat{p}} = 2\sqrt{\left(\frac{N - n}{Nn\bar{M}^2}\right)\frac{\sum(a_i - \hat{p}m_i)^2}{n - 1}} = 2\sqrt{\left(\frac{70 - 10}{70(10)(386.7)^2}\right)\left(\frac{13{,}997.92}{10 - 1}\right)}$$

$$= .0597$$

21.37 Some preliminary calculations:

$N = 180, \; n = 10$

$\sum m_i = 20 + 18 + \ldots + 19 = 220$

$\sum x_i = 530 + 486 + \ldots + 665 = 6964$

$\sum m_i^2 = 20^2 + 18^2 + \ldots + 19^2 = 5036$

$\sum x_i^2 = 530^2 + 486^2 + \ldots + 665^2 = 5{,}083{,}404$

$\sum x_i m_i = 530(20) + 486(18) + \ldots + 665(19) = 158{,}725$

Approximate $\bar{M}$ with $\bar{m} = \dfrac{\sum m_i}{n} = \dfrac{200}{10} = 22$

Estimator of μ: $\bar{x} = \dfrac{\sum x_i}{\sum m_i} = \dfrac{6964}{220} = 31.65$

To calculate the bound on the error of estimation:

$$\sum(x_i - \bar{x}m_i)^2 = \sum x_i^2 - 2\bar{x}\sum x_i m_i + \bar{x}^2\sum m_i^2$$
$$= 5{,}083{,}404 - 2(31.65)(158{,}725) + (31.65)^2(5036)$$
$$= 5{,}083{,}404 - 10{,}047{,}292.5 + 5{,}044{,}674.51$$
$$= 80{,}786.01$$

The estimated bound on the error of estimation is:

$$2\hat{\sigma}_{\bar{x}} = 2\sqrt{\left(\frac{N - n}{N n \bar{M}^2}\right)\frac{\sum(x_i - \bar{x}m_i)^2}{n - 1}} = 2\sqrt{\left(\frac{180 - 10}{180(10)(22)^2}\right)\left(\frac{80{,}786.01}{10 - 1}\right)}$$

$$= 2.65$$

21.39 For a bound of no more than \$200,000, solve the following equation:

$$200{,}000 = 2\frac{s}{\sqrt{n}}\sqrt{\frac{N - n}{N}}$$

For a first approximation, $\frac{N - n}{N} \approx 1$

From Exercise 21.13, we know s = 1,083,162.

$$200{,}000 = 2\left(\frac{1{,}083{,}162}{\sqrt{n}}\right)\sqrt{1}$$

$$\Rightarrow n = 117.32.$$

Now resolve the equation, using n = 118 for the correction factor (from Exercise 21.13, we know N = 1500):

$$200{,}000 = 2\left(\frac{1{,}083{,}162}{\sqrt{n}}\right)\sqrt{\frac{1500 - 118}{1500}}$$

$$\Rightarrow n = 108.09.$$

Now resolve the equation, using n = 109 for the correction factor:

$$200{,}000 = 2\left(\frac{1{,}083{,}162}{\sqrt{n}}\right)\sqrt{\frac{1500 - 109}{1500}}$$

$$\Rightarrow n = 108.798.$$

Thus, 109 large, diverse companies should be questioned concerning expenditures for external audits.

Since she already sampled 32, 109 - 32 = 77 additional firms should be sampled.

21.41 From Exercise 21.24,

$N_1 = 3210,\ N_2 = 2015,\ N_3 = 1740,\ N = 6965$

$s_1^2 = 8.147,\ s_2^2 = 64.075,\ s_3^2 = 61.408$

a. To estimate the mean 1980 income of the head administrators to within \$1000, solve the following equation (the data are in thousands of dollars):

$$1 = 2\sqrt{\frac{1}{N^2}\sum N_i^2\left(\frac{N_i - n_i}{N_i}\right)\frac{s_i^2}{n_i}}$$

For a first approximation, set $n_1 = n_2 = n_3 = n_s$ and

$$\frac{N_i - n_i}{Ni} \approx 1.$$

$$1 = 2\sqrt{\frac{1}{6965^2}\left(\frac{3210^2(8.147) + 2015^2(64.075) + 1740^2(61.408)}{n_s}\right)}$$

$\Rightarrow n_s = 43.70 \approx 44$

Now resolve the equation with $n_s = 44$ for the correction factor:

$$1 = 2\sqrt{\frac{1}{6965^2}\left(\frac{3210^2\left(\frac{3210 - 44}{3210}\right)(8.147) + 2015^2\left(\frac{2015 - 44}{2015}\right)(64.075) + 1740^2\left(\frac{1704 - 44}{1704}\right)(61.408)}{n_s}\right)}$$

$\Rightarrow n_s = 42.75 \approx 43$

Now resolve the equation with $n_s = 43$ for the correction factor:

$$1 = 2\sqrt{\frac{1}{6965^2}\left(\frac{3210^2\left(\frac{3210 - 43}{3210}\right)(8.147) + 2015^2\left(\frac{2015 - 43}{2015}\right)(64.075) + 1740^2\left(\frac{1704 - 43}{1704}\right)(66.408)}{n_s}\right)}$$

$\Rightarrow n_s = 42.77 \approx 43$

Thus, 43 administrators should be sampled from each stratum, so the total number of administrators sampled should be 43 x 3 = 129.

b. To estimate the mean 1980 income of the lead administrators to within \$1000, solve the following equation (the data are in thousands of dollars):

$$1 = 2\sqrt{\frac{1}{N^2}\sum N_i^2\left(\frac{N_i \quad n_i}{N_i}\right)\frac{s_i^2}{n_i}}$$

For a first approximation, set $n_1 = 30$, $n_2 = 30$, and

$$\frac{N_3 - n_3}{N_3} \approx 1.$$

$$1 = 2\sqrt{\frac{1}{6965^2}\left(3210^2\left(\frac{3210 - 30}{3210}\right)\frac{8.147}{30} + 2015^2\left(\frac{2015 - 30}{2015}\right)\frac{64.075}{30} + 1740^2\left(\frac{61.408}{n_3}\right)\right)}$$

$\Rightarrow n_3 = 228.72 \approx 229$

Now resolve the equation with $n_3 = 229$ for the correction factor:

$$1 = 2\sqrt{\frac{1}{6965^2}\left(3210^2\left(\frac{3210 - 30}{3210}\right)\frac{8.147}{30} + 2015^2\left(\frac{2015 - 30}{2015}\right)\frac{64.075}{30} + 1740^2\left(\frac{1740 - 229}{1740}\right)\frac{61.408}{n_3}\right)}$$

$\Rightarrow n_3 = 198.62 \approx 199$

Now resolve the equation with $n_3 = 199$ for the correction factor:

$$1 = 2\sqrt{\frac{1}{6965^2}\left(3210^2\left(\frac{3210 - 30}{3210}\right)\frac{8.147}{30} + 2015^2\left(\frac{2015 - 30}{2015}\right)\frac{64.075}{30} + 1740^2\left(\frac{1740 - 199}{1740}\right)\frac{61.408}{n_3}\right)}$$

$\Rightarrow n_3 = 202.56 \approx 203$

Thus, 203 administrators should be sampled from stratum 3.

21.43 From Exercise 21.26,

$N_1 = 360,\ N_2 = 74,\ N_3 = 95,\ N = 529$

$s_1^2 = 9{,}150{,}500,\ s_2^2 = 25{,}003{,}000,\ s_3^2 = 16{,}801{,}100$

To estimate the mean annual income for households in the community to within \$600, solve the following equation.

$$600 = 2\sqrt{\frac{1}{N^2}\sum N_i^2\left(\frac{N_i \quad n_i}{N_i}\right)\frac{s_i^2}{n_i}}$$

For a first approximation, set $n_1 = n_2 = n_3 = n_s$ and

$$\frac{N_i - n_i}{Ni} \approx 1.$$

$$600 = 2\sqrt{\frac{1}{529^2}\left(\frac{360^2(9{,}150{,}500) + 74^2(25{,}003{,}000) + 95^2(16{,}801{,}000)}{n_s}\right)}$$

$\Rightarrow n_s = 58.54 \approx 59$

Now resolve the equation with $n_s = 59$ for the correction factor:

$$600 = 2\sqrt{\frac{1}{529^2}\left(\frac{360^2\left(\frac{360 - 59}{360}\right)(9{,}150{,}500) + 74^2\left(\frac{74 - 59}{74}\right)(25{,}003{,}000) + 95^2\left(\frac{95 - 59}{95}\right)(16{,}801{,}100)}{n_s}\right)}$$

$\Rightarrow n_s = 42.75 \approx 43$

Now resolve the equation with $n_s = 43$ for the correction factor:

$$600 = 2\sqrt{\frac{1}{529^2}\left(\frac{360^2\left(\frac{360-43}{360}\right)(9{,}150{,}500) + 74^2\left(\frac{74-43}{74}\right)(25{,}003{,}000) + 95^2\left(\frac{95-43}{95}\right)(16{,}801{,}100)}{n_s}\right)}$$

$$\Rightarrow n_s = 47.04 \approx 48$$

Thus, 48 homes from each city section should be sampled.

21.45 Each orange tree would represent a cluster, and the oranges would represent the elements of the cluster. The farmer could randomly select trees and check the damage to the oranges on each tree selected.

21.47 a. n represents the number of accounts receivable selected (n = 100).

N represents the total number of accounts receivable at the department store in Boston (N = 15,887).

b. $\bar{x}$ represents the average age of the accounts receivable selected in the sample of n = 100.

$\mu$ represents the average age of all N = 15,887 accounts receivable at the department store in Boston.

c. $\hat{\tau}$ represents the estimated total monetary value of all N = 15,887 accounts receivable.

$\tau$ represents the actual total monetary value of all N = 15,887 accounts receivable at the department store in Boston.

d. $\hat{p}$ represents the estimated proportion of accounts receivable out of all N = 15,887 at the store that are more than 90 days old.

p represents the proportion of accounts receivable out of all N = 15,887 at the store that are more than 90 days old.

e. $\hat{\tau} \pm 2\hat{\sigma}_{\hat{\tau}}$ represents an approximate 95% confidence interval for the total monetary value of all N = 15,887 accounts receivable at the department store in Boston.

21.49 $N = 3500$, $n = 30$

$$\sum x_i = 10 + 0 + 5 + \dots + 15 + 10 = 633$$

$$\sum x_i^2 = 10^2 + 0^2 + 5^2 + \dots + 15^2 + 10^2 = 39{,}007$$

$$s^2 = \frac{\sum x_i^2 - \frac{(\sum x_i)^2}{n}}{n - 1} = \frac{39{,}007 - \frac{(633)^2}{30}}{30 - 1} = 884.5069$$

$$\bar{x} = \frac{\sum x_i}{n} = \frac{633}{30} = 21.10$$

a. Estimator of $\tau$:

$$\hat{\tau} = N\bar{x} = 3500(21.10) = 73{,}850$$

Estimated bound on the error of estimation:

$$2\hat{\sigma}_{\hat{\tau}} = 2\sqrt{N^2 \frac{s^2}{n}\left(\frac{N - n}{N}\right)}$$

$$= 2\sqrt{3500^2\left(\frac{884.5069}{30}\right)\left(\frac{3500 - 30}{3500}\right)}$$

$$= 37{,}845.89$$

b. $p$ represents the proportion of PAC's that planned to support Reagan.

Let $x$ represent the number of PAC's in the sample that expected to spend money in support of Reagan.

$$\hat{p} = \frac{x}{n} = \frac{21}{30} = .70$$

$$2\hat{\sigma}_{\hat{p}} = 2\sqrt{\frac{\hat{p}(1 - \hat{p})}{n}}\sqrt{\frac{N - n}{N}}$$

$$= 2\sqrt{\frac{.70(1 - .70)}{30}}\sqrt{\frac{3500 - 30}{3500}}$$

$$= .167$$

An approximate 95% confidence interval for $p$ is:

$$\hat{p} \pm 2\hat{\sigma}_{\hat{p}} = .70 \pm .167$$

21.51 Some preliminary calculations:

$a_i$ is the number of employees in plant i that favor the new plan.

$N = 45,\ n = 9$

$\sum m_i = 112 + 75 + \ldots + 83 = 870$

$\sum a_i = 98 + 65 + \ldots + 65 = 752$

$\sum m_i^2 = 112^2 + 75^2 + \ldots + 83^2 = 89,580$

$\sum a_i^2 = 98^2 + 65^2 + \ldots + 65^2 = 66,218$

$\sum a_i m_i = (98)(112) + (65)(75) + \ldots + (65)(83) = 76,889$

$$\bar{m} = \frac{\sum m_i}{n} = \frac{870}{9} = 96.67$$

Estimator of p:

$$\hat{p} = \frac{\sum a_i}{\sum m_i} = \frac{752}{870} = .864$$

To calculate the bound on the error of estimation, first calculate

$$\sum(a_i - \hat{p}m_i)^2 = \sum a_i^2 - 2\hat{p}\sum a_i m_i + \hat{p}^2\sum m_i^2$$
$$= 66,218 - 2(.864)(76,889) + (.864)^2(89,580)$$
$$= 66,218 - 132,864.192 + 66,871.11168$$
$$= 224.91968$$

Estimated bound on the error of estimation:

$$2\hat{\sigma}_{\hat{p}} = 2\sqrt{\left(\frac{N - n}{Nn\bar{m}^2}\right)\left(\frac{\sum(a_i - \hat{p}m_i)^2}{n - 1}\right)} = 2\sqrt{\left(\frac{45 - 9}{45(9)(96.67)^2}\right)\left(\frac{224.91968}{8}\right)}$$
$$= .033$$

21.55 From Exercise 21.54:

$$N = 500,000,\ \hat{p} = \frac{9296}{10,000} = .9296$$

For a bound on the error of estimation of .05, solve the following equation:

$$.05 = 2\sqrt{\frac{\hat{p}(1 - \hat{p})}{n}\left(\frac{N - n}{N}\right)}$$

For a first approximation, $\frac{N - n}{N} \approx 1$, $\hat{p}$ will be estimated to be .5 (to be conservative)

$$.05 = 2\sqrt{\frac{.5(.5)}{n}}$$

$\Rightarrow n = 400$

Now resolve the equation using n = 400 for correction factor:

$$.05 = 2\sqrt{\frac{.5(.5)}{n}\left(\frac{500,000 - 400}{500,000}\right)}$$

$$\Rightarrow n = 399.68 \approx 400$$

Thus, 400 of the magazines Florida subscribers should be included in the sample.

21.57 Some preliminary calculations:

$N = 60,\ n = 12$

$\sum m_i = 8 + 9 + 5 + 12 + 10 + 14 + 3 + 8 + 5 + 10 + 9 + 7 = 100$

$\sum x_i = 45 + 36 + 23 + 55 + 47 + 101 + 16 + 49 + 29 + 62 + 51 + 27 = 541$

$\sum m_i^2 = 8^2 + 9^2 + 5^2 + 12^2 + 10^2 + 14^2 + 3^2 + 8^2 + 5^2 + 10^2 + 9^2 + 7^2 = 938$

$\sum x_i^2 = 45^2 + 36^2 + 23^2 + 55^2 + 47^2 + 101^2 + 16^2 + 49^2 + 29^2 + 62^2 + 51^2 + 27^2 = 29,957$

$\sum x_i m_i = 45(8) + 36(9) + 23(5) + \ldots + 51(9) + 37(7) = 5,196$

Approximate $\bar{M}$ with $\bar{m} = \frac{\sum m_i}{n} = \frac{100}{12} = 8.3333$

$$\bar{x} = \frac{\sum x_i}{\sum m_i} = \frac{541}{100} = 5.41$$

$$\begin{aligned}\sum(x_i - \bar{x}m_i)^2 &= \sum x_i^2 - 2\bar{x}\sum x_i m_i + \bar{x}^2\sum m_i^2 \\ &= 29,957 - 2(5.41)(5,196) + (5.41)^2(938) \\ &= 29,957 - 56,220.72 + 27,453.4778 \\ &= 1189.7578\end{aligned}$$

An approximate 95% confidence interval for $\mu$ is:

$$\bar{x} \pm 2\hat{\sigma}_{\bar{x}}$$

$$\Rightarrow \bar{x} \pm 2\sqrt{\left(\frac{N - n}{Nn\bar{M}^2}\right)\left(\frac{\sum(x_i - \bar{x}m_i)^2}{n - 1}\right)}$$

$$\Rightarrow 5.41 \pm 2\sqrt{\left(\frac{60 - 12}{60(12)(8.3333)^2}\right)\left(\frac{1189.7578}{12 - 1}\right)}$$

$$\Rightarrow 5.41 \pm .64$$

21.59 a. From Exercise 21.33,

$N = 100$, $n = 12$

$\sum x_i = 34.2$, $\sum x_i^2 = 203.18$

Estimator of $\tau$: $\hat{\tau} = N\bar{x}_t = N \dfrac{\sum x_i}{n}$

$$= 100 \frac{34.2}{12}$$

$$= 285 \text{ (in thousands)}$$

Thus, $\hat{\tau} = \$285{,}000$

The estimated bound on the error of estimation:

$$2\hat{\sigma}_{\hat{\tau}} = 2\sqrt{N^2\left(\frac{N - n}{Nn}\right)\frac{\sum(x_i - \bar{x}_t)^2}{n - 1}}$$

where $\sum(x_i - \bar{x}_t)^2 = \sum x_i^2 - 2\bar{x}_t\sum x_i + 12\bar{x}_t^2$

$$= 203.18 - 2(2.85)(34.2) + 12(2.85)^2$$

$$= 105.71$$

$$2\hat{\sigma}_{\hat{\tau}} = 2\sqrt{100^2\left(\frac{100 - 12}{100(12)}\right)\left(\frac{105.71}{12 - 1}\right)}$$

$$= 167.897 \text{ (in thousands)}$$

Thus, $2\hat{\sigma}_{\hat{\tau}} = \$167{,}897$